The collected works of Ruqaiya Hasan

Volume 2 Semantic Variation

Edited by Jonathan J. Webster

Words which, at first sight, seem to be mere adornment and could, in every sense of the word, easily be discarded, become frightening once you start to think about them and realise what they imply.

José Saramago: The Cave. The Harville Press. 2000: 255.

The Collected Works of Ruqaiya Hasan

Volume 2

Semantic Variation

Meaning in society and in sociolinguistics

Edited by Jonathan J. Webster

Dedicated to the memory of my parents

LONDON OAKVILLE

Published by

Equinox Publishing Ltd.
UK: Unit 6, The Village, 101 Amies Street, London, SW11 2JW
USA: DBBC, 28 Main Street, Oakville, CT 06779
www.equinoxpub.com

First published 2009

British Library Cataloguing-in-Publication Data
A catalogue record for this book is available from the British Library.

ISBN 978 1 904768 35 7 (hardback)
978 1 904768 36 4 (paperback)

Library of Congress Cataloging-in-Publication Data

Hasan, Ruqaiya.
Semantic variation : meaning in society and in sociolinguistics / Ruqaiya Hasan ; edited by Jonathan J. Webster.
p. cm. -- (The collected works of ruqaiya hasan ; v. 2)
Includes bibliographical references and index.
ISBN 978-1-904768-35-7 (hb) -- ISBN 978-1-904768-36-4 (pb) 1. Semantics--Social aspects. 2. Language and languages--Variation. 3. Sociolinguistics. I. Webster, Jonathan, 1955- II. Title.
P325.5.S63H37 2009
306.44--dc22

2008032358

Typeset by Catchline, Milton Keynes (www.catchline.com)

Printed and bound in the UK and in the USA

Contents

CONTENTS OF ACCOMPANYING CD

Acknowledgements

Section 2: Questions and answers in sociolinguistic studies

'A sociolinguistic interpretation of everyday talk between mothers and children' co-authored with Carmel Cloran, from *Learning, Keeping and Using Language: selected papers from the 8th World Congress of Applied Linguistics*, Sydney, 16-21 August 1987 edited by M.A.K. Halliday, Howard Nicols and John Gibbons, published by John Benjamins Publishing Co., 1990, pp. 67-99. Reprinted by permission of John Benjamins Publishing Co.

'Language in the processes of socialization: Home and School' from *Language and Socialisation: Home and School – Proceedings from the Working Conference on Language in Education* edited by L Gerot, J Oldenburg and T Van Leeuwen, published by the School of English and Linguistics, Macquarie University, 1988, pp. 36-96. Reprinted by permission of the School of English and Linguistics, Macquarie University.

'Semantic variation and sociolinguistics' from *Australian Journal of Linguistics* 9.2, published by the Australian Linguistic Society, 1989, pp. 221-276. Reprinted by permission of Taylor and Francis (http://www.tandf.co.uk).

'Questions as a mode of learning in everyday talk' from *Language Education: Interaction and Development: Proceedings of the International Conference*, Vietnam 30 March – 1 April 1991 edited by Thao Le and Mike McCausland, published by Faculty of Education, University of Tasmania, 1991, pp. 70-119. Reprinted by permission of Faculty of Education, University of Tasmania.

Section 3: Social hierarchies and the concept of rationality

'Meaning in sociolinguistic theory' from *Sociolinguistics Today: International Perspectives* edited by K Bolton and H Kwok, published by Routledge, 1992, pp. 80-119. Reprinted by permission of Professor Kingsley Bolton.

'Rationality in everyday talk: from process to system' from *Directions in Corpus Linguistics: Proceedings of the Nobel Symposium* 82, Stockholm 4-8 August 1991 edited by J. Svartvik, published by Mouton de Gruyter, 1992, pp. 257-307. Reprinted by permission of Mouton de Gruyter.

Section 4: The world and the world of meanings

'Contexts for meaning' from *Georgetown University Round Table on Language and Linguistics (GURT) 1993: Strategic Interaction and Language Acquisition* edited by James E Alatis , published by Georgetown University Press, 1993, pp. 79-103. Reprinted by permission of Georgetown University Press.

'The ontogenesis of decontextualized language: some achievements of classification and framing' from *Towards a Sociology of Pedagogy: The contribution of Basil Bernstein to Research* edited by Ana Moaris, Isabel Neves, Brian Davies and Harry Daniels, published by Peter Lang Publishing, Inc., 2001, pp. 47-80. (c) 2001. Reprinted by permission of Peter Lang Publishing, Inc.

'The world in words: Semiotic mediation, tenor and ideology' from *The Development of Language: Functional Perspectives on Species and Individuals*, edited by Geoff Williams and Annabelle Lukin, published by Continuum International Publishing Group, 2004, pp. 158-181. Reprinted by permission of Continuum International Publishing Group.

Author's preface

For the work reported in this volume I owe a debt of gratitude to a large number of colleagues and mentors. My first major debt of gratitude is to four intellectual leaders – Vygotsky, Halliday, Bernstein and Labov. It was the thinking of Bernstein and of Labov on the relationship of language and society – and perhaps even more, their sometimes strong disagreements on the extent to which language pervades human life – that initially led me into the exploration of the area I have variously referred to as semantic variation, semantic style, and semantic distance. Vygotsky's concept of semiotic mediation[1] was to capture my attention sometime in the mid 1970's, though I might say that, thanks to Firth, Halliday, and Bernstein, in a very real sense, something akin to this concept has always been present in Systemic Functional Linguistics (SFL) with respect to how language works in the life of its speakers. The Bernstein-Labov controversy on the topic of what is known now as Bernstein's code theory, was the mainspring of the research on semantic variation reported in the present volume. Semantic variation is however not an account of Bernstein's code theory: the code theory, unlike semantic variation, is concerned with all semiotic modalities, not just language. 'Inspired' in the first instance by the code controversy, the research soon became a point of departure also for reflection on the theoretical basis of sociolinguistics, which in the climate of the time has meant Labovian sociolinguistics. The exploration of this vast area required resources. I have acknowledged my debt to the Australian Research Council and to the Macquarie University Research Grant Scheme for funding a body of research which offered me the opportunity to develop my ideas on semantic variation as an important sociolinguistic category; this discourse incidentally got me involved in a critique of some aspects of dominant sociolinguistics – I hope in a constructive vein. The various chapters of this volume present an account of this journey, though focusing mainly on semantic variation as a sociological and a sociolinguistic category, while the accompanying CD describes the range of the research projects the funding had enabled. I would like here to express my gratitude to my colleagues in the department of linguistics at Macquarie University whose encouragement and interest in my work was a source of strength. In particular I again thank Carmel Cloran for her commitment to this research and for her readiness to assist throughout this venture. I regret that much of the work concerning phase two and three of the research projects has not seen the light of day – for this failure, I accept complete responsibility.

As Halliday has often pointed out (Halliday 2007), the parameters of the Bernstein-Labov controversy are complex both ideationally and interpersonally. There are socio-political pressures against recognizing as habitual to the behaviour of a sub-section of the community features which are variants of the privileged variety. Drawing attention to such variation is always problematic, whether the variation happens to pertain to the level of phonology or to those of lexicogrammar and/or semantics; though the former has been the bread and butter of sociolinguistics, the latter is frowned upon. But ignoring systematic patterns of variation at any level simply because it is not 'very nice' to draw attention to them appears lacking in scholarly integrity, and is most probably less than helpful to the welfare of precisely those we would wish to be friendly to. Of course the possibility is always open that the variation under discussion is either factually untenable or theoretically flawed, or the interpretation of the phenomena is not sound. In which case, the hypothesis of semantic variation has to be demonstrated to be wrong not on grounds of etiquette or politically correct speech but on the basis of the principles of scholarly activity. I am grateful to Michael Halliday for offering in his SFL a conception of language, and a sound descriptive framework which I have found enabling: it has, I hope, allowed me to view dispassionately the fact of variation without temptation to treat the variant forms as necessarily 'undesirable'. The model has helped me in conducting this research with a keen awareness of the relationship of language and society, and an understanding of the working of language both in terms of its form and its functions. On a more personal note, I thank Michael Halliday also for discussing with me many of the issues throughout the entire period of researching and reporting.

I am grateful to Jonathan Webster, for his personal support and for the assistance offered to me by The Halliday Centre for Intelligent Applications of Language Studies; in particular to Marvin Lam who advised me in preparing the manuscript and reproduced a number of figures and tables. My thanks are also due to Sandy Lui who cheerfully and quickly produced any figures that defeated my close to nonexistent expertise in the matter. Thanks also to Joey Wong, Executive Officer at the Halliday Centre, for help in the last stages of this lengthy process.

Last (and, as one says, though this time with great truth!) not least, I thank David Butt and Annabelle Lukin (Centre for Language in Social Life, Macquarie University) for their continued encouragement, their linguistic discussions, and for trouble-shooting demanded by recalcitrant computers.

References

Halliday, M. A. K. (2007) *The Collected Works of M. A. K. Halliday, Volume 10: Language and Society* (edited by J. J. Webster). London: Continuum.

Hasan, R. (2005) *The Collected Works of Ruqaiya Hasan, Volume 1: Language, Society and Consciousness* (edited by J. J Webster). London: Equinox.

Notes

1 Most of my interpretations and reflections on the work of Vygotsky – and in passing Luria – have already been published in Volume 1 of Hasan's *Collected Works* (2005); some thoughts on the concept of semantic distance (Hasan 1978) will be found in Volume 3, under preparation, which contains papers on the relationship between society, language, and education.

Editor's introduction

The papers comprising this second volume of Professor Ruqaiya Hasan's *Collected Works* together offer a compelling argument for an integrated sociolinguistics, in which the mutual relationship between the social and the semiotic is investigated, 'reveal[ing] how language and society interact - how language shapes society and how society enters into the process and system of language' (*On Semantic Variation*, Chapter 2). Professor Hasan describes both as cogenetic, language being what it is because of how it functions in society, and societies being as they are owing to the role language plays in their creation and maintenance (*Wanted a theory for integrated sociolinguistics*, Chapter 1).

The investigation of variation in language provides insight not only into the nature of language and language change, but also into the nature of human society. Such studies, as Professor Hasan points out, can also help us understand the role we, as speakers and members of society, play 'in maintaining many of its undesirable traits'. (*On Semantic Variation*, Chapter 2).

Professor Hasan's sociolinguistic investigation of a large naturally occurring sample of mother–child conversation follows the meticulous tradition of variation analysis as introduced by Labov. The semantic analysis of this material is in terms of a set of system networks of semantic features relevant in issuing questions, answers, commands, and other such speech acts. The analysed data was statistically interpreted using Principal Components Analysis. The four chapters in part II of the volume, concerned with mothers' and children's questions and answers, illustrate 'speakers' semantic choices co-vary with some significant social circumstance of their location in society' (*A sociolinguistic interpretation of everyday talk between mothers and children* with Cloran (1990), Chapter 3). In *Semantic variation and sociolinguistics* (1989), Chapter 5, she reports on a study of a large number of semantic features in the spontaneous speech of twenty four mothers and children. The findings from that study revealed 'non random, highly orderly semantic variation'. In another new and previously unpublished paper, *Two social factors in semantic variation* (Chapter 10), Professor Hasan and her co-investigator, Carmel Cloran, note that 'much of the semantic variation which occurs in language is non-arbitrarily related to ideologies of gender and social class... it also concerns linguistic phenomena which are far below the level of speakers' consciousness'.

The findings from Hasan's investigations into semantic variation have prompted her to take issue with Labov's view that sociolinguistic variation is meaning preserving. She argues instead that language is 'an active force that contributes to the making of my environment as I find it' (*Meaning in sociolinguistic theory* (1992), Chapter 7). Hasan contrasts 'a sociolinguistics which grants language its full power, its rightful position in the socio-psycho-historical development of human communities' with 'a sociolinguistics in which language is simply a flow of vocables, and where all linguistic variation is reduced to variation in style, while style itself is seen as meaningless – or at least immaterial to cognition. Sociolinguistics of this kind lacks self-awareness; and it is sociolinguistics of precisely this kind that suppresses any recognition of the linguistic means through which the privileged classes maintain their privilege'. (*Language in the processes of socialisation: Home and School*, Chapter 4).

As the title of the first chapter – *Wanted a theory for integrated sociolinguistics* – suggests, what is needed for integrated sociolinguistics is a suitable theory which acknowledges the mutual relevance between the social and semiotic, and can provide a viable hypothesis to account for the various categories of variation found in language. Professor Hasan draws on two existing theories to provide the theoretical foundation for integrated sociolinguistics. One is Bernstein's theory of the social, the other is Halliday's Systemic Functional Linguistic (SFL) theory of the semiotic.

Though Professor Hasan regards neither as being adequate by itself to serve as a theory for integrated sociolinguistics, together both theoretical approaches have provided Professor Hasan and her co-investigators with a useful theoretical foundation for developing a methodology for studying semantic variation.

This collection of the papers written by Professor Ruqaiya Hasan represents a significant contribution to the ongoing development of sociolinguistic theory, in particular, addressing the need for a theory for integrated sociolinguistics which honestly and courageously faces up to the inequalities in society with the hope that by bringing such inequalities to light, humankind might yet be moved to act.

1

Introducing meaning in sociolinguistics

1 Wanted: a theory for integrated sociolinguistics

1 Introduction

Some fifteen years ago, Jane Hill (1985) had wondered in a review article: 'is a sociolinguistics possible?'. If, to some of her readers, such a question had appeared unnecessarily skeptical in 1985, it would certainly seem even more so today, when sociolinguistics has so firmly established itself as a field of language study. The degree of scholarly enthusiasm, the large number of publications and the popularity of courses on the subject – ours[1] being one relatively humble example – have to be taken as proof not only of its existence but also of its capacity for maintaining itself. But to read Hill as doubting simply the existence or the continuation of the field as we know it today would be a gross misinterpretation: after all, her article was a review of eight publications in the field of sociolinguistics by some very outstanding scholars[2]. In fact, Hill states her real concern quite explicitly in the closing paragraph of her review article (Hill 1985: 470–1; emphasis added):

> The volumes ... give us, then, a profile of the state of the art. Among them can be found work with great quantitative sophistication (...), deep interpretive sensitivity, responsible ethnographic observation, and useful contributions to the empirical foundations of our knowledge. *What is missing from them is a sense of integration*, that the project of one group of workers is attentive to the project of another, that the call for a 'socially contingent' linguistics has produced a unity of view point and approach which is beginning to draw together the various strands of the frontiers of grammar, of sociology, of cultural anthropology into a unified disciplinary project. A decade out from Hymes' manifesto, *it is still not clear that a holistic sociolinguistics is possible.*

Notably, today, two decades out from Hill's call for a 'holistic sociolinguistics', the situation has not changed much. And, despite the fact that the field, judged by usual standards, is flourishing, critique of sociolinguistics – particularly aimed at the paradigm associated with the work of Labov and his collaborators – continues to arrive from different directions; response or attention to any of this critique – even that which comes from within the not too well defined field of sociolinguistics – remains conspicuous by its rarity if not by its complete absence. The multiple enterprises under the banner of sociolinguistics continue in their chosen manner, seemingly unaware of Hill's dream of 'draw[ing] together the various strands of the frontiers of grammar, of sociology and cultural anthropology into one unified disciplinary project'. To my mind, this represents one of the most serious problems a discipline could encounter: today's sociolinguistics[3] appears regrettably unaware of its own true identity – or less metaphorically, the practicing sociolinguists are not aware of the potential of the field properly called 'sociolinguistics'. It is the aim of this chapter to present one image of that 'true' identity by asking a very basic question about the meaning of the label 'sociolinguistics', and pursuing some of the implications of the answer for the conceptualisation of a field deserving of that label.

This very basic but highly pertinent question is: *why would sociolinguistics be possible?* Indeed the rationale for the existence of a discipline called 'socio-linguistics' is not all that evident. The word's own structure –'linguistics' plus the prefix 'socio-' – gives nothing away, except perhaps a simplistic reading according to which in doing sociolinguistics we are actually doing a variety of linguistics which has something to do with society/sociology as suggested by the prefix 'socio-'. Now, so far as the meaning of 'linguistics' is concerned, there can be no question that it refers to a field whose object of study is language[4]: linguistics of any kind that we know today has the aim of modelling human language and of fashioning the description of language according to that model; thus in faulting a linguistic theory we are, in fact, faulting primarily its conceptualisation of language. This much is clear and – dare I hope? – uncontested, but what is not clear is the legitimacy of the original conjunction of 'socio-' and 'linguistics'. Dictionaries will paraphrase the 'word element' 'socio-' as 'of or relating to society'. It is, then, a fair question to ask: how and why would language – a 'mental organ', an autonomous system, a set of (perhaps universal) rules, a stable code, a semiotic modality, call it what you will – come into contact with, or relate to any aspect of human social existence? The question is important for as one interprets this innocent little prefix, so does one prepare the ground for the recognition of a discipline properly called sociolinguistics and for defining its object of study.

1.1 The 'socio-' in today's sociolinguistics

One undeniable historical fact is that from the inception of today's sociolinguistics, most practitioners in the field have interpreted the prefix – at least by implication, if not by assertion – as 'the extra-linguistic entity aspects of which correlate with linguistic variation'. Indeed it would not be far-fetched to suggest that for most linguists this is the main value of the prefix 'socio-'; not surprisingly sociolinguistics has gone about the business of 'explaining' variation by appeal to this entity called 'society' without asking many questions about the entity itself, as if human society, and particularly social groupings of whatever kind, were invented for the express purpose of explaining linguistic variation, be it synchronic or diachronic. With greater sophistication, explanations of a kind began to emerge. Thus beginning with the recognition of the 'functionality' of variation in complex societies (Weinreich, Labov and Herzog 1968), the discipline moved to the 'obvious' fact that linguistic varieties do not simply reflect social hierarchy: they also reveal attitudes to social strata. It turned out that variation could be seen as a device for accommodating others in the society, which, again quite obviously, is important for maintaining society. As sociolinguistics progressed, variation was also found to be indicative of speaker identity[5], and so the list can go on. I am not saying that these 'social facts' are false or even irrelevant; simply that their status as facts was never something to be argued: the facts were taken as just totally obvious. So naturally, 'correlation' was just that – a correlation: one asked neither why there should be such correlation, nor given that there is correlation, what might be implied by it about the relationship of language and society, though this is what might have formed the first steps toward a holistic sociolinguistics. As I remarked (Hasan 1973a) in today's sociolinguistics, the manifest got related to the manifest; deeper questions about the character of the 'socio-' typically failed to engage the mind.

But if 'socio-' is '*of* society or *relating to* society' then this interpretation of their chosen label for the field of study, no matter how convenient it might be for some sociolinguists, would appear to suffer from two serious flaws: on the one hand, it underplays the value of the pre-fix, and on the other it also makes the relation between society and language appear accidental. Thus reading the literature one may be forgiven for thinking that there are two independent processes, namely, that language varies and that people in society fall into groups, and each of these groups has attitudes toward the other groups' values and their vowels. Current sociolinguistics has shown us in a series of brilliant studies that certain linguistic varieties and certain social attitudes happen to go together, and often the variation and/or the attitude correlates with the group's 'social class' – sometimes called SES as if that acronym absolves us from investigating what the expression means in the life of the status holder. However, social class remains a troublesome category: it is treated sometimes as a cut and dried set of categories, and at others, as one whose very existence is open to doubt. Despite this glaring contradiction, there has been no sustained effort to enquire into the basis of the category's emergence, or to problematise its relevance to the life of the social agent: *ex cathedra* declarations sufficed instead[6]. In short, what the practitioners of the discipline have regarded as 'social facts' appears somewhat capricious, a matter of chance: I suggest this has happened so regularly because today's sociolinguistics has put its faith in a model that is opposed to linguistics in a social perspective. Given the discipline's allegiance to the formalistic models the concept of society has remained 'intuitive' and un-analysed. Autonomous language has been wedded to functional linguistic variation. It is hardly surprising that when some 'new' point of contact between language and society is brought to attention, the discipline may either ignore it entirely or go so far as to grant its study the status of another 'strand' (as in Hill) or of a 'trend' (as in Lavandera 1988). From this perspective, the earliest such strand emerged in the work on speech varieties (Hymes 1962); Labov and Fanshel (1977) opened up another new 'trend/strand'; Gumperz on social identities yet another, and so on. In this way, the field becomes a collection of strands/trends, with no principle that has the potential of bestowing upon the body of studies 'a sense of integration'. The irony is that in doing all this, the work of thoughtful scholars has been ignored – true, not in the field of formalistic linguistics but in linguistics informed anthropologically or socially – which had not so long ago indicated valuable directions to discovering richer connections between language and society[7]. As Labov of the earlier days pointed out, one cannot help feeling that the language-society relation deserves better treatment, if for no other reason then simply because it forms the crux of what sociolinguistics as a true study of language in its social context should be about.

I propose to explore the relationship of language and society more deeply in section 2 of this chapter. The implications of the revised model of this relationship will be pursued in section 3. My aim will be to formulate a statement about the central object of an integrated sociolinguistics and to present an indicative outline of the problems which would form its concern. The chapter will conclude with a brief discussion of what kind of theory of language and of society would be needed to support the programme of an integrated sociolinguistics which is itself based on a deeper understanding of the relationship between language and society.

2 Rethinking the relationship between language and society

From a commonsensical point of view, the relationship of language and society poses no problem. It is plain to see that human beings engage in a variety of activities; most of these typically call for 'concerted human action' (Malinowski 1923, 1935); this in turn makes communication with others necessary; language comes into play because it is the most effective modality for such communication[8]. When we use the word 'language' in such statements, we are not talking about what linguists think of as the code or language system – i.e., Saussure's 'langue'; more precisely, our concern is with language in use, i.e., Saussure's 'parole'. So one way of interpreting this situation is to say that society comes face to face not with langue, but with parole, i.e., language in use in social interaction: the emphasis in current sociolinguistics on the study of speech in its social context thus appears fully justified. Of course, as most linguists accept, parole needs langue for its interpretation – in the words of Saussure (1966: 18) 'language [langue, RH] is necessary if speaking [parole, RH] is to be intelligible and produce all its effects'. The power of parole thus derives from the langue. Accordingly, langue remains the undoubted object of study for the science of linguistics, where it is treated as a regulated, rule governed object. It is this system conceptualised as synoptic and stable that is taken to underlie parole as it meets the exigencies of social interaction.

This simple and seemingly transparent narrative appears satisfactory until one happens to wonder what makes it possible for parole to continue to function so effectively as a means of communication. Granted that it relies on langue as an enabling resource, but then the question simply becomes: what kind of resource is langue that it can meet speakers' communicative needs at all times, all places? The situation is especially puzzling because, by contrast with the assumed 'fixed shape' of the code, a careful examination of naturally occurring parole reveals that human communication displays variation along two different lines: first, it varies along the time line from one socio-historical 'age' to another[9], both in its content and in its form; it is this type of variation that provides the measure for deciding what will count as *archaic* or *avant garde* or *normal* behaviour. Secondly, communication varies also along the context line, whereby during one and the same socio-historical stage the content and structure of one verbal interaction will vary from another according to variation in the social context relevant to that interaction; this is what forms the basis for perceptions of degrees of *appropriateness* of behaviour in interactive practices. That these two kinds of variation in the content and form of communication do occur is an empirical fact – this much should be obvious from the examination of records of socially significant parole over time: the Hansard with its political speeches covering the concerns of the community over the last few centuries would be one such record. Faced with this complex heterogeneity, parole appears to function largely without many noticeable problems. Of course there are hesitations as one wonders 'how to put it', but for the most part the flow of speech is unabated. We thus have a conundrum: how does parole playing by the rules of a static, synoptic system manage to retain its efficacy in the face of the volatile, dynamic situation presented by the complex variation that pervades the content and structure of human communication?

The above question could be answered quickly by rejecting the view of langue as a static system rooted entirely in synchrony. Indeed, Weinreich, Labov and Herzog (1968) had cast doubt on such a 'structure': we know that the system of language is subject to ongoing change – its stability is relative. Since parole is guided by langue, what it draws upon is not a static synoptic object but one that is constantly changing; there is, therefore, no mystery about the efficacy of parole. However, this explanation suggests that linguistic change is somehow calibrated with social change. We may go on to assume that this calibration happens simply by chance. Although the assumption has the advantage of preserving the principle of the autonomy of language and so its independence from human environment (see discussion in 1.1), it does smack, in the fashion of classical Greek playwrights, of reliance on the strategy of *deus ex machina*. I am therefore inclined to reject this explanation as fiction and ask: how come change in langue and change in society go hand in hand? Which is just an altered form of the earlier question I raised above: How do human languages acquire those properties which enable the langue of the community to be used with efficacy as parole in a myriad social contexts?

2.1 Langue and parole working in societal contexts

Strange as it may seem the direction for probing into these questions was already indicated in Saussure's seminal text. Often self-contradictory, always thought provoking, this text informs us that (1966: 18–19; *emphasis introduced*):

> … language [i.e., langue RH] is necessary if speaking [i.e., parole RH] is to be intelligible and produce all its effects; but speaking is necessary for the establishment of language, and historically its actuality comes first … *speaking is what causes the language to evolve* … Language and speaking are then interdependent; the former is both the instrument and the product of the latter. *But their interdependence does not prevent their being two absolutely different things.*

It is obvious that Saussure recognises the intimate relationship between langue and parole; but at the same time, he sees no way of accommodating both categories within the scientific discipline that linguistics needs to be. Clearly contraries can be accommodated within the same theory only if one is willing to entertain 'complementarity' as 'scientific' – or one has a more robust idea of what scientific means. Both Firth (1950) and Halliday (1987, 1992b, 2008) refused to accept Saussure's strong classification of the two categories, langue and parole. Halliday in particular engages with the problem of langue-parole because its 'good' resolution is central in explaining how language works. While giving credit to Saussure for problematising the langue parole relationship, he rejects (Halliday 1996: 412) the perspective whereby the two concepts are set up

> ... as if they had been two distinct classes of phenomena ... [*which*] they are not. There is only one set of phenomena here, not two; langue (the linguistic system) differs from parole (the linguistic instance) only in the position taken up by the observer. Langue is parole seen from a distance, and hence on the way to being theorised about.

To elaborate upon the intimate relationship between langue (system/potential) and parole (process/instance), Halliday presents (1987: 121 and elsewhere) the analogous case of climate and weather:

> ...just as, when I listen to the weather report every morning, and I hear something like 'last night's minimum was six degrees, that's three degrees below average', I know that the instance has itself become part of, and so has altered, the probability of the minimum temperature for that particular night in the year – so every instance of a primary tense in English discourse alters the relative probabilities of the terms that make up the primary tense system.

In this view, just like climate/weather, langue/parole are not two distinct sets of phenomena, but the same thing observed from distinct time depths, and just as important, langue is not conceptualised as a 'pre-coded' code – a stable, synoptic structure: it is inherently probabilistic and open to change.

A constant theme in Halliday's writing is that, in order to be able to work as it actually does in the life of its speech communities, the language system must possess the ability to renew itself; this constant evolution of the system is not something 'extra', the description of which can sit at the periphery of our central concerns in 'linguistics proper'; it is in fact a condition for the existence and continuation of that human language which in the end happens to be what the linguistic theory is about. The extract above has indicated Saussure's recognition that instance/parole has a crucial role in enabling the evolution/renewal of langue as an effective resource for meaning in context. Given this, we must reject his recommendation to banish parole from linguistic theory. The aim of linguistic theory is to present a comprehensive account of human language; leaving parole out would turn the linguistic theory into a plot without a hero – the basis for development will disappear. What is needed instead is to conduct a deep examination of how the langue and parole dialectic works; and since parole cannot be dissociated from social context or context from society,

Halliday proceeds to examine the four categories in relation to each other. I present my interpretation of this exploration by starting with figure 1, which is adapted[10] from Halliday (1999: 275).

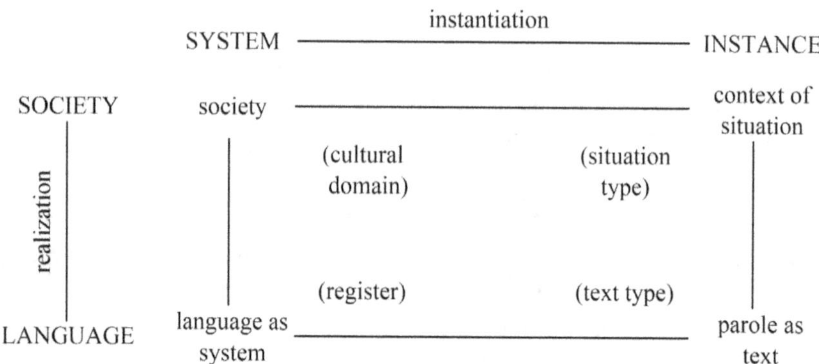

Figure 1: The relationship of society and language: instantiation and realisation

According to figure 1 the four theoretical categories – language system, society, parole-as-text and context of situation – are linked to each other by two kinds of relationship: instantiation, represented on the horizontal axis, and realisation, represented on the vertical. On each axis, the relationship of the categories is analogous. Thus on the horizontal axis, society is instantiated by context of situation, just as language is by parole-as-text, and on the vertical axis society is realised as language just as context of situation is, as parole-as-text [11]; to summarise:

(i) instantiation-wise [society : context of situation :: language : parole-as-text]

(ii) realisation-wise [society : language :: context of situation : parole-as-text]

As the figure shows, each category is connected to the other three either directly or indirectly. To understand the significance of the relationships, we need to examine what role they play in the internal organisation of language, and how they empower the analyst in showing how language works in social life.

As a theoretical concept, INSTANTIATION (Halliday 2008; Matthiessen 2007) permits the analyst a simultaneous focus on the 'potential' and the 'instance': the instance is recognised as 'made intelligible' by reference to the potential, and the potential as a resource constituted by instances. In figure 1, society is said to be instantiated by context of situation. This can be interpreted as claiming that the identity of a specific context is known by reference to that potential which we know as society; at the same time, it is the instances that are in time constitutive of the society. A similar interpretation applies to the other pair on the lower line of the horizontal axis: language system is instantiated by parole-as-text, and parole is constitutive of the system of language. In Halliday's framework the metaphor of rule is avoided because of its 'absolutist' connotations; the potential is a resource permitting its use as the occasion demands. Parole takes shape by speakers exploiting this resource in relation to the needs of their communication – in doing so, they may follow the regularities of the system as they know it, or they may work variations on that regularity, or they may create new pattern(s) by innovating within the frame of the langue. The patterns in parole become intelligible by reference to the system, even as they extend beyond it, even if the pattern maker happens to be an e. e. cummings or a James Joyce. It is in this sense – not simply by using the system as the original that has to be replicated – that language in use in social contexts will maintain and develop the system as resource; without ongoing speaking, language as meaning potential is a desiccated shell, known as a dead language.

The second relation, i.e., REALISATION, is quintessentially semiotic. By definition a semiotic system combines meaning and expression, the two presenting themselves as a seamless flow of meanings to the receiver. However analysis reveals a crucial difference between expression and meaning: whereas expression impinges on the human body, meaning is apprehended by the intellect. They are inherently different, or using more technical terminology, analysis would establish at least two different orders of abstraction: the separation of meaning and expression is thus a product of analysis; their unity is the receiver's subjective experience. A linguistic theory must explain what underlies the receiver's subjective experience of unity. Realisation is the relation postulated to account for the fact that despite the inherent duality, semiosis is apprehended by the receiver as a seamless entity. The theoretical category 'realisation', thus, refers to an inherent bond between these distinct orders of abstraction without this bond language as we know it could not exist[12]. In terms of Hjelmslev (1961), it is a solidary relation; and the theorisation of this bond as 'realisation' allows the analyst to keep the different levels of language in view at one and the same time.

Such orders of abstraction in semiotic systems have always been recognised in linguistics though they have been called by different names in different models, e.g., components, or levels or strata. In the manner of Hjelmslev, SFL divides both content and expression into two strata each. The two strata of content are meaning (semantics) and wording (lexicogrammar), those of expression are sound pattern (phonology) and sound (phonetics). Language is thus a multiple coding system, with four internal strata: semantics realised as lexicogrammar realised as phonology realised as phonetics. The model also recognises a fifth stratum in the theory of language description. This level, called context, is external to language system as such; it functions as an interface between language and reality. With the exception of the lowest two strata i.e., those pertaining to expression, realisation is a dialectical relation: the higher level is the activator of the lower level patterns and the lower, the construer of the higher one[13]; for example, in any act of parole, it is meaning that activates lexicogrammatical form, while the lexicogrammatical form is what construes the meaning. The implication of this postulate is that there is no linguistic meaning without lexicogrammar, and the concept of lexicogrammar without meaning is a contradiction in terms.

Figure 1 indicates two realisational relations: society is realised as language, and context of situation, as parole-as-text. The realisation relation between language and society is what accounts for the fact that we can derive a reasonably good sense of what speakers' society is like from a familiarity with their language system[14], just as given parole-as-text we are able to construe the details of a particular context of situation relevant to that text[15].

It is obvious from the above discussion that each theoretical term in figure 1 is related either directly or indirectly to all the others. Thus if we take parole-as-text as the starting point, it is in direct relation to context of situation on the one hand and to langue on the other: it realises the former and instantiates the latter. Parole as text is related indirectly to society: the relationship is mediated via the category of context which in turn directly instantiates society and is constitutive of it; at the same time society itself is realised as langue, which is of course the resource for parole as text. The immediately following sections will attempt to foreground the centrality of the relationships between the four categories of figure 1 to a deeper understanding of the relationship between language and society.

2.2 Parole in context: the shaping of langue

The density of relationship between the various categories of figure 1 explains how human languages acquire those properties which enable the langue of the community to be used with efficacy as *parole* in a myriad social contexts in different socio-historical environments. The significance of the direct solidary relation of parole both to context of situation and to language system is that parole can never be dissociated from either of these categories – its presence implies the presence of both. Just as it is very difficult to banish parole from the description of langue, so also it is almost impossible to leave out context of situation from the description of parole – whenever this is done, something important about the nature of language as a whole is elided, thus damaging the integrity of the description.

Unlike the 1960s, today the term context is much used in linguistics, and a great deal is being written about it, both in SFL and in other models. Our interest in the category here is particularly from the point of view of the social activity of talk, which is one social activity amongst many. Examination of human activities as a whole suggests that the fundamental elements in the make up of their contexts may be listed under three heads: **A**ction type, including where the actants imagine their action to be 'heading'; **R**elation type, i.e., what are the relationships holding between those engaged in this action; and **C**ontact type i.e., how the interactants become engaged with each other apropos the said action. I coined the acronym 'ARC' for this 'logical structure' which underlies all human social activities (Hasan 2001) – the ARC as a whole must form the backbone of any social activity. For linguists interested in the regularities of parole, one interesting fact is that most human activities, though not all (Hasan 1999 for discussion), implicate parole; conversely parole often, but not always, occurs apropos some material action. Arguably, the best framework for the analysis of the relevant context of discourse which also fits the generalisations for all kinds of human activities is provided by systemic functional linguistics (SFL). The framework recognises three distinct but related vectors[16]: (i) the FIELD OF DISCOURSE, which concerns the nature of the social activity; (ii) the TENOR OF DISCOURSE, concerned with the social relation of the interactants engaged in that activity; and (iii) the MODE OF DISCOURSE, i.e., ways in which interactants come in contact in and for the performance of that activity (Halliday, McIntosh and Strevens 1964).

The justifications for recognising only these three parameters as the elements essential to the understanding of context of situation for discourse are obvious: first, it reflects the basic logical pattern for all social activity: engaging in acts of meaning is one kind of social activity; secondly, each of these vectors may be treated as a 'variable'; thus supposing field of discourse to be pedagogic, this may more delicately be described as presentation or revision, or evaluation, and so on; at the same time, one may need to specify the 'what' of presentation – this could be mathematics, or language arts, or history, and so on. What this means is that the description of each vector is extendable in delicacy (i.e., detail); the field of an activity may be analysed with greater or lesser specificity as the needs of the analysis demand. Each vector can be instantiated by a configuration of values pertaining to it; these values are systemically related to each other in a complex *either/or* and *both/and* relation, which can be represented paradigmatically in a system network (e.g. Hasan 1999). The vectors can thus 'cover' the details of all features of the social situation as required by the increasing depth of delicacy of the analysis[17]; for example, relation/tenor is a highly complex vector subsuming the various aspects relevant to the interactants' social identity e.g., gender, status, age, profession, and ideological stance. Finally, the third justification lies in the remarkable fact that faced with a displaced text, normal acculturated receivers are typically able to derive information precisely about these three vectors from the language of that text. In other words the language of the text encapsulates information precisely about the three vectors listed above – and this is not done by lexis alone. This fact is significant in reflecting both on context and on the system of language.

Context of situation is a 'large word'; it is not easy to specify how much of the materially sens-ible 'scenario' in which the social activity is situated is relevant to the interactants in the performance of the actions they are engaged in; nor are all of the features of the situation material in nature. Consider for example the relationship between the interactants: for some one looking from outside this is not information that can be gathered entirely sensuously though there are features such as sex, age, colour, mode of dressing, comportment that can be 'seen' and their social value as current in the society can be interpreted. But the heart of the information relevant to the relationship lies in the semiotic inter-action of the interactants: what kind of relationship is being negotiated now, at this moment – conflictual or cooperative, 'pulling status' or displaying parity, and so on. The guide to a perception of what will count as the relevant context in the case of discourse is ultimately in the interactants' parole – more specifically in the meanings being exchanged. Assuming that the text is a record of the sayings in the socially situated interaction, the kind of information that is invariably encapsulated in the text could reasonably be treated as construing that part of the social situation which has been treated by the interactants as relevant to the context of their discourse. If so, then in a very important sense, social context of discourse is largely a linguistically construed category. This would make sense because speakers are in the habit of being relevant; they 'cut their parole' to suit the perceived needs of the occasion of their talk. It follows that in their parole-as-text they will attend to various such values of the field, and/or of the tenor, and/or of the mode of discourse. This is what it means to say that *social contexts and parole as text are realisationally related*[18]: the perception of context activates the orders of relevance for the interactants and the text which represents their sayings on the occasion construes the relevant context of discourse for the receiver.

We treat it as established, then, that parole construes the context of situation for the receiver of the ongoing text – which it must, because that is quite obviously a necessary condition for continuing engagement in the 'same' discourse with an other for any duration of time. It follows that if we treat text as the largest semantic unit (cf. Halliday and Hasan 1976, and elsewhere) and proceed to analyse it from the point of view of how the textual meanings are made accessible to the text-receiver, we would establish those lexicogrammatical patterns which have played a part in their construal. An examination of this kind will lay bare the semantic and lexicogrammatical resources exploited by parole as text. And by the same token, the examination of a large corpus of discourses occurring in different types of social contexts would enable us to offer some idea of what kind of resource language is so that it is possible for it to be used successfully in meeting speakers' communicative needs. It is this line of argument that I believe underlies Halliday's schematic characterisation of language as resource in figure 2 (1973b: 353):

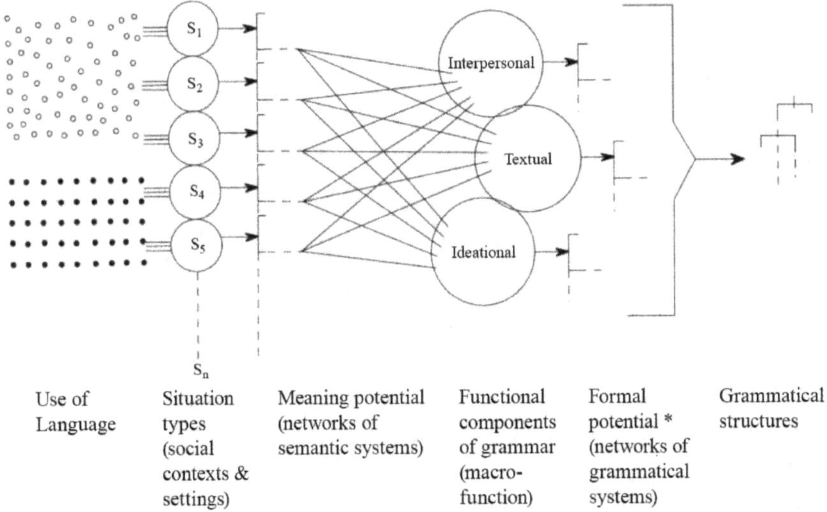

* i.e. meaning potential at the grammatical level, in the system-structure definition of 'meaning'

Figure 2: The evolution of metafunctional resources: from instance to system

The leftmost column in figure 2 presents the different kinds of uses of language in a variety of social contexts; these contexts are indicated in column two as S1 through to Sn. Column three indicates that when the many cases of different types of uses of language are examined, it turns out that despite the fact they belong to distinct types and distinct occasions of talk, they show similarity at a higher level of abstraction: each text 'has' the same three domains of meanings – meanings that relate to the same aspects of human social practice. This similarity is not in types of syntagmatic syntactic structures; rather it can be stated most easily in terms of kinds of meaning and wording. One such kind is relevant to the tenor, one to the mode and one to the field of discourse: which is simply a different way of saying that (i) field, tenor and mode are encapsulated in discourses of various types of meaning and wording, and (ii) that specific to each vector of context are meanings pertaining to certain spheres of human experience of participation in social practices of one kind or another. In column four, Halliday interprets this tripartite formation of worded meanings into specific classes of linguistic function: one class, called INTERPERSONAL, is concerned with tenor i.e.: these worded meanings form the means of negotiating human relations; a second, called TEXTUAL, is concerned with mode, i.e., its function is to realise the ways of discursively organising social practice – for example, were the interactants materially in contact, on this depends the choice between dialogue or monologue, and so on; and the third class of worded meanings, called IDEATIONAL, is concerned with field, i.e., those which construe the acts and their sequences that go into the make up of the activity. The meaning configurations become accessible to the listener only because they are 'coded' i.e., realised as lexicogrammar: no linguistic meaning without lexicogrammar; no lexicogrammar innocent of meaning. This implies that in some sense the lexicogrammar is also specialised: a set of lexicogrammatical patterns best suited to making interpersonal meaning, another to realising textual meaning and yet another for making ideational meanings accessible. However, if lexicogrammar is conceptualised as consisting of syntagmatic structures only, this tripartite organisation of the semantic-formal levels is obscured. What one needs is to see the organisation of language in a paradigmatic perspective, as made available for the level of lexicogrammar in current SFL grammars (Halliday and Matthiessen 2004; for semantics see enclosed CD and Hasan 1983). Halliday schematically presents the paradigmatic organisation of the formal system in column five of figure 2; and it is the options of these paradigmatically organised systems that are actualised as some syntagmatic structure as shown in the last column. This functional resonance creates a strong relation between the three upper strata of SFL theory, namely, social context, semantics and lexicogrammar. Halliday (1999: 274; emphasis original) has remarked:

> As I wrote myself many years ago, language is as it is because of what it does: which means because of what we do with it, in every aspect of our life. So a theory of language [use] in context is not just a theory of how people use language, important though that is. It is a theory about the *nature* and *evolution* of the system, explaining why the system works the way it does.

2.3 Parole in context: functionality in language

It is the kind of functional resonance depicted in figure 2, which has formed the basis for the recognition of linguistic functionality in SFL (e.g., Halliday 1970, 1979a, and elsewhere). The functionality of language forms another constant theme in Halliday's writing, namely that the structure of langue is as it is because the instantiating parole participates in varied social contexts. Parole is able to satisfy the community's needs because thanks to its own participation in the evolution of langue, the latter is inherently functional.

The concept of 'function' when used in SFL with reference to the system of language as a whole is critically different from the concept of 'function' as applied to a speech act such as promising, ordering, etc., or as applied to isolated utterances a la Bühler (1934) for the classification of children's utterances as referential, conative or expressive. SFL uses the term 'metafunction' to distinguish functions of langue system from the 'function' of an utterance. The SFL metafunctions are well known; here a brief word about the three metafunctions to refresh the memory:

(i) IDEATIONAL whereby each language is a resource for construing its speakers' experiences of the world: the meanings and wordings pertaining to this metafunction are critical for construing the nature of the field of discourse; its realisation in language takes the form of systems e.g., those of transitivity, of tense, signification/reference as described in lexis as delicate grammar (Hasan 1985d, 1987a; Tucker 1998), systems of expansion and projection (Halliday and Matthiessen 2004);

(ii) INTERPERSONAL which provides resources for creating, maintaining and changing human relations: it is primarily relevant to the complex construal of tenor of discourse, and its realisation at the lexicogrammatical level takes the form of such systems as those of mood, modality, modulation (Halliday 1994), and so on; and finally

(iii) TEXTUAL which consists in the linguistic resources that enable the weaving of the relevant meanings into an intelligible coherent discourse, while construing information about the mode of discourse such as cohesion, information focus (Halliday 1994).

Bühler thought of functions as operating one at a time; further, his functions were hierarchically ordered, with the referential as the most important. The metafunctions in SFL are not hierarchised; they have equal status, and each is manifested in every act of language use: in fact, an important task for grammatics is to describe how the three metafunctions are woven together into the same linguistic unit.

In linguistics, it is fairly common to view language as active in society: it does something for society. What the above discussion indicates is that society too is active in shaping human language. This reciprocity between the two is, in fact, the essence of linguistic functionality. There exists a view of the notion of functionalism according to which every single unit of language must individually show a cultural significance – if not, then the whole concept of linguistic functionality crumbles! I suggest that the functionalism of language truly resides in revealing a dialectic between society and language system: the system possesses a meaning potential which enables parole to be active in social life, and as the discussion based on figure 2 above indicates the potential itself has taken a specific shape in the system of language due to the traces of human social practice in which parole has intervened. This is relevant to our investigation of the relationship between language and society: first, such a relationship could not reasonably be seen as accidental; we owe the amazing efficacy of language in use to the metafunctional resonance across social context, semantics and lexicogrammar; it is the functional calibration of these that creates the potential; and it is this potential that forms the bench mark for parole working in social contexts. Secondly, the relationship between language and society is not limited to 'speech' and 'its social context'; it goes beyond parole to langue: it actually shapes the langue as resource. In displaying its ability to satisfy its speakers, one thing that parole is doing is bringing back to bear on the social practice what it took from that practice to the language system. But how does parole eventually renew langue? This is where we need to return to parole and socio-historical changes in discourse.

2.4 Parole in context: socio-historically changing discourse

First, let me take a brief look at language change and discursive change side by side, because the two are closely and logically related, but they are also remarkably different. It is obvious that change in discourse subsumes change in language: after all nothing enters into the language system except through the speaking activities of speakers – and that means through the discourses that speakers produce. Thus, logically, discourse is the site both for the actuation and the transmission of language change; but, in practice, consideration of discourse hardly plays any part in the historical study of that change. The one universally undisputed fact about change in the system of language is that it does actually happen. And despite extensive studies, the explanation of change in language probably remains the single most problematic issue, variation theory notwithstanding.

When it comes to socio-historical change in discourse, like language change, it too is readily recognised in a manner of speaking, but to the best of my knowledge no one has systematically examined the phenomenon of discursive change: there exists no branch of diachronic discourse study, though there are sporadic accounts such as the history of some corner of science (Halliday and Martin 1993; Halliday 2004a; Kappagoda 2005). Not surprisingly change in discourse is not a well understood phenomenon; for example, when sometimes we talk about a 'modernised Chaucer', we might mean no more by that description than that the orthography has been modernised, and maybe a glossary of the lexical items is appended. The fact is that at least two aspects of change in discourse take us well beyond change in language: both apply to whole discourse, and neither can be investigated by any methodology employed today in the study of language change. One of these aspects has to do with change in the over-all 'tone' of the discourse, and the other, with what is known as generic structure. For example, when Klemperer (2005) talks about The Language of the Third Reich, although he too proceeds by discussing specific items, his choice of the items is guided by some principle of 'semantic consistency' which is what underlies the 'Nazi tone' as he perceives it. The tone we know as Victorian piety cannot be characterised by a collection of lexical items and/or a set of syntactic structures. As for changes in discursive form, this becomes obvious from a comparison of changes over the last fifty years in various discourse types from personal letters to formal funding applications. Changes of discursive 'tone' and 'generic structure' and possibly other phenomena which happen to pertain to whole texts and whole text types are sometime subsumed under that 'catch-all' term 'style' – a descriptive term that appears deceptively easy to use but has persistently defied clear characterisation (see for example a recent account presented by Schilling-Estes 2002b).

When it comes to the explanation of discursive change, it seems to be quite easy: most people asked why change in discourse comes about, would answer almost without hesitation: 'because society/culture changes'. And our discussion of the relationship between social context and text (section 2.1–2.2) might encourage the belief in the correctness of the answer, one (less than careful) reading of which could be that to say that society changes is to say that (some) contexts change; to say that (some) contexts change is to say that the discourses relevant to those contexts change. The problem I perceive in such a response is not in the mention of society/culture as implicated in discursive change, but in the 'causal linearity' implied by 'because', whereby first society changes and then discursive change follows suit. Our account of the relations of society context and parole has not been causal; it has been presented as forged by instantiation (society and context) and/or realisation (context and text). Neither of these relations inserts 'time' between the two processes; they simply argue their reciprocity. The conception of discourse changing a step behind social change is simply not realistic. Take for example the invention of weapons of mass destruction: there have been perhaps very few events that have changed human societies quite as much as the invention of the atom bomb which was dropped on Hiroshima. Clearly it would be absurd to maintain that during the invention stage, the content and form of discourse stayed in its 'pre-bomb' state, that first the bomb got invented and then the discourse changed.

Our experience of how things work in language as it functions in real life runs counter to such linear explanations: we know – or at least we *ought* to know – that everywhere, at every stage of human history, preachers and politicians have persuaded, and are persuading, their listeners *purely through discourse* to support some line of action which is designed to bring change in society. Obviously such preaching has to precede the social action and its outcome. This makes nonsense of the linear causal explanation. To insist on such causal linearity is to underestimate the power of language in shaping human beings and their universe. The view also poses the unrealistic problem of deciding for each social change the actual point of its onset and completion, which is no less easy to determine than the boundaries of *états de langue* are. It challenges the social subjects' authentic experience of what engaging in parole as text is really like: The fact is that more often than not speakers go on producing discourse almost unaware of aspects of social changes. And this is not a fanciful claim. After all, we do not have any record of English speakers going about 'gob-smacked', as today's popular metaphor would put it, over the long decades when the social institution of marriage was undergoing changes, bringing with it today's wide recognition of *de facto* 'partnership', gay marriage, and instead of 'spouse' the use of the politically correct expression 'marriage partner'. There was no moment in our social-linguistic life when the corporate business revolution, still surging ahead as I write, left us speechless, incapable of describing, furthering or critiquing its variety of 'compassionate capitalism'[19]. Klemperer (1975) was recording the language of the Third Reich even as Germany was developing the Nazi agenda.

What this line of reasoning suggests is that the view of discourse running a step behind the social/cultural change is mistaken. Human society, just like human language, is subject to on-going change. And if we agree with Halliday that there exists a realisational relationship between language and society as shown in figure 1, and that realisational bonds are solidary, then it would follow that the change in language and society is reciprocal. In other words, the relationship between the two is more than skin-deep; it is in fact *dia*-logical: this is another way of saying that their development is guided by a *cogenetic logic*[20]. We know no living language that has existed outside society; and certainly the whole structure of human societies would be fundamentally different in the absence of the participation of human language in social life. The social agent as an interactant does not come to a context without resources; and we have seen above in following up the implications of figure 2, that the resource language offers its speakers is itself founded upon the participation of parole in social life: nothing enters the system of language – the *langue* – except through the working of parole in meeting the realisational demands in the construal of meanings relevant to some context of situation, and what happens in parole is relevant to the evolution of the resources of language system. To the extent that the interactants have active experience of participation in discourse types, and familiarity with the language they propose to use, the scene for interaction is actually set in their favour.

There are of course occasions when social context as instance of constantly changing society might present a face to parole which puts the interactant under semantic pressure, thus in some sense leading to a semiotic struggle in the construal of meaning. Such struggle is perhaps more clearly visible in the communicative patterns of very young children learning their mother tongue: this is so because much of the complex network of regularities built into their mother tongue is not yet accessible to them: children have more work to do to get their meaning across – and even then in early years their communicative success depends much on the cooperation of their meaning group. For the adult using language, the support from the existing system is in direct proportion to how much of the principles governing its dense relationships is internalised, so that its elements have become 'second nature'. The challenge of semantic pressure which changing contexts present to speakers is not necessarily met by 'innovation' i.e., the creation of new lexical items: it may involve semantic shift as in the meaning of 'free' created through the contemporary use of the expression 'free trade' (Hasan 2003); it may involve variation on structural patterns; it may even involve a play on orthography. Renewal of the system has thus many manifestations as historical linguistics so well documents. With discursive change, there is, however, one aspect which neither currently recognised methodologies in Labovian sociolinguistics, nor those in diachronic language change offer any means of analysing. This phenomenon, to which I have referred above as 'discursive tone', is in fact the manifestation of the changing ideology in the speech community. Its analysis appears most amenable in terms of semantic variation (for examples of such analysis, see the chapters of this volume).

2.5 The dialogism of language and society

With the above discussion we have traveled far. We began with language use for social communication as the only link between language and society (section 1.2). Other than this, society had nothing to do with the nature of language, nor had language any bearing on the nature of society – the two simply came together, albeit very frequently, in speech in its social context. But if the language system changes along with the changing society and it is the changes in language use/*parole* that insert themselves into *langue*, becoming a part of it, then something is very wrong with our original model. The idea that the relationship of language and society is accidental with speech skimming on the surface of society loses credibility. Certainly speech/parole is the key to understanding how language is able to satisfy the communicative needs of its speakers. And speech is undoubtedly the locus of the many on-going patterns of variation in language. But to be able to study these phenomena satisfactorily, the value of speech/parole itself has to be understood.

In elaborating the messages of figures 1 and 2 in the above sections, I have attempted to show that the first steps in this enterprise are to understand the nature of the arena where parole works and to examine how parole manages to continue working effectively. An attempt to do just this has brought us face to face with language system and society. Halliday offers an interpretation of langue/system and parole/instance which removes the most fundamental source of contradiction in Saussure's text. For decades linguistics has reified 'the' system of language to the extent that it has seemed to exist independent of the users of that system. Certainly langue is not the property of any single individual, but to the extent that communities are constituted of individuals[21], individuals are central to the evolution of langue. Seeing langue/parole from the SFL point of view leads us to revise the popular view of language system as a homogenous, synoptic object; it turns out that this 'homogeneous synoptic system' is simply a different view of a 'variable and varying dynamic process': language is – to use Lemke's expression (1984) – an open dynamic system. By showing the centrality of the social in the here and now of speaking, and by seeing langue and parole as the same phenomenon, though viewed from different perspectives for purposes of analysis, Halliday has offered a means of exploring the mutual interaction of society and language as it functions in the life of the community. The explorations of the relations of instantiation and realisation which link society, context, text, and language lead to an understanding of the foundation of linguistic metafunctionality. It becomes quite obvious that there is nothing accidental about the relationship of language and society, that the relation is in fact inalienable; and one that concerns language both as system and as process.

At the same time, judging from what we know today about the evolution of the human race, our species has never known language outside society or society outside the reach of language: the developmental stages of both language system and social system have steadily revealed a pattern of cogenetic evolution (Dunbar 1996, 2003; Marwick 2005). By demonstrating the role of the realisational relation between context and text in the genesis of metafunctions, and the role of metafunctions in foregrounding the intimate relation between system and instance, Halliday negates the possibility of doing a viable explanation of any aspect of language – be it syntax or lexicon, discourse or speech acts – without placing language in its social environment. From this point of view autonomous linguistics is inevitably destined for correction, as is also Bourdieu's 'external linguistics' (Hasan 1998). A linguistic theory that fails to account for the nature of language, will also fail in modelling the relationship of language to anything that intimately concerns its speakers: society is one such concern and the making of human mind is another. Of course it still remains to be demonstrated that a correct modelling of the relationship between society and the system and process of language will help bring about a sense of integration to the many strands of sociolinguistics. How can we specify the object of study for an 'integrated sociolinguistics' of this kind? What would its organisation look like? These are the issues I will attempt to address in the next section.

3 An integrated sociolinguistics

The object of study for today's sociolinguistics is variation in the Labovian sense of the term. This was not always the case (for some discussion, chapters 5, 7 and 9 of this volume). In the 1960s when this paradigm had first burst upon the linguistic scene as a breath of fresh air[22], it seemed for a moment that the discipline of linguistics itself was poised to free itself from arbitrary restrictions. However, the scene changed quickly: the orientation of the field altered almost before the 'socio-' had a chance to be taken seriously; instead of concerning itself with the study of language in its social context, which was what it announced to be the aim of sociolinguistics, it has steadily become the study of the significance of synchronic variation for diachronic change in language. Thus the very first sentence of a fairly recent and prestigious publication tells us that 'the core of the sociolinguistic enterprise' is 'the study of language variation and change' (Chambers, Trudgill and Schilling-Estes 2002: 1): the rest is a tangle of other strands, tolerated but not considered significant as sociolinguistics.

Treating 'the study of language change in its social context' (Labov 1972a: 60) as the 'core' of sociolinguistics does leave room for other strands, but it itself has no means of linking these strands to each other. And yet the undeniable fact remains that neither is all language change rooted in variation, especially as variation is understood in variationist theory (for an interesting discussion see McMahon 1994, especially chapter 9), nor can the study of language in its social context be reduced to the single question of explaining diachronic change by reference to patterns of today's variation; so the rationale for making it the 'core' of the so-called *socio*-linguistics is not at all obvious. This is not to deny that diachronic change calls for explanation; nor to doubt the value of the concept of 'variation' as practiced in Labovian sociolinguistics; nor even to deny that in the last resort all/most language change may be 'explained' as social, especially if the social remains an un-theorised, catch-all term. It is simply to say that the object of study for an *integrated* sociolinguistics cannot be as specific, and as narrowly limited as Chambers et al. (2002) ascribe to Labovian sociolinguistics. Clearly, the more limited and specific the 'definition' of a discipline, the more excluding it will become; and more often than not, the excluded has a way of importing chaos into the neat little world built around a narrow concept. So it comes to pass that ironically today's sociolinguistics is more like a strand in some larger discipline – an integrated sociolinguistics, perhaps? – which would have the capacity of showing how the circumscribed area of 'variation theory' can be linked to other areas concerned with the study of speech in its social context. Change in language is simply a by-product of such speech; it is not an independent force; nor is it the measure of the importance of speech in the life of the speaker.

If what we are aspiring to achieve is to create an integrated sociolinguistics, then we must begin by explicitly acknowledging the basis for this integration: in my opinion that basis lies in the reciprocity of language and society. It is the acceptance of this fundamental principle that will allow us to conceptualise sociolinguistics as a field of enquiry whose aim it is to examine the various aspects of the dialogue between society and language. The object of enquiry for such a field has to be the examination of the working of both 'society in language' and 'language in society' in order to explain how they mutually maintain and change each other. This might sound too amorphous an aim for those who like their theories simple, and their goals limited. But if theories with the virtue of simplicity have consistently failed to deliver even those limited goals in a coherent manner, and if we continue to perceive relationships which simple theories are unable to account for, then I fear we have very little choice: we will need to develop a theory which reflects the complexity of the phenomenon, allowing consideration of its diverse aspects in their complexity. Hill (1985: 1) quotes Paul Friedrich (1980: 120) who is worried that such a proliferation 'raises the heretical speculation that "language" (like "culture") is an obsolete folk category, no more appropriate as a "field of enquiry" than is "nature"'. The implicit warning should not be ignored, but instead of abandoning the project it is important to ask whether this undesirable eventuality can possibly be forestalled. Throughout section 2, I have attempted to show that a theorisation of 'taken for granted facts' tends to clarify the picture. It places a grid on a kaleidoscopic scene – even as language does on 'reality' – offering principles which help identify order in seeming chaos. We have theorised speech/parole, social context and other relevant categories in the previous sections. It is worth asking whether by making use of such theoretical categories as have been presented above, it might be possible to organise as a scholarly field that large area I have described above as the study of 'language in society and of society in language'. In the following sub-sections I will attempt to examine the feasibility of this enterprise.

3.1 Parole in context: (i) speaker as social agent

Since it is speech in its social context where sociolinguistics finds its data, it might be reasonable to use social context for placing a grid on the dialogue between language and society. Speech in social context is where their mutual interdependence plays out its entire course. The three vectors of context represent readymade categories which can be used to impose order on the vast area of language-society relationship. The examination of each vector is expected to reveal the diverse ways in which language and society function dialogically; and it is reasonable to suggest that such an examination will not only enable us to predict what the concerns of an integrated sociolinguistics are, but also act as the basis for arguing their inherent interconnectedness. The solution has the merit of avoiding the current situation where each concern is viewed as a 'strand', making current sociolinguistics a wilderness of concerns, where the concerns are without any concern for one another.

I would like to begin this exploration with tenor, which concerns interactant relationships of one kind or another. It has perhaps the greatest significance for sociolinguistics: the interactants are, in a very real sense, iconic of the intimate relationship of language and society in that they are at once social agents and semiotic beings. And above all they constitute the most active element of the social situation. 'Context', as I said above, is a large word: just as its boundaries do not manifest a definite shape without discourse, so also the details of the social practice associated with some context are not inscribed in its material aspects[23]. It is the speaker as a social agent who alone has the capacity to recognise the particular kind of social practice called for by the occasion.

Thus the interactants represent the only element of context to which can be attributed consciousness, the capacity to judge, plan and decide – attributes which presuppose the existence of belief systems and which are relevant to the evaluation of the ongoing activity. These observations about interactants would probably be widely accepted, but there may be less agreement on the nature and ontogenesis of consciousness, on the origins of beliefs and desires and on the formation of ability to judge. Interactants represent that awesome category called 'individual' – and for all its currency in the discourse of social sciences, the popular meaning of the term is surrounded with contradictions. An important questions is: do forms of individuality vary with varying social and semiotic experience?

Saussure described acts of parole as essentially 'willful and intellectual'. This may be so, but experience tells us that in natural language use, deliberation on each element of the saying is an exception rather than a rule. So the question is what will any one 'will' naturally and what saying will present itself to their intellect as normal. Nor can it be claimed that the ability to make use of language is a sufficient condition for engaging in speech. Whorf's 'fashions of speaking', Bourdieu's *habitus* or Bernstein's 'coding orientation' do not refer to a form of premeditated behaviour. A speaker's sayings are not activated from within language, but by the speaker's understanding of what saying the occasion calls for. In the end, the reason why anyone says anything lies in who they are as social beings; this is what guides their recognition of the context and their view of what saying is relevant in that context.

Where do such understandings come from? What naturalises fashions of speaking, so that they may be manifested over a range of different contexts? I doubt if these things are innate. It seems rather that the answer has to be what Bernstein called (e.g., 1990: 13) 'social positioning' – a term that subsumes social class as well as its far reaching consequences for social agents, such as their family, friends, social network, range of expertise, belief systems, and experience of living with others. Social positioning is clearly not something that can be shaken off; one is always positioned in some particular way *vis-à-vis* one's society. In so far as experience is the maker of mind, creating pathways of belief and conviction, the precursors to making judgment and decision, a social agent's individuality and identity is moored in the experiences that their social positioning – itself liable to change – makes accessible. There is thus a logical continuity from a social subject's identity to their social positioning to their ideological orientation to their ways of being, doing and saying – which is what Bernstein's 'coding orientation' was attempting to articulate. We thus have a rich array of questions each of which is of interest to the major concerns of an integrated sociolinguistics. Below I enumerate some of these, using speaker in context as the starting point:

- What are the bases of context recognition and of the formation of judgments regarding what social practice is called for where?
- Given in some sense the same occasion of talk, does the recognition of context or ideas about social practice in that context vary across the society? If so, what does the variation correlate with?
- What variation is found in ways of saying in families, neighbourhood and workplace? What does such variation correlate with?
- What part, if any, does social positioning play in the formation of a social subject's identity?
- How are individuals' belief systems created? How and why do they change? Is there any variation in belief systems across the various segments of a society? Where are these lines drawn, and what is responsible for the drawing of these lines?
- How are social identities forged? What part does language play in it? How do established identities change? What is the difference between social identity and 'face' in Goffman's sense of the word?
- What part does language play in creating, maintaining and changing relationships in family, neighbourhood, and other institutional environments e.g. school, work place, and so on? What are the bases of social network?
- What are the ways in which interactant relationship is negotiated between strangers in the course of carrying out social activities? Do these ways display any variation? How, when, and where?
- What is the importance of managing social distance in the negotiation of interactant relation? What part does language play in this enterprise?
- How are age, status and gender relationships enacted, maintained and changed?
- How does language support hierarchisation, evaluation and presentation of social agents? What part is played in this by the speaker's ways of using language? On what basis are accent, 'grammar' and semantic orientation evaluated?

3.3 Parole in context: (ii) social action

Although social action is something that is brought about by the interactant, it constitutes the point of the activity as a whole. It is to do something that interactants come together and establish a mode of contact. It is immaterial that the idea of what is to be done may not be clear in all its details, that in fact the action may be layered (e.g. playing with the child to make the child happy), that its long term character might be quite different from what the interactants thought it would be (e.g. just chatting with the neighbour might become a source of new and unexpected information). Just as there is a great deal of oversimplification in maintaining that saying is a voluntary act by an individual, so also there is a problem in assuming that 'any one can do anything'. The privilege of participating in various kinds of activity is not equally distributed across any society: who the interactant is makes a difference, but equally it is precisely the activities in which a person can engage that leads to the definition of who that interactant is. Below are some of the issues that an integrated sociolinguistics would need to concern itself with:

- What social activities depend entirely on language for their realisation? What linguistic resources does such realisation demand? What segment of the society exploits which resources most frequently?
- What are the bases for the privilege of participation in the various kinds of activities? How are those interactant attributes acquired which 'qualify' for such participation?
- What human actions do not depend on the participation of language? What role does language play, if used, in the course of such practices?
- Given that the details of social practice are variable within the 'same' material situational setting, how do we account for this variation?
- How do social agents acquire the understandings essential to participation in social activities, especially given that they manifest variant details in realisation?
- What activities are specialised by gender, education, and/or socio-economic status and what kind of linguistic resources does their performance demand? How are these resources distributed to the various segments of a society?

- How are the stages of an activity defined, especially in activities whose realisation depends wholly on language with or without help from other visual semiotic systems?
- What part do accent, grammar and semantics play in the realisation of activities?
- What principles are there for the classification of social activities? Are the activity types hierarchised? On what basis?
- What relationship is there between social institutions and the social practices that are specific to each institution? What part do social practices play in maintaining and developing these institutions?
- What if any is the role of activities in the maintenance and development of society?
- Is participation in social practices relevant to the formation of individuality/personality? Do all social practices have this role or only some? How do they differ?

3.4 Parole in context: (iii) modes of contact

Contact specifies how the interactants come together in and for the performance of the activity. Although contact has a material manifestation, it is its semiotic value that is most relevant for our purposes. Thus co-presence may be thought of as a material phenomenon, but seen as a material phenomenon only, it is not relevant to what goes on in language. At any one point on the shop floor many social agents are materially co-present, but it is the recognition of co-presence by the interactants that is decisive. This as Goffman (1983) pointed out many years ago is what shows that they are attending to each other, that their mutual attention has been 'requisitioned'. Along with this come other sociolinguistic issues. To enumerate a few

- Who acknowledges whose presence where and with what kind of language use?
- How do the possibilities of contact between interactants differ according to whether they are specialised or non-specialised and ritualised or extempore? What are the bases of these differences? How are the differences realised linguistically?
- How have modes of contact changed with changing media technology? How has this impacted on the system of language?

- Under what condition does acknowledged co-presence produce the possibility of dialogue?
- On what basis can dialogue be classified? How do dialogues differ according to activity and/or interactant relation?
- Is there systematic variation in modes of managing the activity across distinct subsections of the society? If yes, what are the details of this variation so far as language is concerned? How does it relate to the enactment of interactant relation?

3.5 The concerns of an integrated sociolinguistics

The issues presented above by reference to relevant elements of the social context – field, mode and tenor – read cursorily, might appear at once too many and too few. They may seem too many because they cover a vast area, and too few because they miss out some important ones. It certainly is true that they cover a vast area. Thus consider under mode the questions concerning dialogue: these questions potentially cover a huge span, allowing the possibility of studying today's chat room dialogues, video link discussions, the as-if dialogues in literary fiction, dialogues with an addressee in absentia through writing and those most primitive of all conversations, namely, mother-infant dialogues (e.g., Halliday 1975b; Trevarthen 1974). Instead of restricting the concerns of sociolinguistics, this mode of identifying the issues actually points to further scholarly fields of enquiry, for example, in what respect are these 'dialogues' alike and how do they differ? If the current theories about the making of human minds are correct, what does variation in the active experience of dialogue mean for variation in forms of human consciousness? Or how might we characterise the segments of a society according to their access to any/all of these modes of contact? Each such issue can be studied in greater or lesser detail, depending on the local aim of that study, but one thing this way of introducing the topics in sociolinguistics ensures is the inclusion of all within the same banner on the basis of a principle that points explicitly to their relationship. I do not see the opening up of such a wide range of enquiries as an undesirable proliferation that obfuscates the scholarly analysis of the relationship of language and society; or turns the enterprise of sociolinguistics into an 'obsolete folk category', which is 'no more appropriate as a field of enquiry'. Instead, it seems to me that the issues indicated above and others implied by them would safeguard against the arbitrary limitation of the object of enquiry in a sociolinguistics that aims to be integrated. The integration of the field is based on the interdependence of two very complex systems – the social and the semiotic; the field is thus inherently complex and the issues mentioned above will form part of a comprehensive investigation of this inherently complex field. The issues, whether stated explicitly or simply implied, may be many, but this is not necessarily a handicap. Given the firm basis of their mutual relationship, their large number and wide scope are actually an asset, pointing to the vastness of the field and the complex relationships within it. It would indeed be quite amazing if an integrated sociolinguistics turned out to be the study of a narrow set of areas.

Do the issues mentioned by reference to the vectors of context exhaustively describe the concerns of integrated sociolinguistics? What is presented here does not necessarily observe the 'fashions of speaking' current in the dominant field; so it fails to mention terms in favour in today's sociolinguistics. For example, the above account has not foregrounded terms such as style, ideology, accommodation, politeness, face, speech variety, social class, SES, and a host of others. But reflection on the issues that have been mentioned will show that each of these concepts will in some way come in for investigation. I have presented the possible concerns of the field as a series of questions; my expectation is that the search for their answers will bring the investigator face to face with the areas referred to by these favoured term. This was partly demonstrated by reference to 'dialogue' in the last paragraph. Or we may take the concept 'style', much discussed in current sociolinguistics, but scarcely mentioned directly in the above questions. The point to be noted is that a careful examination of a questions about variation in 'the recognition of context' or in the 'ideas about social practice' in context would definitely make connection with the concept of style. Take, for example, a context of seeking and giving information (realised semantically as questioning and answering). If across a number of speakers, all else is held equal in the context of discourse except the tenor relation between the interactants, and if in this situation we find that the ways of questioning and answering vary across the speakers such that one group of speakers prefers to question in the negative (*didn't you ask dad?*) while the other questions positively (*did you ask dad?*), and that there exists evidence of robust variation which regularly correlates with the groups' social positioning, we might come to the finding that variation is not only a matter of expression but can extend to content and that (contra Schilling-Estes 2002a) 'group style' is a notion worthy of further examination. Certainly the results discussed in the many following chapters of this volume do fit this description. In short, the limit on the number of questions we can raise with regard to any element of an issue mentioned here is set by how that element actually works in language and/or society. In fact finding variation in ways of speaking simply opens up many questions: Why is style variation important in the life of the individual or in the life of the language under study? What aspect of language-society relationship does style primarily pertain to and what is its scope? The advantage of approaching popular terms e.g. 'stylistic variation' in this manner is that the theoretical place of the term and its realisational nature – how it is manifested in the actual data – are likely to be made far more explicit than they are today. One might venture to add that even the concerns of today's sociolinguistics with synchronic variation might become subsumed within an integrated sociolinguistics; and by being integrated, synchronic variation might find its true location *vis-à-vis* the other relevant areas of enquiry into the working of language and society. This is exactly what an integrated sociolinguistics had set out to achieve.

I am not claiming that every single relevant problem of integrated sociolinguistics has been either explicitly or implicitly presented here. The only general claim I am making is that it might prove a better strategy to treat integrated sociolinguistics as problem centred, with the problems themselves identified by how they relate to the living of life in community – to the logical form of its social practices. What makes a problem specifically sociolinguistic is its significance to some aspect of the semiotic interactions between the members of the community and to their life in society.

4 Concluding remarks: optimal theories for integrated sociolinguistics

This chapter began with an acknowledgment of the need for an integrated sociolinguistics. This led to a close examination of the relationship of language and society. The results of that investigation led to the conclusion that language does not just *happen* to be useful for communication – certainly the usefulness of language is a fact, but if this fairly obvious fact is probed, it turns out that this is not due to chance. The relationship between language and society is in fact inherent so that neither can be ignored without detriment in the study of the other: the social and the semiotic systems are cogenetic in nature. Language is as it is because of the functions it serves when used for the living of life in society, and human societies are as they are because in their creation and maintenance language plays a crucial part. The dialectic between the two furnishes an objective basis for recognising a field of language study which might be reasonably expected to possess the potential of becoming 'an integrated sociolinguistics'. The scope of this kind of sociolinguistics has been discussed in some detail in the sections 3–3.5.

At this point there arises a question whether as a field of study, integrated sociolinguistics must possess an over-arching methodology in the way that Labovian sociolinguistics presents 'variation theory' as a standard for deciding what can be considered as true sociolinguistic data: according to this principle, whatever cannot be analysed under the rubric of 'variation theory' is to be treated as sitting at the periphery of 'sociolinguistics proper'. However, it is important to note that the so-called 'variation theory' is in fact better described as a METHODOLOGY for analysis rather than as a THEORY of sociolinguistics on the basis of which the analyses in the field are carried out. The fact is that theoretical clarity is not an attribute which can be readily ascribed to today's sociolinguistics (for some discussion of this point, see my comments on 'variation', 'variant', 'variable' etc. in the following chapters). In any research, it is the theory that models the object of enquiry; this produces a viable hypothesis about the nature and scope of the data; and it is the nature of the data and the aim of analysis that determine the desirable methodology for analysis. In light of these observations, trying to work out an over-arching methodology for integrated sociolinguistics would appear to be something like putting the cart before the horse. In contrast to Labovian sociolinguistics, the scholarly field of INTEGRATED sociolinguistics as outlined here has not been arbitrarily limited, nor has its scope been defined by the methodology currently available to or preferred by some scholar. Its central object of enquiry has been announced on explicit grounds, a range of problems has been identified as the concern of the field, and the vast scope of these has been predicated upon the kind of relationship between society and language. It is certain that in the probing of these problems actual analysis of linguistic data – and most probably some of the social phenomena – will be called for. We now need to ask where will the methodology for such analysis come from? A good answer to this question can be provided only if that relationship of reciprocity between society and language is taken into account which has resulted in indicating the kind of problems such sociolinguistics will be concerned with. If, as suggested here, we think of this relationship as dialogical whereby the two are implicated in cogenetic evolution, this will carry strong implications for some optimal theory, which can be used as the resource for the exploration of problems of the kind raised above. With reference to this, I would first like to make a general observation, following which I will proceed to a more detailed discussion of the kind of linguistic theory that in my view would be optimal for an integrated sociolinguistics.

One general principle to be observed in probing the specific problems in an integrated sociolinguistics of the kind suggested in this chapter is that both the social and the semiotic must be simultaneously present to the mind of the researcher. And there exist many theories of each of these fields, especially if for 'the semiotic' we read 'the linguistic'. These fields are relevant to an integrated sociolinguistics for it is here that the researcher might find methodologies of description that have either already proved successful or that suggest further possibilities of developing a suitable framework of analysis. However, amongst these theories, there will be some in both domains that either ignore the other domain or by the logic of the syntax of their theory prohibit the acceptance of what has been presented here as the central object of study for integrated sociolinguistics. For example, the sociologist Giddens, almost completely ignores the role of language in the formation or maintenance of society, whereas Bourdieu actively suggests that everything significant in human life is social, and that language brings nothing to the social (Hasan 1998 for critique). This limits their usefulness to doing a viable sociolinguistics. Similarly, the use of those linguistic theories which treat language either as autonomous or as a purely biological phenomenon like the working of the digestive system would be clearly in contradiction to the characterisation of the relationship between language and society on which integrated sociolinguistics rests: to such theories, the shaping of the system, i.e., langue through speech, i.e., parole would most probably be unacceptable. This leads us to anther reason why integrated sociolinguistics must pay attention to those theories of the social and the linguistic which acknowledge mutual relevance: the issues that have been flagged in section 3 will call for the description of aspects of language as well as those of society. Ready made methodologies useful for conducting such analysis can be provided from within sociology and linguistics, as relevant. Clearly, theories acknowledging mutual relevance would be in tune with the central aim of integrated sociolinguistics. One such candidate theory of the social would be the Bernsteinian one. This is not to maintain that Bernstein's theory is either complete or perfect but that it can form a starting point that will be profitable, since Bernstein has a view of society in which social practice, including that of talk, is constitutive of the nature of society. At the same time, integrated sociolinguistics needs in its foundation a theory of the semiotic, especially that of language, which foregrounds the importance of the social in the life of a language. One such theory would be SFL. Again this is not to say that SFL currently addresses all issues such as outlined above. In fact for a theory that introduces itself as a social semiotic one, it is woefully neglectful of specifically sociolinguistic issues; its only substantial contribution is in the field of discourse analysis where it offers a framework for the analysis of social context as well as for that of discourse. However, in both cases, the emphasis is classificatory and concerned with the description of linguistic phenomena rather than sociolinguistic ones; the social enters only somewhat superficially, especially in the description of the vectors of context, making no reference to any sociological framework, and often confusing the description of a phenomenon with its production. But with all their shortcomings such theories will have an advantage over those failing to acknowledge mutual relevance: they will not be in contradiction to the aims of the theory of integrated sociolinguistics, and will often provide suggestions regarding the methodologies suited to the study of problems in the field.

It is clear from the above that the acceptance of a cogenetic relation between language and society has implications for the kind of linguistic theory that is optimally suited for use in integrated sociolinguistics. Such theories will be exotropic (Hasan 2005): they will locate language in the social environment which is the only site for actually witnessing acts of language, where its use makes a difference, and where as a system it is able to evolve. An exotropic theory of language, such as SFL will possess certain features which will facilitate the pursuit of sociolinguistic studies. Tracing the development of the debate in this chapter about the relationship of the social and the linguistic, we note the usefulness of the following concepts:

- Parole as the instantiation of langue;
- Parole as an integral part of the linguistic theory;
- The dynamic nature of the linguistic system; its continued change and renewal by the working of parole in social context;
- The instantiation of society as context of situation;
- The realisational relation of language and society, and of text and context;
- The inherent relationship of language and society;
- Explicit theorisation of strata in language and in linguistics;
- The theoretical concepts of realisation and instantiation;
- The metafunctional nature of language; metafunctional resonance across context, meaning and lexicogrammar;
- The paradigmatic organisation of language with syntagmatic structure as its actualisation;
- The concept of delicacy of description;
- Framework for the analysis of context;
- Framework for the analysis of texture and structure in discourse.

The usefulness of these features in modelling the relationship between language and society and in imposing order on the concerns of this vast and complex field has already been demonstrated in this chapter. The various chapters of this book indicate how these and other design features of a functional model such as SFL prove useful in describing certain novel sociolinguistic patterns. There is no doubt that the nature of the sociolinguistic data will lead to the invention of methodologies which will be specific only to this field, but the adoption of a linguistics that in its design does not militate against the aims of an integrated sociolinguistics will make the task easier, and free of contradictions.

Notes

1 This chapter is based on one section of a course on sociolinguistics that I taught at a Summer Institute at Odense University (Denmark) in June 1999. The content of that course fragment has been further elaborated, specifically with this volume in mind. References will be made to some of the other chapters, where I first began to raise related issues.

2 The publications Hill (1985) reviewed in the article are Chambers and Trudgill (1980); Goffman (1983); Gumperz (1982a, 1982b); Labov (1980); Romaine (1982); Turner (1982); and Swann (1983). See bibliography for details.

3 It is important to use the modifier 'today's' because today's sociolinguistics has adopted a path which is significantly different from that heralded by its leaders in the early days of sociolinguistics e.g., Weinreich, Labov and Herzog (1968), or Labov of the early 1960s. Had Weinreich et al.'s programme of action been followed, today's sociolinguistics would have been a different discipline – it is even possible that it might have been 'holistic' in its approach.

4 Witness the fact that even the most mental linguistics of a few decades back did not begin with an investigation of the structure of human brain, though arguably this might have been one reasonable route to take since language was seen as a 'mental organ'; nor does any functional model of linguistics prioritise the description of social structure over that of language, though all relate the functions of language to speaking in social life, and arguably speaking in social life is closely intertwined with social structure.

5 Though, of course, the chain of arguments that would establish accent as an important element in the perception of the speaking subjects' identity remained un-elaborated.

6 In raising these objections, I have given no specific references to the literature but those familiar with the dominant model's history would definitely have no difficulty in recalling instances of each case. Other chapters in this volume offer these same points of criticism with specific bibliographic references, though one should add that more recently social class has been discussed e.g. Guy (1988) and Ash (2002), but in these writings it is as if no one else has ever thought about the relevance of social class to sociolinguistics, or if they did it is not worthy of mention.

7 I am thinking here of great names such as Boas, Sapir, Whorf, Firth, Pike, all of whom in their different ways tried to show the deeper and more intimate relations between language and society. I believe this literature is suspect, since

accepting those views would bring into question the autonomy of language – a principle cherished by the linguistic model adopted by today's sociolinguistics.

8 I am aware that there are models whose conceptualisation of language as a 'mental organ' would suggest that communication is itself an accidental function of language. Whatever the case, the fact of language active in communication is massively present to human experience.

9 The term socio-historical stage is not an equivalent of Saussure's *état de langue*, though the latter is subsumed in the former: the specific focus is on 'the register repertoire' and the 'register-specific ways of using language'.

10 The adaptation is at two points: the first category on the horizontal axis is called 'culture' in Halliday. I have used 'society' instead as the more inclusive and higher order abstraction than culture. Most human societies are poly-systemic, which is manifested in their multi-culturality. Further instead of the last category on the lower horizontal axis which is called 'text' in Halliday, I have chosen to use the complex expression *parole-as-text*, which is really like saying language-in-use. Language in use in a social context typically counts as text (or text-fragment), as defined in Halliday and Hasan (1976); Hasan (1985a, b, c). All parole in this view is incipient text; it may or may not reach that stage in a manner that produces easy recognition of it as text, but given the conditions for continued discourse, text-hood is what communication strives for.

11 By saying that society is realised as language and context of situation as text I do not mean that language is the only semiotic modality that realises society. In fact, it would be more accurate to say that in the realisation of society as in that of a specific context of situation, many different semiotic modalities co-operate; thus rituals, music, and mime realise aspects of society and texts may be multimodal. However, here our attention is focussed on language, and it is also true that language is a far more pervasive modality in the realisation of both society and text.

12 For further discussion, Halliday (1992a); Hasan (1995a, 1996); Butt (2008a); Matthiessen (2007).

13 Lemke's concept of 'meta-redundancy' (1984) is important but will take us far afield. For discussion see Lemke (1984); Halliday (1992a); Hasan (1995a).

14 In making statements of this kind there is a danger that one might immediately move – as is often the case with linguists – from the assertion of this relation to lexical items and individual structures, vociferously pointing out that 'lexicon' and 'syntax' do not support the claim. But no such claim has ever been made by any serious scholar interested in the relationship of language and society.

15 From time to time, there are of course ambiguities, confusions and misunderstandings, but the relation is robust enough in general.

16 There is a great deal of literature on the notion of context and on the realisational relation between text and context, as any published bibliography of SFL will reveal.

17 Thus the various distinctive features of social context to which Hymes has drawn attention from time to time (e.g., Hymes 1962, 1968 etc.) can be shown to be more specific elements of these three general vectors.

18 For a discussion of the concept of realisation see chapter 2–6 of this volume; for its centrality to the definition of variant/variable in variation theory see chapter 2 especially.

19 See Hasan (2003) for a linguistically oriented account; John McMurty (1999) for a multidisciplinary orientation, and Naomi Klein (2007) for a journalistic approach.

20 Whorf (1956) expressed the same point of view many decades earlier, only the term he used was 'culture' rather than society (cf. 1956: 156 'Which was first: the language patterns or the cultural norms? *In main they have grown up together, constantly influencing each other*'. Emphasis added, RH).

21 In fact Saussure emphatically maintained that *langue* is entirely 'social', that it is the property of the community, as opposed to *parole* which according to him is individual and therefore psychological, i.e., part of the mental behaviour of individual speaker. From this point of view, Saussure's conception of the *langue parole* relation is the opposite of Chomsky's competence performance relation; for Chomsky competence is species-defining, an element of the make up of the human mental system, so not specific to a particular community, while performance is affected solely by speaker's environment, so likely to be local, i.e., social, and specific to some particular community.

22 This is particularly true for scholars who equated 'linguistics' with 'Chomskyan linguistics'. However, neither Prague School linguistics nor Firthian linguistics became dissociated from social concerns of language.

23 The extent to which the material aspect is indicative of the details of the social practice depends on the degree to which the practice is institutionalised (Hasan 1980; Cloran 1999a).

2 On semantic variation

> To come to grips with *language*, we must look as closely and directly at the data of everyday speech as possible, and characterise its relationship to our grammatical theories as accurately as we can, amending and adjusting the theory so that it fits the object in view. (Labov 1972a: 201)

1 Introduction

The central theme of this chapter is taken from a talk I presented at a conference[1] in 1998, where I attempted to place the idea of semantic variation in relation to sociolinguistics. That was nearly a decade ago but although recent sociolinguistic publications (e.g. Chambers, Trudgill and Schilling-Estes 2002) do display an engagement with some of the theoretical problems which were first raised in the late 1980s in several chapters of this volume[2], it appears that so far as the concept of semantic variation is concerned, nothing much has changed over this period. So before turning to the main issue, it is still appropriate today to say a few introductory words on the term *semantic variation,* which still remains a complete non-entity in sociolinguistic literature. First a word here on the origin of the term itself: to the best of my knowledge I am the first person to have undertaken an empirical and systematic investigation into *semantic variation* as a sociolinguistic phenomenon[3]. And yet, it is not I who coined that term: this honour, as much else in sociolinguistics today, rightly belongs to Labov; but, ironically, he introduced the term only to deny it the possibility of any status in sociolinguistics[4]. By contrast, throughout the chapters of this volume I have presented what seem to be compelling grounds for recognising semantic variation as a fact of language use in social contexts of human life. Our findings suggest that the patterns of variation we have investigated at the semantic level are orderly and represent paradigm cases of 'structured heterogeneity' (Weinreich, Labov and Herzog 1968). However, dominant sociolinguistics not just ignores, but expressly rejects semantic variation as a *socio*linguistic concept (Weiner and Labov 1983). Behind this partial narrative is a puzzle: given that in all important respects semantic variation presents a parallel to phonological variation, why is it unacceptable as a sociolinguistic phenomenon? In what way is it not an important aspect of the *study of language in its social context*?

In this chapter, I propose to revisit the concept of semantic variation with two main questions in mind: (i) does the structure of language permit the possibility of semantic variability?; and (ii) if so, what are the conditions under which semantic variation might be seen as a sociolinguistic phenomenon? But before turning to these questions, it will be necessary to examine certain basic terms of the trade, such as *sociolinguistic variable, variant, variation* and *sociolinguistic variety*. In the nature of things, it should not have been necessary to discuss concepts at this very fundamental level: they are, after all, essential to the field of sociolinguistics as work in the Labovian paradigm has so clearly demonstrated. Confusion about these basic terms has arisen for two reasons. In the first place, in current sociolinguistics there is an under-theorisation of the language of description, that is to say, descriptive terms are not theoretically informed. This manifests itself partly in treating the meaning of the descriptive terms at their face value – i.e., taking them to mean just what they are supposed to mean in every day use of language; but then, in the middle of the discourse it so happens that the terms subtly shift their meaning. The confusion that result from such practice should not surprise since what we are engaged in doing when doing sociolinguistics is not just carrying on a non-specialised everyday discourse. Sociolinguistics is, after all, not about common sense; it is about explaining what common sense has begun to reflect on: the slippages in sociolinguistic terminology are simply announcing this fact.

Secondly, as Labov has so convincingly argued, doing sociolinguistics is engaging with the study of language in its social context. The aspects of language which a study in this perspective foregrounds must in turn tell us something about the nature of language itself. It is to be expected that such understanding of language will be a good indicator of the kind of linguistic theory one needs in order to be able to do justice to the study of language in its social context, but the linguistic theory one may actually be using and the view of language it rests on may not be compatible with the pursuit of these aims – whether this is *actually* the case can be determined only upon a conscious and careful examination of how language is conceptualised in the theory which in fact informs the sociolinguists' practice. Despite the early resolutions (see the citation at the head of this chapter) there has been a reluctance in sociolinguistics to consider this possibility, as if a theoretician's ideas about the nature of language bear no relationship to his theory of language and its description: thus, a model of language which was explicitly said to be a-social (Labov 1972a: 185–87) has been adopted to conduct the study of language in its social context. There is no indication that the defects Labov had located earlier in the model have actually been repaired. If so, certainly the literature lacks any explicit discussion of those changes. This chapter will draw attention to a number of the features of the adopted model which are inimical to the study of language in its social context.

2 Variable and variant in sociolinguistics

It is obvious that the concepts *variable* and *variant* are critical to the field of sociolinguistics. However as I have pointed out (see especially, chapter 5 here), statements about the significance or the definition of these terms are less than clear in their formulation. Sometimes, without any supporting argument, it is claimed that the terms are 'not meant to be taken as part of a general theory of language' (see Hudson 1980; for discussion, see chapter 5). This is presented as justification for the lack of clear statements, warranting the assumption that an intuitive, i.e., common sense, understanding of the terms is sufficient. On other occasions clarity is not exactly what could be said to characterise statements about the terms. For example, Chambers and Trudgill (1980: 60) inform us that

> ... linguistic variables can *often* be regarded as *socially different* but *linguistically equivalent ways of doing or saying the same thing, and occur at all levels of linguistic analysis.* [emphasis added, *RH*]

There is much in this statement to deny satisfaction. For example, how should one interpret *often*? Is the *often* subject to some condition or is it a matter of chance? More important still, how much is encompassed in the expression *all levels of linguistic analysis*? Does the scope of its reference include the level of meaning, or is meaning external to language? If meaning is one of the levels/components of language, then clearly linguistic 'variables/variants' would occur on the level of meaning as well, and in that case, it would be rather odd to claim that producing variant meanings as realisation of the 'same' contextual events is a way of *saying* the same thing. Since this would involve contradiction, one might reject this line of reasoning, concluding that meaning is perhaps not supposed to be taken as a level of language – a supposition that would at least offer a logical ground for the rejection of semantic variation as a socio*linguistic* phenomenon. But excluding meaning from 'all levels of linguistic analysis' will raise other questions: after all if 'linguistic variables can be regarded as *socially different ways of doing or saying the same thing*', the social difference indicated by or associated with the linguistic variables presumably creates meaning. We are entitled to ask what kind of meaning it is. If it is social *meaning*, then how do we explain the fact that a linguistic variable creates/construes this kind of meaning, and yet meaning itself is not a component of language? What aspect/component of language relates to meaning, and how? What are the conditions for treating meaning as a level *of* language? These questions are real; they crowd upon us because sociolinguistics has not been explicitly related to any coherently articulated model of language that is capable of satisfying the conceptualisation of meaning demanded by the study of language in its social context.

Returning to the terms *variable/variant*, there is, of course, the simple question of the difference of meaning between *variable* and *variant*. In the literature these terms are used almost interchangeably – indeed, when I first began working in this field, I too followed the dominant fashions of speaking, making no distinction between the terms (see chapters in Part II of this volume) – and yet one might argue quite cogently that it is not the *variable* itself that can be regarded as socially different; it is only the choice pattern of the *variants* that has this privilege. I would blame this confusion on the fact that the terms have 'not been taken as part of a general theory of language': they are under-theorised. Bayley (2002: 117) has recently attempted to repair the situation by placing the terms in relation to language study as a whole:

> … the central ideas of this approach [i.e. the quantitative paradigm. *RH*] are that an understanding of language requires an understanding of variable as well as categorical processes, and that variation that we witness at *all levels of language* is not random. [emphasis mine *RH*] Rather linguistic variation is characterized by orderly or 'structured heterogeneity' (Weinreich et al. 1968: 99–100). That is, speaker's choices between variable linguistic forms are systematically constrained by multiple linguistic and social factors that reflect underlying grammatical systems and that both reflect and partially constitute the social organization of the communities to which users of the language belong.
> …

The move to distinguish variable and categorical processes is certainly desirable. But the problem of the relationship between variable and variant is still unresolved. A variable linguistic form is one that has the *possibility* of variant realisations. Logically on any given occasion, a speaker would choose only one or the other variant. So it seems that variable and variant could not be theoretical synonyms. At the same time, it is also true that to state the value and identity of the variants, they have to be seen in relation to this 'thing' that we are calling 'variable linguistic form'. It seems highly probable that underlying Labov's (socio)-linguistic variable is a stability/constancy – something that is in Bayley's terms 'categorical'[5]. One might go even further and claim that discourse of variability logically implies the recognition of constancy at some point (Hasan 2004a). Obviously, the classification of linguistic processes into categorical and variable is not enough to explain Labov's complex concept: to make sense of it, one needs also to bring the two kinds of process together.

I discussed this issue in the 1980s (e.g., in chapters 3–5 in this volume) by referring to **realisation**, a concept which, according to SFL theory, links the distinct strata of linguistic theory. A similar explanation has arrived in sociolinguistics fairly recently (Antilla 2002: 210):

> Finally, a brief note on the definition of variation is due. One possibility is to regard variation as a form-meaning relation of a special kind. It has been suggested that the form meaning relation in natural languages is ideally one-to-one and that this is the principle that languages strive to satisfy (Antilla 1989). The two possible forms of deviation from this ideal state are illustrated in (6): one meaning (M1) corresponds to several forms (F1, F2), i.e., we have VARIATION; and one form (F1) corresponds to several meanings (M1, M2), i.e., we have AMBIGUITY.

Figure 1: From Antilla (2002: 210): 'Variation and phonological theory'

Antilla's account of variable-variant relation is essentially in agreement[6] with mine (see for example chapter 5, esp. section 3.1)[7] to the extent that it acknowledges the need to recognise the concepts *meaning* and *form* as belonging to two distinct orders of abstraction – two distinct levels of a language's internal organisation. But the two approaches, Antilla's and mine, do differ significantly. For Antilla language is a binary coding system, the two levels recognised are those of meaning and form. By contrast, in SFL, language is seen as a multiple coding system consisting of at least three language internal levels – meaning (semantics), wording (lexicogrammar) and sound (phonology)[8] (see figure 1 in chapter 3). From the SFL point of view, Antilla's 'one meaning … several forms' either elides the level of lexicogrammar or subsumes it with phonology, as if it had no specific part to play in the construal of meaning. However, even a cursory observation of the working of language bears proof to the fact that what *always* makes a difference to the meaning of a sentence is its wording: to recognise meaning as a level of language without recognising the role of lexicogrammar in bringing about that meaning is to ignore precisely that aspect of language which is most central to a language's ability to mean. Units of wording are complex linguistic entities: phonology alone cannot exhaust their description. Simplifying the debate, according to SFL the linguistic unit 'word' has to be viewed from three perspectives: (i) it realises – more specifically, construes – a semantic unit, i.e. a meaning; (ii) it bears paradigmatic and syntagmatic relations to other words, i.e., it enters into lexicogrammatical relations of class and structure with other units at the level of wording; and (iii) it 'has' a phonological form, i.e., it is itself realised – more specifically, signalled – phonologically. Language in use presents itself as a synthesis of meaning, form and sound/graph; if linguistic theory aims to 'explain' the nature of this phenomenon, it will need to recognise all three aspects of the linguistic unit.

Antilla's account bypasses the second aspect, and yet, from the point of view of the present discussion, it seems quite criterial. The linguistic unit 'word' is able to 'have' some specific meaning, precisely by virtue of the relations it enters into with other lexicogrammatical units – a view expressed very clearly in Saussure (1966). The third aspect of the unit word, i.e., its phonological form plays no part in the process of meaning construal: in other words, it furnishes a recognition criterion for the wording, but does not offer any principle for its definition (Halliday 1984b): the same phonic/graphic 'shape' may realise two or more distinct words. For example, despite having the same phonological form, the word *host* in Shakespearean English is not the same word as *host* in today's English – similarly, in contemporary English words such as *pear/pair*, *can* (aux.) / *can* (of Coke) realise distinct wordings. To repeat, meaning is construed not by the phonological shape of the word but by the lexicogrammatical relations a word enters into which is what forges its semantic value. Thus, it is the second and third aspects of the word that are directly relevant to phonological variation. The second aspect of word analysis mentioned above i.e., the word as a lexicogrammatical unit, represents that which is constant; the third aspect i.e., the phonological form of the word, is what is variable. To say that the expression is variable is to say that there is a systematic choice between two or more variant phonological expressions such that each realisation signals the same wording. Since variability is in phonological expression, it is possible to specify in purely phonological terms the specific nature of the environment within which such particular pattern of variance will occur; the variants vary from each other only 'locally' within an identical phonological frame, and irrespective of their meaning difference, the phonological realisations of the words *guard, dark, bark, park* present the same environment in which the wording will 'have' a rhotic or non-rhotic (variant) realisation as so well documented by reference to dialectal varieties of New York English in Labov's work.

I conclude then that the phonological variant's primary relation is to some unit of wording: the wording is constant, it acts as a point of reference, while its phonological realisation is variable. When such variability of realisation obtains, the variants of this variable expression may come to acquire some sociolinguistic value by becoming associated with (some attributes of) certain specific groups of speakers. The above discussion is summed up in the following observations:

(i) The kind of relation of variability generally studied under the rubric of quantitative variation demands the recognition of at least two levels of abstraction in a linguistic theory, both of which are implicated;

(ii) Using the spatial metaphor, the unit at the higher level represents that feature of constancy against which variability may be observed in its lower level realisational pattern[9];

(iii) The lower level is variable, i.e., the realisation of the higher level unit offers a systemic choice: two or more variant realisations of the same higher unit exist. In other words, the variability potential is a feature of the process of realisation;

(iv) All variants will necessarily be commutable within the same structure which is capable of realising the same higher level unit; the pattern of variability is local and explicitly specifiable in linguistic terms;

(v) The realisational variants acquire a sociolinguistic status if (a) the pattern of the variants' occurrence displays an orderly and structured heterogeneity in the speech process of some given (sections of a) society; (b) the selection of variants is 'habitual', i.e., instantiates some 'fashion of speaking' (Whorf 1956); and (c) the recognition criteria for the identification of the variant in the speech process are explicit;

(vi) Observations (i) to (iv) imply that the highest level recognised by a linguistic theory is not capable of displaying this particular kind of variability;

(vii) It follows from the above, that sociolinguistic investigation in this paradigm needs a linguistic theory that (a) is stratified; (b) offers a clear statement of relations between the different strata of the theory; (c) enables a principled way of analysing linguistic data, and (d) is capable of identifying the feature(s) of the social environment which co-vary with variation in the linguistic process.

3 Sociolinguistic variation

The word 'variation' as used in ordinary language simply means departure from established practice/state of being. It, thus, naturally, presupposes a 'norm' or 'standard', which often enjoys the prestige of precedence; and popular attitudes of respect for established conventions translate precedence into 'authenticity'.

This is particularly true when the term is applied to ways of doing and saying things, where this built-in semantics of the word has the potential of displaying bias: someone's norm is talked about as variation from an earlier and more 'authentic' norm, thus assigning 'privilege' – often inadvertently – to some linguistic pattern on the basis of that pattern's 'temporal precedence'. However, as a technical term in Labovian sociolinguistic theory, the semantics of 'variation' has been made more precise by being tied firmly, although most probably without conscious design, to the meaning of 'variable' and 'variant': as Antilla points out (see quote above), one way of 'defining' variation is 'to regard it as a form-meaning relation of a special kind' – of precisely the special kind discussed above as realisation. This is exactly how the term variation has come to be used in dominant sociolinguistics, with the implication that investigations in the framework of variation theory always implicate two levels of linguistic abstraction which are realisationally related as described in the previous section. The claim of functional and structured heterogeneity inherited from Weinreich, Labov and Herzog (1968), has, in theory, moved the discourse of variation to 'synchronic complexity', whereby the different varieties participate in an orderly way in the complex realisational trajectories of some given variable(s). Again, in theory at least, there is no need to assign a (somewhat arbitrary) 'privilege' to some variant due to its 'temporal precedence': all sociolinguistic varieties would be seen as *linguistically* equal[10]. To be considered a variety, each has to display a robust, regular and systematic occurrence of some variant of the same variable, and it is this robustness of the occurrence of the variant in each variety that allows the quantitative studies for which variation theory is so highly regarded. From this point of view, each variant choice has the status of *norm* for some segment of the community 'at this point in time'[11]. And it is expected that such structured heterogeneity would be functional in the wider speech community, i.e., it would play a part in the creation, maintenance and alteration of the speech community's social contexts: the many sociolinguistic varieties are supported by the existing social order while they themselves have evolved to play a part in it, whatever that part may be[12].

Before leaving this discussion of the term 'variation' it is pertinent to raise two relevant issues. First, while the theoretical relation between the terms *variable*, *variant*, and *variation* produces a tight and coherent theoretical structure for sociolinguistics of the dominant type, it does limit the scope of the term *variation* so that such variation can no longer claim to be a comprehensive 'study of language in its social context': to claim this status, it must be supplemented by something that goes beyond 'variation theory'. As Halliday (1975c) points out, there do exist sociolinguistic varieties which do not show variation of the type celebrated in variation theory. Since in fact these 'supplementing' language varieties are based in the social living of life, their study has to be seen as part of sociolinguistics unless the field is arbitrarily limited. The second, and closely related, issue is that when variation studies in this sense of the term are conducted within the framework of the linguistic model that is employed by the dominant sociolinguistics, this inevitably results in limiting the recognition of the possibilities of variation open to language by the logic of their structure. This comes about due to the model's conceptualisation of language and its inward-looking nature. To elaborate briefly, the model recognises semantics, syntax, lexicon and phonology as 'components' of language, but the relationship of these components to each other is not explicitly conceptualised[13], and typically language is presented (whether explicitly or implicitly) as a binary coding system simply consisting of meaning and form (see for example the extract from Antilla above). It should be obvious from the preceding discussion that this under-theorisation of the relations between language 'components' has been instrumental in preventing the clarification of variable-variant relationship for nearly four decades. Then, there is also the linguistic model's assumptions about the nature of what is universal in human language, the significant implications of which no serious sociolinguistics can afford to ignore. The model postulates a universal design in respect of fairly low level linguistic phenomena. It is a tall order to relate such a universally designed language to that real language which plays a crucial role in the social life of the community. However, to justify the socio- in sociolinguistics, in the end, it is precisely this interpenetration of language as active in the life of social subjects, which a serious sociolinguistics must study (for discussion, chapter 1). Not surprisingly, dominant sociolinguistic explanations of what variation does in the life of the speech community have stayed on the surface of human existence as many (e.g., Bourdieu 1990; Gardin and Marcellesi 1987; Williams 1992) have complained; nor has it advanced our understanding of why the system of language supports varieties, or what aspects of the system of language allow variation/varieties to develop.

As evident from the strong divide between 'competence' and 'performance', the model seals off language as system, or 'code' from language as process i.e., its natural use in the contexts of social life, which logically results in an inward-looking account of human language: the complete severance of language from speech has detrimental effects on the explanatory capabilities of linguistic theory itself, but that is not our concern here. So far as sociolinguistics is concerned, what seems to be more significant is the sealing off of language from the very social context in which languages live and die, change and grow, develop the potential of intervening in human activities and of shaping human attitudes to variation. Not viewed as a relevant concept in the model, context largely remains unanalysed and the interpretation assigned to the elements of context continues to be 'intuitive' and commonsensical. This clearly poses a problem when it comes to relating the phenomena of language – including its sociolinguistic patterns – to the social material world. After all, 'social hierarchy' is simply a symptom: underlying it is something far more fundamental. One important question that sociolinguistics must ask is about the part played by language in the organisation of social life – a question that cannot be answered without having some sense of what this organisation is like, and the precondition for developing that sense is the theorisation of the concept 'context'. There are very many ways in which the speakers' external circumstances penetrate their language – both its system and its use; some linguists would argue that even the form of language cannot be adequately described without reference to social contexts of speaking (Halliday 1992b).

Excluding context from linguistic theory naturally means that the highest level of abstraction in the theory is what is called 'semantics'. As the part of language that is concerned with meaning, this component could be seen as the interface between language-internal form and language-external reality. However, the only relation to the massive reality of speakers' life recognised by this linguistic theory is that of language as a surrogate of pre-existing reality, whereby meaning simply becomes naming/correspondence/reference, call it what you will. In terms of SFL this aspect covers approximately the meanings pertaining to the 'ideational' function of language; the model thus ignores interpersonal and textual meanings. This attenuated semantics is what is coded, i.e., realised by (a) syntax and lexicon, and (b) phonology. It follows logically that in view of the nature of variation theory, dominant sociolinguistics can *only* recognise two legitimate types of variation: one, *syntactic variation* e.g. copula deletion, or *that/which* relativisation, where a semantic unit is claimed to remain 'constant' while its syntactic realisation varies (see, however, Romaine 1984); and secondly, phonological variation e.g. —t, d deletion, the presence/absence of rhotic /r/ and such like in carefully specified phonological contexts, where the wording i.e., the lexicogrammatical unit stays constant, while the phonological realisation varies.

Of these two areas, the most remarkable and extensive contributions made by dominant sociolinguistics are in the field of phonological variation, though it has also accommodated 'syntactic variation' (on some problems of which see Romaine's discussion below (section 5.2). The design of the model quite clearly does not allow the recognition of semantic variation. To allow this, the model would have needed to recognise a level of abstraction higher than the level of meaning which would have to be seen as inherently relevant to language. This clearly cannot be done in a model that views the form of language as *au fond* universal, and language as 'autonomous', whatever that may mean. Labov has justified the absence of semantic variation basically on two counts: one, that the level of semantics is concerned only with referential, i.e., truth functional meanings – social meaning which differentiates socially motivated stylistic variation does not represent a semantic phenomenon[14]; and two, that the degree of precision required for variation analysis is in principle not available to semantic phenomena, therefore sociolinguistics cannot extend itself to the study of semantic variation without losing objectivity of analysis. How viable are these arguments? The results of my research which became available from the late 1980s, have forced me to discuss these issues repeatedly (see chapters 3–8 in this volume), and I will return again to some of these points in section 5 below.

4 Variation and sociolinguistic variety

'Variation theory' has enabled impressive discoveries; yet, as I pointed out above, it cannot be treated as a comprehensive 'study of language in its social context'. The simple justification for making this claim is that in every language, there exist, and always have existed, language varieties which do not fall within the rubric of 'variation theory', and yet they are certainly genuine instances of the study of language in its social context: for example, they have obvious origins in the social contexts of speech communities; they display predictable regularities; and they are enormously consequential in power struggles in communities. If such varieties of language fall outside the defined domain of some model of sociolinguistics, then a redefinition of the domain becomes an urgent issue. Labov's attitude to such varieties has been somewhat ambiguous. Consider, for example, the following passage, where an undercurrent of meaning seems to run throughout, suggesting that such varieties perhaps do not belong to the field of sociolinguistics or if they do, their place is definitely not centre stage (Labov 1972a: 184; emphasis mine):

> There is another area of study *sometimes included in 'sociolinguistics'*, that is *more concerned with the details of language in actual use* – the field which Hymes has named 'the ethnography of speaking' (1962) … this field is concerned with describing and analysing the patterns of use of languages and dialects within a specific culture: the forms of 'speech events'; the rules for appropriate selection of speakers; the interrelations of speaker, addressee, audience, topic, channel and setting; and the ways in which the speakers draw upon the resources of their language to perform certain functions.

Hymes' speech varieties (1962, 1967 and elsewhere) are based on systematic differences across different classes of speech events: these differences correlate with differences in the natural social contexts relevant to the speech events.

This is what is known in SFL as register variation, first theorised in Halliday, McIntosh and Strevens (1964), though the concept is rooted in context as developed in Firth (1957) and offers a systematisation of Malinowski's views on context from the perspective of discourse. Although the two concepts – speech variety and register variety – are not identical in all details, there is a good deal of overlap between them. Here, I focus on the SFL concept of register because it is fully integrated into the SFL model of language, being related on the one hand to the context of culture and situation and on the other, to the internal structure of language through the concept of metafunctions, which have their foundation in language use in social contexts (see for discussion, chapter 1 of this volume; also Halliday 1973b, 1979a). A great deal of literature exists on the theory and the methodology for the actual analysis of variation in register. Here I briefly highlight the crucial facts relevant to the concept register variety.

- The semiotic system of language is characterised by its three realisationally related levels of meaning, wording, and sound;
- To explain the evolution and function of this semiotic system, a linguistic theory must invoke the concept of context of culture and situation because *language develops; is maintained and changes only in and by use in the living of life in social contexts*;
- This observation implies that to do descriptive justice to the tri-stratal inner structure of language, a linguistic *theory* must comprise *four strata*: context, meaning, wording and sound; this permits focus both on its semiotic as well as its social aspects;
- Language in use under natural, normal conditions is responsive to three aspects of social context, known in SFL as FIELD, TENOR and MODE of discourse; field refers to the nature of social action in which language in use is playing some part either as an ancillary or a constitutive force; tenor refers to the nature of social relation that exists between the speaker and addressee which is maintained and/or changed via engagement in social practices including that of discourse, while mode refers to the physical and semiotic modes of establishing and maintaining contact for carrying out the business that concerns the participants of discourse on that occasion;
- These three vectors – field, tenor and mode – are vectors of context which act for the speaker as the governing principle for systematic variation in language use; thus different fields call for talk about different things, e.g., discourse of music involves a different referential

domain compared to discourse of volcanoes; different tenor relations will involve different ways of engaging with the addressee, for example, in one kind of participant relation their language will construe respect, in another, banter, and so on; and the difference in modes will go with different ways of organising one's discourse, for example discourse with someone who is physically absent calls for mediated communication; whether this mediation is by writing or by transmission of speech (e.g. leaving a message on someone's voice-mail), it will call for a greater degree of explicitness;

- In this way, each of the three vectors characterising the occasion of language use is responsive typically to a distinct aspect of the language's meaning potential. It is this principle that forms the basis for the recognition of the three metafunctions, known as ideational, interpersonal and textual (Halliday 1973b, 1979a). The aspect of language that pertains to one metafunction is not identical to that which pertains to another. Thus the semantics and lexicogrammar which is the output of the ideational metafunction is what is predominantly active in the realisation of the nature of field; that which is the output of the interpersonal metafunction is predominantly active in creating, maintaining and changing participant relations, while the textual meanings and lexicogrammar play a predominant part in realising mode factors, maintaining continuities in discourse.

These processes create what Halliday et al. (1964: 81–94) have called *variation according to use*, whereas the variation of 'variation theory' was referred to as *variation according to user*. The latter relates to who the user is, where 'who' is identified by location in the social system (Hasan 1973a). All things being equal, this latter kind of variation will characterise most instances of the user's speech. By contrast, the former, i.e., variation by use, relates to what a speaker is doing with his/her language on some particular occasion, and all things being equal, it (or something closely resembling it) will manifest itself again if and only if that particular occasion of use is at issue[15].

A commonsensical approach to register variation would suggest that the user is simply using the resources of his/her language to refer to what needs to be referred to in that situation, with the possible implication that this kind of language use is in no way relevant to *socio*linguistics. But there is more to register variation than reference to different things as the above summary has tried to show. To consider the relevance of register variation to sociolinguistics, one would need to ask questions that go beyond the narrow confines of 'language form'. For example, are all register varieties equally accessible to every member/segment of a given society? If not, what decides this issue?

Sociolinguistic studies have shown conclusively that certain categories of dialect variation function as the reflection of social hierarchy. It does not appear very likely that social practices which form the environment for registers would be socially neutral, so one relevant question is who can engage in which social-semiotic practice and why? What is the constraint and whom does it affect in what way? Further, does the register repertoire of a language change over time? If so, what is the mechanism for this change? If our response to all such questions is to maintain that change in language reflects change in social circumstances and that language itself makes no contribution to social change, then there is something very wrong with our powers of observation and our ways of reasoning. Sociolinguistics has to recognise that there is no one-way traffic between society and language; their evolution is co-genetic; neither can exist without the other as I have argued (Hasan 1984a, 1988 and elsewhere).

Certainly, for one very obvious reason, variety by use needs to be distinguished from variety by user: the criteria for the identification and the methodology for the analysis of register variation differ significantly from those for dialectal variation. For example, unlike the latter, there is no higher level constant in register variation. It is not the case that the field stays the same only its realisation differs: in this sense there are no variant realisations of the same field (however see discussion in section 5.4 below). Rather, the values of the vector of field differ from one instance to another and the realisation will differ not only with differences in field values but also with the values of tenor and mode relations that co-occur with some field values: each register is thus a syncretic realisation of some specific configuration of the values of field, tenor and mode. Thus the identification of a register variety is a much more complex business than that of a dialect variety, first because it does not postulate 'realisational variants' of the 'same' field, tenor or mode separately and/or as a whole, but must take each specific value of each vector as critical, and secondly because it also calls for attention to different aspects of language in use. So the overall structure of the speech event, i.e., its textual structure is as important as (a) how the elements of this structure are realised, and (b) how the various parts of the text hold together, i.e., the texture of the text. By contrast, variation as in sociolinguistic variation theory has no bearing on textual organisation. Predictions about the realisational features of the different register varieties is most conveniently made in terms of semantic categories (Hasan 1973a, 1984b); the recognition criteria for the realisation of these semantic units can be stated in a precise manner using Halliday's descriptive framework for the analysis of wording[16].

Access to social semiotic practices is differentially distributed across the social system. The critical factor is the user's social positioning. There is a bi-directional relationship between an (adult) individual's social positioning and his/her register repertoire: social positioning provides a hospitable environment for the development of the individual's register repertoire, and on-going experience of engagement in that particular register repertoire (both active and passive engagement) further strengthens and defines the individual's social positioning: the repertoires vary with variation in social positioning. Speaking linguistically, power struggle is the struggle to have access to and control of certain categories of information and certain classes of social practice. I agree completely with Labov (1972a: 111) that 'the shape of linguistic behaviour changes rapidly as the speaker's social position changes', but the truly important question is: What changes the speaker's social position? Engagement in certain valued social practices, and access to the means of acquiring certain categories of information seem to be the most important issues. Given these facts, there can be no doubt that register varieties are sociolinguistic in nature. They cannot be abolished simply because their analysis is not as water-tight as that of —t, d deletion; all that I would take this situation to suggest is that every effort should be made to make it more precise: it is absurd to say that since register variation cannot be analysed to our satisfaction today, therefore sociolinguistics is at liberty to leave out any consideration of this aspect of the use of language in its social context.

5 Semantic variation

So what about semantic variation? Is there a *rational* basis for suggesting that the concept is not sociolinguistic in nature? The answer to this depends on what position is taken on the following issues: (i) the existence and nature of the semantic variant; (ii) the nature of the semantic stratum/component; (iii) the readiness of semantics to engage in sociolinguistic variation studies; and (iv) the significance of semantic variation to the field of sociolinguistics. Clearly the issues are inter-related: the place assigned to semantics in language and in linguistic theory is crucial, especially with reference to the first three. The possibility of semantic variation depends on a viable postulate of semantic variant, and the conceptualisation of that notion depends on the conception of semantics. The remainder of this section will consist of the discussion of the first three questions, where some overlap will be unavoidable. The chapter will conclude with a discussion of the possible contributions of semantic variation to sociolinguistics.

The basis for the discussion of issues (i-iii) has already been laid above (see sections 2 and 3) where the exclusion of context from the linguistic model adopted by Labov was brought to attention; the differing conception of semantics in the two models has also been discussed briefly (see section 4). Partial discussions concerning these matters are scattered throughout the various chapters of this volume (see especially chapters 5 and 7). My aim in going over this ground here is to throw some additional light on the centrality of the concept of semantic variation for a field that aims to study 'language in its social context'.

5.1 Semantic variants and linguistic theory

I begin with the nature and existence of the semantic variant as this will bring us face to face with the kind of data which highlights the need for a theory of semantic variation. Do semantic variants exist, and if so, do they display the properties which make them suitable as a tool for sociolinguistic investigation?

In response to the first question, it is true that in terms of the linguistic model Labov uses, the concept of semantic variants does not and *can not* exist: its recognition would be a theoretical anomaly. This non-existence/ non-recognition is a logical consequence of the linguistic model which Labov uses. If semantics is the highest level of abstraction, as it is in this model, then logically there is nothing that semantics in such a model could be said to realise: there is no 'content' whose expression would be a semantic unit; the question of variant 'expression/realisation' does not even begin to arise (see i-vii in section 2 above). While from the point of view of the linguistic theory itself, this chain of reasoning appears impeccably logical, it leaves dominant sociolinguistics with some vexing questions. For example, does the inability of the model to allow semantic variation do justice to the naturally occurring 'data from the speech community'? Does the theory 'fit the object in view' (Labov 1972a: 201)? The *existence* of a pattern in language does not depend on its recognition by some theory; in the end, it is the theory that must fit the data, or it must pay the penalty for not recognising it, as Labov (1972a) points out.

There can be no doubt that there exists a paradigm of variant messages such as *lets wash your hands before you touch that sandwich* v. *wash your hands before you touch that sandwich* v. *I'd like you to wash your hands before you touch that sandwich,* v. *you have to wash your hands before you touch that sandwich,* and so on. How would Labovian sociolinguistics account for the different ways of issuing the 'same' prompt for action? Are the differences across these messages socially insignificant? If not, do they represent 'stylistic variation'? What exactly is stylistic variation?[17] Thinking of 'language as a means of translating meaning into linear form', we do need to ask with Labov (1972: 189) '...where and how do stylistic meanings enter into this process?' The question still awaits a reasoned response: is 'stylistic meaning' and 'stylistic variation' linguistic? The answer to that does threaten to open a can of worms for today's sociolinguistics. Another possibility would be to claim that the difference is not semantic but pragmatic. This has the advantage of leaving intact the status of semantics in this formalistic model: semantics would still remain truth functional, i.e., narrowly referential. But by the same token, instead of solving the problem it simply moves the debate to a different level: how justifiable is the divide between semantics and pragmatics? Is stylistic variation socio-*semantic* or socio-*pragmatic*? Or are there two different categories of stylistic variation – one of them socio*linguistic* in nature, and the other socio*pragmatic*? We thus enter into the domain of 'territorial disputes', and that brings us to ask the most basic question of all: how should one conceptualise the scope of sociolinguistics, which had initially been said to be 'the study of language in its social context'?

But it is not inscribed in the nature of sociolinguistics that it should be investigated only with the machinery of formalistic models; other and more suitable models can be found. I believe that SFL, the model used, in the investigation of semantic variation in the Macquarie studies is one such. The reasoning behind this claim has been presented over the years in the chapters of this volume (see especially chapters 1, and 3–8. The specific features of SFL that appear most relevant to the discourse of semantic variation are summarised below (see also section 4 of this chapter, and the last section of chapter 1).

(i) The theorisation of the requisite levels of abstraction needed for an adequate description of language, yielding an explicit view of stratification in linguistic theory (see section 2 above);

(ii) The explication of the concept of realisation, yielding an explicit view of how the various strata relate to each other (for discussion section 2–3 above);

(iii) The inclusion of context as the highest stratum of the linguistic theory and the theorisation of context, yielding a viable view of the principles for distinguishing material situational setting from semiotically defined context, the latter being that which is primarily relevant to language use (see section 4 above);

(iv) The concept of 'metafunctional resonance' with explicit postulates regarding how context, metafunction, language use and language system are related (see section 4 above);

(v) The equal status of ideational (cognitive) interpersonal (pragmatic) and textual metafunctions realised in the architecture of both the semantic and the lexicogrammatical strata (see section 4);

(vi) The explicit nature of the relationship between syntagm (actual structure) and paradigm (systemic potential), and the clarification of the concept 'delicacy', yielding principles for measuring the relative 'granularity of description' (see chapters 3–5, this volume).

(vii) The concept of 'trinocular perspective' which yields an explicit principle for establishing the definition, recognition and systemic environment of each descriptive category (see discussion of Antilla in 2–3 above).

The realisational relation between the strata of context and semantics implies that contextual acts can be semantically realised. Any such act must be clearly identifiable as an element of some on-going social activity in order to maintain that the 'same act' is being 'done' linguistically. Say, for example, that a speaker may be engaged in the contextual act of attempting to get someone – say, a child – to do something; say, that the something to be done is for the 'child to wash his/her hands before touching some food': these are 'facts' pertaining to the relevant context of language use. For 'doing' this 'thing' linguistically, there exists a system of options; that is to say, there will be different 'valid' semantic 'ways of doing the same thing': the speaker may issue a 'demand for goods/services' which has a [suggestive] meaning, e.g., *lets wash your hands before you touch that sandwich* (see p. 60); or one that is [obligatory] in its meaning, e.g., *you must wash your hands before you touch that sandwich*, and so on. Each variant aims to achieve THE SAME MATERIAL END: each realises the contextual act on the mother's part to get her child to wash his/her hands before touching some food. Each realisation is a message with the semantic properties [progressive: demand: goods/ service], i.e., the context in which the semantic variant occurs is specifiable in semantic terms; and each message differs from the others by virtue of some specifiable element of meaning with a specifiable locus in the structure. In this sense the messages are semantic variants of each other.

But there is more to the relation between the variants than just the point of difference. It is obvious that in the examples under discussion, one strand of meaning remains constant; this is the strand that pertains to the ideational metafunction, consisting of meanings that refer to the details of the material act and the condition under which that act needs to be performed. However, the semantic variant we have identified, i.e., the element [suggestive], is independent of the ideational metafunction; the strand of meaning in whose structure this semantic variant is integrated pertains to the interpersonal metafunction. In SFL, any kind of meaning that language is able to construe is seen as the concern of semantics. The semantic level is where an account of all these meanings has to be presented. So, using those categories, a message may be analysed for each strand of its meaning, each pertaining to some specific metafunction; or, on occasion, only one strand might be analysed if the investigation is concerned only with that kind of meaning elements.

The theory ascribes equal status to all metafunctions; it follows that the choices pertaining to one metafunction are, by default, independent of those pertaining to the others. The interpersonal metafunction to which the variant under discussion pertains does not refer to elements of event structure; it enables the enactment of human relations, construing the interactants' 'face' (in the sense Goffman, e.g. 1967 used the term). And from the point of view of interpersonal semantics, there is no difference between *lets wash your hands before you touch that sandwich* and *lets not play with those marbles when Andrew is crawling about*. Every specific category of semantic variant would pertain to a particular metafunction and would be integrated within a structure which is the output of that metafunction. The categories of the descriptive framework make it clear which structure it is part of; how it is to be recognised; or what it is doing semantically in an utterance. Thus the last two examples realise the same category of contextual act, namely attempting to get some one to do something; both occurrences of the realisational variant have the status of 'message' at the semantic level; both messages count as [suggestive] and both respect the addressee's face by neutralising the distance between command and cooperation.

Examples of semantic system networks and their realisation statements in terms of lexicogrammatical patterns will be found in many of the chapters of this volume. Chapter 7 provides a more detailed discussion and exemplification of the semantic elements pertaining to messages which can realise the contextual act of attempting to get someone to do something, while chapters 5 and 6 offer a discussion of the semantic categories that are active in the realisation of the contextual act of 'attempting to get someone to tell the speaker something'. In keeping with the principle of trinocular perspective, these discussions indicate that the definition criteria for the semantic categories pertaining to messages are derived from the identity of the contextual act – i.e. from the level above; their value – i.e., what they can 'do' semantically' – is forged by their place in a semantic system network – i.e., from the same level; while their recognition criteria are typically furnished in terms of lexicogrammatical patterns – i.e., from the level below.

There is of course no established measure for 'the degree of precision in analysis' but it can be claimed with confidence that semantic variants exist in the natural speech of the community; the semantic environment in which the variant realisations can occur can be specified as explicitly as can the phonological environment for the phonological variant; the semantic variants can be recognised accurately; and can be analysed with at least as much precision as is typical of the analysis of 'syntax', i.e., lexicogrammar – for it is lexicogrammatical patterns that construe meaning: the lexicogrammatical syntagm is an 'actualisation' of semantic choices in social contexts, which have been worded. The wordings themselves are made accessible to the senses by their phonological/orthographic realisation. These comments are relevant to deciding whether the semantic descriptive framework is advanced enough for use in the analysis of natural data (see below). Before moving to any further discussion of the semantic variant, let me first discuss the very different conceptualisation of semantics in the two theoretical frameworks – the one used by dominant sociolinguistics and that developed in SFL.

5.2 Ideas about meaning and semantic variation

The concept of semantic variant, and consequently the variation study in which it participates, can be only as good as the semantic theory underlying this whole enterprise. It is clear that the two theories being compared here are considerably different from each other. Labov has consistently supported the axiom that 'semantics equals truth functional meaning'; and with that axiom comes the entire set of beliefs, e.g., that semantic space is universal. The implication is that the world is the same for all human beings, so if there are semantic differences evident in people's linguistic behaviour, they have to be accidental, dependent on the geographic location, and other such material phenomena. The social meaning of 'who', 'what' and 'where' is not examined, or if it is, and if it draws attention to differences between groups of speakers, the duty for explaining those differences can be relegated to pragmatics. It is not clear where and on what basis one decides whether the nature of the difference is semantic or pragmatic when it comes to a comparison between two likely states of affairs presented as deterrent to doing something, as in (i) *if you play with that sharp knife, I'll clobber you* (a threat) and the other (ii) *if you play with that sharp knife, you will hurt yourself* (a so-called logical reason). Such problems have been often discussed (see especially chapters 5, 7 and 8), and there is no need to repeat them here. What concerns me is how the choice of the model has impacted on the fate of sociolinguistics: it is my view that the original vision of sociolinguistics which was so fervently presented by Labov in *The study of language in its social context* (1972b: 182–259) has been sabotaged. It is not surprising – indeed Labov had already predicted the outcome (1972a: 259) – that there is 'a growing sense of frustration, a proliferation of moot questions, and a conviction that linguistics is a game in which each theorist chooses the solution that fits his taste or intuition', except that with apologies to Labov, instead of blaming the linguist's 'taste and intuition' I might have blamed the linguist's position in the struggle for power.

It is likely that my critique of this model of semantics might be attributed to my partiality for SFL. But, so far as I am aware this is not the case (see chapter 1 for a critique of SFL). Just as I did not coin the term 'semantic variation' so also I am not the first to be confused by the contradictions in the dominant model of sociolinguistics[18]. Lavandera's often confusing and Romaine's carefully argued and constructive critique were both by sociolinguists who are themselves active users of the paradigm (Lavandera 1978; Romaine 1984): obviously, their questions arose in the course of doing their sociolinguistic investigations in the Labovian paradigm, even as mine did. Romaine argued carefully the case for the sociolinguistic significance of syntactic variation, and analysed the problems posed by the axiom that the nature of sociolinguistic variation is inherently meaning preserving. She observed that the problems implicated the foundation of sociolinguistics (Romaine 1984: 26–27; emphasis added):

> What Lavandera (and Dines) are questioning is whether this extension [i.e., the extension of variation analysis to the levels beyond phonology, RH.] requires a modification in the nature of the linguistic variable, i.e., the defining criteria of the variable. I think *it requires much more, namely, a modification in our view of the nature and goals of a sociolinguistic theory and the place of such a theory vis aè vis linguistic theory.*

She quotes (1984: 26) Silverstein's view according to which 'the bias towards pure referential categories is one of the principal reasons why social functions of speech have not been built into our analyses of language'.

Over the years, admirers of Labov such as myself have been frustrated by the underlying contradictions in his not explicitly articulated sociolinguistic theory[19]. In particular what has been most irksome is the woefully under-theorised notion of 'social meaning' which would naturally be said to fall outside linguistics proper, because, of course, social meanings are not truth functional. Can there be a more improper linguistics for doing sociolinguistics than the one which sociolinguists have adopted? Labov claims (1972a: 259) 'I do not believe that we need at this point a new 'theory of language'; rather we need a new way of doing linguistics that will yield decisive solutions'. This is surely curious; what else is a 'theory of language' if it is not a guide to 'doing linguistics' in some particular way; if the solutions a linguistic theory offers are less than satisfactory for the purposes one has already argued as essential, then clearly we need to try another theory of language. As I remarked in introducing this chapter, this is not a possibility contemplated seriously in the dominant sociolinguistic paradigm.

Remarkably, Romaine concludes her critique with the suggestion that perhaps multifunctional theories such as that of Halliday's with their orientation to language use as semantic choice in social contexts might be better suited to doing a sociolinguistics whose scope is not arbitrarily limited by the nature of the linguistic theory. There is no doubt in my mind that a move of this kind will also go a long way towards turning sociolinguistics into integrated linguistics (see discussion in chapter 1) – a dream that sociolinguistics dreamt year ago: after all, as early Labov suggests, there is something very wrong with a linguistics that does not study the language people use in their social contexts of living. It is then disappointing to note that Labov is pejorative in his appreciation of functionalism 1987). With due respect for his achievements, one might point out that functionalism has many meanings: perhaps what is needed is not an easy dismissal but a careful deconstruction of what is encompassed by the word in what theory. Superficial and/or pejorative readings of other scholars by a scholar of Labov's stature is quite unacceptable: that this has happened is obvious from a careful re-reading of Saussure's Course in General Linguistics (Thibault 1997) – especially the relationship of *langue* and *parole*. Contradictions there are in Saussure, but not all the faults Labov assigns to Saussure's 'mischievous' linguistic model are of Saussure's making: many are based on a careless and partial reading.

5.3 Is semantic description advanced enough for use in sociolinguistic investigations?

Like all research, the success of research in sociolinguistic variation too depends on both methodology and on theory: both have to be capable of addressing the issues. The same is true of research in socio-semantic variation, which in my view represents an important aspect of sociolinguistics. Labov has questioned, whether explicitly or implicitly, the possibility of semantic variation on both counts. In the preceding sub-sections (5.1–5.2) I have focussed on certain urgent theoretical issues where I have been quite critical of Labov's theoretical position. By contrast, I am an admirer of Labov's methodology. One very attractive aspect of Labov's ground-breaking work is its uncompromising objectivity in the study of the social patterns of language as they occur in their natural communal contexts. The great care taken in the selection of the linguistic variable in the study of phonological variation has certainly played an important part in this. Let us ask then how 'good' is the semantic variant for engaging in sociolinguistic investigations? Of course, a linguistic variant at any level of language is set up by some investigator; thus, depending on the abilities of an investigator, some specific case of semantic variant may or may not be suitable. So to say that some specific category is not valid is a different issue from one which rejects the entire enterprise on the ground that validity of semantic categories will always be suspect. What we need to establish at this point are the desirable properties of a 'good' linguistic variant, whereby the suitability of a semantic variant must be judged. Here is how Labov (1972a: 7–8) describes the properties of a 'good' linguistic variable/ variant:

> It would be appropriate to ask at this point what would be the most useful properties of a linguistic variable to serve as the focus for the study of a speech community. *First*, we want an item that is frequent, which occurs so often in the course of undirected natural conversation that its behaviour can be charted from unstructured contexts and brief interviews. *Secondly*, it should be structural: the more the item is integrated into a larger system of functioning units, the greater will be the intrinsic linguistic interest of our study. *Third*, the distribution of the feature should be highly stratified: that is, our preliminary explorations should suggest an asymmetric distribution over a wide range of age range or other ordered strata of society.
>
> There are a few contradictory criteria, which pull us in different directions. On the one hand we would like the feature to be salient, for us as well as for the speaker, in order to be able to study the direct relations of social attitude and language behaviour. But on the other hand, we value immunity from conscious distortion, which greatly simplifies the problem of the reliability of the data.

It can be claimed with confidence that in principle there is no reason why semantic variants as introduced above (section 5.1) should not have these qualities. Frequency is not an insurmountable problem for the semantic variant; for example there are innumerable naturally occurring social sites where the variant semantic realisations of the act of 'attempting to get someone to do something' might be encountered. Extracts from naturally occurring discourse included in the chapters of this book (see especially chapters 7–8 for commands and their rationale) and the small sample of recorded and transcribed data in the accompanying CD will support this claim. That the semantic variant is fully integrated in a structure is also not open to question: this has been demonstrated above. Specific critique would be useful, whereas blanket rejections play a different game! The chain of analysis which the analytic methodology provides has the advantage of making explicit the critical linguistic locus in the structure whose realisation is variable as well as the mode of analysis for the recognition criteria for each specific semantic variant of that variable. That the distribution of semantic variants is highly stratified by reference to critical social features of users – in our case, more specifically, social class and gender – is demonstrated in every chapter of this volume by the results of the quantitative analysis of the data. So far as the methodology for the identification of the semantic variant is concerned, this does not pose an issue. How reliable is the methodology for the analysis of semantic data?

Here again, Labov has doubts. In his response to Lavandera's critique, he points out (Labov 1978a) that the analysis of semantic variation cannot be expected to be as reliable as that of phonological variation. According to him by all the criteria cited in the quote above, the 'phonological variables appear to be the most useful' (1966b: 49) – useful in the sense that they display all these characteristics, though he does admit that the non-mechanical recognition of sound by the human ear is substantially facilitated by information about syntax and intended morphemes (1972a: 202; emphasis added).

> The ear is a very poor instrument for judging the absolute quality of isolated sounds. But given an understanding of the syntax and *the morphemes intended*, the ear is a superb instrument for judging *which of several possibilities are realized.*

But the accuracy of the machine's perception of linguistic 'noises' should not beguile us into thinking that in natural language use there are any such things as 'isolated sounds'; language in use always occurs as a synthetic whole, which is comprised of meaning-wording-sound – that is one reason for insisting that the internal structure of language has at least these three orders of abstraction. The task of analysis is to separate meaning from wording from sound, and just as the task of a specialist in phonology is to 'isolate' sound from sound, so also the task of the semanticist is to separate meaning from meaning, i.e., to analyse it, but that is not to say that 'isolated sounds' or isolated elements of meaning are in any way crucial to engaging in linguistic interaction. Naturally, the fact is not to be under-rated that mechanical developments have enabled us to analyse 'isolated sounds' very accurately by the use of the acoustic properties of sound waves as recognition criteria. As against this high grade precision, it is worth remembering that phonological variation is sociolinguistically effective not because it can be so well analysed in terms of physical phenomena, but because the difference between the variants *can* be heard by the naked human ear. This ability to hear and discriminate the sounds of the variant has to be assumed even for the initial stereotyping to become possible in a community. The situation is somewhat similar to the semantic variant as well.

It seems reasonable to suggest at the outset that segmental phonology is criterial neither to the recognition of the semantic variants nor to their semantic value. Nonetheless the question of a semantic variant's recognition criteria is crucial, precisely because unlike sound, which is a *sens-ible* phenomenon, meaning by its nature happens to be purely *intellig-ible*. Both its definition and its recognition criteria can be worked out only by attention to how language produces meaning. This, in turn, implies that the criteria cannot be dissociated from how the theorist conceptualises language, because it is this conceptualisation that forms the basis for his linguistic theory (Halliday 1996; Matthiessen and Nesbitt 1996; Matthiessen 2007). The theorisation of context, realisation, system, structure, delicacy, metafunctionality and trinocular perspective – each of which has been discussed in some details in the pages of this volume – have been developed in SFL in order to describe language. And these are the concepts that play significant part in determining the definition and recognition criteria for the semantic variant, as I have briefly indicated in the discussion in section 5.1–5.2 above. Further details are available from a consideration of the system networks and the realisation statements throughout the many chapters of this volume.

It is true that unlike the phoneme, the analysis of the semantic element cannot be carried out mechanically, but speakers' perception of differing ways of meaning does not depend on the possibility of a mechanical analysis any more than does their judgment of sound: in both cases, the reactions depend solely on whether or not the interactants actually 'get the critical elements of the message'. From this perspective, the behaviour of the subjects whose semantic data is analysed in the chapters of this volume shows clearly that the message does get across. Besides, as I have argued above, semantic variation is a fact of natural language use. In view of this, it is odd to say that we cannot turn to the analysis of semantic variation because there are no descriptive means to hand. Surely there is a constant dialogue between theory and practice: their development is interdependent; descriptive means grow in the service of solving linguistic problems. To wait for the means to first develop is like holding back a child from taking part in linguistic interactions until s/he has 'mastered her/ his mother tongue'.

6 Semantic variation: its contributions to sociolinguistics

Studies in semantic variation are highly demanding in time and labour. In what way do they contribute to our understanding of the relationship between language and society? The research reported in the various chapters of this volume points to significant results yielded by the quantitative analysis of the linguistically analysed data. As a user based variety, semantic variation is indicative of the social classification of speakers; the primary vector of classification turns out to be the speakers' social positioning which is socio-logically reflected in their social class; but the gender of interactants also proves to be a significant vector.

In principle, the statistical results of the research reported herein are in keeping with those of phonological variation in general: like the latter, semantic variation too identifies subgroups each of which coincides with socially defined strata. If this were all that semantic variation were going to tell us, attempting the time-consuming and painstaking analysis would have been something of an over-kill, achieving perhaps no more than the work on accent variation. But semantic variation has a very special position in the discourse of language in social life, and that special position has been accorded to it because of the pivotal role that linguistic meanings play in human mental life.

The separation between what goes on 'inside' the human brain and what 'outside' is perhaps transparently obvious. To act effectively on/in the world, human minds have to 'know the world' in some sense of the word 'know'. Contemporary research in neuroscience (e.g., Boncinelli 2001; Edelman and Tononi 2000; Greenfield 1995, 1997) begins to produce an account according to which the human mind is a 'personalised brain', shaped as it is by the experience of living: experience, if you like, becomes mind. But the nature of what it takes the brain to become mind is not material: as Bateson (1972a) put it, there are no coconuts in the brain; some form of abstraction plays a role in this delicate process. No one would question that language plays a significant part in a wide range of human experiences. This experience is mediated as meanings – and I mean *all* meanings, not just those that are simply limited to representing/referring to information which is the stuff of the experiential metafunction, but also the formation of our subjectivities, that is to say, our interpersonal meanings which concern personal judgements, preferences, beliefs, and attitudes to all that surrounds us and that is inside us.

On the assumption that amongst the many modalities of meaning, language is the most pervasive, the most 'time-binding' and the most competent in translating human sensuous experience into habits of the mind – call it *habitus* with Bourdieu (1990, 1991) if you like – which act as the guiding principle of thought, action and reaction – it would seem to follow that linguistic meaning goes a long way in shaping human minds. This is the logical interpretation of Vygotsky's thesis of 'semiotic mediation' (Vygotsky 1978, Wertsch 1985b) as I have argued over the last couple of decades (Hasan 2005). Cutting a long debate short[20], what this implies is that, for the first time in linguistics, the study of semantic variation might be nudging us one step closer to an answer to the 'fundamental sociolinguistic question that is posed by the need to understand why anyone says anything' (Labov 1972a: 207). Long hours of hard work on the semantic analysis of unself-conscious, naturally occurring data would be worthy of the effort, if we begin to see how an affiliation to ideologies is created and changed by different stable ways of meaning, or different 'fashions of speaking', to use Whorf's terminology. For it seems reasonable to postulate that the grammar and semantics of natural unself-conscious speech is, in fact, simply voicing our ideologies, the attitudes of our mind, as made manifest in the semantic variety of our habitual speech. One – admittedly – small aspect of our results points encouragingly in this direction. It was found that social class and gender based variation existed even in the discourse of child-subjects aged between 3–4 years: and the correlation between the maternal fashions of meaning and children's fashions of meaning is high. In fact we can say with confidence that at this early age, children's 'fashions of speaking' begin to significantly reflect their mother's semantic style (see chapter five for discussion); and the mothers' fashions of speaking as we pointed out earlier are themselves activated by social positioning, specifically by their social class and the gender of their addressees, the children.

During the course of the analysis of the data, a curious interaction between register and semantic variation began to emerge. Given the same relevant context of situation displaying a difference in only one single value[21] – that of the social positioning of the speakers – the tenor enacted on the two sites was considerably different in the two cases (see some discussion in chapter 3). Cloran's (1994) work in semantic variation contributed by drawing attention to another important but related characteristic at the level of discourse: habitual speakers of one semantic variety will classify contexts more strongly; they will make vigorous attempts to keep contexts apart, discouraging any action that might cause interruption, while speakers of another semantic variety will tend to tolerate, with ease, movements from one field to another. The upshot is that the over-all organisation of the activity structures becomes considerably different across the two varieties (Cloran 1995, 1999; Hasan 1999a, 2000). In both cases, conversations become porous, but depending on the speaker's view of what a context is context for – what sayings/doings are 'legitimate' to that occasion of talk – it leads to different degrees and kinds of complexity in the discourse. Remarkably, the generic structure potential of register (Halliday and Hasan 1985) is maintained; but attempts to accommodate a conjunction of contexts or to ensure their disjunction leads to complex textual organisation with overtones of cooperation or conflict (Hasan 1999, 2000) – and with development of information or its curtailment (see chapter 11 here). Further investigations need to be undertaken but the results do suggest that there exists a strong likelihood of being able to accurately predict certain – though not all – characteristics of speakers' discourse, on the basis of their semantic variety.

From the point of view of sociolinguistic theory, the implication of this result appears significant. In earlier sections of this chapter (see 2 and 3), using careful analysis, we have separated variation according to use from variation according to user, arguing that 'variation' as understood in 'variation theory' is an instantiation of the latter. If the only methodology that appears satisfactory for sociolinguistic investigation is furnished by 'variation theory', then clearly register variation which instantiates variation according to use would fall outside this domain, or at best simply tolerate it as not the canonical concern of sociolinguistics. In section 4, I have offered some pertinent reasons for rejecting this position. Now on the basis of empirical investigations, we find a strong indication that semantic variation which conforms in its methodology to 'variation theory' (see especially chapter 7, for parallels) bears a systematic relationship to register varieties, such that given a specific community in Australia speakers grouped by reference to their social positioning are highly likely to be grouped *similarly* by the semantic variety they use; and the semantic variety they use is very likely to correlate positively with the over-all development of the organisation of their discourse arising from the conjunction of two or more fields (Hasan 1999). According to this interpretation, semantic variation displays a systematic and orderly relationship between the different categories of sociolinguistic varieties, which together cover the entire gamut of linguistic variation.

By the same token, semantic variation is a powerful explanatory concept for exploring the near-universal pattern of the valorisation of linguistic varieties. This is because its extra-linguistic correlate is based in the speakers' social positioning. Social positioning is itself a complex notion, comprising social factors which are active in the production and distribution of communal resources. Social class is clearly the primary sociological category that is highly relevant to social positioning, but other parameters of social distinction such as education, family status, gender, age, ethnic and/or religious identity, and so on are also relevant in as much as they relate to the ability to access the community's resources for the production and distribution of 'social good' in a given society. In one community, a particular religious identity might provide better access to these resources, in another this factor might be irrelevant by comparison with a particular kind of educational and technological achievement. But social class is one vector which is itself the product of the workings of the patterns of production and distribution of a community's resources; as such it is a palpable symptom of the play of power; thus it is always relevant to social positioning. There is bound to be a complex pattern of interaction amongst the various factors relevant to social positioning, but this is not the place to dwell on that issue (for discussion, see Bernstein 1990, 2000; Bourdieu 1990, 1991; Giddens and

Held 1982). What appears important is the fact that social positioning is the predictor of the principle of valorisation: it is no secret that power attracts admiration. This has the consequence that the closer a group of speakers is to possessing control over the resources for the production and distribution of the 'social good' the 'better' the varieties in *their* repertoire. This judgment is not based on any linguistic 'facts'; rather, it is a judgment that concerns the community's *attitudes* to social facts whose indices are certain linguistic phenomena. The hackneyed saying holds that power corrupts; this may be true but truer still is the fact that admiration of power corrupts and it corrupts not only the admired but also the admirer by corrupting their ability to distinguish fact from fiction.

The ability to carry out semantic analysis is obviously the one fundamental condition for the investigation of semantic variation. But semantic analysis is itself simply a part of the description of language, just as is the phonology that lies behind investigations of phonological variation. Semantic analysis needs to be accepted as an essential element in sociolinguistics even as that domain is defined today. Consider, for example, the concept of 'stylistic variation': how much of what goes on in linguistic variation is said to lead to 'stylistic variation'? and yet the very concept of stylistic variation, or of style itself is less clearly formulated than the 'linguistic variable': at least the latter had a viable methodology. In the study of style over decades there has never been a more superficial statement than the one borrowed unthinkingly from literary criticism, according to which style concerns simply the 'how' of communication, leaving the 'what' untouched. In today's sociolinguistics, discourse of stylistic variation seems to use style in this same way: it too seems to come about in the context of 'meaning preserving' variation. Here the meaning, i.e., the 'what' consists of 'cognitive' meaning which is of course the content of formalistic semantics, which leaves all else out, as if human cognition works without judgment, without evaluations, without attitudes, and as if in the construal of these phenomena language plays no part. Recent writing is not entirely free of confusions. Thus, in one of the fairly recent publications Schilling-Estes (2002a: 375) tells us that:

> Roughly speaking, stylistic variation involves variation in the speech of individual speakers (INTRA-SPEAKER VARIATION) rather than across groups of speakers (INTER-SPEAKER VARIATION). Intra-speaker variation encompasses a number of different types of variation, including shifts in usage levels for features associated with particular groups of speakers – i.e., DIALECTS – or with particular situations of use – i.e., REGISTERS (e.g. Crystal 1991: 295, Halliday 1978). [CAPS in original]

Are we being told that style is really something that individuals 'tend' to have, rather than groups of individuals? If so, then is it just a different label for idiolect? And what is it that the individual is doing when using this thing called style? One thing the individual is said to be doing style-wise appears to consist in making a collage of features from dialects and registers. What are the dialect features, and where do they come from into the dialect? They are just elements of a group's style whereby the groups are doing the same thing while saying something different. What makes up the group which displays inter-speaker variation? Obviously, individuals speaking in some particular way. Decades of scholarship surrounding Vygotsky's work is lost in one carelessly made easy separation between 'individual' and 'inter-individual' as if human infants are born as ready made individuals. Does it not seem reasonable to suggest that there is need to re-think elements of this discourse concerning the nature of stylistic variation? My response would be an emphatic 'yes': and I would reiterate that style is 'meaningful', and that attention to the study of meaning would definitely contribute a good deal to unravelling the conundrum of what one means by style. The only form of variation we can reasonably describe without 'getting into' syntax and semantics is that of accent. For all else, we need the ability to analyse language as a whole – its meanings as well as its form; and we need to understand not only the inside of language but also the environment – the context – in which it is maintained and in which it changes.

To sum up: investigation in semantic variation has the potential of opening up a new horizon for sociolinguistic theory. The true mission of a sociolinguistics that is worthy of that name is to reveal how language and society interact – how language shapes society and how society enters into the process and system of language. The different kinds of variation we find in language open a window on society – the task of sociolinguistics is not simply to describe those forms of variation to understand the nature of language and language change, but also to use the window opened by sociolinguistic investigations for obtaining a better insight into the nature of human societies. That is a necessary condition for us to be able to understand what it is we contribute as speakers to human society – and also how we largely unwittingly collude semiotically in maintaining many of its undesirable traits.

Notes

1 The reference is to a Symposium on Text, Meaning and Variation, convened by J. R. Martin at the University of Sydney in December 1998. The ideas in the original presentation have been reformulated and further developed here particularly with this volume in mind.

2 I am not implying that these recent discussions are in any way a response to my critique: a voice from 'down under' is literally and metaphorically a distant cry, and, in the nature of things, remains unheard in locations 'up at the top'! However, in this chapter, I shall continue the tradition, I opened in the 1980s, of a (one-sided) dialogue by referring from time to time to the chapters in Chambers et al. (2002) just to update some of my critique of the more modern formulations which, though an improvement on the past state-of-the-art literature, still leave something to be desired.

3 Of course in their seminal work, Whorf (1956), Halliday (1976b), and above all Bernstein (1971a, 1975a) had already pointed in this direction. The groups of researches into the working of semantic variation that I and my colleagues Carmel Cloran (1994) and Geoff Williams (1995) carried out are introduced in the accompanying CD.

4 I am referring here particularly to Weiner and Labov (1983), where the authors specifically discuss the semantics of the term 'semantic variation'. The authors suggest that semantic variation is not sociolinguistic in its nature, though accept the possibility that it may be age-related; children still learning their mother tongue might produce instances of semantic variants. Semantic variation is thus a sign of immaturity!

5 The term 'categorical' is far too strong for describing linguistic forms of any kind, which are typically either 'stable' at some point in time or are 'variable'.

6 Though I would not go so far as to subscribe to his view that 'form meaning relation in natural languages is ideally one-to-one'.

7 It will be noticed that in Hasan (1989), I used the Hjelmslevian terms 'content' and 'expression', where content is synonymous with 'that which is coded'; if wording is coded phonologically, then wording is content and phonology expression. The term 'content' used in this way, is clearly not synonymous with meaning/semantics; all it means is 'that which is coded'.

8 In SFL, the phonetic level has not been always indicated as a separate one, though there are strong arguments for doing so.

9 In terms of Hejelmslev the 'content' is 'the same', the 'expression' varies.

10 Consider in this light terms such as 'copula deletion' which presupposes the universality of copula; or the '*gard* becomes *gad*' which assigns priority to the rhotic variety.

11 Naturally I am not suggesting that historical stages of change should be ignored. However, it is equally important to view a variety in its own right as an 'alternative' code/system.

12 The term 'functional' as used here is descriptive: the various varieties are functional in as much as they participate in the design of communal living. There is no implication that such participation is either inherently good or bad.

13 This must be inferred since to my knowledge there has been no discussion on this issue.

14 Compare this with Labov (1972a), especially chapter 8.

15 For a discussion of 'same register'/'same context' see Hasan (1985a, 1995a, 1999).

16 See for example M. A. K. Halliday and C. M. I. M. Matthiessen (2004) *Introduction to Functional Grammar.* 3rd revised edition. London: Arnold.

17 It has to be said that Schilling-Estes (2002b) notwithstanding, the confusion over stylistic variation remains just as acute as it was when I offered a critique of the notion two decades ago (see Hasan 1992a, 1993, chapters 7 and 9, in this volume).

18 I ignore here the sociological critics such as Bourdieu and Williams because their perspective too is one-sided coming entirely from 'external linguistics' (cf. Hasan 1989): the main question for sociolinguistics is how to combine the external and the internal, how to take into account the co-genesis of language and society, whereby language is in society and society in language.

19 Though I grant that the more recent work e.g. Chambers et al. (2002) is taking steps in that direction.

20 The issue is discussed in some detail throughout the various chapters of this volume. See especially chapters 4, 8 and 9–12.

21 Although I say 'one single value'; this single value has, in the words of Bayley, 'multiple causes', since many factors are active in a social subject's positioning.

II

Questions and answers in sociolinguistic studies

3 A sociolinguistic interpretation of everyday talk between mothers and children [1] [1990]

1 Introduction

Recent work in sociolinguistics has put to rest the fiction of language as a homogeneous system: the heterogeneity that Saussure tried to banish from the concerns of 'linguistics proper' is now at its centre. However, Saussure was a master of antinomies, and amongst the many antinomous pairs he created one, which is particularly relevant to this chapter[2]. We refer here to his contrast between the *social* and the *individual*. He gave substance to these terms (Saussure 1966: 14), as he did to many of his key concepts, by relating them to *langue* (language) and *parole* (speaking):

> In separating language from speaking we are at the same time separating: (1) what is social from what is individual; and (2) what is essential from what is accessory and more or less accidental.

Speaking, for Saussure, was 'an individual act', essentially 'wilful and intellectual', where 'the speaker uses the language code for expressing *his own thoughts*' (ibid.; emphasis added). What according to Saussure banished speaking from linguistics proper was the irregularity and unpredictability of speaking; and yet it is arguable that the idea of talk as irregular, accidental and unpredictable is actually an artefact of his own imagination. Despite his repeated claims about the social nature of language, and the constitutive role of speaking in the creation and evolution of the system of language, Saussure continued to ignore both the social nature of human talk while highlighting individual volition, and the interdependence of the process and system of language. So what is foregrounded is the individual ownership of thoughts, ideas and concepts as perhaps the only important facts about speaking. But how true a model of human talk is this? Is speaking truly irregular, accidental, and unpredictable? Is it truly a-social?

These are the questions we wish to address here by reporting on a small part of a wider research[3]. We shall attempt to show that the nature of human talk is essentially social; and it is this fact which explains its non-accidental and reasonably predictable patterns. The work of such scholars as Labov (1972a, 1972d), Trudgill (1978), Milroy (1980), Romaine (1982a, 1982b, 1984) and others has certainly cast doubt on the veracity of the Saussurean claim. But to show the regular and non-accidental nature of speaking, these scholars have mostly examined the level of sound i.e., the expression plane rather than the content plane of language in terms of Hjelmslev (1961). Our focus is different: we wish to ask whether and to what extent talk is non-accidental and predictable even at the higher level of language, namely, that of meaning.

In adopting this focus, we immediately place ourselves outside that sociolinguistic tradition, which assumes that systematic variation is simply limited to the levels of form and phonology, and could not extend to the level of meaning (Labov 1978a) – a view, questioned recently by some (e.g. Lavandera 1978, 1988; Romaine 1984; Plum and Cowling 1987; Nesbitt and Plum 1988; Hasan 1988, 1992a, 1992b). In the dominant sociolinguistic tradition of today, while the social origins of variation in phonological and syntactic selections is readily accepted (Labov 1972a, 1972d; Labov and Weiner 1977), there is an unwillingness to grant that variation in semantic selections could also have its origin in social factors. The reasons for adopting this position are complex: on the one hand, there is a romantic celebration of individualism, according to which each of us is unique, and our individuality is purely a gift of nature, a manifestation of our 'free will', unadulterated by anything social. It follows that the choice of meaning cannot be granted to be in any way governed by our social attributes! At the same time, there is a tendency to misinterpret statements about what meanings people *actually* mean as a matter of habit: they are heard as claims about these speakers' *inability* to mean any other meanings (Labov 1978a). This interpretation is as unjustified as would be a claim that the habitual deletion of /r/ in the casual speech of the working class East Side New Yorker is of no consequence simply because these same speakers 'can' produce more r-full speech in other environments. The situation is further confused because scholars engaging in these debates have rather different ideas about the nature of language and the place of meaning in language study.

In the following section, we shall briefly outline our understanding of the term *semantic variation* within a functional approach to language, showing how such an approach helps us examine predictable regularities in the patterns of meaning in natural everyday dialogues. We will then go on to present a brief outline of the research together with a fragment of the framework for analysis before presenting and discussing the results of our empirical findings.

2 Meaning and the concept of 'semantic variation'

The idea of linguistic variation, like many productive ideas in the study of language, in fact dates quite far back in time. Humboldt's classic *Linguistic Variability and Intellectual Development*, was first published in 1836; and even while Saussure[4] was actively perfecting his doctrine of language as a homogeneous system, a sophisticated view of variation in language was being put forward, for example, by Mathesius (1964; see also Chloupek and Nekvapil et al. 1987). Within a decade of the appearance of Saussure's *Course*, Firth (1935: 29; emphasis original) had forcefully rejected the idea of homogeneity as even a possible attribute of the system of language:

> Unity is the last concept that should be applied to language. Unity of language is the most fugitive of all unities, whether it be historical, geographical, national or personal. There is no such thing as *une langue une* and there never has been.

Important as the insights of these scholars are, today the study of variation in language is deservedly synonymous with the name of Labov, whose pioneering work gave sociolinguistics its present powerful impetus. Amongst Labov's many achievements, two appear most impressive: his efforts to provide empirical foundations for a theory of language change (Weinreich, Labov and Herzog 1968); and his development of a methodology for an empirical study of sociolinguistic phenomena (Labov 1966a, 1968, 1972a, 1972d). However, the idea of variation in language cannot be separated from one's overall conception of what language is like. On closer examination, it would appear that Labov's ideas about the nature of language, and of the place of meaning in language are sadly out of step with his professed desire to study language in its social context (e.g., in Labov 1972b: 183–259).

Simplifying the debate a great deal, there are at present two opposing views about the relation of meaning (semantics) and wording (linguistic form). In the first view, call it the *externalist view* (Hasan 1988), meanings exist independent of linguistic form; the form simply expresses it. To use current terminology, syntax is autonomous, and the lexicon corresponds to what there exists in the world. This view logically leads to the truth functional analysis of meaning, wherein 'to know the meaning of a sentence is to know under what conditions that sentence would be true' (Kempson 1977: 23), and naturally such 'truth characterization must be responsive to antecedently given facts' (Fodor 1977: 28). With this conception of meaning, it appears valid to ask, as Labov does: 'When a speaker does not choose a passive to express a given meaning, what form does he use?' (Labov 1978a: 94), with the clear implication that meaning is independent of form; what is capable of changing is just the expression, or at best just the 'expressive/stylistic meaning' which one is given to understand is somehow less important to the theory of meaning than cognitive meaning – i.e. meanings to which truth functional analysis can be applied.

There are some severe limitations in such an approach. Specifically, if one is interested in the social motivations for linguistic variation, the limitations of this approach create a closure, making semantic variation a theoretical anomaly. This can be easily demonstrated from a consideration of the nature of the *linguistic variable*. If we wish to maintain that /*gard*/ and /*gad*/ are variants of each other, this is a valid assumption if and only if the two variants bear the same relationship to some higher level constant (Halliday 1975c). That higher level unit here would be the lexicogrammatical item which is orthographically represented as *guard*; it is only the fact that both pronounciations – /*gard*/ and /*gad*/ – are expressions of the same higher level unit *guard* that gives the variants validity as variants of each other, but note that the value of the unit *guard* is defined by its semantics, and constituted by its grammar. The variable is said to be *socio*linguistic, if the choice of the variants correlates with some socially significant circumstance(s) of the speech community (Hasan 1973a). In a model of language where syntax is autonomous, and meaning is correspondence to antecedently given facts, there can *logically* be no higher level constant by reference to which semantic variants could be validated, since from the wording one 'exits' directly into the world of (some set of) objects, events, circumstances etc. of sensuous experience. But these sensuously experienced phenomena *per se* cannot be part of any *theory* of language. Since the theory makes no viable abstraction from these phenomena, it lacks any means by reference to which semantic variants can be validated. The inevitable consequence is that semantic variation becomes a theoretical impossibility, not necessarily because socially conditioned regular and predictable patterns of semantic variation, comparable in all respects to socially conditioned regular and predictable phonological variation, cannot be found in the behaviour of the speakers of a language, but simply because the theory is not equipped to handle this phenomenon.

Opposed to this externalist view is the tradition in which the world of human meanings is seen as an artefact of the various semiotic systems, which evolve in the living of social life. From this perspective, linguistic meaning is constituted by the formal means of a language, with the implication that while signifying language external phenomena – in Saussure's sense of that term – meaning itself remains a language internal fact. In this *internalist approach* (Hasan 1988) the lexicogrammar itself is functional: it is a resource for making meaning. This constitutive view of meaning in language, and of language in society is amply illustrated in the work of many scholars (see, for example, Boas 1911; Mathesius 1964; Sapir 1921; Malinowski 1923, 1935; Firth 1957;

Mead 1934; Wittgenstein 1958; Whorf 1956; Hjelmslev 1961; Vygotsky 1978; Halliday 1970, 1973a, 1973b, 1975a, 1975b; Bernstein 1971a, 1973, 1975a; Bateson 1972a, 1979; Vološinov 1973; Hymes 1971; and many others). Whilst these scholars are not in agreement on all issues related to language, on one fundamental point each holds the same position: every language has a semantics that is unique in some respect to that language. Further, for a majority of these scholars, language plays a central role in constructing the socially significant aspects of the world that impinge on human experience. This turns cognition itself into a socially created phenomenon.

3 Semantic variation and systemic-functional linguistics

Clearly a detailed discussion of any one of these approaches would be out of place here. We will simply note briefly, some important concepts from systemic functional linguistics (henceforth, SFL), which is associated with the name of Halliday. We single out SFL because amongst the many functional approaches, it alone appears to span the wide spectrum from the social to the phonological, thus possessing the potential to link social processes to the processes of individuals' interaction. The theoretical concepts highlighted here are just those most relevant to the study of meaning from a sociolinguistic point of view.

Let us take first the question of the place of meaning in the system of language. Like Prague School linguists, Halliday sees language as a tristratal system, in which the strata of meaning (i.e., semantics), wording (i.e., lexicogrammar, comparable to syntax plus lexicon), and sound (i.e., phonology and phonetics) are realisationally related, as shown in figure 1.

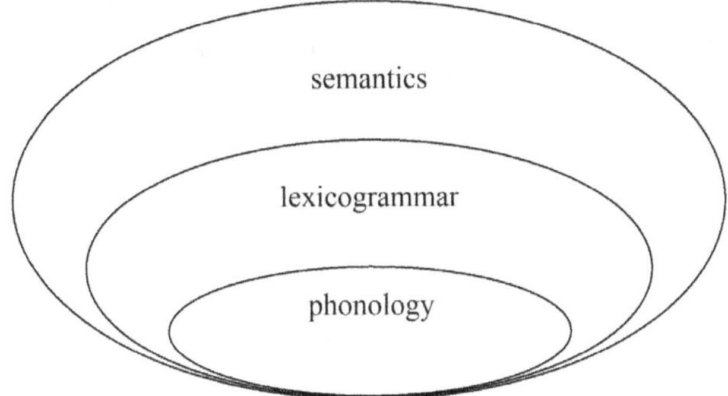

Figure 1: The internal structure of language

What figure 1 does not make clear is the asymmetry of the realisational relation across these strata. According to Halliday, Saussure's line of arbitrariness of relation between the signifier and the signified coincides with the boundary between phonology and the remaining levels of language. In Halliday's view, the relation between the remaining two levels is qualitatively different: 'The relationship between meaning and wording is not, however, an *arbitrary* one; the form of the grammar relates *naturally* to the meanings that are being encoded' (Halliday 1985a: xvii; emphasis ours).

This position is in keeping with the Saussurian principle that linguistic meanings do not pre-date the sign system, and that the value of a signified acts on its referential capacities. It is important to emphasise that the axiom of natural grammar does not entail isomorphism between specific units at the level of semantics and those at the level of lexicogrammar, which is not to claim that such 1:1 relations would be altogether absent. Note also that linguistic form is not a bricks and mortar affair (Hasan 1985d, 1987a), in which elements of the lexicon are cemented together by syntax, with lexicon mirroring the world while syntax remains autonomous. From the formalist approach flow at least two important implications for sociolinguistics; (i) that it is possible to study phonological variation, without necessarily implicating the level of semantics, particularly if the term semantic is equated only with referential correspondence[5]; and (ii) that it is *not* possible to study syntactic variation, as if this too could by-pass the question of semantics. In SFL, by contrast, the question of the relationship of meaning to wording has to be at least treated as problematic; it cannot be just set aside lightly as by Labov (1978a) and Labov and Weiner (1977). As recent critique (e.g., Romaine 1984; Plum and Cowling 1987; Nesbitt and Plum 1988) shows this is precisely an area where sociolinguistics is faced with uncertainties.

If the SFL theory were to stop simply at the claim that lexicogrammar is constitutive of meaning, then by implication linguistic form would turn into a veritable 'prison house', limiting the possibilities of semiosis, and providing no mechanism for the diachronic evolution of human meaning potential. The reason such *stasis* is not found in language is that (a) the relation between the two strata of meaning and wording is not temporal/causal, but dialectical; and (b) that both meaning and wording are functional in nature. The meaning-wording strata of language have evolved dialectically in the service of the speaker's living of life in society (Malinowski 1923, 1935; Halliday 1970, 1973a, 1975a, 1976b etc.). The pressure on speakers to engage in acts of meaning is not exerted because the means for meaning are just lying around as autonomous syntax; the pressures for meaning *cannot* arise from within the language; instead, it is exerted from those social conditions of speakers which exist materially, and/or are imaginable. This perspective introduces two further important concepts: (1) function; and (2) social conditions for linguistic interaction.

Again, like Prague School linguists, Halliday's theory is functional, though there do exist important differences (Davidse 1987). There are three inherently related senses in which the term *function* is used in SFL theory: (i) function as element of structure e.g. Actor is a function in the transitivity structure of the clause; (ii) function as the purpose for which language is being used at some specific time and place between some specific speakers e.g. to flatter, to deceive, to persuade etc.; this is then the function of a spatio-temporally located use of language; and (iii) the functions of language that are not specific to any particular spacio-temporally located use, but which represent a higher order abstraction such that these functions are present in every exchange of linguistic meaning: to mean is to perform such function(s) irrespective of whether one is flattering, deceiving, praising or whatever else. We are concerned here only with the third sense. In this third sense, in SFL, function is now most often referred to as *meta-function*, a usage that is adopted below. The theory recognises three such metafunctions; these are (1) IDEATIONAL; (2) INTERPERSONAL; and (3) TEXTUAL.

The ideational metafunction permits us to make sense of the world. According to Halliday, it has two components: experiential and logical. To say that language has an experiential metafunction is to say that in any linguistic act of meaning, speakers' experience of the material world as well as the inner world of their consciousness will be an aspect of the information being exchanged: the experiential function of language is to encode experience, to refer to the world of things, events etc. The logical function of language is to construct relations between states of affairs, e.g., if this event then that event; or this event and (then) that event; logical relations also exist between objects and therir properties. The ideational meatfunction covers a vast domain of linguistic meaning which makes sense of the world for its speakers, but in the very act of making sense of the world, we use language also to act on others; by speaking we not only make accessible some of our personal experiences, we also create, maintain or change social – that is to say, interpersonal – relations. Each act of meaning is thus a way of acting on others, of revealing our own subjectivity, and our relation to other interactants. Language has therefore an interpersonal metafunction: i.e., it must be able to be used to make such meanings. Finally, no interaction takes place in a social vacuum: forms of talk and the nature of the social process are intertwined. Language, therefore, must have properties which make it possible for speakers to use it to display relevance of their talk both to the frames of social practices and to those parts of the ongoing discourse which relate to the specific social practice in which the speakers are engaged. This is the third metafunction, known as the textual metafunction: human language has the resources for construing relevance within what is being said and between the structure of the social practice and the organisation of the discourse.

There are at present many functional theories of language (Dirven and Fried 1987); but SFL is unique in attaching equal weight to all metafunctions, and in maintaining that in the majority of cases, every message would manifest all four metafunctions. For Halliday, the facts of the semantic level are organised under the rubrics of these four metafunctions; and one way of understanding metafunctions is to say that they are kinds of meaning (Halliday 1970, 1985b). This implies that two messages could have the same meaning from the point of view of some one metafunction, but might differ with respect to the others. Thus *you will see him tomorrow* and *will you see him tomorrow?* display the same experiential (kind of) meaning, but differ from each other in both their interpersonal and textual meanings. It is possible then to maintain that a change of form will typically be indicative of some change in meaning, though the possibility of holding some meaning constant is clearly not denied.

In most current theories today, the term *semantics* means 'the study of meaning', but at the same time the meaning of the word meaning is limited to only *one* kind – that which resembles meanings which SFL would describe as pertaining to the experiential metafunction; so meaning in these theories is purely referential. This explains why in such theories, it is important to recognise additional components for the description of meaning and why these additional components have to be thought of as external to semantics and why they are given distinctive labels such as *pragmatics*, *text linguistics,* and even *sociolinguistics*. In a model where interpersonal and or textual meanings have the same weight and status as experiential or logical and none can be sensically manifested except in union with the others, the question of such separation does not arise. The level of semantics becomes synonymous with what in other models is discussed in fragments under the labels of semantics, pragmatics, or speech act[6].

But if metafunctions are kinds of meanings then they must be relatable to (i) the SOCIAL CONTEXT, i.e., the conditions in which interaction is located and from which the meanings derive their functionality; and (ii) to lexicogrammar, from which the meanings derive their constitutive being. We will examine the first issue first. In modern linguistics, the close relationship between CONTEXT OF SITUATION and acts of linguistic meaning was first explored by Malinowski (1923, 1935). Following Malinowski's lead, Firth (1957) attempted to provide a more abstract characterisation of the concept context of situation . Since then many scholars, including Halliday, have explored this area. Halliday's thinking represents a refinement of both Malinowski and Firth. At the same time, his concept of context of situation is unique because of its relation to the metafunctions at the semantic level, and so by implication, to the lexicogrammar. Looking at context of situation as an abstraction from social process, Halliday identifies three essential parameters of this situation: (1) The nature of the social process: what social practice are the speakers engaged with? This is known as the FIELD OF DISCOURSE; (2) The nature of social relations: how do the speakers relate to each other? This identifies the TENOR OF DISCOURSE; (3) The means whereby the exchange of meaning transpires, and the way the interactants are able to talk and act together: what part does the language play in the social process, and how interaction between the speaker and addressee occurs? This defines the MODE OF DISCOURSE. According to Halliday, these three aspects of the context of situation are always relevant to any exchange of meaning: the text will always reveal the nature of these contextual parameters.

If the meaning-wording levels of language have evolved to serve human needs, it follows that there will be some relationship between the elements of the social processes and the kinds of meanings made by human languages. It is Halliday's claim that the three metafunctions are motivated by and are constitutive of the parameters of the contextual construct. More specifically, it is typically the manipulation of ideational meanings that results in the realisation of specific fields of discourse, while the manipulation of interpersonal and/or textual meanings alone would fail to provide such information. Similarly, the choice of ideational and/or textual meanings would be less relevant to listeners' perception of the social relation between the interactants; rather, this aspect of the context of situation would be realised typically by a patterning of interpersonal meanings. Textual meanings, on the other hand, would be pertinent for the creation of coherence and relevance in discourse. Halliday sees these statements about the relation of metafunctions to the contextual variables as assertions of propensities, rather than as some sort of absolute law[7].

If Halliday's claims are accepted, then it follows that in SFL theory, there exists a level of abstraction above the level of semantics. We shall refer to this as the *contextual level*. The contextual level, unlike the semantic level, is not internal to language; however, the relationship between these two levels is a realisational-constitutive one. The regular and non-accidental nature of speaking is partially explained by reference to this dialectic between the levels of context and meaning. What meanings speakers will mean and what kind of contextual construct others will see them as engaged in are not unrelated phenomena: the majority of listeners are not born with the gift of telepathy, and speakers do not live in a solipsistic universe; the shared knowledge needed for cooperative behaviour is in fact based on engagement in and observation of others' acts of semiosis. We only know what use language is being put to by becoming aware of the meanings being exchanged. The implication is that the nature of context for the use of language and the selection of meanings by speakers placed in that context correlates non-randomly. In fact, it is this non-random correlation that is often known as *speech variety* or *diatypic variation.* Although this is one kind of systematic variation in meaning selection, the main emphasis of our chapter is not on diatypic variation.

Unlike most theories, SFL theory is paradigmatically oriented. It does not start with the question: what do the meanings in this language correspond to? Rather, it begins by asking: what choices for meaning and/or structure making are available in this language for linguistic actions in some specific environment? System networks represent this potential from a paradigmatic perspective. As Halliday (1985a: xiv) points out, in a system network, the description at each level of language is presented as:

> networks of interlocking options: either this, or that, or the other, and so on...(this) means starting with the most general features and proceeding step by step, so as to become ever more specific... Whatever is chosen in one system becomes the way in to a set of choices in another ...

The system specifies environments, in the first instance, by reference to a unit on the rank scale, and then by treating each option as theoretically the point for further options. This latter feature builds in the property of DELICACY OF DESCRIPTION in the model – the description becomes more 'delicate', i.e., more detailed as the systemic description continues. To illustrate these points, it is only at the rank of clause that the systemic choice between [minor] and [major] has any consequence; and it is only if the option [major] is chosen, that some other options become available. The option [major], in turn, is the environment in which it makes sense to say that the clause may have the feature [indicative] or [imperative]; and it is only in the environment of the choice [indicative] that a further option between [declarative] and [interrogative] becomes available; and so on. Here the option [major] classifies the grossest category of clause, and the option [declarative] specifies a far more delicate category. This set of interrelated choices forms one system network at the lexicogrammatical level – that of MOOD. One version of which is shown in figure 2.

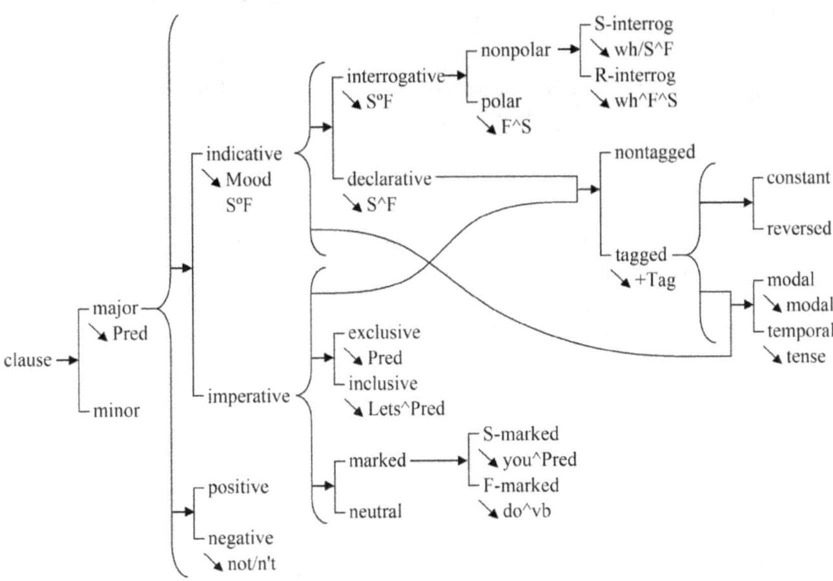

Figure 2: A simplified MOOD system network

The option [*major*] also functions as the environment for some other concurrent systems of options e.g. TRANSITIVITY (Halliday 1966–68, 1970, 1985a etc.) which derives from the experiential metafunction. This implies that the choices in these concurrent systems are available to all clauses with the option [major]; thus underlying each clause is not only a concatenation of choices from MOOD, but also from the other concurrent systems. Figure 3 presents the conventions for reading network notations.

Halliday has claimed that an examination of a system network, e.g., that of MOOD or TRANSITIVITY, would reveal that each such system is prototypically related by realisation to some one metafunction. Thus while the options in the MOOD system realise (some part of the) interpersonal metafunction, those in the TRANSITIVITY system realise (some part of the) experiential metafunction. At the same time, there is evidence (Halliday 1973b, 1979a) that metafunctions are logically related to the contextual variables (as discussed above). This can be taken as evidence that these metafunctions, and only these, need to be postulated to explain how language works in the social life of its speakers.

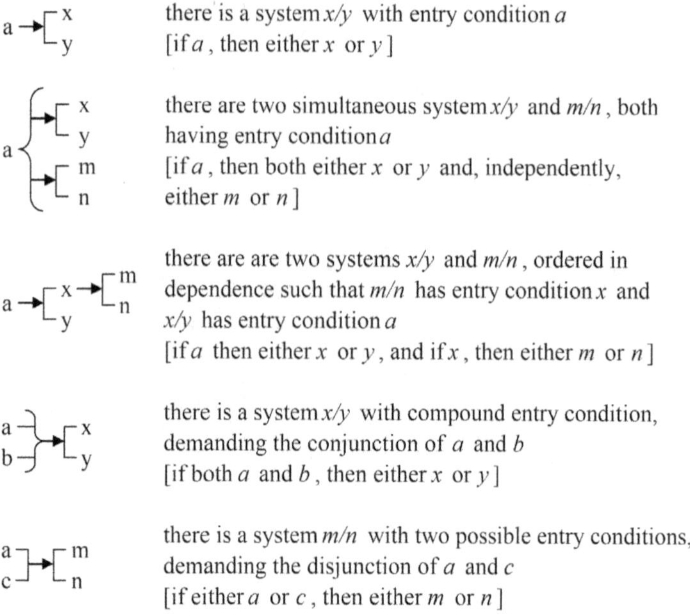

Figure 3: Notational conventions for systemic representation (after Halliday 1973a: 47)

In SFL theory, the shape of the lexicogrammatical structures – i.e. *syntagms* – is said to be realisationally related to the systems of paradigmatic choices. The mechanism for activating this generation is the (set of) *realisation statements*, which specify how the options in the system are finally actualised as a syntagm. For example, the systemic options [declarative] sets in motion the realisation statements which might yield beginnings of a syntagm consisting of the elements Subject^Finite^Predicator in that order. Table 1 indicates some of the steps whereby realisation statements mediate the structural shape of a syntagm, determing its recognition as a category.

Table 1: Paradigmatic motivation for syntagmatic structures: lexicogrammar

Paradigmatic options	Mediating realization statements
1 [major]	(i) insert element Predicator (ii) Predicator preselects verbal group
2 [indicative]	(i) insert element Mood (ii) expand Mood as Subject·Finite (iii) Subject preselects nominal group / nominalization (iv) Finite preselects primary tense / modal
3 [declarative]	Order Subject·Finite as Subject^Finite

The options of each system are accompanied by such realisation statements, from which it follows that each system expressive of a metafunction generates a syntagm of its own, with structural functions specific to that metafunction. Thus a given syntagm manifests more than one line of structure. The hypothesis of multiple structures is in keeping with the hypothesis of the equality of the multiple metafunctions of language. The recognition of multiple structures for each syntagm provides greater resource for the recognition of variation. This can be appreciated from focus on the syntagm *the children are eating ice cream*; figure 4 presents an analysis of this syntagm in terms of MOOD (interpersonal metafunction) and TRANSITIVITY (experiential metafunction).

<table>
<tr><th>The Syntagm</th><td>The children</td><td>are</td><td>eating</td><td>ice-cream</td></tr>
<tr><th>Constituents</th><td>nominal group</td><td colspan="2">verbal group</td><td>nominal group</td></tr>
<tr><th>Transitivity structure</th><td>Actor</td><td colspan="2">Process: material</td><td>Goal</td></tr>
<tr><th rowspan="2">Mood structure</th><td>Subject</td><td>Finite</td><td>Predicator</td><td>Complement</td></tr>
<tr><td colspan="2">Mood</td><td colspan="2">Residue</td></tr>
</table>

Figure 4: Some structural representation of a syntagm

Compare the above with the syntagm *Are the children eating ice-cream.* Following the same method of analysis, its transitivity structure would be identical to that in figure 4. However, there will be a notable difference in its Mood structure, with the Finite *Are* preceding the Subject *the children.* Given such an analysis, it becomes much easier to show at what point and in respect to which feature variation has/has not occurred. The principle of paradigmatic description applies to all levels of language. Thus at the semantic level as well, systems of semantic choices describe the possibilities of meaning within certain formal and contextual environments. And each semantic option is accompanied by some realisation statement(s), exactly as with the lexicogrammatical options (see figure 5 in section 7, p. 101). Claims about variation based on careful criteria such as these are in every respect as objective as those based on phonological analysis: in other words, there is no need to exclude semantic analysis because it is 'vague' and 'uncertain' by its nature, as is sometimes maintained.

How does such an approach to language help in the examination of semantic variation? Each of the characteristics of SFL described above plays an important role. First, it helps preserve the concept of semantic variable by providing a level above the semantic level. The clasim is that if two semantic features are in systemic contrast, they may be said to have the status of variants each of which expresses the 'same' variable. For example, suppose at the level of context, we can recognise a unit of action e.g., *speaker rationalises (i.e., specifies why action is demanded of the addressee)*, then there are a set of semantic variants that could express this contextual unit as in example 1 below:

(1): (if you do such-and-so)

a: you'll get very tired [reason]

b: I won't give you a goodnight kiss [threat]

c: you can have some sweeties later [bribe]

Thus, the contextual unit ACT OF RATIONALISATION may be realised by more than one distinct semantic variants [reason] or [threat] or [bribe][8]. The variants here are semantic features so we cannot say that variation 'preserves' meaning any more than we can say that r-full and r-less variants of *guard* preserve the phonological make up of a unit! The relation of the two semantic variants to their higher level constant is the same as the relation of the phonological variants */gard/* and */gad/* to the higher level constant – the wording unit *guard*. If empirical research were to show that the selection of one semantic variant as against the other correlates non-randomly with some specifiable social circumstance of the speaker, then there would not appear to be any reason for denying the reality of semantic variation.

Secondly, the SFL view of language makes a rich contribution to the concept of meaning. Unlike the formalistic models it does not just privilege referential meanings; it assigns equal status to interpersonal (i.e., social) and textual meanings as well. The immediate benefit of this for the study of semantic variation is obvious. In models with just a truth functional i.e. referential approach to meaning, one is limited to the search for antecedently given concrete phenomena. With the functional approach to language, at least some significant hypotheses can be put forward for the social origin of what in current sociolinguistic studies is known as categorisation, accommodation, pragmatic relevance, and so on. Certainly reference as naming under the rubric of 'categorisation' can be studied with better effects by a sensitive scholar such as Labov, but even then the relevance of any social factors to the acts of categorisation remains something of a mystery (see for example Labov 1973 on cups and mugs). By contrast, in the systemic functional approach, the data for the study of semantic variation do not have to be limited to 'word meanings': meanings construed by grammar may be examined – for example, one may enquire how frequently mothers ascribe the children the role of 'do-er' rather than 'done to'. If it is found that male children are ascribed the doer role significantly more often than the female ones, this would be a fact of a social order indicating one vector of male social power to which female accommodation might be needed. It is only this kind of fully functional focus that will permit us to understand the ontogenesis and maintenance of ideologies. That such a functional perspective explains much about thought and discourse is perhaps evident from the work of scholars such as Vygotsky (1978), Vološinov (1973), Bernstein (1971a, 1973, 1975a), Halliday (1970, 1973a, 1974b, 1975a, 1975b, 1976b) and many others. Since the level of meaning is intermediate between that of social situation and wording, any postulated semantic unit is described twice, once as an expression of some social fact, and again as expressed/constituted by some pattern of wording. This implies that the validity of postulating something as a significant semantic option can be examined both in the social context of the speakers and in the formal structure of their language.

Finally, the fact that the entire description of language takes the form of interlocking systems of options appears highly relevant. In the most general sense, the idea of variation is the idea of choice; where there is no choice there can be no variation (at least of the kind introduced by Labov) whether in meaning or in wording or in sound. However, we are suggesting that it is also possible to examine variation in linguistic behaviour which does not presuppose the existence of alternative expressions of some particular higher level constant: there can be in the words of Halliday variety without (a Labovian type) 'variable' (Halliday 1975c). This happens to be the case with the semantic level. For it would seem possible to examine semantic variation by reference to the notion of *delicacy of description*. Simplifying a fairly complex set of arguments, what is being proposed can be exemplified by reference to example 1 above. If the semantic features [reason], [threat] and [bribe] are in systemic contrast, we may postulate that the systemic semantic environment in which this choice is available is [reasoning], which itself is expressive of a speaker's actual *act of rationalisation*. In this case then the characterisation of message by the semantic feature [reasoning] identifies a more gross category of message than the more delicate feature [reason] or [threat] or [bribe]; at the same time, it is comparable to the classic case of variation in that the act on the higher level of context remains identical, i.e., it is an *act of rationalisation.* What is significant is that now, instead of focussing on variant expressions alone, we are focussing on two more delicate sub-categories of a relatively gross category. In our research, such variant realisations have been taken into account while examining semantic variation.

4 The research subjects

One central concern of the research was to ask: is there any evidence of semantic variation in everyday dialogues? If so, does it correlate with the social class position of speakers? These research questions were embedded in the more general concern with the effect of semantically different interactive practices on the formation of human consciousness, and the possible consequences of the latter on future interaction. To be able to examine these last concerns, we needed to focus on dialogues between dyads, where one member of the dyad would be already 'naturalised' into some socially recognised ways of saying and meaning, while the other would be at a formative stage, and as yet not appreciably influenced by many other significant interactive relations. Clearly, mother-child dyads, with children between the ages of 3;6-4;0 would be suitable subjects. Before the age of four, at least in Australia, peer group influence is[9] not a significant factor in the life of the child, and the mother is the most important 'other' in the child's interactive universe. The average age of the children who acted as subjects in the dyads for this research was 3;8.

The question of social class is very much more problematic, particularly when the subjects are children and (at least some unemployed) mothers. It could be argued that since they do not form part of the labour force, they should not be seen as belonging to any social class (see, for example, Horvath 1985). We suggest that this argument is based on an unviable interpretation of the function of social class in the life of social subjects. Belonging to a social class is tantamount to gaining access to the possibilities for active participation in a specific set of social processes (Connell 1983: 148). These possibilities are non-identical across social classes; further they are not totally exclusive to the bread winning member of the family, but encompass the family as a unit. Thus, for example, infant mortality is much higher in lower class areas of Sydney than in the upper classes; similarly, significant differences will be found in the incidence of unemployment, malnutrition, miscarriages and accidents. When the life chances of women and children are determined by the social status of the family to which they belong, it would seem extraordinary to deny them the privilege of 'belonging' to the social class of that family.

The definition of social class presents yet another problem. Marx criticised 'vulgar common sense' for turning 'class differences into differences in the size of one's purse, and class conflict into a quarrel between handicrafts' (Bottomore and Rubel 1976: 208). Criteria such as occupation, income, education are circular since they are 'implicationally' related. And while they could be used heuristically, to us it appeared best to use more fundamental concepts in the class determination of the subjects for this project. The criterial questions concerned the extent to which a person's position might permit decision making for day-to-day conduct of work-related practices allowing the subject to pass on these decisions to others for execution. Thus it is the exercise of power and access to control of others' activities that decided the class position of the subjects. Clearly this has to do with autonomy at place of work. The answer to these important questions about the subject's autonomy at work, was not a simple *yes* or *no*. Where the answer was *none* or *very little*, as with a council truck-driver or a contract brick-layer, the family was considered to belong to LOWER AUTONOMY PROFESSION (henceforth, LAP); where the answer was *considerable*, as with a bank manager, or a doctor, the family was considered to belong to HIGHER AUTONOMY PROFESSION (henceforth, HAP). The population for this research consisted of 24 mother-child dyads, equally distributed into these two groups. As the interaction of social class and sex has been long recognised in sociological studies, female and male children were also equally represented. All mothers were born and brought up in Australia, and none had lived abroad for a length of time greater than six months. Their first language was English. In effect, in the context of Australia, the implication of these criteria is that all subject dyads are white Australians.

5 Recording mothers and children

Following Labov's lead, it has been generally accepted in sociolinguistic studies that in speaking, the production of phonological patterns is at the lowest level of consciousness. A greater degree of conscious control is assumed both for syntax and for meanings. It is, however, arguable that this position is the natural product of one's view of both syntax and meaning. For example, if meaning is prototypically the referent of some lexical item, one might suppose it to be at a higher level of awareness: indeed this is precisely what Whorf (1956) thought. But in the first place, in SF linguistics meaning is not equal simply to reference or naming; secondly, and more significantly, the concern was with configurations of semantic choices, whose lexicogrammatical realisation would include lexical items but also go beyond them to cryptotypic features. Whorf (1956) had argued that the awareness of such patterns of meaning is likely to be much below that level of consciousness at which might lie the awareness of the meanings of individual isolated (lexical) items. If so, then the possibility of speakers' conscious control on the production of configurations of meanings is about as unlikely as the possibility of conscious control on phonological production.

Clearly for any sociolinguistic research, it is important to ensure the typicality of semantic selections by speakers: the data must reflect habitual linguistic behaviour. Labov (1968, 1972a, 1972d) has shown that, increase in self-monitoring of talk produces significant patterns of variation. If the speakers were required to do something which they would not normally have done at that place, at that time, with that particular other, then the chances of self-monitoring would be considerable; and/or if some outsider, e.g. the researcher, were present in a context of situation which was typically a private domestic one, not open to the prying eyes of an investigator, a certain degree of self-awareness could not be ruled out. We therefore sought the mothers' help in collecting the data: we gave them small and powerful audio-recorders, which once turned on did not need attending to. We asked them to turn it on whenever they felt they would like to when they were engaged in talking to the subject child. Mothers were told that they did not have to worry about turning the machine off and on all the time if the child appeared and disappeared briefly; but to turn it off only when they felt that the child had now become engaged in something else and would not be returning to his talk with her for some considerable time. They were specifically advised to do nothing special to make the child talk since our purpose in collecting the data was to find out what the children say when left to themselves, i.e. not prodded into talking. We, however, did ask them to do the recording at different times of the day so that the children's talk would occur during the different activities in which they engage as a matter of course every day, giving us a wider view of what children like to talk about in their natural contexts of living.

Much to our surprise and delight, we found allies in the little children who unwittingly helped maintain the naturalness of the data. Since the powerful Sony tape recorder was quite inobtrusive, and since there was no researcher/outsider present at the time of the recording, the children had no sense of being in a situation that was in any way other than normal. And whilst mothers did know that whatever was being said was for others' ears, they were unable to act in ways other than usual, because their little children insisted on the same maternal 'face' with which they were already familiar. Further, the mothers were doing this recording at a time when they were engaged in their normal household chores, e.g. attending to the child's toilette, providing snacks, helping with some toy, cooking meals, washing up, and so on. Any one who has juggled the many balls that mothers juggle every day in coping with an immature human in a world of objects and activities would have no difficulty in figuring out how difficult it is to behave other than habitually under such circumstances.

6 The collected data and its contexts

Each dyad was given six hours' worth of recording tapes, but due to the recording instructions mentioned above, there was bound to be some wastage. The total amount of talk collected is approximately 100 real hours. As the resources of this project were limited, and the semantic analysis was labour intensive, all of this data could not be subjected to analysis. Criteria for deriving a viable smaller sample were based on a consideration of the nature of the 100 hours of talk. The SFL model provides a framework for describing the context of situation in which some socio-historically located speaking has taken place. Could the 100 hours of talk be described in general terms, using the framework provided? Recall the three relevant parameters (1) field of discourse; (2) tenor of discourse; and (3) mode of discourse. We will use here the more detailed account of the three contextual parameters following Hasan (1985a, b, c) to examine the nature of the mother-child spontaneous dialogues that we collected.

Beginning with the field of discourse, let us look at the GOAL ORIENTATION of social activity. Over the 100 hours, the social activity would appear invariant if we only consider the LONG TERM GOAL: it could be maintained on reasonable grounds that the activity in which the dyads were engaged was one of socialisation. As long term goals are seldom conscious ones, we suggest that without necessarily realising the fact, the mothers were giving their children early lessons in ways of being, behaving and saying. However, in view of the recording instructions to mothers, not surprisingly, the SHORT TERM GOAL displayed a great deal of variation: they baked cake, they made corn bread, they cleaned rooms, they washed up, they 'read' books, they played all sorts of games, and so on. Each dyad did a myriad things; and no two could be said to be exactly identical in the choice of such activity. However, informally speaking, all 24 dyads were found to interact in somewhat similar MATERIAL SITUATIONAL SETTINGS (Hasan 1973a; Cloran 1994), which can be globally characterised as (a) mother giving care to the child e.g. providing food, giving a bath, dressing etc.; (b) mother and child engaged in some cooperative action, e.g. playing with building blocks, reading picture books, cooking, cleaning up some part of the house etc.; and (c) mother engaged in day-to-day household chores, while child is present in the same location doing something or just watching. It would be wrong to confuse these material situational settings with the notion of social activity relevant to the discourse; rather each situational setting is as general as, say, telephoning, where the social activity may be as diverse as extending an invitation, making a medical appointment, or enquiring about the availability of some goods.

Now it is important to note that the second aspect of field i.e. its EXPERIENTIAL DOMAIN is subservient to that social activity that is oriented to short term goal (Hasan 1994). Thus if the short term activity is to invite someone to a dinner party, the experiential domain relevant to this would be certainly different from that where the short term goal of the activity is to find out the availability of some goods from a department store. This aspect of the field is realised lexicogrammatically, typically via the experiential metafunction, as an organisation of referring to objects, attributes and specific states of affairs (Hasan 1994). I have argued elsewhere (Hasan 1985b, c) that short term goal of activity is typically conscious; by contrast, long term goals of activities often remain covert, and below the surface of participants' consciousness. If the comments about the relationship of short term goal to domain of experience and of the latter to lexical selections are correct, then it would follow that the lexical aspects of a text are the least suitable materials for an examination of semantic variation. In this study, the selection of lexicon is, in general completely ignored, except in as much as it might be implicated in the realisation of some lexicogrammatical configuration. By contrast, the activity of socialisation is a better candidate for the study of semantic variation because of the unconscious nature of its long term goal.

While the material situation settings (a)-(c) introduced above are not such as to indicate the experiential domain, they are not entirely irrelevant to the study. In fact these settings are like malleable frames which are shaped by the workings of the discourse into some specific fields. This possibility is relevant in the context of socialisation. If over an equal amount of talk between the individual dyads, we find some that, for example, use these malleable frames more often for issuing threats, while others use these same frames for providing reasons, then we would be justified in postulating the existence of semantic variation in the socialising activity of the two groups. This strategy has been followed in our study of semantic variation.

The description of the tenor of discourse appears very much simpler. So far as the SOCIAL STATUS relation is concerned, we have a hierarchic dyad formed by (superordinate) mother and her (subordinate) child; and it is in the nature of this relationship that the SOCIAL DISTANCE between the two would be near-minimal. As the long term goal is socialisation, the AGENTIVE ROLES socialiser for mother and socialised for the child appear reasonable. Since in our study, activities with short term goal orientation were ignored, the immediate action based agentive roles are irrelevant. If, then, a pattern of semantic variation is found, such that it exists independent of the variations arising from differences in the experiential domain, it becomes reasonable to ask: what does this variation correlate with, particularly as it would seem that the relation between participants remains invariable?

Finally, the mode of discourse: here, the CHANNEL used is PHONIC; there was in the majority of cases also visual contact between addressee and speaker: the two interactants were where they could see and hear each other. The MEDIUM is SPOKEN and DIALOGIC since the linguistic patterns of the dialogue appeared to conform more to patterns characteristic of speech, and since frequent turn taking as is typical of dialogues took place. Due to lack of space, we shall make no comments on the ROLE OF LANGUAGE, except to add that since the role of language is sensitive, amongst other things, to short term goal orientation, this too varied both within and across the many recorded dialogues. The description of the context of situation for the dialogues is presented in summary form below:

Field of discourse
Long term goal orientation: socialisation into ways of being, doing and saying.
Short term goal orientation: (varied across the various dialogues).
Experiential domain: (varied across dialogues).

Tenor of discourse
Agentive roles: (varied across the various dialogues).
Social relation: hierarchic: mother knowing; child novice.
Social distance: near-minimal.

Mode of discourse
Role of language: (varied across the various dialogues).
Channel of access: phonic with visual contact.
Medium of interaction: spoken and dialogic.

In deriving the sample from the 100 hours of mother child talk, first those discourses were set aside which due to some reason, e.g. household noise, were not intelligible. From the remainder, approximately 45 minutes of talk per dyad was selected as the sample to be analysed. Each dyad was within reason equally represented for each setting (a)-(c), keeping in mind the malleability of the situational settings and the relevance of this to possible variation to context and meaning. All results are based on this sample, which was transcribed as dialogue in ordinary orthography and consisted of approximately 22,000 messages (for transcription conventions, see Hasan 1986a; Butt 1989b; Cloran 1989). Message was defined as in Hasan (1973b mimeo).

7 Analytic categories: an example

Since the principle of paradigmatic organisation applies at all levels of language (see section 3, esp. discussion of figure 2), it is reasonable to suppose that the facts at the semantic level can also be represented as systems of interlocking choices. Our research design demanded a network that represented the semantic choices available to the speakers of English, regardless of the occasion of its use; i.e. what would be described as an *open context system network* of semantic options applying to the potential rather than some specific type/instance of context. In fact, given the relationship between linguistic meanings and context of situation, a particular set of semantic options chosen from such a network in the speech of some speaker could itself be used as a means for identifying the nature of the speech event. This must follow logically, for example, from Hyme's notion of language as constitutive of context as well as from the postulated relationship between meaning and context in the SFL model.

The construction of the semantic networks is one point in the model where Halliday's postulate of both multifunctionality and the equality of status between the multiple functions can be further tested out (Halliday 1973b, 1979a). It transpires that if one is interested in the meanings of the messages, one could not ignore any aspect; nor could one claim greater centrality for one kind of meaning in comparison with the others (Hasan 1985a, b, c): a message packages all kinds of meanings together, and the form of language does not present any viable justification for the recognition of separate 'fields' e.g., pragmatics, speech act analysis and so on. The interpersonal functions of the messages are just as important as the textual functions: it is not much use knowing that some one is making a statement, without also knowing whether the statement is in response to something said by some one else or not. Just as it matters whether the response message is logically related to, say, point of enquiry in a question. And it is also important to know whether messages are used to describe a state of affairs centering round a voluntary action or one that is imposed by some external source. If all metafunctions are seen as equally important to the meaning potential of a language, then the semantic system networks must represent all, as do the lexicogrammatical ones. Such a network was prepared by Hasan (1983). It should be added immediately that the network does not represent all or even *nearly* all semantic options available to the speakers of English, just as no account of speech act analysis is exhaustive with respect to all possible speech acts in using a language. To prepare such a semantic network would be an enormous enterprise, quite beyond the resources of this investigation. A cut-off point in delicacy was chosen such that it would permit us to ask the kind of questions we were interested in exploring. Certainly this cut-off point in delicacy is quite gross, when compared to what would be necessary, if for example, one were to use such a network for the machine generation of meaningful dialogues. Gross though the network is when judged by that standard, it is still too vast to be presented within the scope of one such publication. Figure 5 is a simplified version of a fragment from Hasan (1983), displaying semantic options available to speakers of English for attempting

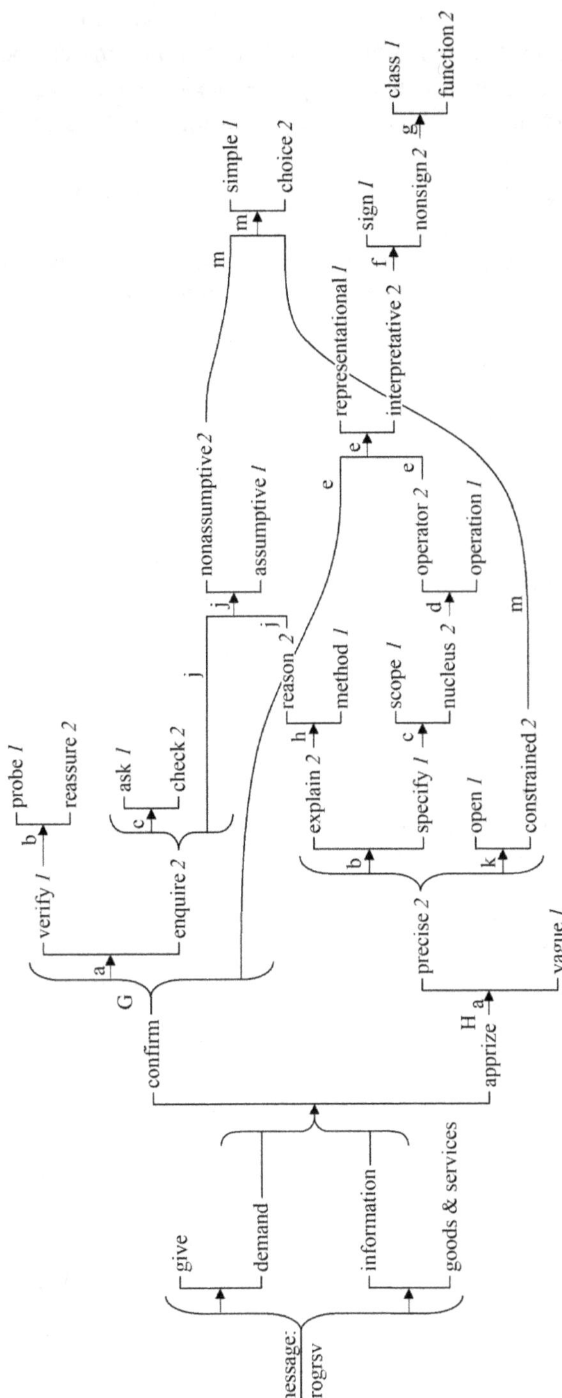

Figure 5: A simplified system network of semantic choices in asking questions

to find out some information from someone[10]. Since the SF model conceives of meaning as constituted by lexicogrammar, it follows that nothing can be entered in the semantic network, that cannot be expressed lexicogrammatically. As Halliday (1973a) points out, to be valid each semantic option in the system network must be accompanied by some realisation statement(s). Table 2 Part I presents the lexicogrammatical realisation statements (column 3) for some of the options (columns 1, 2) from figure 5, while Part II provides examples of the relevant Selection Expressions (SE stand for 'selection expression' and refers to logically possible combinations of options from the system).

Table 2: Realisational statements and examples: H [apprise] as entry condition[11]

PART I: OPTIONS AND THEIR REALISATIONS

ACCESS > H = [DEMAND; INFORMATION; APPRISE]

(interrogative: non-polar; wh- conflated with Theme)

a1	[vague]	ellipsis of Finite and Predicator; AND Theme MUST BE initiated as *what/ how about* with nominal group following
a2	[precise]	interrogative: non-polar
b1	[specify]	wh-element MUST NOT conflate with Circ: Reason OR Circ: Method: Principle
b2	[explain]	wh- is Adj *why/../how/..*
c1	[scope]	wh- is Adjunct; conflates with any Circ EXCEPT Reason or Principle
c2	[nucleus]	wh- is Subj or Comp *who/what../which..*
k1	[open]	interrogative: non-polar MUST NOT be followed IN SAME TURN by an elliptical clause whose single element matches wh-element in function
k2	[constrained]	non-polar interrogative, followed by elliptical clause with single element whose function is the same as that of wh- in the non-polar interrogative; turn change between the two NOT ALLOWED

ACCESS > H a2:k2 [apprise: precise: constrained]

m1	[simple]	elliptical clause MUST NOT enter into parataxis with another elliptical clause with identical structure
m2	[choice]	elliptical clauses MUST enter into parataxis with at least one more elliptical clause with identical structure

ACCESS > H a2:b1:c2 [apprise: precise: specify: nucleus]

d1	[operation]	wh- = *what* is Comp; Lex Vb Pred MUST BE *do/happen/go on*
d2	[operator]	wh- is Subj or Comp *who/what../which..* AND *do* NOT ALLOWED as (non-substitutive) Lex Vb in Pred; *happen/go on* NOT ALLOWED as Lex Vb in Pred
e1	[representational]	Pro [rel: intensv: attrbtv] NOT ALLOWED IF (1) Carr is sign and Att its meaning OR (2) Carr is non-sign and Att its class name

e2	[interpretative]	Pro MUST BE [rel: intensv :attrbtv] AND (1) IF Carr is sign Att MUST BE its meaning OR (2) IF Carr is non-sign Att MUST BE its class name
f1	[sign]	Carr MUST BE a sign e.g. *word/number..* AND Att its meaning
f2	[non-sign]	Carr MUST BE *this/that..* (i.e. implicit reference device)
g1	[class]	Att MUST BE class name of Carr
g2	[function]	wh- = *what.. -for* MUST conflate with Circ: Purp

ACCESS > [apprise: precise: explain]

h1	[reason]	wh- = *why/for what reason/what for*
h2	[method]	wh- = *how/by what method/on what principle*
j1	[assumption]	polarity negative
j2	[non-assumptive]	polarity positive

PART II: SELECTION EXPRESSIONS (=SE) AND EXAMPLES

SEs are grouped together on the basis of some feature(s) common to that group. These features are called assumed options. The assumed options for a group are listed at the head of the group; they are not displayed in each SE individually.

1 Assumed options h [apprise]

SE1 *a1* [vague]

(can't you remember anyone else's name?)
how about the boys?

SE2 *a2:b1:c1:k1* [precise: specify: scope: open]

where shall we put him?/who can I play with?...

SE3 *a2:b1:c1;k2:m1* [precise: specify: scope; constrained: simple]

where shall we put him? up here?

SE4 *a2:b1:c1;k2:m2* [precise: specify: scope; constrained: choice]

where shall we put him? up here, or in your room?

2 Assumed options h a2:b1:c2 [apprise: precise: specify: nucleus]

SE5 *d1;k1* [operation; open]

what are you doing?/now, what's happening here?

SE6 *d1;k2:m1* [operation; constrained: simple]

what are you doing? colouring your pictures?

SE7 *d1;k2:m2* [operation; constrained: choice]

what are you doing? eating or playing with your food?

3 Assumed options h a2:b1:c2;d2 [apprise: precise: specify: nucleus: operator]

SE8 *e1;k1* [representational; open]

who gave you those?/what are you eating?

SE9 *e1;k2:m1* [reprsnt; constrained: simple]

who gave you those? Nana?

SE10 *e1;k2:m2* [reprsnt; constrained: choice]

who gave you those? Nana, or daddy?

4 Assumed options h a2:b2:c2:d2:e2 [apprise: precise: specify: nucleus: operator: interpretative]

SE11 *f1;k1* [sign; open]

what's handsome boy? (= what does handsome boy mean?)

SE12 *f1;k2:m1* [sign; constrained: simple]

what does this say? David?

SE13 *f1;k2:m2* [sign; constrained: choice]

what's this sign? add, or take away?

SE14 *f2:g1;k1* [non-sign: class; open]

what's that?

SE15 *f2:g1;k2:m1* [non-sign: class; constrained: simple]

what's that? a boat?

SE16 *f2:g1;k2:m2* [non-sign: class; constrained: choice]

what's that? a boat, or a catamaran?

SE17 *f2:g2;k1* [non-sign: function; open]

what's that for?

SE18 *f2:g2;k2:m1* [non-sign: function; constrained: simple]

what's that for? for baking cookies?

SE19 *f2:g2;k2:m2* [non-sign: function; constrained: choice]

what's that for? for baking cookies, or scones?

5 Assumed options h a2:b2 [apprise: precise: explain]

SE20 *h1;k1* [method; open]

how does this work?

SE21 *h1;k2:m1* [method; constrained: simple]

how does this work? by battery?

SE22 *h1;k2:m2* [method; constrained: choice]

how does this work? by battery or electricity?

SE23 *h2:j2;k1* [reason: assumptive; open]

why don't you want to kiss me?

SE24 *h2:j1;k2:m1* [reason: assumptive; constrained: simple] why don't you want to go there? because of the other kids?

SE25 *h2:j1;k2:m2* [reason: assumptive; constrained: choice]

why don't you want to go there? because of the other kids, or something else?

SE26 *h2:j2;k1* [reason: nonassumptive; open]

why can you light fires?

SE27 *h2:j2;k2:m1* [reason: nonassumptive; constrained: simple]

why did it die? because it was old?

SE28 *h2:j2;k2:m2* [reason: nonassumptive; constrained: choice]

why did it die? because it was sick, or because it was old?

8 Answer: the point of a question

Although for lack of space, we have presented only that fragment of the semantic choices in figure 5 which realise the act of seeking information from an addressee, the results to be discussed below concern not simply these but also the semantic choices in giving information in response. Thus the focus of the results discussed in section 9 below is on dyadic behaviour: how mothers ask children questions and how they answer their children's questions, and its converse, i.e., how children ask mothers questions and how they answer their mother's questions. Before turning to these results, it may be useful to examine a few extracts to see some of the ways in which questions and answers can be used. The most typical use of a question is to receive as response some information, this being the 'preferred' or 'expected' response (Levinson 1983: 307; Halliday 1985a: 69). And while it may be true that most questions are 'paired' with an answer, the term 'answer' itself is not invariable. So the kind and extent of information received can differ a good deal. Mothers – and children even as young as the ones used as subjects here – can treat a question as a point of departure for providing information that far exceeds what was strictly asked for, as example 1 shows:

Example: 1

Mother: (1) can you try and remind me to ring Pam this afternoon?
Kristy: (2) mm (3) why?
Mother: (4) I'm going to ask her if she'll mind you one night next week
Kristy: (5) mm
Mother: (6) 'cause I'm going out to dinner with some of the ladies from the playgroup (7) because she is leaving
Kristy: (8) pardon? (9) pardon?
Mother: (10) I'm going out with some of the playgroup ladies (11) because Sue is leaving
Kristy: (12) mm

Mother: (13) did you know that they're going to leave?
Kristy: (14) no
Mother: (15) they've been building a house
Kristy: (16) mm
Mother: (17) oh they haven't been building it (18) someone else has been building it for them (19) and it's nearly finished (20) and they're going to move to their house in May
Kristy: (21) why in May?
Mother: (22) they're going to wait until the end of the school term
Kristy: (23) mm
Mother: (24) because Cathy goes to school now (25) and then she will change to her new school after the holidays
Kristy: (26) mm
Mother: (27) if they'd moved earlier (28) she'd only go to the new school for a week or two (29) and then they'd have holidays you see (30) it would mess it up a bit for her

This extract provides a good illustration of the variability of answers. Note in passing that the very first message would not be treated as a demand for informartion, but rather as a particular kind of demand for service, i.e. a consultative command. Kristy's message (2) is thus a case of compliance, since it is a positive response to a command. The mother interprets Kristy's message (3) as a search for explanation; and strictly speaking, her response in (4) does provide this information. But the mother does not stop there; she goes on to give the reason for the already offered reason. The demand for information here produces not simply the information sought, but also information that had not been explicitly sought. By contrast, the mother's own question (13) receives a minimal response in Kristy's (14): the child could not have said less than this without appearing to ignore her mother's question.

As answers, the mother's (4) and (6-7) on the one hand, and the child's (14), on the other, present two extremes: the mother's response in message (6) would be analysed as an *adequate non-minimal* answer, realised by an elliptical clause complex; and yet in (7) she goes on to elaborate upon this by giving more information that is related to the matter in hand, but has not been specifically sought. By contrast, the child provides the barest amount of information that is necessary and sufficient to be treated as a possible answer, and does not go on to add anything else. These two situations appear clearer by contrast with how Kristy's question in (21) is fielded by the mother. Here it is not so very easy to decide what constitutes sufficient information. Perhaps the mother's message (22) is enough? But enough for what? The information that Kristy receives from her mother is seven message long, and it appears to be important to the child – note that she tracks this information closely as evident from her *mm* (23, 26) – the mother's lengthy response reveals to her the significance of May as a time for moving to the new house.

An elaborated answer is then not just 'extra verbiage' and example of 'middle class verbosity' (Labov 1972d: 220). If an answer is an attempt to provide a response that in the respondent's view meets the enquirer's specific need, then elaborated and unelaborated answers display two different estimates of the enquirer's needs. So far as the speakers in a natural dialogue are concerned, in providing elaborated answers, they are not providing information that is 'optional extra' – at least in their own view. Equally, if they do not elaborate, they are not with-holding information that they consider essential to the ongoing discourse. Rather, through the semantic features of their answers, they are indicating what they themselves understood to be the point of the question, and how much information would be enough. Not surprisingly, elaborations typically provide some kind of condition, explanation, reservation, alternative etc. to what would have been 'technically' a necessary and sufficient answer, whether minimal or non-minimal.

Whether an answer would be considered [adequate] or [inadequate] is closely related to the idea of the point of a question. In the analysis of the data for this research we have attempted to keep the idea of adequacy separate from factuality. Consider the following example:

Example: 2

Karen: (1) you read it mum
Mother: (2) it says 'this book belongs to Karen Megan'
Karen: (3) this book belongs to Karen Megan
Mother: (4) that's right
Karen: (5) and that says Karen Megan, doesn't it?
Mother: (6) that's where you scribbled on it
Karen: (7) where? .. (8) where?
Mother: (9) mummy wrote that

Karen's question (5) seeks confirmation, simply needing reassurance that the state of affairs is as she sees it; and it may be that what the mother says in (6) is factually correct: at that particular place in the book Karen might have scribbled. But this statement of the mother's neither supports nor denies the thesis of the child's question, which is simply that at a specific spot in the book there is some mark/writing which stands for *Karen Megan*. Had we not had (7)-(9), we might have been tempted to think that perhaps this is an indirect way of saying: *yes this does say Karen Megan, because that's where you have scribbled (something by way of indicating your name)*. But obviously this is not the interpretation the child is entertaining: she does not recognise the spot that the mother is talking about as identical to the one she herself was talking about. The mother's answer is therefore [inadequate]; it fails to address the point of the question. And, so far as the response to the child's (7) and (8) is concerned, it would be difficult to assign it the status of an adequate answer. A very frequent variety of inadequate answer in our data is that attracted by question whose function it is to seek explanation, e.g. in the following:

Example: 3
Mother: (1) put it up on the stove (2) and leave it there
Karen: (3) why?
Mother: (4) 'cause
Karen: (5) that's where it goes?
Mother: (6) yeah

The mother's (4) *'cause* as an answer to the child's (3) *why* is inadequate, since all it manages to say is something like: *the cause is*. Note how in (5), the child provides what would be a possible, i.e. adequate answer to her own question. Yet another variation on this type of question and answer is provided in the following exchange by the same dyad:

Example: 4
Mother: (1) but you'll be glad (2) when you go back to school, won't you?
Karen: (3) no
Mother: (4) why?
Karen: (5) 'cause
Mother: (6) 'cause why?
Karen: (7) 'cause Rebecca don't go to my school any more

So while it is true that questions are normally used to elicit information that a speaker might need for some purpose or other, the success of this venture depends a great deal upon what the addressee does in response to the question. For example, there are various ways of *responding* but not *answering*: one may simply disclaim knowledge of the facts, and/or plead failure of memory, as in the following exchange between Karen and her mother. Again we are not concerned with the factuality of such assertions; what matters is that so far as the questioner is concerned, behaviour of this kind could very well be a closure so far as that avenue of enquiry is concerned.

Example: 5
Karen: (1) you— you— you try guess a name, alright?
Mother: (2) um .. there's John … isn't there?
Karen: (3) who else?

Mother: (4) I don't know (5) I can't remember

Here, the mother's last two messages disclaim knowledge of fact, and use failure of memory as the reason for not being able to provide the requisite information. There are also occasions in the data, where what looks very much like a disclaimer is actually used as a kind of qualification, warning the questioner that the answer being provided is not necessarily the correct one. This is the case in this short exchange between Nathan and his mother:

Example: 6

Nathan: (1) ah .. yes (2) where is it standing?

Mother: (3) I don't know darling (4) I'm just suggesting perhaps you look there (5) it could be there .. (6) go and have a look.

Here although the mother begins by denying knowledge of the whereabouts of the toy ladder, she does so not, as it were, to evade answering; rather, her message (3) is more like an attempt to absolve herself from being held responsible for what is in her opinion just a guess. In the analysis of the data, such cases would not be treated as evasion.

It is not our intention to identify here all the ways in which an answer may be evaded; however, it is important to point out the logical end-point of evasion. This happens when the addressee, simply ignores the question, failing to give any response whatever, as happens in another exchange between Nathan and his mother:

Example: 7

Nathan: (1) mummy, oh-oh, where does this go?** (2) I know where .. (3) d'you know where this goes?

Mother: (4) no (5) do you?

Nathan: (6) yes .. (7) look

Mother: (7) oh yes

Nathan: (8) that's where [?] (9) what does right in the corner mean? (10) what does right in the corner mean?

Mother: (11) what does right in the corner mean?

Nathan: (12) yeah (13) where's the little bit?

Mother: (14) it means go as far as you can possibly go

Nathan: (15) oh, here's the little bit (BEGINS TO CHANT TO SELF) ..(16) mum see that's the bit up here, isn't it, mum? (17) mum, that's the little bit up here, isn't it mum? .. (18) mum, this is the little bit off there, isn't it mum? .. (19) there mummy lets—

The concept of ignoring is meaningful, if the listener has been given a reasonable chance to reply; the absence of an answer has a different meaning when this opportunity is not present. So for example, Nathan's message (1) is not answered by the mother, but the double asterisk (**) attached to the end of the message (1) indicates that the child did not stop to let the mother answer. When in fact he does so in message (4), the mother provides the answer. By contrast, his questions (16)-(18) are ignored by the mother; there was enough opportunity for her to answer as shown by the absence of the asterisks as well as the presence of the dots at the end of the messages in question, which indicate pauses greater than normal as indicative of turn end. Our data shows that in some families ignoring questions is a typical mode of 'fielding' them. As can be seen from this very short extract, Nathan and his mother are often parties to such exchanges (cf. Nathan's message (9-10)). The effect of such ignoring is typically that the questioner is forced to repeat the question, as Nathan is in example 7, and Karen in example 2 (messages (7-8)). When in an exchange, questions are not being repeated, this raises the possibility that response is being provided.

9 Asking and telling: some results from an empirical investigation

With these brief comments on questions and the response to questions, we turn to the statistical analysis of the semantic features pertaining to questions and to responses to questions. The total number of questions asked by mothers and children in the sample was 3,358, with children asking a little over one third of the questions (1,350) and the mothers the remainder (2,008). This figure does not include those interrogative clauses whose function was to realise some kind of command e.g. message (1) in example 1: *can you try and remind me to ring Pam this afternoon?*, or offer as in *shall I do your laces up?*. Nor does the number include formulaic questions asked by way of channel repair e.g. *what?* or *what did you say?* or its other variants.

A principal components procedure was used for the statistical analysis of variance in the data[12]. The chief attraction of this method was its ability to isolate sub-classes in the research population: it enabled us to answer an important question: if the only criterion used was the habitual selection of some pattern of semantic features, how would the dyads in this research, numbered 1 to 24 in the input, be grouped? Once such groups are identified by the statistical analysis, we could examine how the grouping compared with the grouping based on some extralinguistic criteria (e.g., LAP v. HAP, or male child v. female child). From the total set of semantic features used as input the statistical analytic procedure isolates specific bundles; each bundle is known as a Principal Component or just PC, and subjects are allocated scores on each feature of the bundle. Each Principal Components Analysis (PCA) generates a number of such PCs, with PC1 referring to the bundle accounting for the highest degree of variance. Due to lack of space, the discussion in this chapter will focus only on PC1 of the two PC Analyses that were carried out (1) the semantic features of questions asked by children and the answers to those questions by their mother; and (2) The semantic features of questions asked by mothers and the answwer to those questions by their children. The two analyses are referred to as A1 and A2, respectively. Thus the tables presented below are called PC1-A1 (CQMA i.e., childrens' questions, mothers' answers) and PC1-A2 (MQCA, i.e. mothers' questions and childrens' answers) .

10 The discussion of results: PC1-A1

Table 3 shows the loadings on the features of PC1 of A1 which concerns questions asked by children and the answers to those questions by their mothers. Note that the first letter of each semantic feature in the table is either Q or A: Q stands for a *Question attribute*, A for an *Answer attribute*. Two more points need to be made clear: if a semantic feature used as input is in systemic contrast with only one feature, then entering one such feature as input provides information regarding both. Thus in table 3 Q[explain] is one term in a binary system, the other being [specify] (see figure 5 Ha2b for the system and table 2 for realisation and examples of each term); the loading for Q[explain] is positive at .65; from which we deduce that if, instead of [explain], the feature [specify] had been entered as input, the loading for the former feature would have been negative at -.65, i.e. the exact opposite of the loading on Q[explain]. Thus the semantic features used as input not only state information; they may also imply information that is not explicitly asserted in a table. Below we will discuss some such features in table 3. The second point to note is that not every semantic feature used as input is equally significant to the variance associated with some PC; those features are considered more relevant which reach a certain statistical criterion. In the analyses discussed here, only those features were considered significant which loaded at or above .40. It is important to add that practice in this respect is varied[13]. The semantic features that load criterially on PC1-A1 in table 3 are shown in italics.

Table 3: PC1-A1: children's questions and mother's answers

semantic features	PC1-A1
Q[*repreat*]	-0.85
A[*provide*]	0.81
A[*elaborated*]	0.66
Q[*explain*]	0.65
Q[confirm]	0.37
Q[prefaced]	0.38
Q[ask]	-0.01
A[*adequate*]	0.47
A[assumptive]	-0.08
Q[*related*]	0.44
Eigenvalues	2.98
% Variance	29.90

Before discussing what is implied by the bundle of the criterially loading semantic features in table 3, let us first present a brief discussion of these. Q[repeat], with its negative loading of -.85 implies that subjects scoring high on this feature are highly unlikely to repeat their questions. As argued above in section 5, one important incentive for repeating questions is the absence of an answer. The absence of repeated questions raises the expectation that answers are provided without delay. This expectation is more than justified by A[provide] with positive loading at .81 and A[adequate] with positive loading of .47. These loadings indicate quite clearly that dyads scoring high on PC1-A1 have mothers who answer the child's question without unreasonable delay and provide adequate answers. This is more remarkable in view of the fact that children in dyads scoring high on this PC are more likely to ask *how/why*-questions as predicted by the fact that Q[explain] has a positive loading of .65: these children are quite unlikely to ask questions with the features [confirm] or [specify] (for these terms see figure 5 and for realisations and examples see table 2). That the mothers in high scoring dyads would be highly likely to elaborate their answers is shown by the positive loading of .66 for the feature A[elaborated]. In step with this, children in the high scoring dyads select the feature Q[related] more often than not. This semantic feature is a more delicate sub-set of the feature [elaborated]. What it implies is that the clause realising question is logically related to some other clause by an overt indication of hypotaxis or parataxis. An example of hypotaxis is provided in Kristy asking her mother *why <<if you're on a picnic>> you can light fires too?* (= why can you also light a fire if you're on a picnic?); an example of parataxis is found in Kristy's comment *I'm so quick, aren't I, with this cooking? and I also make scones.* When the features A[elaborated] and Q[related] are interpreted together, the implication is that compared to the low-scoring dyads, those scoring high on PC1-A1 attach more importance to making their meanings specific and explicit by adding and modifying necessary information.

For obvious reasons, it is the PC as a whole that should be treated as *one* complex socio-semantic variable, so long as the variance significantly correlates with some social attributes of the subjects; as explained above, amongst these the criterially loading features are the ones that are most significant from the point of view of the variance associated with it. The bundle of features in column one of PC1-A1 (table 3) account for 29.9% of variance in the data, and correlate significantly with social class, while they are barely short of significant correlation with the sex of the child. On the basis of the pattern of scoring represented in table 3, the high scoring dyads' habitual fashion of meaning may be stated in informal terms as follows:

Child:

- does not repeat her/his questions;
- is much more likely to ask *how/why* questions rather than *who/what/where/when..* questions or *is it/does it* kind of question;
- is more likely to relate her/his question to some other message, so elaborating on the question itself;

Mother:

- is highly likely to answer immediately;
- is much more likely to answer adequately than inadequately;
- is very likely to elaborate upon the necessary and sufficient answer.

The kind of dyadic behaviour specified above turns out to be much more typical of HAP dyads than of the LAP ones (HAP> LAP: p <.01), as figure 6 shows. At the same time, there is a near-significant correlation between this behaviour and the sex of the child. These ways of asking questions and of being responded to are more typical of mother-daughter dyads (=F) than mother-son ones (=M) (F > M: p< .06).

Figure 6 shows the location of LAP (=L) and HAP (=H) dyads by reference to their scores on PC1-A1. The horizontal axis of this figure relates to PC1-A1, while the vertical relates to PC2-A1. Since the horizontal axis shows lowest to highest scores from left to right, the implication is that the higher a dyad scores on PC1-A1, the more to the right that dyad's location would be in the figure. By contrast those scoring high on PC2-A1, would be in the top half of the figure, and the lower scoring in the lower half. We shall not be discussing PC2-A1 here.

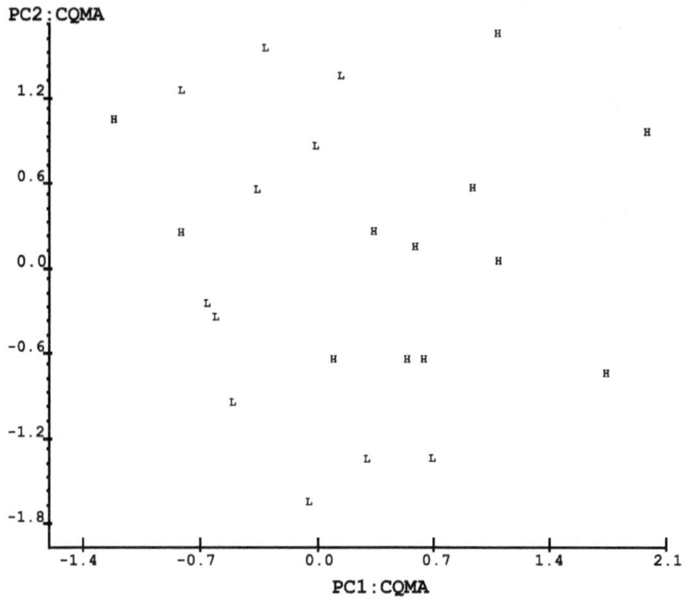

Figure 6: PC1-A1 PC2-A1 scores of lap–hap dyads: children's questions, mothers' answers

11 The discussion of results: PC1-A2

Analysis 2 concerns the results of the second input, which consisted of the same semantic features but this time the features relate to mothers' questions put to children and children's answers. It was found that just like PC1-A1, a socio-semantic variable was constituted also by PC1-A2, correlating significantly both with the social class of the dyad and the sex of the child, while accounting for 32.1% of variance in the data. The total input specification of the loading on the various input semantic features for the second analysis is shown in table 4.

Table 4: PC1-A2: mother's questions and children's answers

semantic features	PC1-A2
Q[*confirm*]	0.73
A[*adequate*]	0.73
A[*elaborate*]	0.67
Q[*assumpitve*]	-0.67
Q[*explain*]	-0.62
Q[*repeat*]	-0.59
Q[*related*]	0.47
Q[*prefaced*]	0.45
Q[ask]	0.11
A[provide]	0.11
Eigenvalues	3.21
% Variance	32.10

In PC1-A2 only the last two features do not reach the criterial loading of .40 or above. Most of the terms in tables 4 have already been discussed in connection with table 3. The only exceptions are the terms [prefaced], and [assumptive]. The feature [prefaced] is an option in a system pertaining to the logical metafunction. A message is said to have the semantic feature [prefaced], if it is introduced as some saying, thinking, preference, evaluation etc. Thus in example 6, Nathan's mother produced a message with the feature [prefaced], when she said *I'm suggesting perhaps you look there*. Here *perhaps you look there* is prefaced by *I'm suggesting*. This projection clause complex is treated as one [prefaced] message. Similarly in examples 8 and 9, we have answers that are [prefaced]; the preface component is shown in italics:

Example: 8

Mark: (1) why are you putting the torecaider (=taperecorder) upstairs?
Mother: (2) oh *I just thought* I'd bring it up

Example: 9

Mother: (1) that might be enough for two sandwiches there mightn't it?
Kristy: (2) mm .. *I think* a little bit more lettuce [?I might have] (3) 'cause I love the lettuce and blue vein mum

The feature [assumptive] is an option in the [demand;information] network (see the system labelled j in figure 5, and their realisation in table 2; examples are provided in SE23–28).

The semantic features that make up PC1-A2 are in some respects like those in PC1-A1. Thus just as in the high scoring dyads for PC1-A1 children are not likely to repeat their questions, so also in the high scoring dyads for PC1-A2, mothers are not likely to repeat their questions, with the same expectation that their questions are responded to in some (satisfying) way by their children. Further, just like the children in the high scoring dyads for PC1-A1, mothers in the high scoring dyads for PC1-A2 are likely to relate their questions to some other message. However, the semantic features of children's question and those of mothers' do differ in some respects: as tables 3 and 4 show, children in the high scoring dyads PC1-A1 are more likely to ask *why/how*-questions than either *who/what/when …* or *yes/no*-questions. This tendency is reversed for the mothers in the high scoring dyads for PC1-A2: here mothers are not very likely to ask *how/why*-questions, which have a negative loading (-.62), thus implying that questions with the semantic feature [specify] – i.e. those with *who/what/where..* – are more likely to be asked; further in the mother's sayings, questions with the feature [confirm] – i.e. yes/no questions – are very much more likely to occur (positive loading .73). We have noted in the results a differential selection and patterning for the *how/why*-questions: in mother's talk such questions are more often than not associated with challenge, and so they tend to occur in a control situation with direct commands that do not allow discretion (Hasan 1988; Cloran 1989). An example is provided below, where the mother had been trying to get Karen to go to bed; she had reasoned, scolded and slapped her to make her obey but Karen was still resisting:

Example: 10

Mother: (1) Karen do as you— (SLAPS CHILD) (2) put your legs down (3) or I'm going outside right this minute without a kiss (4) now put your legs down (ANGRY VOICE)
Karen: (5) mmhm (PROTESTING NOISES)
Mother: (6) now give a kiss good night
Karen: (7) I'm not (=I won't/ I'm not going to)
Mother: (8) you're not gonna kiss me?** (9) *why?*
Karen: (9) 'cause
Mother: (10) 'cause why?
Karen: (11) 'cause I don't like you (IN VERY LOUD VOICE)

It is clear from the mother's threat in (3) and from the form of her question in (8) that she assumes the child would want to kiss her. The *why* in (9) is thus a prompt for explanation but at the same time a challenge in as much as the mother assumes that kissing her is a 'must' for the child; the same position obtains for (10). Note in passing that (8) is a good example of a question with the feature [assumptive]; the hidden thesis of this question is *I assume you're going to kiss me good night.* The selection of the feature [assumptive] typically implies a closeness of relationship by virtue of which another's beliefs, attitudes, motives and actions are treated as if they were knowable without semiotic action and did not need to be made explicit. Such questions therefore do not act as the opening of a negotiation in the speakers' actual social practices. Two other semantic features which characterise the mother's questions if they belong to the high scoring dyads for PC1-A2 are [assumptive] and [prefaced]; both of these have been exemplified above, and neither is criterial for high scoring children's questions in PC1-A1. Note that [assumptive] has a negative loading (-.67), so that high scoring mothers would be quite unlikely to choose this feature; however, the feature [prefaced] has a positive loading at .45 and is thus likely to be present in the talk of the high scoring mothers. When we turn to the attributes of the answers given by children of high scoring dyads, it is notable that the answers are very likely to have the feature [adequate] and [elaborated]. Recall that table 3 had indicated that answers to children's questions by their mothers had also displayed these characteristics. On the basis of the pattern of scoring represented in table 4, the high scoring dyads' habitual fashion of meaning may be stated in informal terms as follows:

Mother:

- is highly likely to ask yes/no questions;
- is not likely to ask why/how questions, which implies that she is more likely to ask questions that seek specification of who/what/when …;
- is not likely to make unspoken assumptions in asking;
- is not likely to repeat her questions, which implies responses are readily provided by her child;
- is likely to relate her questions to other messages, thus elaborating on its thesis;
- is likely to introduce the question together with someone's point of view, by presenting the question as a saying or an idea.

Child:

- is highly likely to offer adequate answers;
- is likely to elaborate her/his answer, so that the sayings provide much more information than is simply necessary and sufficient to address the point of the question.

This dyadic fashion of meaning is more likely to characterise the HAP dyads than the LAP ones (HAP > LAP: p<.002); further, mother-daughter dyads are more likely to behave this way than are the mother-son ones (F > M: p<.02). Figure 7 presents the plotting of the HAP and LAP dyads by reference to PC1-A2. The conventions for reading figures 7 are the same as for figure 6.

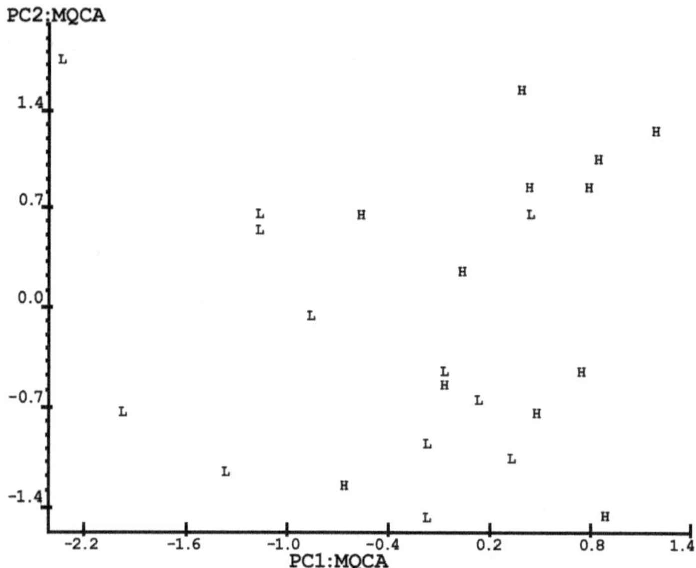

Figure 7: PC1-A2 and PC2-A2 Scores of lap – hap dyads: Mothers' questions, children's answers

Figure 8 presents the location of the mother-daughter (= F) and mother-son (= M) dyads by reference to PC1-A2. The conventions for reading figures 8 are the same as for figure 6 and 7. Figure 8 shows that the scoring position of mothers on PC2-A2 correlates with two social factors (1) the social class of the family; and (2) the addressee child's sex.

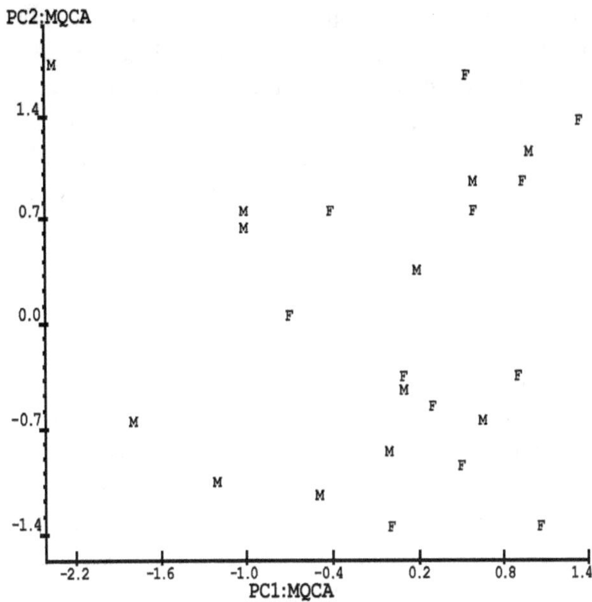

Figure 8: PC1-A2 and PC2-A2 scores of F (mother-daughter) and M (mother-son) dyads

If there is this degree of closeness between the two results of PC1-A1 and PC1-A2, it would be reasonable to expect that a high positive correlation would obtain between them; and this is indeed the case (PC1-A1 v. PC1-A2: r =.59). The semantic coherence of the two factors discussed shows that a specific kind of orientation to meaning is to be found in the two groups identified by their semantic behaviour. Thus for example, the kind of responsive behaviour that is displayed by high scoring HAP dyads would be inexplicable, if in the contextual act of making children do what the mothers want them to do, the HAP mothers used [threats] rather than [reasons], or did not elaborate their commands or the rationale for the command. For this would indicate critical semantic dissonance between the mothers' questioning-answering behaviour and their control behaviour. This is of course not the case. The control behaviour of mothers is also a socio-semantic variable, with significant difference between the HAP group and the LAP group (Hasan 1992a, 1992b). When the mothers' question-answer behaviour is correlated with their control behaviour, not surprisingly, there too a high correlation is obtained (r =.68), while children's question-answer behaviour also correlates positively with their mothers' control behaviour (r =.69). Due to lack of space, it has not been possible to compare our results with those cited in Turner and Mohan (1970), Turner and Pickvsance (1973), Robinson and Rackstraw (1972), Wootton (1974) and others who have worked with Bernstein's code theory. The degree of semantic consistency found in the behaviour of the two social classes requires a higher order concept than semantic variation. Such a concept, we suggest, is *semantic orientation*[14] which is directly deriveable from Bernstein's theory of *codes*.

12 Conclusion

We would conclude that the above results provide convincing argument for the recognition of semantic variation as an important sociolinguistic phenomenon. Thinking of the semantic category *question* as the realisation of the contextual act of *attempting to find out some information* and *answer* as the realisation of the contextual act of *giving some information to satisfy a demand for information*, we can look at the various semantic features of questions and answers as variant expressions of these higher level units. And when we do so, as in this research, we find that speakers' semantic choices co-vary with some significant social circumstance of their location in society. To us it appears that this is a classic case of sociolinguistic variation, provided the theory of sociolinguistics is not hegemonically closed to suit one theoretical position. The variation here is not just an expressive, stylistic matter, totally empty of cognitive content; rather, through such features as [*assumptive*], [*adequate*], [*related*], [*prefaced*], and [elaborated] at least some categories of meanings that are normally thought of as cognitive have been implicated in the findings. In any event the idea that cognition excludes everything except referential meaning is itself open to question[15]. We therefore question Labov's thesis that sociolinguistic variation is inherently meaning preserving.

Our results incline us also to reject Saussure's belief that in parole the individual is the master. In the first place we have demonstrated that belonging to a particular social class makes the selection of certain semantic features highly probable, which in turn has repercussions on the habitual use of lexicogrammatical patterns; and secondly, it has to be recognised that the individual is after all not simply a biological organism; important features of our individuality derive from our belonging to some specific position in some human community. We must conclude, therefore, that speaking is essentially social, irrespective of which stratum of language is examined and despite the fact that it is carried out physically by one single organism: the only part where the 'individual' is the master – in the sense that he alone has the 'executive capacity' – is the actual phonation; the choice of what sounds should be produced is a matter of what variety of language the individual has grown up with – in its phonation alone the community does not directly participate. Unless we characterise speaking in this way, we cannot conceive of any means whereby the system of language itself comes to be social, as Saussure apparently wanted it to be. The meanings people 'choose' to mean by virtue of who they are and what the system of their language is like cannot be seen either as accessory or accidental. Following the drift of Saussure's thought, it would seem that he wished to point out the accidental nature of phonation as a sign-manifesting modality. This may be so, but speaking is not simply phonation. Its essential character resides in its meaningfulness, and the meanings selected in speaking can not be typically described as unpredictable, accidental, or wilful.

Nor do we feel convinced that Saussure's emphasis on the individual ownership of thoughts, beliefs, attitudes etc. is above question. This debate is complex, but at least two remarks are necessary. First, we agree with Vygotsky (1978) that in the life of an individual, all higher mental functions must at first have been external – i.e. social – before they become internalised i.e. a part of the individual's inner make-up. Second, if the speaker's 'own thoughts' are the instance of higher mental functions, and if our higher mental functions are socio-genetic, it would seem to follow that they are not as much an individual's own possession by an act of nature, as they are a social gift. And if they are social gifts, then it is important to understand where such gifts come from, what is the means by which the social structure, the semantic orientation of communication and the inner consciousness of speakers are linked to each other. By closing with this issue, we wish to signal how central to this research are the three conceptual frameworks provided by Vygotsky and those provided by Bernstein's theory of code and Halliday's SFL.

Notes

1 This paper was co-authored by Ruqaiya Hasan and Camel Cloran.

2 An abridged version of this chapter (first written in 1987) was published in 1990 in Halliday, Gibbons and Nicholas (eds) *Learning Keeping and Using Language*, Vol 1. (pp. 67–100). Amsterdam: Benjamins. I am grateful to my co-author, Carmel Cloran for permission to include the paper here in a revised version of the original MS.

3 The research project (1983–1986) was supported by the Australian Research Grant Scheme, and by Macquarie University Research Grant, both acknowledged with gratitude. It was initiated and directed by Hasan, who was responsible for the overall research conceptualisation and design and for the preparation of the analytic framework in terms of which the semantic analysis of the data

was conducted. Cloran was responsible for the linguistic analysis of the entire sample data for Phase I and for the application of the statistical procedures. The interpretation of the statistical results was often conducted jointly by Hasan and Cloran; I accept the responsibility for any errors therein. We received help from too many colleagues to permit mention of each name here; but at Macquarie University our special thanks are due to Anne Eyeland and Allan Taylor for help with statistics, to David Butt, Michael Orlemans, Rhondda Fahey and staff of the Speech, Hearing and Language Research Centre, in particular John Telec and Harry Purvis. We also thank Barbara Horvath, Gregory Guy and Chris Nesbitt at Sydney University for advice on statistical matters.

4 Though in fairness to Saussure it must be granted that in the same Course in General Linguistics (1966) he also included chapters on language variation and language change.

5 This is precisely what has been done in sociolinguistics for many decades with great success.

6 We are aware that these views of Halliday's have been questioned (Leech 1983; Butler 1985). Since this is not an appropriate place to discuss these criticisms, we refer the reader to Hasan (1995a) where the issues are addressed in some detail.

7 This approach has also been criticised by colleagues as 'non-scientific'; again, the reader is referred to Hasan (1995a).

8 There is no implication that these three variant features exhaust the choice at that point.

9 This was certainly true in the early 1980s; more recently we have witnessed babies as young as 6 months being sent to the crèche on a regular basis.

10 In fact the fragment presented here was Mark 1; it was revised on the basis of the first run of analysis. Chapter 4 also uses this same network. The revised version is presented in chapter 5 of this volume.

11 Abbreviated terms in these tables can be interpreted by reference to Halliday (1985a).

12 For a more detailed discussion, see Horvath (1985); Cloran (1989); and Cloran in accompanying CD.

13 For example compare Horvath (1985); see also a more up to date account in Cloran's contribution in the accompanying CD.

14 More recently, I have come to think of ideology as the underlying factor which, according to Bernstein (1990), stands in a dialectical relation to the social subject's social positioning.

15 Recent work in neuroscience such as that of Damasio in particular (e.g., Damasio 2000) would suggest that emotions and feelings are basic facts of cognition.

4 Language in the processes of socialisation: home and school [1988]

1 Introduction

The main concern of this paper[1] is to explore the role of language in the processes of socialisation, with special reference to home and school – the two places, where at least in Western cultures, most of the talk in the life of young individuals occurs. I shall present my views on socialisation in the following section, where I will try to point out why a particular theory – that of Bernstein's (1971a, 1975a, 1982, 1986, 1987a) – appears to me most fruitful in exploring patterns of socialisation. Section 3 will raise the question: what has our conception of language to be like, if this view of socialisation is accepted? In section 4, I will describe the outline of a research, which examines ways of talking at home and in the first year of schooling in order to show how the abstractly stated processes of socialisation are actually constructed largely by everyday talk. The results of the research are presented in section 5. The paper will close with a discussion of the implications of the positions adopted here in respect to both socialisation and language.

2 Socialisation

I use the term 'socialisation' to refer to a multiplicity of interactional processes through which persons develop the ability to interpret their environment and to participate in social practices in such a way that both their interpretations and their actions are seen as meaningful by other members of the community at least in their own speech fellowship (Firth 1957). Recalling Connell's comments (1988) on community I must add that for me, as for perhaps most linguists, 'community' is a relative concept: the boundaries of a community cannot be fixed once and for all. Nor was any positive loading intended in using the term 'meaningful' above: I simply mean that through the socialisation processes, the actions and interpretations of one member of a community become something to which some meaning can be attached by others in the community. This presupposes neither consensus nor conflict, approval nor objection; but is itself a necessary pre-requisite for any of these reactions. However, it needs to be emphasised that this ability in the members of a community to interpret others' behaviour in some specific way(s), is far from being a simple matter. For it can only come about under a complex set of conditions, namely that the socialised persons construct for themselves, in interaction with others, some model(s) of ways of being, doing and saying that bear a systematic relation to those acts of being, doing and saying current among the members of their immediate community. So, in terms of Basil Bernstein (1987b) in any study of socialisation, we are necessarily concerned with trying to find out 'How does the outside become the inside and how does the inside reveal itself and shape the outside?'

This elegant and beguilingly simple formulation puts the debate at a higher level of abstraction, drawing attention to the centrality of the relationships that exist between social structure and the forms of consciousness that are created through the processes of socialisation and that, in their turn, act upon the socialising social structures. According to Bernstein (1971a: 172)[2], the theory of socialisation is concerned with providing an explicit account of the processes that underlie 'this social structuring of experience'.

2.1 Socialisation and society

Let us begin with one of the earliest statements by Bernstein about socialisation (1971a: 174):

> I shall take the term [i.e. socialization] to refer to the process whereby a child acquires a specific cultural identity, and to his responses to such an identity. Socialization refers to the process whereby the biological is transformed into a specific cultural being. It follows from this that the process of socialization is a complex process of control, whereby a particular moral, cognitive and affective awareness is evoked in the child and given a specific form and content.

Bernstein goes on to identify the basic socialising agencies in contemporary societies as the family, the peer group, the school and the workplace. It is through experiences in these social locations that particular forms of consciousness are created, maintained and altered. Let us for a moment focus just on the family, keeping in mind Bernstein's comment (ibid.) that '... the focusing and filtering of the child's experience within the family in a large measure is a microcosm of the macroscopic orderings of society'.

Now, although at a first glance, it may seem that at least in the kind of societies that we are familiar with, any one family is a free-standing unit, with more or less complete autonomy of decision and action, this first impression would have to be revised as soon as we look more closely into the matter. It would be silly to suggest that the family is like a puppet controlled in every respect by strings held in the hands of some external agent, but it would be equally silly to suppose that the family is an atom, entirely self-sufficient unto itself – and even the atom is not that! – totally unaffected by what surrounds it. For example, taking our own local contexts, think of a family's decisions about its children's education: how much autonomy does a family possess? What are the factors that will affect one's decisions? Where do these factors originate from? And how is it that a family has come to accept these factors as legitimate forces that have the right to control its decisions? As soon as we begin to examine these questions more closely, we find that a family, in the modern society at least, is not a free-standing unit; it does not have a free choice to the extent that it can autonomously decide exactly what kind of medical facilities, leisure occupations, community centres, child care facilities etc. it will enjoy. Limitations are placed on the range of its choices by phenomena, which in the last analysis, can be traced to what sociologists describe as the social division of labour, and hence to the distribution of power.

An acceptance of this position implies that forms of socialisation within families cannot be discussed in separation from the social positioning (Bernstein 1982) of the family through its relations to the social division of labour. Our question then becomes: what is the exact nature of these relations? Much of radical contemporary sociology – and certainly that of Bernstein's – is an attempt to provide answers to such questions, for the relations between social division of labour and specific groups of persons, individual institutions etc. are not transparent. Instead they must be traced through a series of steps where at one end, are highly abstract concepts such as the distribution of power, or class relations, while at the other end lie structures of actual human practices – something that impinges directly upon human beings. What I am calling a series of steps is not to be understood as necessarily moments in a temporally ordered cause-effect relation, capable of being described as first A happened then as a result B happened. Rather, the relation is often one of 'coding' or realisation, in the sense in which these terms are used by Halliday (1961, 1970, 1973a, 1975b, 1978, 1985a, 1992a, b, 1996) to describe the relations between strata in the structure of language. So, for example, one possible coding of the distribution of power is social class hierarchy, which is itself expressed by, say, differential possibility of control over resources.

Clearly the series of steps that cover the vast area between the social distribution of power and the experiences of individual (groups of) men and women cannot be discussed here in detail. Let me add that over the years, Bernstein's writings have repeatedly traversed this space. Indeed, one of the directions in which his theory has developed is precisely its ability to describe with a greater delicacy of focus the specific kinds of relations that link the distribution of power with the way patterns of human praxis are likely to be organised in a community (see especially Bernstein 1982, 1986). One reason I began this discussion with extracts from his earlier papers was to indicate that this preoccupation with describing the nature of the relationship between the macrocosm and the microcosm is nothing new to Bernstein. It is important to emphasise this point in order to counter the myth that 'changes' in Bernstein's theory have been major departures from his initial theoretical position, and that these departures have rendered his idea of codes vague and unstable (Edwards 1976: 90ff.). It is certainly true that the theory has not stayed rooted in one stage (see Bernstein 1987b for a detailed account). Indeed, considering that even by 1976, Bernstein had been writing for a decade and a half, a complete absence of change from the 1960s would have been far more alarming, as indicative of intellectual stagnation. Whatever the nature of knowledge, it certainly is not impervious to change; so, for me at least, it is difficult to sympathise with criticisms leveled against 'change in framework' as such. And as for Edwards' claim that the 'changes' qualitatively altered the concept of code, rendering it vacuous, I would suggest that the claim is based on a genuine misreading of the literature.

2.2 Socialisation and the concept of code

But how does the concept of code enter into the discussion of socialisation? According to Bernstein (1971a: 145) 'The concept of code, refers to the principle which regulates the selection and organization of speech events'. Today, instead of saying, just 'speech events' Bernstein would talk, perhaps more explicitly, about both physical and discursive resources – subsuming all forms of being, doing and saying (Bernstein 1982, 1986, 1987b). But even this is not a qualitative shift. For example, based on Bernstein's own writings Hasan attempted to point out that the concept of code was essentially sociological (Bernstein 1971a: 174); that its sociolinguistic aspect derived from its sociological nature (Hasan 1973a). To understand the centrality of the concept of code to any discussion of socialisation, we must probe into the meaning of the claim that code 'regulates the selection and organization' of social practices: we need to examine how microcosmic social phenomena are linked to 'the macroscopic orderings of society' (Bernstein 1971a: 174). Since detailed examination of these relations is not possible here, I present a series of almost axiomatic assertions. This naturally does not mean that the issues are closed – that they are not open to scrutiny and discussion; simply that, this is a stage I am by-passing for lack of time.

To begin with, then, my claim would be that social practices of being, doing and saying are constitutive of the social system (Hasan 1984c); it is through these practices that social systems evolve; it is through them that they are maintained; and, it is these practices that sow the seeds of change. On the other hand, practice implies beliefs and knowledge as well as desires and attitudes. I suggest that these mental dispositions on the one hand motivate social practices, and on the other they themselves are created and maintained by social practices: the interdependence between these mental dispositions and social practices is an interdependence between strata, characteristic of what Lemke refers to as 'dynamic open systems' (Lemke 1984). Mental dispositions are not static; they evolve even as the practices they 'motivate' unfold. Let me refer to this ever evolving mental map as consciousness. Consciousness is, then, this ever evolving dynamic system of beliefs, knowledge, desires and attitudes. If my arguments are accepted, then it follows that whatever 'regulates' consciousness thus defined, also regulates social practice; and whatever regulates social practice, also regulates the social system – its creation as well as its evolution. Following this reasoning, one of the most important questions is: what is it that regulates consciousness? – that shapes the inside? I understand that in asking these questions we are raising the issue of the ontogenesis of ideology (Bernstein 1982, 1986, 1987a; Halliday 1975a; Hasan 1986a; Cloran 1989).

The question about the nature of consciousness – like most important questions – has not been given one simple answer. According to one school of thought – i.e. German Idealism of the past and 'cognitive science' of our day – consciousness is epistemologically prior: mankind orders its world of reality, guided by this innate, subjective mental power; consciousness itself has an autonomous existence. It is well known that in his *German Ideology*, Marx criticised this approach as 'descending from heaven to earth' (cited in Bottomore and Rubel 1976: 90), claiming that if we began from 'real active men and from their real life-process', 'ascending from earth to heaven' (ibid.), we would find that:

> Morality, religion, metaphysics, and other ideologies, and their corresponding forms of consciousness, no longer retain … their appearance of autonomous existence. They have no history, no development [i.e. of their own]; it is men, who in developing their material production and their material intercourse, change, along with their real existence, their thinking and the products of their thinking. Life is not determined by consciousness, but consciousness by life.

This same view is articulated by Marx in his *Preface to the Critique of Political Economy*, cited in McLellan (1975: 40):

> In the social production of their life men enter into definite relations that are indispensable and independent of their will … The sum total of these relations of production constitutes the economic structure of society, … to which correspond definite forms of consciousness. The mode of production of material life conditions the social, political and intellectual life process in general. It is not the consciousness of men that determines their being, but on the contrary, their social being that determines their consciousness.

It would be wrong to give the impression that Marx's view of human beings ignored the subjective side of the individual. On the contrary, granting that the first premise of all human history is 'the existence of living human individuals', he recognised the need to take into account 'the physical constitution of these individuals', and the primacy of 'sense experience' as the necessary basis for all science. As recorded in Bottomore and Rubel (1976: 82), he criticised Feuerbach's views on materialism:

> The chief defect of all previous materialism (including that of Feuerbach) is that things, reality, the sensible world, are conceived only in the form of objects of observation, but not as human sense activity, not as practical activity, not subjectively … The materialist doctrine concerning the changing of circumstances and education forgets that circumstances are changed by men and that the educator must himself be educated.

If we find it difficult to reconcile Marx's view that 'circumstances are changed by men' with his view that men's 'social being … determines their consciousness', this may be because of our insistent reduction of all relations to the one relation of cause-followed-by-effect in a uni-linear progression of time. It is a conception that has played havoc with the idea of dialectic as it has done with that of realisation in linguistics, which is not surprising since the two have a good deal in common. Be that as it may, Marx (cf. McLellan 1975: 43) saw no inconsistency in his position, maintaining that:

> Men make their own history, but they do not make it just as they please; they do not make it under circumstances chosen by themselves, but under circumstances directly encountered, given and transmitted from the past.

We must assume that among the circumstances that are 'directly encountered', the most important is the economic structure of society, for according to Marx it is to this aspect of human existence that 'definite forms of consciousness' correspond. And we have already seen that consciousness is as inalienably related to practice, as practice is to change as well as maintenance of that set of circumstances and conditions of human existence the aggregate of which we refer to as the social system.

2.3 Socialisation, consciousness, and concept code

I am aware that the question I raised at the beginning of section 1.2, namely, *what has code to do with socialisation?* has not yet been answered. So far I have argued that socialisation is a process through which individuals acquire specific modes of interpreting and participating in social practices; and that all forms of being, doing and saying – all practices – inevitably imply consciousness; from which it follows that socialisation must be implicated in the formation of a subject's consciousness: in fact, I would go so far as to claim that the terms socialisation and consciousness refer to two perspectives on the same phenomena. If, then, we accept with Marx, that it is men's 'social being' – their economic structure – that 'determines their consciousness', then we are back with Bernstein's question: how does the outside – the socio-economic structure of a society become the inside – the definite form of the consciousness of a subject? The quotations from Marx point in rather general terms to his answer – that 'the mode of production of material life conditions the social, political and intellectual life in general'. Put beside such general remarks, today Bernstein's theory of socialisation, if I read it correctly, goes beyond hinted implications. It puts forward a series of specific hypotheses to explain 'how the outside becomes the inside …', and in this explanation, the concept of code plays an important part.

Code is crucial to socialisation because it is crucial to the shaping of specific forms of consciousness. It enters into discussions of socialisation, because it is the active principle in the set of processes we refer to as socialisation. I hope that your reading of Bernstein (1986, 1987b) agrees with my interpretation. These are of course more recent pieces; so let me go once again to an earlier exposition (Bernstein 1971b: 144) as an economical demonstration of the fact that the perspective presented above is not a recent addition to the theory of code:

> … the particular forms of a social relation act selectively upon what is said, when it is said and how it is said … The different forms of social relation can generate very different speech systems or linguistic codes.
>
> … different speech systems or codes create for their speakers different orders of relevance and relation. The experience of the speakers may then be transformed by what is made significant or relevant by different speech systems. As the child … learns specific codes which regulate his verbal acts, he learns the requirements of his social structure. The experience of the child is transformed by the learning generated by his own, apparently, voluntary acts of speech. The social structure becomes … the substratum of the child's experience essentially through the manifold consequences of the linguistic process. From this point of view, every time the child speaks or listens, the social structure is reinforced in him and his social identity shaped. The social structure becomes the child's psychological reality through the shaping of his acts of speech.

We have here a theory of socialisation that highlights the role of social factors in the genesis of human minds by making interaction crucial to the formation of consciousness – of what is also called 'cognition'; it is, moreover, a theory in which interaction is not naively seen as uniform, invariable and indifferent to the social conditions in which the interactants find themselves. Depending on their social conditions, their own orientation to meanings – i.e. the social subject's own coding orientation – will be different (Bernstein 1982: 310):

> The simpler the social division of labour, and the more specific and local the relation between an agent and its material base, then the more direct the relation between meanings and a specific material base and the more restricted the coding orientation.
>
> The more complex the social division of labour, the less specific and local the relation between an agent and its material base, then the more indirect the relation between meanings and a specific material base and the more elaborated the coding orientation.

The power and control relations that inhere in the social division of labour are translated by the abstract principles of classification and framing into specific interactional practices. Classification refers to the creation and maintenance of boundaries between categories: how things, identities, positions differ from each other. Classification is a function of power. Framing refers to the pacing of interaction; it is a function of control through which access to classification is provided. Either can be strong or weak. Classification is said to be strong when the insulation between categories is strong; it is weak when this insulation is reduced. Bernstein (1987a) suggests that

> ...if there is strong insulation then positions have unambiguous identities, sharp boundaries, specialized practices ... if the insulation is weak then identities are more generalized, boundaries reduced and practices more integrated.

Strong framing locates control of the pacing and form of communication with the dominant interactant. Thus in a socialising context, strong framing would locate the control of communication with the socialising agent, the transmitter, while weak framing would place this control, in some measure, with the acquirer.

These two concepts – classification and framing – act as the links between the 'macroscopic orderings of society' – its macro structures – and the practices of microcosmic agencies e.g. the family by focusing on interactional practices. So while from one point of view different coding orientations are an expression of an agent's differing location within the social division of labour, from another, complementary point of view, the different coding orientations are indicative of different interactional practices. To say that codes regulate the selection and organisation of discursive and non-discursive social practices is to say that it is the coding orientation of speakers that defines for them what would count as a legitimate way of being, doing and saying in a particular context. In fact since the recognition of a context implies an understanding of the possibilities of the selection and organisation of meanings, it is obvious that codes must be active in the very recognition of a context (Bernstein 1982, 1987a). It follows that if there exist in a community two different coding orientations – e.g. elaborated and restricted – then these different orientations are simply an expression of speakers' differential location in the social division of labour. From this point of view there is nothing to choose between the two; neither is inherently superior to the other; both are crucial to the formation of consciousness and both are symbolic indicators of social subjects' particular location in the social structure. The privileging of one coding orientation over another, the hierarchisation of one form of communication over the other, does not, in my opinion, arise from the inherent attributes of this code as against the other (Hasan 1987b). It arises from the fact that, because of their symbolic relation to economic structure, specific coding orientations become symbolic of dominant and dominating social relations in class societies. As Marx remarked in German Ideology (cited in Bottomore and Rubel 1976: 93):

> The ideas of the ruling class are, in every age, the ruling ideas: i.e. the class which is the dominant material force in society is at the same time its dominant intellectual force ... The dominant ideas are nothing more than the ideal expression of the dominant material relationships...

Bernstein has often referred to the 'invidious positioning' of subjects which arises from social class domination but which is wrongly perceived as the direct consequence of differing coding orientations, legitimising the meanings of the few, invalidating those of the others.

I see then in Bernstein's theory of socialisation an analysis of social relations, beginning with the distribution of power – the basis of class domination – and ending with tangible, sensible (i.e. capable of being sensed) practices. In the range of these practices it is the interactional practices that are more crucial from the point of view of socialisation, since it is these that are in the Marxist sense truly 'human' i.e. socially regulated. And I believe that amongst the interactional practices themselves, it is the discursive ones that have a special significance. I make this claim for at least two reasons. First, talk, the use of language, appears so effortless that perhaps for this very reason it is ubiquitous to a degree that no other kind of human practice is. Secondly, as Hjelmslev (1961) remarked language is invisible: we use language all the time, but we hardly pay conscious attention to it; to most of us language appears simply as an epiphenomenon, a secondary flow, a side-kick of the somehow more robust extra-linguistic activities. This common-sense perspective is shared even by some sophisticated scholars. For example, we are warned by Atkinson (1985: 68) that 'Language – and this cannot be said too often – is subsidiary, in that it is a means to understanding social relationships, structures, and processes'. But Atkinson is not alone in holding this view: he is in the good company of highly renowned philosophers and linguists (for some details, see Hasan 1984a, c, 1987b). It is not my intention at this point to refute this view of language, mistaken though I believe it is; my intention is to use it as evidence of a claim I am about to make.

The fact that language is invisible, the fact that the sounds and meanings that we produce appear subsidiary, simply 'reflecting' reality – this widely held conception of language has far reaching consequences. If the words are only expression, if that which they refer to is really real and such that language itself has no power over it, then it follows that what we do with our language – our discursive practices – will have to be denied the power of bringing about any change in 'reality'. Later I will argue that the view of language simply as expression is a misconception (see section 3 below). But if the view is a misconception, and reality is to a large extent defined by language, then the illusion of the powerlessness of language in construing reality, quite paradoxically, becomes the greatest source of its power: it becomes the most powerful instrument for the maintenance of ideology; it becomes an active principle in the formation of human consciousness, while all the time it is being overlooked as 'merely' a secondary flow – we are not even aware that the words that surround us are in fact instrumental in turning us into what we become. This situation is further compounded by the fact that individuals embark on this process of exchange of meanings from a very early age (Trevarthen and Hubley 1978; Halliday 1973b, 1975b, 1979b, 2003; Lock 1978). No matter how far back we cast our minds, not one of us knows, or has known, a language-less world. This illusion about language that it is simply a neutral medium of some kind which permits the real categories of our social and physical universe to shine through is perhaps essential to our continued use of language for the living of life (Hasan 1984c). But it does have one serious consequence. The folk view becomes so firmly entrenched, that a great deal of analysis is needed to break through this illusion of being in direct contact with nature. In fact, it takes a Wittgenstein, a Halliday, a Bernstein to articulate that difficult dual perspective which at once affirms the active power of language as well as its semiotic value, in relation to culture. One important fact about discursive practices is that in them there operates the complex system of language which is itself a semiotic.

And the highest level of this semiotic – the level of meaning – is as relevant to the analysis of social structure as it is to the analysis of linguistic structure.

If Bernstein's theory of socialisation is attractive to me, this is because it is the only theory I know that neither trivialises social facts nor language, that presents a dynamic view of socialisation without ignoring the consequences of socially created forms of inequality – unlike Mead (1934), for example, though he was a giant among scholars. Further, it is a theory that has the conceptual power to throw light on all major socialising agencies. Perhaps the work of Vygotsky (1962, 1978) and Luria (1976) is the closest to Bernstein's in its insistence on the centrality of interaction, on the relevance of social systems to forms of interaction, and on the dynamic function of language in social processes. However, neither Vygotsky nor Luria are concerned to the same extent with the articulation of a theory of socialisation with the wide scope, characteristic of Bernstein's work; at the same time, the social system described in the work of these Russian post-revolution scholars is of course qualitatively different from our own. By contrast, Bernstein's work is concerned with the workings of our own social structure, thus making it more relevant to the realities of our social life. A question may be raised here: what does my acceptance of Bernstein's view of language imply about my attitude to the critiques of his discussion of linguistic features of code? This is an important question but I shall not deal with it here. Let me say that the aspects criticised are concerned with facts of a different order about language, than those that are the focus of my attention in this paper. Before I turn to this discussion of language, I will draw attention to two other important issues.

2.4 The reproduction metaphor

In his opening address to this conference, Halliday expressed discontent with the term 'socialisation':

> Like acquisition, socialization is a flawed metaphor. Both these terms tell us that there is something 'out there' that pre-exists, called society or language: by implication, an unchanging something to which children are gradually moulded until they conform.

The problem with such a view is that neither society nor language is invariant: not only does each change over time, but at any given moment each displays co-existing variants. The idea of 'getting' something that is 'out there' negates the possibility of change. Socialisation, in the sense of reproduction, if the term is taken literally, would certainly not account for change over time. As Connell (1983: 145) points out:

> The continuity, the persistence through time with which theory is concerned, does not have the ontological structure of a reproduced identity, but that of an intelligible succession. It is not a relation of similarity between the structure today and the structure yesterday that is the point, but a relation of practice between them, the way one was produced out of the other.

Continuity should not be confused with replication, for replication negates evolution. A theory of socialisation that could not account for the relation between the continuities and discontinuities of social structures over time – that could not throw light over evolution – would be a dangerous distortion, just as a theory of language would be a distortion if it presented language as an idealised, homogeneous, non-changing system.

Although over the last decade, the metaphor of reproduction has come to be used increasingly in Bernstein's writing (Bernstein 1975a, 1982, 1986, 1987a) – note also the full title of Atkinson's explication of Bernstein (Atkinson 1985) – I would suggest that, despite this, Bernstein's view of socialisation does not aim at 'reproduced identity', at replication. Indeed, Bernstein has always been concerned with 'the question of change in the structuring of experience' (1971a: 172; see also 1975a: 110–11). Throughout Bernstein's writing from the early seventies to date, one would find observations on the mechanism of social change. While the suppression of contradictions, cleavages and dilemmas that inhere in classification maintains continuities, the acquisition of the strategies of challenge and opposition, of questioning and scrutiny which are associated with a particular kind of framing (Bernstein 1987a) will open up that closure created by the suppression, thus providing a powerful mechanism for evolution. Further, the selective creation, production and changing of texts could become a means whereby the positioning of subjects is changed (Bernstein 1982: 307; see also p.325). In short there is ample evidence that Bernstein has developed a view of socialisation in which the socialised is not a 'clone'; today's social structure does not replicate that of yesterday's.

It seems to me that at least in one sense the reproduction metaphor is well justified. Although the material details of class domination might vary between yesterday's and today's social structures, the principle of class domination and the patterns of control over privileging, legitimate meanings that flow from such domination continue unchanged. This brings us to the question of co-existing variants. I do not need to labour the point that Bernstein's theory has been a theory of social variation – what is sometimes referred to as 'sub-cultural differences'. His theory of differing coding orientations with all the implied antecedents and all the entailed differences in social practices is certain proof that for Bernstein the social structure is not a monolithic, homogeneous whole.

It is an interesting idea that if the social structure is a semiotic of essentially the same kind as language, then the very presence of synchronic variation might act as a powerful instrument for diachronic evolution (see, however, Halliday 1975c); the presence of variants today at least raises the possibility of a changed form tomorrow. I feel tempted to add that the issue is not replication: there will be change. The issue is rather that of the value of that change, what that change might signify (Bernstein 1987a).

2.5 Socialisation, social structure, and the subject

Closely related to the issue of socialisation as reproduction in this narrower sense, is yet another concern. The nominalised form *socialisation* is a grammatical metaphor (Halliday 1985a) for a transitive process *to socialise*: this implies that some being socialises some other being. There is the active agent – the socialiser – and there is the passive 'patient' – the socialised. It is as if into the very grammar of this process were built in a relation of domination as Wexler points out (1982: 276):

> The category of socialization affirms the powerlessness of the individual against a reified collectivity, a system which purportedly reproduces itself ... [it] surrenders in advance the human capacity for appropriation and transformation...

Connell (1983: 149) voices the same misgivings, though with a different emphasis, when he cautions that

> We cannot treat social structure as something persisting in its identity behind the backs of mortal people, who are inserted into their places by a cosmic cannery called Reproduction.

But perhaps the most fashionable view is that expressed by Mackay, who goes so far as to suggest that (1974: 180) the notion of socialisation is simply an adult conspiracy in order to deprive children of their social power and status:

> To observe that change takes place after birth is trivial, but the quasi scientific status of the term *socialization* marks this triviality. In fact, the study of these changes as socialization is an expression of the sociologists' commonsense position in the world i.e. as adults. The notion of socialization leads to theoretical formulations mirroring the adult view that children are incomplete beings. Investigators have consequently been distracted from the important area of study which is adult-child interaction and the underlying theoretically important problem of intersubjectivity implied in such interaction.

Indeed, the possibility of treating socialisation as a process with but a single active agent acting on a passive patient certainly exists. So it is interesting to note that in his writings Bernstein has often explicitly drawn attention to the active role of the subject being socialised, as in Bernstein (1975a: 11; emphasis added):

> ... It ... becomes important to understand the different forms of socialization into distinctive underlying rules. For these underlying rules are not learned as a consequence of any one practice, but they are somehow inferred by the socialized from a range of social relations. In this sense, *the socialized is always active in his own socialization. He both acquires the ground rule and he responds to it...*

In fact, it is more typical for Bernstein to use the terms 'transmitter' and 'acquirer', giving both members of the dyad an active status rather than 'socialiser' and 'socialised'. For Bernstein, reproduction does not work by stealth; it works by the active participation of historically located agents. If there is a force external to the members of this dyad it is the same social condition which according to Marx makes 'men enter into definite relations that are indispensable and independent of their will'; but in this respect neither the socialiser nor the socialised is entirely free.

Whatever the dangers in the use of the term socialisation, it is difficult for me to sympathise with Mackay's view of it as a systematic process of the usurpation of a child's power. Indeed I find his claim that 'To observe that change takes place after birth is trivial' somewhat puzzling. Socialisation does not refer to just any kind of change, but to a specific kind that creates a systematic relation between a subject's consciousness and the social practices of the subject's community. If Mackay's claim is that such a change will come about as a result of biological growth without the participation of other human beings, particularly adults, it would be rather difficult to test such a hypothesis except by extrapolation from the cases of feral or isolated children; and these would surely not provide great support for Mackay's hypothesis. If the idea is to claim that the adult does nothing 'intentional' by way of socialisation, this too is puzzling, for there is no necessary assumption that socialisation is always and only self-aware instruction. Why attack a claim that has never been made? It is equally odd to be invited to study adult-child interaction in order to explore the 'important problem of intersubjectivity'. The study of socialisation is necessarily a study of interaction and there is no reason to assume that the problem of intersubjectivity is not really the problem of socialisation. Indeed a good case can be made that socialisation is the creation of intersubjectivity. The sweeping generalisation about the common adult stereotyping of children as 'incomplete beings' too surprises me; but perhaps I am not a common adult or maybe I understand something different from 'incomplete'.

It is obvious that I do not find Mackay's views on socialisation, or interaction or intersubjectivity very illuminating. The only reason I have spent this much time looking into his ideas is because his position reminds me of the position of certain educationists who believe that any form of instruction is an insult to the child's intellect, an attack on his integrity as an individual, and an obstacle to his free growth. In the concluding section of this paper I shall put forward a view which questions the wisdom of this Romantic Liberalism.

In closing this section, I should perhaps add a warning: what is presented here as Bernstein's theory of socialisation is naturally my interpretation of that theory; even as such it is not a complete account. The selection and re-organisation of its elements is naturally conditioned by my perception of the needs of this discourse! So, as Atkinson would remark, it is another 'secondary re-contextualization' (1985: 172) of Bernstein. But I do hope it is not contributory to his 'unfortunate fate' (ibid.): in the first place, I have presented here what in my understanding is the right reading i.e. that which, hopefully, corresponds to Bernstein's own. The accuracy or inaccuracy of my interpretation is, however, less the point than the possibility that through my talk I may have provoked you to go directly to the source itself (and that is really not such a bad fate to befall a writer!).

3 Language

I have argued that socialisation involves the shaping of definite forms of consciousness, that the typical context in which socialisation unfolds is interactional, and that interaction implies overwhelmingly more often than not the use of language. It follows logically that in the shaping of consciousness language must be a primary active force. Once we have gone this far, we would have to accept that in order to perform this function language must have certain essential characteristics, in the absence of which it could not act as a primary force in the shaping of consciousness. What are these characteristics?

It may sound paradoxical, but the very first requirement would be that such a language should not be just a means to an end: it should not be simply a 'mirror' passively reflecting something that exists independent of it. If language is capable of playing an active role in the formation of consciousness, then it should also be an active force in the creation of that reality which its use makes accessible. It should not be simply a means to understanding and/or expressing already existing social relations and processes. If language is capable of playing a part in socialisation, then it should also be instrumental in fashioning these very social relations and processes. When in these assertions, I use the modal 'should' I do not imply a moral necessity, but a logical one. So it is legitimate to ask: what logical reasons are there for suggesting that the simple 'mirrorite' approach (Butt 1984) to language would be in conflict with claims about the centrality of language in socialisation?

3.1 Meaning in language: the externalist approach

When language is assigned a subsidiary role so that it is simply a means to understanding or expressing something, then it is logically implied that the thing to be understood or expressed is independent of language, that language has played no part in bringing about the existence of this thing. If the word 'meaning' is glossed as that which is understood or expressed through the use of signs, then obviously in the approach under discussion, meaning must remain external to language, since language is simply a secondary flow of expressions. I will refer to this as the *externalist* approach. In this approach language is reduced to a naming device: it becomes a set of 'names' that label pre-existing things, properties, events, actions, and so on. It is a condition of naming that the phenomena named should exist and be recognisable as having specific identities quite independent of the 'names' that the speakers of the language choose to give them. In this externalist approach to meaning, the meaningfulness of language consists merely in providing labels that will correspond to phenomena which in their turn are so clearly categorised prior to language that there could be no question about their identity.

Enough has been written about the difficulties inherent in this approach (Hjelmslev 1961; Saussure 1966; Whorf 1956; Wittgenstein 1958; Hasan 1984a; Butt 1984), but here let me draw attention to an issue central to the present discussion. It is sometimes argued that concrete things such as mountains, trees, rivers etc. have a physical existence that is quite independent of language, and so at least in these cases language simply reflects a pre-existing reality. However, there are problems in conceding this point even in the case of physical existents. (How does one know what is a mountain? What is in common to Mount Kosciusko and Mount Kilimanjaro?) We do not know prior to language which aspects of physical reality are relevant to the identity of that class of things which is known to the speakers of English as a mount(ain). Moreover, there appear to be no principles by reference to which generalisations can be made about practices of classification across the languages of the world; and it is well known that these practices are not uniform. It would seem that the criterial physical attributes of the thing in question are not easy to specify;

that in the last resort, a mount(ain) is that which is not a hill, or a mound, or a slope…; in other words, it is the relations internal to 'language English' that determine the referential value and identity of *mound, hill, mountain.* So the view of language as an inventory of names has to be abandoned; instead, we need to see language as a system of relations, which serves as the most powerful device for the very identification of what we think of as real.

If a discussion of concrete, physical phenomena has forced us to acknowledge this much about language, then a consideration of essentially non-concrete phenomena e.g. rights, obligations, social relations and such like will make us appreciate the power of language even further. If we see language as 'subsidiary, in that it is a means to understanding social relationships, structures, processes' (Atkinson 1985: 68), then we imply that language has no place in the creation of these phenomena. Now unlike physical things, these phenomena are not even lying around anywhere to be sensed, such that they could be said to 'exist' (cf. the mountains) whether human beings were around or not. Relationships, structures, and processes are peculiarly human; and I would agree with Marx that being peculiarly human, these phenomena are also social. But how is it that these social phenomena come into being? How do they become part of an individual's consciousness? Generally, the answer to these questions is: 'through interaction'. And certainly this is the answer suggested by Bernstein since the earliest days of his writings. But with the externalist approach to meaning, this answer gives rise to problems. Surely, interaction is largely language operating in contexts of situation. If it is through interaction that these social phenomena come into being, then how is this coming into being effected without the complicity of language? If language is denied an active role in the creation, maintenance, and alteration of 'social relations, structures, processes', then it makes nonsense of the claim that interaction is central to socialisation, or that socialisation is the shaping of consciousness.

In the externalist approach, language is logically prevented from being granted an active, creative role. It is seen simply as an 'empty formalism'; it becomes contentful because it 'names' something, corresponds to some extra-linguistically identified facts, themselves knowable without language. Language, to echo Derrida's critique, is a diaphanous robe through which shimmers extra-linguistically validated reality, which reality is the real, the true meaning. Thus in this approach, the concept of meaning is truly a form of the 'transcendental signified' which Derrida (1974) has so skillfully attacked. It is important to point out that when language is approached in this way, its essentially social nature is all but denied; for the sociality of language in this view consists only in observing the convention of using the same expression for the same referent. Classification itself becomes a 'natural' activity, not one which is informed by social relations or economic facts. It is easy, then, to maintain the illusion, that reality is somehow pre-ordained, independent of what we say or what we hear others say. It is indeed difficult to see how such language could 'shape the child's social identity', or how its use could 'turn the social structure into the child's psychological reality' (cf. Bernstein 1971b: 144; see extract above). It is not simply that this externalist conception of meaning in language is incoherent with Bernstein's sociology; the fact of the matter is that it negates the possibility of any real sociology whatever; it does this by implying a world of human action in which discursive human practices are alienated from other modes of social action; and language remains impotent to create any change. The fact that many philosophers and sociologists have held and at present hold such somewhat naïve views about language, does not thereby bestow validity on these views. A better test for the validity of an approach to language would lie in how far the approach is able to account for the working of ideology by relating it to the power of language. Judged by this standard, the externalist approach fares not at all well.

3.2 Meaning in language: the internalist approach

So we need to abandon the externalist view that meaning is something external to language. We need, instead, an approach that is capable of doing two seemingly disparate things at once: first, we need to show that meanings are the very artifact of language, and so are internal to it; and secondly, that these linguistically created meanings nonetheless pertain to our experience of the world around us and inside us, giving this experience an intersubjective objectivity which forms the basis for our perception of the possible and the impossible, the same and the different, the appropriate and the inappropriate, the coherent and the incoherent.

But what evidence is there to allow us to say that meaning is internal to language? I will try to answer this question from the perspective of the Systemic Functional theory of language. To examine this problem, let us turn once again to the central concept of interaction. Imagine a specific case of interaction; imagine also that in some recorded form we have access to the text which was the realisation of that unfolding interaction. Looking into such a recorded text we would find a dense semiotic structure. This structure would be a coding of meanings that are recognisable to at least some segment of our society as indicative of a particular social situation. To the socialised reader, the meanings of a text will provide certain kinds of social information, which may be listed as follows:

1) What kind of social relations obtained between the interactants;
2) What was the nature of the social process in which the interactants were engaging apropos which they produced the language;
3) What mode of message transmission was employed.

The fact that these strands of meaning can be gleaned from a recorded text is evidence that a certain structure of meanings – a certain social situation – has been recreated by language. I use the word re-created, which implies that there did exist something prior to this reading – namely the (imaginary) interactive situation in which the (imaginary) text had unfolded. But what about literature, where there is no re-creation, but simply creation? Such creation would be impossible if meanings were not internal to language, or if language were simply a mirror reflecting what physically surrounds it. Without this ability to create meanings, languages would be useless for most purposes for which they are used daily, whether in ordinary day-to-day life or in highly specialised areas.

We tend to behave as if social context is a piece of material reality and the job of language is to reflect it. However, the relation between language and social context is very much more complex. For, it has to be recognised that the identity of a context is not established simply by reference to the physical attributes of the material situation: rather, this identity is known by the meanings at risk in a context, by the selection and organisation of meanings specific to it (Bernstein 1982, 1986, 1987b; Firth 1957; Halliday 1973a, 1975a, c, 1977; Hasan 1973a, 1978, 1979, 1980, 1985a, b, c). Contexts validate meanings, but configurations of meaning identify contexts. This implies that language has to be able to construct meanings, for it is this that would enable the interactants to keep track of the ongoing (or shifting) contexts. If contexts are identified by linguistic meanings then it follows that the construction of linguistic meanings themselves occurs not as a result of language reflecting the immediate situation, but because the meaning-making potential is inherent to language as a structure. Human language is not a mechanism for generating formal structures, which first get generated and then become meaningful. Rather the very generation of such structure is an act of meaning.

The meanings created by language are not a reflection of some immediate situation; neither do they correspond to some esoteric metaphysical entities that exist independent of language. The meanings in language relate closely to the concerns of the living of life by humans. This is made obvious from an examination of the three strands of meaning which represent three highly general functions served by human languages. For most of us, language becomes an important means of establishing some relation with others: we ask and respond, offer and demand; we let a person in into our attitudes, evaluations and estimates. By these and other such 'actions' – which are performed with language – we forge new social relations and maintain or break or alter old ones. This is the INTERPERSONAL function of language. The fact that language is able to constitute meanings of this type is why a discourse manages to contain in it information about the nature of the social relationship obtaining between the participants. The technical term that refers to this set of social facts is TENOR OF DISCOURSE. So, a specific kind of tenor, e.g. a 'teacherly' one, is brought into being by the selection of certain interpersonal kinds of meanings. If I wish to play the game of being a teacher, then I have to make use of my language in such a way that it will make certain meanings which meanings the members of my community will see as typical of the social relation of teacherness.

While the interpersonal function of language is important in that it creates, maintains and/or alters social relations which occupy an important place in the life of any community, an equally important part is played by language when it becomes the means of defining our experience of the world. We use language to say who is doing, thinking, saying etc. what to whom, and where, when, why and how these processes may be being enacted. But being able to say these things implies that we can recognise discrete classes of things – that we know the principle of separation between afternoon and evening, walking and striding, man and woman, employment and exploitation, and an almost uncountable number of such classes. In the preceding section, I tried to show that the classification of non-linguistic reality is not a 'natural' operation; it is a well known fact that human beings the world over do not classify the non-linguistic universe in the same way. Classification is done semiotically; and language is used in the creation of these classes, as well as for the relations between classes. This is the IDEATIONAL function of language.

Although classification as used above is not identical with Bernstein's more specific, technical use of the term 'classification' (Bernstein 1975b, 1982, 1986, 1987b), there is a good deal in common to both. The ideational function of language participates in the creation of a community's body of knowledge – whether it is knowledge in the specialist sense or knowledge for everyday living of life. The fact that language constitutes meanings of this kind – setting apart buying from borrowing, teaching from learning, work from leisure, and so on – is the fundamental reason why from the language of a text, we are able to say what was the nature of that social activity in which the interactants were engaged, and apropos of which occurred that particular interaction. This kind of information about the context of a text, we refer to as FIELD OF DISCOURSE. So the social activity of teaching geometrical shapes (Butt 1989b; Butt and Cloran 1988) is brought about by the selection and organisation of certain meanings of this kind. Martin, Wignell, Eggins and Rothery (1988) show what meanings had to be made to create the field of pedagogic presentation of geography and history. Halliday (1988) shows how language constructs the discourse of physical science.

But what about the third strand of information? How do speakers come to infer this? To answer this question, we need to recognise a third function of language – called the TEXTUAL metafunction. Speakers normally use their language in such a way that the meanings they select suit their perception of the occasion for saying, thus displaying the relevance of language to non-linguistic phenomena. Not only this, but language has to be used so as to enable the speakers to indicate the identity, similarity, and the interconnections between the various parts of the ongoing talk. It is through the selection of certain kinds of meanings that such relevance is created. Textual meanings become a means of indicating some important aspects of interactive contact – i.e. how the sayings of one interactant become accessible to the other participants. This aspect of the situational information is known as MODE OF DISCOURSE. Typically, mode of discourse is linguistically produced by meanings of the textual kind.

3.3 Context, function and language form

In the above section I began with the question: what evidence is there for saying that meaning is internal to language? I answered this question by showing that (i) language can be used to re-create a past context as when one recounts; so it cannot be solely a reflector of the here-and-now; (ii) it can be used to create a context which never existed as in literature; so it is not bound by historical factuality; and (iii) above all, the very identity of social context is defined by reference to linguistic meanings. It is an empirical fact that members of a community tend overwhelmingly to recognise the identity of social contexts in which they find themselves; the stronger the group identification, the truer this observation. It is important to add that other modalities of meaning co-occur with language, particularly in face-to-face interaction, e.g. expression (gesture etc.), appearance, physical location. However, material attributes of the situation cannot unmistakably convey the information about the identity of the situation – a church is not always for godly acts, or a shop for economic ones (Hasan 1980; Cloran 1987) – therefore, the means for arriving at such information must lie somewhere else. I have suggested above that this source is language: it is linguistic meanings that transform a material situational setting into some socially significant context – a site for the enactment of social relation, and for the performance of social process. Clearly language could not act in this capacity if it were not a meaning-making system, if meanings were not internal to it. It is the structures of linguistic meanings that provide information along three dimensions, giving us a triadic model of context of situation at an abstract level:

1) tenor of discourse i.e. the nature of social relations;
2) field of discourse i.e. the nature of social process;
3) mode of discourse i.e. the nature of verbal contact.

That language is capable of being used this way is indicative of both its creativity and its sociality. In my view, it is a wrong strategy to underplay the role of language, simply in order to emphasise the importance of social phenomena; a better strategy would be to show how language and social phenomena are closely aligned by what we might call their co-genetic logic. Despite the fact that language is not subsidiary to social facts and relations, the kind of meanings it makes are deeply responsive to speakers' social environment. The essential character of language is functional: it is a meaning potential and the kinds of meanings languages are used to make – the interpersonal, the ideational, and the textual – are precisely the ones that construct the identity of a social situation. Thus there is a close relationship between the three functions of language and the three parameters of situation, central to the identification of a context (Halliday 1975b, c, 1977).

These statements should not be seen as implying a one-way causal deterministic relation, which would grant a temporal or logical priority to either language or to social situation. The dependence of language and social context is mutual; there is a deep interpenetration of language by social context, and of social context by language; so much so that it is difficult to think that one could evolve without the other. To understand the source of this interdependence, we must turn to the nature of language itself. The fact is widely recognised that language is a semiotic system. One necessary characteristic of a semiotic system is that it must establish contact with some phenomena which are essentially different in kind from the elements of the semiotic system itself. So, for example, the semiotic system of language makes contact with non-linguistic reality. But just because language and reality are not one and the same thing, there has to be some central concept which would explain the nature of their response to each other. The idea of naming was one mistaken attempt to provide such a central concept. I believe a much better solution was found by Malinowski (1923, 1935) through his notions of context of situation and context of culture (Hasan 1985e), notions which have been developed by Firth (1957) and particularly by Halliday in his numerous writings.

In the Systemic Functional model, the concept of social context is an integral part of the theory of language. As a concept, it is used to explain some of the most essential aspects of language; for lack of space, these issues cannot be discussed here in detail. But I would like to draw attention to two of the most important contributions of this concept. First, it provides that frame of consistency in which the elements of the semiotic system of language are brought into contact with phenomena that are essentially different from the elements of the semiotic system itself. The concept of context helps to show how reference – the relation of the linguistic signs to the non-linguistic phenomena – is not a metaphysical but a social act. A second and equally important contribution of context of situation is that it emphasises the centrality of the speakers, and so of speech. These speakers are, ultimately, the creators of their language. This implies that speech plays an active role in the creation, maintenance and alteration of a language system. Further, if we ask: why do speakers create a language? The answer is not: because language is an aesthetically satisfying formal system for the creation of structures etc. Rather the answer would be that speakers make a language evolve through innumerable acts of speaking because they – the speakers – are social; their sociality demands semiosis – i.e. acts of meaning to others. So it is within the context of communality that speakers speak to exchange meanings, and so infuse linguistic meanings with sociality. Language is a resource for making meanings, but the roots of the linguistic meanings themselves lie in the social life of the speakers of the language; and it is through the patternment of social context that the linguistic sign and the non-linguistic referent of the sign become associated with each other.

In this phase of the discussion, I have said more than once that language is functional, that it is a resource for making meanings. Let me elaborate on these assertions a little. The functionalism of language does not consist in the simple recognition that language is useful, that we use words to do things with them. This very obvious fact does not need linguistic theory to proclaim itself. A truly functional approach to language is one that shows how the acts of meaning are constituted by the selections of meaning and wording. Halliday has suggested that the structure of language is as it is because of the functions language is used to serve in the life of a community. From this point of view neither the evolution of the functions, nor that of lexicogrammatical form is fortuitous. The functions relate directly to the social contexts, but the meanings specific to each function are constructed by the lexicogrammatical form, which is itself 'informed' by function. If this is true, then we would expect the lexicogrammar of a language to fall 'naturally' into three relatively distinct components; each of these components would be the active means for creating the meanings pertaining to some one function, as Halliday has argued (1970, 1973b, 1977, 1978, 1979a). Time and space do not permit an exploration of this issue here, but there is more than just an indication to suggest that the lexicogrammar of languages is, indeed, organised precisely in this way (see especially Halliday 1979a).

This hypothesis about a triadic organisation at the level of lexicogrammar is of special interest to my arguments. If it is true that the lexicogrammar of a language is 'informed' by the three functions, and that the functions themselves are in a realisational-constitutive relation to context of situation, then we can claim that the living of communal life – its social character – pervades the very form of language through the continuities of these connections. This claim about the interpenetration of social context and linguistic form is extraordinarily important. Its importance lies in the part that linguistic form – lexicogrammar – plays in defining the identity of the signs that constitute the semiotic system of language. If we think of the lexicogrammar of a language as sets of related systems, each of which (systems) consists of mutually exclusive choices, then we can begin to see how this aspect of the lexicogrammatical organisation of a language would define the meaning potential of a linguistic sign. For example if we have a system with the choices 'singular' or 'plural', the one term can be defined as not the other: so if 'singular' means 'one', then 'plural' means 'more-than-one'. This is the case with English. But consider now an Aboriginal Australian language in which the system consists of not just singular or plural but of three terms: 'singular' or 'dual' or 'plural'. In this system the meaning potential of 'plural' is defined differently from English: it must now mean 'more-than-two', and not just 'more-than-one' as in English. Languages develop their own systemic relations which the systemic linguist represents in system networks, or speaking more accurately and less metaphorically, I should say that speakers develop systems of choices that are specific to their language, which is what one describes as a linguist. If the lexicogrammar is the resource for identifying linguistic signs and for defining the meaning potential of the signs, then it is the resource for making meaning. On the other hand, if what goes into the systems of this lexicogrammar is that which is 'informed' by the sociality of the speakers that arises from the concerns of their daily life, then we can see that in the end linguistic meaning, and social existence are two aspects of the same 'reality'.

It will have been noticed that there are many points in this entire discussion of context and meaning where I could have referred directly to Bernstein's work. This is because the model of language I have presented is one which by its nature is well-suited to his theory: it is a model that would allow language to bear the weight that Bernstein's theory places on interaction. Language can be so effective in socialisation, because it has 'connived' at the making of society itself. The meanings made by any language, including English, are not universal, not impartial, not innocent of the consequences of social division of labour. These meanings are saturated with the patterns of our living of life. So the linguistic and politico-economic systems interpenetrate. Through its role in socialisation, language gives back to the community, what the speakers of the community put into the system in the first place. It is important to recognise the power of language, the role of speakers and therefore of speech in creating the language. This is so because, in the end, language is in the hands of its speakers and it is certainly a possibility that change in forms of discourse may create certain changes: a possible example of such change in recent years is the feminist discourse.

4 Language and socialisation

One challenge posed by Bernstein's sociology is to develop some strategy for the examination of orientation to meanings. My research[3] at Macquarie University, supported by the Australian Research Grant and Macquarie University Research Grant, has been an attempt to meet this challenge. Section 1 has hopefully indicated the vast scope of Bernstein's theory; and although my own research was inspired by his hypotheses, its scope is much narrower. So it is important to say a word about the relationship of my research – The Role of Everyday Talk between Mothers and Children in Establishing Ways of Learning – to Bernstein's theoretical framework.

I have argued in section 1 that in Bernstein's theoretical framework, language has a crucial place in the processes of socialisation, and hence in the formation of consciousness. The importance assigned to language is the primary justification for a linguist's entry into this exciting though hazardous area of enquiry. However crucial language may be to socialisation, Bernstein has argued that the very structure of communication – the selection and organisation of meanings – is regulated by social relationships. Consideration of these relationships leads us, by steps in the argument, to the recognition of the fact that in Bernstein's words (1987b: 37) 'Without a shadow of doubt, the most formative influence upon the procedures of socialization, from a sociological point of view, is social class'. It is 'the fundamental dominant cultural category' (Bernstein 1975a: 175); and it 'acts crucially on all agencies of cultural reproduction and therefore on both family and school'. He adds (1987b: 37):

> The code theory asserts that there is a social class regulated unequal distribution of privileging principles of communication, their generative interactional practices and material base with respect to primary agencies of socialization (e.g. family) and that social class, indirectly, effects [sic] the classification and framing of the elaborated code transmitted by the school so as to facilitate and perpetuate its unequal acquisition.

My research is concerned with the theoretical and empirical linkages between three concepts: (1) social class; (2) code; and (3) consciousness. More specifically my interest is in the role of language in creating and maintaining these linkages. While the macroscopic aspects of Bernstein's sociology are highly relevant to my research, the research was not designed to test any of these aspects. It had a much more limited aim: to carry out an empirical examination of the linkages between the three concepts named above. If the macroscopic aspects of Bernstein's theory enter my research, this is because of the hypothesised relations between social class, distribution of power, and the social division of labour which penetrate acts of communication. My research is also limited in another respect: if we grant that not all communication is linguistic, it would follow that as regulator of the structure of communication, codes would be realised not simply linguistically, but also by other, non-linguistic, modalities. My research is concerned only with the modality of language; it seeks to answer the question: does the selection and organisation of linguistic meanings vary in correlation with variation in social class? If yes, then how can that variation be interpreted? There is not enough space here to enter into the confused and confusing debate about codes and language variety (see, for some discussion, Bernstein 1987b: 574). I will simply declare that if the selection and organisation of linguistic meanings varies systematically in correlation with some specific social circumstance(s) of the members of the speech community, there remains no logical reason for denying the variants the status of language varieties. Labov's theoretically unsupportable claim that variation in language is 'meaning preserving' (Labov 1972a, 1972b) arises from his impoverished conception of meaning as simply referential and of form as an autonomous structure. The situation is made worse by his almost exclusive focus on variation at the level of phonology. Semantic variation, i.e. systematic differences in selection and organisation of linguistic meanings, bear all the necessary characteristics of language varieties (Hasan 1973a, 1984a, 1987b, 1989; see also chapter 3 of this volume) and should be so treated. The relevance of this discussion is to establish that my research is not concerned with the entire realisational spectrum of codes: it is concerned only with that part of the realisation of code varieties which I refer to as semantic variation, or variation in semantic orientation. The tripartite focus of my research on semantic variation, social class and consciousness determined the research design.

4.1 Research design: the subjects

It is a well known fact that the definition of class presents problems. Marx criticised 'vulgar common sense' for turning 'class differences into differences in the size of one's purse, and class conflict into a quarrel between handicrafts' (Bottomore and Rubel 1976: 208). Such attributes as occupation, income and/

or education as 'definers' of class suffer from a circularity common perhaps to all definitions. As pointed out above, one central question my research was intended to explore was: does orientation to linguistic meanings vary with variation in social class? It was therefore necessary to ensure that the subjects represent some systematically defined classes. I am aware of the objections raised (e.g. by Horvath 1985) against class allocation of women and children on the basis of the husband and father's class position. These objections do not appear to be grounded in a coherent sociological theory. A detailed discussion of the issues cannot be undertaken here for lack of space. Briefly, despite the locative metaphors used, class is not a material location: it is a dynamic concept, involving active participation in social processes (Connell 1983: 148). The possibilities open for participation are not specific to just the 'bread winner'; rather, they encompass the family as a unit. Both gender and biological maturity interact with, and redefine, these possibilities (Bernstein 1977, 1975, 1982; Butt and Cloran 1988; Cloran 1989). In other words, just because wives and children are themselves not engaged 'in the labour force', we cannot assume that they have no social class position, or even that their social class position would be qualitatively different from that of the bread-winning 'man of the family'.

Following the implications of some of Bernstein's statements (e.g. Bernstein 1982: 310, 1987b: 571–73), I took 'the relationship between agents of production and the object and means of labour' (Poulantzas 1981: 143) as critical to the categorisation of the subjects in this research. In practical terms, for the family of each 'subject dyad' we asked the following questions:

(a) how possible is it for the bread winner of this family to make work-related decisions which could/would affect the policy and/or day-to-day conduct of the work related practices of others in the work place?

(b) how possible is it for the bread winner to pass on these decisions to others in the work place so that those decisions might be executed?

Clearly the answer to these questions would determine the degree of autonomy enjoyed at work by those in question. Further, the answer would not necessarily be a simple 'yes' or 'no', but could be ranged on a continuum. Where the answer was 'none' or 'very little', as would be the case with, say, the Council truck driver, or a bricklaying contract labourer, the family was considered to belong to a Lower Autonomy Profession (= LAP). If the answer was 'considerable', or 'a great deal', as would be the case with a bank manager or a medical practitioner or university lecturer, the family was considered to belong to a Higher Autonomy Profession (= HAP). It is, of course, not a matter of sheer coincidence that parents in a LAP family tended to have neither higher education, nor advanced technical training; in particular, none of the mothers had any experience of tertiary education. By contrast, at least one, if not both, parents in HAP families possessed higher education, and many mothers had had professional training as a doctor, a teacher etc. The level of education was treated as an associated attribute of the families that participated in the research. It is obvious from the discussion that the LAP family in this research is equivalent to the working class, and the HAP, to the middle class.

As social class is an important concept in this research, care was taken to ensure that macroscopic factors affecting behaviour should not vary randomly. Australia is a multi-ethnic country, with many far-flung cultures being brought together, e.g. the Lebanese and the Vietnamese. There exist families, where the 'natural' language for day to day interaction is not English: the study of semantic variation would become highly complex if the semantic system of more than one language had to be calibrated. For these reasons, it was required that both parents should have been born and brought up in Australia; neither should have lived abroad for a period of more than six months; and that both parents should be users of English as their mother tongue. Because of Australia's social history, these requirements effectively ensured that the population of 24 families (12 LAP + 12 HAP) for the project was drawn from amongst White Australians.

The second central question this research was intended to explore was: Do different semantic orientations create different forms of consciousness in the socialised? The scope of this enquiry is vast; the precautions needed in the selection and observation of the population alone are daunting. The resources of this project did not allow the kind of longitudinal study which is suggested from a combined consideration of the work of Mead (1934), Vygotsky (1962, 1978), Bernstein (1971a, 1975a, 1982, 1986, 1987a), Halliday (1973a, 1975b, 1979a etc.), Trevarthen and Hubley (1978), Lock (1978) etc., as this would have involved a study of socialisation from early infancy to at least the upper primary schooling stage. The design of my research is indeed very modest. In order to examine the two central questions, the enquiry was divided into two stages: Phase I and Phase II. The former was designed to answer the question: does semantic orientation co-vary with social class? The data base for this was natural mother-child interaction in everyday life. Phase II was concerned with the second question: does experience of different semantic orientation create different forms of consciousness? The data base for this enquiry was the child's subsequent interactions with other members of the community, including the school.

For Phase I the starting point was socialisation in the family. The study began with an examination of the interactive experiences of children between the ages of three and a half to four years (3;6—4;0). Why this age? I wished to collect data only by audio-recording in a situation as near natural as possible, which ruled out the presence of any outsider, including the researchers, on the scene of recording. On the other hand, when the immediate situation is not shared, then the child must be at least about 3 years old to be intelligible on audio-recording. The upper limit of four years was determined on the argument that children of this age range have usually not developed very close peer group ties. Most of their interaction has been within the family. In all probability up to this point in a child's life the most significant socialising agency would be the family; and within the family, the person most closely involved would be the mother. In fact, it so turned out that in the LAP families, either there was no (surrogate-)father, or if there was, he was out to work early and back so late that on most working days there was not much interaction between the father and the (subject) child. And even where some child care arrangement was used, the mother remained the most significant 'other' who engaged with the child in the majority of social processes that the child was capable of entering into. It seems therefore valid to suggest that in the socialisation of children of this age range, the mother best represents the family as a socialising agency. For these reasons, in Phase I the study focused on interaction between mothers and their 3;6—4;0 year old children. Bernstein has often drawn attention to the interaction between social class and sex (Bernstein 1971a, 1975a, 1982), so the two sexes were equally represented in the child population for each class. The population for Phase I consisted of 24 mother-child dyads, with the children divided equally by sex and social class.

In Phase II, one third of the children (2x2x2) were followed at the age of 5;0–5;6 years. The decisive factor for the commencement of recording was the child's entry into the school. This event removed the child from the immediate home and neighbourhood environment, placing her/him into some hitherto unfamiliar social processes with other participants most of whom would also be unfamiliar to the child. It was argued that this would place the child under a certain amount of pressure; and that coping interactively with this pressure would reveal how/if socialisation at home bears any systematic relation to what goes on in a young child's life outside the home, the family, and the neighbourhood. The children were recorded in four broadly materially defined situation (1) in the classroom; (2) in the school playground with new peers; (3) at the child's home with old peers, i.e., their neighbourhood friends; and (4) in dialogue with the researcher, David Butt, at the child's own home. Interaction in each of these material situations was recorded twice: first within the first four weeks of the child's entry into school; and again within the last four weeks before the end of that school year. Because of my keen interest in comparing the semantic orientation of teachers in the KG classroom with that of the HAP and LAP mothers' in talking to their young children in everyday home environments, the classroom data was augmented at a later stage by recording 16 more teachers in precisely the same conditions as those for the earlier eight teachers. We thus have data of teacher talk from 24 KG teachers, 12 of whom taught in schools in areas predominantly inhabited by LAP families, while the other 12 taught in HAP catchment areas.

4.2 Research design: the data

If the aim of a research is to examine a subject's or a dyad's, habitual orientations to meaning, it is obviously important to ensure that the corpus to be examined is as close to their habitual ways of saying and meaning as possible. Labov (1968, 1972a) has shown that increase in self-monitoring of talk produces significant patterns of variation. Labov's work was, of course, limited to the phonological level. It has been generally assumed in linguistic discussions that in speaking, the production of phonological patterns is at an appreciably lower level of consciousness than that of meanings themselves. However, Whorf (1956), whose main concern was with semantic variation across languages, provided a deeper analysis of 'awareness of meaning', according to which, awareness of meaning is not uniform for a whole level of language's organisation, but varies depending on the way categories of meanings are realised. Lexical meanings are uppermost in consciousness – their realisation is highly overt and segmental – while meanings which are constituted by 'configurative rapport' are at the deepest layer of consciousness – their realisation is covert and non-segmental; they are created by the patternment of wordings, but the underlying principle of that patternment is not present to speakers' consciousness (Whorf 1956; Halliday 1973a, 1976b, 1978; Hasan 1984c, 1986a; Cloran 1989).

These observations lead to two conclusions: if we are to examine interaction, the interaction itself should not be self-monitored. Nor should it be simply a simulation of the real, as in Labov's 'transformation of personal experiences' (1972e), but rather the 'real' everyday stuff which happens naturally in the living of life. Secondly if we are interested in interaction from the point of view of habitual orientation to meaning, then the focus should be on the least conscious aspect, viz. the patternment of meanings rather than individual lexical items, relations etc. Bernstein (e.g. 1982) claims that the unit for the study of his theory of coding orientation is the whole discourse, not single utterances. The reason for this is obvious: evidence of meanings below the conscious level is not to be found in isolated lexicogrammatical units. The first of these conclusions determined the mode of data collection, while the second determined also the methods of analysis. In collecting data for research, I had to ensure (a) that the collected data was representative of unself-conscious, everyday interaction, and (b) that the duration of the interaction was not mechanically determined as it was, for example, in Wells' data (Wells 1981, 1985); rather it should reflect boundaries as perceived and/or created by the participants, for it is only under this condition, that we stand a good chance of encountering complete texts (Hasan 1978, 1979; Halliday and Hasan 1985). In maintaining the unselfconsciousness of the data, I found unexpected allies in the subject children themselves. These children were too young to permit the mother to put on a qualitatively different 'face' for the recording occasions; because the mother's unfamiliar face defied intelligibility for the children, they insisted on the return of the face they were familiar with. Secondly, the recordings were made by the mothers themselves on a small, unobtrusive but powerful tape recorder. No outsider was present on the occasion. The instructions given to the mother emphasised

(1) our interest in finding out what little children talked about in everyday familiar situations with some one close to them such as the mother;

(2) therefore, the need to collect instances of everyday talk in which the mother was not doing anything special to make the child talk, but letting the talk happen as it normally did in everyday life;

(3) mothers were advised to turn the tape recorder on when she felt she and her child were in a situation of talk; there was no need to turn it off at every small interruption, silence etc., the recorder was to be turned off only when it became evident that the child has disengaged from talk for some indefinite time;

(4) the mother was requested to consider recording the talks with her child at different times of the day so as to capture a range of the child's different interests.

No other contextual restrictions were placed on the mothers. Each dyad was given six one hour cassettes for recording; the mothers were to get in touch with us when they had finished recording all the tapes. Dyads took approximately four weeks to finish the recording and on average each recorded circa four real hours of speech thus producing close to 100 hours of naturally occurring speech; the length of individual recorded events varied enormously within and across the 24 dyads, ranging from 2.5 minutes to over 20 minutes.

The data of mother-child natural dialogues thus collected revealed that certain material situations were in common to all families, e.g. care-giving, playing together, cooperative household activity, eating a meal together etc. Each such material situation is, as it were, a malleable entity, which is shaped by the workings of the discourse into contexts that are more specifically describable as those of, for example, control, play, or instruction etc. It follows that if each dyad were equally represented for some commonly occurring material situation, then their selection and organisation of meanings would be indicative of what this malleable material situation was transformed into – what specific discourse relevant contexts were recognised and constructed by each dyad. Accordingly such a sample was drawn from each dyad. The total number of messages analysed for the 24 dyads over all the material situations was well over 22 thousand for Phase I.

As mentioned above, there were four recording environments in Phase II. As I shall only have time to refer to the classroom interaction, it is unnecessary to describe the considerations that governed the selection of each recording environment. The collection of the classroom data was presented to the teachers as aid to a research undertaken to examine inference making on the part of the children, which again justified emphasis on letting children talk in their usual manner. By this method, it has been possible to obtain normal classroom talk from the teachers themselves. In obtaining samples of teacher talk, one main intention was to conduct an overall comparison of ways of talking at home and in school. I am aware that functional equivalence of meaning across largely distinct contexts is questionable: it is one thing to find direct commands in a leaflet, instructing installation of a household gadget, and it is another to find direct commands in regulative discourse in the pedagogic context. There have, however, been attempts (e.g. Edwards 1976; Rosen 1972) to question Bernstein's claim (Bernstein 1971a) that the elaborated coding orientation is characteristic of the educational context. Like Labov (1969), these authors' claims seem to be based on an analysis of language that, in my view, is far from viable. It was natural to ask if Bernstein's claim would fare differently when classroom interaction is analysed using more semantically sensitive categories, such as I believe were the ones designed to analyse data in my research (Hasan 1983 mimeo).

4.3 Research design: semantic system networks

I hope, by now, it is obvious why I prefer to use the term semantic orientation (Hasan 1984a, 1986a; Hasan and Cloran 1990), rather than Bernstein's 'coding orientation': the latter is much wider in its scope, involving all modalities of semiosis; the former – semantic orientation – is restricted to language alone, assuming that isolating one modality of semiosis from the others which typically co-occur with it is viable. I have proceeded on the assumption that this is indeed the case; otherwise one would have to deny the possibility of linguistics, and by the same token deny any specificity to language *per se*. on the basis of previous discussion, it should also be obvious that the focus of the analysis had to be the level of semantics. Given the conception of language in section 3, at least three things follow:

(i) Linguistic meaning is not monolithic; every message is a configuration of at least three distinct 'kinds' of meanings: interpersonal, textual, and ideational. To be viable, a framework for the semantic analysis of the data should permit the identification of all three strands of meaning in every message.

(ii) If the identity of a linguistic meaning (a signified) is known by its relation to other meanings (other signifieds), and if this relation is paradigmatic and syntagmatic, and if the paradigm and syntagm are so related that a particular syntagm is the specific actualisation of one of the possibilities opened up by the choices in the relevant semantic paradigms, then it follows that the semantics of a language can be represented as a set of systems of choices. Together, these networks of choices would, represent the meaning potential of a language. A system network of this kind is necessary for the semantic analysis of any data.

(iii) If linguistic meanings are constituted by lexicogrammar, then the recognition criteria for a semantic option in a system network would have to be provided by explicit statement in terms of some lexicogrammatical pattern(s) which realise it. Hasan (1986b) demonstrates that so long as lexicogrammar is seen as multifunctional, such explicit statements of realisation can be provided.

Both Halliday (1973a, 1978, 1985a etc.) and Bernstein (1973a, 1982, 1987b etc.) have argued that the semantic systems of a language are context specific. However, I take the position that, since, for all active purposes, the specificity of contexts must be a relative matter rather than a categorical one, it must be possible to construct a relatively 'context-independent' semantic network. i.e. a network, which up to a certain degree of delicacy, displays all possible semantic choices in the language, such that it is the configuration of choices from such a network that in the last resort becomes a heuristic device for the definition of a specific class of context of situation. Such a network would be an account of the meaning potential of a language. I do not have the time here to develop the arguments in favour of my position. Nonetheless experience based on research suggests that it is possible to isolate 'context specific' systems of meaning from such a context independent network. Keeping in mind the three conditions ((i)–(iii)) above, I have constructed such a context independent network describing the semantics of message in English (Hasan 1983). (For a definition of 'message', see Halliday 1984a, 1985a; Hasan 1973b.) This network is metafunctionally organised, and contains:

(1) systems of textual meanings, e.g. choices concerned with topic maintenance, topic change, etc.;

(2) systems of interpersonal meaning, for example, choices concerned with speech role exchange such as asking, replying etc.;

(3) systems of ideational meaning, which, following Halliday (1976b, 1977, 1985a etc.), can be seen as falling into (a) logical meanings, e.g. cause, consequence etc.; and (b) experiential meanings e.g. types of doings, doers, undergoers etc.

Realisational statements are attached to each semantic option, and are in principle treated as the recognition criteria for that option. Although I have presented this network as context independent, I must hasten to add that, quite obviously, it does not represent all or even nearly all that needs to be known about the meaning potential of English, because its cut-off point in delicacy is fairly gross. However, two important points appear relevant: (i) that extensions of the network may need to 'presuppose' the systems of options already built into this semantic network and (ii) that a context specific network can be seen as a partial abstraction from the network constructed for the research. Clearly the presentation of the whole network in one article is an impossibility. A fragment of the 1983 semantic network, together with a two-part table displaying realisation statements and examples of selection expressions have already been presented earlier in this volume (see chapter 3, figure 5 and table 2; pp 101–106)[4]. Each message was analysed in terms of approximately 70 semantic variables. The analysed data was subjected to Principal Component Analysis (Horvath 1985; Cloran 1989; see also the account in chapter 3 and Cloran's contribution in accompanying CD).

5 Some results: on teachers' and mothers' semantic orientation

The statistical analysis of the data from Phases I and II produced a vast number of results. Keeping the focus of this occasion in mind I have decided to present the results of only two analyses both from Phase II, both comparing mothers and teachers. The research population for these analyses is 48 with 24 mothers and 24 KG teachers. The 24 teachers were evenly dividend between the LAP and HAP catchment areas, which represent the areas of residence for the LAP and HAP mothers of Phase I. The school data included in this analysis represents teacher talk in the KG classroom during such activities as picture reading, number talk etc., and is taken solely from the first run of data collection. In other words, the teacher talk included in this analysis is talk which young children (approximately 5 years old) would encounter within three to six weeks of having joined the school. One very important factor that could influence the nature of children's own participation in the classroom discourse is their degree of familiarity with the teacher's semantic orientation. And this familiarity will naturally be greater where the mother's semantic orientation is more like that of the teachers'. If linguistic interaction plays a part in shaping consciousness, then it follows that different habitual semantic orientations will at least create a somewhat differing sense of what counts as 'normal', 'expected' and 'legitimate' response to objects, persons and processes. Countless studies have shown the centrality of shared assumptions as an important element for sustained participation in discourse; and without doubt, our assumptions are largely fashioned through our interaction with significant others. For these reasons alone, a comparison of the semantic orientation of mothers' and teachers' talk could be interesting. There are of course related, and much stronger arguments for such comparative studies. These arise from the role of the school as a significant socialising agency, and the place of the institution of education in the distribution of social power. The arguments for these claims are no longer as rare as they were when Bernstein began to draw attention to them.

5.1 PC1: Analysis I: the construction of individuation

Table 1 presents the details of the first factor – PC1 in Analysis I. This PC will be called PC1-AI. This is a PC, where each of the semantic features entered in the analysis is relevant to the structure of the factor, since each has loaded at .5 or above. Thus PC1-AI is constituted by the entire set.

Table 1: PC1 – Analysis I (= PC1-A1)

VARIABLE	PCI
Inherent reason	.58
Child as senser	.86
Hypotheticality	.64
Actuality	.63
Usuality	-.67
Possibility	-.83
Necessity	-.78
Eigenvalue:	-3.69
% Variance:	52.70

PC1-A1 accounts for 52.7% of variance in the data, the chances are very high that the set of semantic features as a whole would function as a sociolinguistic variable, distinguishing sub-classes in the population. Figure 1 shows the location of each speaker (24 teachers + 12 HAP mothers + 12 LAP mothers) as determined by their scores on both PC2-AI and PC1-AI, with PC2-AI displayed on the vertical axis. Clearly subjects scoring high on this factor would be in the top half of figure 1, those scoring low would be in the bottom half.

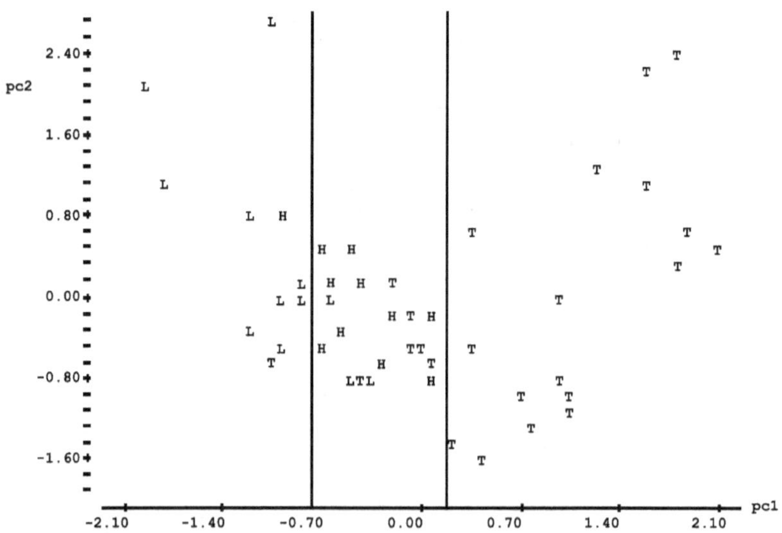

Figure 1: PC1-A1 and PC2-A1: speaker scores

(Key: L = LAP mother; H = HAP mother; T = Teacher)

Our concern here is with PC1-AI, which is displayed on the horizontal axis of the figure; the lower a subject scores on this variable, the closer that subject's location would be to the left end of the figure, and vice verse. The two vertical lines in the figure, divide it into three unequal columns: note that LAP mothers cluster primarily (9 out of 12) in the left-most column, showing that their scores on this variable are low. By contrast, the majority of teachers (18 out of 24) cluster into the right most column indicating that their scores on this variable are highest, while the HAP mothers (11 out of 12) occupy a mid-way position. The bar graph in figure 2, displays the mean scores of the speakers in the three groups:

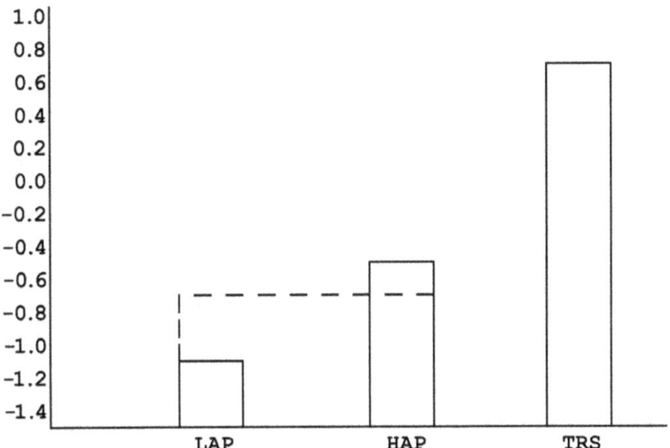

Figure 2: Mean scores of speakers on PC1-A1

The dotted line indicates mean score for mothers as a whole.

The mean scores of the mothers as a whole compared to the mean scores of the teachers on PC1-AI show that teachers will choose this sociolinguistic variant significantly more often than mothers as a whole (p=.000). The comparison of the mean scores of HAP and LAP mothers shows that HAP mothers choose the sociolinguistic variant significantly more often than the LAP mothers (p=.001). However, when HAP mothers are compared with teachers, teachers show a significantly higher selection of this sociolinguistic variant (teacher > HAP mothers: p=.000). Exactly the same results are obtained when teachers are compared with LAP mothers (teachers > LAP mothers: p=.000). It is clear then that on this measure, teachers' classroom talk differs from all mothers' talk, with the obvious implication that the classroom semantic orientation would be unfamiliar to both HAP and LAP children. Nonetheless, because there does exist a statistically significant difference on this same measure between the

LAP and HAP mothers (HAP mothers > LAP mothers: [=.001] we may be justified in concluding that the degree of unfamiliarity might be somewhat greater for the LAP child than for the HAP one.

Statistically, then, PC1-AI isolates one highly significant variable that accounts for semantic variation in the way teachers, HAP mothers, and LAP mothers interact with small children. But how is this factor to be interpreted? What are these semantic features that enter into its structure? Given the restriction of space, I provide examples of each feature, beginning with the very first [inherent reason]. So we are concerned with identifying those messages which function as 'logical' or 'rational' reason; this contrasts with such 'irrational' reasons as threat, bribe, appeal to authority etc. Speakers produce a 'logical' reason by way of justifying some such dialogic move as commanding, offering, generalising etc. Here is an example from the data, where the mother is attempting to get her child to go to bed:[5]

Example: 1

Mother: (1) Karen, come on into bed please … (2) quick … (3) come on (4) you've gotta go to school tomorrow Karen (5) now move! … (6) into bed!

Karen: (7) Mum! (CALLING ATTENTION)

Mother: (8) you won't be up in time to go to school (9) if you don't get into bed…

Here the consequence in (8), which is conditioned by (9), functions as inherent (often called 'logical') reason justifying the set of commands and assertions produced by the mother in (1)-(6). The entire command-justification complex is summarised in 1a.

Example: 1a

Mother: Karen, come to bed quickly because if you don't you won't be able to get up in time to go to school and you've got to go to school tomorrow.

Like many meaning features used often in description, [inherent reason] is a complex notion, characterised by a certain combination of choices from interpersonal and logical metafunctions, whose lexicogrammatical realisation has been explicitly stated elsewhere (Hasan 1983). As pointed out earlier, the message function called 'inherent reason' is in systemic contrast with such message functions as threat, bribe, blackmail, appeal to authority either communal or personal, and tautology. In each of these, the reason is not inherent/ logical/ 'rational', but rather taken to be external or 'irrational', as may be clear from a comparison of Ex: 1 with Ex: 2; the latter forms part of the same dialogue as Ex: 1 some 40 messages later:

Example: 2

Mother: (1) Karen, do as you— (SLAPS CHILD) (2) put your legs down (3) or I'm going outside right this minute without a kiss (4) now put your legs down (ANGRY VOICE).

Note the common belief that there is a non-accidental relation between someone going to bed early and getting up early; the same cannot be said about a child not tucking her legs under the blanket and her mother walking out on her without giving the child a kiss. For principal component Analysis I, the message function 'reason' was treated as a conjunction of two mutually contrasting categories: inherent reason and external reason. Each subject's choice of inherent reason was expressed as a percentage of all reasons chosen by that subject. The semantic feature inherent reason has a positive loading of .58 in PC1-AI (see table 1 above), with the implication that subjects scoring high on this PC – e.g. teachers in this project – would select inherent reason more often than external reasons such as bribes, threats etc. The reverse behaviour would be expected of subjects scoring low on this PC; according to figure 1, these would be LAP mothers.

The second entry in table 1 is child as Senser. Those familiar with SFG (e.g., Halliday 1985a) will recognise the term Senser, as a Participant function associated with Mental Process. Thus it is a lexicogrammatical term, deriving from transitivity. This transitivity function, Senser, is one of the main lexicogrammatical functions that is realisationally related to a semantic feature with a longish label: 'experiencer of inner, ego-based doings and happenings', such as thinking, knowing, seeing, watching, listening, hearing, hating, loving etc., most of which are instances of Mental process. The term [Senser] is used in this table as a practical convenience both because of its size and its mnemonic value. When this kind of experiencer status is ascribed to someone what is highlighted is their unique subjectivity – their ego-based experiences – in a way that is absent when they are seen as the doer of some concrete deed such as walking, driving, fighting etc. For the analysis under focus, the choice of the role 'experiencer of ego-based activities' for the child was expressed as a percentage of the choice of all other -er roles (Hasan 1985f) ascribed to the child. As table 1 shows, this feature has a positive loading of .86. So subjects scoring high on this PC – and they are teachers – would ascribe this status to the children more often than would, say, LAP mothers. Consider, for example, the following dialogue from one classroom:

Example: 3

Teacher: (1) Well now, here's another picture (2) now what do you think this is a picture about? (3) have a look at in.

Pupils: (4) a bus.

Teacher: (5) yes, it's a picture of a bus (6) all right, well, who do you think is going to catch the bus? (7) who's catching that bus?
Pupils: (8) kindies
Teacher: (9) you think it might be kindies (10) what about you Tony?
Tony: (11) um … school [?girls]
Teacher: (12) you think it could be a school bus (13) I think it could be, too … (14) have a good look at it … (15) what do you think, Kim?
Kim: (16) I think it's preschool
Teacher: (17) you think it could be preschool (18) might be preschool … [8 messages later]
Teacher: (27) tell me all the things you can see in it [i.e. the picture] … (28) right … Len?
Len: (29) people
Teacher: (30) you can see people in the picture … [approx. 20 messages later]
Teacher: (50) how many children can you see, sitting in the bus? (51) see if you can count them.

In this set of extracts from one classroom interaction the teacher ascribes to the children the status of experiencer of inner, ego-based processes repeatedly, e.g ... *do you think* .. (2), (6), (9), (12); *you can see* (30), *can you see* (50) and *see* (51). The class room data from which the above example is taken is not extraordinary: it bears considerable resemblance to other classroom data cited in other studies e.g. Rosen and Rosen (1973), Stubbs (1983), Wells (1981, 1985), and Sinclair and Coulthard (1975).

The third semantic feature entered in table 1, [hypotheticality] refers to the character of the message as hypothesis. A message with such a feature does not relate to what Whorf would call 'sensed' time, but rather to a hypothetical, imaginary time. The lexicogrammatical realisation of this semantic feature is complex, involving certain combinations of conditionals, modals, or secondary tense. Their detailed description here would take us too far afield, but the following examples might give an idea of what is at issue:

Example: 4

Julian: (1) when I get old as you (2) and [?Maree likes me] (3) could we Marry each other?
Mother: (4) no (5) because Maree's your cousin.
Julian: (6) oh
Mother: (7) 'cause cousins aren't allowed to marry
Julian: (8) why?
Mother: (9) 'cause the law says they're not.

In this example, both messages (1) and (2) will be said to have the semantic feature of [hypotheticality]: they constitute the hypothetical condition under which the question of the possibility of Julian getting married to Maree arises. In example 5, which is taken from our data of classroom talk, there occur several messages with this semantic feature:

Example: 5

Teacher: (1) you look at how tall the little girl is ... (2) she can only just reach that saucepan (3) what might happen to her?
Alan: (4) burn herself (5) burn herself
Teacher: (6) why do you think she might burn herself? (7) how ... how would she burn herself?
Alan: (8) [?if she be big] ...
Teacher: (9) you're right (10) just tell me again (11) I couldn't hear
Alan: (12) if she be big ...
Teacher: (13) if she was big ... ? (14) well she's just a little bit tiny isn't she? (15) she ... what if .... You know how sometimes you're just trying to reach something (16) and you can't quite reach it (17) and your hand slips (18) what do you think will happen (19) if her hand slips? (20) what will that saucepan do (21) if her hand slips, Suzie?
Suzie: (22) burn herself
Teacher: (23) how will she burn herself (24) what will the saucepan do?
Suzie: (25) tip down (26) and burn herself
Teacher: (27) right, the saucepan will fall (28) and tip things all over her (29) and << (30) if the things in that saucepan are all hot >> then she will ... (31) Alan?
Alan: (32) tip it over her
Teacher: (33) tip it over her ...

Like the first two features, the semantic feature [hypotheticality] too loads positively at .64; and again subjects scoring high on this PC – here the teachers – are very likely to select this semantic feature much more frequently than those who score low.

On the axis of time, [actuality], the fourth semantic feature in table 1, contrasts on the one hand with [hypotheticality], and on the other with [usuality], which is the fifth semantic feature in the table. More specifically, in messages with [hypotheticality], time is not time that is seen as open to sensuous experience but is imaginary; by contrast, both in [actuality], and [usuality] time is real and open to sensuous experience. With the feature [actuality] time has either been sensed in the past or is being sensed here and now in the present moment of the speech. By contrast, in [usuality] the entire span of time – past, present, and future – is implicated; as Whorf (1956) remarked time is experienced not only as memory, and present experience but also as anticipation. Instances of these semantic features can be located in the examples provided above. Thus the reference to time here and now of (1) *is*, (6) *do ... think*, and (9) *are* in Ex: 5 represent the feature 'actuality'. Note how each of these messages is 'about' a unique event; thus ... *do you think ...* or *you're right* refer to specific events/happenings; they are not generalisations going beyond the speakers' here and now. Contrast this state of affairs with Ex: 4, (7) ... *cousins aren't allowed to marry* (9) *'cause the law says they're not*; each of these represents a generalisation and the feature of 'usuality' is present in each – covering past, present, and future. In PC1-AI, the semantic feature [actuality] loads positively at .63, while [usuality] is negatively loaded at -.67. This is to be interpreted as indicating that those who score high on this PC make a frequent choice of the semantic feature of [actuality], thus they are concerned with specific events; further they are unlikely to choose [usuality], so it may be assumed that they are not concerned with generalisations.

The remaining two semantic features – [possibility] and [necessity] – can again be discussed together. Lexicogrammatically, their realisation involves the selection of options from the systems of modality and modulation (Halliday 1985a). A choice of low value modal, instantiated by *can, could, might, may*, also metaphorical realisations e.g. *it's possible/likely that ...* realise the semantic feature of 'possibility'. A single glance at the classroom interactions will provide instances of this semantic feature both in Ex: 3 and 5. The semantic feature [necessity] is realised most frequently as a choice of high value modal e.g. *ought, have (got) to, must, should.* An instance of this feature is found in message (4) of Ex: 1: *you've gotta go to school tomorrow*. The selection of the feature [possibility], clearly, leaves 'avenues open', permitting alternatives. This point is illustrated very clearly by Ex: 3. To the teacher's question: *who* ***might*** *be catching the bus*, different children give different answers. The teacher is able to accept all of them as possible alternatives. The rather restrictive nature of the semantic feature [necessity] is perhaps obvious enough: the selection of necessity constructs situations which offer little or no discretion, since the availability of choice is synonymous with discretion, and this is precisely what is denied with the selection of [necessity]. It should be clear from these remarks that these two features are diametrically opposed to each other; it is, therefore, not surprising to find that while the former – [possibility] – has a positive loading of .83, the latter, i.e. [necessity], has a negative loading of -.78. These loadings suggest that subjects scoring high on PC1-AI – in our case the teachers – will select [possibility] very frequently, thus allowing discretion; by contrast, they would be far less likely to select the feature [necessity]: together the two choices imply that teachers are quite unlikely to impose a set choice, or to disallow room for negotiation.

When each individual semantic feature of a PC is discussed in isolation from the others, there is quite unavoidably an aura of some fortuitousness about their being grouped together as constituents of one factor. What does it mean to say that speakers who score high on this factor will typically

- choose to give reasons that are considered [logical];
- treat the child verbally as the possessor of a unique subjectivity, with a capacity for thoughts, feelings, sensation;
- draw attention in their speech to specific states of affairs, and not be concerned with routines;
- permit discretion to entertain alternatives, and not constrain choices by presenting something as unavoidable.

Is there a higher order semantic abstraction that can be used to characterise this bundle of semantic features as a whole? Is there a principle that breathes unity into it? I believe such a semantic abstraction can be found in that ideology which attaches a great deal of importance to the uniqueness of the individual, where each person is viewed as a differentiated 'other'. The underlying principle is Durkheim's 'organic solidarity' which produces and is produced by 'individuated' social subjects, each differing from the other, but all working together. Note that a semantic orientation that is characterised by this set of semantic attributes must 'presuppose a sharp boundary or gap between self and others, which is crossed through the creation of speech which specifically fits a differentiated 'other''; as Bernstein (1987: 147–48) reminds us this is a quality of the elaborated code, the code that is 'oriented toward a person rather than a social category or status' (ibid.). The emphasis on rationality, on the unique sensing self, on the juxtaposing of the hypothetical and the 'real', and on the recognition of discretion – these are indeed important elements in our educational ideology. In our frequent discussions about educational issues, we may not use such 'strange' expressions as one might think are being used here, but when we claim that the aim of education is to 'nurture each child's *own* personality', to have 'a high regard for each child *as an individual, precious and unique*' (Ashworth 1973; emphasis added), or that the aim is to develop 'cognitive ability', or that true education is a 'widening of horizons', we are saying in effect, that in classroom discourse such a bundle of semantic features must appear with some reasonable degree of frequency so long as this conception of educational goals does not change. It is in fact language such as this, with meanings such as these, that enables the fulfilment of these aims. If my interpretation is correct, then this factor is concerned with the construction of *individuated selves*. On this measure, at least, it would appear that classroom interaction is more exaggeratedly oriented to elaborated code than is HAP mothers' discourse, while the subjects who do show the lowest degree of orientation to elaborated code on this measure are, reasonably enough in view of Bernstein's hypotheses, the LAP mothers.

5.2 PC1: Analysis II: the construction of the pedagogic subject

Table 2 displays the details of PC1 and PC2 in Analysis II. Following the convention established earlier, I shall refer to PC1 of this analysis as PC1-AII, and to PC2 as PC2-AII.

Table 2: PCs 1 and 2 – Analysis II

VARIABLE	PC1	PC2
Non-interpretation questions	-.87	-.09
Non-assumptive questions	.83	.08
Supportive responses	.70	-.38
Inherent reason	.72	-.40
Additional information	.86	.29
How/Why questions	.13	.47
Direct commands	.12	.83
Eigenvalue :	3.26	1.34
%Variance :	46.70	19.20

So far as PC1-AII is concerned, the last two semantic features in that table are not relevant to the variation since for this factor the loading on these features is much below .5; in other words, their contribution to the variation in the data is negligible. The factor is, then, constituted by only the first five semantic features and accounts for 46.7% of variance in the date. Scores on this factor correlate with the social position of the speakers (24 teachers, 12 LAP mothers, and 12 HAP mothers). So, just like PC1-AI, this bundle of semantic features has the status of a sociolinguistic variable. Figure 3 below shows the mean scores of the various groups:

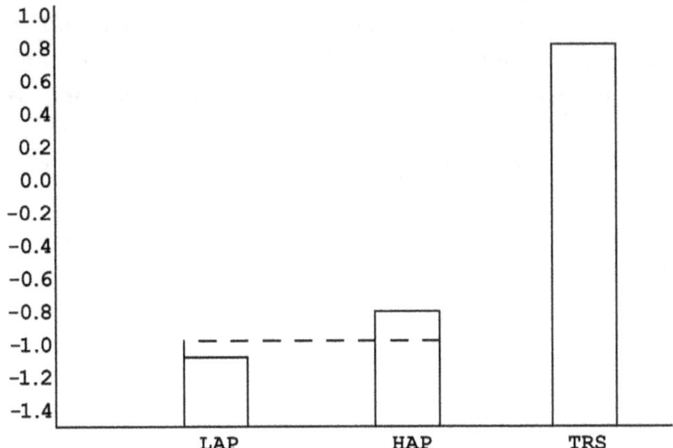

Figure 3: Mean scores of speakers on PC1-AII

The dotted line indicates mean score for mothers as a whole

These differences in the scores are statistically highly significant. Teachers score higher than mothers as a whole (teachers > mothers: p=.000); ('mothers' here refers to both LAP and HAP mothers). Thus teachers score higher than HAP mothers (teachers > HAP mothers: p=.000), as they do when compared with the LAP mothers (teachers >lap mothers: p=.000). Nonetheless, there is significant difference between the HAP and LAP mothers (HAP mothers > LAP mothers: p=.009). In this respect, PC1-AI and PC1-AII appear quite alike: there is sufficient justification for claiming that in respect of both of these sociolinguistic variables teachers present an extreme position, just as the LAP mothers do: these two groups – the teacher and the LAP mothers – represent the two end points of a scale. However, while HAP mothers do not replicate teachers' behaviour, they also differ significantly from the LAP mothers, tending more in the direction of the teachers. We can claim, then, that compared with the LAP child, the HAP child will have significantly greater familiarity with talk characterised by both of the sociolinguistic variables which are captured by PC1-AI and PC1-AII, even if it remains true that teacher talk must appear relatively unfamiliar to both groups. I believe there is an implication here that both these factors are, in some sense, germane to the pedagogic context. Let us, then, take a quick look at the five semantic features that constitute PC1-AII presented in table 2.

The first semantic feature is [non-interpretation seeking] questions. If the message function, question, is viewed as a demand for information, further semantic attributes of a question can be established by examining the kind of information that is sought. Under certain conditions, the information sought could call for the interpretation of a sign or an object. The two conditions under either of which the possibility of seeking interpretation exists are that either (i) the demand can be met by a yes/no answer i.e. the speaker is seeking to confirm (see figure 5 systems a, b, c, in chapter 3), or (ii) the demand can be met by specifying the answer to *what/who, what ... does, what ... for* etc. as opposed to *why/how* (see figure 5 representing semantic choices in asking questions, and their realisation as shown in table 2, part 1, in chapter 3). The following extract provides an example of a yes/no 'interpretation seeking' question:

Example: 6

Mother: (1) ah the pictures have dots (2) to show you where the stick-on pieces go

Kristy: (3) mmm (4) so *do the dots say where the stick on pieces go?*

Mother: (5) the dots don't say it (6) they're not a special kind of writing, or anything.

In this example, (4) is a yes/no [interpretation seeking] question; and note that the mother does give a 'no' by way of answer. More technically message (4) in the above extract has the semantic features [demand; information: confirm: interpretative]. Had Kristy asked: *what do these dots say/mean*, then her saying would have been treated as a question seeking interpretation through an answer to *what*. More technically, this made-up alternative would have the semantic features [demand; information: apprise: precise: specify: nucleus: operative: interpretative]. Kristy's question (4) in Ex: 6 contrasts with Julian's question (3) in Ex: 4: *could we marry each other?* This is a question about how things are or could be i.e. it 'has' the semantic feature [representation], whereas Kristy's question *do the dots say ...* is a question about what something means i.e. it 'has' the semantic feature [interpretation]. When the entry in the factor reads [non-interpretation seeking] questions, this refers to both the yes/no – i.e. confirm – and that category of *wh*— question, here labelled apprise, which has the systemic option [representation] as opposed to [interpretation]. The binary systemic contrast between these two semantic features means that if one is selected then the other is not. In PC1-AII, [non-interpretation-seeking] question – which is to say, [representational] question – loads negatively at -.87. Thus subjects scoring high on this PC, i.e., the teachers – will tend predominantly to select the feature 'interpretative' question. In other words, the focus of such speakers is on eliciting 'meaning' or on making verbally explicit their understanding of objects and processes; their focus is not on the non-semiotic.

The second semantic feature called [non-assumptive] question is one option in a binary systemic contrasting with [assumptive]. As the system network in figure 5 of chapter 3 shows not all questions 'enjoy' this systemic choice – only those with the feature [enquire] or with [apprise: precise: explain: reason] enjoy this privilege. An example of each case with the feature [assumptive] is provided below in Exs:7 and 8, respectively:

Example: 7

Karen: (1) how did you get that? (ALLOWS NO TIME FOR ANSWER)
(2) you didn't get out of [?]
Mother: (3) I walked over (4) and got it (5) didn't you see me?
Karen: (6) nup
Mother: (7) you must be blind

Example: 8

Mother: (1) d' you love daddy? .. (2) d' you love daddy?
Julian: (3) mmm (POSITIVE)
Mother: (4) d' you love Rosemary?
Julian: (5) no
Mother: (6) why don't you love Rosemary?
Julian: (LAUGHS)
Mother: (8) you're a [?ratbag] (REALISES CHILD IS TEASING)
Julian: (9) I do
Mother: [?]
Julian: (10) who else do you want me to love?

In Example 7, there is an assumption behind the mother's question (5) *didn't you see me?*: she expected Karen to have seen her; this is obvious from the mother's comment (7) *you must be blind* at being told that her assumption underlying (5) was not correct. Thus (5) is a message with the semantic features [demand; information: confirm: enquire: assumptive]. In Ex: 8, the message with feature [assumptive] is (6; 7) *why don't you love Rosemary?*, there is again an implication that the mother assumes Julian should love Rosemary, his sister. That the child has interpreted his mother correctly – as someone who has certain assumptions about whom he should or should not love – is clear from his question (10) *who else do you want me to love?* Messages (6) and (7) of Ex: 8 will then be said to have the following semantic features [demand; information: apprise: precise: explain: reason: assumptive]. Compare these messages with message (2) of the following example, which forms part of the same dialogue as Ex: 4 and Ex: 8.

Example: 9

Mother: (1) I love you
Julian: (2) why
Mother (3) 'cause you're my boy.

Here Julian's (2) *why?* Is an elliptical clause which can be expanded as (2a) *why do you love me?* This contrasts with Ex: 8 message (6,7) *why don't you love Rosemary?* and would be semantically described as having the feature [non-assumptive]. This description is correct on the assumption that by asking Ex: 9 (2a) *why do you love me?* Julian is not implying that the mother should not love him. As with the previous semantic feature, the existence of a binary systemic contrast between [assumptive] and [non-assumptive] implies that the loading on one would be the reverse of the other. On PC1-AII, the semantic feature [non-assumptive] has positive loading of .83, with the implication that subjects scoring high on this factor, i.e., teachers are highly likely to ask [non-assumptive] questions. The choice of this feature in turn means that they do not act as if certain premises are so self-evident that they do not need to be made verbally explicit. The recognition of 'otherness' discussed in connection with PC1-AI appears to be relevant to PC1-AII as well.

The label for the third semantic feature in table 2, [supportive responses], appears transparent enough. In a Sinclair and Coulthard (1975) kind of analysis, an important subcategory of such messages would invariably occur as Follow-up in an IRF (Initiate, Respond, Follow up) triad, where Initiate is often a question and Respond an answer while Follow up is some kind of evaluation. This is most typically the case in my data, where classroom talk is concerned. However, the occurrence of [supportive response] is not limited to this function alone. So in the following dialogue several messages would be said to have the feature supportive:

Example: 10
Julian: (1) I dropped it (2) and it went like this ..
Mother: (3) did it?
Julian: (4) yep
Mother: (5) oh, that's good isn't it?
[5 messages later]
Julian: (6) this closes that door all by itself
Mother: (7) does it?
Julian: (8) yep, it goes bang
Mother: (9) yeah?
Julian: (10) it just went like this (11) when it was – when it was going down
Mother: (12) did it?
Julian: (13) yep
Mother: (14) wow! what else can it do?

Julian is playing with a toy, manipulating it to make it do various things. While the mother's messages (3, 7, 9 and 12) might in isolation appear as if they had the feature [demand: information], the ongoing context of the talk shows perhaps quite clearly that these messages do not function as questions but rather as an empathising comment. In her message (5) we find a positive evaluation – not of any answer, nor of any compliance – but of something that the child has been doing on his own, while in message (14) there is clear encouragement to the child to continue. The mother's messages thus 'tell' the child that the mother is listening, that she is interested, that she wishes him to go on talking, all of which may be taken to display the semantic property of [supportive response]. An adequate response to a demand may also be viewed as supportive. Many instances of messages with this feature – more specifically with 'agreement' and 'positive evaluation' – will be found in the classroom talk presented in Ex: 3 and 5. As table 2 shows this semantic feature has a positive loading of .70. On this basis we may conclude that the feature has occurred frequently in the speech of those who score high on PC1-AII, namely, the teachers. Such speakers are concerned with what Goffman (1967) describes as face maintenance; talk of this kind, it may be justifiably claimed, assists in shoring up the interactive other's self-esteem.

The fourth semantic feature [inherent reason] has already been discussed above (5.1). As in PC1-AI, so here too [inherent reason] has positive loading (.72), which implies that subjects with high score on PC1-AII have a strong tendency to give rational reasons. The final semantic feature constituting PC1-AII is [additional information]. With some oversimplification, one may gloss this category as follows: when in a dialogue a speaker goes on voluntarily to give more information than the interactive other's sayings strictly necessitated, then the messages will belong to this category. Thus these messages provide an elaboration, the specific form of which may be the steps in an argument, or the details of some physical phenomenon, or the recall of further (relevant) events etc. Consider as an example the following extract.

Example: 11

Kristy: (1) was that a baby one (= moth) or a big one?
Mother: (2) no (3) moths are um – (BANGING NOISE) (4) hey don't bang the oven (ADDRESSING RUTH, KRISTY'S YOUNGER SISTER) (5) moths are quite old .. (6) when they are little (7) they're little worms (8) and um well you know the book about the hungry caterpillar that you've got?
Kristy: (9) yes
Mother: (10) he ate and ate (11) until he became a big fat caterpillar
Kristy: (12) mmm
Mother: (13) and then he built himself a cocoon (14)**and um—
Kristy: (15)**mmm

Mother: (16) and then he came out of the cocoons (17) but they –
(MESSAGE INTERRUPTED AS MOTHER TALKS TO RUTH)
(18) they only come out of their cocoons (19) to lay their eggs
(20) and <<(21) after they lay their eggs>> they die .... etc.

Strictly speaking Kristy's question in (1) could have been answered by simply confirming one or the other alternative: *yes* (i.e. *it was a baby moth*) or *no* (i.e., *it was not a baby moth*). Though this would have strictly speaking answered the question, apparently, in the mother's opinion it would not have been sufficient. She went on to provide a great deal of information about the life-cycle of moths. So all of the mother's messages to Kristy have the semantic feature [additional information]. It is obvious that speakers who score high on this PC, choose very frequently to provide [additional information] since this category has a positive loading of .86. Talk characterised by additional information is instrumental in constructing much of what is today fashionably called 'knowledge of the world' or 'cognitive content'. Summing up the behaviour of high scorers, i.e. teachers, on PC1-AII, we may claim that

- they show a lack of concern with the substantive aspects of everyday experience and a deep preoccupation with interpretation of phenomena;
- in the context of making enquiries, they do not behave as if certain necessary premises are shared and so self-evident as much to the addressee as to the speaker ;
- they justify their assertions, questions, commands etc. with 'rational', 'logical' reasons;
- they are purveyors of a constant flow of cognitive content, with a high degree of what Bernstein referred to as elaboration in his description of codes; and
- in the environment of the above behaviours, they issue agreements, positive evaluation, and encouragements to continue interaction.

The principle of coherence for PC1-AII may be expressed, following Bernstein's arguments (Bernstein 1971, 1975, 1986) as the creation of pedagogic consciousness. The claim is simply that this factor will *contribute* to the process, not that there is no more to the creation of pedagogic consciousness than this factor. The title of this sub-section is 'the construction of the pedagogic subject': this title is not fanciful. The significance of this factor covers the meaning of the ambivalent expression 'pedagogic subject' in both senses:

first, it refers to the instructional discourse (Bernstein 1986) specific to the pedagogic environment – what are the abstract attributes in common to most specialist subjects in the sense of 'disciplines' or 'branches of knowledge'; and, secondly, the term 'pedagogic subject' refers to the acquirer, the pupil whose very identity is being shaped through classroom interaction.

The factor under discussion, PC1-AII, thus draws attention to some of the most widely valued elements of our educational ideology. For example the view is held quite widely amongst those who find themselves competent to pronounce on curricula, that education is about 'mastering' specialist knowledge. It is not concerned with ordinary happenings and doings – with familiar everyday knowledge (see Butt and Cloran 1988). Education is really concerned with the essence of things, with acts of interpretation; these acts naturally cannot be dissociated from those foundations for knowledge construction that we know by the name of 'definition' and 'classification'. Scientific knowledge, as we know it, is made of discourse of this kind; see, for example Halliday (1988b) and also Martin, Wignell, Eggins and Rothery (1988c, 2004a). Quite irrespective of the levels of success in actual performance, one of the cherished tenets of educational discourse is to state one's premises clearly, not simply to presume that others share them. Both the distancing from everyday experience, and that from the 'other' by not assuming shared self-evident knowledge are essential ingredients of that other highly prized quality of ideal knowledge, which we know by the name of 'objectivity'. And this impression is further strengthened by the emphasis on the 'rationality' of argument within the context of providing the so-called higher order, specialist knowledge, which at this stage of education is just a transformed reproduction of the already legitimised knowledge. That the conception of knowledge and learning just described is highly valued is indicated, for example, by Donaldson's claim that 'much that is distinctively human depends upon it', it being 'our ability to deal, in cold blood, with problems of an abstract and formal nature' (Donaldson 1978: 24). The factor indicates also that in this context of abstract, rational, and objective knowledge construction, one will find gestures of encouragement to draw forth the required information, frequent legitimizing and responsive moves, agreements and positive evaluations, which will, together, make the essential nature of educational knowledge explicit to the acquirer, while meeting a demand, which we think is obviously 'quite reasonable': namely that the pupil's self-esteem as a unique individual should be nurtured.

It is remarkable that as with PC1-AI, so also with PC1-AII, the teachers, who score the highest on both factors, differ significantly from the mothers as a whole, as they do also from each subgroup of mothers, whether HAP or LAP. And this difference is in all cases highly significant as the following summary shows:

Table 3: Teachers and mothers PC1-AI and PC1-AII

PC1-AI (mean scores)	PC1-AII (mean scores)
Teachers > mothers (all): p=.000	Teachers > mothers (all): p=.000
Teachers > HAP mothers: p=.000	Teachers > HAP mothers: p=.000
Teachers > LAP mothers: p=.000	Teachers > LAP mothers: p=.000
HAP mothers > LAP mothers: p=.001	HAP mothers > LAP mothers: p=.009

The conclusion is unavoidable that teachers are, as it were, a class apart from other mortals. What can make them so significantly different? I suggest that here in teachers' behaviour we have an effective demonstration of what it means to say that education is a powerful instrument for socialisation. Through their own training as teachers, in readiness to act as the transmitters of our dominant ideology of knowledge, teachers have become significantly differentiated from that other class – mothers – who pay at least equally as much attention to small children, and teach them much they need to know – but in everyday environments, not within the official education frame. Table 3 shows that HAP mothers too display these behaviours significantly more than the LAP mothers do. On this basis it seems reasonable to suggest that the orientation to meaning which characterises the HAP group is likely to create a more receptive audience for those teachers who teach HAP children. And, indeed, our results (not discussed here) do show that while there is hardly any significant difference between the teachers in HAP areas as opposed to those in LAP areas, there are some interesting differences in the behaviour of the HAP and LAP classes of children in the classroom. This is not surprising. HAP children's experience of ways of meaning is significantly closer to the teacher's ways of meaning in the classroom than is the LAP child's experience. This is not an issue about language deficit as it has been wrongly suggested (Stubbs 1983; Edwards 1976 etc.) in the literature: it is an issue about what appears relevant to whom and why.

5.3 PC2-Analysis II: control in the classroom

PC2 in Analysis II, which will be referred to as PC2-AII, differs from the two PCs discussed above. As table 2 shows, it is one of those cases where the entire factor is composed of one single semantic feature, 'direct command', which loads at .83. All other semantic features are irrelevant to the variance of the data with respect to this factor since their loading is below .5. The semantic feature [direct command] is realised lexicogrammatically by the selection of a specifiable sub-category of imperative clause (Hasan 1983); or by a declarative with high modal e.g. *got to, have to, must, should, ought to.* PC2-AII is a sociolinguistic variable, accounting for 19.2% of variance in the data and correlates significantly with the speaker's social position, as is evident from figure 4, which shows that the results on this PC are significantly different from those summarised in table 3 above. So far as 'direct command' is concerned, LAP mothers score significantly higher than HAP mothers (LAP mothers > HAP mothers: p=.000); they also score higher than teachers (LAP mothers > teachers: p=.02); and teachers score higher than HAP mothers (teachers > HAP mothers: p=.000). Thus in respect of [direct command], teachers are more like LAP mothers, than they are like HAP mothers in that both groups of speakers favour direct command, even though it still remains true that teachers differ significantly from LAP mothers as well.

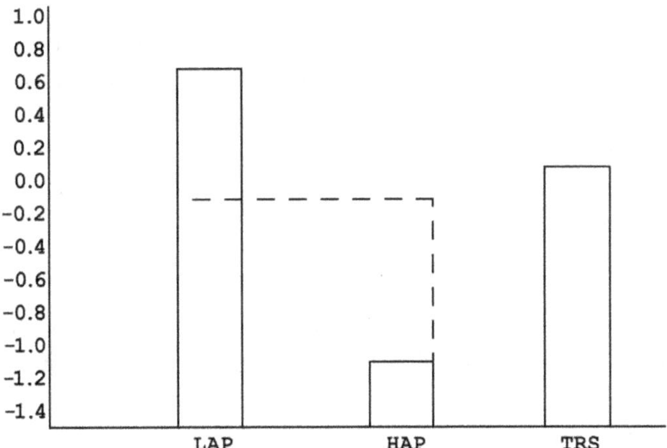

Figure 4: Mean score of speakers on PC2-AII

The dotted line indicates mean score for mothers as a whole

Turning to the interpretation of this finding, first note that the scores of the two groups of mothers and teachers here differ from those on PC1-AI and PC1-AII, showing a reversal of the earlier trends, as the following summary shows:

(a) PC1-AI and PC1-AII: Teachers score higher than HAP mothers who score higher than LAP mothers

(b) PC2-AII: LAP mothers score higher than teachers who score higher than HAP mothers.

Since on PC1-AII, teachers' score is significantly lower than that of the LAP mothers, we may claim that they incline in the direction of the HAP mothers, just as the HAP mothers had inclined in the direction of the teachers with regard to PC1-AI and PC1-AII. An important fact to note is that [direct commands] issued by teachers typically differ from those issued by both LAP and – to a lesser extent – HAP mothers. If Ex: 1 and Ex: 3 are compared, it would be found that the former (LAP mother's talk) has six direct commands. The Process in each of the six clauses is either overtly or implicitly of the material kind *come, go, move, get (into bed)*. In Ex: 3 (presented earlier), there were the following direct command messages:

Example: 3

(3) have a look at it

(14) have a good look at it

(27) tell me all the things ...

(51) see if you can count ....

It appears that this is a fairly typical situation: teachers' [direct commands] require either some form of ego-based, *intra*-subjective activity typically realised as mental process e.g. *look, see, think*, or they require *inter*-subjective activity involving semiosis, often calling for the use of language e.g. *say, tell, explain* etc. I shall not be able to provide specific figures here in support of this claim but would draw attention to PC1-AI where teachers score high and are shown to be inclined to frequently ascribe the child the status of experiencer of ego-based inner processes.

The fact that teachers issue many [direct commands] in the classroom has not gone unnoticed. Edwards (1976: 175) comments that 'in most classrooms most of the time, it is tempting to describe control as positional'. I would be reluctant to give in to this temptation, if for the simple reason that positional control involves also the absence of discretion giving; it implies, further, that, verbally, the controlled is not constructed as a unique person. I believe that these points are made quite clearly by Bernstein in various of his writings. Now, the twenty four teachers whose classroom interaction we have examined, do grant their pupils discretion (cf. PC1-AI); they also treat them as unique persons (cf. PC1-AI and PC1-AII). So, at least so far as the evidence of this research goes, it would seem not justifiable to claim that their control strategy is positional. The reason Edwards offers for putting forward his view does not appear to me very convincing. According to him it would be justifiable to see classroom control as positional because 'the main justification for the teachers' commands is inherent in the role-relationship, and the norms regulating it' (ibid.). If one were to accept this argument, it would have to be conceded also that from a purely common sense point of view command is inherent to the mother-child relationship as well, particularly when children are as young as ours in this research were. But our results show clearly that not all mothers are equally inclined to control positionally (further discussion in chapters 7–8).

I would explain this frequency of [direct command] in teachers – which it should be recalled is still significantly less than in LAP mothers' discourse – by the need to orchestrate the behaviours of so many persons within the constraints imposed by the complex material conditions of teaching. The expression 'material conditions' does not refer simply to the constraints on time, space, or the number of pupils to be 'gathered up'. It refers also to the kind of constraints to which Bernstein has drawn attention in his analyses of classification and framing in educational knowledge (Bernstein 1971a, 1975b, 1986 etc.). Clearly the stage of educational process from which my classroom data is collected is one where in terms of specific 'contents' what is taught is already-produced knowledge. But, while seen as content what we have in the early kindy classroom is a re-play of already produced knowledge, there is more to the process when seen from the point of view of socialising the social subject into the ways of engaging in educational discourse: in the former perspective we have simply talk re-producing knowledge; in the latter perspective we have talk aiming to produce subjects socialised into the role of 'pupils'. Teachers' talk has within it properties that, given certain conditions, would produce new apprentices to the current ideology of educational discourse. Naturally, the new apprentice's finished picture of educational discourse would be no more identical to his teacher's, than is a child's language to that of his parent's. The fact that typically the teacher's 'direct commands' are demands on the pupils for a specific kind of 'intellection' and 'communication' is, I believe, an important argument in favour of this position. In fact, when it comes to control of the pupil's personal conduct in the classroom, teachers of even such very young children, seldom issue direct command. When Daniel mimics the teacher repeatedly, she does not say *don't mimic me* or *stop that*, much less (the 'full-blown' positional) *you mustn't mimick your teacher* or *stop doing that or I'll punish you*. She says simply *oh Daniel you are very mouthy today*. This is not to claim that teachers, or even HAP mothers, would never use positional control; such a claim would be just as absurd as the claim that the upper class members of New York city never display non-rhoticity. The essential nature of language, both the system, and the process, is probabilistic (Nesbitt and Plum 1988); neither codes, nor dialects, are amenable to a categorical/absolute characterisation.

6 Concluding remarks

I have argued that social interaction is the means whereby human beings' consciousness is shaped. While consciousness is fundamental for the creation, transformation and regeneration of the conditions of social life, every aspect of human existence, including social interaction – and, hence, consciousness – is deeply compromised by the actually existing conditions of social life. The process whereby in Bernstein's words the 'outside becomes the inside' or in Vygotsky's words the 'internalization of the external' comes about – is this dialectic between social structure, semiotic mediation and human mind, or as some prefer to put it, between culture and cognition. For Vygotsky 'Any higher mental function was external because it was social at some point before becoming an internal, truly mental function. It was first a social relation between two people' (Vygotsky 1978: 162). Leont'ev (1981: 167; emphasis added) summed up the position succinctly:

> This means that humans' mental processes (their 'higher psychological functions') acquire a structure necessarily tied to the sociohistorically formed means and methods transmitted to them by others in the process of cooperative labour and social interaction. But it is impossible to transmit the means and methods to carry out a process in any other than in external form – i.e. in the form of action or *external speech*.

In this paper, I have focused on 'external speech', on social interaction by means of language, because language, due to its inherent attributes as a semiotic system of a specific kind, occupies the most important position in this complex transaction between the levels of what Lemke (1984) calls the 'dynamic open systems'. But if these premises are accepted, then certain conclusions follow automatically, and these are:

- should material conditions of social life differ markedly either across cultures, or across strata within the same culture, then the form of social interaction will also differ;
- if social interaction differs across segments of the same society, then different forms of consciousness will arise;
- since consciousness is central to carrying out social functions, different forms of consciousness will find expression in (amongst other things) different orientations to meaning; in such societies semantic variation correlating with speakers' social position is logically predicated;
- communication between speakers with distinct semantic orientations will give rise to problems, for the words of one will be filtered through the divergent view point of the other (see, for a telling example, Hasan 2004b).

I have presented a set of three results. These results showed that in keeping with the above arguments, social class of speakers – LAP v. HAP mothers – correlates with significant differences in orientation to meaning in all of these results. And whilst I was not able to develop the arguments presented by Bernstein about the nature of pedagogic discourse and its relation to social structure, I believe my results, particularly those on PC1-AI and PC1-AII, showed quite clearly (1) that a significant degree of difference exists between classroom talk and every day dialogue; (2) that the HAP mother's orientation to meanings is more like that of the teacher's, and (3) that it differs significantly from the LAP mothers' orientation to meaning, which is least like that of the teachers'. It does seem to follow from this set of findings that in our community there will be children for whom teachers' orientation to meanings will be a source of problem. In making sense from other's wordings, we do not listen to those wordings as absolute, immutable containers of unique determinate meanings; we bring our entire life experience to bear on the process. Thus it can come to pass that the same utterance by a teacher can appear to say and mean one thing to one class of children and another to another. We, who are inordinately proud of our egalitarian educational system, need to ask what we mean when we talk of educating 'the child'. Which child? For I know of no western society today where those coming to be educated can so blandly be described as 'the child' as if each had the same mental disposition, the same universe of reference to experience.

There are of course those amongst us who would argue that either differences of the kind I have described in section 5 do not exist, or that if they do, they are unimportant; thus Wells (1977: 22) suggests that

> those who wish to show that the language of lower-class children is different, will always find evidence to prove their point, but it does not follow that such differences necessarily put these children at an educational disadvantage – unless they trigger off expectations that all too easily become self-fulfilling.

Wells' article was addressed to Joan Tough's work, with which I am not familiar; however, the position he adopts is quite typical. There is much that I find disturbing in this passage. First, it seems to be implied that those who find evidence of difference between the varieties used by children of different social classes do so somehow by a sleight of hand, by using research methods which are less reputable than those of truly scholarly scholars. Of course, following Labov (1969), scholars have drawn attention to the nature of the data used in the studies of code orientation, which was collected in an experimental setting. And yet it is data of precisely this kind, for example, in Lenneberg

(1975) or Brown and Lenneberg (1954) on the basis of which many of us are quite happy to subscribe to an a-historical, a-social, and an a-semiotic view of human cognition. I am tempted to suggest that the research one accepts as valid does not depend simply on the 'objective' merits of the research; it is also a function of the judging scholar's belief system. If this is true then I can say in an equally disdainful and superior tone that those who wish to deny the close bond between a person's language and her socio-historical background, those for whom language is simply wording whose meanings are external to the system itself, will always reject out of hand any evidence of semantic variation, no matter how well-founded it is. Further, for their own ideological reasons, their own intellectual identifications they will accuse those of divisiveness who draw attention to significant semantic differences between social classes: for it is acceptable to draw attention to phonological, non-semantic differences between social classes; it is acceptable to talk of differences between men's and women's talk, both their wording and their meaning; however, it is immoral to show that different classes may have a different picture of rationality, for did not the good God give us all exactly the same rationality? The same set of meanings? The hidden arrogance of this attitude most probably escapes these scholars' attention, for of course the rationality they consider universal is identical to theirs! It is interesting to note that just as Bernstein has been accused of middle class prejudice, so also Luria's important research with the Uzbeks was suppressed 'as evidence that Luria was denigrating the people among whom he had worked' (cited in Cole 1976). And yet curiously the responsibility for denigration lies with those who believe that, for example, to appeal to 'rational' reasons is better than to appeal to a convention, or to make your premises explicit is better than to just assume shared knowledge.

In one respect Wells is right. Of course, from the characteristic orientation to meaning displayed by members of the LAP class, it does not follow that such children are necessarily at an educational disadvantage. If our conception of the nature of knowledge and of educational discourse were different, if we were to give up our adoration of uniqueness of each individual, if we were to reject Popperian conceptions of rationality – and this is not impossible; there are societies where such is the case; only we describe them as 'emerging nations' – if our educational ideology were to be different in these ways, then, of course, the LAP child would be at no disadvantage whatever. It is somewhat ironic that precisely those scholars who reject the hypothesis of semantic variation, also subscribe enthusiastically to those ideological positions which are typical of the middle class consciousness. There is yet another condition under which, even with the educational system as it is, the working class child might not be put at a disadvantage: if we had clear descriptions of what the requirements of educational discourse are, and what sociolinguistic (specifically semantic) features characterise lower class language, it may be possible to train the teachers to meet the needs of different classes of children. This means of course a somewhat better 'analysis' of academic language than that which was carried out by Labov (1969) and a somewhat deeper analysis of classroom interaction than is customarily conducted by scholars in the field. When such explicit descriptions are available, it may be easier to establish both the nature of the privileging meanings, and the nature of the distinct departure points from which children are made to travel in the direction of those privileging meanings. The system of education has a chance of becoming egalitarian only if the existing differences are recognised, *without being treated as irreversible*.

I suspect that these suggestions will not be well received by many colleagues, who seem to believe that the problems of education arise largely because of teachers' attitudes (Wells 1977; Stubbs 1983). Note, for example, how in the above quote Wells claims – in an almost throw-away comment – that even if the working class child's language differs, this difference itself is immaterial – what would really disadvantage the child is the teacher's negative attitude. Of course in one sense this is very true. Even if the teacher had a good idea of the goal toward which the child should be moving to master our idea of educational discourse, and even if she knew explicitly how to help the child get there, things would not work out at all well, if she devalued the child himself. But Wells' comment presents a simple explanation for a highly complex situation, and succeeds in giving the impression that if only the teacher could somehow get rid of this unfortunate propensity to denigrate the underprivileged child, all would be well: the fault, it would seem, lies entirely with the teacher. This position is both facile – it fails to appreciate the active role of meaning and wording in learning (Vygotsky 1962, 1978; Donaldson 1978; Halliday 1973a, 1975b, 1979a, 1980) – and it is unfair to the teacher. Even with the best of intentions, as things stand today, a teacher would still not be able to help the child simply by having good will towards the child. This is because she does not know explicitly what characterises educational discourse, nor what the child's own point of view is, what his own language is like, and why. And the teacher does not know this because there seems to be a consensus that there is nothing 'to be know'd' here. I believe that the results I have discussed throw some doubt on this complacent attitude. If we really want to make sure that the different semantic orientation which the working class child brings to the class does not disadvantage him, then we need to train teachers so that they can work out how to meet the needs of children of all classes rather than just those who show some familiarity with the principles of educational discourse.

This recommendation implies that I believe teachers have an important – indeed a central – role to play in the classroom. Certainly, there is no doubt that peer-group interaction in or outside the classroom is a generative influence on the mental functions of children, and so it should be encouraged as Burton (1983) argues, but it would be wrong to imply that the teacher's role is simply that of an observer or dispenser of materials – and that the children through their amazing inborn capacities will manage the rest. If we believe this to be true, we should agitate for immediate de-schooling of the society. It seems to me that peer-interaction and teacher guidance are not, or at least need not be, mutually exclusive. While neither can replace the other, because of the socio-historical dimension of socialisation, the adult has an important role to play. To accuse adults of conspiring to usurp children's rights (Mackay 1974) appears simplistic; and to blame teachers for all that goes wrong in the classroom seems to be a rather superficial response. But if we want the teacher to take the central role that should be hers, then she does need to find out about the character of educational discourse, and about variations in semantic orientation. I am not impressed by horror stories of how 'a garbled account' of Bernstein's theory has caused havoc in schools (Rosen and Rosen 1973; Burton 1983 etc.); how it has vitiated teaching; and how it has made them denigrate the working class child. It is not that I doubt the veracity of these reports: these things may well have happened, but they are not logically inherent in Bernstein's theory. Much more to the point is the question: where do teachers get this 'garbled account' from? How is it that after years of academic preparations, teachers apparently still come to their classrooms with deplorably naïve attitudes to language and to society? What have the teacher educators been doing? Why don't they teach them better? Why should teachers be held responsible for the deficiencies of those who educate them? What do these educators themselves think of language? What is their view of the creative power of language? To me it seems shortsighted, not to say dishonest, to hold the teacher responsible while exonerating those who fail to educate the teacher. I agree with Stubbs (1983) that teachers need sociolinguistics, but for my part, I would choose a sociolinguistics which grants language its full power, its rightful position in the socio-psycho-historical development of human communities – I would avoid a sociolinguistics in which language is simply a flow of vocables, and where all linguistic variation is reduced to variation in style, while style itself is seen as meaningless – or at least immaterial to cognition. Sociolinguistics of this kind lacks self-awareness; and it is sociolinguistics of precisely this kind that suppresses any recognition of the linguistic means through which the privileged classes maintain their privilege.

Notes

1 The contents of this chapter were first presented as a plenary talk at The Working Conference on Language in Education, Macquarie University, 17–21 November 1986. It was published in *Language and Socialization: Home and School*, edited by Linda Gerot, Jane Oldenburg (Torr) and Theo van Leeuwen. The present chapter is a slightly revised version. At the time of the conference, the term 'socialisation' had not yet been so discredited as to fall into disuse. I have retained the term. To me as a non-sociologist, the term is apt for what it refers to – the process of becoming naturalised in the ways of being, doing and saying common to one's society.

2 Page references to those of Bernstein's papers which are included in *Class, Codes and Control* Vols 1 and 3, are to these volumes, irrespective of their original place of publication. For a good bibliography of Bernstein, see Atkinson (1985).

3 For help at various stages of this research I am indebted to many. Special thanks are due to Anne Eyland (School of Economic and Financial Studies, Macquarie), and Andrea Coutts-Stern (Systems Analyst, Macquarie), to Harry Purvis and John Telec (Speech, Hearing and Language Research Centre, English and Linguistics, Macquarie), and to Chris Nesbitt (Sydney University). To Barbara Horvath (Sydney University), for bringing to my attention principal components analysis. I owe many thanks to my colleague Dr David G. Butt, and to Alan Taylor (School of Behavioural Sciences) for his help with statistical analyses. My greatest debt of gratitude is to Carmel Cloran; without her excellent help this research would have been much poorer.

4 At this point pages containing such information were deleted from this chapter to avoid unnecessary repetition.

5 The conventions used for transcription of examples in this chapter are as follows:

(WORDS IN CAPITALS)	Situational commentary based on evidence from audio-recording (including both language or non-language evidence e.g., screams, giggles, clatterings etc.).
(1) numbers in parentheses	Identify message number in the example.
(11) <<(12)>>	Message 12 occurred before the completion of message (11); see for example messages (29) and (30) in Example: 5 in this chapter.
...	Greater than normal pause.
** and he went ** was he...	Messages paired by double asterisks show point of overlap in the dialogue.

5 Semantic variation and sociolinguistics [1989]

1 Introduction

Let me begin this chapter[1] by agreeing with Weinreich, Labov and Herzog (1968: 101) that 'in a language which serves a complex (i.e., real) community, it is the *absence* of structured heterogeneity that would be dysfunctional'. Certainly, the claim has observational adequacy: its thesis actually corresponds to our untutored perception of how systematic variability in the use of language operates in everyday social life. It is, therefore, all the more important to note that the acceptance of this claim raises some serious problems for sociolinguistics as it is practised in the dominant Labovian model. The critical problem arises because the orthodox position refuses to grant the possibility of socially significant 'structured heterogeneity' at the semantic level – what is referred to as semantic variation (Weiner and Labov 1983: 31). This naturally raises a problem: in complex communities, where communication across distinct social groups is normally perceived to be problematic, it would be logical to expect structured heterogeneity at the level of meaning, because communication cannot be separated from meaning. On what ground can the absence of semantic variation be seen as functional? A more recent stance to the concept of semantic variation (Weiner and Labov loc. cit.) leads to greater contradiction, an issue to which I return briefly in the concluding section.

In this chapter I will argue that the theoretical position implicit in the Weinreich, Labov and Herzog claim is a more viable foundation for sociolinguistic studies than is the Labovian reduction of all sociolinguistic variation to variable ways of saying the same thing (Labov 1978a). I believe that the latter proposition is questionable both on empirical and on theoretical grounds. By reporting on an empirical research conducted at Macquarie University, I will attempt to show that in fact there is evidence of systematic sociosemantic variation, thus throwing doubt on the established view that sociolinguistic variation is necessarily meaning preserving. I will argue that unless the concept of meaning is arbitrarily constrained, the possibility of the occurrence of socio-semantic variation must form an essential part of any rational theory of sociolinguistics if it is to be seen as 'the study of language in relation to society' (Hudson 1980: 1).

This theoretical orientation has determined the structure of the chapter. In section 2, I shall provide some initial details about the subjects and the data used in the research, findings from which are used here to support my theoretical claims. Section 3 presents a discussion of the fundamental concepts of semantic variation and of linguistic variable, indicating briefly the kind of linguistic phenomena which in my view are relevant to the study of the former phenomenon. Section 4 is concerned with the methodology for the analysis of semantic variation in naturally occurring mother-child dialogues; it also reports some of the results from this study. The final section will briefly examine the theoretical implications of the findings.

2 The research

The research[2] described here forms the initial part of a much larger effort which began in 1983. Its inspiration derives from the Vygotskian theory of the role of semiotic mediation in the development of cognition (Luria 1976; Vygotsky 1962, 1978; Wertsch 1985a, 1985b) and from Bernstein's compatible theory of the role of linguistic interaction in socialisation (1971a, 1975a, 1982, 1987). As a whole, then, this research goes beyond the issue that concerns us here, namely the possibility of sociosemantic variation. The research presented here relates only to Phase I, and concerns dialogues between 24 mother child dyads. The research design has been described in some detail (see chapters 3 and 4 of this volume). Here I add further comments on the troubled and troublesome issue of social class, and the validity of the collected data as representative of mundane routines of subjects' lives.

2.1 The subjects: their social classification

In assigning subjects to this social class or that, one is always confronted with problems of the definition of social class. As Connell (1977: 3) points out:

> … there is an enormous range of theory and speculation about class. This is to be expected from its importance, complexity and opacity, not to mention the struggle of classes and their intellectuals to define the social world in ways that are friendly to their own interests.

Various ways have been devised for rendering this complex concept simple so that it can meet the much valued – one might even say, grossly over-valued – criteria of explicitness and quantifiability. There are the well-known Registrar-General's class categories, which were devised for purely administrative reasons and have no pretensions to theoretical validity even though they have been pressed into the service of academic investigations; there are others devised for social surveys where class has been simply reduced to the scales of income, occupation etc. (for discussion, Connell 1977: 26); there are more theoretically inspired models, for example that of Goldthorpe (Marshall, Rose, Newby and Vogler 1988: 22). Many studies of social class approach the concept through the already recognised socio-economic strata; what is problematised is not how the strata came to be, but rather the manifest dimensions of differentiation (Connell 1983: 84ff., for critique). The fact that strata are differentiated by reference to a plurality of dimensions, which do not always coincide, has lead to the belief, as Connell (1977: 27) points out, that social class is at best a diffuse concept and at worst simply the machination of a divisive imagination that 'perpetuates the mythology' of class, a view disputed by the empirical research conducted by Marshall et al. (1988: 3). As against these approaches, there are traditions inspired by Marx: these typically problematise the very existence of strata and classes. The history of social strata – what they are and what they might become – is traced to the market place, where labour power is sold for wages. This emphasis on relations of production and distribution, which arguably yields the most sophisticated class analysis, reveals quite understandably the complexity of the concept, rather than providing us with a clear-cut set of categories into which individuals can be easily inserted. Thus, to the extent that modern complex societies are not polarised, to that extent sections of the society will be found to stand in a complex relation whereby from one perspective they will be dominating agents, and from another, dominated ones (Marshall et al. 1988: 23). The Australian Vice-Chancellors in the Dawkins era would be a poignant example of such a category.

This is not an easy situation: an honest linguist aspiring to study language in its social context and not wishing to enter the arcane sociological debate – though in fact it is hardly more arcane than the debate about the variants of a variable vowel – is caught between the intractability of the notion of social class and the dominant ideology of the discipline of linguistics according to which categories are (must be?) discrete, with well-defined boundaries. At the same time, thanks to feminism, ethnicity, and other overt but possibly less contentious manifestations of asymmetry in social relations, it is possible for the sociolinguist to continue producing publications on language in its social context; but there is no exaggeration in claiming that in class based societies such as ours, 'without a shadow of doubt, the most formative influence upon the nature of verbal interaction, from a sociolinguistic point of view, is social class (Bernstein 1971a: 175), a view fully endorsed by Labov who too points out that 'socio-economic class is one of the most important elements of social structure in complex urban communities, and correlation with the linguistic variables immediately shows a strong relation' (Labov 1966b: 12).

The implication is quite obvious: contentious though the category of social class may be, it cannot be entirely ignored in sociolinguistic studies. Faced with this dilemma, sociolinguists have adopted such strategies as have suited their beliefs and purposes. To me it seems that defining class by income, education and occupational labels is like describing language without reference to meaning. I have therefore devised some means of operationalising class in a way that captures at least some of its theoretical bases (see the discussion of the origin of HAP and LAP categories in chapters 3 and 4). Note that the breadwinner(s) of none of the 24 families had control over the means of production: they varied with respect to whether they themselves could exercise control over others. The possibility of such control was almost non-existent for the LAP group, while for the HAP group there was considerable scope for the exercise of power and control over decisions. This operationalisation of social class, in some respects, resembles that of Wright (see Marshall et al. 1988: 24ff.) who argues that:

> the relational properties of exploitation and domination … can be tapped by means of information about ownership of productive means, the degree of autonomy exercised by individuals at work, and their involvement in decision-making and supervision of other employees …

One might question the validity of using the breadwinner's social class position for assigning mothers and children to the two groups, when many mothers themselves were not employed, and the children were too young to be implicated in such matters. These objections appear cogent only if social class is 'objectified', an approach against which I have argued elsewhere (Hasan 1992a). True that children and many women are not in the work force; the same criteria of autonomy and exercise of power on subordinates do not apply to them. However, these criteria are not important in and of themselves as attributes of persons; rather their importance lies in the fact that they permit participation of the family in certain social processes, and make its entry into other processes comparatively less likely. And it would be indeed somewhat difficult to argue that access to social processes for members of a family is determined afresh for each individual member, as if the destiny of each were totally, or even largely, independent of that of the others. I have also provided an account of how in the practical life of 'un-employed' women and small children, the social class of the family becomes a potent and decisive influence. On these grounds, it has seemed reasonable to treat the mother-child dyads as belonging to LAP or HAP groups.

2.2 The data: naturally occurring dialogue

It is widely accepted that the methodology of modern sociolinguistics owes nearly everything to Labov. The design of his researches suggested highly imaginative and certainly far more reliable ways of collecting, analysing, quantifying and interpreting the data of linguistic variation than were known to traditional dialectology. Like most researches in the field, mine too has benefited from his example. For this reason, although the same view was voiced long ago, for example, by Firth (1950), I would refer here in particular to Labov's comment (1972a: 184) that: 'It seems natural enough that the basic data for any form of general linguistics would be language as it is used by native speakers communicating with each other in everyday life'. Certainly any study with the aim of examining degrees of semantic consistency or variation in a group of speakers must make use of language data that occurs naturally within identifiable social contexts, that are the natural contexts of living for those speakers. The data for phase I was collected following this principle (see chapters 3 and 4 for some details).

The mothers were given the option of listening to any part of the recording and of erasing or withholding such parts as they wished not to be known to the researchers. Therefore, the research data represents what the mothers were willing to reveal as their public face. It is valid to ask: is this data natural, and free from that kind of self-monitoring which according to Labov should be avoided? In answering this question, three considerations appear relevant. First, mothers were not entirely free to choose their own public face. They were after all engaged in dialogues with their children, and as is becoming obvious from the growing industry of conversational analysis, face in a dialogue is managed cooperatively. The children were too young to take in the implications of the dialogues being recorded. So even though the mothers were aware that what was passing between them and their children would be revealed to some outsider, the children had no such awareness. Thus their behaviour remained unaffected by such considerations, and acted as an effective pressure on the mothers to behave as their children expected them to behave. The children, thus, unintentionally contributed to maintaining the naturalness of the data.

The second factor ensuring the near-naturalness of the data is the pattern of what I have referred to as woman's work (Hasan 1986a). In their normal natural day-to-day life, mothers of very small children juggle many balls simultaneously: they are cooking a meal; they are watching over the physical safety of their small children; they must look out for that downpour if the washing is on the line; given that they are the embodiment of nurturing love, they must not forget the individual needs, likes and dislikes of other members of the family while shopping, cooking, clearing up etc.; they must not let that shop close before they get the ingredients for tonight's dinner, and so on and so forth. In the middle of all this are the questions, the statements and the personal needs of her child (the subject of this research) who is in dialogue with her. Each of these forms of work made a demand on the mothers' attention. If, as is generally believed, telling the truth is more natural in most circumstances, and therefore simpler than lying, then this is certainly the kind of circumstance in which acting naturally rather than posturing is almost a condition for survival! There is here not much possibility of sustaining a self-consciously adopted dramaturgical role, and the data collected in this phase speaks for itself (see, Butt 1989a; Cloran 1989; and other publications cited here and in the CD).

Finally, from conversations with the mothers, it appears that most of them considered these dialogues totally trite and incapable of revealing much. Whether this was because in the recording instructions, so much emphasis was placed on the child's talk, or for some other reason, is not relevant: what is relevant is the fact that, far from worrying about what kind of self-image was being projected by what they had said during the recording, the mothers tended to think of the goings on as routine, pedestrian and more or less lacking in significance. This is in keeping with women's ideology about talking to little children according to which what is said to a child can have no intellectual value (Hasan 1986a: 134); at the same time, it corresponds to the general ideology about language itself as mere clothing, thus rendering the workings of language in daily life invisible, all of which potentially, makes the material more powerful as indicator of ideologies, which are simply naturalised. These beliefs, coupled with the naturalness of the data (see accompanying CD for a sample), suggest that during the recordings the mothers were not attempting to project a self-image which had been consciously adopted for the purpose of showing them to advantage.

The 100 hours of collected data is contextually homogeneous (Halliday and Hasan 1985) with regard to TENOR and MODE; but clearly, the FIELD varies (for discussion see chapter 3 here). Ignoring what the talk is about, and taking into account only the material goings on within which the talk is embedded, three global types of domestic activities can be identified: (1) mother giving care to the child e.g. bathing, dressing; (2) mother engaged in some household chore e.g. cooking, sewing, while the child is around – just playing or watching her; and (3) mother and child engaged cooperatively e.g. cleaning a room, baking, hanging out clothes etc. Since our resources were limited, a representative sample was constructed as described in chapters 3 and 4 of this volume. This sample consists of 20,544 messages (in formal terms, a message is typically realised as a ranking clause defined as in Halliday 1985a). All results presented here are based on this sample.

The sampling technique has some significant consequences. The concrete activities described above do not depend totally for their identification on the use of language: for example, anyone present on the scene would have known without reference to the ongoing talk that mother and child were eating together. The significance of this comment is highlighted by comparing such concrete activities with the totally discursive ones, for example, greeting, lecturing, announcing etc. where the dissociation of language and action in this way is not possible. This is just another way of saying that, in general, language is not actively involved in identifying the nature of concrete activities (1) – (3), with the implication that it can therefore be used for whatever else might engage the speakers' interests during such occasions. This in turn implies that the one and same material situational setting can be used for talking about different things: so one mother might use the activity of putting her child to bed for teaching that child rules of obedience, another might use the same activity as an occasion for talking about what happened during the day, or for reading a story. If the dyads have equal representation in terms of the three concrete activity types described above, then it is valid to ask: how do mothers use this time? Do they inform more than they scold; instruct more than control; praise more than threaten or ignore? If there is significant variation between mothers in any of these respects, then we can go on to ask: what does this variation correlate with? If, say, all mothers praise an equal amount, it is valid to enquire whether they praise the same things? If not, what does this latter difference correlate with, if anything? Thus, the sampling technique facilitates the examination of semantic variation.

3 Semantic variation: conceptual foundations

This brings the discussion to semantic variation itself. Can one examine semantic variation in ways analogous to those in which, say, phonological variation is examined in current sociolinguistics? Curiously, the answer to this question could be either *yes* or *no*, depending on one's understanding of the expressions (1) linguistic variable, and (2) meaning in language. Let me develop this point.

3.1 The linguistic variable

There can be little doubt that the concept of linguistic variable is crucial in quantitative variation studies of the type first made familiar by Labov's work in Martha's Vineyard and in New York City. However, the ways in which the term linguistic variable has been used in the literature is usually far from illuminating. Take Labov himself: his pre-occupation is typically methodological, and an examination of his statements (e.g. in Labov 1966a: 49, 1966b: 6-7, 1972a: 7-8) will reveal that the problem engaging Labov's attention is: how do we decide which variable is worth the effort of studying? This is certainly an important question, and the properties of the variable Labov identifies are important to the success of a research. But equally important, if not more, is the question: where and how does the notion of the variable fit into our conception of language? what gives it its validity as a category in sociolinguistics? On these issues Labov's perspective is, perhaps, expressed by remarks of the following kind (1978a: 1):

> Linguistic variables or variable rules are not in themselves a 'theory of language'. They are all heuristic devices. But it is not accidental that linguistic theory has profited from the analysis of variable ways of saying the same thing.

I have no difficulty in accepting that 'linguistic variables ... are not in themselves 'a theory of language'': there is certainly more to the 'theory of language' than just the linguistic variables. Nonetheless, by its very nature the concept is hardly likely to be 'theoretically innocent'. For example, if one claims, as Labov does, that the variants of a linguistic variable simply represent variable ways of saying the same thing, then one is already invoking some theory of language. In the context of such a theory of language, if the agentless passive is considered as a variant of some linguistic variable (Weiner and Labov 1983), then logically only three possibilities would seem to be open:

1) the grammatical form of a language, or at least some explicitly specifiable part of it, has nothing to do with meaning; **OR**

2) the postulate of agentless passive as a linguistic variant is not viable; **OR**

3) the assertion that linguistic variables are always meaning preserving is not viable.

No matter which of these possibilities is accepted, it says something about one's theory of language, however poorly articulated that theory may be. The fact that a theory is unarticulated does not make the consequences of that theory disappear; it simply sows confusion. Because of the refusal to engage with the theoretical status of the linguistic variable, often its discussion leads to serious contradictions. Consider the following statement (Chambers and Trudgill 1980: 60; emphasis added):

> Linguistic variables can often be regarded as socially different but *linguistically equivalent ways of doing or saying the same thing, and occur at all levels of linguistic analysis*.

The obvious question is: how many levels of linguistic analysis are there, and what are they? Is meaning one of those levels? If so, what would it mean to claim linguistic equivalence for two semantic variables? What does linguistic equivalence consist of? Thus anyone who accepts the above characterisation of the linguistic variable, must believe that meaning is not a level of linguistic analysis; otherwise they must see the propositions as involving contradiction. I would agree with Hudson (1980: 157) that sociolinguists who use linguistic variables have made no attempt to define them rigorously, but I would find it difficult to accept that:

> Fortunately, the notion 'linguistic variable' itself is not meant to be taken as part of a general theory of language, but rather as an analytical tool in the sociolinguist's tool chest, so we need not worry unduly about such problems of definition.

Labov makes use of linguistic variation to explain serious issues, such as diachronic linguistic evolution, or the underlying form of language. Curiously, despite the socially significant orderly heterogeneity whose absence we are invited to consider dysfunctional (cf. the opening quotation), on examination the underlying form of language turns out to be entirely homogeneous once we look below the surface (is this an affirmation of the principle of a variable parole/performance and an invariable langue/competence?), a conclusion which one might well question, as Le Page and Tabouret-Keller appear to do in their introduction (1985: 5ff.). To the extent that variation studies are used to support these momentous theses, the notion of linguistic variable is necessarily implicated in the debate and plays a decisive part. It seems extraordinary to consign it so lightly to a tool chest, as if it were quite as extraneous to one's model of language as an electrician's tool kit is to the circuitry.

Ignoring the wider issue of the relationship of the linguistic variable to the overall model of language, it would be useful to highlight those aspects of the term which are relevant to the concept of semantic variation. In order to do this we need to have some hypothesis about the nature of the linguistic variable particularly in relation to the modelling of language. To begin with, then, the idea of linguistic variable depends on at least two design features of language: (1) language is stratal; and (2) the relation between the strata is one of coding. Conventionally, the coded stratum is referred to as CONTENT, the coding one as EXPRESSION (cf. Hjelmslev 1961). The variants of a variable form a system of mutually exclusive choices at some level of expression, such that no matter which choice is selected, the higher level element coded by it remains constant. This constancy of content is purely a formal construct and it is best not to confuse the expression 'constancy of content' with the ordinary expression 'identity of meaning'. So for example, the lexico-grammatical unit *guard* is the higher level constant, which can be expressed as either the rhotic phonological syntagm or the non-rhotic one. It is not any positive property of the acoustic image represented by the rhotic or non-rhotic syntagms that bestows on them the status of mutual variants: their validity as variants derives entirely from the fact that in the content-expression cycle, they are the expression of the same content. The variable itself is thus an entirely abstract entity – a set of linguistic variants allowing the possibility of choice within a specifiable context or a potential, as Mathesius (1964) suggested. The variants of a variable are not 'free variants' precisely because the probability of their occurrence is conditioned by the linguistic and/or social environment, as all sociolinguists are agreed, thanks to Labov's brilliant researches. The pre-fix *socio-* is applied to the linguistic variable where the probability is socially conditioned, as many have pointed out.

3.2 Linguistic variable and semantic variation

If language is thought of as only bi-stratal, consisting of the two strata of form and phonology, then clearly the very question of semantic variation is ruled out. But this exclusion would be as ex cathedra as Saussure's exclusion of parole from linguistics proper, unless the adequacy of the model which entails it can be demonstrated. Without going into details, then, it should be noted that a linguistic model without meaning would be incapable of explaining either the production or the comprehension of discourse; and that most modern theories have found it necessary to accept that meaning is an integral part of language. So the exclusion of the possibility of semantic variation on the above basis would be simply an artefact of an inadequate theory of language. But even the recognition of a third stratum – that of semantics – does not by itself improve the situation.

Implicit in the idea of semantic variation are the claims that (a) there is a stratum higher than the semantic one, which forms the content that is expressed by semantic choices; and (b) there are variants of a semantic variable such that they represent a system of mutually exclusive choices, where the selection of any member of the system codes the same higher level constant. It follows that the idea of semantic variation is not available to any model in which language is viewed as an autonomous, impermeable object, which has nothing to do with the social life of its speakers. Putting the same view positively, we may claim that the idea of semantic variation can be entertained only in those models of language where the relation between linguistic meanings and some semiotic representation of the environment, such as context of situation, is considered to be an essential aspect of the design feature of language, so that the relations between the two strata are systematic and not *ad hoc*. One such theory is put forward by Barwise (1988, 1989) with a concept of situation which is narrow and rather restricted (cf. Jackendoff 1988) though enjoying the precision of formalisation; another such theory is presented by Halliday (1968, 1974b; Halliday and Hasan 1985) where the concept of context of situation is much wider and so capable of yielding quite rich explanations even if it lacks formal rigour.

Theoretically, apart from the stratum of phonology, the postulate of semantic variable implies a recognition of three other strata: (i) context of culture and situation, (ii) meaning and (iii) wording. Features of the context of situation are coded as systems of semantic options, while the latter are coded as choices at the lexicogrammatical stratum. This latter statement is essential because semantic phenomena are knowable only by reference to the network of relations at the lexicogrammatical level of language. This is a typically European perspective (Eco, Santambrogio and Violi 1988: 19-22) according to which the objective world is inter-subjectively construed and inter-subjectivity itself is semiotically constituted, language being just one, though very extensive, mode of semiosis. Note that these three strata are essential to account for the intellig-ible aspect of the linguistic sign. The phonological stratum, by coding the lexicogrammatical features, creates them as material objects. This materiality of the signing construct is an essential condition for its production as well as its reception. Phonology, thus, accounts for the sens-ible aspect of the linguistic sign.

Although phonological features and constructs serve as the expression of lexicogrammatical forms, the relation between the two is not one of construal, but mainly of manifestation. The dividing line between phonology and lexicogrammatical form coincides with the Saussurean line of arbitrariness (Romaine 1984; Halliday 1973a, 1992a, b; Hasan 1985e): what this means is that phonology cannot be said to define the identity of a lexicogrammatical category. It is this characteristic that explains Saussure's insistence on the purely conventional bond between the signifier and the signified. The principle of arbitrariness is important to the present discussion, even though its scope of operation in the structure of language is limited. In the first place, it follows from this principle that, in general, phonology would itself not be directly implicated in the study of semantic variation; and secondly, an understanding of the principle reveals the complexity of the debate about meaning and sociolinguistic variation. Most studies of linguistic variation have been concerned with phonological phenomena, the system of variants under examination being located at that stratum. The claim that sociolinguistic variation (in phonological coding) does not involve variation in meaning is not only understandable, but, in general, also demonstrably accurate. However, as soon as, in accordance with Sankoff's recommendation (1973), sociolinguistic studies move from this level to higher strata, the problems arising from the lack of a theoretical understanding of the concept of linguistic variable crowd upon us, as witness the writings of Lavandera (1978), Romaine (1984), Plum and Cowling (1987), and Nesbitt and Plum (1988). However, this is not the only impediment to the study of semantic variation: some of the problem lies also in certain conceptions of meaning, as I will attempt to show below.

3.3 Meaning and semantic variation: view 1

Any discussion of the claim that linguistic variation is necessarily meaning preserving – 'variable ways of saying the same thing' – immediately encounters the problems posed by the varied interpretation of the word 'meaning', sometimes even by the same author. Some of these problems have been highlighted by Romaine (1984) in her valuable discussion of the Lavandera-Labov controversy. My aim here is not to go over the same ground but rather to show how two different theoretical approaches to meaning – the one recommended by Labov (1973, 1978a) and the one recommended by Halliday (1970, 1977, 1985a) – inevitably create somewhat different possibilities for the study of semantic variation.

With a certain degree of oversimplification, it may be said that Labov recognises two categories of meaning: (1) social meaning; and (2) truth functional meaning. The phonological variation found in the speech of the various communities Labov has studied is not gratuitous: it has social meaning in the sense that it displays systematic social motivation. So, for example, if in BEV, one considers the choice of *de* as opposed to *the* (Labov 1972a: 189), then the frequency with which these two variant forms are selected, and the pattern of the switch from one to the other, would be indexical of the speaker's social circumstance. This circumstance may be explained by reference to social strata, and/or by reference to the speaker's self-identification with some group of speakers, and/or by the speaker's desire and/or need to accommodate to the listener. Labov attaches a good deal of importance to this aspect of meaningfulness in language, and saw his methodology as correcting the mistaken practices of earlier linguists by restoring to their rightful place the socially significant elements of human speech which, he maintained (Labov 1966a: 48) 'have been traditionally relegated to a kind of linguistic scrap-heap under the name of 'free variants', 'social variants', 'expressive variants' and similar terms'. And again, reviewing the pattern of the selection of *de* and *the* in Boot's discourse, he makes the following comments (Labov 1972a: 189):

> Without any clear way of categorizing this behavior, we are forced to speak of 'stylistic variants', and we are then left with no fixed relation at all to our notion of linguistic structure. What is a style, if not a separate sub-code, and when do we have two of them? We normally think of language as a means of translating meaning into linear form. Where and how do stylistic meanings enter into this process?

Here Labov draws attention to a problem which according to my reading has remained unresolved throughout his work: a quarter of a century later it is still not clear how he would integrate social meaning into his over-all model of language. Rather, there are disturbing hints that the importance of the concept of social meaning may be being eroded; witness, for example Labov (1978a: 2):

> Though formal linguistics recognizes the existence of expressive and affective information, these are in practice subordinated to what Bühler (1934) called 'representational meaning' or what I will call 'states of affairs'. To be more precise, I would like to say that two utterances that refer to the same state of affairs have the same truth value, and follow Weinreich (sic!) in limiting the use of 'meaning' to this sense.

It would seem that Labov's idea of meaning has become increasingly more restricted than it had been in the early sixties. Thus Weiner and Labov (1983: 30) claim 'It seems to us preferable to restrict the term 'meaning' more narrowly to designate the coupling of a given sentence with a given state of affairs'. The justification for taking this position is the unquestioning acceptance of a linguistic tradition (Weiner and Labov 1983: 30):

> In this respect, we are continuing in the tradition of Weinreich's efforts to restrict 'meaning' to significata that are shared throughout the speech community... Weinreich pointed out that descriptive semantics must deal with the 'constant, institutionalized aspect of the meaning of signs... without denying the existence of a non-institutionalized margin of meaning'.

As a result of this redefinition of the term meaning, the position of this word in the phrase social meaning becomes even more ambiguous. As Romaine (1984) has also pointed out, it is no longer clear how the term should be interpreted. The relationship between the two types of meaning seems to be a curious sort of opposition: it would seem that the more you have of social meaning, the less you can have of the significative (Labov 1978a: 2-3), as if social meaning bore no relation to reality, referred to nothing whatever in human life.

The relevant question here is: what consequences does such an approach to meaning bear for the concept of semantic variation? In answering this question, I shall ignore social meaning whose linguistic status itself is so uncertain that it is difficult to say what it might or might not entail. But the second, more restricted sense of meaning is different: here linguistic meaning is equated with representational meaning, which by implication limits the investigation of semantic variation to that of variability in denotation. In effect, one is constrained to look simply into the boundaries of words and their meanings (Labov 1973), asking, for example, whether the significata of 'common sense' and 'mother-wit' are the same or not (Labov 1968). The main problem with this approach is of course that it effectively excludes meaning as a level of language, since one exits directly from words into the world, a view from which at least some modern truth functional semantics would appear to dissociate itself (Barwise 1988, 1989; Barwise and Perry 1983). One of the reasons for this dissociation is that despite its sophisticated formalisations, the classical view smacks somewhat of the simplistic naming theory of language. Clearly, in this approach to meaning the question of a semiotic representation of context does not even begin to arise. No viable study of semantic variation such as I report on below, can be carried out under this rubric of meaning, and to the extent that the truth functional theory of meaning is inadequate as a semantic theory, to that extent the limitations placed on semantic variation by this theory are open to question in the same way as are limitations placed on the term 'linguistics' by brilliant minds with limited aims, such as Saussure or Chomsky both of whom Labov has rightly criticised for unjustifiably limiting the field of linguistics.

3.4 Meaning and semantic variation: view 2

The positions taken by the functional models of language present a contrast to the above view. There are many functional models in linguistics today, each with a slightly different orientation (Dirven and Fried 1987). The view presented here is that of Halliday's systemic functional model (see Halliday 1970, 1977, 1979a). According to this model one goal of a semantic theory is to specify the bases for the intersubjectivity of linguistic meanings. As with the first view so here too I shall oversimplify, mentioning briefly only those aspects most relevant to the concept of semantic variation. The model, as I see it, recognises five strata: (i) *context* (see chapter 1 in this volume for discussion); (ii) *semantics*; (iii) *lexicogrammar*; (iv) *phonology*; and (v) phonetics.[3] Of these, as indicated above (section 3.2), criterial to semantic variation are the three strata of situation, semantics and lexicogrammar. Further, these strata are linked to each other by *realisation*, which is a dialectical relation: the identity of a context of situation is largely constituted by meanings at risk, while the speaking subject's view of meanings at risk is activated by his/her perception of the context of situation. Similarly, the meaning potential of a language is constituted by the lexicogrammatical form of that language, while the lexicogrammatical form itself is a response to semantic pressures exerted on speakers over time. Thus, as pointed out (section 3.2), a content-expression cycle unites the three strata under focus.

This conceptualisation of meaning as defined simultaneously by situation and linguistic form has some important implications. First, if the relation of semantics to the other two strata is dialectical, then it follows that there would exist certain reciprocities across these strata. Let me elaborate on this. Halliday has argued that at the level of semantics the organising concept is that of *metafunction*. Briefly, four metafunctions are recognised: (i) *experiential* (ii) *logical* (iii) *textual*, and (iv) *interpersonal*. The experiential metafunction enables a symbolic representation of the inter-subjectively objective experience of goings on, of objects, abstractions and properties etc. It is thus closest to, though not identical with, Bűhler's representational function. The logical metafunction construes relations between states of affairs, objects, their properties and states etc. Together the two are referred to as *ideational*, and cover the range of meaning traditionally recognised by philosophers and logicians, and some times referred to as 'cognitive meaning'. The textual metafunction creates relevance both within the on-going discourse and between the discourse and the occasion for the discourse; it thus covers the kind of meanings that in other models might be referred to as pragmatics (e.g. Leech 1983). Finally, the interpersonal metafunction concerns meanings that represent the speaker's subjectivity and modes of discursive action; this metafunction is closest to Bűhler's other two functions – expressive and conative – but (contra Leech 1983) it is not identical to them. If the strata of semantics and context of situation are related by realisation as defined above, then there should be some evidence of the reciprocal relation between the two. Halliday argues that this is the case: the four metafunctions are essential to the general characterisation of the semiotic structure of the contexts of situation within which the exchange of meanings between speakers is embedded (Halliday 1974b, 1977; Halliday and Hasan 1985). What is being claimed is that it is through these four kinds of meanings that the general nature of the context of talk is created, interpreted and defined. It is important to emphasise that contrary to some readings (e.g., Berry 1982; Butler 1985), Halliday does not claim a simple and absolute correspondence between *some specific* metafunction and *some specific* contextual variable, as if one mirrored the other; he does, however, claim that typically the ideational metafunction is constitutive of field, the interpersonal of tenor and the textual of mode.

Turning to the relation between semantics and lexicogrammar, two points are important. First, a similar compatibility, without total correspondence, is to be found again between the two strata. Halliday (1970, 1977, 1985a) argues that when the grammar of a language is envisaged as networks of interlocking options, then those systemic options which are constitutive of a specific metafunction reveal closer relation to each other than they would to options which might constitute some other metafunction. These system networks are the most abstract form of a grammar, specifying the language's potential for the generation of structures. It is Halliday's claim that the type of structures generated by a system network constitutive of one metafunction differ from those generated by system networks constitutive of other metafunctions (Halliday 1977, 1979a). Thus lexicogrammatical structures which express the interpersonal metafunction are in general prosodic, while those expressing the logical metafunction tend to be iterative, and so on. The second point to note is that since all four metafunctions are equally relevant to the exchange of meaning, a lexicogrammatical unit such as a clause will represent choices from each, and therefore display multiple structures, each the expression of a distinct strand of meaning. In view of Labov's disdain for functional explanations (Labov 1987), quite ironically this is the kind of view of language that would go a long way in lending coherence to Weiner and Labov's claim that the passive counterpart of an active sentence 'says the same thing' at least some of the time (Weiner and Labov 1983: 30): it does, but only with regard to the experiential meaning; it does not do so in regard to textual meaning.

This conception of the place of meaning in human language opens a genuine possibility for the study of semantic variation. If some feature in the context of situation is treated as the content, we can ask what are the variant semantic options for expressing that feature. The system of semantic options available for expressing that content can be thought of as the semantic variants. For example, imagine that a feature in the situation is ACTION OF COMMANDING, then it is possible to choose as expression a message with the semantic option [exhortative] as when Pete's mother says to him: *listen, you behave yourself and just cut it out please* or [consultative] as when Steve's mother says: *can you get me a tissue please?* or [assertive] as when Davie's mother says *you mustn't hit girls*. Being variants, each expresses the same content, i.e. the situational ACTION OF COMMAND; but because these variants are located at the stratum of semantics, it would be absurd to maintain that their meaning is the same.

These semantic variants differ from each other in a systematic and orderly way: the choice of one excludes the choice of the others. Now, in illustrating the variant expressions of the ACTION OF COMMAND, I have not attempted to hold all other kinds of meaning constant in the above messages. But this is no more problematic than illustrating the rhotic variant by the item *guard* and the non-rhotic by the one which rhymes with *dock*. Obviously, it would be possible to present the choice of variant expressions for COMMAND, in such a way that the variants are identical on all other dimensions of meaning. This is a possible but not necessary strategy if the metafunctions are seen as having equal status, rather than as competing (cf. Labov's view of social and referential meaning) or mutually exclusive (cf. Bühler's three functions). When each metafunction is seen as playing an equally important part in specifying the total meaning of a message, and each has a mode of expression which is identifiable in the structure of the clause, it is possible to examine variation in one metafunction, ignoring the others. For example, if the content under focus is COMMAND, then, since it is a discursive action, the variants will be specified by a system of options which represents that particular component of the interpersonal metafunction which is related expressively to discursive action. Other metafunctions would be only marginally, if at all, implicated in the expression of this content. And since all metafunctions have an equal status, the command-expressing options are equally independent of, say, event-expressing options just as the latter are of the former. For example, most linguists would maintain that *you get me a tissue* and *can you get me a tissue* are experientially (i.e. referentially) alike; as evidence one would cite the fact that the analysis of both in terms of Process-Participant configuration (Hasan 1987a) – or Predicate Argument, if you prefer – would be the same. However, the two clauses differ interpersonally; as evidence note that their mood choices are different. Similarly, it seems also reasonable to maintain that interpersonally *get me a tissue* and *be very quiet* are alike; note that their mood choices are identical – both are *jussive imperative* – though the Process-Participant configuration is different – the Process in the first is *material* and *benefactive*, while in the second it is *relational*. And since the metafunctions have an equal status, there is no reason for attaching greater importance to one kind of similarity or difference in meaning, and treating the others as not so important.

Linguists in overwhelming numbers believe that semantics is concerned only with representational – i.e., experiential and possibly logical – meanings; all other kinds of meaning are an undifferentiated mass called pragmatics. It follows from this view that the examples of variation I have described above will be seen as cases of pragmatic variation, rather than that of semantic variation. It would, therefore, be appropriate to make a few comments in anticipation of this stance, which raises at least two separate questions. First, how valid is it to limit the term meaning in such a way that meaning equals semantics equals representational meaning, leaving every thing else that appears significant under the rubric of pragmatics? Secondly, does variation of the kind exemplified above also apply to representational meaning?

3.5 Meaning: the semantic pragmatic dichotomy

It could be argued that underlying the clear distinction between representational and pragmatic meanings is a real difference: the former kind of meanings are dictated by nature; they just exist independently of semiosis and are entirely objective. By contrast, the latter kind of meanings are dictated by convention; they do not exist prior to semiosis and are entirely subjective, or at best inter-subjective. It has also been argued (e.g. by Leech 1983) that the expression of the meanings of the former kind is grammaticalised, while that of the latter kind is not. Underlying these positions are complex debates about the nature of reality and of grammar, but this much should be obvious that if semantics is the study of meaning in language, and meaning in language is limited to being representational in the above sense, then it would follow that language is just a secondary flow, a mirror that faithfully reflects a reality the identity of which is pre-linguistically knowable. The debate turns on whether the reasons for accepting this view are more compelling than those for rejecting it. Without repeating the arguments, I am inclined to agree with those who reject this view as somewhat simplistic in its assumption that the classification of sense data is a socially neutral process, driven entirely by the objective attributes of real, physical phenomena.

If representational meanings alone are treated as internal to language, it is implied that pragmatic meanings somehow fall outside the system of language. So a curious position arises whereby that kind of meaning which is integral to language-as-code/system – i.e., semantics in this view – is simply onomastic just pointing to what there supposedly is, while the kind of meanings that are extrinsic to language-as-code/system – i.e., pragmatics in this view – are precisely those without which no discourse could be constructed and no meanings whatever could be exchanged. And yet the former, which is not expressible without the latter, is treated as real linguistic meaning, the latter as if it were not linguistic meaning, but something else which is like real linguistic meaning without being quite it (perhaps, some scrap-heap of communicative relevance or social significance). The acceptance of this position would appear more rational if it could be demonstrated that the system of language is more efficacious in pointing to reality than it is in creating intersubjectivity or that it displays greater regularities in the formal expression of the so-called semantic meanings than in the expression of those meanings referred to as pragmatic. Naturally such demonstration itself depends upon being able to clearly differentiate that which is real in the sense of pre-existing language from that which is construed merely intersubjectively.

We encounter then yet another problem: how do we know what is inside semantics and what is outside it? Are we, for example, constrained to treat such forms as *perhaps, probably, of course, naturally* as not semantic but only pragmatic since these are without doubt expressions of a speaker's subjective estimate of possibilities, certainties etc., and are far from being representational in the sense of corresponding to some existent? Let us suppose for the sake of argument that we do treat them as pragmatic as some scholars have done (e.g. Holmes 1988 in her treatment of *of course*). But how different is *perhaps* from *possibly*, how different is the latter from *possibility*, and how different is that from *common sense* in these respects? How objectively based is the meaning of *common sense*, and what existent does it correspond to? How do *perhaps, possibility* and *common sense* differ from those items which Sapir (1944) thought were inherently relational e.g. *big* and *small*, *few* and *many*? Are the problems of these quantifiers even remotely like those we might encounter in comparing *hill* and *mountain*? If it is granted that the boundary between the pre-existing objective phenomena and the subjective evaluative ones is fuzzy, then clearly their mutually exclusive assignment to either the semantic or the pragmatic type of meaning is open to question. One might grant that the recognition of pragmatics as a legitimate concern in the study of language was an extremely significant concession wrested from a conservative autonomous linguistics at a moment when it dominated the scene and was least willing to entertain the validity of interpersonal or textual meanings. This was certainly a big step forward, but it could be that in thinking of representational meaning – semantics – as somehow inherent to language and interpersonal and textual meaning – pragmatics – as somehow adventitious and independent of linguistic form, we are once again creating another ill considered dichotomy in the study of language, which is likely to prove as problematic for linguistics as the Saussurean dichotomy of *langue* and *parole* has done. The popular conceptualisation of the status of semantics and pragmatics *vis-à-vis* each other appears to me to constrain the concept of semantics arbitrarily. If on the basis of such conceptualisation, the examples of semantic variation provided so far are discounted, this would imply a basic disagreement about the nature of language rather than a simple dismissal of the concept of semantic variation.

3.6 Variation in ideational meaning

Let me turn now to the question whether semantic variation as I have defined it above applies to representational meanings as well. The answer depends on whether the model of language incorporates the level of context. If no stratum of context is recognised and semantics is itself equated with lexical meaning alone, then there would be no semantic variation in the sense in which the term was defined above (sections 3.2 and 3.4). This does not preclude the possibility of studying variability in the referential scope of lexical items, as studies of lexical equivalence across dialects demonstrate. If we refer to this as semantic variability, then in such models, the study of semantic variability would be limited to examining the relation between the lexical item as a name tag and some piece of human experience as a pre-linguistically identified phenomenon to which the tag is attached by convention. Sometimes the issue would be: what are the different name tags for the same phenomenon? Sometimes the question would be raised: given a name tag, what is its scope of application to the world of reality? This methodology has been masterfully demonstrated by Labov (1968, 1973). The approach raises some interesting questions about the idea of meaning (for some discussion see for example Jackendoff 1988; Fauconnier 1988; Cummins 1989).

When, however, the model recognises situation as linguistically construed, semantic variation in the specific sense of variation in the choice of ideational meanings need not be so restricted. Instead it is possible to think along the lines argued in 3.2 and exemplified by the discussion of the situational ACTION OF COMMAND in 3.4. Let me provide an actual example. First, suppose a feature in situation is RATIONALISATION OF COMMAND – let us refer to this as RATIONALE. Its semantic expression can be achieved in a number of different ways. For example Alan's mother chooses to say: (a) don't make a mess with it (b) or you'll get a smack, while Helen's mother tells her: (a) oh, well, don't wave that around (b) you're gonna spill it. Here, in both cases, the (b) messages are variant expressions of the contextual content RATIONALE: in both the speaker is coding reason for the addressee to act in a particular way.

As variant semantic expressions of RATIONALE, the two differ from each other. To be more precise, Alan's mother produces a message with the semantic features [external: threat], while Helen's mother utters something which has the semantic features [inherent: logical]. In either case a RATIONALE has been expressed linguistically. If we now ask: what is the basis on which the two variant expressions differ from each other as reasons, the answer would take us to certain ideational meanings which relate the reason to the COMMAND at issue. An [INHERENT] reason must refer to a state of affairs whose eventuation depends on the state of affairs referred to by the message functioning as command; moreover, this dependence arises from the logic of physical forces. The semantic relation between the two is roughly of the kind to which Schank and Abelson (1977: 11ff.) refer as 'conceptual dependency'. By contrast, [external] reason must refer to a state of affairs whose eventuation depends, once again, on the state of affairs referred to by the message to which it stands in a reason relation; but in this case the dependence arises from the logic of interpersonal relations (for further discussion, Hasan 1992a, b).

This has at least two important implications for the semantic make-up of [EXTERNAL] reason: (i) the event in the [EXTERNAL] reason has to be one which is attitudinally salient e.g. *smack, please, make angry, tell off*..., and (ii) the event must be such as to call for at least two human actants, of whom one actant is typically the addressee. Further, if we are interested in differentiating between reason and consequence, then reference to time must be taken into account. This is obvious from a comparison of Helen's mother's utterances with the following:

Example 3: (a) you were waving it around (b) so it spilt

Example 4: (a) if you wave it around (b) it will spill

Hopefully, this very condensed discussion has succeeded in showing that it is, indeed, possible to identify semantic variants whose status as variants is determined by choices in experiential and logical meanings, and which are cases of different ways of expressing the same situational content, viz., RATIONALIZATION OF COMMAND.

While it is possible to attempt the semantic analysis of single messages in terms of the choice of experiential, logical, interpersonal and textual meanings that have combined to give the message both its individuality as that specific message, and its generic quality as that specific type of message, semantic analysis remains incomplete (Firth 1935: 27ff.) until the individual messages are seen in relation to each other and in relation to the social activity that is going on. This, then, brings in the dimension of text, i.e., the over-all ongoing organisation of sayings that both express and construe the nature of the social activity in question. In this analysis, it becomes necessary to recognise 'stages' (as in Mitchell 1957: 178) or 'scripts' (cf. Schank and Abelson 1977), or elements of the 'generalised structure potential' (=GSP) (Hasan 1978, 1979; Halliday and Hasan 1985). This provides another environment in which the question of semantic variation can be raised. Suppose there is a social activity that we may refer to as MATERNAL CONTROL OF CHILD'S BEHAVIOUR, then it is significant to ask: does this social activity have one singular script, one single schematic structure (cf. Martin 1985; Ventola 1987), or is it a structure potential such that variant expressions of the same content – the same social activity – might be found to occur, yielding variant text structures, as Bernstein would predict? This discussion is relevant to the issue of variation in ideational meaning. Suppose for example that the expression of the activity of controlling children covaries systematically with some social attribute of the mothers, the question is whether this varying expression of the same contextual activity content could come about without the complicity of ideational meanings. A priori, there is no reason to assume that systematic and orderly variation would only occur in textual and interpersonal meanings but not in the ideational ones. This has already been demonstrated by some of the results obtained in this research, which is reported in chapters 7 and 8 below.

4 Socio-semantic variation: an empirical study

Hopefully, the preceding section has succeeded in establishing the viability of semantic variation as a theoretical concept. To turn this theory into practice, one needs to be able to specify the systems of semantic variants choice amongst which is available to speakers of a language. When the data is analysed in terms of the variants chosen, the question can be raised whether the choice of variants is orderly or random. And if it is orderly, we may ask whether this orderliness is explained by reference to language-internal phenomena and/or by reference to social phenomena.

4.1 Analytic categories: the idea of semantic networks

If semantics is an account of the meaning potential available to the speakers of a language, then it follows that at least one aspect of the semantic description of a language would be a specification of such choices. In the systemic functional model, with its paradigmatic orientation, this specification will take the shape of networks of interlocking semantic options. Halliday (1973a, b) suggests the desirability of making semantic system networks context-specific, and the earliest such networks devised by him (Halliday 1973) and by Turner (1973) were an attempt to represent the meanings relevant to maternal control as predicted by Bernstein's theory of socialisation (1971). The basic assumptions underlying context-specific semantic networks are implicit in the systemic functional theory of language, specifically in the conceptualisation of how strata are related through realisation. If a context is defined by the meanings at risk in it, then using a specific context as a point of departure, one may arrive at a systemic account of those very meanings which are relevant to that context. This, in essence, is also the kind of assumption made by Schank and Abelson (1977) in their account of how comprehension becomes possible through a knowledge of scripts and plans and goals, though they present the relationship between meaning and context as a matter of human knowledge structures, without raising the issue of their ontogenesis.

The data of my research was only partially context-specific: while we know that it consisted of dialogues between mothers and their small children, the social activities in which the mothers and children engaged were varied, e.g. cooperative play, book reading, and cooperative engagement in domestic chores of various kinds. (For further details, see chapters 3 and 4). An obvious implication is that the research design demanded a system network that would represent the semantic choices available to speakers of English regardless of the occasion of language use – in other words, it was necessary for the networks to be context-independent.[4] However, if the realisation relation between the strata of context and semantics is as described above (section 3.4), then patterns of choices from such a context-independent network would themselves become indicative of the nature of the speech environment. This is the assumption underlying Hymes' (1971) claim that language is constitutive of context.

In practice, the preparation of a fully context-independent semantic network is a highly exacting demand, as it calls for the representation of the entire semantic potential of a given language; and the network prepared for the research (Hasan 1983) was certainly not designed to reach this ideal. A cut-off point in the delicacy of description was chosen such that it would still permit the examination of the questions central to the research. Despite this relative grossness of the descriptive categories, the network is too extensive to present in a chapter of this scope. It will however be useful to discuss some small segments to give an idea of the nature of the semantic categories in terms of which the data was analysed. The network was designed to capture those semantic options whose point of origin is MESSAGE (see chapter 4). Using the four metafunctions as an organising principle, the contents of the system network can be stated as follows:

1) system of interpersonal meanings, for example options in message function (questioning, informing, commanding…), options in personal evaluation, point of view etc.;

2) systems of experiential meaning, for example the ascription of actional, evaluational etc. roles, identification, definition; construction of time etc.;

3) systems of logical meaning, for example cause, condition, and meta-textual relations etc.;

4) systems of textual meanings, for example options in topic maintenance, topic change etc.

Attached to each option in the network are realisation statements. If the option in a system is itself thought of as content, then the realisation statements provide details of how this content is expressed at the level of lexicogrammar.

The details provided fall into two categories: first, the facts of one stratum of language are re-stated as facts of another one. For example, the semantic unit message is realised as clause at the lexicogrammatical level. Secondly, paradigmatic facts are re-stated as syntagmatic ones, thus translating system into structure. This translation of system into structure shows how (with apologies to Mathesius 1964) 'the potentiality of the phenomena of language' is turned into the actuality of an instance in use – in other words how *langue* and *parole* are related. To give an example, the primary systemic option originating from the semantic unit 'message' is a simple one as shown below in figure 1:

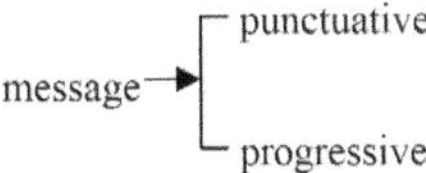

Figure 1: A primary system in message functions

If the option [progressive] is chosen, then the set of realisation statements presented in table 1 will apply. These will refer to lexicogrammatical features (a) which pertain to the unit clause and (b) form a necessary condition for taking that clause as realising the semantic option in question:

Table 1: Realisation statements for semantic feature [progressive]

1)	preselect option [*major*];
2)	insert element Predicator;
3)	preselect (an instance of) verbal group at Predicator.

Both the options in figure 1 can potentially function as the ENTRY POINT to some more delicate options. Ignoring certain possible intermediate options, imagine that our concern is now with choices in MESSAGE FUNCTION – i.e., what it is that the speaker could achieve discursively by acting on the addressee through language. Seen thus the message is not a 'speech act' but an 'inter-act' (Halliday 1985a), in that simply by choosing to discursively act this way or that, the speaker creates a context in which the interpretation of the addressee's silence as well as speech is necessarily refracted through the speaker's act. The reciprocity of message function suggests the following options in meaning:[5]

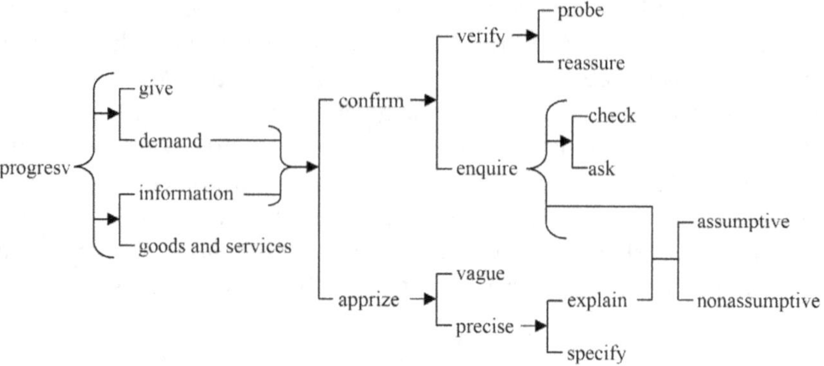

Figure 2: Options in expressing questions: a simplified fragment

The treatment of speech acts such as command and question etc. by linguists has proceeded in general as if these were unanalysable concepts. The approach adopted in this research departs from that assumption. Figure 2 presents a highly simplified fragment of a network according to which the category question would be the least delicate. The network claims that just two semantic options – viz., [demand; information] – underlie every question in English. Each additional system in the network specifies a semantic parameter by reference to which questions may be further distinguished from each other. Once the idea of variable delicacy of description is applied to messages that realise such basic categories as question, command, offer, reply etc., it becomes possible to state how these options are expressed in the lexicogrammar. For example, the simultaneous selection of the options [demand; information] can be seen as an instruction to enter the system network of MOOD at the lexicogrammatical stratum. The selection of these two options furnishes the CONJUNCT ENTRY CONDITION to a more delicate systemic option between [confirm] or [apprise]; and the choice of the option [confirm] permits entry into a more delicate system whose mutually exclusive terms are: [verify] or [enquire]. Suppose the former option is selected, then one realisation requirement would be that the clause expressing this option must have the MOOD features *declarative:tagged*. These lexicogrammatical features in turn imply that the structure of the clause must have the concatenation of elements Subject^Finite….Finite^Subject as instantiated in *you did…,did you?*. (The dots indicate the possibility of the occurrence of other elements of structure, which are however not motivated by the semantic option under focus and so not specified at this point). The option [verify] acts as an environment for a systemic choice between [probe] and [reassure]. Suppose the former option is chosen, then the clause capable of expressing the choice would have the MOOD features *declarative:tagged:marked*. The MOOD feature *marked* in this selection expression would be realised by the tag polarity matching the polarity in the main part of the clause, as in *you did painting today, did you?* where both *you did* and *did you* display positive polarity. If the option [reassure] were selected, then the clause capable of expressing this choice would have the MOOD features *declarative:tagged:unmarked*, in which case the feature *unmarked* would be realised by the tag polarity contrasting with the polarity in the main clause, as in *you wouldn't want to hurt her, would you?* or *I'm so quick, aren't I, with this cooking?* Note that in these messages the polarity selection in the tag *would you* and *aren't I* contrast with the polarity in the clause *you wouldn't...* and *I'm...*, respectively. The option [enquire] is expressed by the choice of *indicative*; a further specification takes place with the choice [check]: a clause realising the latter feature would have MOOD features *declarative:untagged*, and a KEY feature which is itself expressed by Tone 2 (Halliday 1967: 56-57); an example would be *you don't like the ice-cream?* on a rising tone. The contrasting option [ask] would be realised by a clause that is *interrogative:polar*, as for example in *didn't you see me?*, where the element Finite precedes the element Subject.

The option [apprise] is realised by a clause with the MOOD feature *interrogative:non-polar*, often referred to as wh- interrogative, because typically there is a wh- element and it occurs as Theme of the clause as in *what's that?*. As for the choice between [vague] and [precise], the former is realised by a clause with Mood and Predicator ellipsis (Halliday and Hasan 1985) where Theme is *how/what about*. For example when Karen's mother appears not to remember the names of any of her girl friends at the play centre, Karen asks *how about the boys?*, which given the co-text would be expanded as *how much do you remember about the boys?*. The option [precise] is the environment for a more delicate choice between [explain] and [specify]. The former is expressed by a clause whose Theme is *why* (or equivalent expression e.g., *what for*) as in *why are they moving in May?* or *how* which sometimes functions in lieu of *why*. The option [specify] is expressed by clauses whose Theme may be a wh-participant or wh-circumstance (see chapter 3 in this volume) as in *what's handsome boy?* or *where does this go?* etc.

Although this exemplification of the categories for the semantic analysis of messages is of necessity both brief and highly simplified, (for an earlier version of this system and list of realisation statements see the last two chapters), hopefully it is sufficient to indicate the kind of linguistic analysis on which the results are based. In presenting the results below, there will be further examples and discussion of the significance of these semantic options. The messages in the sample were analysed for semantic options pertaining to all four metafunctions, though the results presented here will be concerned with options mainly deriving from the interpersonal and textual metafunctions. A principal components analysis was used for statistical processing of the data.

4.2 The statistical procedure

There were two reasons for wishing to adopt a principal components procedure for the statistical analysis[6] of the data. It is an effective method of data reduction – an obvious advantage, given the detailed analysis of large numbers of messages (for details, see Cloran in accompanying CD). In the case of this research, the procedure reduced the large number of variant semantic features to a smaller number of clusterings of derived ones. (Each such clustering is called principal component or PC.) Secondly, this statistical procedure also assigns a score to each subject on each PC which thus forms the basis for ranking the subjects *vis-à-vis* each other. If this ranking clusters a group of subjects by reference to their scores on some PC, we can ask whether a specific group of subjects differs from another by reference to some social attribute such as social class, the child's sex, its sibling position etc. Should a significant correlation be found between some social attribute of a group of subjects and their scores on some PC, we would be justified in treating that PC as representing a clustering of the variants of a COMPLEX SOCIO-LINGUISTIC VARIABLE.

Despite these advantages, this statistical procedure is not an unmixed blessing, in that it poses a problem because of a restriction on the number of variable features in relation to the number of subjects: the former can never be in excess of the latter. For my research, the ratio of subjects to variable features was set at around 3:1. As is evident from the discussion of the population and the analytic framework, it then became necessary to establish some rational ground for deciding which semantic features would be entered together with which others for statistical processing. Two strategies were used to determine the input pattern: (i) using those options which pertain to some explicitly specifiable part of the network e.g., all those options which can be traced back to [demand; information]; this strategy would net in all variant expressions of the situational feature, in this case, question; or (ii) using a clearly identifiable social activity e.g., replying to questions, which would net in semantic features relevant to the expression of questions as well as their replies. The results presented below are based on the latter kind of input.

In preparing this second kind of input, two alternative approaches are available: (a) one can use as input the semantic choices in the dialogue of the dyad e.g., choices in mother's questions and in children's answers may be used as input, or (b) one can simply focus on individual behaviour, e.g. choices in mother's questions and mother's answers or in children's questions and children's answers may be used as input. Obviously, the significance of the two inputs is different; for example, in the context of questions and answers, an input of type (a) is indicative of the quality of dialogic cooperation – how the two members of the dyad keep in step. By contrast, in that same context, the input of type (b) is capable of shedding light on the individual's own semantic orientation – how that individual's own choices of meaning might be characterised. This does not mean that in the latter type of enquiry, the individual speaker's dialogic behaviour is seen as independent of the moves of their dialogic partner – a possibility that must be discounted, particularly in the case of dialogic data of the type used in this research. Rather, there is simply a difference of emphasis between the two approaches whereby the latter enquires into the consistencies and contradictions found within the dialogic strategies of one group of speakers without assuming that these will be the same as those found in the dialogic behaviour of the other group who act as their conversational partner, by contrast, the former enquires into how the two partners position each other through their discourse.

Both these approaches were adopted in the research, but since the results of the dyadic approach have been presented elsewhere, I shall devote the following sections to a presentation and discussion of semantic variation in mothers' questions and mothers' answers on the one hand and children's questions and children's answers on the other.

4.3 Questions and replies: mothers

The total number of questions asked by mothers was 2008. This number excludes clarification questions, ritual questions of the type *you know what?* as well as those messages which would be generally described as indirect command or offer. Table 2 presents the results of the principal component analysis of mother's semantic choices in asking questions and giving answers. In this table, the prefix Q and A indicate that the semantic options in the relevant brackets pertain to the expression of the situational category question and reply, respectively.

Table 2: Mothers' questions and mothers' answers

Semantic features	PC1	PC2	PC3
Q[prefaced]	0.69	0.17	-0.13
A[related]	0.68	0.48	0.06
A[responsive]	0.67	0.19	-0.01
Q[related]	0.65	0.53	-0.26
A[adequate]	0.56	-0.37	0.34
Q[assumptive]	-0.52	0.71	0.17
Q[ask]	0.21	-0.47	0.27
Q[confirm]	0.37	-0.14	0.73
Q[explain]	-0.32	0.58	0.64
Eigenvalue	2.72	1.84	1.27
% variance	30.2	20.5	14.2

I shall restrict myself to a discussion of PC1 alone, referring to it as PC1-MQMA (=mothers' questions, mothers' answers). As table 2 shows this PC accounts for 30.2% of variance in the data; it also correlates significantly with mothers' social class (see discussion in 4.5 below). Before discussing the results, I shall briefly describe and exemplify each semantic feature. Sections 4.3.1–4.3.3 describe semantic features pertaining to QUESTION, sections 4.3.4–4.3.5 to features pertaining to answer, and section 4.3.6 to features shared in common by both questions and replies.

4.3.1 Q [prefaced]

The semantic option [prefaced] is open to all messages that are [progressive] (see figure 1 and table 1 in section 4.1), though for this input it was calculated only for questions, since what was at issue was the attributes of questions. The feature derives from the logical metafunction, and its typical lexicogrammatical realisation is through choices in PROJECTION (Halliday 1985: 227–51), though there are other modes of prefacing. Dialogue 1 contains some illustrations:

Dialogue 1

Mother: (1) can you try and remind me to ring Pam this afternoon?
Kristy: (2) mmm (POSITIVE) (3) why?
Mother: (4) I'm going to ask her if she'll mind you one night next week
Kristy: (5) mm
Mother: (6) 'cause I'm going out to dinner with some of the ladies from playgroup (7) because Sue is leaving
Kristy: (8) pardon? (9) pardon?

Mother: (10) I'm going out with some of the ladies (11) because Sue is leaving
Kristy: (12) mm
Mother: (13) did you know that they're going to leave?
Kristy: (14) no
Mother: (15) they've been building a house
Kristy: (16) mm
Mother: (17) oh they haven't been building it (18) someone else has been building it for them (19) and it's nearly finished (20) and they're going to move to their house in May
Kristy: (21) why in May?
Mother: (22) they're going to wait until the end of the school term
Kristy: (23) mm
Mother: (24) because Cathy goes to school now (25) and then she will change to her new school after the holidays
Kristy: (26) mm
Mother: (27) if they'd moved earlier (28) she'd only go to the new school for a week or two (29) and then they'd have holidays, you see (30) it would mess it up a bit for her

In this dialogue, messages (1), (4) and (13) have the semantic feature [prefaced]. Message (1) is a [consultative] expression of a COMMAND, which as pointed out above (4.3) would not have been included in the input for the above PC analysis of messages treated as question. Message (4) has the function of answer, and (13) of question. Simplifying, each has two distinct parts: for example, in (13) there is a sort of preface - *did you know* - which, as it were, ushers in the remainder of the message *(that) they're going to leave?*. The option [prefaced] is closely associated with the expression of point of view, since messages with this option present a state of affairs as if it were someone's *[locution]* or *[idea]* which is refracted through some verbal process as in (4) above *I am going to* ***ask*** *her...*, or through the mental processes of cognition as in (13) *did you* ***know****...*, or perception as when Pete says to his mother *did you* ***see*** *how high it went?* or affection as when Laura's mother tells her *today I don't* ***want*** *to be anywhere*, or through the process of ascription as when Cameron's mother asks him about his strange-looking ice-cream *you* ***(are) sure*** *its nice?*.

The loading on this semantic feature is positive, which suggests that mothers scoring high on PC1 tend to ask questions with messages that are [prefaced], so that the children are likely to be exposed to another's point of view.

4.3.2 Q [assumptive]

The feature [assumptive] is in a systemic contrast with [non-assumptive]; the choice becomes available either in the context of the semantic option [enquire] or that of [explain] (see figure 2). A message with the feature [assumptive] has an unvoiced thesis – an assumption, in fact, that something is/should be the case to which direct reference is not made by the wording of the question. Dialogues 2 and 3 illustrate this phenomenon:

Dialogue 2

Karen: (1) how did you get that?** (2) you didn't get out of [? UNINTELLIGIBLE]
Mother: (3) I walked over (4) and got it (5) didn't you see me?
Karen: (6) nup
Mother: (7) you must be blind

Dialogue 3

Mother: (1) d'you love daddy? .. (2) d'you love daddy?
Julian: (3) mmm (POSITIVE)
Mother: (4) d'you love Rosemary?
Julian: (5) no
Mother: (6) why don't you love Rosemary?
Julian: (LAUGHS)
Mother: (7) why don't you love Rosemary?
Julian: (CONTINUES TO LAUGH)
Mother: (8) you're a [?rat-bag] (REALISES THAT CHILD WAS TEASING)
Julian: (9) I do
Mother: [UNINTELLIGIBLE]
Julian: (10) who else do you want me to love?

The features [enquire: ask: assumptive] occur in Karen's mother's question (5) *didn't you see me?* – it asks a yes/no question with negation – and in doing this also implies that Karen is sure to have seen her. This is obvious from her comment (7) *you must be blind* on finding out that her unspoken assumption was not correct. Since Karen is not blind, it is obvious that her mother believed Karen should have seen the mother walk over. In dialogue 3, the mother's question (6) has the feature [assumptive]; Julian is quick to note that the mother has opinions about whom he should or should not love; this is implied in the child's final question (10) *who **else** do you want me to love?*. It appears reasonable to suggest that speakers who are likely to produce such messages would tend to believe that they know the addressee's state of knowledge, belief, feelings as well as what is an appropriate internal state for the addressee to maintain.

Since the feature has a negative loading, the implication is that high scorers would tend not to choose this semantic feature. This in its turn implies that they do not presume knowledge about the other's beliefs, affect etc.

4.3.3 Q[confirm], [ask] and [explain]

These three options have already been described above (see figure 2, section 4.1). The following dialogue between Cameron and his mother provides an example of the interplay of particularly the first two semantic options:

Dialogue 4

Mother:	(1) well you sit up (2) and eat it (3) you sure its nice?
Cameron:	(4) yeah
Mother:	(5) don't want your mum to eat it for you?
Cameron:	(6) nup
Mother:	(7) sure?
Cameron:	(8) no.. (9) you wouldn't like it mum
Mother:	(10) oh I'm sure I would
Cameron:	(11) no you won't
Mother:	(12) oh I was sure you wouldn't like it..
Cameron:	(13) I do like it so (14) but what— .. mum what's that?* (15) oh… mum you don't like the eyes.. **(16) they're -
Mother:	**(17) they're Smarties … aren't they?
Cameron:	(18) there you go
Mother:	(19) you don't like the ice-cream?
Cameron:	(20) there you go (21) you can have it
Mother:	(22) you don't like it.. (23) is that right? (24) you don't want to eat it?

The messages relevant to this discussion are (3), (17), (19), (23) and (24). Since one heuristic criterion for distinguishing between [ask] and [check] is the order of the elements Subject and Finite *vis-à-vis* each other, (3) poses a problem through its ellipsis of Finite: it might be read as *are you sure*… i.e., *[ask]* or as *you are sure*… on rising tone i.e. [check]. However, a message with the option *[ask]* is the most unmarked expression of a yes/no question, with the implication that this is the most neutral way of finding out information, whereas the selection of [check] might be paraphrased in some such way as 'I have some reservations against conceding that this is the true state of affairs: tell me what you think'. The co-text for dialogue 6 suggests that (3) should be treated as an expression of [check]; note both the mother's persistence and her (12) *oh I was sure you wouldn't like it*, which shows that she had some reservations about Cameron's approval of the ice-cream. In message (17), the mother is not so much seeking to find out some new information; rather she is seeking to be reassured that the child's perception of the situation is the same as hers. This message would be analysed as expressing the options [confirm: verify: reassure]. Presumably as the child extends the ice-cream towards the mother, she produces her next message (19) *you don't like the ice-cream?* The semantic options [confirm: enquire: check] underlie this message. Since the child does not respond directly to this question, the mother, in her next turn, first presents the same information as an existing state of affairs (22) *you don't like it…*, waits for the child's response and then in (23) asks a question with the feature [enquire] *is that right?*, which is the most explicit way of checking on the yes/no status of a thesis! And in the last message of her turn (24) *you don't want to eat it*, she as it were, sums up her concerns. One aim in presenting this (partial) analysis is to show how the same situational content – i.e. QUESTION – is realised as so many different semantic variants.

The location of [explain] in figure 2 shows it to be dependent on [apprise: precise]; the option itself is in systemic contrast with [specify]. The option [explain] is chosen in two of the dialogues above. In dialogue 1 in Kristy's (3) *why?* or her (21) *why in May?*, and in dialogue 3 Julian's mother's (6) and (7) *why don't you love Rosemary?* The option [specify] is present in this latter dialogue in Julian's (11) *who else do you want me to love?* Other examples of wh-questions are provided in the following two sections.

As table 2 shows none of these three semantic options loads criterially for PC1-MQMA. The implication is that these options are irrelevant to any covariance accounted for by this PC. The members of the two social groups are not differentiated by their choice of any of these options.

4.3.4 A [responsive]

Every [progressive] message in a dialogue can be viewed from two mutually non-exclusive perspectives: (i) what is the preceding textual environment for the message, and (ii) what textual environment the message itself creates for the addressee. For example, in examining a question we may ask what message that question is itself preceded by – a question following a question will typically have a different significance from that which it would have when following an assertion or a command or offer. And, equally, we may ask what is the fate of a question, how is it fielded by the person to whom it is addressed. Normally, when a question is asked, this creates a textual environment with the expectation that the addressee will respond; and of course normally this expectation is satisfied. However, this is not always the case. Simplifying the discussion a good deal, the semantic feature [responsive], which pertains to answers and is in systemic contrast with [non-responsive], refers to these two possibilities. A few examples illustrate the latter feature:

Dialogue 5
Mother: (1) was it nice down the beach?
Janet: (2) oh a little bit hot and a little bit cold..
Mother: (3) what, hot and cold?
Janet: (4) whose's this Anna (MOTHER'S NAME IS ANNA)
Mother: (5) that's daddy's

In message (3) the mother asks a question which has itself arisen from Janet's rather equivocal description of what it was like on the beach. The expectation of an answer is however not met, as (5) shows Janet's attention is diverted to something else. In this example both dialogic partners take a turn, and so it is possible to use the saying of the two speakers as evidence that Janet's attention is no longer engaged with what she and her mother were talking about earlier. Sometimes, however, the evidence is of a different kind, as exemplified in the following:

Dialogue 6
Karen: (1) that- I'll get that off, my lipstick
Mother: (2) no, you can't have this
Karen: (3) what?
Mother: (4) OK?
Karen: (5) what? .. (6) what, mummy?
Mother: (7) this blue thing
Karen: (8) why?
Mother: (9) 'cause << (10) if you tried to do this >> you'd poke your eyes out .. (11) see?
Karen: (12) yep

In this dialogue, the child's first question in (3) is interpreted not as a channel repair but as one seeking to establish the referent of the implicit *this* in mother's (2) *you can't have this*. In (4) the mother is still continuing with her earlier saying. So from the point of view of Karen's question, mother's (4) is [non-responsive]. In (5) Karen repeats her question which receives no reply. The dots after (5) show that she allows a little more than normal pause at the end of this message. Despite this clear indication of turn assignment from Karen, the mother, who is preoccupied with her make-up, does not respond at all, and Karen has to ask her question a third time before she gets a reply in (7) *this blue thing*. Both message (4) in dialogue 5 and message (4) in dialogue 6 have the feature A[non-responsive]; neither bears any relevance to the question as such. By contrast, when the message has the semantic feature A[responsive]; it shows varying degrees of relevance to the question. Note for example the cohesive relations between (4) and (5) in dialogue 5, and between Karen's repeated *what?* and *mother's this blue thing*. The following section develops this point further.

4.3.5 A [adequate]

The option [adequate], which is in systemic contrast with [inadequate], is applicable to any message with the feature A[responsive]. I have shown above that not all questions are replied to. But even the fact that a message has the feature A[responsive] does not necessarily mean that the information sought in the question is actually provided. The options A[adequate] and A [inadequate] capture the possibility that a message may have the feature A[responsive] without necessarily providing an answer; it may instead provide a disclaimer (Halliday 1985a: 69) or a non-answer (Levinson 1983: 336). The following dialogue provides examples of both options:

Dialogue 7
Mother: (1) but you'd be glad << (2) when you go back to school >> won't you?
Karen: (3) no
Mother: (4) why?
Karen: (5) 'cause
Mother: (6) 'cause why?
Karen: (7) 'cause Rebecca don't go to my school any more
Mother: (8) who's Rebecca?
Karen: (9) this little [?girl] in my school
Mother: (10) did she leave?
Karen: (11) yeah
Mother: (12) why?
Karen: (13) 'cause ..
Mother: (14) how come she left?
Karen: (15) I don't know ..

The feature A[adequate] does not refer to either the factuality or the quantity of information provided. Instead a replying message is judged to have this feature if it provides some information which addresses the question's QUERY POINT. For example, the query point of a message with the option [confirm] is: tell me yes or no. So in the above dialogue, Karen's reply (3) although minimal has the feature A[adequate], as it does address the query point in the mother's question. On the other hand, her message (5) *'cause* would be said to have the features A[responsive: inadequate], for although Karen's reply is cognisant of the query point – she recognises a reason needs to be supplied – she gives no information that can be counted as reason. This contrasts with her message (7) where a reason is given and the message is A[responsive: adequate], as are her next two messages (9) and (11). But to the mother's next *why* in (12) she gives a reply that is A[responsive: inadequate] as is also her response in (15). It will be seen that when a message has the feature A[non-responsive], it, as it were, misses or ignores the query point as in dialogues 5 and 6. And while all messages with the feature A[responsive] address the query point, only those are said to have the feature A[adequate] which provide some information relevant to the query point, saying *yea* or *nay* to the yes/no question, and specifying *who, what, which, where, why, how* etc. in the case of *wh*-questions, more examples of which are given below:

Dialogue 8
Karen: (1) who are my mummy (2) when I was a little baby?
Mother: (3) me (4) I was always your mummy.

Dialogue 9
Mother: (1) where did you find that picture?
Janet: (2) in a magazine

Dialogue 10
Janet: (1) what's his birthday called?
Mother: (2) his birthday is in November (3) yours is— yours— your birthday is in **July
Janet: **(4) in July
Mother: (5) and that's— that's coming up soon

This semantic option has a positive loading on PC1-MQMA, implying that high scoring mothers would tend to produce A[adequate] replies.

4.3.6 Q/A [related]

Like the option [prefaced], the semantic option [related] pertains to the logical metafunction, and applies to all messages with the option [progressive]. It points to particular kinds of logical relation between the states of affairs referred to by the clauses that realise the messages so related: these are relations of condition, cause, consequence, sequence, addition etc. Consider for example Karen's mother's reply to Karen's *why?* in dialogue 6. She could have said simply: *'cause you would poke your eyes out .. see*, and this would have been a reply with the feature A[adequate], without the feature A[related]. However, Karen's mother relates her reason why Karen should not have this blue thing to a condition *if you tried to do this (you would ...)*. So the mother's response here would be said to have the semantic option A[related]. The selection of this semantic feature is indicative of additional information, which, as it were, elaborates upon information so making the domain of the elaborated thesis more precise and narrow. The mother is not making a universal statement: Karen would not *always* poke her eyes out; only ***if*** she did something with this blue thing. Similarly in Karen's question to her mother in dialogue 8, Karen is not wondering about who was her mother but only about who was her mother at a particular point in time. Structures which are motivated by logical meanings tend to be ITERATIVE, so at least in theory, the number of individual messages that could be related to a question or to an answer is, potentially, unlimited. In dialogue 1, Kristy's mother's reply to Kristy's (21) why in May? has the following set of messages which have the feature A[related]:

Example 1

Mother: (22) they're going to wait until the end of the school term
(24) because Cathy goes to school now
(25) and then she will change to her new school after the holidays
(27) if they'd moved earlier
(28) she'd only go to the new school for a week or two
(29) and then they'd have holidays you see
(30) it would mess it up a bit for her

The longest such sequence contained 21 messages and occurred in the context of maternal control, though a sequence of 2 to 4 is more frequent. Table 2 shows a positive loading for this option. The implication is that high scoring mothers would be likely to provide additional information to explicate and make precise the referential application of their questions and replies.

4.3.8 The social correlate of PC1-MQMA

PC1-MQMA provides evidence of variation in mothers' choice of certain semantic features in their dialogues with their children. However, we know that not all linguistic variation need correlate directly with the social attributes of speakers (Weiner and Labov 1983: 31). Figure 3 presents the location of each mother as determined by her score on PC2-MQMA by PC1-MQMA (consult chapters 3 and 4 above; see Cloran in accompanying CD, on conventions for locating subjects by their scores). Ignoring PC2-MQMA, for which a mothers' position by her score is displayed on the vertical axis, consider the horizontal axis, where lowest to highest scores for PC1-MQMA are ranked from left to right. Thus lowest scoring mothers would be located left-most, and highest right-most. The letter L stands for a LAP mother, and H for a HAP one. The point need not be laboured that the mothers' scores on the semantic features of PC1-MQMA do co-vary with their social group. HAP mothers are more likely to select these semantic features than LAP ones (H > L: $p < .0003$).

The fact that PC1-MQMA correlates significantly with the social class of the speakers gives it the status of a complex socio-linguistic – or to be more precise – socio-semantic variable. It is important to emphasise that the social class of the speaker cannot be said to co-vary with any one single feature of PC1-MQMA. However, the PC as a structured unit, delineates a pattern of semantic choices, which as a whole covaries with the speakers' social class. Quite irrespective of how we interpret the pattern of semantic choices delineated by PC1-MQMA, the tendency for its choice is far from random. My results would support the claim that orderly heterogeneity does occur at the semantic level; and, therefore, contra Labov, not all sociolinguistic variation can be described as variable ways of saying the same thing (Labov 1978a: 1).

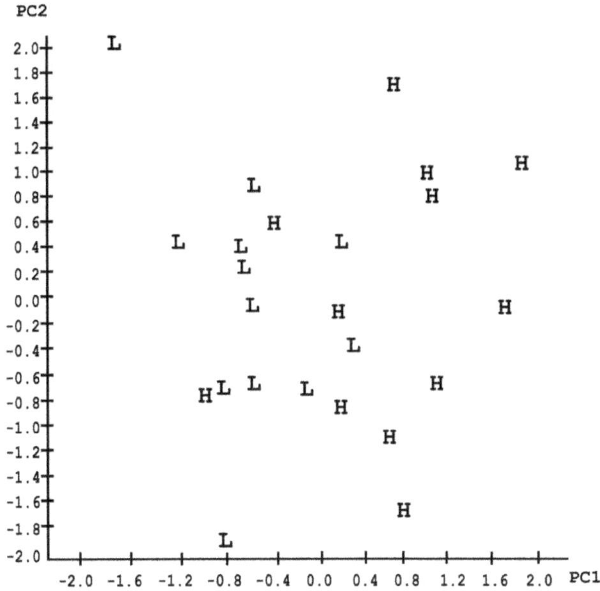

Figure 3: PC1-MQMA: mother's location by social group

Before discussing the significance of this result, let me first present the results of the analysis of children's questions and children's answers in the following section.

4.4 Questions and answers: children

Table 3 presents the results of the PC analysis of children's questions and replies. The total number of children's questions statistically processed for this PC analysis was 1,350. As will be noticed the set of semantic features is in common to both, and as with mothers, so here too certain ritualistic categories of questions were excluded from this count, e.g., framing questions *you know what?*, clarification questions arising from channel failure *what did you say?*, and those which would normally be described as indirect commands or offers.

Table 3: Children's questions and children's replies

Semantic features	PC1	PC2	PC3
A[related]	0.74	0.30	-0.29
Q[related]	0.63	0.42	-0.25
Q[confirm]	0.60	0.01	0.44
Q[prefaced]	0.58	-0.31	0.17
A[adequate]	0.55	0.20	0.15
Q[assumptive]	-0.51	0.51	0.32
A[responsive]	0. 34	-0.71	0.25
Q[ask]	-0.12	-0.56	-0.01
Q[explain]	0.00	0.25	0.86
Eigenvalue	2.37	1.57	1.32
% Variance	26.4	17.5	14.7

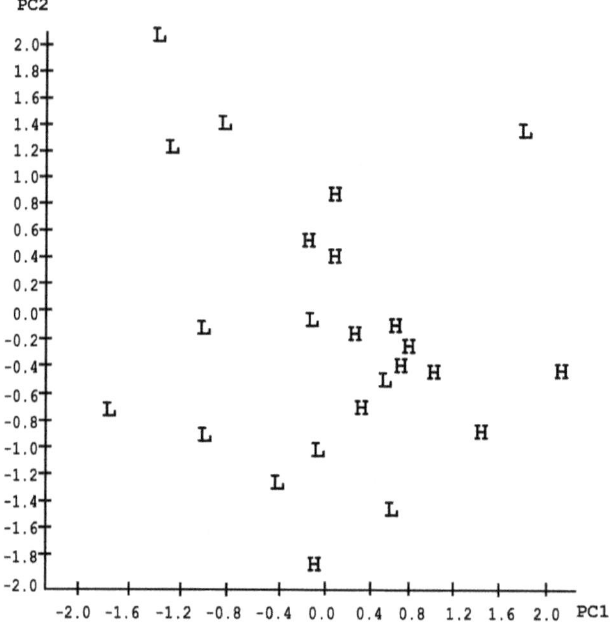

Figure 4: PC1-CQCA: child's location by social group

As with MQMA, here too I will discuss only the first PC, referred to as PC1-CQCA (=children's questions, children's answers). This PC accounts for 26.4% of variance and correlates with social class. Figure 4 presents the location of the children from the two social groups by reference to their scores on PC2-CQCA by PC1-CQCA, the letters L and H indicating LAP and HAP, respectively.

It is again quite obvious that HAP children are more likely to be high scorers on PC1-CQCA than are the LAP ones, the level of significance being $H > L: p < .009$. This is a lower level of significance than that obtained for PC1-MQMA ($H > L: p < .0003$), but it is still sufficiently high – particularly given the age of the children – to raise questions about the effects of social environment on semantic orientation. Results such as these might be seen as retrospectively justifying the decision to ascribe social class position to women and children despite the fact that they are not in the work force and have no independent income.

4.4.2 PC1-MQMA v. PC1-CQCA

Although the two PCs delineate a slightly different picture of semantic choices, given the dialogic nature of the data, it is important to examine them also in relation to each other, for in the over all interpretation of the semantic patterns delineated by the two PCs an understanding of the effects of interaction will be an advantage. In this respect, both the similarities and dissimilarities between PC1-MQMA and PC1-CQCA could be relevant. The loadings of the semantic features for PC1 of both MQMA and CQCA are presented in table 4 below.

Table 4: PC1-MQMA v. PC1-CQCA

PC1-MQMA	Semantic features	PC1-CQCA
0.67	A[responsive]	0.34
-0.52	Q[assumptive]	-0.51
0.69	Q[prefaced]	0.58
0.37	Q[confirm]	0.60
0.56	A[adequate]	0.55
0.65	Q[related]	0.63
0.68	A[related]	0.74
-0.32	Q[explain]	-0.00
0.21	Q[ask]	-0.12
30.2	per cent variance	26.4

In this comparison, it is not the actual figures at which a semantic feature loads that is important; rather, the significant questions are: are the same features criterially loaded? and is the positive or negative sign the same for the criterially loading feature(s)? One outstanding difference between the two PCs will be noted immediately: the features A[responsive] loads criterially on PC1-MQMA but not on PC1-CQCA. And while the feature Q[confirm] loads criterially on PC1-CQCA, it just fails to reach the criterial point for PC1-MQMA. For the remaining features, there appears to be remarkable similarity between the two PCs, with the positive and negative signs remaining consistent across the two results.

4.5 Interpreting PC1-MQMA

To interpret the results, let me first briefly summarise the pattern of semantic selections identified by PC1-MQMA. Mothers who score high on this PC will show the following inclinations:

- they are unlikely to ask questions with an assumed but unvoiced thesis;
- the thesis of their questions is likely to be presented as someone's Locution or Idea;
- they are inclined to give additional information relating to their questions and answers, so that the thesis of both is modified and made more precise;
- they are inclined to address the query point of their children's questions; and
- the replies they give are likely to give information that is relevant to the query point.

The higher the score of a mother, the more likely she is to choose this complex pattern of semantic features; the lower the score the less likely she is to choose these meanings. But what does it mean to say that this or that choice is found or not found in the dialogue of this or that mother? When the choice of semantic features is inventoried one by one as above, it is not easy to see its contribution to the discourse as a whole. We need to ask: in what way is the tendency to choose any one semantic feature in this PC compatible with the tendency to choose any other criterial semantic feature of this same PC? If the PC is a complex sociosemantic variable, are the various elements of this complex variable related to each other? If so, how? Is the inclination to choose this semantic feature rather than its opposite in the environment of the remaining features of this complex variable governed by a higher order principle? The postulate of a higher order principle, such as accommodation theory (cf.

Labov) or code orientation (cf. Bernstein) would have an obvious advantage: it would make the overall pattern intelligible so that tendencies for the choice of individual semantic features need not be seen as adventitious, simply triggered by individual events in the life of the speakers. It is in interpreting the findings that the debates about the relationship between social condition, interaction and the development of human cognitive abilities become relevant to semantic variation studies of the kind reported here.

The pattern delineated above characterises HAP mothers, and given the covariance of social group with PC1-MQMA, it can be deduced that the semantic choices made by the LAP mothers would contrast with the HAP pattern of choices. Despite this dissimilarity there are certain respects in which the two groups are alike in the meanings they chose in questioning and answering their children. Let me turn first to this interesting finding of invariance: the results show that irrespective of their social class, mothers use questions to seek similar kinds of information. There is no significant difference between them in asking yes/no questions (Q[confirm] 0.37), or in asking neutral yes/no questions (Q[ask]O.21), and somewhat surprisingly, even how/why questions do not contribute to variance (Q[explain] - 0.32). One might be inclined to argue that this semantic homogeneity across the social groups has a natural explanation in the homogeneity of biological development. The mean age of the children was 3;8, with a narrow range of 3;6-4;2. If we assume that the patterns of cognitive growth are in general uniform, and that mothers automatically adjust their discourse to the child's abilities, then it follows that there should be uniformity in mothers' questions. I find this explanation unconvincing for two reasons. First, if the premise of developmental uniformity and the naturalness of maternal adjustment are granted, this would imply that semantic heterogeneity in maternal discourse is either irrational or at least inexplicable, not to speak of the hidden though discredited assumption that biological equals chronological. Secondly, the explanation treats precisely those issues as unproblematic which are themselves in need of explanation: why does the mother automatically adjust her discourse to her child's abilities? Is she programmed biologically to do this? How specific and detailed is this programme? How does the child's own cognitive development come about? How credible is the time-bomb model of human cognitive development according to which the hidden innate cognitive abilities suddenly explode into sight at appointed intervals in a predestined order? These seem to me to be strong enough reasons for rejecting the above natural explanation. I would rather turn to the role of language in the living of life (cf. Firth 1957) to account for this invariance. Perhaps this uniformity can be explained more effectively by examining the nature of talk as it unfolds in the material conditions of mothers' and children's everyday life.

Speech act analysts have argued that the typical motivation for asking a question is the speaker's desire to find out some as yet unknown information. If that is so, then speakers wishing to find out some information can be expected to direct their questions to some one who is likely to know. Seen from this perspective the question is: what is it that the children know which their mothers would not know? The conditions of their daily life narrow the range of such knowledge. And it is noticeable that mother's questions in this data typically tend to have some reference to the play centre which their child attended, or the child's personal likes, dislikes, needs etc., or what the child may be engaged in at that moment. That mothers do not vary in the kinds of information they seek from their children indicates that they desire to find out similar kinds of things from them. And this might be because the kind of knowledge their children possess and which the mothers themselves do not possess is almost uniformly the same; further, the occasion for seeking this kind of information from their children is probably the same. If it is true that mothers and children live their lives in such close contiguity so much of the time in the early years of the child's life, then it would be quite reasonable to expect that the mothers as the socially maturer dialogic partner would be good at adjusting to the child's meaning-making strategies. Those strategies are pretty much known to the mother, since it was mainly interaction with her in the first place that was instrumental in creating those strategies. It is not simply the biological condition of being a mother that enables the mother to adjust to the child's meaning-making strategies: anyone who spent so much time interacting with the child as mothers of small children tend to do would enjoy the same facility.

It would seem then that whatever differentiates the LAP mothers' question-answer discourse from her HAP counterpart, it is not the fact that she is less involved with the child or that she is less given to encouraging her child's curiosity about the nature of the world. So then what is it that differentiates them? Let us continue with QUESTIONS before turning to REPLIES. The three Q features that load criterially are Q[prefaced] (.69), Q[assumptive] (-.52), and Q[related] (.65). In describing the first of these, I pointed out that this feature is an important element in the creation of point of view (cf. 4.3.1 above). In questions with a preface, reference is made to states of affairs as if they were someone's verbal or mental representation of reality – a saying or an opinion – rather than an objective version of it. There is a difference between asking *have they left?* and *do you think they have left?*. The former has to do with the world of objective phenomena; the latter is primarily concerned with the world of your opinion. One consequence is that saying yes/no to the latter technically does not commit you to anything in reality: what you say is your subjective opinion. But this is not all: presenting theses about the world as someone's saying or opinion is a way of revealing that person's inner self. I am not claiming that the inner self so revealed is real, whatever that may mean: the claim is simply that this is an inner self that becomes known to the addressee. Of course different evaluations of this feature will arise from different ideologies (for discussion, chapter 7), but what does not seems controversial is the fact that the tendency to choose this feature implies an acceptance of others as persons with their own subjective experience, and a unique inner self which is not known until revealed by the person so addressed. This in turn implies an acceptance of the discreteness of persons, and an affirmation of their autonomy. If this is true then it should follow that speakers who tend to choose this feature will tend NOT to choose the feature Q[assumptive], because the tendency to choose the latter feature implies the speaker's presumption to know the addressee's state of knowledge, belief, feelings etc. (see 4.3.2 above). Note then that the loading of this feature is negative. These two features taken together can be interpreted as indicative of a regard for individuality, a belief in the uniqueness of persons, and a readiness to grant that states of affairs can be viewed from different angles. The HAP mothers' tendency to make these two choices – two of those that differentiate them from LAP mothers – in asking questions reveals them as well adjusted middle class women displaying the same semantic orientation that characterise other members of her group: with them she shares the middle class emotional investment in upholding the sanctity of individuality, and in legitimating the uniqueness of persons. The LAP mothers do not share this middle class ideology: they do presume to know others' state of knowledge, belief, feelings etc. and they do not place a great deal of premium upon uniqueness of personal intent, opinions etc. It is not that one view is better than the other: it is simply an informal everyday version of the contrast so familiar to sociologists who identify one kind of approach to social phenomena as methodological individualism and another as collectivism (Knorr-Cetina 1981: 7). The middle class mother has the informal version of the former; the working class mother that of the latter. Although this leaves the third feature Q[related], which I propose to discuss with the answer feature A[related], I would conclude this discussion of the mothers' questioning behaviour by claiming that the features of questions in respect of which these middle class mothers differ from the working class ones have little to do with the nature of objective knowledge: in that respect both groups are alike; where they differ is what they tend to 'teach' their children about individuation.

It is a commonplace of scholarly writings to emphasise the relevance of questions to the growth of human knowledge and to the development of an individual's cognition (Robinson and Rackstraw 1972; Goody 1978; Popper 1979). But quite obviously this growth and development must depend at least to some extent on what the replies are like. When we look at PC1-MQMA from this point of view, then a third interesting fact becomes obvious: all three semantic features relevant to replies load criterially and positively. Very simply, the picture is this: HAP mothers will tend to give replies which are [responsive] (.67) and [adequate] (.56). This means the mothers' replies not only address the query point of their children's questions but also provide the required information. I would suggest that it follows that mothers who tend to address informatively the query point of their children's questions show greater engagement with the on-going dialogue (see discussion of the feature [nonresponsive] in section 4.3.4). The positive loading of the feature A[related] (.68) shows that more information tends to be added to what would by itself have been just sufficient. In fact since Q[related] also loads positively (.65), we may say that while the two groups of mothers do not differ in the kind of information they seek from their children, there is evidence that they differ significantly in information they provide to their children both in the context of replying to the child's questions and in the context of asking questions of the child, so that questions put to the child become a vehicle for conveying additional information which makes the intent more precise than it would have been if the additional information had not been supplied.

It seems reasonable to suggest that PC1-MQMA identifies a higher order principle that may be called INDIVIDUATED INFORMATIVENESS, where both parts of the characterisation are equally important. It is not simply that the HAP mothers' questions in building point of view and in avoiding presumption of access to private knowledge legitimate the specific middle class view according to which the autonomy of the individual is sacred; it is also noticeable that in her tendency to reply relevantly to the child's questions, she validates the child as a dialogic partner, who can expect to claim the mothers' attention. This is individuation in action!

4.6 Interpreting PC1-CQCA

If we turn now to the high scoring children, the structure of PC1-CQCA differs in some important respects from that of the mother's – i.e., PC1-MQMA. Let me first summarise briefly the pattern of semantic choices identified by PC1-CQCA in asking questions and giving responses. Those who score high would display the following pattern of semantic choices:

- they are unlikely to ask questions with an assumed but unvoiced thesis;
- they are likely to present the thesis of their question as someone's Locution or Idea;
- they are likely to ask yes/no questions;
- they are likely to relate their questions and answers to other additional relevant information;
- when they reply, their answers will tend to give the kind of information sought in the question;

Although the semantic features used as input for the two PCs were the same, the structure of the PC is not identical (for details see section 4.4). I shall try to show whether these dissimilarities create any significant differences in interpretation, and if so how.

Let me first examine the features pertaining to replies. Of the three relevant features, the children are like their mothers in respect of two, differing from them in respect of one i.e., A[responsive] (0.34). This is also a feature that does not load criterially thus implying that it is not a feature that contributes significantly to variation between the two social groups of children. While all children will display the same tendencies in addressing the point of the mother's question – A[responsive] (.34), only the HAP children will typically tend to give replies which are [adequate] (.55) and also [related] (.63) i.e., provide additional and more precise information. In these respects the HAP children vary significantly from their LAP counterparts. In other words the extent to which children will attend to their mothers' questions is invariable across social groups, but there is a social class effect on the nature of information supplied in replies.

Questions, too, present a somewhat similar picture. If we look into the kind of information children seek, their behaviour is something like their mothers without being identical. Like the mothers, the two social groups of children do not vary in their choice of Q[ask] (-0.12) and Q[explain] (0.00). However, unlike the mothers, the feature Q[confirm] (.68) turns out to be positive and criterial. That is to say, one respect in which the LAP and HAP children vary is the tendency of the latter to ask yes/no questions. It seems reasonable that children should seek information from their mothers, since their need for information is patently obvious and since mothers could be expected to know. However, two points should be noted: first, it is remarkable that the questions are not of the type which are particularly associated with search for knowledge i.e., how/why ones (cf. Popper 1979). And secondly, it is a measure that contributes to differentiation between the two social groups: in other words, the difference cannot be explained by appeal to maturational stage. I would suggest that the difference in the children's semantic choice might be a response to maternal semantic orientation. I have argued above that HAP mothers are more informative, show greater engagement with the dialogue, and tend to shore up the child's self image in significant ways. This creates an environment in which questions acquire greater legitimacy than they would have in an environment where either the mother ignores the question or fails to provide the information sought.

It is interesting to note the children's reproduction of the maternal semantic orientation in respect of the two features Q[prefaced] (.58) and Q[assumptive] (-.51). Learning how to mean is also learning the ideologies that are created, maintained and changed through the social organisation of the life of individuals. This social organisation itself impinges on individuals through significant forms of action. Speaking is one such action. The ways in which mothers talk appears to have some consequence for how their children talk. The HAP mothers, I argued, are more informative relative to LAP mothers; the HAP children we now note are more informative than the LAP ones. HAP mothers, more than LAP ones, through their choices of meaning celebrate the importance of the individual; HAP children more than LAP ones show similar tendencies. Taking into account these differences and similarities between the high scoring mothers and the high scoring children, it would seem appropriate to suggest that PC1-CQCA should be interpreted as INDIVIDUATED INFORMATION EXCHANGE.

5 Semantic variation and sociolinguistic theory

In closing this chapter, I would like to claim, with apologies to Weiner and Labov (1983: 29), that by examining a large number of semantic features selected in spontaneous speech, together with messages that show their opposing choices, I have been able to throw some light on the crucial and contentious question of semantic variation in sociolinguistic studies. I believe I have demonstrated that non-random, highly orderly semantic variation occurs in the speech of the 24 mothers and children whose everyday dialogues were recorded and analysed for this research. It remains now to draw attention to some of the most important implications of this research.

First, let me return to Weinreich et al. quoted earlier who quite unequivocally claim that in a language serving a complex (i.e., real) community, it is absence of structured heterogeneity that would be dysfunctional. To any one who holds this view, a sociolinguistic theory that denies the possibility of semantic variation poses an immense problem. The functionality of language is much more manifest and much more readily relatable to its level of meaning than to its level of sounds: this is one of those rare axioms on which linguists who are willing to accept any relation between language and society would seem to be in accord. It is then legitimate to ask why, of all the levels of language, the level of semantics is the one that should remain immune to variation? why it should be possible to grant that variation in phonological expressions is functional in a complex society, but impossible to grant functionality for variation in the choice of semantic expressions. If it is true that social pressures are continually acting upon the structure of a language (Labov 1966a: 4), how is it that the very *raison d'être* of language – namely, meaning – defies these social pressures? Assuming that social pressure acting upon the structure of language would manifest itself in variation in the linguistic structure, why would the level of meaning remain unaffected?

The post-Lavandera decade from 1978 has seen a further source of contradiction: on the one hand, the arbitrary restriction of meaning to referentiality has been more explicitly advocated (Labov 1978a; Weiner and Labov 1983), and on the other hand it has been granted that there could be some environments such as, for example, the early stages of language learning which according to them 'inevitably involve variation of a meaningful kind' (Weiner and Labov 1983: 31). And while variable elements are found at all levels of the internal structure of language (loc. cit.), the reservations against semantic variation continue. One reason advanced (Weiner and Labov 1983: 31) is that:

> ... the possibility of accurate measurement is less immediate with semantic variation. We obviously have a much better chance of getting intersubjective agreement in identifying formal variants than semantic variants.

There is no doubt that the identification of semantic variants is not as clear-cut an issue as the identification of phonological units, particularly when the latter happen to be segmental. On the other hand, if semantic variation is an important phenomenon for understanding some of the problems of communication and of exploitation, and if understanding the social motivation for a particular kind of semantic orientation is a step toward the empowerment of the less privileged segments of the society – and I believe it is both these things (Hasan 2004b; see also chapter 4) – then ignoring semantic variation simply because precise measures are not available is hardly likely to appear a good enough reason for not doing anything. Until the problem is seen as a valid one rather than as a manifestation of middle class prejudice (Labov 1972b, d) or the result of a poor linguistic model (Weiner and Labov 1983), improvements in the research methodology in this area will hardly occur. Even if one were to grant that the concept of semantic variation is speculative, this does not necessarily deserve the neglect or the hostility with which any work in this area is generally greeted.

There are many areas of linguistic endeavour just as speculative if not more so. Consider for example the debate about language as a mental organ; after three decades of persistent enquiry, no common agreement has emerged[7]. However, engagement in that enterprise hardly draws the violent reactions reserved for any work in the area of sociosemantic variation. At the same time, the difficulties in researching semantic variation, even if real enough, can be exaggerated – and often are – thus becoming another powerful means to keep hidden from our consciousness the ways in which middle class ideology somewhat mindlessly and often in ignorance perpetuates its position of dominance and exploitation. The discussion of semantic variants presented above hopefully shows that there are ways of conceptualising semantic phenomena which might reduce reliance on vaguer criteria and that the possibility exists of a much greater degree of precision in the study of semantic variation than has so far been granted.

As argued above, the recognition of semantic variation calls for a specific conceptualisation of the nature of language. I believe that it is a mistake to imagine that the social significance of language is limited simply to Bühler's expressive and conative functions, or that the relationship of language and society is fully accounted for by this ritual bow in the direction of sociality. What we need is a model in which the meaning of linguistic variation is not limited to subserving the social functions of identifying the social position of speakers or adjusting to the social position of listeners and audience (sic) (Weiner and Labov 1983: 31). The social meaning of language resides in its power to create, maintain and alter images of social reality by which human communities live (Fairclough 1989). To be able to describe this, we need a model where social organisation, social context and language are related to each other in a non-ad hoc manner. The model used in the research meets this requirement by recognising a stratal organisation of language which links it to society. The dynamic element in this model of language and society is provided by the inter-stratal relation of realisation, where realisation is not simply the expression of pre-existing content but itself plays a creative part in giving it its identity – a process that Lemke (1984) describes as the exchange of information between the interlocking parts of a dynamic open systems. This exchange of information permits the various interlocking components of a dynamic open system to maintain their identity even while they evolve. It can be argued convincingly that language and society do form parts of such a dynamic open system (cf. Halliday 1987). The model I have presented here is compatible with this assumption. It is also a model of language as a potential for meaning. This implies that at each of its levels, language is seen as paradigmatically organised with systems of options that represent the potential of choice within fairly explicitly specifiable contexts. In a model of this kind, concepts such as those of system, choice, alternation and delicacy of focus are the natural and necessary elements for the description of language; and these concepts are hospitable to the idea of linguistic variation, which naturally includes the idea of semantic variation.

This approach is in fundamental opposition to models where language is seen as an autonomous structure, a biological organ which is deep down the same for every one not simply in the capacity it gives potential access to but in the actualisation of that capacity e.g., in its fairly concrete details of structure formation (see, for example, Sells 1985). The shared representation of the structure of the world which we inhabit and the innate structure of language are conceptualised in such models as growing independently of each other. It is not surprising, therefore, that meaning becomes objectified, and semantics is reduced to simply the correspondence of words to the world, i.e., to just referential meaning. In this approach, quite obviously, the idea of the sociality of language is simply an anomaly. By these steps, a large part of the essentially human element of language structure is conceptualised as falling outside linguistics proper, in zones whose relation to language is left ambiguous. These zones are given respectability by appeal to discredited antinomies e.g., system versus process; their acceptance appears to be motivated more by the politics of academic discourse than by a desire to understand why any one says anything or how process and system may be related to each other in a dynamic flow of mutual activation. However well such conceptions of language might accord with the logician's ideas about language, or the philosophers' views of innate rationality, they do not appear to be well suited to that kind of sociolinguistics which *aspires to be simply* ***linguistics*** *... with a broader social base* (Labov 1972b: 184).

Notes

1 This chapter was first published in the *Australian Journal of Linguistics* No 9, 1989. It appears here in its original form except that some parts were expunged from sections 2.1 and 2.2 in order to avoid repetition. My thanks are due to Michael Halliday and Carmel Cloran who had commented on the earlier draft. I alone am responsible for the opinions expressed here.

2 The research project was called The Role of Everyday Talk between Mothers and Children in Establishing Ways of Learning, Phase I and II. Funding by the Australian Research Grant and Macquarie University Research Grant for its entire duration (1983-1986) is gratefully acknowledged. I have been fortunate in having Carmel Cloran as my research assistant, and would like to take this occasion to thank her for her valuable help. Thanks are due also to David Butt,

Michael Oerlemans, and Rhondda Fahey who have each made valuable contribution

3 The view of strata has been updated; for a discussion of the first three strata see chapter 1 here.

4 The expression 'context independent' is capable of being misunderstood. In more recent work, I have preferred to refer to such semantic networks as Open Context semantic networks.

5 Note that this system network has been further 'simplified' than those presented in chapters 3 and 4.

6 I thank Barbara Horvath, Greg Guy, and Chris Nesbitt for helping in the early stages of statistical analysis. I am deeply indebted to Alan Taylor who has given valuable time and advice, and to Anne Eyeland without whose help I could not have continued. I also acknowledge with gratitude the help and support I have received throughout the research from Harry Purvis and John Telec of the Speech, Hearing and Language Research Centre at Macquarie University.

7 Interestingly, today as this volume goes to press, the reverse is the case! In light of neurological research, it seems to be more widely accepted in the late twentieth and early twenty-first century that far from language being a mental organ, language and human brain have co-evolved; there is no evidence of language being 'hard-wired' in the human brain, but there is a good deal of evidence of experience of interaction being an essential condition for cognitive development.

6 Questions as a mode of learning in everyday talk [1991]

1 Introduction

Teaching and learning have always been organised around talk. There was a time when talking in the class room was largely a teacher's prerogative: pupils were supposed to listen and learn. But over the past few decades this trend has changed: today, in the ideal class room teachers and pupils interact; they negotiate; and there is a feeling amongst educators that no matter what the subject, learning is better if the learners are active participants in their own education. Interaction is a central concept in education today as evident from the title of our conference[1]. My paper will be concerned with the acknowledged importance of interaction – though viewed from a somewhat different point of view. First, unlike most people here, I shall not be discussing interaction in the class room; instead, I shall be concerned with interaction in everyday life. Secondly, although like many here, I too will be concerned with language, my concern is not directly with the teaching or learning of some language – at least not in the sense in which language learning is usually understood. Instead, my concern is with an exploration of how the experience of engaging in everyday interaction – the experience of *languaging* in everyday talk – might prepare one for participation in the discourses of knowledge. Put very simply, the question I am asking is: does the experience of languaging in everyday interaction bear any relation to learning and to knowledge?

From one point of view, it could be claimed that the act of experiencing life in its many aspects – of interacting and acting with others – is the most effective mode of learning: the COMMONSENSE KNOWLEDGE that is thus experienced and internalised is something entirely indispensable for the continuation of human life. And the relationship of everyday interaction to learning and knowledge, in this perspective, is so very obvious that it seems superfluous to raise the question I posed above: language as the medium of the message and knowledge as its meaning made of worded information are clearly two aspects of the same phenomenon, as many have pointed out.

However, terms such as 'learning' and 'knowledge' themselves need to be examined closely, partly because most societies seem to operate with two distinct conceptions of knowledge: the apparently effortlessly gained *commonsense knowledge* of the type I have just mentioned, and the specialised, deliberately gained UN-COMMONSENSE KNOWLEDGE which not all members of the society are expected to possess – or at least not to the same extent. Irrespective of the politico-economic structure of societies, the latter sort of knowledge has always claimed higher prestige: be it the shaman's knowledge, the priest's, or the modern specialist's, to have knowledge of this kind is to possess a social good. But even within this larger category of un-commonsense knowledge, by consensus, expert opinion has carved out yet another division: there is the intuitive, magical or *qua si* religious knowledge of the medicine man, the shaman, the priest; and there is the rational, *objective knowledge* of the modern specialist – particularly in the domain of the physical sciences, mathematics, logic, and so on. It is this latter 'rational' 'objective' knowledge that holds the place of pride among all forms of human learning. Little wonder then that many areas of enquiry in the social and human sciences (*sic!*) invest a good deal of energy in proving their scientific credentials.

The valuation thus placed on the terms 'knowledge' and 'learning', sets objective knowledge and learning apart from all other forms of knowledge so much so that for most of us, particularly in the context of scholarly discussions such as the ones we are engaging in at this conference, the terms *learning* and *knowledge* are not likely to be confused with the everyday commonsensical stuff, or with the systems of beliefs possessed by priests and shamans: for us, the terms refer unambiguously to objective knowledge – knowledge of the type we endeavour to impart and to (re)produce in our educational institutions. This separation between the two kinds of knowing, the two modes of learning, is so much part of our common wisdom, so taken for granted that we pass over the distinction without giving it a thought. The question I want to ask is: are the two forms of learning and knowledge – commonsense knowledge and objective knowledge – truly as remote from each other as we are led to believe? Or, is there perhaps reason to think that in some sense the knowledge and learning we gain from everyday talk shapes the possibilities of not only our engagement with objective knowledge but also our participation in its production?

To suggest an answer to this question, I shall look closely at one aspect of everyday talk between some Australian mothers and their small children. More specifically, the aspect of talk, I will examine here concerns questions and answers that pass between mothers and their children. Current attitudes to questions and answers provide good reasons for thinking that this is an important area when it comes to knowledge and learning. For example, in linguistics, those studying the illocutionary force of utterances (e.g. Austin 1980; Searle 1969) are agreed that the *raison d'etre* of a question is to find out something that one did not know, i.e., to remedy one's state of ignorance;

if this is so then one might concede that questions and answers are important to learning and knowing. The special position of at least certain categories of questions for the advancement of human learning has been pointed out by many philosophers: Popper, one of the most famous philosophers of our time, has declared that all pure knowledge is based on *why* and *how* questions. This assigns such questions an important role in the life of humanity, the more so because it is believed that the evolution of knowledge is itself synonymous with the evolution, even survival, of human species: the *homo sapiens* evolve not by physically adapting to their external environment but by figuring out how to adapt the physical environment to suit the human body (Medawar 1982; Popper 1979; Popper and Eccles 1977); and this end could not be achieved without asking *why* and *how* questions. Again, scholars interested in the mental development of children have commented on the relation between the asking of questions and mental development: thus Piaget (1960: 162) claimed that 'there is no better introduction to child logic than the study of spontaneous questions': he is convinced of the association between mental maturity and the ability for asking serious questions seriously. In view of the importance assigned to questions in human life and learning, it seems reasonable to ask: what are the children learning by asking and by being asked? The answer to this question might enable one to address other questions, such as: is this learning relevant to the learning of objective knowledge? If so, how? But before starting this enquiry, let me say a word about the mothers and children whose questions and answers I intend to examine in this paper.

2 Subjects in dialogue: the speakers and the data

The questions and answers I discuss today are taken from an empirical research[2] I directed at Macquarie University. The title of the research was *The Role of Everyday Talk between Mothers and Children in Establishing Ways of Learning.* As the research design, methods of data collection, and other such issues have been discussed in some detail in chapters 3–5 of this volume, I shall give the barest essential details for convenience of reference. The research was divided into phases 1 and 2. The first phase examined some of the semantic properties of naturally occurring dialogues in the home environment of the mothers and children; the second, with the semantic analysis of class room talk as well as peer group discourse among children. Though at a later point I will refer briefly to phase 2 class room data, the dialogues on which I mostly draw for this paper are from phase 1.

2.1 The subjects

The subjects in phase 1 were 24 mothers and their 3;6–4;2 year old children from the Sydney area (children's mean age 3;8). All the mothers were native speakers of English, born and brought up in Australia and without significant experience of living in any other culture. The mothers were equally distributed by social class, referred to as HAP and LAP[3], as were the children by sex and class.

2.2 The dialogues

Before beginning the collection of data, my research assistant, Carmel Cloran, and I first interviewed all the mothers individually. On this occasion, we informed mothers that we were interested in collecting samples of children's talk because we were keen to find out what very small children talk about when they are in their everyday familiar environment, and when no one is actively prodding them to say something. We suggested that the dialogues where the children were talking to their mothers in familiar home surrounding without the presence of outsiders would serve our purpose very well. The mothers who volunteered to participate collected the data while engaged in various household chores. From approximately 100 hours of mother-child dialogue, a sample consisting of 20, 544 messages was selected for analysis. The statistical results presented here (section 5) are based on the questions and answers that occurred in this sample.

3 A model for the analysis of meaning in dialogue

The kind of analysis that needed to be carried out was in fact determined by the aims of the research: to find out if, and how, everyday dialogue plays any part in establishing ways of learning. Given this aim, the main focus of our analysis had to be on the meanings being exchanged (for discussion chapters 4, 5 and 7). What was needed was a viable and explicit framework for the analysis of meaning. However, even after nearly a century of modern linguistics, the analysis of meaning poses problems.

The notion of meaning, and therefore the methods for its analysis, have traditionally been equated in linguistics with focus on lexical content, and/or truth-functional or simply representational semantics. The inadequacy of these approaches is increasingly recognised in the literature (Eco, Santambrogio and Violi 1988; Barwise 1989; Hasan 1984a,1984b, 1989); the need to make appeal to *pragmatics* as something over and above linguistic meaning (Levinson 1983; Leech 1983) can be taken as an indirect evidence that this conception of linguistic meaning is flawed. Analysing meaning in language by simply examining lexical content, or by reference to some variety of correspondence theory, or by factoring meanings out into linguistic meaning and pragmatic meaning as if the two were, in principle, unrelated to each other, misses out on important aspects of linguistic meaning – particularly since quite often the term pragmatics is used as a catch-all expression, covering almost any aspect of language in use.

3.1 Modelling language in context

In devising the framework for the analysis of the linguistic meaning of messages in dialogue, I have used the insights of Michael Halliday's systemic functional model. It is not possible here – or even necessary – to discuss the model in any detail; let me just draw attention to those design features of the model which are most pertinent to the problems that concerned my research in general and the topic of this paper, in particular.

First, as was evident from Halliday's address (Halliday 1999), this linguistic theory attempts to explain, on a non-ad hoc basis, the continuities between language and the social systems of a speech community. The community's talk – their discourse – is related to the system of language which functions as the enabling resource for speaking; the two are related as instance is related to its governing principle, or system. And the latter two – the instantiating texts and the enabling system – are in turn related to the situations of talk and to the community's culture, the latter giving the situation its identity and its value as a social situation.

This perspective yields a stratal linguistic theory, whose four strata are: CONTEXT – social situations instantiating culture; SEMANTICS – the linguistic meaning potential; LEXICOGRAMMAR – the resource for linguistic meanings; and PHONOLOGY/GRAPHOLOGY, which is the *sens-ible* stratum of language that gives access to the *intelligible,* i.e., the worded meanings.

3.2 Realisation: the active relation

The *second* relevant feature of this linguistic model is the conceptualisation of the relation between these strata: they are said to be related by REALISATION – a concept that Halliday has discussed in some detail in his address (Halliday 1999). He suggests that at the higher levels of language, it is 'a relationship that can be traversed, or activated, in either direction'. So culture is construed by the system of language, while the system of language is itself culturally activated; similarly linguistic meanings at the semantic level are construed by lexicogrammar, while the latter itself is semantically activated (Halliday 1970, 1979a, 1992a etc.). The concept of realisation is, thus, quintessentially semiotic; it attempts to capture the creative nature of language. By creativity of language I do not mean only the possibility of producing a longer sentence than the last known longest one: this is a formal and limited notion of creativity, which says nothing about its relevance to any one who actually uses the device. By calling language creative, I mean it is unavoidably implicated in the creation, maintenance, and change of all our systems of belief as well as institutions, in all impulse to concerted action – in short in everything that involves an *other*. (Berger and Luckman 1971; Bernstein 1971a, 1971b, 1971c; Malinowski 1923, 1935; Mead 1934; Vygotsky 1962, 1978; Whorf 1956; Wittgenstein 1958.) To be creative in this sense, language must naturally have certain formal capacities, but such capacities cannot be simply limited to the possibility of producing iterative structures. This issue is important to my research in the following three ways.

First, if it is granted that language is creative in this sense of playing an important role in the construction of systems of belief, and other such mental states, then my original question becomes: do the systems of belief and mental states created by the language of everyday talk relate to the systems of belief that we refer to as *objective knowledge*, and so to those mental strivings which we talk of as *learning*, and if the answer is 'yes', then how does this relation work. By building a non-ad hoc principle for relating language to cultural systems, the systemic functional model makes it possible to explore questions about the relationship of language and reality which could not be meaningfully raised in a linguistic model that views language as a surrogate of already existing reality: if language is simply a mirror, then logically it can have no part in the creation of that which it mirrors (Butt 1989a; Hasan 1984a). Second, the two attributes of the model discussed so far are important to my discussion because of the light they shed on the nature of linguistic meaning. Linguistic meaning, in this view, is construed by the lexicogrammar: tautologically, whatever cannot be worded is not linguistic meaning. It follows then that, to be explicit, an analysis of meaning must be anchored in the lexicogrammar. And finally, linguistic meanings are said to be construed not simply by lexis but by the working of lexicogrammar as a whole. So the analysis of meaning cannot be simply the analysis of 'content words' as in the study of cups, mugs and bowls (Labov 1973; Wierzbicka 1984). The terms meaning and semantics have a different meaning in the systemic functional model.

3.3 A functional view of meaning

This brings me to the *third* important feature of the model – its conceptualisation of the linguistic meaning potential. In most linguistic models, the term 'semantics' is largely equated with referential meaning – what is some times called 'cognitive' or 'representational' meaning. By the logic of this position, knowledge and classification are prior to language; linguistic meaning becomes glorified naming, albeit under different labels e.g., correspondence, truth etc. When other distinctions of meaning come to attention which are essentially non-referential, such as the difference between *John smokes habitually.* and *does John smoke habitually?* (cf. Searle 1969), they are relegated to some other branch of study – such as, perhaps, pragmatics, often with the implication that this is not a part of 'linguistics proper' (Leech 1983). The systemic functional model does not subscribe to this practice. Instead it uses the notion of *metafunction* as an organising concept to account for phenomena at the level of semantics. The four well known metafunctions (1) the EXPERIENTIAL (2) the LOGICAL (3) the TEXTUAL, and (4) the INTERPERSONAL (Halliday 1970, 1973b, 1977, 1979a etc.) together account for the meaning distinctions that in other models are distributed under semantics (covering cognitive/referential meaning, approximately metafunctions 1, and 2); pragmatics (approximately the third metafunction) and illocutionary meaning (approximately the fourth metafunction). By comparison with other models, whether functional or formal, the concept of semantics is richer in the systemic functional linguistics as it integrates all those meaning distinctions which are linguistically construable. Moreover, among the current models, this model is unique in refusing to consider any one kind of meaning as linguistically more important than the others. According to this approach, it is equally important to know whether someone is making a statement or an offer (an interpersonal meaning distinction); whether the statement is responsive to some demand made by another or not (a textual distinction); whether it relates logically to another message as for example cause relates to effect, or condition to consequence (a logical distinction); whether the message represents a voluntary action or one that is imposed externally (an experiential distinction); and so on. Since in processing a message each such semantic aspect must be attended to, there seems to exist no justification for maintaining that some meanings, such as the referential ones, are more important, more central, than the others.

While there appears to be no convincing argument to treat referential meaning as in some way more linguistic than any other kind of meaning, support for viewing all metafunctions as having an equal status is found in the lexicogrammar. Systemic functional theory claims that the lexicogrammar of a language is realisationally related to the different components of the language's meaning potential: each of these metafunctions activates some specific part of the lexicogrammar of a language; and, significantly, the grammatical description of a unit such as the clause shows evidence of more than one structural line in operation. So in clause grammar, transitivity choices are activated by the experiential metafunction: it is from these choices that we construe such meanings as who did what to whom where when how and for what purpose etc. The relation of clauses to each other is activated by the logical metafunction: dependence between two states of affairs, and the projection of one state of affairs by another are relations that are construed by choices in the system of taxis, i.e., subordination and coordination. Mood and modality choices are activated by the interpersonal metafunction: it is from these choices that we construe such meanings as the speaker's speech role – asking for something or giving it – or the speaker's assessment of possibility etc., while the choices of theme, information focus and cohesion are activated by the textual metafunction: the relevance of one message to another in the economy of the on-going discourse is construed by these choices (Halliday 1970, 1979a, 1985a). If 'linguistic meaning' is a term that refers to this range of meanings, it follows that a comprehensive analysis of meaning in dialogue will involve analysing the data from all these points of view; on the other hand, the metafunctional approach to meaning also offers a reasonable principle by which the goals of the analysis may be limited.

3.4 Language as meaningful choice in context

The fourth and final design feature of the SF model I will discuss here is its conception of language as a vast *network of systemic choices*: the lexicogrammar and the phonology of the language have been represented in this model as systems of interlocking choices – what options speakers of the language enjoy in a given environment at these two strata of the language's internal organisation. Thus taking the English clause again as an example at the lexicogrammatical level, the clause would be regarded as the point of origin for a set of system networks. Potentially each option in a system network acts as the environment for further options (Halliday 1973, 1976, 1977; Halliday and Martin 1981). So as the system network is traversed, each subsequent choice represents a move in DELICACY – i.e., it indicates greater specificity of the description. The description of language is thus *paradigmatic*. Attached to each option in this paradigmatic representation are some *realisation statement(s)*; these statements specify the recognition criteria for the description, and in doing so they also specify the shape of the syntagm – i.e., how each option is expressed in a *syntagm*. Thus it is from the paradigmatic systems that the syntagms – that is to say, structures – are generated via the realisational statements attached to the systemic options (Halliday 1969, 1977; Hasan 1987a, 1985a, b, c, 1992a; Martin 1987; Matthiessen 1992).

System networks representing choices at the levels of lexicogrammar and phonology have been in evidence since the early 1960s (Halliday and Martin 1981), semantic networks have been much less common. It is assumed that, at least in theory, the meanings the speakers of a language can mean are also amenable to being represented as systems of paradigmatic choices. In fact, in the late sixties and early seventies, semantic networks were already being produced by, for example, Halliday (1973a) and Turner (1973). (For a discussion of Halliday's semantic system networks, Hasan 1996.) Following these leads, I prepared a semantic network (Hasan 1983) for the analysis of the dialogic data in my research.

3.5 A semantic network for the analysis of dialogue

The design features of the SF model described here imply the presence of certain properties in a semantic network if it is to succeed in representing the meaning potential of English. It must represent *all choices of meaning for each metafunction, taking as points of origin each of the recognised units at the semantic level*, such as, perhaps, text, message, entity, event etc. And given the assumptions in the model, a semantic network would be pointless unless its options could be shown to be related in a non-ad hoc way by realisation to lexicogrammar. These are exacting demands. In the first place, an exhaustive system network of this kind which can be said to represent *all* the meanings of any one language, however justifiably predicted in theory, in practice appears as unattainable as the exhaustive description of the lexicogrammar of any language: we do not know everything about the grammar of even the best described language in the world today, viz., English. The network that I prepared is not intended to capture the entire meaning potential of English. One obvious way in which its scope is limited is that its point of origin is the unit *message*: the network is intended to represent the meaning options that are applicable to English messages, rather than to, say, entity, quality, or event. I would characterise message as the *smallest semantic unit capable of entering into the structure of a text*. Lexicogrammatically, message is typically realised as a (ranking i.e., non-rank-shifted) clause; exceptions to this generalisation are explicitly specifiable.

The decision to use message as the point of origin for the semantic system network does limit the scope of the network. But even so, what remains is an enormous enterprise. Halliday (1973b) suggested that in practice it might be best to produce semantic networks that represent the choices relevant to some specific contexts: if this suggestion is adopted, then unlike lexicogrammatical and phonological networks, which are not context specific, the semantic networks would be context specific. Halliday's own semantic network (1973b) represented the meaning potential associated with the context of maternal control.

The data collected for analysis in the two phases of my research ranged over a large number of contexts; or to be more precise, some features of the context varied a good deal while others did not (for discussion, chapter 3 in this volume). For example, the MODE OF DISCOURSE in both phases of the research remained dialogic, with face-to-face contact between the speakers. In phase I, some elements of the TENOR OF DISCOURSE too were invariant: the speakers stood in the relation of mother and child with minimal SOCIAL DISTANCE (cf. Hasan 1973a). It was mainly in respect to the FIELD OF DISCOURSE that the dialogues varied a good deal, ranging over instruction, control, nurturing etc. The network I prepared was oriented to the two relatively constant vectors of the context of situation. However, this same network, with some minor adjustments, has been successfully used in phase II, where the tenor relation for some of the dialogues was that of teacher-pupil, and for others that of familiar peers. The same network with some modifications is currently being used for the analysis of legal discourse (Maley and Fahey 1991) and for other class room discourses. Since the network has so far not been used to analyse either the semantic choices in messages in monologues or in the written medium, any claim of context-independence would be premature. However, one might be justified in claiming that it appears fairly adequate for analysing dialogic messages. Further – though this aspect was not pursued in my research – the network would also permit the coding of exchange structures, with certain advantages that appear to be absent from other frameworks created for the specific purpose of analysing exchange structures in dialogue (e.g. Berry 1981; Martin 1985).

The message semantics network does represent choices from all four metafunctions (discussion in chapters 3–5). Thus, in examining a message that 'has' the interpersonal function of question, the network would allow, *up to a certain degree of delicacy*, the specification of what category of experiential phenomena such as event or action or state the question was about; whether it was logically related to some other (subsidiary) message as cause, consequence, condition etc.; whether textually it was topic maintaining or initiating; and so on.

Since in this model linguistic meanings are said to be construed by the lexicogrammatical form of the language, the analysis of meaning goes beyond an intuitive labelling of units: only those meaningful phenomena have the status of semantic option whose lexicogrammatical realisation is explicitly stateable. Associated with each option in the network are realisation statements (for some examples see chapters 3; 4; 5 and 7), which specify what lexicogrammatical patterns construe what semantic option. Thus the criteria for claiming that a specific semantic option is present in some message are made far more explicit than in any other model for semantic description that is known to me.

The fact that the meaning of any one message is being examined from four distinct points of view permits a principled account of both the points of similarity and dissimilarity between the messages analysed. While all questions are alike in being questions, they can vary from each other on one or more of the meaningful dimensions, mentioned above. So, for example, if we have two *why* questions, one might be topic maintaining (e.g., *why here?*) the other not; one might be 'conditioned' (e.g., *if you wanted it yourself, why did you give it to him?*), another not; and so on. The concept of delicacy is also relevant: depending on the need of the analysis, one may compare all questions with all statements; but for some other purpose, it may be relevant to compare yes-no questions with why-what questions. This possibility of varying the degree of delicacy in the semantic description of the data provides greater flexibility in the description, and becomes central to the study of variation in the data. Limitations of time and space do not permit a demonstration of the network; however, parts of the semantic network with realisation statements have been presented elsewhere[4]. In the following section I shall present some semantic features of questions discursively rather than in a network form.

4 Some semantic attributes of questions

The discussion in this paper is based on the analysis of 3,358 questions, and their answers. This number refers exclusively to questions; for reasons given below (section 4.3), it does not include any count of answers. Approximately two-thirds of the questions were addressed to the children by their mothers (exactly 2,008), while the remaining third (exactly 1,350) were asked by the children.

4.1 Questions with a difference

The term 'question' itself is used somewhat loosely in the linguistic literature. Throughout this paper I shall make a distinction between the semantic category of question and the lexicogrammatical term 'interrogative'. Neither all questions are interrogatives, nor all interrogatives function as questions. In keeping with the principles of paradigmatically oriented descriptions, the definition of question 'resides' in the system of semantic options: a question is some specific configuration of a set of options 'legally' permitted by the form of the network pertaining to the system of 'role allocation'; it is such configurations of semantic options that the members of the community regard as question. Informally, a question calls upon the addressee to provide a semiotic response: it cannot be directly answered by some physical action. Even under this definition, the questions under discussion in this paper do not include all the questions that mothers and children asked in the analysed sample; much less all the interrogatives produced. Excluded from this count are the following categories of messages:

i) Clarification question: these are questions asked to get the previous speaker to repeat what was said before, sometimes referred to as (a kind of) channel repair. Examples: *what did you say?, daddy said what?,* or just elliptically *what?.*

ii) Consultative command: where the structure of a clause is interrogative, but semantically instead of demanding information (i.e. functioning as a question), the point of its utterance is to demand goods and services (i.e. to call for a physical response) – it thus functions as a command/request of the kind commonly labelled indirect command; an example would be *can you try and remind me to ring Pam this afternoon?* (see dialogue 4 below), where 'yes' does not mean 'I agree this is the case' but rather 'I agree to comply/act as you wish'.

ii) Gambits: certain formulaic questions, which function as some kind of prompt to the addressee, acting as a cue for the addressee to produce as her next move a ritualistic message which in turn permits the first speaker to relay some information in a manner which foregrounds it textually. Here is an example from the data:

Mother: you know what you would have done?
Cameron: what?
Mother: you would have run to mummy, crying really loudly, shouting, and you didn't .... etc.

Clarification questions are excluded as they are provoked mostly by material conditions of communication: if one is in a noisy environment, or shouting across rooms – as happens sometime in the data – one might miss the question and request a repetition. Such questions bear very little relevance to the concerns of this paper. Gambits were excluded as they appeared to be closer to an attention fixing device than to a question; moreover, gambits are highly formulaic, and are not likely to provide the possibility of open enquiry. The reason for excluding consultative commands is obvious; although such commands may be often followed by a linguistic response, eliciting such response is not the point of the message as pointed out above.

4.2 The meanings in questions

Turning now to the questions included in the present data set, let me begin by talking about one meaningful distinction between questions which is widely recognised: this is the distinction between [demand; confirmation] as opposed to [demand; information] (for a more detailed account, see the last three chapters). The speaker chooses the semantic option [confirm], hoping to elicit a yes/no answer, which agrees or disagrees with the 'thesis' of the question; the semantic option [apprise] construes attempt to elicit some specific element of information. Both these choices are instantiated in the following dialogue[5] between Karen and her mother:

Dialogue 1

Karen: (1) who are my mummy (2) when I was a little baby?
Mother: (3) me (4) I was always your mummy
Karen: (5) no (6) when you was a little girl
Mother: (7) when I was a little girl (8) you didn't have a mummy (9) you weren't there
Karen: (10) mm (SHOWING DISBELIEF)
Mother: (11) oh you can't be here all the time you know
Karen: (12) well somebody must be my baby— (CORRECTING HERSELF) mummy (13) 'cause I couldn't stay home by myself (14) I didn't have a father
Mother: (15) you didn't have a father? (16) you've got a father
Karen: (17) I have (18) when I was a little baby (19) I didn't... (20) I was home by myself...(21) wasn't I, mum? (22) wasn't I?
Mother: (23) you was home by yourself?
Karen: (24) yeah .... (25) how did you get that?...
Mother: (26) mm?
Karen: (27) how did you get that?** (28) you didn't get out of [?]
Mother: (29) I walked over (30) and got it (31) didn't you see me?
Karen: (32) nup
Mother: (33) you must be blind

In the above dialogue, message (31) *didn't you see me?* has the semantic feature [confirm], while questions (1), (25), and (27) have the semantic feature [apprise]. There are two more questions in this dialogue with the feature [confirm]: messages (21) and (22) are like (31) in that they realise the semantic option [confirm]. They differ from (31) in that they are elliptical but this does not affect their status as questions with a particular semantic make up as the expansion of the ellipsis will demonstrate. It is not my concern here to foreground the multifunctional orientation of my message semantic network, but note that the ellipsis in (21) and (22) realises the option [topic maintaining] in the semantic system of continuity which through the co-selection pattern here is indicative of the fact that the questions under focus are the continuation of some preceding part of the dialogue. Note also that at message (25) Karen changes the topic and that this is not the point where she could have produced a message with the feature [topic maintaining] realised as some elliptical message such as *how did you?* This is not to say that questions introducing a new topic will never be realised by an elliptical clause but normally ellipsis would be rare in any clause realising [topic initiating]; if this did happen, the ellipsis would be highly likely to be exophoric.

The semantic options [confirm] and [apprise] in their turn act as the environment in which other meaningful choices become available. The option [confirm] permits a choice between [enquire] and [verify]; a message with the option [enquire] may either select the feature [ask] or [check], while those with the option [verify] may select [probe] or [reassure]. The option [apprise], by steps leads to a choice between [explain] and [specify]. Most of these options are exemplified in the messages of dialogue 2:

Dialogue 2

Mother: (1) d'you love daddy?... (2) d'you love daddy?
Julian: (3) mm (AGREEING)
Mother: (4) d'you love Rosemary?
Julian: (5) no
Mother: (6) why don't you love Rosemary? (REPROVING TONE)
Julian: (LAUGHS)
Mother: (7) why don't you love Rosemary?
Julian: (CONTINUES TO LAUGH)
Mother: (8) you're a [?rat-bag] (REALISES CHILD WAS TEASING)
Julian: (9) I do
Mother: (10) [?]
Julian: (11) who else do you want me to love?
Mother: (12) you can love whoever you want to
Julian: (13) can I love Peter?...(14) can I?

Mother: (15) no (16) I think that's more like friendship
Julian: (16) pardon?
Mother: (17) thought you'd say that (18) it's like friendship, isn't it?...(19) you are friends with Peter, aren't you?
Julian: (20) yep... (21) mum!
Mother: (22) yes (ATTENDING)
Julian: (23) when I get old as you (24) and [? Maree likes me] (25) could we marry each other?
Mother: (26) no (27) because Maree is your cousin
Julian: (28) oh
Mother: (29) 'cause cousins aren't allowed to marry
Julian: (30) why?
Mother: (31) 'cause the law says they're not
Julian: (32) who is that?
Mother: (33) the law?
Julian: (34) yeah
Mother: (35) the policeman...
Julian: (DRINKS NOISILY) (36) what if we got married – (37) what if we— if they saw we were already married?
Mother: (38) I don't think so (39) because <<(40) when you get married >>, you've gotta have a licence
Julian: (41) why?
Mother: (42) 'cause you do (43) **so that they know who got married and who hasn't
Julian: (44)** mummy
Mother: (45) mm (ATTENDING)
Julian: (46) where am I gonna get my licence from?
Father: (47) the [? motor transport] department (LAUGHS)
Mother: (48) you don't get it from the transport department
Julian: (49) will you get me one?
Mother: (50) what for? (51) what sort of licence do you want? (53) a driving licence?
Julian: (54) yeah
Mother: (55) no (56) you're too young to have a driving licence
Julian: (57) well when I get big
Mother: (58) when you get big (59) you can get your own licence
Julian: (60) where do you get them from?
Mother: (61) daddy just told you
Julian: (62) from the lottery game
Mother: (63) (LAUGHING) you don't get it from the lottery game
Julian: (64) you do... (65) where do you get them from then?
Mother: (66) you get them from the department of motor transport

To begin with those options that ultimately depend on [confirm], messages (1), (2), (12), (13), (14), (25) and (49) of dialogue 2, realise the semantic option [ask]. The semantic options [demand;information:confirm:enquire:ask] are realised lexicogrammatically by a clause whose mood choices are [indicative: interrogative:polar]: as the examples indicate, this is the most neutral way of attempting to elicit a yes/no response. The option [ask] is in direct contrast to [check]. This latter semantic feature is realised by a clause on a rising tone, whose MOOD choices are [indicative: declarative:untagged]. The option is exemplified in dialogue 1, in the mother's incredulous messages (15) *you didn't have a father?* and (23) *you was home by yourself?*, where she is not saying: *tell me what is the case* or *I didn't hear you*, but rather: *I can't believe that you can think such an amazing thing.* A question with this semantic feature is either attitudinally marked, as demonstrated by the mother's questions here, or it attempts to draw an attestation from the addressee as in message (5) in dialogue 3 between Karen and her mother:

Dialogue 3
Mother: (1) put it up on the stove (2) and leave it there
Karen: (3) why?
Mother: (4) 'cause
Karen: (5) that's where it goes?
Mother: (6) yeah

Strictly speaking it is not true that Karen does not know whether or not the propositional content of (5) is true, thus putting in question the preparatory condition specified by speech act analysis whereby '*S* does not know the answer …' etc. (Searle 1969: 66); it is far more reasonable to interpret this interaction as indicating that she does know her proposition to be true. All she is doing by asking (5) is drawing her mother out – trying to get her to attest to the truth of that proposition.

The semantic option [verify] permits a systemic choice between [reassure] and [probe]. Messages with these semantic options probe the veracity of a presented thesis, or seek to be reassured about its veracity between the interactants; thus in their meaning they are closer to [check] than to [ask]. In both cases, the clause realising the semantic option must have the lexicogrammatical systemic properties [indicative: declarative: tagged]. However, if the feature [reassure] is selected, then the realising clause must have the lexicogrammatical features [...tagged: reversed]: in other words, the polarity choice in the clause capable of realising this option is the opposite of the polarity in Mood Tag. The option [reassure] is illustrated in dialogue 2 by messages (18) *it's like friendship, is**n't** it?* and (19) *you **are** friends with Peter, aren**'t** you?,* where the clause polarity in (19) and (20) is positive, while that in the Mood Tag is negative. By contrast, if the semantic option [probe] is selected then the realising clause must have lexicogrammatical features [...tagged: constant], where the polarity of the clause and the Mood Tag remains the same. Compare *you like sugar, do you?* which exemplifies the choice [probe] with *you're friends with peter, aren't you?* which exemplifies [reassure]. There are of course many more semantic systemic options pertaining to questions with the option [confirm], but most of these are not relevant to the present discussion, except one systemic contrast, viz., [assumptive] v. [nonassumptive]. However, before turning to these, I will discuss some questions with the feature [apprise].

The semantic feature [apprise] is in systemic contrast with confirm (see figure 2 in chapter 5). Skipping some systems in between, let me draw attention to the systemic choice between [specify] and [explain] which ultimately depend on [apprise]. Both these options are exemplified in the above dialogues. The feature [explain] is exemplified by messages (6), (7), (30), and (41) in dialogue 2, and by message (3) in dialogue 3: these are then the familiar *why/what for* type of question. The option [specify] is exemplified by such messages as (1) and (27) in dialogue 1, and (11), (32), (36), (37), (46), (50), (51), (60), and (65) in dialogue 2. Again it is obvious that [specify] questions are the familiar *who/what/where/when/how* questions. Questions with the feature [explain] have the potential of a further semantic distinction, the nature of which may be highlighted by a comparison of (6) and (41) from dialogue 2. As (41) is elliptical, the ellipsis will be expanded here to highlight the semantic contrast under focus. The messages put side by side are:

(6) why don't you love Rosemary?

(41) why have you got to have a licence?

Here both messages have the semantic feature [explain]; but there is a difference between them. The question in message (41) is a simple search for explanation; by contrast, the question asked in message (6) gives rise to the inference that Rosemary is to be loved: the mother has a thesis, which she is not voicing but simply assuming it to be the case. This point is not lost on Julian: having satisfied his mother that he does love Rosemary, he goes on to ask in (11) *who **else** do you want me to love?*. This can only be interpreted as: *who else **apart from Rosemary** do you want me to love?* Systemically, message (6) has the semantic feature [assumptive]; message (41) has the feature [nonassumptive].

The feature [assumptive] is realised by the choice of negative polarity *in the clause*. It is important to emphasise that in the context of [apprise], this option is available only to questions with the semantic feature [explain]; it is not available to those with the semantic feature [specify]. This is not to claim that lexicogrammatically negative polarity cannot be chosen – is *ungrammati-*

cal – in non-polar interrogative except where the *wh-* element is instantiated as *why/what for*. The claim is, rather, that the meaning of *not, n't* in these cases would be appreciably different. Indeed, the fact is that most questions with the feature [specify] are much more likely to be positive; they either sound bizarre or require a rather specialised context if the realising clause has negative polarity. Consider, for example, *when/where can't I get my licence? what haven't you eaten? what aren't you doing?* There are, however, contexts where a specific pattern of this kind is perfectly 'normal', as for example a teacher checking about an exercise set to be finished in the classroom *who hasn't finished?* Messages such as these are typically interpreted as demand for a specific category of information, not as making some specifiable assumption; indeed it would be difficult to say what assumption can underlie a question of this kind uttered in this kind of context. That said, a good deal of work remains to be done to determine the meanings of negative polarity. For example, it is notable that if a negative polarity is selected with *how*, the question seems to make sense only if the *how* can be interpreted as *why*, as in *how doesn't it work?* In other words there is a difference between the meaning of how depending on whether it colligates with negative polarity or with positive. This is made quite clear from a comparison of the meanings native speakers ascribe to *how does it work?* by contrast with *how doesn't it work?* In the research reported here the latter clause type is treated as realising the semantic feature [... specify: explain: assumptive]. It is very likely to be interpreted as a speaker assumption that the 'it' in question ought to be working.

There is one other semantic context which allows the systemic choice between the options [assumptive] and [nonassumptive] as a consideration of the following extract from dialogue 1 shows:

Extract from Dialogue 1
Karen: (25) how did you get that? ...
Mother: (26) mm?
Karen: (27) how did you get that?* (28) you didn't get out of [?]
Mother: (29) I walked over (30) and got it (31) didn't you see me?
Karen: (32) nup
Mother: (33) you must be blind

Here the mother's message (31) *didn't you see me* would normally be interpreted as implying that Karen must have seen the mother go out, without actually making this claim in as many words. In this respect, it resembles message (6) in dialogue 2. That the mother was making some such assumption is clear from her response to Karen's negative reply to her question. We can read mother's (33) as saying: *anyone who is not blind would have seen me go out; since you are not blind, I assume you saw me go out.* If some such reading of (33) is correct, then there are two alternative environments in either of which the systemic choice between [assumptive] and [nonassumptive] becomes available: the choice applies to those questions where either the feature [explain] has been selected OR to those where the feature [enquire] is selected. Using the semantic features that have been discussed above, the mother's message (31) would be analysed as displaying the following systemic options [confirm: enquire: ask; assumptive].

The systemic option between [assumptive] and [nonassumptive] is not available to questions with the feature [verify]. So if we compare *didn't you see me?* with *you aren't friends with Peter, are you?*, the claim would be that despite the negative polarity of the clause in the second example, the message has no feature [assumptive]: it is not so much that an unvoiced assumption is being made; it is that a thesis is being asserted in as many words and verification is being sought, at the tag end. Before leaving this discussion, it is perhaps worth pointing out that there has been a good deal of interest in the negative as a politeness device. However, examples of [assumptive] questions to which I have drawn attention here would seem to indicate that contrary to such suggestions (Leech 1983; Brown and Levinson 1983), negation in questions at least does not have the function of politeness. In fact it would appear that the semantic value of negation is subject to the environment in which it occurs. But in this respect negation is not exceptional: lexicogrammatical patterns do not have an invariant, core meaning, which persists in some sense in every occurrence of that pattern. Meaning is a matter of semantic context; and what the paradigmatic systemic representation of semantics does is to specify contexts for meaning.

All the above systemic options apply exclusively to questions; in other words there are no statements, commands, offers which may be said to have such features as [confirm] or [apprise] or [explain] or [assumptive] and so on. I now draw attention to some semantic systems that are not exclusively applicable to questions because they relate to other metafunctions. First, another dialogue:

Dialogue 4

Mother: (1) can you try and remind me to ring Pam this afternoon?
Kristy: (2) mm (=YES) (3) why?
Mother: (4) I'm going to ask her if she'll mind you one night next week
Kristy: (5) mm
Mother: (6) 'cause I'm going out to dinner with some of the ladies from the playgroup (7) because Sue is leaving
Kristy: (8) pardon?* (9) pardon?
Mother: (10) I'm going out with some of the ladies (11) because Sue is leaving

Kristy: (12) mm
Mother: (13) did you know that they are going to leave?
Kristy: (14) no
Mother: (15) they've been building a house
Kristy: (16) mm
Mother: (17) oh they haven't been building it (18) somebody else has been building it for them (19) and it's nearly finished (20) and they're going to move to their house in May
Kristy: (21) why in May?
Mother: (22) they're going to wait until the end of the school term
Kristy: (23) mm
Mother: (24) because Cathy goes to school now (25) and then she will change to her new school after **the holidays
Kristy: (26)** mm
Mother: (27) if they'd moved earlier (28) she'd only go to the new school for a week or two (29) and then they'd have holidays you see (30) it would mess it up a bit for her.

In message (13) of dialogue 4, the mother asks Kristy a question, the expected answer to which is *yes/no*. But the question is not *are they going to leave?*, which would be like other questions with the options [ask] that I discussed above. Question (13) is not asking whether a state of affairs obtains; rather it is asking about Kristy's state of knowledge with regard to that state of affairs. Other examples would be *did dad say he would get it for you? do you remember what I told you the other day? did you think you had lost it?*, and so on. Questions such as these have the semantic feature [prefaced]; their [unprefaced] counterparts would be *will dad get it for you? what did I tell you the other day?* and *had you lost it?* A message with the semantic feature [prefaced] is the projection of someone's idea, opinion or locution. When the feature [prefaced] occurs in the environment of a question, the question is not about what the world is like; it is rather an enquiry about someone's – and quite often in my data the addressee's – 'mental representation of that world'. The question is an attempt to elicit what someone knows, believes, thinks, remembers etc. Typically this semantic feature is lexicogrammatically realised by a clause complex, where the logical relation is that of one clause projecting the other(s) (for clause complex and projection, see Halliday 1985a).

The second semantic feature to be discussed here is called [related]. First, I present two examples of messages with this feature, one from dialogue 1, the other from 2:

Dialogue 1

(1) who are my mummy (2) when I was a little baby?

Dialogue 2

(23) when I get old as you (24) and [? Maree likes me] (25) could we marry each other?

In the first example, the message that realises the question and its meanings is (1) *who are my mummy*; the second message is subsidiary to it: it 'acts on' the meaning of (1) making it more precise. The question is not simply: *who was my mummy?* but specifically *who was my mummy at a particular time namely when I was a little baby?* Here message (1) would be analysed as a question that has the semantic feature of being [related]. This feature is lexicogrammatically realised by an actual or potential (i.e., overtly expressed or covert/implicit) expansion; if a clause complex (cf. Halliday 1985a) occurs, then the clause realising the question itself would be non-hypotactic though related by taxis to the other members of the complex. The logical meaning relation between the elaborated question and the messages that elaborate it is varied: it may be causal, conditional, concurrence, and so on.

As is obvious from the above discussion, elaboration is an iterative relation and so it can vary in extent. In phase I data, the most extensive case of elaboration within one speaker turn involved some 21 messages; but there are many where only a single clause realises the feature. The elaboration in the first example is minimal. By contrast, that in the second example is less so, since there the message functioning as question *could we marry each other?* is itself elaborated by messages which are in a complex relation to each other. Like the semantic feature [prefaced], the feature [related] is not exclusively applicable to questions. Thus answers to questions too may be either [related] or [unrelated], as the discussion in the next section will attempt to show.

4.3 Some semantic features of answers

It is certainly true that the asking of questions can itself be a clear indication of the desire to know some new information (though as pointed out above this is not always true); and so questions may be the first step toward knowledge. But by the same token, answers to questions too must play a significant part in the development of a person's knowledge. And just as questions can differ from each other semantically, so can their answers. Here the first issue is whether or not a response is provided: the fact that a question has been asked is no guarantee that it will also receive an answer; on the other hand, the fact that an addressee may begin by saying *I don't know* does not necessarily mean that the question is going to remain un-answered, for a disclaimer of this kind may be followed by another message that does constitute an answer. These facts make it somewhat difficult to calculate the number of answers given. A disclaimer is a kind of reply, but not all questions receive a reply: they may draw no response whatever. This may happen in everyday talk because sometimes the person asking the question 'finds' the answer even while asking it; so sometimes, the addressee may be given no opportunity for replying; sometimes the addressee may be distracted; at other times the addressee may show a complete disregard for the speaker. Most of these phenomena can be exemplified from the following dialogues:

Dialogue 5

Nathan: (1) what does right in the corner mean?** (2) what does right in the corner mean?

Mother: (3) what does right in the corner mean?

Nathan: (4) yeah (5) where's the little bit?

Mother: (6) it means go as far as you can possibly go

Nathan: (7) oh, here's the little bit (SINGING TO SELF) (8) mum, see that's the bit up here, isn't it mum? (9) mum that's the little bit up here, isn't it mum?... (10) mum this is the little bit off there, isn't it mum? ... (11) there mummy, lets –

In dialogue 5, Nathan allows the mother no opportunity for answering his question the first time, but simply goes on to ask the same question again. And having confirmed in message (4) that the mother's understanding of his question was correct, he moves to the next question in (5), to which he himself finds an answer in (7) meanwhile possibly not paying any attention to the mother who just finishes answering (in message 6) the question he had posed first. Piaget might have described these questions by Nathan as 'psuedo-questions' on the ground that he does not seem to care whether or not he has received a response to his question. Nathan goes on to ask a fresh question in (8) which he repeats three times, without receiving an answer, which in view of Piaget would again be classified as a 'psuedo-question'. One might, however, wonder why Nathan repeats his questions if he does not care to know the answer. Or perhaps, Nathan's mother too thinks that Nathan's questions are psuedo-questions and not worth taking seriously. Or, is it possible that Nathan has developed this mode of asking questions precisely because his questions have not been readily answered?

Dialogue 6

Mother: (1) oh hurry up… (2) quick… (3) sit down… (4) you're gonna have your hair washed now… (5) look –
Karen: (6) what? (7) what mummy?…(8) what?
Mother: (9) nothing
Karen: (10) why did you say 'look'?
Mother: (11) alright lay down (12) and I'll wash your hair

In dialogue 6, the mother draws Karen's attention to something by saying (5) *look*—, a message that she leaves incomplete. When Karen wants to know what her attention is being drawn to, she has to ask her mother three times in messages (6, 7 and 8), before she is given an answer. That answer does not satisfy Karen, so she asks another, a more explicit question in (10); that question is ignored by the mother, just as Nathan's last three questions are in dialogue 5. So one vector of variation is whether in the next speaker's turn, the message is [responsive] or not; if it does not respond to the question, this might take the discourse in some other direction. However, even when the message has the feature [responsive], this is not the end of the story: the [responsive] message may be either [adequate] or [inadequate]. Consider dialogue 7:

Dialogue 7

Mother: (1) wait (2) till Daniel comes home or daddy
Pete: (3) he won't come home
Mother: (4) yes he is
Pete: (5) when?
Mother: (6) he's coming home this afternoon
Pete: (7) when is it gonna be this afternoon? (PETE IS CRYING FOR A BALL HE HAS LOST)
Mother: (8) yeah he'll get it this afternoon
Pete: (9) when is it gonna be this afternoon though?
Mother: (10) oh a long time
Pete: (11) oh no
Mother: (12) oh yes (13) oh yes (14) what time is it? (SPEAKING TO SELF)
Pete: (15) can I play with [?]
Mother: (16) no
Pete: (17) oh why not?
Mother: (18) no
Pete: (19) oh (CRIES AGAIN)

In this dialogue, Pete's question in message (5) is answered by the mother in (6) *he's coming home this afternoon*; the answer would be treated as [adequate]. The semantic feature [adequate] is not defined by reference to the objective nature of the world or by any consideration of truth; instead, the definition is semiotic: an answer is said to be [adequate] if it addresses the point of the question. Pete's question demands information about Daniel's time of arrival; the mother's answer specifies a time. Whether Daniel is *really* coming back then or not is beside the point. Similarly, in dialogue 2, when the mother answers Julian's question (30) *why (aren't cousins allowed to marry?)* by saying (31) *cause the law says they're not*, the issue is not whether she has got the NSW legal system right: the answer she provides is capable of being a cause of (30), and addresses the point of that question. Compare this with Pete's mother's answer to Pete's (17) *oh why not?* Her answer cannot be [adequate]: her (18) *no*, when expanded would be something like *you cannot play because you cannot play*. Her answer in (18) fails to address the point of Pete's question; it would thus be said to have the semantic feature [inadequate]. If we go back to dialogue 3, we will find another answer that has the feature [inadequate]: I am referring to Karen's question (3) *why?* to which the mother's answer is just (4) *'cause.*

Just as with questions so also with answers, there are many more semantic choices, but the last one to which attention is drawn here is the feature [related]. This semantic feature has already been discussed above with reference to questions. An example of answers with this semantic feature can be found in dialogue 5, where the mother answers Kristy's (3) *why?* with the following (for this reconstruction, I ignore Kristy's supportive acknowledgment in (5)):

> (4) I'm going to ask her if she'll mind you one night next week (6) 'cause I'm going out to dinner with the ladies from the playgroup (7) because Sue is leaving.

She provides an even more elaborated answer to Kristy's (21) *why in May?*, producing seven messages (22, 24, 25, 27, 28, 29, 30) which together form the answer to that question.

5 Questions and answers: two profiles

As I have pointed out repeatedly, the semantic features discussed above represent a very small proportion of the total set of features in terms of which the messages of everyday dialogue between mothers and children were analysed. But the above description provides sufficient foundation for asking: do mothers vary in the questions they ask and the answers they give? If so, in what respect?

And what significance might one attach to those variations? To answer these questions we needed to carry out a statistical analysis of the linguistically analysed data.

5.1 Principal components analysis

The analysed cases were statistically processed by a Principal Components Analysis (PCA); (for a discussion of this procedure, see Cloran 1989; also in accompanyng CD) the results of the principal components analysis were validated by subjecting the analysed data to a cluster analysis as well[6]. Let me present the results of that part of the PCA which uses as input the semantic features discussed above in terms of their relative frequencies in Mothers' Questions and Mother's Answers (MQMA). The focus of the discussion will be on PC1 only, the loadings for which are represented in table 1.

Table 1: Mothers' questions and mothers' answers [MQMA]

Semantic features	PC1
Q[prefaced]	0.69
A[related]	0.68
A[responsive]	0.67
Q[related]	0.65
A[adequate]	0.56
Q[assumptive]	-0.52
Q[ask]	0.21
Q[confirm]	0.37
Q[explain	0.32
Eigenvalue	2.72
% variance	30.2

As table 1 shows, PC1 accounts for 30% of variance in the data: that is to say, the semantic features that load criterially here are the ones in terms of which the two groups of mothers in this research differed most from each other where the question-answer meanings are concerned. In this PC analysis, all features loading at 0.4 or above were considered criterial, implying that such features are relevant to the variance in the data whereas those with a score below this level on this PCA will make little or no contribution to variance in the analysed data: members of the population do not differ significantly from each other on these non-criterial features in the context of the input package. One aspect of the interpretation of PC1 in table 1 is that the 24 mothers do not differ from each other significantly in the frequency of their selection of the semantic features [ask], [confirm], and [explain]. Whatever difference exists between them would be accounted for by the frequencies of the remaining semantic features in the table. Note that although the table contains only nine semantic features as input, the results are based on more features than just these. This situation comes about because the loading on each feature in the PCA implies a result for its logical 'opposite' as well. So it follows that the features in the table implicate some others which are not mentioned in the table but which are systemically related to those shown in the table. This is true of all the input features, whether they are criterial or not. For example, take the non-criterial feature [ask]: since its frequency was computed as a percentage of all its systemic opposites, this implies that the frequency of the mothers' selection of features [check], [probe], and [reassure] is also non-criterial: mothers do not differ significantly from each other by virtue of their pattern of selection for any of these semantic features. Similarly, since [confirm] was computed as a percentage of [confirm] and [apprise], the non-criteriality of [confirm] implies the same for its opposite term, just as the non-criteriality of [explain] implies the non-criteriality of [specify]. If on the other hand, we take the criterially loading semantic feature [adequate], we can assume that its 'opposite' semantic feature [inadequate] is also relevant: those who score high on PC1 are likely to select the feature [adequate]; they are **not** likely to select the feature [inadequate]. The reverse is true of the low scoring group.

5.2 Profile one: the mothers

It is obvious from the above comments that the mothers do not differ significantly in respect of *any of the systemic choices that are exclusively applicable to questions* (see section 4.2). There is one single exception to this generalisation. That exception is the semantic feature [assumptive], which *does* load criterially, the implication being that the pattern of its selection will contribute to variation in the data. However, note that the loading is negative at -0.52. When the loading of a feature is negative, this implies that those who score high on the PC are *not* likely to select the feature in question. So mothers who score high on PC1 will typically produce questions that are not [assumptive].

Two other semantic features pertaining to questions load criterially: [prefaced] and [related]. The loading of both features is positive, at 0.69 and 0.65 respectively, implying that mothers scoring high on this PC are very likely to ask questions which have these semantic features. Thus so far as questions are concerned, only these three semantic features will account for variance in the data: high scoring mothers' questions will be typically [prefaced], [related] and typically they will **not** be [assumptive]. As to the features relevant to answers, the table shows criterial loading for [responsive] (0.67), [related]

(0.68), and [adequate] (0.56). Since the loading is positive, the implication is that the high scoring mothers' answers would typically have these semantic characteristics.

5.3 Interpreting PC1

An interesting observation about this result is that the high scoring mothers' question answer strategies – the set of six semantic features as a whole – can be explained by one powerful principle, namely the principle of individuation. According to this principle, each of us as an individual is a unique being, and the intentions, beliefs, opinions of each one of us are private to each; they are, in principle, inaccessible to our conversational *others* without verbal mediation. Unless relatively specific and explicit verbal exchanges occur, the *other's* subjectivity cannot be accessed: one cannot assume a *reflexive relation*, acting on the presumption that the other is just like us, therefore fully knowable. This principle will explain why the mothers' questions are the way they are; and why their answers have the attributes that they have. This statement is further developed below.

I have argued (see section 4.2) that a [prefaced] question seeks not so much to know what the world is like as it seeks to know what someone else's view is. Those who habitually produce questions with this semantic feature may be said to be 'giving off' (Goffman 1967) a meaning of a more abstract order. They may be implying that *access to others' beliefs, opinions, attitudes, and knowledge etc. depends on what is/has been explicitly communicated; another's subjectivity is not knowable without specific locutions.* If so, then it is reasonable to expect that such speakers would tend to display explicitness and specificity in their own sayings.

The feature [prefaced] is a direct means of eliciting what someone else thinks, believes, judges to be the case while the feature [related] makes the meaning of the elaborated message more precise by adding some relevant modifying information to it. It seems logical then to expect that the speakers who are more inclined to select the feature [prefaced] should also be the ones who are inclined to select the feature [related]. And this is precisely the pattern ascribed by the statistical result to those mothers who score high on PC1. We may hypothesise then that the high scoring mothers' ways of asking questions show them to be governed by the underlying principle of individuation – a point that was made a long time ago by Bernstein (1971a, b, c) though not formulated in these linguistic terms. But what about the negative loading of the feature [assumptive]?

The feature [assumptive] would be used by a speaker who feels justified in believing that she knows the other interactant so well as to assume knowledge of the likely, normal, and/or desirable behaviour on their part. Messages such as *why don't you love Rosemary? why won't you kiss me? why don't you like nana? didn't you see me? haven't you finished your tea yet?* appear mundane and insignificant; but they add up to building an orientation to a certain perspective: the speaker is implying that there are commonly accepted ways of being, thinking, reacting, and sensing that are known to everyone, including the speaker and the addressee. It is in the fitness of things that both the speaker and the speaker's conversational other would know without needing to be told such obvious facts as who should be loved, liked, kissed, and what the pacing of an activity should be. And since the code of conduct is self-evident, there is little need for explicit verbal communication. If this is a correct interpretation of the semantic feature [assumptive] then this feature runs counter to the features [prefaced] and [related]; and if that is so, then we ***should*** find that those who habitually select the last two features do not select the feature [assumptive]. The negative loading of this semantic feature on PC1 is in keeping with this expectation.

Following this line of reasoning, there exists no great mystery about the positive criterial loading of the semantic features relevant to answers, since those three features quite clearly enhance the possibility of initiating and maintaining verbal communication. The questions are relatively explicit, ensuring a good chance of the successful initiation of communication. A message with the feature [responsive] in the answer will contribute to topic maintenance; if in addition, answers also have the property of being [adequate] and [related], then the answers of the high scoring mothers ensure that the unique individuals can 'come together'; being unique would not preclude the possibility of knowing the other; their daily interaction can reveal their selves to each other: languaging is an essential aspect of their being.

There is an inherent problem in this social construction of the unique individual. Our experience of the world forces us to recognise at least some measure of *the non-uniqueness of individuals*; since, to a large extent, the success of our actions depends on calibration with others, we stand in need of *reflexivity* – that is to say, we need to know what the other is like; if each individual remains unique and un-knowably different, then social existence becomes highly problematic if not impossible. Knowledge of the other is necessary not simply for engaging in concerted action; the latter so overtly require cooperation from others, that the need for calibration would be granted by even the most confirmed individualist. But those actions and strivings which do not call for overt cooperation from others, are still far from being ego-limited; by *ego-limited* action I mean actions that can be taken without any regard for the other, to which the other's opinions, attitudes and evaluations etc. are entirely immaterial, so that the entire structure of the action is limited simply by the ego of the actor[7]. In this sense, then, almost every aspect of our social being – our decisions, actions, seemingly natural impulses and dispositions, as well as our self-esteem, our 'face' as Goffman (1967) put it – are, as it were, our social others reflected in us.

But such calibration with others depends on the presence of a reflexive relation; its roots clearly lie in access to others' subjectivity, in the possibility of making assumptions about what they believe, what they know, how they will react and so on. If more of our social being requires calibration with the other than not, then for us to continue as a member of the community engaging in its ways of beings, doing and saying (Hasan 1984a, c), the socially constructed unique individual has to become a relatively open book that can be read with ease. Herein lies the inherent paradox in the social construction of the uniqueness of individuals: it is a fragile concept, maintained at the expense of considerable energy through intense semiotic mediation. The maternal behaviour delineated by PC1 in table 1 shows some of the properties of that semiotic mediation. The semantic features of questions and answers by the mothers who score high on PC1 construct their children as unique individuals, whose subjectivities can only be reached through such verbal processes. What purpose is served by such social construction of individuality, in the social economy of human societies, is a separate question, which cannot be raised here for lack of space.

While, hopefully the above discussion explains the principle which underlies the behaviour of the high scoring mothers, the discussion also shows clearly that subscribing to this principle is not the only route to reflexivity, and that reflexivity is a crucial requirement of social existence. The mothers who do not score high on PC1 are mothers who find the primary source of reflexive relation in the shared experience of practical living: for them the basis for assuming knowledge of the other lies not in the verbally revealed selves, but in the shared patterns of practical existence; what creates and maintains reflexivity for these mothers is not talk as such, it is the experience of living and sharing contexts as members of a collectivity. If the former group of mothers subscribe to the principle of individuation, acting as if hardly anything can be taken for granted between persons, then the latter group of mothers (those who do not score high on PC1) subscribe to the principle of naturalised reflexivity, acting as if most things can be taken for granted between persons who share the contexts of living with each other. These are two different orientations to what appears relevant: neither is better or worse; each is maintained at some expense.

It now remains to ask whether these two groups of mothers who are differentiated by their semantic choices are also differentiated by some definite social attribute. PCA can point to an answer by 'plotting' subjects *vis-à-vis* each other by reference to their scores. For each PC that is isolated by this statistical procedure, the analysis assigns each of the 24 mothers a cumulative score by reference to the total package of the features used as input. Using this score, the subjects can be positioned *vis-à-vis* each other. Figure 1 presents such a plotting of the subjects by reference to two factors – PC1 and PC2. The relative position of the mothers on PC1 is indicated on the horizontal axis, with the lowest scores on the left and the highest at the right end; their relative position on PC2 is shown on the vertical axis, the lowest at the bottom and the highest at the top. The letters L and H stand for LAP and HAP subject respectively. Figure 1 shows many more HAP mothers than LAP ones positioned in the right half on the horizontal axis; thus mothers' scores on PC1 correlate with their social class position (HAP mothers > LAP mothers: $p < .0003$). HAP mothers favour individualism; they prefer to (re-)constitute non-verbal experience verbally, making it self-conscious and open to reflection in the process. LAP mothers favour collectivism; they prefer to rely on shared practical experience as the constructor of their conversational other.

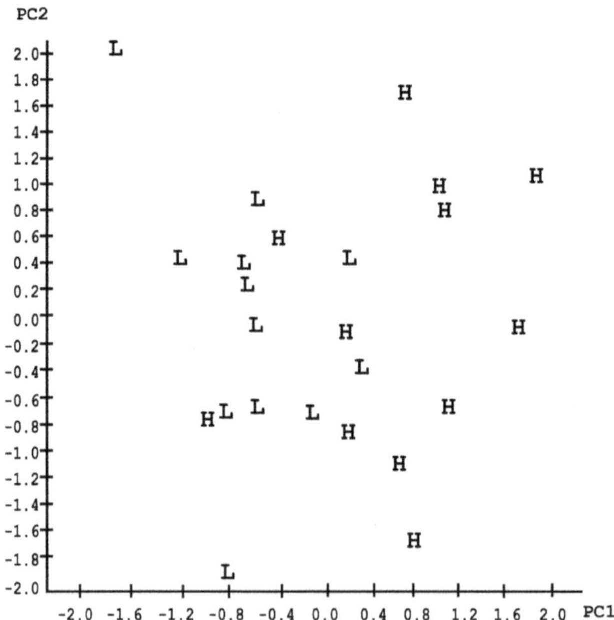

Figure 1: Mothers' position by social group on MQMA

5.4 Profile two: the children

The above discussion has established a significant difference in the question answer strategies of the mothers from the two social groups. It is legitimate to ask: how is this finding relevant to the question I posed in opening this paper? In my view, there are two distinct perspectives from which this question can be answered: one at the level of *what*, and the other at the level of *how*.

To take the first perspective first: there is the widely accepted, and no doubt largely correct, claim that questions are designed to find out something: one learns from a question in as much as the question is answered adequately. When typically questions are not answered – i.e., the semantic features [responsive] and [adequate] have a low frequency in the environment of answers – it would seem reasonable to suggest that in such interactions, less learning would be taking place than would occur in environments where these features have a higher frequency in answers. This way of approaching questions is oriented toward the experiential component of the meaning of those messages which function as questions and answers. And while it is true that many of the mothers' and children's questions are in themselves entirely mundane, concerned with highly local matters such as what jumper to wear, where the school shoes are, or whether daddy is back yet etc., it is also true that even the most simple question can be, and often is, used as the occasion for providing information that is not local in its character. In other words, some mothers do often go beyong the information sought. So for example, when Carol asks a question which in Piaget's view might have quite a dubious status as a question: *do pussy cats die when people die?*, her mother answers the child's question in a way that explains something about the principle of mutability (Hasan 1984a); Kristy's mother describes the life-cycle of a moth, apropos of a question about the death of a specific moth; the same dialogue takes them through to a discussion of the nutrition cycle; on another occasion, the nature of climatic changes is discussed (see Butt 1989b); Janet's mother informs her about criteria for species identification; Steve's mother explains why a mandarin tree is not likely to grow from a pip that comes from the mandarin Steve is now eating (Cloran 1999); and so on. In short, children's questions present a context in which mothers can take on the role of an instructor (Hasan 1986a); it is abundantly clear from the data of this research that some mothers do construct systems of knowledge – or if that seems too pompous a term for such modest beginnings – at least they begin to lay the foundation of such knowledge, initiating the child in 'knowledging discourse'. But there are at least two vectors of variation here: first, quite obviously, in those cases where mothers typically either do not answer, or give answers that are inadequate (e.g., tautological), such foundations of knowledge are not being laid; and secondly, mothers differ in the sort of knowledge that they choose to talk about at some length.

I do not wish to under-estimate the importance of the above kind of difference in learning through everyday talk. But it is easy to exaggerate that importance, and I suspect that this has been the case in education, where debates have centred around the absence of this pattern of language or that; this piece of information or the other. To me it seems that the second perspective – that of asking what, if anything, is learned by how questions are answered – is perhaps equally important, if not more so. But this aspect has gone largely un-noticed, perhaps because its character is not easily examinable. To explain what I mean by these comments, let me go back to the example of an interaction in which typically questions are not responded to; or if they are, the answer tends to be inadequate. Looking at this situation as one of learning *what* – i.e. learning some item of information – one tends to regard this kind of interaction as a situation of non-learning: I suggest that this is a *mis-description*. What we do with language, never ends in nothing. And this is true here too. The children learn something from the typical absence or irrelevance of what mothers say apropos of their questions: one thing they might learn is that questions are not an effective mode of learning; that they are not a context for the construction of systems of knowledge. A why-question may be the foundation of pure knowledge as philosophers and logicians have proposed. But if a *why* typically draws no answer, or if it draws the simple response *'cause*, then it is really unreasonable to expect that the recipient of such responses will go on believing in the efficacy of *why* as a mode of learning. Is the asking of *why?* so instinctive, so ingrained that no matter what our practical experience, we are impelled to ask that question as we are impelled to breathe? I very much doubt that.

In describing how 'the tree of knowledge' grows – how systems of human knowledge evolve, maintaining a momentum of their own – Popper (1979) suggests the possibility of knowledge 'without a knowing subject': what he is drawing attention to is the fact that as the systems of knowledge grow, and as they become part of a community's heritage, they become available to other members of the society; they exist independent of individual minds; as systems of knowledge they have an existence which is quite unaffected by individual consciousness; there inhere problems in those systems, potentialities which may or may not be discovered by us at some stage of our evolution. Quite irrespective of that, the potential of its growth is there, whether it is being exploited or not. By analogy, I suggest that in the experience of everyday living, a great deal of teaching goes on 'without a knowing, conscious teacher': the semiotic mediation that Vygotsky talked about is not limited to only that interaction which is consciously undertaken with reference to some specific learning problem valued highly in our educational systems. That the children learn from their mothers is evident from the fact that when the children's own questions and answers are examined, using the same semantic features as input, the result very closely resembles those of the mothers' questions and answers which have been discussed above. This can be seen from table 2, which presents the results of the PCA for children's questions and children's answers, using the same features as input.

Table 2: Children's questions, children's answers

Semantic features	**PC1**
A[related]	0.74
Q[related]	0.63
Q[confirm]	0.60
Q[prefaced]	0.58
A[adequte]	0.55
Q[assumptive]	-0.51
A[responsive]	0.34
Q[ask]	-0.12
Q[explain]	0.00
Eigenvalue	2.37
%variance	26.4

A comparison of tables 1 and 2 will show close similarities in the structure of PC1 for both (for more discussion, see previous chapter): the main point of difference is that in the context of children's questions and answers, the high scoring children are very likely to ask yes/no questions as opposed to who/what questions[8] while with mothers, no exclusive features of questions were relevant, apart from [assumptive]. Here, in table 2, we find that high scoring children are likely to ask questions that like their mothers' questions are [prefaced], [related], and **not** [assumptive]; like their mothers, the children too would tend to be [responsive], provide answers that are [adequate] and [related].

Figure 2 plots the children's position by reference to their scores analogous to the way mothers' positions are plotted in figure 1. As in figure 1, so here the significant social variable is social class: HAP children score higher than LAP children (HAP children > LAP children: p <009).

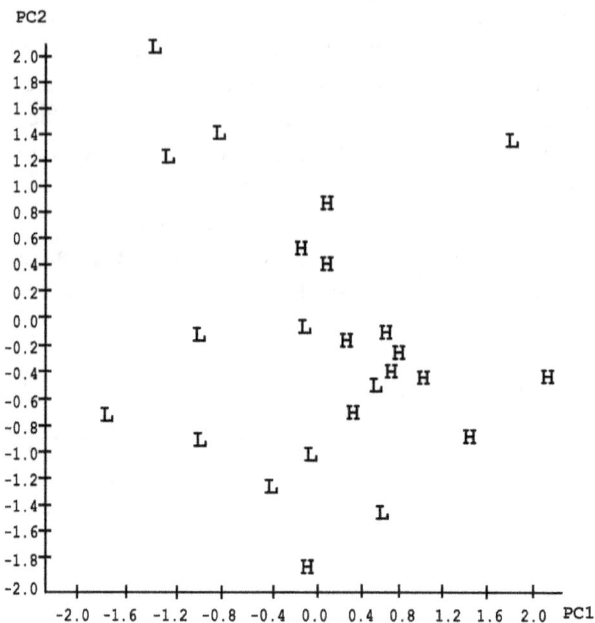

Figure 2: Children's position by social group on CQCA

I interpret this result as evidence that everyday interaction teaches, despite Popper's derisory remarks about commonsense knowledge. The children are not simply learning *what* or failing to learn *what* – a matter very much easier to control and to change – but they are also being schooled in *how* to ask and *how* to *tell*: they are learning modes of interrogating the community's existing knowledge so as to create that which Popper might describe as 'objective knowledge'. And to the extent that their experience of everyday interaction is different, to that extent this aspect of their learning is different. If the results of this research are treated as indicative of what actually happens in life, then the question is not whether or not we learn from everyday talk to infer, to surmise, to extrapolate from what we know; the question is not whether our experience of interaction creates in our mental dispositions or orientation to certain orders of relevance (Bernstein 1971b, 1971c, 1987). The *real* question is whether the difference in orientation to individualism or to collectivism discussed above bears any relevance to engagement with objective knowledge. It is this question the answer to which would link my findings to the question of participation in objective knowledge.

An overwhelming consensus exists among scholars that the possibility of objective knowledge is predicated on belief in the efficacy of enquiry, in the development of an orientation toward precise formulation; above all, a commitment to semiotic mediation, rather than a reliance on practical everyday experience. That teachers begin to inculcate these features in their young pupils from the very early stages appears to be the case from data collected in the second phase of this research (Hasan 2004b, 1988). Teachers questions tend to be an exaggerated version of the HAP mothers questions, displaying a high frequency of the feature [prefaced], and almost entirely eschewing the semantic feature [assumptive] (see chapter 4 here for detail). The answers they evaluate as 'good' must at the least be [adequate]; the extent to which they insist on providing proof for assertion, in getting the children to make hypothetical deduction from what is to what might be – all of these features are features that the learner will need to develop: at this abstract level teaching is not simply the teaching of *what*; it is in fact what Bernstein calls the construction of the pedagogical subject, the development of a disposition, the creating of an orientation toward how the what has to be constituted; in short, it is the shaping of consciousness. If the orientation to negotiating information differs markedly, the teaching and learning of a specific element of knowledge cannot be treated as a straight forward matter. It does not seem too far fetched to suggest that a child who brings to the school a disposition that is already congruent with the disposition the schools are aiming to create stands a better chance of succeeding in constituting the *what* of knowledge in ways that through the ages have been considered essential to it. The expression very much in fashion today in educational discourse is 'equality of educational opportunity': I want to put it to you that the concept of equality in human societies – which are typically non-egalitarian – is a problematic one. It requires much deeper reflection than it has received so far: for one thing, equality might not consist in giving everyone the same thing where the thing given is biased in favour of some recipients only.

6 Conclusion

I opened this discourse with a question: does the experience of language in everyday interaction bear any relation to learning and to knowledge? In attempting to answer that question, I have suggested that there is good reason to believe that where ways of saying and meaning differ there learning by experience will differ; that what is learnt from questions and answers is not identical in all cases: the difference permeates both the learning of *what* and *how*. I suggested that the *how* difference could be more serious than the *what* difference, since the how difference creates a disposition towards both the experiential content of knowledge, and towards the efficacious means of participation in the discourse of knowledge, on which depends the 'acquisition' of the content of knowledge. The differences in habitual modes of interaction give questions and answers different values: one form of interaction facilitates effective participation in the kind of knowledge that is celebrated in schools. Of course, we could change the nature of knowledge instead (as implied by Labov 1969); but in decades following that valiant suggestion, I have seen no moves in that direction. A pertinent question is do we know how to change the nature of the discourses of knowledge, so that it becomes neutral, permitting all participants to participate in it on equal terms, no matter what habits of the mind they bring to it.

In opening this conference, our Convener Mike McCausland, described the conference as one 'about crossing boundaries'; the official address from the host country emphasised that the mastery of communicative means contributes to thinking, cognition and learning. Many of my colleagues, in discussing multicultural education here, have pointed out how important it is for teachers to understand and familiarise themselves with the cultures to which their pupils belong. Candlin talked about 'learner-centred' teaching and learning. In closing this paper I would like to raise three questions that link my paper to these themes, by raising three questions which seem to link the present discussion with their recommendations:

i) What kinds of boundaries do we willingly recognise in our complex societies? And how do we propose to cross those boundaries the existence of which we are not willing to grant in the first place?

ii) Why is it legitimate and desirable for a teacher to try and understand, say, the Japanese culture so as to make that student's learning effective, when it is not legitimate to recognise, much less to try to understand, the sub-cultural differences within a complex culture such as Australia – particularly when the sub-culture in question is that of the less privileged segments of population in our community?

iii) How is it possible to create a learner-centred learning situation, when there seems to be no valid account of how learners differ? Is it possible to produce a learner-centred curriculum which will suit every learner? Could this be a contradiction in terms?

My aim in raising these questions is not to criticise in order to negate the value of my colleagues' suggestions: it is, rather, to try to understand how my interest in education is linked to the interests of my other colleagues in the same field of education – how the teaching and learning of specific subjects and the orientation to learning and knowledge through the experiences of life might be related to each other.

Notes

1 The title of the conference was The International Conference on Language Education: Interaction and Development, held in Ho Chi Minh City, Vietnam March 30-April 1, 1991; Convenors Thao Lê and Mike McCausland, University of Tasmania.

2 The research was funded by the Australian Research Council and the Macquarie University Research Grant from 1983–1987. My thanks are due first and foremost to Carmel Cloran who assisted with this research throughout its entire duration; I thank also David Butt, Michael Oerlemans, Rhondda Fahey for helping at various stages of the research. For help with data entry and retrieval, I am grateful to Anne Eyeland (Behavioural Sciences), Harry Purvis, and John Telec (Speech Hearing and Language Research Centre, all at Macquarie University). For advice about statistical processing I am indebted to Allan Taylor (Behavioural Sciences, Macquarie). These generous colleagues have played an important part in the successful conclusion of this research.

3 I have presented arguments supporting (a) the criteria for social class demarcation, and (b) the decision to treat the family as a unit implicated in the social class position (see chapters 4, 5 and 7 of this volume). Recently Gordon Wells has objected (oral communication) that the data of this research is not suitable for making any claims about social class variation since it does not represent the entire range of the gradation of professional autonomy. I believe this objection is spurious: to accept this would be like agreeing that one could not profitably compare or discuss the differences between the language of 5 year olds and that of 12 year olds unless one compared all the intervening chronological stages in between.

4 While the semantic network prepared for the analysis of the research data is far from exhaustive, it is still too extensive to be presented within the scope of a paper such as this. Chapters 3–5 of this volume present some fragments of the system network pertaining to questions, response, while Hasan (1992a) is a more detailed discussion of semantic options relevant in demanding goods and services.

5 The transcription conventions used here are as follows:

(1)	numbers in parentheses refer to message number in consecutive order in the dialogue;
(LAUGHING)	words in capitals are contextual comments based on the context/co-text;
**abc	double asterisk followed by words indicates the beginning of overlap; overlap similarly identified in next speaker's turn;
[?abc]	items so enclosed were not readily audible; interpretation is based on context/cotext;

[?]	this inaudible stretch could not be interpreted even with help from context/cotext;
...	a pause greater than would be normal between such (parts of) utterances;
ab?**	speaker did ask a question but allowed no time for response before proceeding.

6 I acknowledge with thanks the advice and assistance given by Peter Freebody (University of New England) for cluster analysis of the data, which though not presented here corroborates the PC analysis.

7 And even this leaves the problem of how an ego becomes what it is. This is too complex a debate to introduce here. The interested reader is referred to the work of such scholars as Bernstein, Bourdieu, Cicourel, Halliday, Luria, Mead, Vygotsky on the one hand and on the other hand, to the work of Cazden, Inhelder, Lenneberg, Piaget, and many others.

8 I have discussed the significance of this difference in chapter 5.

III

Social hierarchies and the concept of rationality

7 Meaning in sociolinguistic theory [1992]

1 Introduction

In *The Study of Language in its Social Context*, Labov (1972b: 185) draws attention to a contradiction between principle and practice in the Saussurean model of language:

> Saussure conceived of linguistics as one part of 'une science qui etudie la vie des signes au sein de la vie sociale'. Yet curiously enough, the linguists who work within the Saussurean tradition (and this includes the great majority) do not deal with social life at all: they work with one or two informants in their offices, or examine their knowledge of langue. Furthermore, they insist that explanations of linguistic facts be drawn from other linguistic facts, not from any 'external' data on social behaviour.

This situation leads to what Labov calls the 'Saussurean paradox'. The aim of this chapter is to report on a sociolinguistic research which draws attention to a somewhat similar contradiction in the Labovian paradigm of sociolinguistics. As Labov has pointed out repeatedly, the consequence of Saussure's limiting of linguistics to the study of *langue* was 'to exclude the study of social behaviour or the study of speech'. I believe I am right in saying that throughout the chapter to which the above extract belongs as well as in most of his writings in the sixties and mid-seventies, Labov consistently leads his reader to conclude that such an outcome is to be deplored, claiming that the basic data for any form of general linguistics ought to be 'language as it is used by native speakers communicating with each other in everyday life' (Labov 1972b: 184), and that (*loc.cit.* 187):

> ... it is difficult to avoid the common-sense conclusion that the object of linguistics must ultimately be the instrument of communication used by the speech community; and if we are not talking about that language, there is something trivial in our proceedings.

Respect for naturally occurring communication is thus evident in Labov's work, but language as it is used by native speakers in communicating with each other is not simply a patterned flow of phonological or morpho-syntactic forms; it is, in fact, first and foremost an attempt at the exchange of meanings. From the point of view of communication, the level of meaning is, then, as integral a part of language as are the levels of wording and sound, and like these other levels, it, too, is subject to change and evolution, even if the rate of such change and evolution might be different (Hudson 1980; Romaine 1984). Due to its similarities to other levels in these respects, it would seem reasonable to suggest that the possibility of sociolinguistic variation is at least as open at the semantic level as it is for the syntactic one (Labov and Weiner 1977). However, there has been a refusal in Labovian sociolinguistics, to grant this possibility: it has been simply assumed that all sociolinguistic variation can be described as 'variable ways of saying the same thing' (Labov 1978a).

In this chapter, I shall report some results from an empirical research which throw doubt on this easy assumption, and raise some serious questions about sociolinguistic theory. In presenting this material and the arguments based on it, I shall use the textual strategy of *re-contextualisation* (Atkinson 1985; Bernstein 1986), borrowing from Labov's sociolinguistic studies (e.g., Labov 1966a, b, 1968, 1969, 1972a, d, 1973, 1978a, b; Weiner and Labov 1983 etc.). The discerning reader will find many echoes of Labov throughout this chapter, though the majority of overt citations are from that well-known piece to which I have already referred above, namely, *The Study of Language in its Social Context*. By using this method, I hope to highlight the ways in which my research has faithfully followed the methodology recommended by Labov for the study of sociolinguistic variation. This similarity in methodology will, perhaps, draw attention more forcefully to a significant point of contrast: the results of this research reject the description of sociolinguistics as variable ways of saying the same thing. My claim is that as Saussure limited the domain of linguistics, so also Labov limits the domain of sociolinguistics, which reduces it to 'social diagnostics', ignoring deeper issues of the role of language in the creation, maintenance and change of social institutions. This implies that the mistaken conception of language as 'form for the sake of form' continues. It needs to be pointed out that these limitations draw Labov into self-contradictions: for example, on the one hand he wishes to suggest that sociolinguistics is not 'something apart from "linguistics" ' (Labov 1972: 183). On the other hand, because of the narrowing of sociolinguistics as defined by Labov, the field cannot be equated with linguistics. Or if it is, then one would have to concede that 'as a theory of language this approach is seriously defective' (Labov 1972b: 200).

The organisation of the chapter falls naturally into two parts, each with one dominant thread. The first part lays an empirical foundation on the basis of which some theoretical questions are raised in the second part. As I begin, it will soon become evident that an empirical fact is not like Newton's apple: in the absence of theory, a fact might not necessarily hit scholarly consciousness. Often something assumes the status of a fact because one has a hypothesis; it is naive to assume that if we could just be empirical enough to take care of the facts, theory will follow faithfully. Throughout this chapter the two threads of fact and theory will certainly intertwine.

2 Part one: empirical foundations

This first part presents a brief account of the empirical research mentioned above. The focus of the research, relevant to this chapter, is highlighted, and important aspects of research methodology are described, including the framework for the semantic analysis of language in use. Finally one fragment of the results obtained is presented, before moving to part two.

2.1 The focus of the research

In giving a title to the research project under focus[1], I have followed the useful Australian tradition of finding a transparent descriptive name, which in its literalness provides some idea of the nature of the research problems. The title I chose was The Role of Everyday Talk between Mothers and Children in Establishing Ways of Learning. As an enquiry into the relationship between ways of talking and ways of learning, the interests of this research reach out into a wide area, of which the following three need mention:

i) the relationship between everyday language use and socialisation (e.g., Bernstein 1971a, 1973, 1975a, 1982, 1986, 1987a, b; Halliday 1972, 1973a, 1974a, 1975a, b, c, 1976a, b).

ii) the relationship of language to cognitive development (Luria 1976; Mead 1934; Vygotsky 1962, 1978; Whorf 1956).

iii) the role of language in human evolution, what Medawar (1982) refers to as *exogenetic evolution* i.e., the non-hereditary transmission of successful adaptive strategies from one generation to the next (Popper 1979; Popper and Eccles 1977).

Needless to say, these three areas are not unrelated; they are concerned with the same general issue, namely the semiotic origin of human conduct. I mention these momentous areas of enquiry first, to place my own study in its scholarly context, but secondly and more importantly as an indication of what it might mean to conduct the study of language in its social context, a theme to which I return in my concluding remarks.

There are certain advantages in the way the research title was formulated: it shows that the study must focus 'upon language in use' (Labov 1972b: 183) within a well-recognised 'social context of the speech community' (Labov 1972b: 184). Further, and equally important, it narrows the vast area covered by the expression focus on language in use: whether or not everyday talk between mothers and children plays any part in establishing children's ways of learning, it is quite certain that the specific characteristics of the mothers' vowels and consonants could not bear any direct relevance to this issue. Rather, if such a relationship could be shown to exist, then the relevant aspect of mother's talk is far more likely to be the semantic one. We are concerned then not with just any aspect of language in use, but specifically with what characterises it semantically.

Because the focus had to be on the semantic analysis of the mother-child talk, the research presented a framework within which the issue of the possibility of semantic variation could be empirically examined. And while there are other aspects of this research which I believe are germane to sociolinguistics of the kind that I believe is needed to throw light on the nature of human language, for the purposes of this chapter, it is the possibility of semantic variation that forms the central concern. It is from this point of view that I proceed to describe who the speakers were, how the data of everyday talk was collected, and what categories were used for the semantic analysis of the data.

2.2 About the subjects

Where in his pioneering text, Saussure (1966) had presented everyday talk as chaotic, un-orderly, and unpredictable, Labov (1966a) in his seminal study, conclusively established the largely predictable and orderly character of everyday talk. The orderly heterogeneity of everyday talk makes itself manifest as soon as the speaking individuals are placed within the context of their speech community. The factors which bring order into the potentially chaotic data of language as it is used in everyday life are the socially identified attributes of speakers, for example their social class position, their sex, their age and kin relation. The explanatory efficacy of these social parameters has been admitted in many studies (e.g., Horvath 1985; Lieberson 1966; Romaine 1982b; Scherer and Giles 1979; Shuy, Wolfram and Riley 1967; Trudgill 1974, 1978, to mention but a few names at random). In selecting speakers for my enquiry I have naturally kept these parameters in mind. As is obvious from the research title, the kin relation is already built into the project design: the speakers are mothers and their children. The research subjects were 24 mother-child dyads; 12 of the children were female and 12 male. The decision to use only 24 dyads was governed by the material resources available, though encouraged by the suggestion that 'basic patterns of class stratification, … emerge from samples as small as 25 speakers' (cf. Labov 1972b: 204; Shuy, Wolfram and Riley 1967). Because the focus of the study was on the relevance of a mother's ways of meaning to her child's ways of learning, it was important to ensure that the child's experience of participation in meaning should be largely with the mother. This meant selecting children who as yet had no regular significant contacts with other socialising agencies such as peer group, neighbourhood, or the school. Accordingly, the age of child population ranged between 3 years 6 months to 4 years 2 months, the mean age being 3;8. All mothers were born and brought up in Australia; their mother tongue was English and, in general, they did not have any experience of living in other cultures. But what about social hierarchy?

2.3 Social class: an excursus

Sociolinguistic studies have generally supported Labov's (1966b: 12) claim that:

> … socio-economic class is one of the most important elements of social structure in complex urban communities, and correlation with the linguistic variables immediately shows a strong relation.

And yet, a newcomer to the field of sociolinguistics would be somewhat surprised to find the 'keep off' signs that surround the concept of social class. Consider, for example, the following comment from Trudgill (1974: 35):

> The whole question of social class is in fact somewhat controversial, especially since sociologists are not agreed as to the exact nature, definition or existence of social classes.

Without more specific references, it is difficult to comment on the claim that sociologists (as a whole?) 'are not agreed as to the … existence of social class'; and as for the problems in defining and determining its nature, social class as a crucial sociological concept does not appear to be very different from many crucial concepts in other disciplines. Take for example the concept of meaning in linguistics. In one of the recent publications, Barwise (1988: 23) opens a debate by asking 'Where is meaning anyway, in the mind of the speaker or author, or in the world shared by a speaker and his audience and an author and his reader?'

The entire introduction of that volume (Eco, Santambrogio, and Violi 1988) wherein Barwise's question occurs is taken up with the discussion of the different conceptions of meaning that are entertained in linguistics. This, however, does not mean that in 'doing' linguistics one could, and much less that one should, avoid the controversial notion of meaning, or even that one should view with suspicion anything that is contaminated by the idea of meaning. To me the notion of social class appears comparable. In Connell's rather effective formulation (1983: 148), whatever the philosophical uncertainties about social class, 'people are constantly doing class' all around us, with consequences that are hardly short of terrifying.

This disdain for social class in sociolinguistics deserves a separate investigation; here, let me simply agree with Robinson (1979: 214) that the casualness with which the term has been used in our studies of language in its social context is, to say the least, unsatisfactory. Class has been equated with the categorial referents of occupation, and/or income and/or education; this has yielded that handy, somehow completely un-controversial acronym of Socio-Economic-Status, called SES that everyone can now use without a qualm of conscience. We have not considered it necessary to look into either the mutual relations between these three terms, or the relation of this trinity to any theory of society. To do this, we would have needed some familiarity with sociological debates. However, we have been assured by our intellectual leaders in the field that the tedious business of crossing the gulf between sociology and linguistics is quite expendable (Labov 1978b). Little wonder that our perception of social class suffers from objectification in the Whorfian sense of the term: the parameters of SES are seen as naming certain objects whose value in the world remains constant; they thus become things, containers in which individuals can be placed. We can then quite legitimately raise the question: should women be *in* the lower SES, if they have no occupation, no income? Should children be in any SES, if they have no *location* on any of these parameters?

There may well be sociologist who as Trudgill maintains doubt the existence of social class, but even a nodding acquaintance with the sociological theories of those who do use such concepts would have revealed that this objectification has led to quite the wrong conception of social class. On the criterion of observational adequacy alone, it would be better to think of membership in social class as the possibilities open for participation in social processes. And with that view, it would be hard to maintain that the bread-winners' position in the social division of labour plays no part in specifying the possibilities open to the members of their family. After all, not every aspect of the behaviour of women and children can be explained simply by their desire to *accommodate* their providers – and let me hasten to add that there is nothing at all simple about the fact of any human being accommodating any other: a large part of such behaviours are a subject's response to the fact that, like any other identifiable unit in a society, s/he too plays a part in maintaining and altering the system of processes and institutions to which we refer as *society*. When a report commissioned by the Australian Commonwealth on poverty and opportunity, claims that 'child assaults occur more often among families living in poverty, six to eight times more often' (*Sydney Morning Herald* April 16, 1988), it seems strange to claim that children belong to no social class, because they themselves are neither poor nor rich. Here is another segment of the same serialised report (Sydney Morning Herald April 6 1988):

> ... for the death of every professional or executive, there were two deaths among unskilled or manual labouring workers. One study shows that death rates among men in the class with the lowest occupational prestige were 1.54 times higher for cancer than for men from the highest class; 4.88 times higher for mental disorders; and 2.86 times higher for accidents... Other studies have shown a correlation between suburban stillbirth rates and socioeconomic status of the suburb... women in poorer areas had a much lower rate of pap smear checks, and the immunization of children was related to the educational level of their mothers.

The report of the commission is remarkable in the extent to which it shows the essential interdependencies of human destiny, the extent to which an individual's position in the social universe is defined not by what is *in* that individual, but by that individual's relation to others in the community, and by the possibilities of his/her action, non-action and exploitation.

I am not convinced that any method of creating groupings of human beings – be it social networks, ethnic or racial demarcations – will avoid the issue of hierarchisation. Social class as a term refers to a complex, and variously interpreted, principle of hierarchisation. Following the reasoning articulated very clearly in Bernstein (1986), whose logically pursued steps in the argument are crucial to the central problems raised in my research, I have found myself in agreement with Poulantzas (1981: 138–39) in maintaining that 'a social class is defined by its place in the ensemble of social practices, i.e., by its place in the social division of labour as a whole'.

Since 'place in the social division of labour as a whole' is in the last resort related to the concept of power as defined by Lukes (1974), I have attempted to devise a method by which the family's place in the division of labour is identified by reference to the breadwinner's ability to exercise power in his/her place of work. The responsibility for attaching such weight to this parameter is entirely mine, and I do not assume that any of the three scholars named above necessarily agrees with my approach. In effect, my suggestion is that the answer to a two-part question would be crucial in identifying the position of each family from which the mother child dyad would be drawn:

i) how possible is it for the breadwinner to make work-related policy decisions which would affect any aspect of the work-life of others in his/her place of work?

ii) and if the breadwinner does have the possibility of making such decisions, how possible is it for him/her to pass on such decisions to others who could then act as instruments for the execution of these decisions?

Clearly the answer would not be 'yes/no' but rather 'more/less'. The acronym LAP derived from the expression Lower Autonomy Profession was used where such possibilities are relatively attenuated. This contrasts with the acronym HAP which stood for Higher Autonomy Profession, where the possibilities for such exercise of power are higher. Hopefully, the steps in the argument indicate clearly that the degree of autonomy does not inhere in the name of the profession; it is one thing to be a truck driver employed by a County Council, and a somewhat different thing to be a truck driver in a business that you yourself own.

2.4 The social position of the subjects

The 24 mother child dyads acting as subjects in the research were equally distributed between the LAP and HAP categories. None of the LAP or HAP families were self-employed. Not surprisingly, the LAP/HAP position of the families co-varied with the mother's educational level: none of the LAP mothers had qualifications exceeding High School Certificate, whereas most HAP mothers had some professional training and/or a university degree.

2.5 The nature of the data

Given the focus of this research, it became necessary to avoid all those situations which might lead to the self-monitoring of what was being said, for example by requiring the dyads to do certain things they would not normally do at that time, in that place or in that company. Naturally, no outsiders could be present. This ruled out elicitation as well as techniques of situation-simulation such as employed by Labov (1969). Instead, I chose to seek mothers' help in collecting the data.

Each mother who agreed to participate in the research, was given a small but powerful audio recorder, which did not need attending to once turned on; nor did the subjects need to wear a mike. We asked mothers to turn the recorder on whenever they felt they would be able to record while talking to the child who was the other member of the dyad. They were told not to worry about turning the recorder off and on if the child disappeared only briefly. They were also asked specifically not to do or say anything special in order to make the child talk, since our purpose in collecting the dialogues was to find out what small children talked about when left to themselves in their daily environment, without any prodding. We however did ask them to do the recording at different times of the day so that the children's talk would be represented over the range of activities they would normally engage in during the day such as, playing with mother, having a bath, getting dressed, being put to bed, or whatever the normal activities of the household were.

It so turned out that the social immaturity of the children worked in our favour in maintaining the naturalness of the data. The audio-recorder was unobtrusive, and above all, no outsider was present during the recordings. So these very young children had no sense of being in a situation that was other than normal. Whilst the mothers did know that the sayings would be exposed to others' ears, they were unable to act in ways other than usual, since – to use Goffman's metaphor (Goffman 1967) – their children recognised only that maternal face which they were already familiar with. Moreover, the recordings were made over a period of approximately four to six weeks, during times when mothers were also engaged in their normal household chores. This further reduced the possibility of self-consciously controlled presentation of the self by the mothers. Each dyad was provided with six hours' worth of audio tapes, but some wastage arising from the recording instructions was to be expected. In fact, the total amount of talk collected was around 100 real hours.

Although this 100 hour data is relatively homogeneous – it is dialogic and the relation between participants may be said to be comparable – nonetheless quite understandably, it varies within and across dyads with respect to what the talk is about, since the mothers had not been constrained in this respect. (Chapter 3, for further discussion on relevant context.) Using the concept of material situational setting, the data was classified into three types of domestic activities: (1) mother giving care to the child, e.g. bathing, providing food, dressing etc.; (2) mother busy with some other household chore, e.g. cooking, sewing, ironing etc., while child is present in the same location either doing something on his/her own or just watching; and (3) mother and child engaged cooperatively, e.g. playing together with building blocks, reading together from a picture book, cleaning/tidying up, baking etc. Since an in-depth semantic analysis of the type envisaged was labour intensive, a representative sample was devised by selecting just over 45 minutes of talk per dyad, which was within reason equally divided between the three above situational categories. The results reported below are based on this sample. The sample was transcribed as dialogue in ordinary orthography (for details of transcription conventions see Hasan 1989; Butt 1989b; Cloran 1989), and consisted of 20,544 messages. Message, defined as the smallest unit capable of realising an element of text structure, formed the unit for semantic analysis.

A word should be said about the significance of this sampling technique. The three activities mentioned above can be identified by those *in situ* without reference to language: if we are on the scene, we do not need to hear what a mother is saying in order to know whether or not she is dressing her child. This has an important implication: such activities can function like malleable frames within which different things can be talked about. So, one mother might use the eating time for telling her child how to conduct herself at table, while another might use it for giving information about how rottenness in fruit and death in animals are alike and different (Hasan 1984a). If in the sample the dyads have equal representation in terms of these activities, then it is valid to ask: how do the mothers use this time? Do they control or inform an equal amount? If not, what does this variation correlate with? If yes, do they control and/or inform in the same ways? If not, what does that variation correlate with? This point is directly relevant to the analysis of the sample discussed below.

2.5 The semantic debate

Like the term *social class*, the term *semantic* is highly controversial (Eco et al. 1988). On the one hand, there exists a rather narrow perspective, in which meaning is primarily lexical and/or truth functional (Labov 1968, 1973, 1978a; Weiner and Labov 1983), on the other hand there is a much wider perspective where meaning is multifaceted, as in the writings of Firth and Halliday. Interestingly, the latter perspective has been gaining steady momentum as a result of disillusionment with interpretative semantics. The former position is, of course, inadequate for the purposes of my research. If meaning were to be considered merely truth functional (for some arguments against the orthodox versions of this approach, see Eco et al. 1988; Barwise 1989) and a matter of simply the lexicon of a language (a view against which see Halliday 1961, 1970, 1973a, 1975a, b, 1977, 1979, 1985b; Hasan 1984a, b, 1987a, 1988; Whorf 1956), then the analysis of meaning would consist of an examination of the referential scope of sentences and particularly their constituent lexical items. However, theoretically, such a model of meaning is impoverished; and not surprisingly, it would be difficult to provide a convincing sociolinguistic interpretation of variation in referential scope should any such variation be found to occur (see for example Labov 1968, and also 1973 where no interpretation is provided). My research problem was to find out whether what mothers say bears any relevance to what strategies children develop for learning. It would have been absurd to reduce mothers' sayings to a string of lexical items, as if the contribution of grammar to meaning is nil; and, notably, if that approach to meaning had been taken, there would have been no point in conducting the enquiry, since the answer to the research question would quite obviously have been 'no', not because meaning is itself irrelevant, but because this concept of meaning is so untenable that it would always prove irrelevant to human communication. Nor could we view mothers' sayings as simply correspondence to a limited aspect of objective reality, since such (ideational) meanings cannot be interpreted until they combine with the interpersonal and textual meanings. It would seem then that to examine the efficacy of mothers' sayings as meanings, it is necessary to abandon both the pillars of the traditional correspondence-to-reality approach.

I have adopted an approach to meaning articulated by Halliday (see especially 1973b, 1975a, b, 1977, 1979a), where the semantic level of language is a meaning potential, which is itself constituted and expressed by the form of language. From this point of view, it is the lexicogrammar as a whole, not just the lexicon, that functions as a resource for meaning construal. The semantic level is metafunctionally organised into four components:

i) EXPERIENTIAL MEANING, subsuming reference to objects, events, circumstances, attributes, states of affairs etc.;

ii) LOGICAL MEANING, subsuming relations between states of affairs e.g., a cause and its effect and between phenomena e.g. an object and its property;

iii) INTERPERSONAL MEANING concerned with speaker's subjectivity and the enactment of speaker-addressee relations in interaction; and, finally,

iv) TEXTUAL MEANING concerned with the relevance of sayings to each other and to the context of situation in which they are embedded.

In this model, context itself is constituted at least partially by speakers' acts of linguistic meaning (contra Barwise 1989). Since these meanings are not simply expressed by the form of language but are also constituted by it, two important arguments follow: (i) the organisation of the lexicogrammatical form of language acts as witness to the metafunctional organisation of the semantic level (Halliday 1970, 1979); this implies that linguistic form is highly diagnostic of that level's organisation without being isomorphic with it; and (ii) postulating some element of linguistic meaning calls for the specification of some lexico-grammatical form or relation which is the condition for the existence of that element of meaning and is thus able to express it. This again does not exclude the many-to-many relation between the units of the two levels.

2.6 Semantic system networks

As a meaning potential, the semantic level must specify the possibilities of meaning – i.e., what the speakers of a language CAN mean linguistically. Since the principle of paradigmatic organisation applies to all linguistic levels, one form that specifying the possibilities of meaning can take is that of a system network displaying interlocking choices (Halliday 1973a; on the nature of networks, see Halliday and Martin 1981; Halliday and Fawcett 1987; Hasan 1987a). The preparation of an exhaustive semantic network for any language is perhaps even more daunting than attempting to represent the entire lexicogrammar of a language. Strictly context specific semantic networks will be found, for example, in Halliday (1973b) and Turner (1973). To a certain extent these networks formalise the views of Bernstein (1971) on the options in meaning available to mothers in the context of controlling their children. The mother-child dialogues in the research sample were not limited to just this context; in fact, the social activity aspect of the dialogues were quite wide ranging. It follows that a context specific semantic network would have been inadequate for the analysis of such data. I, therefore, prepared a relatively context-free semantic network for English (Hasan 1983), keeping in mind the fact that my sample consisted of dialogues between mothers and children. This network was flexible enough to be used for teacher-child interaction (Hasan 1988) as well as for peer (child) interaction[2].

This system network specifies choices in each of the four metafunctional components, using the semantic unit message as the point of origin. To each option in the network are attached realisation statements, which specify the lexicogrammatical consequences of the choice of that option. Realisation statements re-express (1) facts of one stratum of language into facts of another one e.g., MESSAGE at the semantic level is typically realised as a ranking clause at the lexicogrammatical level; and (2) paradigmatic facts as syntagmatic ones, 'translating' system into structure, to show how the potential is related to the instantial. For example, if with message as point of origin, the option [progressive] is chosen, then the following realisation statements will apply:

i) preselect option [*major*][3] at rank clause;

ii) insert element Predicator in clause;

iii) pre-select (an instance of) verbal group at Predicator.

Through its realisation statements, the semantic option [progressive] has implied that these meanings are expressed and constituted by the lexicogrammatical unit 'clause' such that the clause has the systemic feature [*major*]. And this feature in turn implies that in the structure of the clause occurs an element

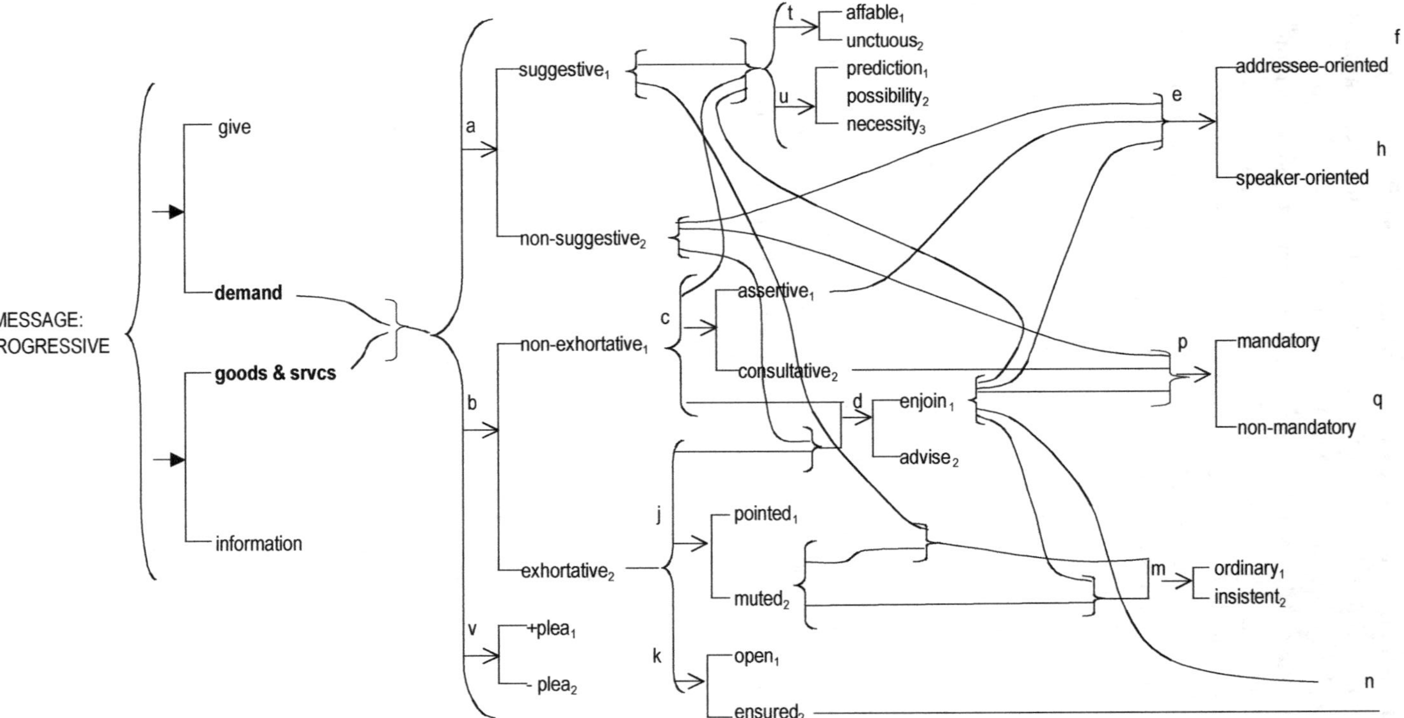

Figure 1: A network of semantic options in making people do things

with the function Predicator; and, further that the element Predicator is itself expressible only by the occurrence of some instance of a unit lower than clause such that it belongs to the class of unit 'verbal group'.

Each message of the sample was analysed in terms of options pertaining to its experiential, logical, interpersonal, and textual meanings. Some adjustments had to be made for the statistical analysis; these are described below. While I would emphasise that the semantic network prepared for the research was very far from representing the total meaning potential of English, it is still too extensive to be presented within the scope of this chapter. A fragment pertaining to the interpersonal meaning is presented in figure 1, which specifies semantic options in demanding goods and services. One way of reading this network is to think of it as an analysis of the concept *command* as used by Halliday (1984a, 1985a), which is wider than *order* or *request* as used in most pragmatic studies. The realisation statements for the options, then, specify those lexicogrammatical properties of a clause which make one category of command similar to as well as different from another. Table 1 presents some examples of the realisation of semantic options from figure 1. The table is divided into three parts: part A lists the classes of realisation statement so far recognised in SFL theory; part B provides an option by option realisation statements for a few of the options from figure 1, while part C 'deconstructs' the instantiation of a few (partially entered) selection expressions (Halliday and Martin 1981; Hasan 1987a).

Table 1: Realisations statements[4]

Part A: Classes of Realisation Statement

(i) structuring	(a) insert element Mood
	(b) expand Mood as Subject and Finite = S^F
	(c) order S to precede F = S^F
(ii) layering	conflate S and Actor = S/Ac
(iii) pre-select	(a) between ranks at the same stratum
	(b) between distinct strata

Part B: The Realisation of Some Semantic Options from Figure 1

message semantic features are DEMAND; GOODS & SERVICES,
realised as options from MOOD system network

(1) b1 NON-EXHORTATIVE

preselect clause features [major: indicative]

insert Mood; expand Mood = S^F

verbal group preselects features finite and indicative

(2) b2 EXHORTATIVE

preselect clause features [major: imperative]

insert Finite

verbal group preselects features [finite: imperative]

(3) a1 SUGGESTIVE

if NON-EXHORTATIVE

nominal group at S preselects features [1st person; plural] = item (*we*)

if EXHORTATIVE

preselect clause features [imperative: inclusive]

insert element S

nominal group at S preselects [1st person; plural] = item (*lets*)

(4) a2 NON-SUGGESTIVE

if NON-EXHORTATIVE

nominal group at S preselects feature [2nd person] = item (*you*)

(5) b1c1 NON-EXHORTATIVE: ASSERTIVE

preselect clause with features [major: indicative: declarative]

order elements S•F•Predicator as S^F^P

(6) b1c2 NON-EXHORTATIVE: CONSULTATIVE

preselect clause [major: indicative: interrogative: polar]

order elements S•F•P as F^S^P

(7) b1d1 NON-EXHORTATIVE: ENJOIN

verb at F preselects low modal = item (*will/'ll/would…*)

(8) b1d2 NON-EXHORTATIVE: ADVISE

verb at F preselects modal = item (*had/'d better*)

if EXHORTATIVE

insert Mood Adjunct

Mood Adjunct 'is' item *better*

(9) a1b2j1 SUGGESTIVE; EXHORTATIVE: POINTED

preselect clause [major: imperative: inclusive: marked: person]

S 'is' 1st person plural + stress = item (*let **us***)

(10) a2b2j1 NON-SUGGESTIVE; EXHORTATIVE: POINTED

preselect clause [major: imperative: exclusive: marked: person]

insert S

nominal group at S preselects feature 2nd person = item (*you*)

(11) a1b1d1t2 SUGGESTIVE; NON-EXHORTATIVE: ENJOIN: UNCTUOUS

if c1 ASSERTIVE

preselects features [declarative: tagged]

insert Mood-tag; expand Mood-tag;

order F and S as F^S

Mood-tag polarity [positive]

if c2 CONSULTATIVE

Mood-tag polarity [negative]

Part C: Selection Expressions with Examples

EX (1): a1b1c1d1 SUGGESTIVE; NON-EXHORTATIVE: ASSERTIVE: ENJOIN

we'll just do this first

SUGGESTIVE	Thing in nom gp at S pre-selects features [1st person plural]; item *we*
NON-EXHORTATIVE	insert Mood
ASSERTIVE	order Mood elements as S^F
ENJOIN	Finite preselects modal; (modal is weak form of *will*); items *we'll*

EX (2) a1b1c1d2 SUGGESTIVE; NON-EXHORTATIVE: ASSERTIVE: ADVISE

we'd better just do this first

SUGGESTIVE	as above
NON-EXHORTATIVE	as above
ASSERTIVE	as above
ADVISE	Finite preselects modal; (modal weak form of *had better*); items *we'd better*

EX (3) a1b1c2d1 SUGGESTIVE; NON-EXHORTATIVE: CONSULTATIVE: ENJOIN

shall we just do this first

SUGGESTIVE	as above
NON-EXHORTATIVE	as above
CONSULTATIVE	order Mood elements as F^S
ENJOIN	Finite preselects modal; (modal is *shall*); items *shall we*

EX (4) a2b2j1d2 NON-SUGGESTIVE; EXHORTATIVE: POINTED: ADVISE

You'd better just do this first

NON-SUGGESTIVE	Thing in nom gp at S cannot 'be' 1st person plural
EXHORTATIVE	clause features [imperative: exclusive]; insert P
POINTED	clause has features [...marked: person];
	Thing in nom gp at S has features [2nd person sing]; item *you*
ADVISE	Finite preselects modal;
	(modal weak form of *had better*) items *you'd better*

2.7 The statistical analysis

A principal components procedure was considered appropriate for the statistical analysis of the data[5] for two reasons. First, it acts as an effective method of data reduction, reducing, in this case, the frequency of the occurrence of a large number of semantic options to smaller clusterings of derived variables i.e., principal components (=PCs); and secondly, in doing this, the procedure assigns a score to the subjects on each such clustering, or PC. It is thus possible to arrive at the clustering of subjects on the basis of their ranking on their scores for any one PC. We can then examine whether the clustering of subjects on the basis of their score on some PC – i.e., on some complex of semantic features – correlates with any socially identified attribute(s) of the speakers. If so, then the PC scores can be tested for significance of the said social attribute(s). Should the correlation be significant, we would be justified in claiming that the PC in question is a complex sociolinguistic variable, and like other sociolinguistic variables, it helps to describe systematic, orderly variation in the use of language in its social context.

Whilst the principal components procedure had these advantages, it also posed some problems because of a restriction on the number of variables in relation to the number of subjects. There does not seem to be complete agreement on this issue; however, for the batch of results discussed here, the ratio of subject to variable is maintained at around 3:1. This had another consequence: it became important to establish some rational ground for deciding which semantic options would be entered with which ones for statistical processing. Now, even though the network in figure 1 by no means exhausts the semantic options available to speakers in issuing commands (so, for example, it will not 'generate' a command – if it is a command – of the type *what the hell do you mean by leaving all this mess around*, which of course no mother said, not very surprisingly!), the network was still too delicate (see Halliday 1961 on delicacy) for statistically valid use with only 20,544 messages. It became necessary to move back in delicacy. For example, the contrast between ENJOIN and ADVISE was abandoned. This meant that the semantic options in terms of which the sample was actually statistically processed were far more 'gross' – i.e., less delicate – than those in terms of which it was actually analysed and those that were represented in the network. This 'grossing' of the options naturally implies that there were fewer options to be statistically processed. Even so, these 'gross' semantic features were too many to be used as one single input. To determine the input pattern, in general, we have used two ways: (1) using the options pertaining to some specifiable portion of the network, e.g., options dependent on DEMAND;INFORMATION which specify the semantic characteristics of questions; or (2) using a clearly defined situational description, e.g., exchange of information between mother and child – in other words, the patterns of seeking information and the addressees' response to that search (Hasan 1988; Hasan and Cloran 1990). The result presented below is based on an input of the second kind, using those semantic options which were available to mothers in attempting to control their children (on maternal control, Bernstein 1971a; Turner 1973; Halliday 1973b).

2.8 The context of maternal control: some examples from the data

Before turning to the results, let me give a few examples of dialogues embedded in the context of control. The first two dialogues cover practically the entire control episode as it occurred naturally. I will return to them in characterising the nature of the context of control in section 3.

Dialogue 1
(Mother is bathing Karen)
Karen: (1) mum, could you get me my toys… (2) could you, mum… (3) have a little play… (4)**can you, mum
Mother: (5)**it's too cold for your toys, Karen (6) 'cause the water's getting cold
Karen: (7)**no, it isn't for me
Mother: (8) it is
Karen: (9) mum, put [?them] down
Mother: (10) no
Karen: (11) yes
Mother: (12) tomorrow (Karen begins to cry)
Mother: (13) y-e-s
Karen: (14) 'cause [?water] will be cold tomorrow too
Mother: (15) no it won't
Karen: (16) yes it will
Mother: (17) no it won't
Karen: (18) yes it will (19) I want my toys now (20) I'm not getting out, mum
Mother: (21) I beg your pardon?
Karen: (22) I'm not getting out
Mother: (23) you'll get out
Karen: (24) no, I won't
Mother: (25) yes
Karen: (26) no
Mother: (27) yes
Karen: (28) I'm not standing up

Mother: (29) I'll drag you out (30) if I have to
Karen: (31) I won't stand up mum
Mother: (32) I'll drag you out then
Karen: (33) no, not out of the bath
Mother: (34) yeah, won't I
Karen: (35) no
Mother: (36) you watch me
Karen: (37) mmm (protesting noise)
Mother: (38) come on up (39) and I'll dry you (40) and you can have some powder on
Karen: (41) no
Mother: (42) come on
Karen: (43) no mummy
Mother: (44) yes (45) don't tell me "no" all the time (46) just do as you're told ...
(mother takes Karen out of the bath and begins to towel dry Karen)

Dialogue 2

(Mother is bathing Donna)
Donna: (1) mum I need my towel
Mother: (2) you want to get out, do you?
Donna: (3) yeah, now... (4) bring the ladder
Mother: (5) (mother laughs; moves something) there you are
Donna: (6) [?need] to close the door (7) doesn't close (?trying to close the door)
Mother: (8) no (9) well, it's just as well you don't have to have a bath in that every night (10) come on (11) can you pull the plug at the same time too, sweetie
Donna: (12) no
Mother: (13) of course you can
Donna: (14) because I haven't got any arms (15) look
Mother: (16) oh, you lost them this afternoon, did you?
Donna: (17) yeah
Mother: (18) left them on the train?
Donna: (19) pardon?
Mother: (20) did you leave them on the train, did you?** (21) oh well, do it with your toes then, would you?
Donna: (22) no (23) I - I -I left them on the train
Mother: (24) you tell me when you're ready to get out
Donna: (25) o k (26) now!
Mother: (27) you're not ready (28) until the plug's out

Donna: (29) well, I lost my hands and foots
Mother: (30) then you'd better find them
Donna: (31) ooh, they're in the front (32) so I'm getting out
Mother: (33) no you're not (34) please pull the plug out Donna…
Donna: (35) can't feel it (36) 's not anywhere… (feeling for it under the water)

(37) I feel it now (noise of water running out)
Mother: (38) good (39) I thought you'd see it my way
Donna: (40) I can get down now
(Donna giggles as mother rubs her dry with the towel)

Dialogue 3

(Davie has hit his sister; mother compares his behaviour with that of the local terror, Dean, by way of telling him not to misbehave in future)
Mother: (1) you told me that Dean is a bully (2) is that right?
Davie: (3) no
Mother: (4) is Dean a bully?
Davie: (5) no
Mother: (6) he's not?** (7) that's what you told me the other day
Davie: (8) yes
Mother: (9) that Dean's a - (10) d'you want to be a bully too?
Davie: (11) no
Mother: (12) well don't you— (13) you stop hitting Rebecca then (14) because < (15) if you keep doing that > then you're a bully too… ok?
Davie: (16) mmm (agreeing with mother)
Mother: (17) now, don't you dare hit Rebecca
Davie: (18) no
Mother: (19) or anybody else for that matter
Davie: (20) no
Mother: (21) especially girls (22) you don't hit girls

Dialogue 4

(Pete is moving about energetically while holding a glass full of juice)
Mother: (1) don't do that … (waits for Pete to respond; he doesn't) (2) now look, you'll get it all over me
Pete: (Pete just laughs and continues moving about)
Mother: (3) it's not funny (4) what's funny about that?** (5) you do it again (6) and I'll whack you

Dialogue 5

(Mother has been trying to get Karen into bed; she has reasoned, scolded, threatened and slapped her to get her to obey).

Mother: (1) Karen do as you— (slaps Karen) (2) put your legs down (3) or I'm going outside right this minute without a kiss (4) now put your legs down

Karen: (5) mmhm (refusing to comply, but mother fixes her into bed)

Mother: (6) now give a kiss goodnight

Karen: (7) I'm not (defiant)

Mother: (8) you're not gonna kiss me** (9) why?

Karen: (10) 'cause

Mother: (11) 'cause why?

Karen: (12) 'cause I don't like you (very loud voice)

2.9 Meanings in control: a sociolinguistic variable

Table 2 presents the result of the statistical analysis of mothers' semantic choices in the context of controlling their children. The main focus of discussion in this chapter will be PC1. Note that of the nine semantic features entered as input, the loading of all but one – C[action] – shows their relevance to PC1; and that PC1 accounts for 45% of variance in the data.

Table 2: Meanings in maternal control

	PC1	PC2	PC3	PC4
C [indirect]	0.84	-0.32	-0.14	0.25
S [supportive]	0.83	0.06	-0.01	-0.23
C [suggestive]	0.82	-0.38	-0.00	0.10
C [elaborated]	0.77	0.29	0.02	0.13
R [logical]	0.64	0.20	-0.07	-0.31
R [elaborated]	0.62	0.35	0.19	-0.45
Q [explain]	-0.50	0.60	-0.11	0.11
C [action]	0.34	0.24	0.75	0.45
C [prefaced]	0.44	0.37	-0.60	0.38
Eigenvalue	4.04	1.07	1.00	0.83
% Variance	45.00	12.00	11.10	9.20

Before attempting an explanation of the semantic features that were used as input, or trying to interpret PC1 as a whole, let us ask if subjects' ranking by their scores on this PC correlates with any known social attributes. Figure 2 shows how the 24 mothers are positioned *vis-à-vis* each other by virtue of their scores on PC2 and PC1.

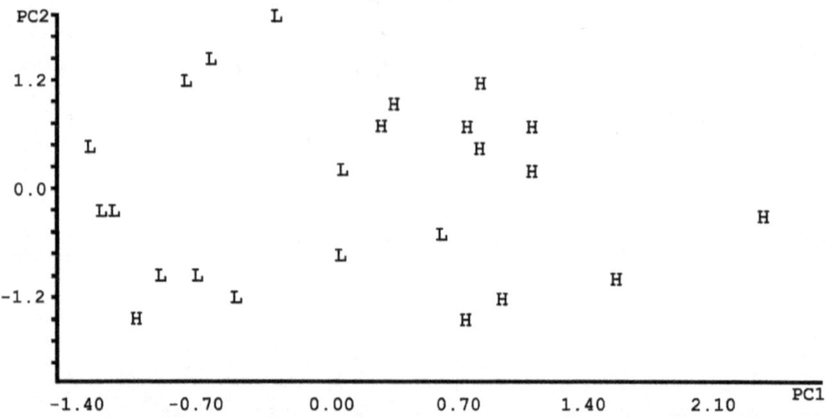

Figure 2: Meanings in control and social class

In figure 2, mothers who score high on PC1 would be in the right half of the space indicated by the horizontal axis, while those who score low would be in the left half. L stands for LAP mother and H for HAP mother. It is obvious then that by reference to their score on PC1, the 24 mothers can be clustered into two groups, and this grouping has been arrived at on the basis of their semantic choices; it thus correlates with their social class position (p. <.0002). This implies that PC1 is a strong candidate for the status of a complex sociolinguistic variable. Therefore it would be profitable to look more closely into the semantic features that make up this complex sociolinguistic variable.

2.10 The semantic features explained

In table 2, the semantic features are enclosed in square brackets, each of which is preceded by a capital letter where C stands for command, S for statement, R for reason, and Q for question. Two of the semantic features in the table –[indirect], and [suggestive] – are in fact based on the network presented in figure 1. For lack of space the details of the calibration of options which are thus renamed cannot be discussed fully, though I will try to show at least some connections. Each feature will be exemplified from the research sample, except where indicated otherwise. The feature [indirect] is present in Karen's message in dialogue 1, when she asks for her toys *(1) Mum, could you get me my toys …* As the dots indicate Karen waits for her mother to respond and on not receiving any response, she produces another message with this same semantic feature in *(2) could you, Mum …* and yet again in *(4) can you, Mum.* Message (11) in dialogue 2 also displays the same feature, as does (30). The semantic feature [indirect] is in binary contrast with [direct], and so the loading for the latter can be deduced from table 2 (in fact, it would be an exact opposite at -0.84). Several examples of the feature DIRECT can be found in the dialogues. Thus in dialogue 1, we find Karen saying *(9) Mum, put [?put] them (ie toys) down*, and the mother closes the verbal debate with *(45) don't tell me 'no' all the time (46) just do as you're told*, while in dialogue 2, Donna commands *(4) bring the ladder*. Another example of the feature DIRECT worth pointing out is again from dialogue 1 and 2. In the former, Karen's mother says *(23) you'll get out*; in the latter Donna's mother says *(33) no you're not (coming out)*. In terms of figure 1, (starting at labelled systems), the semantic options embodied in these message are (=a2;b1:c1;d1:e1:f1), which in words represents the following selection expression:

> [non-suggestive: non-exhortative: assertive; enjoin; addressee-oriented: authoritarian]

To simply state to the children what they will or will not be doing is in fact an imposition of authority on the mothers' part. The network in figure 1 distinguishes this highly authoritarian command from the ordinary ones such as (45-46) in dialogue 1. However, in the 'grossing' of the semantic options such finely distinct choices are collapsed into one category called [direct]. Consider two other examples of this same (gross) semantic feature [direct] in dialogue 3, where Dean's mother says *(13) you stop hitting Rebecca then* and *(17) now, don't you dare hit Rebecca.* Hopefully, these examples show that a command with the semantic feature [direct] grants the addressee little or no discretion, whereas with [indirect] commands the addressee is treated as if they have the right to demur. This is one reason why the latter category of command is normally perceived as 'polite', while the extreme example of the former appears almost 'imperious'. It follows then that those mothers who score high on PC1 are the ones who will grant discretion to their children more often than those who score low. According to figure 2, the high scoring mothers would be predominantly HAP ones.

The semantic feature [suggestive] contrasts with [non-suggestive]. All examples cited above have the latter feature. Dialogues 1-5 do not contain any example of a command that has the feature suggestive. If in dialogue 2, instead of saying *(30) then you'd better find them*, a [non-suggestive: direct] command, which in terms of figure 1 has the semantic option [advise], Donna's mother had said something like *(30a) lets stop fooling around sweetheart (Mum's got lots of things to do)*, then the first part of this saying would have been a [suggestive] demand for the child to do something. A command of this kind blurs the boundary between cooperation and demand, thus underplaying the power relation between the controlling agency and the controlled. A literal indication of this is provided in dialogue 6, where the mother is attempting to get Mike dressed in his day clothes, which he is resisting:

Dialogue 6

Mother: (1) well, you can't wash your cars in your pyjamas (2) you've got to come and get dressed, **O K
Mike: (3) **what?
Mother: (4) come on, we'll go and get dressed
Mike: (5) are you going to get dressed?
Mother: (6) I'm already dressed (Mike cries)

Here message (4) has the feature [suggestive]. Note due to the presence of this semantic option, the child is led into thinking that possibly the mother too intends to change; however, the mother's response shows that in fact it is Mike alone who is being required to do so. The selection of this feature is conducive to the suppression of distinctions between authority and benefaction, between command and offer, between coercion and cooperation. Depending upon our own ideology, we may see such behaviour either as diplomatic – it avoids conflict – or as deceitful – it suppresses unpalatable 'facts'. Whatever our ideological stance, it would seem reasonable to suggest that a command with the feature [suggestive] shows a recognition for the addressee as an individual in his/her own right who needs to be supported in his/her belief that he/she enjoys parity with the speaker. It is not my claim that the choice of this feature is only made when this relationship obtains in reality; rather, my claim is that such a choice shows that this is how the speaker would like to be seen in regard to the addressee. Of course, sometimes the speaker's 'bluff' – if it is a bluff – can be called as in dialogue 6. If these arguments are accepted, then it would be reasonable to suggest that mothers who score high on PC1 are also mothers who do not verbalise clear-cut status boundaries, so that the power of authority remains invisible, in the sense in which Bernstein uses these terms (Bernstein 1971a, 1975a, 1986). We may conclude on the basis of figure 2, that the invisibility of authority is predominantly a feature of HAP mothers' control.

Two of the semantic features in table 2 – [elaborated] and [prefaced] – derive from the logical component of the semantic network (Hasan 1983). First, a few words about the feature [elaborated]. One example of a command being elaborated is provided by Davie's mother when in dialogue 3 she says *(17) now, don't you dare hit Rebecca (19) or anybody else for that matter (21) especially girls*. Here (17) is a [non-suggestive; direct] command; the last two messages (19 and 21) will be analysed as elaborating the command in (17). Their effect is to add to the command, so that it is generalised by (19), and then a specific condition is set in (21) for the demanded action: a rough paraphrase of (17, 19, 21) would be: 'Rebecca should be immune from

Davie's violence as should every one else; but Rebecca doubly so, because she is a girl since girls in general are not to be hit'. Elaborations are thus alternatives, additions, contrasts, special conditions etc. From one point of view, one could see the reasons offered for a command as an elaboration of that command. For the analysis under focus, however, the reason given for a command has not been treated as its elaboration, but rather as representing an element in the Generalised Structure Potential (=GSP) (Halliday and Hasan 1985) of a text produced in maternal control. As table 2 indicates, [reasons] too can be elaborated. An example would be (13-15) from dialogue 3, where *(13) you stop hitting Rebecca then* is a command, whose reason is *(14) because if you keep doing that (15) then you're a bully too*. The desire (ascribed by the mother to Davie) not to be seen as a bully is a reason for not hitting Rebecca; there is a risk of Davie being seen as a bully only under certain conditions; it is this condition – *if you keep hitting Rebecca* – that is an elaboration of the reason. Again the category [elaborated] is 'gross' compared with the options in the system network e.g., [condition], [concurrence], [addition], and others, which were all collapsed into one gross category.

However, this is less serious an issue, than the possible confusion of [elaborated] with verbosity, or with wandering away from the point, which might well happen if one followed Labov's (1969) value-laden characterisation of Bernstein's term elaborated. The fact that they are made from the stance of championing the down-trodden does not ensure their greater objective validity, much less that hereafter it would become possible for all of us who are sympathetic to the cause of the disadvantaged to conduct our discourses of knowledge without elaboration, as this term is described above with reference to framework presented here. Semantic features such as [condition], [concession], [concurrence], [apposition] and so on are neither textually unnecessary, nor are they optional extras for those mothers who habitually use them to show how states of affairs referred to by their commands and reasons are logically related to other state of affairs. It may be that persons who use these related states of affairs – which is really the primary issue of elaboration, not the presence or absence of logical connectives themselves – see them as constituting the ground against which the figure(s) of command and reason stand out clearly, making the commands more explicit. Equally mothers who do not elaborate their commands and reasons are not with-holding information; they have a different conception of the ground against which the commands and reasons stand as figures. The smaller the degree of elaboration, the greater the likelihood of an assumption that the addressee already knows, through some other source than the present discourse, how the states of affairs referred to by commands and reasons are related to any others which might give them their validity; or, equally, there may be an assumption that it is immaterial if the addressee does not know these 'details'. It follows that mothers who score higher on PC1 are those who believe that more information relating their commands and reasons to other states of affairs is a necessary ingredient of control, and that they cannot take for granted their child's access to such information without its being said explicitly by them here an now. These as we know from figure 2 are predominantly HAP mothers. They are prone to laying out the argument explicitly rather than taking it for granted that the argument is already known without being worded.

A message is said to have the feature [prefaced] when it is introduced as a saying – as report or quote – or as a percept or a concept – in short, as an idea. This semantic feature is lexicogrammatically realised through projection (Halliday 1985a), which is derived from the logical metafunction. In the dialogues presented above there are no examples of any commands with this feature, but the following extract is taken from a dialogue between Karen and her mother. Karen, who doesn't want to eat the food she has been given, tries to divert her mother by turning the situation of control into one of play:

Dialogue 7

Mother: (1) now eat your tea
Karen: (2) try to get my spoon
Mother: (3) you spill that food off that spoon (4) and I'll smack you (5) now eat it
Karen: (6) **try to get—
Mother: (7) **I don't want your spoon
Karen: (8) try to get it
Mother: (9) no I don't have to try to get it (10) because I don't want it
Karen: (11) try to get [?the lid]
Mother: (12) no I don't want the lid (13) all I want is for you to eat your tea.. (14) all I want … is for Karen Megan to eat her tea (15) you're making me upset (16) d'you know that?

In this dialogue the mother's demands (13) and (14) for Karen to eat her tea have the feature [prefaced]. Again, just as different evaluations of the feature [suggestive] would arise from different ideologies, so also one might view the feature [prefaced] as one which imposes the dictum and desire of another on the addressee, thus bolstering their authority, or as one of the features that is crucial to the construction of point of view (Cloran 1989). Note how in the above dialogue, the preface in (13, and 14) helps in building the mother's perspective on the situation. The selection of this semantic feature, then, is one of the verbal strategies by which an addressee may be sensitised to someone else's point of view on some given state of affair. Our evaluation of such sensitisation may be negative; i.e., we may believe that it is a way of highlighting another's dictum and desire, suppressing the addressee's own interests. Or we may view this sensitising positively; we may believe that it is a way of creating an awareness of other's beliefs and desires which after all is one effective basis for the development of reflexivity. But what cannot be denied is that its use must assume separate, individuated selves (cf. Bernstein 1971a), whose beliefs and desires are not necessarily accessible to others without being verbalised. If this line of argument is correct, then it follows that mothers who score higher on PC1 would view their children not as an extension of themselves but as separate selves, or to use Bernstein's terms as 'unique person'.

The semantic feature [action] is derived from the experiential part of the semantic network, where meanings pertaining to objects, events, states of affairs etc. are represented up to a certain degree of delicacy. Referentially, those processes which are concrete – i.e., they are undertaken visibly, using visible parts of a concrete body – are said to have the feature [action]. Thus the word *get* in *get me my toys*, *pull* in *can you pull the plug…*, *hit* in *you stop hitting Rebecca* etc. are all examples of the feature [action]; these contrast with features such as [talk] e.g., *tell* in *don't tell me 'no'…*, and [sensing] e.g., *think, remember, look at* or *love* as in messages (not cited from the research data) such as *think again, try and remember, look at this picture carefully*, or *love thy neighbour as thyself,* and so on. This is not a complete account of the options in the semantic network relating to activity, but hopefully it is sufficiently detailed to show where a semantic feature such as [action] derives from. Commands with this feature are obviously demands on addressees to do or not to do certain concrete acts; they are not demands to conduct oneself e.g. *be good* or to engage in a sensing activity e.g., *try and see if you can remember what I told you*, and so on. This feature is not relevant to the complex sociolinguistic variable identified by PC1. (It must be added that the input figure was calculated only on the basis of explicit selection of a word referring to some activity.)

In demanding goods and services, speakers usually ground their demands in some assertion which is presented to the addressee as the motivation for complying with the demand. Such an assertion is what is referred to in table 2 as reason. A reason with the semantic feature [inherent] is one that is ideationally related to demand as a cause is to its effect. For example, in dialogue 4, when Pete's mother demands that he should stop dancing around with a glass full of juice, offering as reason *(2) now look, you'll get it all over me*, the latter message describes an outcome that potentially inheres in Pete's 'doing that'. The historical truth or scientific validity of a reason is quite immaterial to its status as [inherent]. Taking the above example, the possibility exists that the juice might not spill; or that neither mother nor Pete have ever seen it do so: what makes the reason inhere in Pete's action is in principle the physical nature of the universe; it is based on a 'theory' of what the physical world is like. Yet another basis for a reason being inherent can be seen in an example from dialogue 3, where the mother claims that keeping on hitting Rebecca (who is a female, and therefore at least by convention weaker than Davie) would make Davie a bully; once Rebecca is seen as a weakling, the relation between the two propositions would inhere analytically by the social conventions and the conventions of the English language. Contrast this with Pete's mother's reason in dialogue 4 when she says *(6) and I'll whack you* and Karen's mother's reason in dialogue 5 where she threatens *(3) or I'm going outside right this minute without a kiss*, both of which are [non-inherent] or [external] reasons with the specific feature of [threat]. The link between spilling juice and being whacked or disobeying mother and being deprived of her kisses is not as direct as in the previous two cases. For example, Pete's being whacked and Karen's being deprived of mother's kisses depends on the mother witnessing the child's misdemeanour, whereas whether any one finds out or not does not alter the very high probability of spilling liquid from a violently jerked glass or getting the status of a bully from hitting the weak. Another example of [external] reason which differs from the last two is given by Karen's mother in dialogue 7 when she says *(15) you're making me upset*. This is a variety of reason that Bernstein (1971a) would refer to as 'emotional blackmail'.

With very rare exceptions, philosophers and logicians have always considered the use of [inherent] reason as a mark of rationality. In fact my extension of the term 'reason' to refer to threats, bribes etc. might be strongly objected to by some, simply on the ground that these are not really reasons. This philosophical view has entered into the consciousness of the educated segments of the community, and needless to say that the choice of the feature [inherent] reason and rationality have become synonymous. But if rationality is synonymous with giving and accepting [inherent] reasons, then by our own logic we are forced to say that mothers who score higher on PC1 are more rational than those who do not. However, this is not the only possible way of interpreting the findings of this research. Consider the fact that a reason is [inherent] if it appeals to physical or symbolic phenomena; so far as I can see there is no justification for maintaining that appeal to physical and symbolic phenomena is necessarily more rational – more reasonable – than appeal to interpersonal relations, which would usually form the basis for [threat] where speaker has more power relative to addressee, [bribe] where speaker has to know what addressee likes, [blackmail], where addressee must care for speaker's feelings, [cajolement], where speaker knows addressee's positive self image, [authority], where speaker stands in a definite relation of superiority to addressee, [tradition], where addressee wishes to be seen as a normal member of the community; and so on. In each case the success of these forms of reasoning depends on some interpersonal relation to other(s); this clearly indicates the nature of such reasons as rooted in natural phenomena. We can thus sever the usually unquestioned tie between rationality and appeals to physical or symbolic phenomena. We can interpret the results shown in table 2 and figure 2 as indicating that mothers who score high on PC1 are those who have greater respect for physical facts and symbolic orders than they have for interpersonal relationships, particularly those arising from authority, power, and regard for community. The high scoring mothers are predominantly HAP ones. By contrast low scoring LAP mothers prioritise interpersonal relations, ignoring the 'logic' of the physical and the symbolic.

Just as there is a possible element of the GSP of control called reason, so also we may recognise another element which may be referred to as support. These are again assertions, which may have the semantic feature [supportive] or [non-supportive]. A [supportive] statement is one in which the speaker actively contributes to the maintenance of the addressee's face. For example, consider Donna's mother's messages (38-9) in dialogue 2: *good, I thought you'd see it my way*. Donna's obedience of her mother is being presented to Donna by her mother as something that Donna herself has done voluntarily on the basis of a belief in the rightness of that action. This contrasts with [non-supportive] statements found in dialogue 1, where a confrontation and direct contradiction of each other occurs almost as a prosody throughout the piece. In concrete terms the outcome of the two episodes is alike, in that Karen too does what her mother wants her to do – she finally gets out of the bath without having played with her toys – but the framing (Bernstein 1975b, 1986) of this discourse is such that it would be difficult for anyone, Karen and Karen's mother included, to suggest that she has done this voluntarily. Again, depending upon our ideology, we may criticise the supportive maternal behaviour on the ground that it hides from the child the fact of his/her being manoeuvered into submission, or we may claim that statements with the feature SUPPORTIVE will tend to reduce the possibility of conflict, thus leading to a smoother tenor of relation. Whatever our ideological stance, it would be hard to deny that in issuing [supportive] assertions a mother does foster self-esteem in the child to the extent that she contributes to his/her positive face, while minimising the force of authority. If this is so, it would follow that those who score high on PC1 are very likely to suppress the force of authority, as well as the possibility of conflict, and to contribute to the self-esteem of the child. And as pointed out, the high scorers are HAP mothers.

This leaves the entry Q[explain] to be discussed. This feature derives from that part of the interpersonal network, which is concerned with proposition (cf. Halliday 1985a) – i.e., the exchange of information, rather than proposal – i.e., the exchange of goods and services, as in commands, requests, offers etc.

However, while in the context of information exchange, e.g. in the classroom or at home when mothers and children are engaged in perhaps reading a picture book, the *wh*-question, particularly the *how/why*-question, is a search for specific information, in the context of control, the function of the *wh*-question in general and, of *how/why*-question in particular, can be that of challenge rather than a search for information. For example, in dialogue 5, Karen's mother throws such a challenge to Karen in (9) and (11). It is thus a semantic feature, the choice of which one would expect to be congruent with the choice of the feature [non-supportive], especially in the context of control. Note that the feature [explain] (realised by a *why*-question) loads negatively in table 2; this is in keeping with the above expectation, since there is a positive loading for [supportive]. If this interpretation of the choice of the feature [supportive] is accepted, then it would follow from HAP mothers' higher scores on PC1 that they are fairly unlikely to engage in confrontational behaviour with their children in the context of control.

3 Part two: theory from practice

Although the previous part of the chapter has been concerned mainly with empirical matters, as I had pointed out earlier, it was not possible to exclude theoretical considerations, whether of a very general kind, e.g., the concept of social class or of meaning, or more specific, such as in interpreting the implications of mothers' scores for each semantic feature used as input for table 2. This second part of the chapter (section 3) will be concerned with an examination of the interpretation of the complex sociolinguistic variable delineated by PC1, to see whether the total structure made up by the individual semantic features entering into this variable is informed by a unifying principle. If the answer is 'yes', we can then ask whether the kind of sociolinguistic explanations current in the field today will be able to make any sense of the findings reported here. Before embarking on this move, I should emphasise that because of the need to conduct an in-depth analysis of a fairly large sample – over 20,000 messages – with limited resources, I have had to decide to limit the number of speakers to 24 dyads; this made it possible to use a fairly representative sample of what each dyad's talk is like. Obviously, it is desirable to conduct such studies over a larger population of subjects and therefore of messages to check whether the results of this research are replicated. The findings of this research can certainly be compared with those of other researches; however, limitation on space does not allow such a discussion, especially since the conception of the problem as well as the analytic framework for the various research projects is substantially different.

3.1 Invisible control: the meaning of PC1

Let me summarise quickly the results of PC1. The loadings for the individual semantic features for PC1 and the interpretation of the feature provided above, indicate that subjects scoring high on this PC would be:

- highly likely to issue [indirect] and [suggestive] commands; the implication is that they would give greater discretion to their children, blurring the status boundary so that the essentially coercive nature of their authority is made invisible;
- strongly inclined to [elaborate] both their commands and their reasons, though the tendency to elaborate commands will be higher, thus showing that they consider it essential to prepare and make explicit the ground for both commands and reasons by relating them to other explicitly cited states of affairs;
- likely to give more [inherent] reasons for the commands they issue, showing greater respect for physical and symbolic phenomena, than for interpersonal relations, thus attaching greater importance to the material and symbolic world than to the place of strictly personal relation to others in the community;
- somewhat inclined to [preface] their commands as a saying or an idea, not viewing the child as an extension of self but as a separate being, who must be made aware of others' point of view through verbalisation;
- highly likely to make [supportive] assertions, thus contributing to the child's positive face, while at the same time softening the force of authority;
- quite disinclined to issue challenge to the child, thus positively avoiding conflict.

Once the summary is laid out like this, it seems reasonable to suggest that PC1 isolates a pattern that could be justifiably called *invisible control* (cf. Bernstein's 'invisible pedagogy'). It is obvious from the subjects' scores that a vast amount of the HAP mothers' energy is devoted to making their authority invisible, in gaining their objectives through diplomacy and manoeuvrings rather than through an open appeal to their own authority, much less by setting themselves up openly as the child's adversary. In the process they also transmit to the child a particular picture of how the world is organised and the place of the child's self in relation to that world. These are certainly important elements of the discourse of their control, but let us ignore these issues for the time being and look more closely at the descriptive expression 'invisible control'. I realise that all summary statements, because they leave out the finer details, are capable of being misinterpreted, but this in a nutshell is the main difference between the HAP and the LAP mothers' semantic choices in the context of control: the former make their control as invisible as possible, the latter act so that it cannot fail to engender a recognition of what counts as authority, so that authority cannot remain hidden from the child's consciousness, and so that its irrationality must become a part of the child's primary experience of life. At the same time, quite significantly, LAP mothers place no taboo on conflict, so that conflict is not something that must necessarily be avoided. I should state quite clearly that I am not presenting these maternal behaviours as the result of conscious planning; rather, extrapolating from some Whorfian terms, these are just 'habitual fashions of meaning'. What this result indicates, then, is that given the same context – that of control – the two groups of mothers systematically differ in what meanings they consider relevant.

3.2 Semantic variation: data in search of theory

Having interpreted the meaning of PC1, let me ask two simple questions: (1) how might one explain the kind of semantic variation indicated by PC1? And (2) is this highly systematic and orderly variation sociolinguistic in its nature? Turning to the first question first, it may be that I am mistaken in my interpretation of the notions of identification and accommodation (Labov 1978a) by reference to which sociolinguistic variation is typically given its social significance in the current literature. But I fail to see how either of these notions can be deployed for explaining semantic variation in the use of language by mothers in the context of controlling their small children. What group are the mothers identifying with? If we say that the pattern of their semantic selections is motivated by their need to 'keep in' with their own respective groups, or that they speak thus because they belong to a particular social group, what have we said? It seems to me, we have said precisely nothing. For we must now raise the question: why did some ur-group begin to mean these meanings in the first place? Was it an arbitrary choice? If so, do people mean just any meaning arbitrarily, irrespective of who they are, and how they are positioned in the society? Or should we perhaps take seriously Marx's claim (see McLellan 1975: 40) that *It is not the consciousness of men that determines their being, but on the contrary their social being that determines their consciousness*.

Be that as it may, it seems to me that the notion of group identification, while it has worked well as an explanation for speakers' maintenance of certain variant forms, cannot be used to explain semantic variants: unlike the relation of sound to wording, the relation of wording to meaning is not arbitrary (Halliday 1979a). We may treat the variant semantic features as social markers of Australian English, but this label does not explain why they are there; their *raison d'être* cannot be to simply act as social markers. I should make it quite clear that I am not denying the validity or usefulness of the concept of social markers of speech to sociolinguistic studies as a whole; I am simply claiming that if semantic variants are treated as social markers, unless one is able to show wherein their social nature lies, the description lacks explanatory adequacy.

The notion of accommodation does not seem to fare any better either. If we say that the mothers' varying semantic choices are motivated by a desire to accommodate their children, we are immediately faced with an untenable position: we would seem to imply that the LAP and HAP children as two distinct groups carry in themselves certain distinctive attributes which motivate their mothers' distinct semantic selections as a way of accommodating to the children's differential attributes. But surely this is not the end of the story; for now we need to ask: what is the origin of these distinctive attributes? Since the children are so small, should we say, perhaps, that these attributes are innate? I myself should certainly resist going down that slippery path! But perhaps, we could be more general. Could we, perhaps, maintain that the mothers' behaviour is an accommodation to their position in the community? This is, however, rather a vague description, and means the same as identifying the speaker's social position. What does position in community mean? And what does accommodation to position in the community mean? If we reflect carefully on this question, we would come to the conclusion that in the last resort this general description says no more and no less than that the mothers respond to their social class position. In other words, accommodation to being a LAP mother produces LAP meanings. This does not explain anything; it is simply another way of claiming that social class correlates with semantic variation; only it makes the fact of social class rather invisible. Of course, we have been warned by Weiner and Labov (1983: 31) that:

> we must not conclude that all linguistic variation subserves the social functions of identifying the social position of speakers and adjusting to the social position of the listeners and audience. Variable elements are found at all levels of linguistic structure. Some variation is the result of articulatory constraints on grammatical processes; some reflects a variable recognition of grammatical boundaries; some appears to be the residue of historical processes which persist long after the social conditions that gave rise to it have disappeared.

It does not seem to me that any of the explanations mentioned as alternative to identification and accommodation will fit the kind of variation under focus. And although Weiner and Labov (ibid.) generously grant that 'Studies of the development of phrase structure rules in the early stages of language learning inevitably involve variation of a meaningful kind', this is of no comfort in the present case, since whatever the nature of the present study it is certainly not concerned with developmental linguistics. I have deliberately laboured these points, because it seems to me important to show that sociolinguistic theory as it is conceived today is incapable of making any sensible pronouncements about semantic variation of the kind described above.

3.3 Basil Bernstein on class and control: visible and invisible

And yet it is not as if there never have been any theories to explain why the same context might elicit different 'orders of relevance' (Bernstein 1971a: 144). Since the early 1960s the writings of Bernstein have consistently attempted to clarify the logical links between the position of speakers in the division of labour, the relevance of this to human relationships, the relevance of human relationship to forms of human communication, and the relevance of forms of communication to the shaping of the developing child's consciousness. The conceptual problems that Bernstein has attempted to illuminate are complex, and his arguments have not always been understood (see for example the misinterpretations by Labov 1969; Weiner and Labov 1983; Trudgill 1974; Dittmar 1976; Edwards 1976 etc.). Nonetheless, if we are looking for a theory that will explain the variation in the discourse of control between LAP and HAP mothers, then we need to understand the sequence of his arguments. It was Bernstein who through his theory of elaborated and restricted codes drew attention to the underlying principles which explain the semantic selections of both groups of mothers. He was able to predict those social conditions under which 'status differences are less clear-cut' (Bernstein 1971a: 158) 'there is the appearance of the child having a choice' (ibid.) where 'the mother, so to speak, lays out the situation for the child', 'The rule is, so to speak, achieved by the child. The child, given the situation and the explanation, opts for the rule'. (ibid.) In these phrases which, for lack of space, I have plucked out of their context, Bernstein is describing the person-oriented form of elaborated control, which is characterised by weak classification and weak framing (Bernstein 1975b, 1986). According to Bernstein, if classification is weak, then boundaries between phenomena are blurred; when framing is weak, then the rules for carrying out some activity are treated as negotiable. Bernstein makes these generalisations on the basis of a sociologically powerful theory; he is not proceeding on the basis of actual observation of my research data. After my detailed discussions above, it is not necessary to labour the very obvious point that though Bernstein has not seen my data, it is his descriptions that fit its nature; and they illuminate the nature of the mothers' discourse by reference to the underlying social conditions that give rise to the discourse. Consider for example the following (Bernstein 1971a: 159):

> In the case of person-oriented appeals, the rights of the controller or parent which inhere in his formal status are less likely to come under attack than under positional appeals. For in the case of personal appeals, what may be challenged are the reasons the controller gives or even a specific condition of the controller or the parent.…Thus personal appeals may act to protect the normative order from which the controller derives his rights. For here there is an attenuation of the relationship between power and the rule systems. In the case of positional appeals which shift rapidly to the imperative mode of control, the formal rights of the controller or parent may well be challenged, and with this the whole normative order from which the controller derives his right can come under attack. Imperative/positional forms of control under certain conditions may lead the socialized to turn to alternative value systems.

In the light of these (rather scanty) extracts from Bernstein, even a quick look at dialogues 1 and 2 reveals how successful the theory is at making predictions about which mothers are likely to say what kinds of thing to their children in the context of control. I have deliberately quoted from some of Bernstein's earliest writings as a means of demonstrating that in many respects the critique of Bernstein by sociolinguists was undertaken even more casually than that of the notion of social class. When Bernstein claimed (1971a: 176) that 'elaborated codes draw upon rationality', he was not showing his alleged deep prejudice against the working class speakers; if the results of my research are to be given credence, he was simply describing the fact that certain middle class speakers were far more inclined to give [inherent] reasons than were others. The evaluation of rationality as good or bad, is not Bernstein's invention. But, certainly, it is his contribution to show that we are likely to view rationality as desirable or undesirable depending upon our social position. When he claims (1971a: 177) 'where codes are elaborated the socialised has more access to the grounds of his own socialization', he is not extolling the alleged middle class habits of verbosity; he is saying simply that orientation to elaborated code leads a person to talk as if they believed that the situation must be laid out explicitly for the addressee, because the addressee is a separate individual, not an extension of the speaker's self. A way of interpreting this is to say that middle class people prize individuality above community – an aspect of middle class ideology that can hardly be denied. Note how we all consider it praiseworthy to strive to be unique individuals, different from everybody else. From this point of view, it is quite unsatisfactory to damn elaboration as an easily dispensable attribute of discourse, without asking if the tendency to elaborate has contributed to our own power, whether in academia or in some other domain.

If, as Labov (1972b) maintains, the fundamental questions of sociolinguistics are posed by why any one says anything, and if saying has anything to do with meaning, then it seems to me that we do need a theory such as Bernstein's that is sociologically informed. The full scope of this theory is not revealed by the discussion presented here; because my concern has been to simply highlight the class-sensitive semantic choices of control. It would seem to me that Bernstein's is a theory in whose power it is to show the deep motivations of our choices of meaning; that can reveal the extent to which our concepts of individuality as god-given need to be reconsidered. A theory such as Bernstein's certainly has distinct advantages over a somewhat naive do-it-yourself sociology that underlies much of the discussion about 'the social significance' of language in use. One of its prime contributions is to show that much of what we are and what others are is not decreed entirely by innate mechanisms, but is our own and our immediate meaning group's responsibility. As Halliday (1975c) commented we need Bernstein's sociology to give Labovian sociolinguistics its foundation, not the other way round as implied in Weiner and Labov (1983).

4 Coda: the subject-matter of sociolinguistics

I have argued above that sociolinguistic theory as it stands today, cannot provide an explanation for the kind of semantic variation described in this chapter. There are at least two ways of handling this situation: one is to modify the theory; the other is to define the field in such a way that irksome phenomena of this kind can be excluded. For example, we might deny that the kind of analysis indicated here is in fact semantic, or we might argue that it contributes nothing to our understanding of the nature of language and is thus not a part of sociolinguistics proper. However, such a response would inevitably raise the question of the definition of 'semantics' and 'sociolinguistics'. And as is perhaps evident to all (socio)linguists, the boundaries of words and their meanings are not given by nature; they are created by our own discourses – this is one reason why Saussure's exclusion of discourse (*parole*) from linguistics causes such a major problem. It should not be assumed that in this respect technical terms differ from cups and mugs, or from wisdom and mother-wit; for they too are given their meaning through discourse. But in the case of the definition of semantics, the ascription of meaning to the term is conscious: it has been developed so as to maintain the term in harmony with what our theories can do.

The issue of whether the categories in terms of which I have analysed my data are semantic or pragmatic or some other kind of creature altogether can only be answered within the framework of some specific theory; which is to say, in the end, the issue is decidable only by reference to our ideas about language itself, for it is this that a theory is designed to explain. If I see language not as an elaborate naming system, not as a structure of form that passively reflects the universe, but as an active force that contributes to the making of my environment as I find it, and as I can construct it through the use of my linguistic resources, then the Labovian view of semantics would appear to me inadequate. My semantic analysis would therefore have to be different from the item-based, referential analyses which he might regard as semantic. This implies that in order to exclude this study from consideration either it should be argued successfully that language is not an active force in social life, or that the kind of semantic analysis I have conducted is less suited to the analysis of language as an active social force than the item-based referential analysis. Or perhaps, we should take seriously the comments made by Gardin and Marcellesi (1987: 23) who point out:

> predominating sociolinguistics did not give its attention to the examination of a relationship other than the arbitrary one… yet works by Bernstein urged the study of variation at a semantic and cognitive level and its connection with the place of the subjects in the social division of work. … If it is not forgotten that it is through linguistic interaction that humanity constitutes itself… (and that) at the same time linguistic interaction faces, analyses, and transforms reality, then sociolinguistics can define its explanatory specificity and can effectively become 'linguistics put back on its feet'…

My study in semantic variation is a modest attempt to fill the gap which Gardin and Marcellesi deplore and the absence of which leaves sociolinguistics open to criticism. If 'true' sociolinguistics is that study of language in its social context, which makes some contribution to the general theory of language – as demanded by Labov (1972a, d) – perhaps one might point to the fact that a study of the present kind does precisely that. It does this by recognising the deeply social nature of language, by restoring it to its rightful place in human communication; it raises human communication above a set of patterned noises to an effective instrument for changing those very social divisions, those very social contexts which have been created and maintained through the complicity of language use. These divisions and cleavages do not disappear because we in a mistaken sentimental interpretation of egalitarianism refuse to recognise them; rather, like invisible control, they are simply made invisible; but those whom we profess to champion continue to bear the consequences of that control!

Notes

1 The research was funded by the Australian Research Grant and Macquarie University Research Grant Schemes. Throughout this research I have been fortunate to have the valuable help of Carmel Cloran, who analysed the entire corpus for the phase of the research under focus, and carried the responsibility of the research during my unavoidable absences.

2 The semantic network is currently being used in researches by other colleagues and postgraduate research students at Macquarie University for studies in various fields e.g. second language development, class room discourse, and legal discourse.

3 Terms enclosed in square brackets e.g., [progressive] here refer to an element of the semantic level, those in italics in square brackets e.g., [*major*] represent a systemic option in some lexicogrammatical system network.

4 Throughout this table, the semantic features are in capitals letter and the grammatical within square brackets.

5 I thank Barbara Horvath and Greg Guy (Sydney University) for their advice in the early stages of statistical analysis. My thanks are also due to Alan Taylor (Macquarie University) for help with the statistical analysis, though the responsibility for input criteria and for the interpretation remains mine. Thanks are also due to Ann Eyland, whose brilliant help in the early stages got the analysis set up and to Harry Purvis and John Telec for their valuable assistance through the most difficult periods of this research.

8 Rationality in everyday talk: from process to system [1992]

1 Introduction[1]

Since revolution is a favoured term in the historiography of linguistics, let me begin with the remark that unlike the much publicised Chomskyan revolution in modern linguistics, the revolution that is corpus linguistics occurred without any noticeable flourishes. In fact, I am not even sure that those who did most to bring this revolution about – such as Francis, Kučera, Leech, Quirk, Svartvik – saw themselves in the early days of corpus linguistics as engaged in a deliberately iconoclastic enterprise. However, the successes of corpus linguistics have thrown into question some of the most cherished beliefs that form the foundation of the dominant linguistic approaches of this century. Take, for example, the Saussurean dichotomy of langue and parole, a distinction which in some form or other remains crucial for all linguistic theories. The seemingly unbridgeable gap that Saussure created between these two complementary aspects of language now appears – thanks to the revived respectability of interest in working from corpora – to be an artefact of his conception of what language in use is like. Granted that in parole there are elements of willfulness, of idiosyncrasy, of individuality, as Saussure maintained, this is still far from the whole story: after the pioneering work of Labov, it seems impossible to deny that like the chaos of chaos theory (Gleick 1987), parole is inherently orderly. But this orderliness becomes visible – again, like the presence of order in chaos – only from an examination of massive data. The true nature of parole is not revealed by simply consulting one's intuition; it is only when parole is seen through the eyes of sizeable corpora of naturally occurring language that it becomes possible to appreciate the true nature of human talk – and by talk I mean any exchange of meaning whether by writing or by speaking. Since understanding the efficacy of human talk is a condition for understanding the nature of language itself, corpus linguistics is in a position to study the nature of language by examining human talk from two closely interwoven perspectives.

The first perspective concerns the examination of that aspect of parole which relates most directly to 'the fact that natural languages are essentially pragmatic languages' (Bar-Hillel 1970: 208). The universal characteristics of parole – its orderly variation, its flexible regularities – are functional (Halliday

1970): they have their origin in the relations of parole to the community's living of life, while at the same time, the various dimensions of a community's social contexts of living depend on parole for their creation, maintenance, and evolution. Language as a social semiotic is predicated on this mutual relation between parole and social contexts. The second perspective on the efficacy of talk is furnished by an examination of language as system: granted that the system of language qua system is invariant in respect of the features that make that system a system – e.g., its functionally based organisation, its realisationally linked strata, and the *or* and *and* relations manifested in the paradigmatic and syntagmatic pattern formation – this is certainly not all that we mean by language system. The lie to the complete invariance and constancy of what we understand by language is given by the very recognition of the concept of *etats de langue*; and it is certainly not necessary to labour the point that the move from one *etat de langue* to the next originates in parole. It follows that language as an already produced and an evolving system is predicated on the symbiotic relation between parole and langue – between process and its product – so we may claim that the system enables the efficacy of process while process fashions the very rules by which it attains this efficacy. Clearly the two perspectives are essential to each other: language could not be a static product if it is to remain an effective social semiotic since the social dimensions of human communities are not static; process could not be entirely idiosyncratic or individualistic if it is to furnish a system displaying large scale regularities. Corpus linguistics has in its hands the unique possibility of revealing both the invariant qualities of language as a system for semiosis and the variation inherent in language because of the fact that language systems live in and through the practice of semiosis. Since the practice of semiosis is of necessity embedded in the social living of life, corpus based linguistics can be a powerful means of revealing the details of this complex situation.

Because naturally occurring use of language inevitably leads into the social contexts of a community and because it is in using language that we most naturally display our sense of the internalised system, corpus based linguistics permits enquiry into language from both perspectives – that of language as social semiotic system and that of language as a product inscribed in the social process of speaking. However, it seems to me that the advances in corpus linguistics have not seized the opportunities inherent in the approach. Instead, the size, the storage, and the retrieval of data seem to be some of the primary concerns in the field. In the area of description, the formal analysis of the 'material' occupies the centre of attention, without any concern with the social context, the traces of which must arguably exist in the corpus, as debates about that very difficult issue of representativeness of the data indicate. It would be presumptuous of me – particularly since according to certain definitions I do not even deserve the title of corpus linguist – to suggest that issues such as predominantly occupy corpus linguists today are either immaterial, or not deserving of attention. The point I want to make here is simply that these preoccupations do not represent the full gamut of what can be achieved through an examination of the rich corpus of naturally occurring language; and I would hazard a guess that if certain problems do not receive attention, this may not be for lack of power and sophistication in the present day technology, but rather because the traditions of autonomous linguistics still dominate our thinking: the long shadow of the Saussurean dichotomy still obscures the most central and dynamic aspects of human language. It is always easy to postpone those problems of the analysis of language, which appear less central. Certainly, it is my impression that the socio-semantic analysis of corpora has been one such problem.

In this chapter I shall attempt to present one approach to the analysis of meaning in everyday language, keeping in mind the fact that naturally occurring corpora are, above all, the use of language by socially positioned speakers. For this socio-semantic study, I shall examine the data of everyday talk between mothers and children: more specifically, my interest will be in the kinds of reasoning the mothers employ in talking to their children. Some of the questions I shall raise are the following: if reasoning is to be taken as a textual strategy, what categories do we need to describe its nature? What is its semantic structure? How is this structure realised lexicogrammatically? How is the social positioning of the speakers manifested, if it is, in the mothers' reasoning? If there is evidence of variation, is it simply idiosyncratic, or does the corpus display the traces of the potency of social context in a systematic manner? Most of the practical details regarding the research project have been described above in chapters 3-6. The data used here comes from Phase 1 of the research and the methodology used for the analysis of meaning is the same as described in the previously mentioned chapters[2]. However, an indication of the framework for the analysis of reasoning needs to be provided in section 2, followed by some cases of mothers' reasoning which will indicate the range of reasons mothers use. Section 4, will conclude the discussion by commenting on the kind of variation my corpus reveals; and the implications of this study from a social and linguistic point of view.

2 Reasoning and rationality

In the literature on reasoning, a distinction is made between various kinds of reasoning, the one most often invoked being that between inductive v. deductive. This chapter will be concerned primarily with deductive reasoning, which is based on inference (see section 4 for justification). The close relation between reasoning and rationality is so well accepted that it need not be argued, but it would be instructive to take at least a brief look at some of the terms associated with both these words. To do this, let me first consult another corpus-based source, viz., the dictionary. We may grant a dictionary's claim to play the role of '…a useful guide to writing and speaking … as well as an aid to reading and understanding' (Sinclair 1987: xv); but if so, this is only because the claim is grounded in the fact that by definition a dictionary is a conventionalised record of how (some sections of) the community understand the words and vocables of some language. The dictionary is a guide because it reflects the community's usage; it presents a record of not only (some section of) the speech community's classification of experience but also how these classes of experience are valued in the community. In examining the terms reason and rationality, both the classificatory (i.e., ideational) and the evaluative (i.e., interpersonal) aspects of the meaning will be relevant.

2.1 Reasoning in community

Part of the entry for rational as 'adj.' in the Shorter Oxford English Dictionary reads as follows:

> . adj. 1. Having the faculty of reasoning; endowed with reason. b. Exercising one's reason in a proper manner; having sound judgement; sensible, sane 1632. 2. Of, pertaining or relating to, reason 1601. 3. Based on, derived from, reason or reasoning 1531. 4. Agreeable to reason: reasonable, sensible; not foolish, absurd, or extravagant 1601. …

Note here the near equation of rationality with soundness of judgement and its absence as synonymous with foolishness. It follows that if on some agreed definition of rationality, some one were to lack this attribute, then such a person could be legitimately considered foolish. So it is important to understand what would count as exercising one's reason in a proper manner. Part of the entry for reason as substantive reads:

> I.1. A statement of some fact (real or alleged) employed as an argument to justify or condemn some act, prove or disprove some assertion, idea or belief… b. *Logic.* One of the premises in an argument; esp. the minor premise when placed after the conclusion 1826…

The account proceeds to link *reason* to constructions such as *why, wherefore, that*; *of, for; to*... etc. We find that reason is the 'intellectual power or faculty … characteristic of mankind … which is ordinarily employed in adapting thought or action to some end; the guiding principle of the human mind in the process of thinking'; the term can be equated with *sanity*. As process, reason is seen as:

> . 2. *intr*. To hold argument, discussion, discourse, or talk *with* another -1671. b. To argue, discourse, converse, talk -1667. c. To employ reasoning or argument with a person in order to influence his conduct or opinions 1847. 3. To think in a connected, sensible or logical manner; to employ the faculty of reason in forming conclusions 1593. 4. with object-clause: a. To question, discuss *what, why*, etc. 1529. b. To argue, conclude, infer *that*, etc. 1527. …

Grammatically, to reason is an intransitive process. Like sleeping or laughing it does not extend beyond the doer. But unlike the latter verbs, it resembles those verbal processes which have the potential of leading to interaction thus influencing an other. Any sustainable account of reasoning will need to take note of the fact that being rational is a desirable attribute, since it is the opposite of foolish; that the exercise of reason often involves discursivity; that it is fashioned to suit some end. This brief look into the dictionary provides some non-specialist senses of the relevant terms. Let us turn now to the specialists – the philosophers and logicians – since the analysis of reasoning is considered their special purview.

2.2 A notional account of reasoning

In the logico-philosophical literature the use of the terms discussed above stands in a complex relation to the 'guidance' provided by the dictionary. It will surprise no linguists that typically the usage is congruent for the most part with the views expressed in the dictionary; this is particularly so where the evaluation of rationality is concerned. The main difference seems to be in the narrowing of the definition of rationality itself. Let me emphasise that what follows is not a review of this learned logico-philosophical literature: this is frankly beyond my competence. To an outsider such as myself, the disagreements amongst logicians and philosophers on notions connected with reasoning and rationality seem just as important as the agreements; and both can be equally mystifying – could it be because one is perhaps not being rational? My aim in this discussion is to tease out some of the important attributes of reasoning identified in the literature. The review and discussion of these attributes can then function as a basis for further description.

Although in the logico-philosophical literature, the terms reasoning, and rationality are often used as if they were one and the same thing, there appears to be an important difference between the two: rationality, like reasonableness, is inherently good and desirable. The same cannot be claimed of reasoning, *per se*: an act of reasoning is not necessarily inherently good. One is not reasonable or rational simply because one reasons; one is reasonable and rational because one reasons well. As Pole (1972: 155) points out: 'Irrational people will reason. They reason indeed, but reason badly (their distinguishing feature)…'.

Note that whereas the Shorter OED presents *having the faculty of reasoning* as a possible paraphrase of rational, the acceptance of Pole's view would deny this possibility; rather, it would require 'exercising one's reason in a proper manner' as a necessary condition for attributing rationality to someone. If this distinction between reasoning and good reasoning is important, then we need not only to specify what will count as an act of reasoning, but also what will constitute good reasoning. On what basis would we decide that reason is being used in a proper manner. One of the clearest statements about (good) reasoning was provided by Peirce (1955: 7):

> The object of reasoning is to find out, from a consideration of what we already know, something else which we do not know. Consequently, *reasoning is good if it be such as to give a true conclusion from true premisses, and not otherwise* (emphasis mine. RH). Thus the question of validity is purely one of fact and not of thinking. A being the fact stated in the premisses and B being that concluded, the question is, whether these facts are really so related that if A were, B would generally be. If so, the inference is valid; if not, not. It is not in the least the question whether when the premisses are accepted by the mind, we feel the impulse to accept the conclusion also. It is true that we do generally reason correctly by nature. But that is an accident; the true conclusion will remain true if we had no impulse to accept it; and the false one would remain false, though we could not resist the tendency to believe in it.

According to this view, reasoning is good only if two kinds of truth are simultaneously present: true premises and true conclusion. However, it is arguable that (a) these two kinds of truth are independent of each other, and (b) that they differ qualitatively. So far as true conclusion is concerned, there is an element of necessity about it: given certain premises, (good) reasoning logically and inexorably leads to a certain conclusion. So, to take a hackneyed example, if we believe that (1a) *all men are mortal*; and (1b) *Socrates is a man*, then from the belief in these premises follows the necessary conclusion that (1c) *Socrates is mortal*. But the necessity of the conclusion is not affected by the truth or falsehood of the premises. Thus suppose someone were to say: (2a) *all men are immortal*; (2b) *Socrates is a man*; and therefore (2c) *Socrates is immortal*, then so far as the necessity of the conclusion is concerned, this latter piece of reasoning is as impeccable as the first one. Whether or not a conclusion is true is independent of the truth/falsehood of the premisses; as Pole points out (1972: 161): 'To recognize that *p* implies *q*, I need not myself accept *p*'. I take this to imply that it is not necessary for *p* to be true – whatever that may mean; it is sufficient for some one to believe that *p*. A true conclusion is then what follows necessarily from believing that *p*, irrespective of whether or not *p* is true. Conversely, if a conclusion drawn by someone is false/invalid, this does not necessarily imply that the premises are thereby rendered false. For example, if instead of (1c), someone were to say (1c') *(therefore) Socrates wears clothes*, then this is a conclusion that does not follow necessarily from the given premises; it is an invalid conclusion because it cannot be derived from the terms of the premises. However, the invalidity of this conclusion does not render (1a-b) false.

To my mind, these examples show two things: first, it is possible to appreciate the unblemished character of someone's reasoning even if one disagrees with the initial premise. We may fail to understand how anyone can come to believe premise (2a), but we cannot fail to accept the logicality of their conclusion, the correctness of their inference, so long as disbelief in (2a) is suspended. Secondly, an invalid conclusion does not imply that the premises themselves were either invalid or untrue. I conclude that the truth of premises and the truth of conclusion are independent of each other and that for the purposes of analysis it is best to dissociate them.

My second claim was that the two kinds of truth are qualitatively different. A hint of this difference is provided in the above discussion. A true conclusion is true by necessity: as such, it is the essence of reasoning. With apologies to Peirce '...if A, the premise, were accepted, B, the conclusion, would necessarily have to be': we are not concerned here with historical truth; rather our concern is with inferential truth. In fact, it could be misleading to use the term truth to refer to a necessary inference; a more precise term would be valid conclusion. Let me refer to this attribute of reasoning as INFERENTIALITY. If there is a truth here, it is presented as truth by derivation – a truth that is implicit in the semantico-logical relation (Halliday 1985a: 203ff.) between the messages. The derived truth of (1c) *(therefore) Socrates is mortal*, presented as a conclusion is not the same as the truth of the assertion *(1b) Socrates is a man*. So I am claiming that by contrast with true conclusion, the truth of a true premise is presented as a primary fact, having its roots in the world being (perceived as) such and so. I shall refer to this kind of truth as VERIDICALITY. Veridicality is essentially spatio-temporal in nature; a universally true assertion still refers to infinite time. Inferentiality is not so constrained; something could be inferentially true in a universe that has no spatio-temporal existence, but exists simply in our imagination. From this follows an important difference between these two kinds of 'truth'. As the Peirce extract implies the acceptance of the first kind of truth – inferentiality – is in no way affected by our personal taste, desire, conviction, or attitude, and so on. The acceptance of the premise is sufficient to safeguard its truth. This is not so with veridicality. So given the assertion *capitalism is exploitative*, or *the nature of authority is coercive*, the acceptance of the truth/falsehood of these assertions does appear to be subject to our political convictions. The importance of this difference will hopefully become obvious at a later point. Let me now return to the question of reasoning and good reasoning.

According to Peirce, good reasoning calls for both inferentiality and veridicality. Leaving the question of good reasoning aside for the moment, I am going to argue that so far as reasoning itself is concerned, it is only the attribute of inferentiality that is criterial. This attribute is widely recognised as a *sine qua non* of any discourse that deserves to be called reasoning – the one defining characteristic in the absence of which no reasoning can be said to have taken place. The case is different for veridicality. Something may lack veridicality, but it could still be viewed as a case of reasoning. This is illustrated by (2a-c), where veridicality was absent, but which still represents a case of reasoning, even if a bad one by Peircean standards. By contrast, a number of true assertions in a row will not be constitutive of reasoning so long as the attribute of inferentiality is not present. As an example, consider the following:

> (3a) on Friday, March 26, 1991 I parked my car in the Gordon shopping centre car park at 1:45 p.m. (3b) but when half an hour later, I returned to the car park, the car was no longer there (3c) I reported this incident to the Pymble Police Station by phone (3d) and they asked me to lodge a report in person.

It is highly unlikely that (3a-d) would be regarded as a case of reasoning. This is not because it is illogical in the ordinary sense of the word; but its logic is the logic of temporal sequentiality, not of inferentiality; and it is this lack of inferentiality that prevents it from being seen as a case of reasoning. Since I know from personal knowledge that (3a-d) are a faithful account of true events as they occurred, it follows that the attribute of veridicality is not sufficient by itself to cause something to be seen as an act of reasoning.

It may be argued that the truth of (3a-d) is different from that of (1a). In the latter case it transcends 'the this, the here and the now' (Peters 1972: 210), whereas the truth of the former is historically specific: it concerns the this, the here and the now of a past moment in a specific person's life. In the literature on reasoning and rationality, it seems to be generally accepted that the major premise is better for being universal, and for possessing general applicability. Thus one reason for Jarvie's (1976) scathing criticism of Toulmin (1958, 1972) is the latter's suggestion that other than universally true assertions, such as *scarcely any Swedes are Roman Catholics* (Toulmin 1958: 109) could function as a major premise in rational argumentation. The distinction between a universally true and a 'locally true' premise is linked in the literature to that other important distinction between deductive and inductive reasoning, respectively (see for example Overton 1990: 3). The major premise in deductive reasoning is universal. All this is fairly familiar, but note first that a universally true assertion must still make reference to time and space; moreover, an assertion may be universal in its scope without being true as for example (2a) *all men are immortal*; and, finally, Peirce talks not simply of a true premise, but rather of 'true premisses'. In the kind of reasoning illustrated by (1a-c), only (1a) *all men are mortal* is universal; (1b) *Socrates is a man* can justifiably be said to be an assertion about a specific being. What I have referred to as veridicality – i.e., the truth of premises – comprises both a universally true assertion and a locally true one.

It is to be noted that veridicality – whether it is universal or not – is, by itself, not sufficient for something to be even seen as connected discourse. This will be evident from a consideration of: (4a) *all men are mortal* (4b) *precious metals do not rust*; (4c) *the present Prime Minister of Australia is called Bob Hawke*. In (4a-c) each assertion has veridicality; but the set as a whole is not a case of normal connected discourse: we cannot easily imagine a situation in which (4a-c) would be said one after the other by one and the same person as part of the same discourse. It follows that we cannot sensibly debate the status of (4a-c) as an instance of reasoning; this is purely because the assertions are not connectable. This conclusion demands the recognition of yet another attribute of reasoning, viz., DISCURSIVITY: After all, to reason is, as the dictionary informs us, *to hold argument, discussion, discourse with someone*; and we can do none of these things without being discursive. Further, the presence of veridicality is by itself not sufficient for something to have the quality of discursivity.

So far I have mentioned three attributes of reasoning: (i) inferentiality; (ii) veridicality; and (iii) discursivity. What is the relation of these attributes to each other? Of these three, discursivity would appear to be the most general: any set of messages possessing inferentiality must also possess discursivity, but the reverse is not true. This formulation implies that discursivity is a necessary but not a sufficient condition for some saying to be regarded as a case of reasoning: something may have discursivity, without also being an act of reasoning. So for example, (3a-d) have discursivity; however, the messages are not a case of reasoning because there is no inferentiality. Discursivity is an attribute of all classes of texts and/or textual strategies. The attributes of inferentiality and veridicality are independent of each other, as I attempted to argue with (2a-c). As for veridicality and discursivity, again there seems to be no necessary connection between the two: (4a-c) shows that something may be true without possessing the attribute of discursivity. On the other hand, the presence of fictive discourse makes it obvious that discursivity does not entail veridicality. Taken together, these observations lead to the conclusion that every case of reasoning must have discursivity and inferentiality; that inferentiality is the criterial attribute of reasoning; and that it is immaterial whether veridicality is absent or present. But if so, what, if any, role does truth play in reasoning?

Such literature as I have been able to consult, I have found not clear on this issue. On the one hand, it is obvious that experiments on reasoning (e.g. those reported in Nisbett and Ross 1980; Overton 1990; Stich 1990; Wason and Johnson-Laird 1968, 1972 etc.) make use of premises which are only as-if-true assertions, in the sense that at least some of them are not, in truth, true. If the results can be taken as an indication of the extent of subjects' ability to reason, then clearly veridicality is not an essential ingredient of reasoning. On the other hand, there seems to be a general agreement that veridicality is a highly desirable attribute of reasoning: in fact, there are scholars (e.g., Jarvie 1976; Kekes 1979) who would treat (2a-c) as a piece of defective reasoning purely on the ground that its major premise is false. Note, however, that even if (2a-c) are taken as an instance of bad reasoning, the 'bad-ness' of reasoning here would still be of a quite different kind from that in Bateson's example: (5a) *men die;* (5b) *grass dies;* therefore (5c) *men are grass* (Bateson 1987). The explanation for the badness of reasoning here will have to be granted as arising from the invalidity of inference, not in terms of the lack of truth of the premises, notwithstanding the qua si metaphorical nature of dies in (5b).

There is yet another problem to be considered: to require veridicality even as an attribute of good reasoning has obvious implications for the interpretation of rationality. If the mark of rationality is good reasoning and good reasoning requires beginning with true premises, then it follows that rationality cannot be correctly attributed to any reasoner who fails to begin with true premises. Rationality will clearly be impossible to attain, unless one is in possession of the truth. This, in turn, has certain disturbing implications: either the domain within which good reasoning might occur would be extraordinarily limited (e.g. empirically proved phenomena), so that one would reason only from indisputable, hard facts, or it must be assumed that the truth/falsehood of all primary assertions is a simple issue, displaying a uniformity of belief in all members of a community. But since this latter assumption is without basis (e.g. consider the claim about the exploitative quality of capitalism), this raises the vexing question: whose truth?

The three attributes I have identified here are not presented as an exhaustive account of concepts relevant to reasoning; in fact, I shall need to add to these attributes, but this addition will be made more easily once I have presented my views on the structure of reasoning.

2.3 The structure of reasoning

As the Shorter OED suggests reasons and reasoning are closely associated with *why? Wherefore?* etc. The importance of *why* is not simply because it enters into a construction with reason; in fact *why* is criterial to any discussion of the structure of reasoning, in as much as it can be justifiably regarded as the harbinger of reasons themselves. This is not to say that every reason offered actually follows a *why*. In everyday talk between mothers and children, mothers do not wait for their children to put 'a proposition into the interrogative form' (Peirce 1955: 11); some mothers will seize any opportunity that appears suitable for giving reasons. Consider the following example[3]:

Extract 1

Julian: (1) when I get old as you (2) and [? Maree likes me] (3) could we marry each other?
Mother: (4) no (5) because Maree is your cousin
Julian: (6) oh
Mother: (7) 'cause cousins aren't allowed to marry
Julian: (8) why?
Mother: (9) 'cause the law says they're not
Julian: (10) who is that? [= who is law]
Mother: (11) the law?
Julian: (12) yeah
Mother: (13) the policeman …

Here after answering the child's question in (4), the mother goes on immediately to offer a reason in (5) by way of justifying that answer, even though the child has asked no *why* question. When, in (6), Julian makes a bemused acknowledgment of this bit of unsolicited reasoning, she produces yet another unsolicited justification in (7), as if there were an unspoken question in the air asking: *why shouldn't I marry Maree simply because she is my cousin?* This second unsolicited reason from the mother does draw an actual *why* from Julian in (8): and the mother again provides a reason for the reason that she had given earlier. If this is typical of reasoning, it would be wrong to suppose that an overtly asked *why* question is necessary for reasoning to occur. But if so, why should *why, wherefore* etc. be regarded as important to reasoning? What role do they play in the reasoning game? Let me use the same example to comment on these issues, using *why* as the prototypic item; hopefully, in the course of doing this, I shall also be able to present my view of the structure of reasoning.

First, the very reciprocity of *why* and *because* is important; and this is true irrespective of whether or not either of the terms is overtly present. This is tantamount to claiming that in principle every *because* is a *response* to some *why*; and, potentially, every *why* is a call for a *because*. It would follow that, wherever in a discourse, there is the possibility of a *why* occurring, this represents a point where reasons can legitimately be introduced. While this may be true, it is important to realise (a) that *why* is not free to occur just anywhere in a dialogue; and (b) that its 'reason-demanding' function is not entirely identical in all cases of its occurrence. For example, my data reveals that *why* and its other variants e.g., *what for*, are much more likely to occur following a statement or a command; their occurrence following an offer or a question is far less frequent. It is not entirely clear to me why this should be so. I suggest tentatively that, in general terms, a statement is a claim that something is the case, while a command is produced in the expectation that something will become the case. Perhaps because of this, both the claim of an actual state and of an expected one lay themselves open to a demand for validation[4]. By contrast, a question neither claims nor necessarily expects something to be the case, while an offer only anticipates the addressee's satisfaction, and so neither is hospitable to the demand for justification. Also in both these environments – that of a question, and that of an offer – the terms *why, wherefore* etc., when they do occur, appear to have a slightly different function. Consider, for example, an exchange in which A says to B *are you driving to town today?*, to which B's response is *why?*. This use of *why* is different from Julian's use of the word in (8) above. Thus it makes sense to expand Julian's query as *why aren't cousins allowed to marry?*; it would be a travesty of B's question to expand it as *why am I driving to town today?*. Julian's why metaphorically demands: *how do you justify your assertion?*, while B's *why* asks: *what makes you ask this question?* (For a discussion of this difference, see Halliday and Hasan 1976.) Very often, a *why* following a question or an offer is perceived as a challenge (chapters 5 and 7, this volume). The difference between these two environments – that of assertion and command as opposed to that of question and offer – has other consequences. If some one gives a reason justifying an assertion or command, then this giving of reason is perceived as normal and unremarkable even if the justification had not been sought. But if a justification has been sought, then the not giving of justification is seen as lacking in cooperation. Thus in extract 1, it seems 'quite natural' for the mother to offer reasons in her (5) and (7) even though Julian had not asked for it; but had she refused to give a reason after its explicit demand by Julian, this would have been very noticeable (for a case of this see extract 7).

A noticeable feature of the piece of reasoning in extract 1, is the iterative character of reasons where one reason is justified by another reason, which in turn is justified by another one. This iterative giving of justification is, in fact, the essence of inferentiality in reasoning. Although in classical illustrations, particularly of the syllogistic kind, most of the reasoning procedure remains hidden (Toulmin 1958), in actual fact the reasoning of extract 1 has much in common with that of a syllogism. To demonstrate this, let me present this structure in a formulaic form:

Table 1: The structure of reasoning

(i)	you are not to marry x
	why can't I marry x?
(ii)	because x is your cousin
	why is her being my cousin a reason for my not marrying x?
(iii)	because cousins are not allowed to marry
	why are cousins not allowed to marry?
(iv)	because this is a legal requirement.

In table 1, I have identified four steps in reasoning[5]; each of these steps, is an element of the structure of reasoning; and each, except the last one, is followed by a demand for justification. I will refer to the first step as Claim. A Claim as I suggested above, 'is a' statement or it 'is a' command. The second step supplies a justification for making that Claim. I shall refer to this element of the structure of reasoning as simply Reason. Reason, unlike Claim, is restricted to being assertive. Very often in everyday talk, reasoning is minimal in the sense that it consists only of Claim and Reason. But Reason, being assertive, itself needs some kind of backing, which would serve to validate it. This validation is provided by the third step, which I shall refer to as Principle. If I am not mistaken, what I am calling Principle is very much like what Peirce called the 'leading principle' (1955: 129ff.). It is that part of the chain of reasoning where a generalisation is made: a Principle asserts a state of affairs which is regarded as universally applicable in the speech community. Thus in extract 1, the Principle moves away from the specific cases of Julian and Maree; it now applies to all cousins, no matter who they are and where they are in the community. But, even a Principle is open to enquiry. One may ask for the basis of that Principle: where does it draw its authority from? The answer to this is provided by the fourth and final element of the structure of reasoning. This is where we have the cause of causes – the final dictum. It is where 'the chain of reasons has an end' (Wittgenstein 1958: 326). For want of a better word, I use the term Grounding for this final step. A Grounding specifies the source of validity for the Principle.

It is commonly supposed (Jarvie 1976) that no justification can be sought for the Grounding assertion, though perhaps it would be more accurate to say that a why question at this point leads to something more elaborate and rather different from reasoning. Thus if one asked: *why is there such a legal requirement?* or *why is a legal requirement binding?* (cf. the example in table 1), then any attempt to answer such questions will draw us into an analysis of un-commonsense knowledge. Consider, for example, Durkheim's view of how crime and punishment are constituted (Durkheim 1964). This is not the place to follow this line of argument, but it does seem that so far as the immediate chain of reasoning begun by the initial Claim is concerned, the act of reasoning is completed with the final step of Grounding. Grounding points to the basis being invoked to ascribe legitimacy to the chain of reasoning: a chain of reasoning will be more legitimate than another – all else being equal – to the extent that the assertion which expresses its Grounding is viewed as legitimate. Thus, if the legal institution is itself viewed as legitimate, then any reasoning which follows correct inference etc. and which appeals to that institution will be viewed as legitimate.

Now, precisely the same structure as the one described above can be shown to underlie syllogistic reasoning despite its truncated classical form, as is evident from a comparison of table 1 with table 2 below:

Table 2: The structure beneath a syllogism

(i) gold does not rust
why does gold not rust?

(ii) because it is a precious metal
why does its being a precious metal stop it from rusting?

(iii) because precious metal does not rust
why does precious metal not rust?

(iv) because this is a law of nature.

It is hopefully obvious that so far as the structure of reasoning is concerned, there is no difference between the two tables. Where there is difference is in the state of affairs that is referred to in the two cases. The initial Claim in these two acts of reasoning points to different domains, and through their logical steps of justification, the two reasonings arrive at two very different bases for legitimation. It so happens that the notion of veridicality can be much more easily applied to the Principle in table 2, than to the Principle in table 1. Or perhaps it might be more accurate to say that today an appreciably wider section of the human community would accept the legitimacy of a Principle whose Grounding is in nature (cf. table 2). By comparison, the legitimacy of the Principle whose Grounding is in some social system e.g. the legal one (cf. table 1) will in the nature of things be accepted only by that segment of humanity where the legal system is actually in force.

The third feature of reasoning can be best described by a consideration of tables 1 and 2. By introducing a *why* question after each step except the final, I do not wish to imply that these *why* questions are always or even typically voiced at every point where they are shown in the table. On the contrary, people do not even go around saying things like: *because precious metals do not rust and because gold is a precious metal therefore gold does not rust*; the most likely locution is some such as: *gold does not rust; it's a precious metal*. In dialogue, the possibility always exists of the addressee raising a *why* between the last two messages, but it is relatively rare to find a case where the *why* is overtly pressed into service at every possible point. So, *why* is important not because it must occur, nor even because it is always satisfied if it occurs, but simply because it remains the underlying impetus, therefore a logical possibility. It is this potentiality of *why* that is important to the theory of reasoning: wherever a *why* can occur, there exists a point at which an addressee can justifiably demand further justification, and thus invoke an element that will contribute to the structure of reasoning. And yet, paradoxically, it seems that while *why* 'carries forward' the reasoning, the *why* query itself, as it were, sits outside the reasoning procedure. Reasoning is an act of legitimation: the *why* provokes the procedures of legitimation, without forming a necessary part of it. This I see as the theoretical role of *why* in reasoning.

It is perhaps obvious from the above discussion that nearly all elements of the structure of reasoning 'are' assertions; the sole exception is Claim, which I have suggested might be either assertion or command. So to the three characteristics of reasoning identified above (see section 3.2), we may now add a fourth: reasoning is predominantly assertive. The question of where universal or local truths operate in reasoning is best addressed by reference to what part an assertion might be playing in the structure of reasoning. Typically, assertions in Claim and Reason can be and often are historically specific, whereas those in Principle and Grounding are universal – or at least more widely applicable.

2.4 The lexicogrammar of reasoning

In sub-section 2.1, I provided an account of the communal view of reasoning and rationality; in 2.2, I have outlined my understanding of the most important aspects of these concepts as put forward by philosophers, who claim to understand more about reasoning and rationality than any other segment of our society; in 2.3, I have attempted to show that the structure of the classic form of reasoning is essentially the same as that which underlies mundane, everyday reasoning. In this sub-section, I will describe in broad terms those elements of the linguistic system (of English) that are implicated through realisation in acts of reasoning. To do this, I shall make use of Halliday's systemic functional model (for the design features of the model, see Halliday 1970, 1979a, 1985a; Hasan 1995a; Martin 1991; Matthiessen 1991, 1992. I alone am responsible for the account presented here).

What does the system of language have to be like in order to meet the human need for reasoning with others? Ignoring such preliminaries as the need for a system of meaning and wording that is largely in common to the reasoner and her addressee, let me go directly to the important attributes of reasoning which are identified above on a the basis of meaning. To say that the attributes identified are meaning-based is to say that they specify (some of) the semantic properties of reasoning. If it is true that the resource for the construal of linguistic meaning is the lexicogrammar of a language, then for any given language, it should be possible to identify those aspects of the lexicogrammar which are realisationally related to each specific attribute, so long as it is a semantic attribute i.e., one that pertains to linguistic meaning. The statements made here are with regard to English, though they might hold good for other languages to the extent to which (a) the semantics of reasoning is in common to the two; and (b) the various relevant semantic properties are realised by the same lexciogrammatical pattern(s) as in English.

First, then the attribute of discursivity, without which nothing that we say could possibly be taken as reasoning. As a semantic notion, this attribute is a more specific concept pertaining to the textual metafunction. For a set of messages to function as reasoning, it is necessary that they possess the semantic attribute of texture (Halliday and Hasan 1976, 1985): the expressions *quality of connectivity, texture*, and *discursivity* refer approximately to the same phenomena that underlie connectedness in discourse. Semantically speaking, reasoning messages will be 'connected' to each other by the relations of *identity* and/or *similarity* of meaning (Hasan 1984b, 1985b). Therefore, in its lexicogrammar, we should expect to find the use of such coding devices as (cohesive) reference, substitution and ellipsis as well as patterns of lexical connections across the messages. Leaving those trivial cases aside, which linguists frequently dream up as examples, there is no form of normal, non-pathological discourse, which lacks the property of discursivity – i.e., texture. At the same time there is no text type – i.e., register – whose identity as that text type/register can be established solely on the basis of the presence or absence of discursivity, *per se* (Halliday and Hasan 1985). Reasoning as a textual strategy is no exception. In their recent studies, Halliday (1987, 1988b) and Martin (1988) have demonstrated that the lexicogrammatical realisation of discursivity differs across distinct registers.

It is likely then, that reasoning too displays lexicogrammatical patterns that are specific to the discursivity typical of this particular textual strategy; if so, this is as yet a closed book.

A more precise definition of inferentiality would draw on both components of the ideational metafunction: viz., experiential and logical. Semantically when some state of affairs is inferred from some other, then between them there could hold relations such as those of condition, entailment, conclusion, contingency, dependency, conjunction and disjunction. These and other such relations form part of the logical metafunction. Messages linked by such relations constitute what in the systemic functional model is known as rhetorical structure (Mann and Thompson 1987; Matthiessen and Thompson 1989). The lexicogrammatical expression of these semantic relations may be overt; if so, we would expect to find the iterative structure of expansion (Halliday 1985a) where some subordinating conjunction, as exemplified by the following structures *if x (then) y; because a (so) b; if (either) x or y (then) z; if (both) m and n (then) p;* and so on will indicate the integration of two (or more) messages as a logically joined entity. On the other hand, it is well known that many of these semantico-logical relations – in fact, most – may remain covert; they may not be realised lexicogrammatically by the occurrence of such 'logical connectives' as *and, but, so, therefore, if* and so on. In these cases, the relations of condition, conclusion etc. are understood on the basis of an understanding of the experiential and textual content of the messages in question. For example when a mother says to her child: *You can't use that knife. It's very sharp. You'll cut yourself*, the logical relation of these messages will be obvious to a normal speaker of English. The common wisdom is to maintain that the logical relations can be derived from an understanding of the 'propositional content' – i.e., experiential content – of the messages. More specifically, such content concerns states of affairs, the elements that make up the structure of events, actions, states etc.; and these pertain to the experiential metafunction. They are expressed lexicogrammatically as transitivity structures and as reference (i.e. signification in Saussure's terms).

It should be obvious that the possibility of inferring the requisite logical relations between messages in the absence of logical connectives cannot be attributed entirely to propositional content / experiential meaning, since the understanding of textual meaning is equally as important for making such inferences. So, for example, the identity of reference for *you*, for *knife* and *it* as well as the relation of meaning between *use* and *cut*, and between *knife*, *sharp* and *cut* are essential to a correct understanding of the above example. It is possible for messages to have propositional content, without having textual meaning – i.e. without having the connectivities that will permit inferential relations between them. This point was illustrated by (4a-c) above (see section 2.2). To conclude, inferentiality is a complex notion: it is construed jointly by transitivity structures, signification, and cohesive ties. Expansion, which is the lexicogrammatical expression of the logical relations under discussion, is itself dispensable. So, by a paradox, although the attribute of inferentiality is essentially logical in nature, and although it is the *sine qua non* of an act of reasoning, an act of reasoning does not necessarily depend on the overt presence of logical connectives. Moreover, since traditionally, in the description of language, the grammar of textual relations has not been foregrounded, the origin of the inferential relation is seen by most linguists as inhering entirely in the 'propositional content', i.e., in what SFL would refer to as 'states of affairs' – things being so-and-so. But it is clear from the above discussion that this view is open to question.

The experiential metafunction is also relevant to the attribute of veridicality. It is not that there is any part of the lexicogrammar of any language that is so designed as to *always and/or only* express the property of veridicality (as, for example, the grammar of expansion always expresses logical relations). But the structures of transitivity and signification have the potential of coding what from a commonsense point of view is considered 'true' – whether locally or universally. It seems to me that the notion of truth as referring to something invariant that exists in and of itself and exercises some control over the nature of meaning in language has been somewhat diluted by the concept of possible worlds. To quote Overton (1990: 4):

> The truth of a sentence or a proposition in a deductive argument is best understood through the concept of possible worlds. Roughly, a possible world is any situation that is conceivable or imaginable .... This means there are many possible words [*sic*! RH] (e.g., the worlds of novels, films, myths, etc.). The commonsense familiar world – called the actual world – is one of these worlds. *A sentence is true in a given possible world when the sentence correctly describes that possible world. Furthermore, a sentence is logically or necessarily true when it is true in all possible worlds*. [emphasis on last two sentences mine. RH]

But the possible worlds of novels etc. are construed by the meaning making potential of lexicogrammar; to say that a sentence is true in some such world if it 'correctly describes that world' is to say hardly more than that the sentence means what it means in that language, and that its meaning is congruent – i.e., non-contradictory – with respect to the meanings construed by other sentences in the same discourse. So the sentence is true not because there is any actual necessity by truthfulness, correspondence to fact, or whatever but purely because the form of language is meaning making. The worlds of fiction do not have to be congruent with the world of our sense experience; any state of affairs can be construed through language so long as the mind can imagine it and the language can be made to mean it. What language 'reflects' of these worlds, therefore, is precisely what it has itself created: language offers us one representation of reality (Hasan 1984b). In the end, then, what is 'true in all possible worlds' including the actual one, and therefore 'logically or necessarily true' is some state of affairs which no one's imagination and/or locution has yet conclusively contradicted – such as the proposition about the flatness of the earth, often cited as a classic case of 'untrue' would have been for those who lived in the medieval ages. This means that truth is socio-culturally located: although veridical states of affairs can be lexicogrammatically expressed in transitivity structures, the latter themselves do not bear any indication of whether in the actual world of time and space such things are or are not. From *John has left*, one of the things we infer – i.e., understand – is that John is no longer where the speaker is. The inference will remain the same whether the states of affairs referred to corresponds to a situation that exists at the moment of speaking in the so-called actual world or whether it is simply imagined or deliberately fabricated by the speaker. There are then no lexicogrammatical structures that exist solely to express the attribute of veridicality. Truth is not an organising concept at the semantic level of natural languages (see also Santambrogio and Violi 1988: 5); rather, truth, in the sense of correspondence to (perceived) reality may be simply an interactive convenience created by the meaning construing power of language.

Turning to universality, it too is a more specific concept within the experiential metafunction. Notions such as class exhaustiveness, and of time-less-ness are realised by structures relevant to Thing and Tense in the grammar of the nominal and verbal group, respectively. Local truth, on the other hand, requires a 'definite description' for at least one participant, and temporally specific reference to the action, event, or ascription of some state.

As for the two message functions – or speech acts, if you prefer – that typically make up the structure of reasoning, these relate to meanings which fall within the interpersonal metafunction. No major premise could take the form of a demand for confirmation; and even though the why and wherefore incite steps in reasoning, in principle the questions themselves fall outside the reasoning process (see discussion in section 2.3). To put it in Peirce's quaint terminology, the *why* and *wherefore* are indicative of the 'mental irritation', the resolving response to which is the act of reasoning. Technically, the lexicogrammatical realisation of the assertive quality of most reasoning messages is expressed by the declarative mood of the clause, though in Claim other mood choices are possible (for more detail chapters 3–5 here).

Typically in the logico-philosophical discussions of reasoning and rationality, there is no indication of the structure of reasoning. Statements about the form of reasoning, when they are found, do not connect easily with considerations of the part played in reasoning by language. There are some notable exceptions to this formal approach (e.g., Habermas 1970a, 1970b, 1984; Toulmin 1958, 1972). In fact, the structure of reasoning presented in section 3.3, despite significant differences, has a good deal in common with the framework suggested by the discussions both in Habermas and in Toulmin. However, even these scholars pay hardly any attention to the essential role of language in reasoning. It seems to me that actions, desires, attitudes, beliefs etc. are not reasons, *per se*. They can be presented as reason; but this calls for a certain way of 'languaging'. And in the absence of such languaging, actions, desires etc. cannot be definitively seen as having the function of reason. For this reason, I have attempted to give some indication of how the semantics and the lexicogrammar of language is implicated in human acts of reasoning. I am aware that the account is anything but complete; and also that the limits of one chapter such as this will not permit detailed demonstration of how the above information can be operationalised in the analysis of reasoning in the data.

3 Reasoning in everyday talk

To say that two or more discourses are cases of reasoning implies that they share something in common. In sections (2.3), I pointed out one source of similarity, namely the structure of reasoning which can be stated in terms of just four elements: Claim, Reason, Principle, and Grounding. This naturally does not mean that there are no differences between actual cases of reasoning. For example, with respect to structure itself, it may be that some elements are *always* present, others might or might not be: the *generalised structure potential* (GSP) of a text type for all registers so far examined calls for the recognition of both elements that are obligatory and those that are optional (Hasan 1985a, c). Again the very same elements of structure may not be realised in the same way across different cases of reasoning. So, an element may be realised by one message, or by a set of logically related messages; or to take another example, the basis for Grounding might be different. In the following sections, I shall briefly consider the question of structural variation before turning to the differences in realisation, and more specifically to differences in the kinds of Grounding mothers provide.

3.1 The structure of everyday reasoning

In extract 2, I present an example of reasoning which highlights all three issues mentioned above: (i) are all elements of the structure of reasoning always present? (ii) are all elements realised in the same way? and (iii) is there variation in the sort of Grounding that mothers provide?

Extract 2

Mother: (1) don't do that ... (mother waits; Pete pays no attention) (2) now look, you'll get it all over me
Pete: (Pete laughs; still continues to move energetically)
Mother: (3) it's not funny (5) what's funny about that?* (6) you do it again (7) and I'll whack you

This dialogue takes place as Pete, holding a glass full of orange juice, is moving around energetically (the details are clear from the wider co-text, not reproduced here). The mother produces a command in (1), which I take as the Claim. The Claim here 'is a' command. Now, to interpret (2), we must infer that she implies: because the juice will spill. It is only on this assumption that (2) makes sense. (2) then forms part of Reason. Reason here consists of (A) because you'll spill it (B) (with the result that) you'll get it all over me. (A) and (B) together form a 'logical' unity, consisting of action and consequence; the two together form the Reason for the mother's Claim. So the element Reason in this case is realised not by a single message, but by two logically integrated messages, whose logical relation remains covert.

If this analysis is accepted, then in these two messages produced by Pete's mother, we have an overt realisation of Claim, and a covert or in terms of Whorf (1956) a 'cryptic' realisation of Reason. It might be objected that there is, in fact, no Reason here; that Reason is being imputed by the analyst. This objection does not seem reasonable. If the mother's first message is 'heard' by the child as *do not shake that juice about*, then the second message, in the absence of some other good reason, will be heard as *you will get that juice all over me*; and this does give us warrant for suggesting that there is an implied part to this Reason, namely *(because) you will spill that juice*. But what about Principle or Grounding? Would it be justifiable to postulate some Principle, and some Grounding to Pete's mother's reasoning simply on the basis of our understanding of the Reason she has given, or should we say that this Reason has no Principle to support it and no source from which it derives legitimacy? It seems to me that at least two considerations are relevant here. As Pollner (1974) points out, in everyday reasoning – what he refers to as 'mundane reasoning' – one hardly ever presents an immaculately organised explicit chain of reasoning: the expression is usually cryptic or condensed. If because of this condensation of meanings, we were to say that no reasoning is occurring here, then it would turn out that most of our everyday talk will require to be treated as habitually un-reasonable, or at least un-reasoning. By implication reasoning and rationality become the privilege of those who produces discourses of specialist knowledge. This is a somewhat questionable conclusion.

On the other hand, if we ascribe all steps of reasoning to every such case as is illustrated by extract 2, then it becomes difficult to differentiate those who typically reason by maintaining more steps than those who do not. And this may be an important distinction, displaying systematic variability in language use. My solution to this dilemma is to recognise that reasoning has a *generalised structure potential* (GSP): in producing the text types that we think of as reasoning, there exists the possibility of choosing all four elements of structure; but choice also implies the possibility of not choosing all four elements. We can go further than this: we can hypothesise (see section 2.3), that to be seen as a case of reasoning, the discourse must have at least two elements, viz., Claim and Reason, however cryptically these might be realised. Their occurrence constitutes the minimal structure of reasoning. They are two obligatory elements of the structure of reasoning, in whose absence reasoning cannot be said to have occurred at all. So in extract 2, Pete's mother's reasoning is minimal; it is not developed to its fuller potential.

This account seems quite straightforward, but it does raise one problem: are we to say that the Reason Pete's mother has given lacks any general Principle as support, and that there is no source for its legitimation? Clearly this is not so. It is in the nature of things that liquid will spill if it is shaken about in inadequate-sized containers. This outcome is not affected by whether or not Pete's mother fails to recognise and/or voice her recognition of the Principle. In this particular case, it seems reasonable to even ascribe at least a tacit knowledge of this general rule to Pete's mother, since it is hard to imagine that her experience of living has not equipped her with this knowledge. It would, however, not be valid to suggest that she actually intends to voice any such Principle, much less to suggest that she is implying it cryptically, since there is nothing in her saying that would support this claim. Unless a Reason is tautological (see 4.5 below), it must derive its legitimacy from some Principle and that principle itself must have a Grounding. If these arguments are valid, then it seems best (i) to suggest that Pete's mother's reasoning in the segment under focus offers evidence of an actually minimal structure; and (ii) to assume that underlying her reasoning is a Principle and a Grounding, even if an intention to bring this to the child's attention cannot be imputed to her. In this view, the fully expanded structure of her reasoning will be said to have the following schematisation:

Claim: don't shake that juice about

Reason: it will spill and so will get all over me

Principle: liquid spills if shaken about in (inadequate sized) container

Grounding: this is a law of nature

This schematisation, which in the final analysis owes its origin to the information provided in Reason, places the reasoning in messages (1–2) of extract 2 on an equal level with the reasoning in the syllogism (see table 2, section 2.3), and in extract 1. But at the same time, the actual structure of reasoning in these three cases is different, thus serving to illustrate the point made about structural differences: Extract 1 has – i.e., displays in its actual structure – all the elements; the syllogism has only three – typically it does not have the element Grounding, while extract 2 has only two elements – its actual structure neither has Principle, nor Grounding. We may claim then that in contrast to the other two its actual structure is minimal. So far as Grounding goes, again there is a difference between extract 1 and 2: while the Grounding in extract 1 is social, that in extract 2 as supplied above is 'physical'; like the syllogism, it is made 'legitimate' by reference to our ideas about the nature of the physical universe. Extract 2 has also provided a hint of variation in the realisation of elements: an element may be realised by a single message or by a number of messages in some logical relation. When this happens, then the realisation may be cryptic or elaborated. Extract 2 is an example of cryptic or condensed (realisation of some element of) reasoning. I will return to extract 2 shortly to discuss the mother's messages (3)-7), but fist a brief discussion of an example of a considerably elaborated realisation.

3.2 Elaboration and the structure of reasoning

Extract 3 is from a dialogue between Janet and her mother. Janet is cross with her mother because the mother had stopped her from playing with marbles. She draws an unflattering picture, which she shows to her mother; it is at this point that Extract 3 begins. Andrew is Janet's baby brother:

Extract 3

Janet: (1) that's you (2) because you don't want me playing with marbles

Mother: (3) Chicky I don't like you playing with marbles (4) when Andrew is around (5) that's all… (6) and you know what, yesterday I found a marble right there (7) when Andrew was crawling around (8) now it was one of those marbles that you were supposed to put back and you forgot

Janet: (9) and—
Mother: (10) and that's why – that's just why I've got to have a rule about it Chicky
Janet: (11) he has – he hasn't swallowed it?
Mother: (12) no (13) well, I just happened to find it (14) before he did (15) before he found it (16) because <(17) if he swallowed it> he would choke (18) and that's why we have to be very careful (19) and when you have the marbles – (20) I don't mind you having the marbles (21) as long as he is asleep – (22) and then we check (23) and make sure that all the ones you have, have gone back in the bowl ... (24) that's a pretty fierce looking drawing
Janet: (25) it's you
Mother: (26) (laughs) I know

One important point to note about extract 3 is that its structure is in fact minimal; in this respect it is like extract 2, having simply the elements Claim and Reason. Principle and Grounding are not articulated by Janet's mother any more than they are by Pete's mother. And if the fact of this similarity is not immediately obvious, this is because of the difference in the way that the elements are realised in the two extracts. While the realisation of the minimal structure in Pete's mother's reasoning is simple in the element Claim and cryptic in Reason, the realisation of both these elements in Janet's mother's reasoning displays a great deal of elaboration. Let me display this schematically:

Claim: you are not to play with marbles
when Andrew is around
BUT I don't mind you having marbles
so long as Andrew is asleep
BUT if you have the marbles
you must put them away
when Andrew wakes up
and (before putting them away)
you should check
to make sure that all marble are safely in the bowl

Reason: if he finds marbles lying around
he will swallow them
if he swallows them
he will choke
(if he chokes he could die)
AND your behaviour in the past suggests that unless we are careful such an accident could occur

Though as in extract 2, so also here Principle is not offered, it is possible to frame it something as follows: babies being immature need to be provided a safe environment by their care-givers in order to avoid accidental injury, while the Grounding of such a Principle would be located in the organisation of the universe by nature. So like extract 2, the ultimate legitimacy of this reasoning too is grounded in the nature of the physical universe. A comparison of extracts 2 and 3 shows how two cases of reasoning might be similar in certain respects, and yet different in others. Both display minimal actual structure, which is typical of 'casual' everyday reasoning, though there are exceptions as extract 1 demonstrates. Both 2 and 3 are grounded in the nature of the physical universe, and again present a contrast to the reasoning in extract 1. But extracts 2 and 3 too differ from each other; the latter presents an example of fairly elaborated reasoning; by contrast, the former is condensed.

Elaboration as I have implied above is an optional property of reasoning. In this respect it is somewhat like veridicality: neither is a sufficient or necessary condition for something to be taken as reasoning; and both are aspects of the realisation of some element of structure. So for example, a reasoning will be seen as reasoning (cf. extract 2) whether the realisation of its elements displays elaboration or not, just as it will retain its character as reasoning irrespective of whether the premises are true or not. What defines something as reasoning is not affected by the presence or absence of elaboration though I am tempted to add that perhaps elaboration is a more important quality of good reasoning, than is veridicality. If extract 3 is examined closely it will be seen also that the realisation of Claim and Reason is not discrete: it is not the case that one first methodically says everything that may be considered to be a Claim and only then does one proceed to state Reason. Rather, the realisation of the various elements of a text's structure is typically interspersed – this is certainly true of texts in the spoken mode, and truer still of those spoken and dialogic. So far as the order of the elements of structure in reasoning is concerned – which element precedes which? which might be interspersed with which? – this requires further research, and for this what we need is not just the logician's or the philosopher's stylised formulae, but also evidence from large scale corpora.

3.3 Social and logical grounding

It should be obvious from a comparison of extracts 1 and 2 that not all the reasons mothers provide are legitimised by appeal to the physical nature of the universe. It is not that the physical nature of the universe prevents cousins marrying each other; it is simply that the legal institution prevalent in the community prohibits such union. The legitimation, in the last analysis, is by reference to a socially sanctioned system which is designed to regulate individual behaviour. This appeal to the social nature of the universe differs from Pete's and Janet's mothers' appeal to the physical nature of the universe. The Grounding of the latter kind is typically said to be logical. I shall refer to the Grounding of the former kind as social. Below I present some more cases of social reasoning in mothers' talk.

3.4 Social grounding in mothers' reasons

Extract 4 is taken from a dialogue between Cameron and his mother. Cameron's family is visited by a certain Mr. Box, who happens to have three little children. One refers to them naturally as 'the three little Boxes'; and not surprisingly, Cameron finds this hilarious. In the extract below the mother is offering her reasons why Cameron must not laugh at the mention of 'the three little Boxes' when old Mr. Box is visiting:

Extract 4

Mother: (1) now you can't laugh about his name (2) when he comes, right? (3) because people's names are important to them, right? (4) and people don't like others laughing about their names … (5) we do think it's funny though, don't we?

The following is an interpretation of the structure of this piece of reasoning, using the same GSP which is applied in the above cases:

Claim: don't laugh at Mr. B's name

Reason: since people's names are important to them, people do not like others laughing about their name, so (I deduce) he will not like you to laugh at his name

Principle: one respects others' feelings

Grounding: this is a social requirement

Like the Grounding in extract 1, the Grounding in extract 4 is also social, but we need to note two points: first, the Principle makes reference to feelings; and secondly, it would be hard to maintain that it is backed by any particular social institution, e.g. the institution of law. I do not think that the requirement that reasoning is not subject to feelings and emotions is threatened by Cameron's mother's reasoning. So long as one accepts the major premise – i.e., the Principle – irrespective of one's taste one must also accept the validity of the Claim and the Reason. Neither the legitimacy of the Reason nor that of the Principle is less binding in character than those offered in earlier examples whose Grounding was logical. Like the Principle in logical reasoning, here too the Principle is being presented as a universally applicable assertion. If we discount such Reasons and Principles simply because of their reference to feelings, or on the basis that the Principle may not be acceptable universally, what significance would such an embargo have in terms of how we think, reason and act in everyday life? We may refuse to admit such Reasons and Principles into the pantheon of real, logical reasons; but this will not gainsay the fact that in social life it has a force, and that force is hardly less definite than that of liquid spilling or gravity pulling, men dying or babies choking to death.

Let me turn now to another case of socially grounded reasoning, which differs in some ways from the above.

Extract 5

Mother: (1) go to your room! (angry voice)
Davie: (2) no! (defiant)
Mother: (3) I beg your pardon! (4) you do what I say (5) or I'll smack you (6) now do you want maca- do you want sandwich or not?
Davie: (7) yes (stamps angrily) … (8) peanut butter… (9) peanut butter … please mummy (in chastened voice)

The background to this confrontation is that Davie having first refused to eat macaroni which mother had prepared turns up asking for some macaroni, at a time that in his household is not taken as the time for eating cooked meals. The mother offers him various items, which Davie rejects. By the point where the above extract begins, the mother is really angry, instead of food Davie finds himself at the receiving end of punishment: the mother's first message is really a punishment which imposes confinement. Davie is rebellious; and the mother is indignant. I would schematically represent her reasoning as follows:

Claim: if you don't do my bidding, I shall hit you

Reason: I have authority as your mother

Principle: authority must be obeyed

Grounding: this is in the nature of authority

Against this analysis it may be objected that the interaction is an example of coercion rather than that of reasoning. It is then important to point out immediately that coercion is perhaps an evaluative term for a kind of reasoning which too has some 'logic' underlying it. By treating this interaction between Davie and his mother as a case of reasoning I do not imply either approval or disapproval of this mode of reasoning, any more than assigning an analysis to the transitivity structure of an obviously false claim would imply that I approve or disapprove of uttering lies. There may be some sort of an ideal about 'how people should reason', and such a requirement might be based on someone's idea of what reasoning should be like. But this is not very different from the writing of prescriptive grammars according to which the rules of the grammar define what counts as grammatical, and the rules themselves are based on someone's conception of what it is to be grammatical. Such ideals have not proved binding for human practice, though they have proved useful for creating classes of the privileged and the not-so privileged speakers. Human practice is responsive to human social positioning: that is to say it is largely practical. If one has the experience of authority as coercive, and if one should know it to be a fact of one's own experience that force is difficult to counteract, then one might consider it very reasonable and practical to use force oneself precisely where one is able to do so with impunity. It is a question then whether what is at fault is the reasoning ability of the reasoner or those social conditions which produce systematically distorted communication, as Habermas (1970b) would say. In taking extract 5 as an instance of a particular kind of reasoning, and in assigning it a specific structure, I am suggesting simply that if one reasons this way, then the reasoner's Reason could be 'justified' by this Principle; and the acceptance of the Principle would imply just this kind of Grounding: I am not claiming that these justifications will meet my approval or yours; or even that the use of these sorts of justification makes the world a desirable place for you and me to live in. All I am claiming is that this chain of reasoning can be carried through to its final point: if someone uses coercion then this is what they must believe. By taking it as a piece of reasoning, I am also suggesting that such reasoning does occur in our society. In fact, it is not very different from that method of enquiry which Peirce described as 'the method of authority' (Peirce 1955, 14). Peirce offered reasons why such a method for the fixation of belief was not desirable. But does it follow that because the method is not desirable it is not practiced? One only has to look at the political disposition of the world at present – especially from the point of view of the so-called emerging nations – to realise that this question is simply rhetorical. An analysis of this kind has at least the merit of making us recognise the extent of our collaboration in the exercise of authority.

If extracts 1, 4, and 5 are compared, we can immediately begin to see the variety in social reasoning: 1 is a case of legally based reasoning; 4 is co-operative reasoning, while 5 is coercive reasoning. But at a higher level of abstraction they are all social in as much as they are predicated on how human beings interact to maintain themselves as individual systems in the face of their natural need for interdependence. Before leaving the discussion of coercive reasoning, it is worth pointing out that the Claim in such reasoning is typically logically complex. So in the above example we have: *do as I say or I'll smack you*. The two messages are related and lexicogrammatically realised as a clause complex. Returning to extract 2, we note Pete's mother says: *you do it again and I'll whack you*, which has a similar semantic composition and which too is realised as a clause complex (see also extract 7, for another similar example). In lay terminology, coercive reasoning is referred to as THREAT. I suggest that this view needs revision: for coercive reasoning can take an apparently benign form, as when a mother says *if you're very good, mummy will buy you an ice-cream*. This is commonly known as BRIBE. However, threat and bribe are both essentially coercive: The former forces by exciting fear; the latter forces by tempting with the promise of gratification. By analogy, at the level of interstate relations, we can threaten the use of the latest armament as an instance of the first case, in the second, we can offer millions in aid. The result is the same – an invasion of integrity, an exploitation of dependence. A similar sort of reasoning is to be found when a mother says *you're going to make mummy very sad if you don't listen*. Following Bernstein (1971a) – on whose analysis of rationale most of this discussion is based – I would refer to this reasoning as an instance of emotional blackmail. Emotional blackmail is a case of coercive reasoning on the ground that it forces by playing on the addressee's desires and affections.

3.5 Tautological reasoning

Despite the arguments I have presented above, it will have to be granted that the literature on reasoning would most probably not include threat, bribe, or emotional blackmail as any kind of reasoning at all; controversial as these 'reasons' are, there is one kind which would be even more controversial in the scholarly circles. Consider extract 6. It is taken from a dialogue between Karen and her mother. Karen is playing with a torch; her mother would prefer her to put the torch away:

Extract 6
Mother: (1) put it up on the stove (2) and leave it there
Karen: (3) why?
Mother: (4) 'cause
Karen: (5) that's where it goes?
Mother: (6) yeah

Karen's *why?* here is perhaps one of those questions which Piaget (1960) might have regarded as a pseudo-question. The idea that a question is asked solely for the purpose of acquiring information that is not available to the questioner is, however, rather naive. Even if this were the case, there is the possibility of turning this to 'good advantage', which many mothers do. But apart from this, there may be a sense in which the confirmation by reiteration of a known fact may be as important a purpose for a child asking a question as any. This seems to be the case here with Karen, since it is quite obvious that she, in a manner of speaking, knows the answer to her own question. My concern here is both with the reason that she knows to be the reason, and the way her mother responds to her why question.

First, then, the mother's response to Karen's *why?*: the ellipsis of the simple *'cause*, could technically be expanded to make it read as: *'cause (I want you to/ you should) put it up on the stove and leave it there*, on the assumption that Karen's question is: *why do you want me to /why should I put it up ...* etc. In the analysis of my data such responses have been coded as cases of tautological reasoning. It has been suggested that from the point of view of experiential content a syllogism too is tautological: it gives no new information. However, this is an unjustifiably narrow view of 'information'; the inferential reasoning that is part of the syllogism is itself a significant informative element. As Peirce (1955: 59) remarked:

> It is a matter of real fact to say that in a certain room there are two persons. It is a matter of fact to say that each person has two eyes. It is a matter of fact to say that there are four eyes in the room. But to say that if there are two persons and each person has two eyes there will be four eyes is not a statement of fact but a statement about the system of numbers which is our own creation.

This argument applies equally to a hypothetical syllogism: *if all men are mortal and Socrates* ...etc. No such relation seems to obtain between the parts of the discourse in extract 5. It seems as if it fails the crucial requirement of having the attribute of inferentiality. Now, when we look at sequences of this kind from the point of view of learning, we often simply imagine that nothing is being learnt. I suggest that this is not the case: language is like matter; it does not destroy; it reappears in some other form in the consciousness of the interactants. So, for the mother to say that *(I want) you (to) do x because (I want) you (to) do x*, is to 'teach' Karen something, viz., things do not have to have reason. Turning to Karen's second question (5) *that's where it goes?*, it shows that Karen has understood the mother's reason at a fairly deep level. For she, too, is saying something like: *should it go there because that's where it goes?*, which is another form of tautology: do things this way because we do things as we do them, and that's all there is to it.

It may be thought that this is too fanciful an interpretation of what is going on; that an importance is being attached to the 'tautological reason' that it does not deserve. Rather than argue the case, let me just reproduce another dialogic extract that might speak for what I have argued above. Extract 6 is again from the Karen dyad. Karen's mother is trying to put Karen to bed, she has reasoned, humoured, and scolded to get Karen to go to bed; Karen keeps resisting; the extract begins where the mother has become quite angry:

Extract 7

Mother: (1) Karen do as you're— (SLAPS KAREN) (2) put your legs down (VOICE ANGRY) (3) or I'm going to go outside this minute without a kiss (4) now put your legs down (VOICE ANGRY)
Karen: (5) mmhm (REFUSING TO COMPLY)
Mother: (6) now, give a kiss goodnight
Karen: (7) I'm not
Mother: (8) you're not gonna kiss me?* why?
Karen: (9) 'cause
Mother: (10) 'cause why?
Karen: (11) 'cause I don't like you (VERY LOUD VOICE)

I am tempted to suggest that Karen is beginning to learn her lessons well: she does not have to give her reasons. It is not that she does not have a reason, as is obvious from the last message in the extract; it is just that reasons do not have to be given. Possibly another perspective on tautological reason is that it is the extreme degree of condensed reasoning, so much so that it is impossible to suggest any content for the various steps in reasoning. Tautological reason implies that it is not necessary for reasons to be explicitly articulated between the interactants: their minds are revealed to each other without the mediation of verbal communication.

If it is agreed that the minimal structure of reasoning is Claim and Reason, then it may be argued that tautological reasoning is, indeed, a sort of reasoning, the most abstract form of which is: *Do this (this way) because it should be done (this way)*. We may disapprove of such reasoning as standing in the way of human progress but we can hardly deny it a discursive status purely because of our disapproval. If, however, the category of tautological reasoning is recognised it will be one of the very few cases where it seems almost impossible to seek out a derived Principle or the Grounding for the Principle. From this point of view, it differs significantly from reasoning with minimal structure. In the latter, although, Principle and Grounding may not be actually present, it is possible to derive them from an understanding of the Reason. With tautological reasoning, I have not found it possible to postulate any Principle, much less the Grounding of the Principle, which is not a reiteration of the tautological Reason. In one sense, the problem of deciding whether or not this is a species of reasoning is severe only if the term reasoning itself is given the kind of valuation that the dictionary and the logico-philosophical literature gives it, whereby reasoning is reasoning only if a particular class of reasons is given. If we think of reasoning as a textual strategy, we do not need to accept the valuation as an integral part of it: reasoning is simply argumentation; it is neither inherently good nor bad any more than an assertion has to be true in order to be an assertion. As a textual strategy it is employed to achieve some social goal; and as such it is best to talk about its efficacy in the achievement of that goal rather than as a sign of mental prowess, moral strength, or whatever. And it may be that tautological Reasons do achieve some social goal for the speaker.

3.6 Logical versus social grounding

The above account represents the main kinds of reasoning mothers do with their children: leaving aside tautological reasoning, they give one variety or other of logical reason; or they give some kind of social reason. Interestingly, the reasoner is never at a loss for reason: hardly any mother says *such and so is the case; now let me see why it is the case*. Everyday reasoning comes effortlessly; that being the case, it must draw upon the speaker's internalised view of what the world – physical and social – is like. Reasoning thus becomes diagnostic of what Bernstein (1982, 1987b) has referred to as 'orders of relevance', which are responsive to one's social positioning. As one measure of systematic variation in the daily exchange of meanings amongst my subjects was the frequency of logical v. social reasoning, it would be useful to say a few words about the general nature of these two kinds of Grounding.

Typically reasoning with logical Grounding is considered superior to reasoning with social Grounding; the reasons offered for this valuation of logical reasoning celebrate its 'scientific' i.e. empirical nature. Logical reasons are like hard currency; they are supposed to be redeemable everywhere where methods of experimentation and falsification are accepted[6]. This use of the term logical implies that the basis of logicality resides only in the natural disposition of the universe as it is discovered by science. It could be argued, however, that this misappropriation of the term by logicians and philosophers narrows it to suit their own convenience: by this re-classification, logical becomes what logicians, philosophers, and scientists do. To say that science is in search of truth is one thing; but to claim that all scientific 'findings' are truths – logically superior because they are the findings of scientists – is quite another thing. In fact, it is highly doubtful that the physical nature of the universe as it is accessible to us is anything other than a communally accepted fiction, having the quality of *pro tem* truth. Some examples of such grand, incontrovertible truths accepted 'universally' were, for example, the flatness of the earth, the hypothesis of 'humors', of racial inheritance, and that of creationism. Each of these at some time or other has been seen as reflecting the nature of the universe *per se*. Social Grounding is, arguably, just as logical since reasoning that is grounded in the social nature of the universe also appeals to systems and conventions created on the basis of theories about human beings as interpersonally dependent. Human nature requires the creation and maintenance of social systems as a necessary condition for the survival of humanity. What could be more logical, in a practical sense, than to recognise this fact in exercising the faculty of judgement?

In examining cases of reasoning, it appears that by comparison with social grounding, reasoning with logical grounding has a much wider scope: it can subsume reasons of very different classes. Thus, even when, experientially speaking, the facts are of a somewhat different order – e.g., human mortality, as opposed to the behaviour of liquid, as opposed to properties of precious metal – all are treated as if they were part of the same grand scheme. If a mother says *don't touch that, it's hot*; or *don't force the doll in there, it'll break*; or *put on your socks, otherwise you'll catch a cold*; the final court of appeal for each is the physical nature of the universe. Each is a logical reason in that sense, despite the fact that the Principle invoked in each case is a distinct one. By contrast, the term social is not as widely construed. So for example, in extract 1 the social reason is grounded in the institution of law. This reasoning is very likely to be treated as an altogether different kind of phenomenon from the other categories of social reasoning. Further, like logical, the term social too has a valuation; and in keeping with this valuation, certain kinds of social reasoning are not treated as any kind of reasoning at all, to which attention has been drawn above. So, when a mother says as Pete's mother does: *you do it again and I'll whack you*, many would deny this the status of reasoning; bribe and emotional blackmail would meet the same reaction. But as I have argued above (see section 3.4), this confuses someone's ideal of how people 'should' reason with how people actually do their reasoning. Social Grounding is ultimately social in the sense that it presupposes the necessity of inter-dependence. This interdependence may take the form of coercion or co-operation; it may be ratified by the creation of a social institution, or it may be a local convention – e.g. don't do that, because in this family girls don't do that – irrespective of these distinctions, the reasoning is social in the sense that it is predicated on interdependent social relations. And it could be argued that those who more frequently employ social reasoning than the logical are probably much more aware of the interpersonal dependence of human beings.

3.7 Everyday reasoning: from process to system

The attributes of reasoning and its structure identified in the above sections are not limited to everyday maternal discourse only. Though in classical examples nothing resembling tautological reasoning occurs, approximately the same description can be extended to syllogistic reasoning. Where classical syllogistic reasoning differs most from everyday reasoning is in the choice of Grounding: everyday reasoning displays tautological reasoning where identifying a non-tautological Grounding becomes problematic as well as the other varieties which do have some Grounding. The contrasts discussed in the above sections can be represented as a system of options as in figure 1:

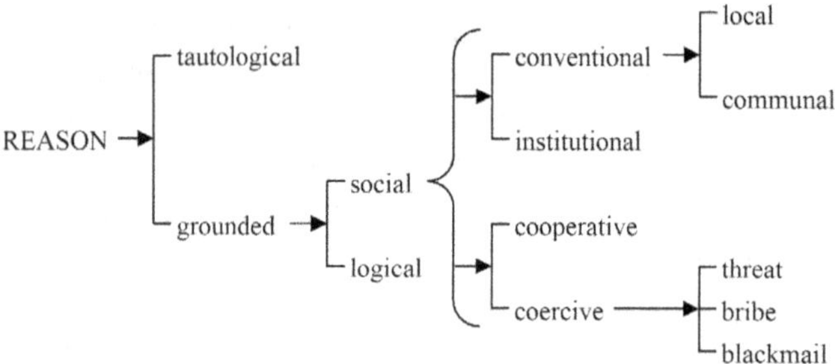

Figure 1: A simplified system of choices in reasoning

Obviously, it is possible to introduce more delicate options. For example, is threat by reference to speaker-as-authority, e.g., *I'm gonna go outside this minute without a kiss*, or by reference to someone else, e.g. the father in the context of my data? Such a choice would be at the intersection of [local] and [threat]. A message such as *the police will come and take you away* is an [institutional; threat]; and again, other more delicate choices are possible. So the system above is presented as a simplified account of the range of possibilities.

It is relatively easy to set up 'notional' choices for some environment. For a purely notional notion to acquire the status of a 'semantic' value, it is necessary to show how such an element of meaning is construed by the lexicogrammar. Attached to each option in a semantic system network is a (set of) realisation statement(s), indicating how a particular semantic option is realised. To specify the realisational patterns for each of the options in even a simplified system of the type presented in figure 1 is an enormous enterprise. Some idea of its enormity can be gained from my very condensed account of the realisation of some of the semantic choices in asking questions (discussion in chapters 3–6, this volume). An example of a semantic system network for rationale with relatively explicit realisation statements is found in Halliday (1973b: 72–102), which furnished the model for Patten's (1988) work on the generation of problem solving texts. The point that I would emphasise is that it is possible to provide explicit accounts of semantic categories. An account of this kind will be complex; it will involve not just identifying simple contrasts of the kind [singular] v. [plural], but rather it is likely to call for an examination of a syndrome of features. This syndrome will cover patterning of varied kind. For example a message functioning as [threat] must be realised by a clause that is [*transitive*]; its process must be [*material*] – a much greater specificity of process choice can be achieved when lexis is treated as most delicate grammar (Hasan 1985d, 1987a); the clause must be logically related – overtly or covertly – to a [command]; and so on. I find that the types of 'information' that is needed to decide whether or not a message can be said to be functioning as [threat] ranges over the four metafunctions discussed earlier (see section 2.4).

I have argued the relevance of different bases for legitimation. In some respects, my approach is close to Toulmin's (1958) and Habermas's (1984). The structure of reasoning presented here approximates Toulmin's (1958: 109ff.): For example, his Conclusion is approximately my Claim; his Warrant is close to my Principle. Toulmin was, however, concerned with probabilistic Claims rather than absolute ones. I have not addressed this problem. Habermas links his notion of 'validity claims' to the kind of speech act that is performed in uttering what I have called the Claim. Thus in making the Claim that 'the new version of King Kong makes more psychological sense than the original' (Habermas 1984: 36), one is 'making an evaluative statement' (ibid.: 39). The Grounding for such a Claim should establish the preferability of certain values. My approach is quite close to this, but again it is not easy to pinpoint specific similarities and dissimilarities between the two approaches since very few detailed analyses are provided by Habermas.

A characteristic emphasised here is the minimal structure of reasoning in everyday discourse. In fact, it is highly likely that with the exception of specialist domains, reasoning will tend to display actual minimal structure. An important variable is the presence or absence of cryptic quality: obviously, nearly every mother reasons cryptically at some time, but this does not mean that mothers' behaviour is uniform in every respect. The degree to which mothers are prone to elaborate the various parts of their reasoning varies in a systematic manner as do other aspects of their reasoning. I discuss some of these vectors of variations below.

4 Reasoning, rationality and humanity

In analysing everyday reasoning, I have deliberately used syllogistic reasoning as a paradigm case. This is because of the privileged position of such reasoning as an example of deductive reasoning, and because of the privileged position of deductive reasoning as a sign of rationality, and because of the place of rationality in our notions of humanity. As Luria (1976: 101) points out psychologists have regarded the steps of deductive reasoning 'as basic properties of human consciousness … assuming implicitly that they exist in the same form at all stages of history', in all human beings. In fact, belief in the innateness of the processes of deductive reasoning argues that rationality is a species-specific quality. It is like competence in Chomsky's linguistic theory: human beings, by definition, are rational (Cohen 1981). The view inherits the problems of the nativist approach: if we interpret this as a claim that whoever is human is rational, and if we believe that rationality is a quality manifested in humans by their reasoning – rationality is competence while reasoning is performance – then it follows that the concept of rationality is 'incorrigible' (see endnote 6), and that we have a grammar of rationality which permits the distinction between 'surface' reasoning – which may show ungrammaticality, infelicity, slips and what not – and 'deep' rationality which is not infected by these accidents of performance. The problems of determining the relation between competence and performance are serious enough with regard to language; they would be severely aggravated in the case of rationality and reasoning (see for some comments the discussion of Cohen 1981). If rationality is taken as an innate human attribute, then it follows that whoever is not rational could reasonably be said to be not human. This makes the problem of determining the set of rules that will be said to constitute the 'grammar of rationality' a socially sensitive one. It is not at all clear what would count as 'correct intuition' and who would be regarded as the native reasoner capable of producing 'unimpeachable data' through introspection. Whoever else might have this distinction, it is hardly likely to belong to the underprivileged members of our community!

More recently, with the work of Piaget, the nativist view has been somewhat modified. Now the ability to arrive at a necessary conclusion from the knowledge of some fact(s) purely through deductive reasoning is seen as a mark of intellectual maturity. Overton (1990: 22ff.) provides details of experiments showing that the 'systemic availability' of the full range of deductive reasoning occurs only in a certain sequence with other forms of mental development, and only at a certain maturational stage. The implication is unavoidable that intellectual maturity and rationality are intertwined.

Apart from its psychological interest, deductive reasoning has long held an exalted status as a mode of general enquiry (see for example, Peirce's hierarchy of the methods for the fixation of belief. Peirce 1955: 11ff.); its role in the exogenetic evolution of humanity has been more stridently proclaimed by Popper (1979). In short, from the writings of a number of influential logicians, philosophers, and psychologists, it would appear that deductive reasoning is the pinnacle of perfection toward which the human intellect is straining – or if it isn't, then it should do, if it were rational. By comparison, the principle of inductive reasoning can be dismissed under pejorative descriptions such as 'the bucket theory of mind' (Popper 1979: 61): in this view, inductive reasoning does not lead to the growth of human knowledge; it is based on local, specific experience, whereas deductive reasoning is preferable because it is based on universally true facts. In examining mothers' reasoning with their children, a question that needs to be raised, then, is: is the mothers' reasoning deductive? And if rationality is defined as just the quality of reasoning deductively, then the question becomes: are all mothers rational, or only some? And if, by any chance, it is this same type of rationality that is innately ours, then the question becomes: are all mothers human, or only some of them? This confusion inheres in the assimilation of the normative and the prescriptive, irrespective of whether the prescriptive is rationalised by appeal to innateness or to elitism of the scientist, the logician and the philosopher.

4.1 Order in chaos: the pattern in parole

In opening this chapter I argued that corpora have a privileged position in the study of parole: their study can reveal the patterned quality of linguistic interaction. The semantically analysed cases of reasoning were statistically processed using a principal components analysis. Table 3 presents the PC1 loadings on some of the variable features of reasoning as a whole but only with reference to those cases where the Claim in the reasoning is itself a command. In table 3, the letter C stands for the message function [command]; in an act of reasoning, such a message would realise the element Claim; R stands for Reason; S for statement; and Q for question.

Table 3: PCA for commands and their reasons

	PC1
C [indirect]	0.84
S [supportive]	0.83
C [suggestive]	0.82
C [elaborated]	0.77
R [inherent]	0.64
R [elaborated]	0.62
Q [explain]	-0.50
C [action]	0.34
C [prefaced]	0.44
Eigenvalues	4.04
% Variance	45.00

The feature S[supportive] identifies messages which encourage the child to comply by praising and/or giving hints, whereas Q[explain] identifies a message that raises a how/why question. A question of this kind said by the mother to the child in the course of getting the child to do something which the child is resisting functions invariably as a challenge. Compare for example the mother's *why* in extract 7 with Karen's *why* in extract 6. Only the former is construable as a challenge to the child who is refusing to do what the mother wants her to do. C[indirect] is self-evident; it refers to orders such as *could you help, I'd like you to help…, would you mind helping…*etc. in common parlance these are known as 'polite commands' or 'requests'. C[suggestive] is another variety of indirect command; an example would be *lets not make all this mess here*. These semantic attributes of [command] are interpersonal and display a systemic contrast with C[direct] (see discussion below). The feature C[elaborated] is self-evident (see 3.2); it pertains to the logical metafunction, as is the feature C[prefaced]. The former is lexicogrammatically realised as some form of expansion while the latter feature is typically realised by the logical relation of reporting (or quoting) locutions or ideas, i.e., it is projection of one kind or another (see Halliday 1985a for the sense in which these terms are used here). C[action] is experiential; it refers to the nature of the process the child is being asked to engage in or to desist from. For example, *don't do that* is a case of C[action] whereas *be very careful* is a case of C[conduct]. The features R[logical] and R[elaborated] are hopefully self-evident from previous discussions. Since each of the features is a term in some system, and since the input to the PC analysis is in terms of frequency calculated as a percentage, the table above gives more information, by implication, than is displayed in the table. For example, the fact that R[elaborated] loads positively at 0.62 implies that the other term in the system, i.e., R[cryptic] would load negatively at -0.62.

Cutting the discussion short (for a more detailed discussion, see previous chapter), the mothers who score high on PC1 would typically not challenge their children; they would tend to be supportive; they would largely avoid bald orders; their reasons are more likely to be grounded in the objective, physical nature of the universe than in social institutions, conventions etc.; both, their reasons and their commands are likely to be elaborated. Most readers will not be surprised to learn that the mothers scoring high on PC1 are likely to be the HAP ones ($p < .0002$). It follows that there is a systematic, orderly variation in reasoning between the two social groups; that LAP mothers will tend to choose reasons that are mostly social. Looking at the disposition of the data, it becomes obvious that the LAP mothers are also much less likely to choose cooperative reasons than coercive ones. Further, where an explicit demand for justification is made by asking *why?*, these mothers are much more likely to offer tautology. Their reasons tend to be cryptic, rather than elaborated. And their commands are typically not [indirect] or [suggestive] but [direct], often bordering on imposition: e.g., *you are going to your room this minute.*

4.2 Interpreting the results

Although the above picture is very close to the community's stereotype of reasoning in the course of control in the working class families, when the results of an empirical project present such findings they are often attacked on the ground that the results are based on the stereotype. The impression is given that only if the researcher had not been prejudiced the results would have looked quite different. The implication is obvious: if the researchers' false ideology does not obfuscate issues, it would be revealed that all human beings, irrespective of their socio-historical positioning must, and will act in the image of the middle class, presumably because the middle class, particularly the well-educated section of it is the true arbiter of good sensible behaviour! It does not take much reflection to recognise that this is the other face of middle class prejudice. The privileged position of the middle class ensures that their values would have a privileged position; if others are shown to differ from them then either these others are wrong, or the researchers are wrong. By these steps, the debate gets buried in a mire of irrelevancies; it becomes almost impossible to pursue any crucial research questions. For example, what reasons can be postulated for the variation in patterns of reasoning, which co-vary with speakers' social positioning?

To answer this question we need to interpret the choices. If coercive reasoning is the favoured basis for justifying commands, it implies that the power of authority is considered to be such that it can constrain others' behaviour. I would suggest that the social position of the LAP families provides them with sufficient personal validation of this principle. So it is not accidental that the patterns of reasoning in the LAP group show the power of authority in a naked form: if commands are likely to be direct rather than suggestive or consultative, this is indicative of the fact that the person giving the command has a position of dominance; if coercive reasoning is employed more often than in the HAP group, this is because the person giving the reason wishes to emphasise the fact of power which can constrain. In short, as Bernstein said, the principles of control in the working class are visible: the controlled persons know what is the ground on which they are being controlled. Reasoning then becomes a means of 'teaching' the child the nature of power and authority: clearly this is not irrelevant to the expected – and statistically validated – life patterns of the working class members.

By contrast the HAP groups' reasoning in the environment of control tends to be invisible. The child is typically not directed but is manoeuvred into acting in the required way. It is objectively not the case that mothers in the middle class have less authority, less power over their children; it is simply that this authority and power remain invisible. Explicit elaboration of both Claim and logical Reason takes precedence. The power of authority need not be tested, need not be made visible. In fact, it would be dysfunctional to sensitise the child to issues of domination: this could conceivably get in the way. I am suggesting that if you are in the social position of largely being subjected to the power of authority, then you need to be able to recognise it. If, on the other hand, you are in the social position of exercising power of authority, then it is far more 'sensible' to learn to mask it as something that is dictated by 'reason'. Both the HAP and the LAP groups are adjusted to their social positioning: *in natural everyday discourse, speakers will speak their social position.*

Let me conclude by saying that variation in language is functional in a rather deep sense: it is functional not in the sense of being useful for you or me; it is functional in the deeper sense of permitting one to both create one's reality and to come to terms with it. I believe that the LAP orientation to the kinds of reasoning that is overwhelmingly employed by the mothers is a good example of this principle. It makes their child aware of the nature of authority – something that that child is very likely to have to come to terms with. Making the principles of control visible serves another purpose. In my data, the LAP children rebel; they challenge the awesome authority of the mother; so, consider Karen's refusal to ingratiate her mother. The HAP children do not rebel: there is nothing visible to challenge. Instead, they attempt to control in the invisible ways in which their mothers have been controlling them: consider Janet's unflattering portrayal of her mother!

4.3 Socio-semantic analysis and corpus linguistics

In the opening section of this chapter, I suggested that corpus linguistics is indeed well placed to study how system is created in the process – how langue is in the deepest sense the gift of parole, and how the nature of parole is orderly. In my account of reasoning in everyday talk between mothers and their small children, I have presented an example of how a system can be constructed by reference to the process of talk. I have attempted this in two ways: by presenting a systematic account of the structure of reasoning and by presenting a system network representing choices available to speakers at some point in the process of reasoning. The literature on reasoning and rationality is largely an idealised account of someone's view of how reasoning should be done, and what would count as being reasonable. My partial systematisation of the process of reasoning took the form of identifying the possibilities of its structural shapes – its GSP – as well as the typical actual structures found to occur in most everyday cases of reasoning. This account does not begin with a system that is *sui generis*; it is an account that is based on an examination of a large number of cases of reasoning: this is how in our community reasoning is done by most members. The hypothesis about the structure of reasoning is hopefully clear enough to be questioned and refuted. I have also attempted to present a minute system of the choices available to Reason and Grounding. This system is simplified; but the descriptive reach of even a simple system of this kind is considerable. Although an instance of each of the choices in the system can be found in my data, the corpus is not large enough to display statistical regularities for the more delicate options. In fact, for the purposes of statistical processing, this simplified system network needed to be further simplified into just a binary choice between [logical] v. all other kind of reasoning dubbed [nonlogical]. To show regular, statistically valid patterning of more specific choices in reasoning such as, say, [cooperative] v. [coercive] would requires the analysis of much larger corpora than my project was able to undertake due to lack of funds. It seems to me that some comments pertinent to doing corpus linguistics can be made on the basis of my experiences, even though both the framework and the point of departure for me are so different from those for the typical corpus linguist.

The first question I would raise is that of the analysis itself: the justification for corpora is some analysis which will throw light on the nature of language. If scholars such as Whorf, Firth, Wittgenstein, Halliday, Hymes etc. are right then the essence of linguistics is to develop ways of analysing meaning. The analysis of the semantic patterns in corpora may be a very demanding task; but this task cannot be shelved aside, except on the assumption that language is basically a formal algorithm. It may be that corpus linguistics wishes to embrace this last perspective, but if so, it is not yet free of the constraints imposed on the study of language by Ferdinand de Saussure. My analysis of the semantic attributes of reasoning is a modest and incomplete illustration of one way of going about it. The framework is not automated: there is no programme for mechanical semantic parsing. But this is not to say that such a programme is in theory not feasible; and the degree to which it is feasible will become evident only when semantic analysis of data is considered one of the important goals of corpus linguistics. Arguments for the importance of semantic analysis arise from all directions: whether we are concerned with understanding how persons in a society interact, or with teaching the foreigner how to talk to a doctor, or with teaching a student the 'art' of writing a 'good essay', or with finding out how to go about the machine generation of text etc., we need to analyse and understand the semantic nature of human discourse. More recently, automatic speech recognition studies have come to recognise the importance of semantic information for the correct recognition of phonological units. There are many other practical reasons for this much needed development in corpus linguistics.

The adequacy of corpora is an important issue. My experience shows that this issue cannot be judged in *vacuo*. The important question is: adequate for what? Suppose my interest had been to ask: what is the frequency of pronominal Subject in English?, it is conceivable that 22,000 clauses might constitute adequate evidence. But given my interest, and my desire to analyse data semantically at a certain degree of delicacy, it turned out that 22,000 messages were not adequate for checking variation in the more specific, more delicate points of semantic contrast. To actually produce a statistically viable result for such delicate choices as institutional threat v. conventional, local threat v. conventional, communal bribe, I would need a much larger corpus. There is also another aspect to the question of adequacy: the sorts of question I have asked could not be asked even with a trillion word corpus culled from newspaper feature articles alone. Such a corpus is not likely to show variation in social positioning as clearly as my data does. To be adequate, corpora must be matched to the aim of analysis; and at the same time, corpora must instantiate ways of speaking, which are not restricted to some specialised variety. A million examples of logician's cases of reasoning cannot reveal the nature of everyday reasoning prevalent in the community.

The interest in language as a means of creating and maintaining society is a valid concern: increasingly, talk about ideology has become fashionable. However, it is very seldom that assertions about ideology, power, authority etc. are explicated by reference to how they are manifested in the daily verbal interaction of the members of society. Even less often is the material analysed from a semantic and a lexicogrammatical perspective. But it is a study of language from these perspectives that would reveal the deep relationship between language as form and language as process in social contexts. Much of social context is about the maintenance of human relation: in the end, human relation has to be seen as responsive to the position of members in their community; and language is deeply implicated in the creation and maintenance of human relations. Linguists have avoided and/or condemned studies of variation in ways of meaning, especially if such a study is class-based. There has been, to the best of my knowledge, no rational discussion as to why social conditions of human existence should leave the domain of meaning completely untouched. By a tacit agreement in the establishment of linguistics, it turns out that to get into this field is to invite either silence from one's peers or a resounding denunciation. Both are undesirable, but the first is worse, because it systematically distorts academic communication, preventing it from understanding one of the most pressing issues: is hierarchic exploitation a necessary accompaniment of social existence? I am aware that in my study I have raised contentious issues. It has seemed necessary to do this: it so happens that we do live in a non-egalitarian society; simply to pretend that certain things do not happen in our 'nice' civilised world, just because they upset our delicate sensibilities, does not seem very rational. We can hardly deny that the nature of the societies in which we live today is oppressive. To understand how this oppression is maintained, and what part the relatively privileged play in it, is important: in my view such understanding might bring us to a stage in human evolution (cf. Popper) which would most probably surpass in importance that aspect of our evolution which has enabled us to understand the physical forces of nature sufficiently well to create effective ways of maintaining and annihilating human life.

Notes

1 I thank my colleagues Carmel Cloran, Rhondda Fahey, Theo Van Leeuwen, Yon Maley, Geoff Williams, and Colin Yallop for their comments on the first draft of this chapter. The responsibility for the views expressed here remains mine.

2 The original section 2 was deleted at this point to avoid repetition regarding research design subjects and other such details.

3 The following transcription conventions will be employed in presenting the dialogues:

(1)	the number in round brackets consecutively number the messages within any one extract;
(AB)	AB is contextual comment or interpretation of some item(s) of saying by reference to context and/or cotext;
**ab	indicates overlapping talk;
**xy	
[?ab]	items in square brackets were not readily intelligible; this interpretation given by reference to co-textual, contextual and/or the way of saying (intonation, stress, voice quality etc.) clues;
[?]	this stretch of the recording was not intelligible; no clues for interpretation;
.	a pause greater than normal between such messages;
?*	after this question, speaker did not allow addressee time to reply.

4 In this connection it is interesting to note that the cases discussed by Habermas (1984: 34ff.) for different kinds of validity claims are all either statements or commands: there are no questions and no offers.

5 In some respects this schema is very much like Toulmin's suggestion (1958: 101ff.), though there are some significant difference, which I refrain from describing for lack of space.

6 Pollner (1974: 43) refers to the work of Gaskings (1965), who claims that certain mathematical notions are 'incorrigible', in the sense that they can never be falsified. An example would be '2 + 2 = 4'; every time a calculation produces a result other than shown, it is the result that will be considered wrong; not the proposition. Pollner suggests that much of our social construction of reality is incorrigible precisely in this sense. This is an interesting view, which questions the idealised picture of rationality in science. My comments in the preceding paragraph indicate my agreement with Pollner's view.

IV

The world and the world of meanings

9 Contexts for meaning [1993]

1 Introduction

Let me begin by problematising the relation between language and communication, two of the three terms that form the theme of this Congress. I will present a reinterpretation of this relation, which in my opinion has important implications for the interpretation of the third term in the Congress theme, viz., *social meaning*. My claim will be that all meaning is social. If so, then the modifier *social* in the expression *social meaning* is either a tautology, or worse still it is a potential source of what Bourdieu (1977) refers to as *méconnaissance*, misleading us into thinking that meanings could be other than social. I will suggest that the current interpretation of *social meaning* particularly as that term is used in sociolinguistics today is theoretically misleading. Belief in the validity of this term leads to a refusal to recognise certain kinds of linguistic variation whose ideological power is, thus, permitted to remain invisible and entrenched, while the study of language in society is prevented from a deeper understanding of how language is used for the living of life, how it acts in the creation, maintenance and alteration of human relations, which range from consensus to conflict, from cooperation to exploitation, and from accommodation to submission.

I shall begin this chapter by presenting in section 2 a partial history of how the relation between language and communication has typically been conceptualised in the dominant strands of modern linguistics. Thanks particularly to the seminal work of Labov (1969), we are familiar with some of the shortcomings of that conceptualisation. However, it is my belief that Labov's own methodology for bringing language and communication together is not free of problems. The section will conclude by developing this view. Section 3 presents an account of the relations between language and communication as developed by other modern linguistic theories which reject the views based on the dominant model. More specifically, the section will represent the position taken by systemic functional linguistics (henceforth SFL) as that theory has evolved over the years. In section 4, I will turn again to the notion of *social meaning* to see how the SFL view of this concept compares with that of linguistic meaning / social meaning presented in section 3. In section 5, I will discuss some results of a research in linguistic variation which was carried out at Macquarie University. My aim in presenting the findings of this research is to indicate how the reinterpretation of communication and language enhances the scope of sociolinguistics.

2 Language and communication: the dominant perspective

Returning to language and communication, I suggest that in fact these terms foreground once again the dichotomy invested in that extraordinary Saussurean pair langue and parole – extraordinary, because surely there is no other pair of terms in modern linguistics that has been christened and re-christened at the altar of so many different linguistic theories. We have met the pair some time under the guise of system and process, or as language system and language use, some time as competence and performance, or as language and speaking or as language and speech, some time as the potential and the actual, and some time as just language and communication – as in the theme of this Congress. I certainly do not intend to imply that the relations of the terms to each other remain identical across theories: Each re-exploration represents a somewhat different conceptualisation and the new names assigned to the two terms are indicative of this difference. Nonetheless, there still remains a good deal in common even across very distinct theories, from which, one may be entitled to draw certain conclusions. For example, the reiterated affirmation of this binary division points, at the least, to a conviction among linguists that in order to understand the nature of verbal semiosis, it is necessary to recognise the separateness of these two aspects of the over all experience of human language. But it probably points to something else as well: It shows, perhaps, that we have not yet fully worked out all the significant relations between the two terms – we have not yet 'cracked the code', as Halliday put it in his speech. That is why decade after decade, theory after theory, the terms need to be re-visited, re-explored, and re-conceptualised. And because linguistic theories since Saussure have agreed in emphasising the distinction between langue and parole, foregrounding their separateness, it seems only reasonable to suggest that what has remained unclear, what has been pushed in the background and so has forced linguists to revisit the concepts so frequently, is some relation that undermines this claim of simple separateness between language and communication. The history of linguistics lends further credence to this view: From time to time, linguists have argued that language and communication are not just two separate aspects, simply needing to be divorced from each other in the interests of doing true linguistics; they have at least hinted at some positive relation that ties the two together, thus throwing doubt on the wisdom of emphasising only half of the truth, namely their separateness. It is not fanciful to suggest that it is here – in the examination of the non-separateness of langue and parole – that we might be able to find a more satisfactory interpretation of the mutual relationship between the first two terms of the theme of this Congress.

What are these relations of non-separateness, and who advocated them? Surprising as the claim may sound, their first advocate was the great master himself, who while insisting on the importance of the distinction between langue and parole also drew attention to their *interdependence*: It was Saussure who claimed that

> language is necessary if speaking is to be intelligible and produce all its effects; but speaking is necessary for the establishment of language, and historically, its actuality always comes first. How would a speaker take it upon himself to associate an idea with a word-image if he had not first come across the association in an act of speaking? Moreover, we learn our mother language (sic!) by listening to others; only after countless experiences is it deposited in our brain. Finally, speaking is what causes language to evolve … Language and speaking are then interdependent; the former is both the instrument and the product of the latter. But their interdependence does not prevent their being two absolutely distinct things. (Saussure 1966: 18–19; see also Harris 1977: 19)

The distinction between these two 'things' appeared so absolute to Saussure that he despaired of the possibility of studying them together within the same theoretical framework:

> We must choose between two routes that cannot be followed simultaneously; they must be followed separately. One might if really necessary apply the term linguistics to each of the two disciplines and speak of a linguistics of speaking. But *that science must not be confused with linguistics proper, whose sole object is language.* (Saussure 1966: 19–20; emphases added)

I do not quote these passages because I agree with everything Saussure has to say, but because such passages show that the original architect of the famous dichotomy did not simply insist on the separateness of language and communication, he also recognised certain strong positive relations that tied the two together. The problem of how to describe the mutually supportive relations of language and communication engaged the attention of some of the best known European linguists: Mathesius, Hjelmslev and Firth. Mathesius attempted a functional explanation, and amongst his peers came closest to devising a dialectic approach (Mathesius 1964; Daneš 1987); Hjelmslev (1961) attempted to unite system and process by creating analogous categories for their description within the same analytical framework, and by other such formal means (Hasan 1995; Martin 1992); Firth (1957), inspired by Malinowski's ethnographic studies, turned to the notion of context, as a solution to the problem. But with the rise of the dominant transformational generative model of the late fifties and early sixties in the United States, these views either lost salience or were pejoratively dismissed, hardly ever receiving a fair interpretation. This was only to be expected since none of these earlier linguistic frameworks shared the fundamental assumptions that characterise the TG of the late fifties – early sixties. Let me turn briefly, then, to this dominant model in order to see how language and communication fared there.

It is commonly believed today that Saussure's langue (language) and *parole* (speaking) are interchangeable with Chomsky's competence and performance. There certainly are some similarities between the two linguists: Both assume the homogeneity of langue/competence; both prioritise langue/competence as the object of true linguistics; and both concede (reluctantly, perhaps?) the possibility of studying parole/performance so long as it stays somewhere beyond the fringes of 'linguistics proper'. However, in the context of the present discussion there are important differences as well: Note for example that Chomsky perceives little positive relation between language and communication. In this, he is far more logical than is Saussure in his recommendations: The idea of language as 'the product' of communication must remain foreign to the conception of language as a mental organ. In a model where details of formal structure itself – rather than the human capacity for verbal semiosis – is treated as innate, language change and language variation must pertain only to 'surface' matters (such as, perhaps, 'social meaning'?); and there can only exist an irreversible temporal linearity between language and communication: One can view language as an 'instrument' for communication, one can point out that the nature of this instrument is not perfectly reflected in communication, but one can hardly concede that language is the 'product' of communication or that communication plays any significant part in shaping or evolving language. Unlike Chomsky, Saussure thought of language as 'essentially social' – an assumption shared by Mathesius, Hjelmslev and Firth, which brings them closer to the spirit of Saussure's approach, but less to some of his words. And while Saussure saw communication as 'psychophysical', he still thought of it as rooted in this socially created language. So he could grant an interdependence between *langue* and *parole* – and he did so with a clear voice. But it is precisely this step together with his conception of 'linguistics proper' which leads to contradictions. As I see it, Saussure's position embroils him in theoretical incoherence, whereas Chomsky's claims are lacking in observational adequacy: The empirical fact is that language, in a non-trivial sense of that term, is not homogeneous. Synchronically, it shows variation; and diachronically, it is subject to change. A linguistics that cannot explain why intuitions about the well-formedness of a sentence differ across the various historical stages of a particular language is inadequate in terms of its own goals, its own standards of evaluation. So, language and communication are, in the end, problematic notions for both of the structuralist formal models, but the nature and origin of the problems is not the same. This analysis bears relevance to my critique of sociolinguistics as practised today, a theme recapitulated in the closing remarks of this section.

It is not necessary to repeat here Labov's masterly critique of these two linguistic theories. This critique did not dwell on the differences between the two models; it focused, instead, on what lay in common between the Saussurean and Chomskyan conceptions of 'doing linguistics'. Weinreich, Labov, and Herzog (1968) and Labov (1972b) forcefully and convincingly brought to our attention the problems and paradoxes that inhere in the assumption of linguistic homogeneity, and in the attempt to study language in isolation from communication. The name of Labov is rightfully associated with this sociolinguistic turn. It was Labov who presented evidence of 'orderly heterogeneity' in language, and skilfully demonstrated 'the use of the present to explain the past'; it was from him that we learnt that no study of language is viable except in its social context; that 'the basic data for any form of general linguistics would be language as it is used by the native speakers communicating with each other in everyday life' (Labov 1972: 184). It was not that Labov was the first to have stumbled upon these profound truths: The ideas were well accepted by many, even in America. What carried greater conviction was the particular combination of careful empirical research and theoretical reflection which Labov brought to his discourse of the mid to late sixties. At that point in the history of linguistics it seemed as if a major step was about to be taken in creating a linguistics which would pay due respect to the interdependence of language and communication while still acknowledging their specificity. Saussure had declared 'we must choose between two routes', because in his opinion both could 'not be followed simultaneously'. For a moment, it seemed that Saussure was to be proved wrong; linguistics was to become an integrated study of both language and communication. It is not my intention to underestimate the importance of Labov's work when I say that these promises remained promises; the expectations did not turn into reality. What actually happened was something rather different: Sociolinguists ended up doing diachrony by synchrony and sociolinguistic variation was carefully restricted to surface phenomena (Hasan 1989, 1992a). Let me explain what I mean by these claims.

Labovian sociolinguists – and the name of Labov stands here for all who follow his methodology, which in practice amounts today to most main stream sociolinguists most of the time – study language change by describing what could justifiably be seen as a particular *état de langue*, and confronting it with a similar description of another specific *état de langue*. True that the Labovian *état de langue* in contrast to Saussure's langue and Chomsky's competence displays 'orderly heterogeneity' since what forms the basis of description is 'language ... used by the native speakers communicating ... in everyday life', but the problem of creating a linguistics of human verbal semiosis such that it provides a viable description of the relation of interdependence between language and communication is not resolved simply by using naturally occurring language as the data against which the observational adequacy of our claims may be checked. Certainly the use of such data is a large step in this direction and Labov must be thanked for turning the tide against navel gazing in favour of audio-taping, but this step by itself is not tantamount to creating an integrated linguistics of language and communication. In one respect these studies of diachrony via synchrony are disturbingly like traditional philological studies: The study of language change is here transmuted into the study of the stages of item change. Thus one examines how a particular consonant gives way to another consonant; how one vowel, over time, becomes another; one 'word-image' acquires another phonological shape as its expression. Whatever the faults of the Saussurean views on language change, his criticism of this mode of describing language change was cogent, and we might be well advised not to disregard them. Accounts of such atomistic changes can hardly be expected to reveal the nature of the massive interaction between communication and language that has to be postulated to account for their interdependence.

Where Labov came nearest to integrating the two perspectives was in the observation that synchronic variation and diachronic language change are two facets of the same phenomenon. This is a valuable insight but the effectiveness of this insight is compromised by Labov's view of synchronic variation: We are told that synchronic variation, particularly of the sociolinguistic kind, is relevant only to social meaning. It concerns the how, not the what of saying: What Labov refers to as 'referential meaning' – the real stuff of linguistic meaning that constitutes semantics (Weiner and Labov 1983) – is said to fall outside synchronic variation; there is no social variation in 'semantics proper'. But if so, what mechanism do we have for diachronic semantic change such as in the case of the items *silly*, *host*, and so on? We could say – following the logic of autonomous linguistics – that change and variation in language are limited to surface phenomena, not reaching the deeper level of semantics. Ironically, we do not need to go far in search of arguments and evidence to refute this kind of claim: Labov's own arguments used against the claim of linguistic homogeneity will do beautifully! It might be argued that the Labovian methodology for the study of language in society is the best we have at present; this may be so, but it can hardly be a reason for stopping one from suggesting that we need something better. Saussure restricted linguistics to the study of language alone, thus denying the possibility of combining the two perspectives; Labovian methodology allows us to describe both but only up to a point: The fact of the matter is that its acceptance of some of the basic assumptions of a model that treats language as an a-social and arbitrary system (Gardin and Marcellesi 1987), prevents it from providing a consistent framework for studying the interdependence of language and communication. Saussure conceptualised this interdependence in terms of determination: Language is not only an 'instrument' but also the 'product' of communication. The metaphor of determination highlights causality, and the causal perspective is, to use Markova's terms, perforce 'mono-logical' because it is a perspective in which two 'things' are brought together in a cause-effect logic (Markova 1988). This is what militates against devising a linguistics which will account for both simultaneously. To achieve this we need to adopt a 'dia-logical' perspective, which emphasises the co-genesis of communication and language: Instead of seeing them as two independent things which come together by what one does for the other, the co-genetic perspective emphasises the fact that in a rather important sense the two are inherently united; one does not determine the other: They co-evolve; unless one exists the other cannot. If we are to create a linguistics that follows the 'two routes' of language and communication 'simultaneously', then we must at one and the same time see language as a system that underlies communication, and communication as the impetus for the genesis of that system. It is this perspective that will explain why the structure of language is as it is and why language is able to meet the communicative needs of its speakers to the extent that it does.

3 Communication and language: a functional perspective

In order to create integrated linguistics, we need to interpret the term *communication* in a specific way. As it happens, the interpretation that is needed is not a new one: The view is, in fact, widely accepted that communication is not merely 'uttering … noises of certain types, belonging to and as belonging to, a certain vocabulary, conforming to and as conforming to a certain grammar' (Austin 1980: 95). Rather, communication is first and foremost an act of meaning, an exercise in intersubjectivity. But an explicit acceptance of this view raises an important question: What forms the basis of intersubjectivity, what makes the act of meaning possible? Dominant linguistics has an ideological commitment to the uniqueness of individuals, which leads it to insist that meanings are ***in*** speakers; however, the postulate of intersubjectivity demands that, for any communication to occur, meanings must be ***across*** speakers – they must be share-able and shared. But if meanings are specific to individuals, then what makes it possible for any sharing to occur? One answer has been to cite shared context as the basis for intersubjectivity. But where there is an assumption of the purely individual nature of meaning, the viability of this answer will itself demand a particular view of context: It will imply that context is something concrete and physical whose recognition calls for nothing other than the physical senses, and the 'vocables' are simply 'names' for the elements of this physiologically accessible context. The grandiose catch-all label of *shared world knowledge* – as if the world was as free of variation as language – is not unmotivated. If we can assume that by virtue of being human, we all apprehend the same 'things', and that the 'vocables' of a language are names for these things, this helps explain the currency value of the vocables in the exchange of meaning. By these steps, language becomes nomenclature, semantics is restricted to being referential, and the notion of reference is reduced to a variety of association or correspondence.

Much has been written against the 'view that every meaningful word is a name and that every sentence is a description' (Baker and Hacker 1988: 13), and clearly this is not the right place to pursue this lengthy debate. The point, however, needs to be made emphatically – and has been made, amongst others, by Bernstein, Gumperz, Halliday and Hymes, and many others – that context in the sense of 'occasion for talk' (Hasan 1995a) cannot be seen as a concrete, physical construct: It is itself semiotically constituted, and by this I mean two things. First, it is not the physical phenomena themselves but their interpretation in a community that is relevant to our 'perception' of the nature of context; and secondly, the identity of some context as an occasion for this kind of talk or some other is, in the last resort, defined by the linguistic meanings being exchanged. So, to repeat a simple example, if while I am browsing in a shop, the assistant says to me *Can I help you?*, this broaches a context of shopping; if my reply to this is *No, thank you. I am only looking.*, this redefines the context as not an occasion for shopping talk: the concrete physical situation has remained virtually unaltered, but two distinct contexts have been 'recognised' by the speakers largely on the basis of what is said.

Simple as in many ways this example is, it hopefully succeeds in making the point that the idea of a language-independent shared context as the explanation for the possibility of the exchange of (individual-internal) meanings poses serious problems: It appears that the sharing of meaning is itself essential to one's perception of context. So, instead of equating context with concrete, physical phenomena – with material situational setting (Hasan 1973a) – it is best to think of it as part of a theory of how speakers and addressees position and reposition their world by their acts of meaning. And the word meaning as used here refers to a more complex notion than the relation of naming or correspondence. The act of meaning, which is to say communication, is not isolated items of the lexicon or single simple sentences (with an imagined corresponding situation): The act of meaning is in fact text-forming. 'The text is the linguistic form of social interaction. It is a continuous progression of meaning' (Halliday 1975a: 37). This implies that it is the text that identifies the nature of its context. To claim that context is known by text is to say with Hymes that language in use reconstitutes context: communication as exchange of meaning is an on-going record of the contexts being 'created'. This turns context into a semiotic construct, whose value and identity is known by the meanings that are meant: context and text are really two sides of the same coin – two functives of the same function of semiosis. The signified context and the signifying meanings in the shape of text are related to each other by realisation. This is an interesting conclusion: it implies that the nature of context can be revealed in the act of meaning itself.

So what do contexts look like when seen through linguistic meanings? Granted that each occasion of talk is distinct from every other, is there anything in common across these myriad individual contexts? We are familiar with certain frameworks, such as that of Hymes' (1962, 1967), which identify contextual parameters that are relevant at an abstract level to every occasion of talk. These share a good deal with the Hallidayan framework which builds on the work of Malinowski and Firth. Most readers will be familiar with Halliday's notion of context of situation as a tripartite construct consisting of *tenor of discourse* i.e., the nature of social relations between speakers, *field of discourse* i.e., the nature of the social action engaging the speakers, and *mode of discourse* i.e., social contact which plays an important part in the semiotic organisation of social action and social relation. My aim is to highlight certain, perhaps, not well understood aspects of this conceptualisation. In the sixties, Halliday's framework did not differ very significantly from that of Hymes': Halliday's three contextual parameters had differently aligned most of the contextual features which Hymes' schema had divided variously on various occasions. But even at this early stage one difference was noticeable: from the very beginning, Halliday has attempted to relate context of situation to the wordings of the text (Halliday, McIntosh and Strevens 1964: 74–110). With the development of functional perspective (Halliday 1970, 1975, 1977, 1985, 1991), this aspect of his approach has become increasingly explicit: Halliday argues a 'natural', i.e., non-arbitrary relation between the structure of context and the organisation of language. Given the claim about the semiotic nature of context, this is a significant development, and it may be helpful at this point to spell out the steps in this argument.

Consider first two well recognised facts about texts: each text is an 'individual'; as pointed out (Halliday and Hasan 1985) each has a distinct identity, in the sense that it is not the replication of any other text. And no text can be a complete record of all the meanings that can possibly be meant using some given language: its meanings will be a 'selection made by the speaker from the options that constitute the *meaning potential*' (Halliday 1975: 37; italics in original). The claim that text is a selection, and (partial) instantiation of the meaning potential, is important for three reasons: *first*, it is a claim that a text is interpretable only in light of the systems as they are shared by the speakers. This does not mean that everything in the text necessarily *conforms* to such system(s). As Sinclair (1991: 492) points out, 'language users use the regular patterns as jumping off points, and create endless variations to suit particular purposes. The variations are not random, but are rule governed, like the underlying patterns'. However, the idea of language as system is essential to even recognise variation: concepts such as *same, different*, and *original* as applied to language are unintelligible without some idea of what is possible and what is typical in what environment. It is this sense of the possibility of meaning that underlies the postulate of language as a meaning potential. In other words, human language acts as a resource, a meaning potential, whose actualisation in texts is a necessary condition for the construal of contexts, on the understanding that contexts are semiotic in nature. *Secondly*, if despite being an 'individual', each distinct text reveals the abstract structure of context, then this argues that over and above those specificities of meaning which individualise texts, it is possible to recognise a more abstract level of meaning, as some type of meaning rather than a specific element of meaning. The capacity of different individual texts to construe context indicates that what is relevant to the construal of context is the abstract type(s) of meaning. This takes us to the *third* point. If we say that every text 'has' these categories of meaning, we must imply that the entire meaning potential can be described in terms of this abstract organisation, otherwise individual texts that are only a selection from it, an actualisation of it, could logically not display within them these categories of meaning. We conclude then that it is a characteristic of the meaning systems of human language – the meaning potential as a whole – that it will make possible the construal of the ***field***, the ***tenor*** and the ***mode*** of speakers' discourse. This returns us to the original claim: *the meaning system of human language is not arbitrary; it is functionally specialised with respect to context.*

But this in its turn, poses a further question. What is the explanation for the presence of this functional organisation in the meaning potential of human language? It seems that the choice of answers is limited: either we must maintain that linguistic meanings are as they are because they are the signifier of the context of social interaction, or we must rely on serendipity. Systemic functional linguistics adopts the first solution, thus subscribing to the view that the cultural systems of a community are created, maintained, and altered by its semiotic systems: they enter into the cycle of semiosis. Just as text is an instantiation of the meaning potential of language, so also context of situation is an instantiation of the context of culture: a particular context of situation is interpreted by reference to the underlying system – i.e., context of culture; and just as the text's meaning selection realises the context of situation, so the meaning potential of the language as a whole realises the context of culture. The functional specialisation of the meaning potential is explained by this semiotic relation between language and context. The meaning system of human language is organised the way it is since language and context are united dialogically: linguistic meaning construes context, and context activates linguistic meaning. This dialectic between linguistic meaning and social context is one important part of Halliday's claim about the functional nature of language. However the full significance of this claim can be understood only when a critical question is addressed: how are linguistic meanings produced? What part, if any, does the form of language play in the production of linguistic meanings.

In formal models, linguistic meaning is some glorified variety of the naming relation. This assumes that things, properties, processes etc. can be itemised, and their boundaries identified, without any semiotic mediation. The form of language – its lexicon and syntax – are simply labels to refer to 'what there really is'. Given these assumptions, it is logical for such models to present the relation between meaning and form as arbitrary, arising purely from conventional association. These views are incompatible with a semiotic view of context. In an account of language as social semiotic, it is incoherent to suggest that we can know without semiotic mediation 'what there really is'; according to this approach, what we are destined to consider real in the living of life is at least as much semiotically construed as it is sensuous, with the significant difference that only the semiotically construed has any value in social exchange. So far as interaction is concerned, the currency value of private, un-sharable sensuous experience is nearly nil. Linguistic meaning is an interface between the world as we experience it and the interpretation of that world as it is construed by the form of language (Matthiessen 1991). In an important sense then the abstract relation of coding which links context and meaning is recapitulated in the relation between meaning and wording. So with some oversimplification it may be claimed that context is realised as meaning; meaning is realised as wording, or lexicogrammar. The creative power of language resides largely in the lexicogrammar, for it is the lexicogrammar that produces meaning, and this is tantamount to producing semiotic constructs of reality. It is through the realisational relation between meaning and wording that the world of human experience enters into discourse. Given this stance, the relation between meaning and form cannot be that of conventional association between the name and what the name names, since neither meaning nor form can be said to precede the other: they co-evolve, just as culture and meaning potential, and context and text co-evolve. I understand this to be the heart of Halliday's functional hypothesis, according to which the higher linguistic strata – those of meaning and wording – are functionally organised with respect to context: the form of human language is as it is since it co-evolves with the meanings which in turn co-evolve with the community's contexts of social interaction. This is what links the social existence of speakers to their verbal syntagms confirming the non-arbitrary, functional nature of the higher levels of linguistic organisation.

An attractive aspect of Halliday's functional hypothesis is that it is open to empirical examination. To begin with, if context is a semiotic construct realised by meanings as construed by wording then in texts as its realisation there will exist evidence of what the abstract form of context is like: a hypothesis about the abstract nature of context would be seen as viable only if the meanings of the text will bear testimony to it. Leaving metaphors aside, what would count as evidence for the functional hypothesis? In systemic functional linguistics this is taken to mean that the abstract organisation of each of these levels of linguistic description would echo the organisation of the other two. So, for example, if Halliday claims that context is a semiotic construct consisting of three abstract parameters, this can be rewritten as a claim that the higher strata of meaning and wording display a similar organisation. So given the tripartite structure of context, if it is taken as the starting point, then the linguistic levels of meaning and wording should also be describable as comprising three subsets – or clusters of system – such that they would possess the following properties:

1) Each specific contextual parameter would be realisationally related to a specific cluster of meaning systems; the implication is that meanings are functionally specialised *vis á vis* context;

2) Each such cluster of meaning systems would in turn be realisationally related to a specific cluster of lexicogrammatical systems; the implication is that the lexicogrammar is functionally organised with respect to context realising meaning systems.

The claim of systemic functional linguistics is that indeed such a fractal organisation does exist at the higher levels of language. To appreciate these claims, it is necessary to understand the concept of system.

The three notions fundamentally relevant to the understanding of system are the potentiality of choice in some environment. A system 'is a' set of interlocking options which represent what is 'possible', i.e., the potential, under some explicitly specified condition. To take a fairly obvious example, in the environment of interrogative – i.e., where a clause 'has' the feature interrogative – there exists the potential of choosing between the features polar (construing typically demand for confirmation: *is it?* or *isn't it?*) or non-polar (typically construing demand for information: *why/where/when did you?*). To say that the level of meaning has a tripartite systemic organisation is to maintain also that the choice of options in one system is relatively independent of choices in the other two: the choice of polar v. non-polar from the system of mood is not constrained by the choice of transitive v. intransitive from the system of transitivity. Consider, for example, the following pairs: *are you going?, where are you going? did you see him?, when did you see him?, did he read your application?, what was he reading?, were you driving his car? why were you driving his car?* And each of these lexicogrammatical systems construes a specific system of meaning which is realisationally linked to some specific contextual parameters. For each contextual parameter, there is, as it were, a mini-semantics and for each system of meaning, a mini-lexicogrammar. These points can be illustrated by using the information in table 1, where the contextual features and some of the realising systems of meaning and wording are tabulated. But before that let me make two points. First, realisation is not a simple relation of replication (Halliday 1991a, 1992b); the requirement of a strict one to one correspondence contradicts the need for the recognition of distinct strata as distinct orders of abstraction (Hasan 1995a). Secondly, talking about systems of meaning and wording is crucially different from talking about isolated individual elements of meaning or wording: characterising a system of meaning or wording as a whole is to deal with categories of a higher level of abstraction, as was pointed out earlier. To take an example, instead of being concerned with a specific meaning, e.g., statement, we are concerned with a system of meaning, e.g. speech role exchange whose specific terms are statement, question, command, acceptance, amongst others. Similarly, the concern is not with an isolated entry in the lexicon such as *pain*, but with the systems of the lexicon as significative resource; nor are we concerned with specific structures such as declarative clause, but rather with the mood system as a whole.

Table 1: Metafunctional resonance: The co-genesis of context, meaning, and wording

<table>
<tr><th>METAFUNCTION</th><th>CONTEXTUAL VARIABLE</th><th>MEANING SYSTEM</th><th>WORDING SYSTEM</th><th>WORDING STRUCTURE</th></tr>
<tr><td>interpersonal</td><td>social relation
(=tenor)</td><td>role exchange;assessment of probability, obligation</td><td>mood system (e.g.,declarative v. interrogative...);
systems of modality, modulation</td><td>prosodic</td></tr>
<tr><td>experiential</td><td rowspan="2">social action
(=field)</td><td>states of affairs
classification of phenomena</td><td>transitivity system (e.g., material v. verbal....);
lexical systems.....</td><td>segmental</td></tr>
<tr><td>logical</td><td>relations of states of affairs
relations of phenomena</td><td>expansion, projection systems
modification...</td><td>iterative</td></tr>
<tr><td>textual</td><td>verbal action and contact
(=mode)</td><td>point of departure; news
focus points of identity, similarity</td><td>thematic, information systems
cohesive connections</td><td>periodic</td></tr>
</table>

As table 1 is dense with information, let me provide a brief illustration of how a contextual parameter, a category of meaning, and of wording are realisationally related. In each case I shall restrict myself to using as example only part of the social facts relevant to the contextual parameter under focus and the meaning-wording systems which construe it. We can begin with tenor, and within tenor with that aspect of social relation which translates into a sense of our rights and obligations as interactants in the same social activity. Obviously the modality choices are relevant in the construal of this aspect of tenor, but the system of speech role exchange is equally important, if not more so (Halliday 1984a, 1985a). The choices available here are those of demanding or giving, and what is demanded or given could be either information or goods-and-services. If the speech role of demanding goods-and-services is adopted, further choices become available, such as direct order, e.g., *cook those potatoes!* or consultative order, e.g., *could you cook those potatoes?*, or assertive desiderative order, e.g., *I'd like you to cook those potatoes.*, and so on (both the examples and the terminology are simplified; further discussion, chapter 7, in Part III). Which of the options is chosen is relevant to what social relation already exists between the speakers and/or what social relation the speakers wish to enact now. These systemic meaning options are lexicogrammatically realised as choices in mood, with such options as imperative (*cook those potatoes!*), or interrogative (*could you cook those potatoes?*), or declarative (*I'd like you to cook those potatoes.*), and so on. It is not the case that every text will 'have' in it an imperative or an exclamative; simply that typically communication involves making some choice from this system. SF linguists refer to the cluster of systems of meaning which construes the tenor of discourse as interpersonal meanings, and to that cluster of systems of the lexicogrammar which construe such meanings as interpersonal lexicogrammar. The contextual parameter of tenor, interpersonal meanings, and interpersonal lexicogrammar are related to each other functionally. The interpersonal metafunction of language consists in this relation. To say that human language 'has' interpersonal metafunction is to say that in every language there is a set of lexicogrammatical systems which construes systems of meaning that contribute to the production, maintenance and alteration of social relations between interactants, and to making the 'inner self' of the speakers accessible intersubjectively.

The system of meanings to which table 1 refers as 'states of affairs' concerns goings on: doing, sensing, saying, being, which imply the involvement of participants such as 'doer', 'done-to' etc., and circumstances such as those of time, place, manner, etc. This is one of the systems of meaning that is relevant to the construal of social action. For example, *cook the potatoes in boiling salted water for 20 minutes until soft* construes part of the social action of instructing someone how to cook something. Lexicogrammatically, such meanings are realised by choices in the system of transitivity, and by 'lexical' reference as is perhaps evident from this example. The type of meaning that (partially) construes social action, and that is itself construed by transitivity and lexical reference may be referred to as experiential. However, social action is not typically construed simply by reference to 'simples': speakers also need to refer to complex entities and complex states of affairs – e.g., not just *water* but *salted water*, not just *salted water* but *boiling salted water*, not just *cook potatoes …*, but also *cook potatoes ... until soft*. What is achieved here is greater specificity through relating things to properties and some state of affairs to some other(s). The meaning systems that form the basis of such relations are known as logical meanings and they are construed by logical lexicogrammar, e.g. systems of expansion and projection (Halliday 1985a). The logical and experiential systems of meanings and wordings are together active in the construal of social action. The relation that links logical experiential meanings and wording to the contextual parameter of social action is referred to as the ideational metafunction of language. The recognition of the ideational metafunction of language is a recognition of the fact that in every language there exist systems of wording which construe meanings, that in turn form the expression of the speakers' experience of the world, both the external world of sensuous experience and the internal one of imagination, cognition, reflection, and emotion.

Turning to the third contextual parameter, it is difficult to illustrate briefly – and without trivialisation – how linguistic meanings construe the semiotic organisation of human relation and action. What is at issue is the ongoing organisation of the interpersonal and ideational meanings into an accessible flow of communication. This involves the identification of the phenomena of the world that are entering into the discourse as the same happening or entity e.g., ***the*** *potatoes…*, (i.e., definite, identified as same individuals rather than just any members of the class *potato*), or indicating differing degrees of similarity e.g. ***another*** *potato* (identical class but distinct member), or *some* ***onions*** (a distinct class which pertains to the same general domain as *potato*). Additionally, it involves judgements of what information is accessible from what source; for example using the expression *the potatoes* where there has been no previous mention of *potatoes*, as opposed to in a recipe as in the original example where the ingredients mention *new potatoes 1 lb*. The semiotic organisation of information also involves decision about what needs foregrounding: compare *into the salted boiling water drop the peeled potatoes* … as opposed to *the potatoes should be cooked in* ..., as opposed to *cook the potatoes in*.... Each of these expressions is grammatical so far as the individual clause is concerned but the textual environment in which one is more likely to occur than the others will be governed by such considerations as how topic is to be organised. The inability to make appropriate judgements for the semiotic organisation of interpersonal and ideational meanings so as to make communication easily accessible to one's addressee is one of the underlying problems of what is known as 'disordered communication'. The lexicogrammatical systems which construe such meanings are those of phoricity, lexical-field formation, theme and information focus development. Such meanings and wordings together construe the mode of discourse, and their relation is recognised as the textual metafunction of language.

Just as there is no social context that consists simply of social action or of social relation or of semiotic organisation, so also there is no text which displays just one kind of meaning, just one kind of wording: the three metafunctions operate in unison. So an utterance such as *cook the potatoes in salted boiling water until soft.* 'has' interpersonal meaning; it has an exhortative command realised as a jussive imperative. It also 'has' an experiential meaning, displaying a state of affairs that involves acting on something realised as material process *cook,* with *the potatoes* as goal, and so on. The logical and textual meanings and wordings of the syntagm in question have already been briefly alluded to. The grammar of a language is a device for the calibration of the distinct metafunctional strands into one and the same syntagm. So we do not have texts and/or messages that are simply interpersonal, or ideational, or textual: they are functional in all three ways at once. In this respect, the systemic functional concept of metafunction is significantly different from that of, say, Bühler's to whom most ideas about linguistic functionalism can be traced (Dirven and Fried 1987). Bühler's functions unlike the systemic functional metafunctions were mutually exclusive. The discussion in this section is not presented as an account of functionalism in systemic functional linguistics: this is a large issue that cannot be developed here (see Halliday and Hasan

1985). It was necessary to bring in the notion of the functional organisation of language and the simultaneity of metafunctions in order to pave the way to a reinterpretation of the relations of language, communication, and social meaning. This will be the concern of the next section.

4 Functionalism and social meaning

Although I have presented a highly condensed account in the above section, it hopefully does suggest that linguistic form is functionally organised with respect to systems of meaning and systems of meaning with respect to the context of communication. Let me clarify what the acceptance of this approach implies for a revised understanding of the relations of the three terms in the theme of this Congress. First, take the claim of co-genetic relation which links context, communication and language. This is an attempt to do justice to the specificity of communication and language while also recognising their deep interdependence. It is implied in this claim also that functionalism is not an attribute of any one level of language; it is neither intrinsic nor extrinsic: It is a relation that links the material conditions of human social existence to human verbal semiosis. This is why the resonance of the metafunctional principle is felt through the context of communication to language use through to language system. This perspective is capable of explaining why the potential for being useful inheres in human language: language is able to meet the needs of its speakers because the wordings and meanings of a language are not arbitrary with respect to the community's living of life. Society, in a very real sense, is operative 'in' language just as much as language is operative 'in' society. If we find 'the reflection of social processes in linguistic choices' this is because the roots of communication are in the social living of life, and because the form that human communication takes is text, and because text is to language as an instance is to a system. It is only in this kind of approach that doing sociolinguistics can equal doing linguistics. Saussure had doubted the possibility of creating a linguistics which would at once respect the distinct identity of language and communication and yet illuminate their deep interdependence: it seems to me that the functional approach I have described here goes a considerable way towards meeting that challenge. This resolution is made possible in fact by following Saussure's hint – by taking him more seriously than he took himself when he suggested that linguistics was a species of semiology, concerned with one semiotic system among many others in the community. But whereas Saussure thought of the various semiotic systems as simply co-present, systemic functional linguistics attempts to integrate language as a semiotic system with other semiotic systems in a community. It is clear that the claim of co-genesis itself rests on that of the semiotic relation of coding which integrates the context of culture and situation with language and communication. In taking this step we have found it necessary to reject Saussure's entirely sequential way of looking at communication and language (see quotes in section 2).

By these steps we have arrived at a point in this discussion where the concept of social meaning can be re-viewed. The relation of semiotic construal of context, communication, and language denies the possibility of recognising a causal determinative relation between these terms. Clearly, in a linguistics of this kind, those referential theories of meaning are unacceptable where every word names some pre-identified thing and every sentence mirrors some actual state of affairs. I argued in section 3 that the construal of context calls for interpersonal, ideational, and textual meanings, and that all three types of meaning are construed simultaneously by lexicogrammar. If so, then there seems no justification for claiming that the linguistic level of meaning – its semantics – is just referential and that other kinds of meaning can be excluded from semantics. From a functional point of view, all three kinds of meaning are equally socially motivated, and together they constitute the semantic level of language. This removes the justification for making a distinction between meaning that is social and meaning that is semantic. It might be argued that the concept of social meaning is required because the attitudes of the community valorise something which in itself has no meaning, namely, the phonological variants. I do not find this justification very compelling. In the first place, variation invites valorisation; phonological variation is no exception to this rule. Secondly, it would be an error to give the impression that if value in the sense of prejudice or praise is attached to meanings – and it certainly is – this is because these values inhere in the nature of those meanings in some non-social natural way just as gravity inheres in matter. Nothing could be further from the truth. The valorisation of meanings depends on the attitudes of the community as much as the valorisation of the phoneme does. Our failure to recognise this is not activated by some scientific principle; it simply confirms the power of ideology. So to single out the valorisation of phonological variation as social meaning and to claim that it is this meaning that is the true concern of sociolinguistics is to deny the possibility that meanings are subject to a similar valorisation. This leaves our ideological allegiances unexplored; it encourages simplistic solutions to highly complex problems – one example is the unqualified claim about the equality of languages (see Hymes 1993), another is to say that semantic variation is not social (Weiner and Labov 1983), and if someone attempts to record its social nature, this is simply because such researchers are prejudiced, or their linguistic techniques are inferior. These attitudes to semantic variation leave us with a serious problem: if it is believed that in a complex society such as ours, phonological variation is 'functional' in the sense of being practically useful (Weinreich, Labov and Herzog 1968: 101), then how is the absence of the variation in meaning to be explained? Since meaning is what our social universe is made of, why would there exist no variation in that sphere of language? Why would there be no valorisation of experiential meaning? In the following section I present the findings of a research in semantic variation, which demonstrates that semantic variation is not only a possibility but that it is an actuality, and that in a manner of speaking this variation is 'functional': it plays an important part in maintaining the inequalities of our 'egalitarian' societies.

5 Semantic variation: the ideological power of worded meaning

The details of the research one fragment of which I discuss below are provided in earlier chapters (3–5). Close to 20544 messages were analysed semantically and statistically processed using PCA. Table 2 displays represents the loadings on the input semantic features in PC1, which accounts for 45.00% variance in the data. The input features in this case had consisted of some semantic choices relevant to maternal control.

Table 2: Socio-semantic variation in maternal control

	PC1	PC2	PC3	PC4
C [indirect]	0.84	-0.32	-0.14	0.25
S [supportive]	0.83	0.06	-0.01	-0.23
C [suggestive]	0.82	-0.38	-0.00	0.10
C [elaborated]	0.77	0.29	0.02	0.13
R [logical]	0.64	0.20	-0.07	-0.31
R [elaborated]	0.62	0.35	0.19	-0.45
Q [explain]	-0.50	0.60	-0.11	0.11
C [action]	0.34	0.24	0.75	0.45
C [prefaced]	0.44	0.37	-0.60	0.38
Eigenvalue	4.04	1.07	1.00	0.83
% Variance	45.00	12.00	11.10	9.20

The majority of the features in table 2 are semantic choices in making command (=C), though two are features of reason (=R), while Q(explain) stands for challenge and S(supportive) for supportive comments. PC1 of table 2 claims that subjects scoring high would be highly likely to issue [indirect] and [suggestive] commands (e.g. *could you take this stuff to your room?* and *we'll get dressed* / *How about taking this stuff to your room now?* respectively). The features indirect and suggestive are in systemic contrast with [direct] commands such as *take this stuff to your room* and impositions e.g., *you will take this stuff to your room now.*, with the implication that those who score high on the former two must score low on the latter, and vice versa. So mothers who score low on indirect and suggestive are highly likely to make direct commands or impositions. High scoring mothers are also highly likely to make [elaborated] commands, where the command is related to some other message which expresses a condition, concession etc. as in *could you stir the mixture as I pour the milk in?* High scoring subjects are also reasonably likely to make prefaced commands, where the command is projected (Halliday 1985) as a locution, desire, or idea etc. as in *I want you to stir the mixture as I pour the milk in* where the command to stir the mixture is projected as the speaker's desire. I ignore C[action] since its loading is not criterial on PC1. Turning to reasons, high scoring mothers are very likely to give [logical] reasons – reasons that are grounded in the physical nature of the universe, e.g., (*don't touch that*) *because it's hot*. Such reasons contrast with those whose grounding is social. Social reasons range from convention e.g., *because that's how we do it* to threat e.g., *because I'll hit you.* So PC1 scores indicate that the low scoring mothers are very likely to give social reasons. High scoring mothers are also very likely to give [elaborated] reasons, as in *because it's Rebecca's doll and if you break her she'll (i.e. Rebecca will) be very upset.* Q[explain] refers to a why-question, which when addressed to the child by the mother in the context of control, is seen as a challenge. For example when Karen refuses to comply with the mother's order to kiss her goodnight, the mother says *you're not gonna kiss me? why?* This feature has a negative loading, with the implication that high scoring mothers are not likely to challenge their children in the context of control. The remaining feature S[supportive] refers to such remarks as *I know you'll understand* which express confidence in the child's ability to act 'reasonably', 'judiciously', etc., and this feature has a high positive loading implying that high scoring subjects are highly likely to issue supportive statements in the context of control.

The statistical procedure assigns an overall score to each subject. Figure 1 identifies the position of the 24 mothers by reference to their scores on PC1 and PC2.

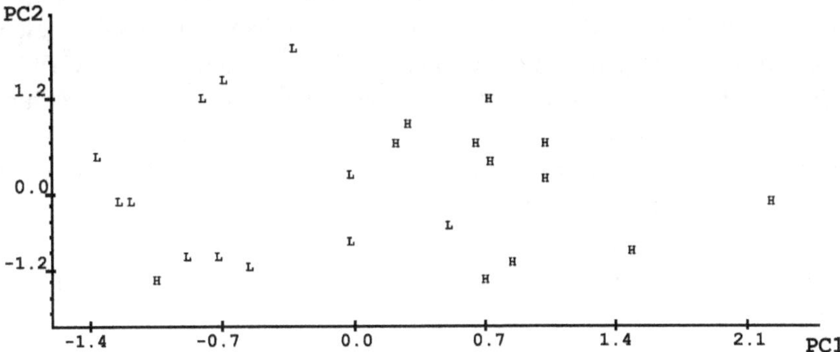

Figure 1: Social class and maternal control

In figure 1 the location of mothers is determined on the vertical axis by reference to their scores on PC2, so high scorers are placed at the top and low ones at the bottom end of the vertical axis. The mothers' position on the horizontal axis is relevant to the present discussion as this position is determined by reference to their scores on PC1. On this axis, the leftmost point indicates the lowest score viz., -1.40 and the rightmost, the highest viz., 2.10. So the lower the mother's score on PC1 the more to the left her location would be in figure 1, and the higher her score, the further to the right she would be positioned. The letter H in figure 1 indicates a HAP mother, the letter L a LAP one, and it is quite clear from the figure that the HAP mothers are the ones who have, on the whole, scored higher than the LAP mothers on PC1. This should not be taken as a claim that HAP mothers invariably act this way any more than the high frequency of r-fullness could be taken to imply that speakers of a rhotic dialect invariably produce /r/. What is being identified is a fashion of speaking, a coding orientation which occurs significantly often to become associated with a particular social group. Nor am I claiming that every single mother in these two social groups will behave in conformity with the group's practices. My claim is simply that in the context of control, there is far greater likelihood of a HAP mother than of a LAP mother displaying orientation to the cluster of meanings identified by PC1 (p (HAP > LAP) <.0002). A cluster analysis of the data produced the same results.

But what is the interpretation of this result? What does it mean to say that HAP mothers control their children's behaviour by giving indirect or suggestive commands, and so on? To interpret the results of PC1 we need to ask what principles governing behaviour are indicated by this semantic orientation. What is the representation of these habitual meaning selections in the interactants' consciousness? What experience of the world is construed by this fashion of speaking? The semantic features [indirect] and [suggestive] command underplay the speaker's privilege to command; they permit a sense of discretion to the addressee. It is important to point out that neither group of mothers is willing to 'let the child get away with it'. In the majority of cases, mothers in both groups get the children to act in the way that they themselves desire. But for the HAP child the mother's power remains invisible, whereas the LAP child is left in no doubt whatever about the mother's power to get him to act as she thinks best. When it comes to reason, we find a similar pattern: a [logical] reason that is grounded in the physical nature of the world appears to have an objective character; the effectiveness of a social reason such as threat, convention, or bribe resides once again in the relationship of the reason-giver *vis á vis* the addressee. The HAP mother's authority remains 'safely' masked; the LAP mother's authority is flagrantly obvious. Commands and reasons with the semantic feature [elaborated] possess greater verbal specificity. The greater the degree of empathy between the speaker and addressee, the less need there would be for verbal specificity. A higher degree of elaboration implies that the speaker is less willing to act simply on the assumption of shared knowledge with the addressee. The interactants are thus construed as individuals 'in their own right', with thoughts, beliefs, feelings that are inaccessible to others without speech. This interpretation of elaboration is further supported by the fact that mothers given to elaboration are also those whose commands tend to be [prefaced]: a preface such as *I'd like you to ... do you think you could ...* etc., is making one's own subjective position verbally explicit or seeking the addressee's subjective position. Which is to say, the speaker is not willing to assume or allow shared knowledge of the conversational other's subjectivity. The HAP child is thus socio-semiotically produced as an individual with his own unique subjectivity, the sharing of which is within his personal discretion. This granting of unique individuality, the masking of maternal power, and the granting of discretion combine to produce a sense of the world under one's control, where the external control on the child's actions is rendered invisible, its motivation being presented as either above human manipulation (reasons are 'logical', guided by 'unavoidable rational principles') or as self-regulated (the child has discretion and own judgement). The LAP child is socio-semiotically produced as someone whose experience of the collective is an aspect of his subjectivity, the sharing of which does not depend on his personal discretion; the control on the child's action is quite visibly external. The power that controls his actions is derived from the speaker's social position *vis á vis* the addressee. But this position itself is not unique to the speaker: it is the condition of being a mother – a status recognised by the community – which gives the speaker greater discretion than the child. The child's actions are quite clearly under the control of this greater power.

When couple of decades ago Bernstein (1971a) drew attention to the variation in coding orientation he was, in my view, unfairly attacked as displaying social class prejudice. In the flurry of the debate a rather interesting issue got lost. Let me point to that issue by taking the two pictures I have presented above – one that is created by HAP fashions of speaking, the other created by LAP fashions of speaking. The kind of result that I have reported here has often been said to be motivated by the prejudice of the researcher. It is, however, ironic to reflect that I can be accused of prejudice against the LAP group, ***only if*** the somewhat smug assumptions of my hypothetical accuser are accepted: the accusation of prejudice against the LAP group will hold only if it is granted that the HAP ways of meaning are indeed the better ways of meaning. I submit that this is by no means a necessary assumption in the description of socio-semantic variation than it is in describing stigmatised accents as different from privileged ones. This raises the question: on what basis do we valorise human behaviour, particularly of the semantic type, which underlie our beliefs, ideas etc.? I am forced to agree with the claim that 'the ideas of the ruling class are in every epoch the ruling ideas, i.e. the class which is the ruling *material* force of society, is at the same time its ruling *intellectual* force' (Marx and Engels 1985: 64; emphases in original). Which means that there is at least as much, if not far more, prejudice in granting the superiority of HAP behaviour than there is in describing LAP behaviour as different! The unquestioned assumption that the HAP construal of social consciousness is in fact natural is capable of being far more pernicious because it is not even perceived as prejudice. Later I will argue that this assumption has a role in our society, but for the present let me ask, how is this orientation to meaning on the part of these two groups functional in a complex industrial society which, claiming to be egalitarian, bristles with inequality? Here is a speculative answer.

HAP ways of behaving appear highly functional in the HAP station of life. If you have sufficient autonomy so that you can take significant decisions about your environment, and you can use others as the instrument for the execution of those decisions, then you are in a position of control; you are controlling others' actions in order to get them to do things you consider 'reasonable'. When control is invisible, when reasons are 'in the nature of things', the chances of open conflict are reduced: the person giving rise to such conflict is invariably viewed as 'unreasonable'. The data shows that HAP children cry; they complain; they even retaliate symbolically because they feel the pressure of authority; but they seldom challenge the mother's authority, and they certainly do not directly reject their mother's commands, though they have other ways of displaying their resentment. From the point of view of middle class ideology, the HAP mother is polite, she is 'reasonable', she gives the child a positive face, and so on. But let us not forget that her behaviour is well suited to efficient subjugation, where the subjugated becomes a willing accomplice in his/her own subjugation. This is true power, and for an apprenticeship to the middle class stations in life its functional value can hardly be questioned!

But what about the other side of the picture? There are contradictory messages in the control practices of the LAP group, one which celebrates the power of authority and the need for obedience, and another which lays authority bare as an open target for attack. One might ask, how can a flagrant parading of authority be functional? I am inclined to suggest that it depends on who you are, what degree of autonomy you possess, how far you control, and how far you are yourself controlled. It is certainly true that in most societies the autonomy of members will vary from context to context. One could be more autonomous with respect to some, less with respect to others. Nonetheless, some of us may be less autonomous with respect to a good proportion of the community's contexts, and the LAP subjects in my research belong to that category. Under these conditions, the maintenance of social existence will involve entering in relations of submission – relations that are independent of our will, relations the basis of which lies in the other's power. The recognition of authority could then be criterial; the inculcation of the idea that the nature of control is external would be an entirely beneficial perspective. If authority is visible, if the source of control is tangible, one can hit back: the data shows that LAP children will often rebel; they will attempt not to comply with the mother's commands, and sometimes they are willing to 'take her on' physically. If the views presented here are accepted, it would seem that a tension exists in our society: middle class practices are geared to maintaining hierarchy by making subjugation invisible; working class practices are geared to challenge subjugation, albeit in the end it is authority that might often win! And it is here that we can highlight the function of an unquestioned belief in the superiority of the middle class practices.

The positive evaluation of the middle class practices makes any divergence from those practices questionable. Logicality and rationality, as we understand these terms, are fashioned to fit middle class practices; it is not that members of the middle class never submit to authority or that they never support acts of violence – it is significant that our sense of outrage at violence or exercise of authority is itself so selective, so self-serving! Similarly, the importance of the collective is not altogether absent from middle class contexts; it has 'naturally' to be disregarded if it runs counter to 'self-fulfilment': 'I' before 'we', as

Bernstein pointed out. This supports the highly valued 'free competition' – a principle extraordinarily well understood by the middle classes. The higher valorisation of middle class practices is a powerful deterrent to challenge.

I am aware of the provocative nature of my comments, so for good measure let me close this discussion of socio-semantic variation by saying that the examination of this kind of variation is a key to the conflicting ideologies in our modern complex societies; its recognition is a challenge to our facile belief in the benevolently egalitarian nature of the society we live in; and that at this moment in the history of the world when we are rather inclined to congratulate ourselves on the continued success of our economic order and on our admirable democracies, the need is more urgent than ever before to pay attention to the challenge which the sociolinguistics of semantic variation is capable of revealing. A sociolinguistics that is able to reveal the power of language and communication in the creation, maintenance and alteration of the world we live in demands a theory of meaning that goes beyond meaning as correspondence to facts; what it demands instead, is a theory of meaning which is based on the recognition of the functionalism of language, a functionalism of the kind which explores the deep interdependence between communication and language, which in the last resort arises from the fact that human life as we know it is fashioned in the dialectic processes of both language and society; *all* meanings are social and *all* meanings are cognitive: they represent the semiotic face of our social processes.

6 Synopsis

In this chapter I have argued that current conceptions of the relationship between language and communication are flawed, and in turn they flaw our understanding of the scope and power of human language. I have argued that communication is the act of meaning, characterised by intersubjectivity. To account for intersubjectivity we need to grant the semiotic nature of context, which in turn implies a co-genetic relation between context and linguistic meanings. Where context is a semiotic construct, there linguistic meanings cannot be seen as a naming relation linking the form of language to the world of experience. Linguistic meanings are construed by lexicogrammar. From the semiotic nature of context and from the construal relations of context, meaning and wording flows the metafunctional hypothesis. This approach puts in doubt the division of linguistic meaning into social and semantic. It permits us to recognise the possibility of semantic variation, thus revealing to us the power of our communication in the creation, maintenance, and change of the social world in which we live.

10 Social factors in semantic variation[1]

1 Introduction

One wonders what the development of sociolinguistics would have been like if it had been founded on a conception of language as a meaning potential which both helps to produce society and is itself developed within society. As it happened, sociolinguistics borrowed the view of language as an autonomous system while its point of departure into the field lay in dialectology – the discipline which studied differences amongst the various dialects of a language by enumerating the inventory of their variant synonymous forms or, in terms of Abercrombie (1965), paid attention simply to different accents for expressing the same lexicogrammatical items. If at any point an attempt was made to explain the patterns of divergence, as for example between rural and urban dialects, the explanations dialectology found were always sociologically innocent, celebrating commonsense: so for example, the vocabulary relating to livestock *obviously* had to be more developed in the rural dialects. In dialectology, meaning equalled naming, so, for example, *pip, pit* and *stone* referred to the same thing. Meaning difference across dialects was never an issue for dialectology; phonological, morphological and lexical difference was. Modern sociolinguistics has inherited most of these stances. For example, in the seminal work of Labov (1966a), the 'inventor' of modern sociolinguistics, this same disdain toward meaning is maintained. His definition of sociolinguistic variation as different ways of saying the same thing seems to have sealed the fate of any study dealing with semantic variation. Many years ago, with the inception of TG, pioneering work in semantics such as Whorf's (1956) was discredited as lacking in scientific sophistication. Some two decades later, in the heyday of sociolinguistics, when it came to the evaluation of Basil Bernstein's code theory's suggestion that linguistic meanings play a crucial role in shaping persons or their relations to the world they live in, the brave new science of sociolinguistics treated it as a divisive act rooted in social prejudice. Sociolinguistics never asked why language should vary phonologically, morphologically and lexically, but *never* semantically, even though the *raison d'être* of language is arguably to permit the exchange of meanings.

In this chapter we dissociate ourselves from these dominant preoccupations of sociolinguistics whereby vowel differences across the distinct varieties of a language are treated as indicative of a community's values and as reflecting the fact of social hierarchy, but the differences in semantic choices and the social significance of those differences are required to be invisible, or consigned to an ill-defined notion of 'style' which apparently bear no relevance to the shaping of 'cognition'. Our views on language in relation to society have been discussed in some detail in earlier chapters of this volume. Our claim is simply that given the same general environment for speaking, speakers of a language will show an orderly, systematic variation in the meanings they will mean, and that this variation in meaning will relate significantly to their own social attributes, specifically to their social positioning. In the following sections we will present some findings of a research[2] the details about its design, subjects and analytical frameworks have been described elsewhere in the preceding chapters of this volume. Our focus is once again on the sample consisting of 20,544 messages from Phase I of the project.

2 Gendered talk: an ethnographic description

The talk that passes between mothers and children in the privacy of their home suggests that despite the so called 'sexual revolution' of the latter part of the twentieth century, gender still serves as a criterion in everyday life of the community for distinguishing ways of being, doing and saying. Indeed, by three and a half years of age children have learned that various aspects of the world are differentiated on the basis of gender; that gender is, in fact, an essential element of their own identity and that of the other members of their immediate fellowship (Cloran 1989). Not surprisingly, they use it to establish the identity of their toys (*Is teddy a boy or a girl?*) and their pets; example:

Extract 1[3]
Mother: oh look at that black kitten! isn't she beautiful!
Colin: no, it's a boy

These young children learn early that their own gender identity and that of their interactional partners determines how they may describe an entity – a male kitten cannot be called *beautiful* – a distinction that shows a remarkable sense of discrimination, considering the children's age. They also learn what behaviours are the preferred ones in relation to which sex:

Extract 2
Colin: we punched her, don't we?
Mother: you don't punch girls, do you?

The same mother makes no such comments when Colin promises to kick Kevin up the wall (sic!) and thus make him go crashing into the water:

Extract 3

Colin: and Kevin smacks me on the head
Mother: does he?
Colin: and I - I will - I kick him up the wall .. and he went [?crashing down] and he will go (CRASH) in the water
Mother: oh will he?
Colin: yeah, but I will kick him up to the sky and then he will fall in the water …
Mother: have you finished your drink?

Clearly so far as the mother is concerned, the aggression Colin as a male can exercise on another male is one thing and how he behaves to a female is quite another. We are not concerned with the im/morality of any stance brought to the child's attention; our concern is simply to emphasise the sociogenetic nature of sex-based distinctions. Extract 4 appears to be an early inculcation of sexuality:

Extract 4

Julian: how much do I love you?
Mother: you don't love me .. you don't love me
Julian: yeah
Mother: why?
Julian: because I'm your boy ..
Mother: do you love daddy? .. do you love daddy?
Julian: mm
Mother: do you love Rosemary?
Julian: no
Mother: why don't you love Rosemary? (CHILD LAUGHS) Why don't you love Rosemary? (CHILD LAUGHS) You're a [?ratbag]
Julian: I do
Mother: [?]
Julian: who else do you want me to love?
Mother: you can love whoever you want to
Julian: can I love Peter? .. can I?
Mother: no. I think that's more like friendship
Julian: pardon?
Mother: thought you'd say that. It's like friendship, isn't it? .. you're friends with Peter, aren't you?
Julian: yep .. mum!

Mother: yes
Julian: when I get as old as you and [? Maree likes me] could we marry each other?
Mother: no, because Maree's your cousin

Julian must love Rosemary, his sister, but the freedom to love 'whoever else he wants to love' does not include loving Peter or any other male; that the child has 'got' this message is indicated by his last utterance in this extract, where he is exploring the freedoms of heterosexual love. We are not implying that Julian is aware of the complex issues but that the prohibition concerns male not females appears obvious from his question.

Gender socialisation is most probably aided by the human propensity to use classification as a means of learning about the world, and attributes associated with the two gender classes are no exception. Mothers of boys tend to explicitly point out the various kinds of attributes and also the specific behaviours expected of their sons. The emphasis with girls seems to be not so much on attributes as it is on behaviour, and the behaviour most often inculcated is that of nurturing the other:

Extract 5

Mother: what is the lady doing?
Carol: um pouring out um coffee or tea for father.

Extract 6

Father: look at you! You look like you've been making mud pies or something and eating them.
Carol: mum, you better wash my face.

In extract 5, the picture does represent the act of pouring coffee but that it is *for father* is an inference presumably based on what ladies such as Carol's mother 'naturally' do in everyday life; in 6, Carol assumes the nurturing role to be part of 'woman's work': it is the father who points out she needs cleaning; the person she expects to do this job is her mother; her experience has told her that giving care is a mother's business. Occasionally, mothers will explicitly recommend such behaviours, reinforcing the inevitability of the female child's assumption of a nurturing role in her adult life:

Extract 7

Mother: if you don't do your own work now, when you grow up and have your own little babies you won't know how to look after them, will you? So you'll have to learn how to do those things when you're little, won't you?

It is relevant here to say a few words about how mothers present themselves to their children. Hasan (1986a) points out that the value attached to the work men and women do places women's work in the less desirable category: this is obvious from the material gains associated with the two spheres of action. Indeed what is arguably the most important job of all – the traditionally exclusively female role of nurturing the partner, the young, growing up generation or the ageing parents[4] – is unpaid, and attracts no privilege. Given the economic definition of labour as 'bodily toil for the sake of gain or economic production' (cf. The Macquarie Dictionary), woman's nurturing work does not count as labour at all. In a curious reversal the moral good is downgraded in preference to the material good: the highly exacting work of nurturing becomes invisible; it is either 'not work' at all, or it is work of the kind that is best avoided. This ideology is often expressed by the mothers themselves, as our data shows:

Extract 8

Alison: is Pop home?
Mother: no .. they're all out. they're all at work
Alison: Bob and Mark are working
Mother: yes, Bob's at work. Mark's at work. everybody's at work
Alison: I not at work
Mother: no, you're only little
Alison: [are] you at work?
Mother: I don't work. I look after you…
Alison: who's playing with Pammy?
Mother: nobody. who'd look after you if mummy went to work .. eh?

The task of 'looking after' the family involves the mother in a number of disparate activities. Hasan (1986a) identifies three such areas: (i) as a manual labourer, doing the washing, cleaning, cooking etc.; (ii) as a counsellor/companion, providing emotional support for the children (and probably others in the family!); and (iii) as teacher, instructing the child in the ways of being, doing and saying specific to the (sub)culture of the family's speech fellowship. The necessity of such 'non-work' is repeatedly mentioned by the exhausted mothers. Thus David's mother, after bathing him, exhorts him to hurry since she's *got to* get the dinner ready; Stephen's mother announces that she *has to* take the baby for his immunisation shot; and Sam's mother is pleased that he has learnt to push himself on the swing since it means that she will no longer *have to* do it for him. While acknowledging this necessity, mothers often disparage the work they do:

Extract 9

Mother:	[?you'll probably] have to get changed into your work clothes later because daddy's going to the tip.
Cameron:	what for?
Mother:	daddy needs a helper
Cameron:	oh.
Mother:	when he goes to the tip.
Cameron:	what?
Mother:	daddy needs a helper when he goes to the tip.
Cameron:	oh I want to play on my bike. I don't want to go to the tip.
Mother:	you do?
Cameron:	I want to stay here [?]
Mother:	you haven't been to the tip [?with your daddy] for a long time.
Cameron:	no.
Mother:	it'd be much more interesting going to the tip than helping mummy do the vacuuming
Cameron:	mm.
Mother:	because that's a boring job isn't it?

The mothers do not just disparage the work they do; they also disparage themselves, explicitly or implicitly:

Extract 10

Helen:	today you should have got my painting
Mother:	but you said you didn't do one
Helen:	no, the last day I forgot my painting
Mother:	oh I see. Well we'll have to have a look for it next time – next week ..
Helen:	and don't go without it
Mother:	oh I'll try and remember but I've got a – I haven't got a good memory, have I? ..

Extract 11

Donna: now could I have your metal plate now?
Mother: yes. oh dear, I've just turned the oven off, silly mummy!

Extract 12

Mother: how come I can't do that?
Julian: what?
Mother: [? wink with both eyes]
Julian: I don't know .. because I'm clever .. [? that's clever]
Mother: oh

Julian: you just have to wink [?like] this ..
Mother: the other one like that?
Julian: why?
Mother: I don't know. You must be clever .. maybe you got it from your Dad, eh?

As one encounters these scattered comments in the environment of everyday talk, they appear quite harmless – just things one normally says, but it is not fanciful to suggest that in speaking as they do, the mothers are simply being faithful to their social positioning! The attitude of denigration for women and their work pervades all areas of female social existence. And although women are becoming more and more visible in the labour market, here too gender is used in just about every society as a basis for differentiation, both in the kinds of labour they may engage in and the sorts of economic returns they may claim, as well as the age at which they may/must retire. Nonetheless, the traditional boundaries based on gender difference are weakening, a fact that too is reflected in our data; one example:

Extract 13

Mother: don't put her head in there. you'll break her and Rebecca will get very upset
David: no she won't
Mother: yes she will
David: no she won't
Mother: she sure will. It's her doll
David: my doll
Mother: don't be silly! boys don't play with dolls
David: yes they do and girls have to play with trucks .. nana said .. they have to

By the same token, there is some evidence that female children are being prepared for the possibility of taking on employed positions (just like males) but this is invariably *in addition to* their traditional role in the house:

Extract 14

Donna: I want to go to high school
Mother: well, you have to be Miranda's age to do that – 13 or 13 or 15 or 16 or 17 or 18 and after that, you can go to university or you can go .. er, to do something else
Donna: I'm not gonna do any thing after that
Mother: aren't you?
Donna: no

Mother: how do you know?* how do you know what you'll feel like doing, when you're eighteen?
Donna: er ..
Mother: it's a long time till you'll be eighteen, isn't it?
Donna: well, I have [?a] — I'll do the cooking
Mother: you'll do the cooking mm, well you can still do that and go to university too, you know ..
Donna: [?why]?
Mother: well, you've always got to eat and if you don't live here and have me cook for you, well, you'll probably get a flat some day with a friend and do your own cooking .. you can't go and eat in restaurants every night, can you?

But when it comes to boys, this mastery of the double universe interestingly does not appear to be encouraged. For example Cameron's mother does not envisage any other role for him than the traditional ones, which 'naturally' lie outside the home; when Cameron suggests that he might work in the home the mother simply fails to 'hear' him:

Extract 15

Mother: and what about if there were lots of firemen .. and they didn't need any more fireman so you couldn't be a fireman and you couldn't be a construction worker
Cameron: I would be .. instead of those two .. – um what else at home?
Mother: what else – ?
Cameron: what else at home?
Mother: a policeman .. an [? ambulance] B
Cameron: yeah .. I be a policeman .. and I don't – if I couldn't be a policeman I'd be a fireman .. or um an ambulance man
Mother: yeah

3 Visible and invisible gender discrimination

The examples of gendered talk presented so far are relatively easy to detect by simply reading/listening to the interaction, since they are directly related to the issue of gender. Even so, the gender-differentiating nature of such talk typically goes unnoticed because, thanks to the pervasive nature of gender ideology, such behaviour appears just normal: the elements of gender ideology are unquestioningly accepted as self-evidently natural (Douglas 1975; Elshtain 1981). As Hasan (1986a) points out a pervasive ideology of this kind penetrates deeply into all aspects of social life, shaping our ways of being, doing, saying, and meaning. So far we have exemplified explicit reference to gender, but where language is concerned, this gender differentiation goes beyond such explicit direct references: side by side with the kind of discriminating talk presented above, we also find more cryptic ways of maintaining the difference. This is done by the choice of semantic features where the choice systematically correlates with gender difference but the variable features themselves do not transparently or directly refer to gender as such. There is no talk of boys and girls, dads and mums, pretty and handsome. Instead, it is as if gender difference is taken for granted and the unquestioning acceptance of the position acts as the point of departure for the meanings that are meant. The issue of gender is as it were made invisible, and yet mothers systematically tend to choose different meanings in talking to their sons as opposed to their daughters.

These ultimately gender differentiating features of meaning have another remarkable quality: they are not isolates, with one feature having nothing to do with the other(s). Rather, we find certain constellations of semantic features, which display a *configurative rapport*, a certain *consistency* in Whorf's sense of the term (1956: 41; 81; 158 etc.). Access to the elements of such constellations and to the principle(s) underlying their consistency cannot be achieved simply by informally scanning the dialogues, picking out lexical items which either directly or indirectly relate to gender differences. There is, however, a methodology for investigating the working of such constellations: for example, we may identify some environment which is in common, such as, say, that of a mother answering children's questions, or herself asking them questions. We may then enquire whether the frequency of mothers offering a response of the same kind, say, *adequate* response, is the same for children of both sexes? Do they attend to the child's question or *ignore* it to the same extent across the two sexes? Is there any variation in the degree to which answers to the two groups of children are *elaborated*? We suggest that the clustering of such elements of meaning has a significance that is greater precisely because it does not have any obviously discernible conjunction with sex difference as such; it comes across as just the natural way of talking and is therefore not subject to conscious deliberation or traditional patterns of identification such as are found in the referential scope of, say, *handsome/beautiful*. In fact, when differences of the kind we mention above are pointed out, this arouses incredulity, if not indignation. Despite such reactions, the data speaks for itself: when such constellations are examined, we do find that the principle of their configurative rapport inheres in what is taken for granted with respect to the two sexes. The interpretation of the statistical findings of our data leads us to conclusions that make sense only if we appeal to these taken for granted beliefs and attitudes that are current in our community.

The incidence and significance of constellations of this kind can be revealed with the use of multivariate statistical techniques. The technique is no less effective or viable here than, for example in corpus studies such as has been conducted by Biber (1988) where factor analysis has been used to identify linguistic patterning in corpora. In the research reported here a related technique called principal components analysis (PCA) was employed. As with factor analysis, this procedure[5] mathematically clusters a number of variables. Whereas the units for Biber's analysis are of necessity based on 'word forms', the unit of analysis for us are categories of semantic 'feature' 'option'; our point of departure is an element of meaning not the form of a word or the substance of some 'grapheme(s)'. Through a principal components analysis we have identified clusters of semantic features on the basis of the frequency of their co-occurrence in the messages of speakers. While a number of PC analyses were undertaken in the research on semantic variation, our discussion here will focus only on two PCAs. Both centre upon the semantic features of messages issued by speakers in the environment of information exchange, i.e., asking and answering questions.

Multivariate statistical analyses such as PCA not only identify the clusters of features associated with systematic variation in the data, but also assign scores to speakers on the basis of these identified variable clusters, known in the analysis as principal components (PC). Since the scores are distributed on the basis of a constellation of features used by the speakers, the distribution can be examined to ascertain any co-variance in terms of speakers' social attributes, e.g., the sex of the child or the family's social class provenance, or the child's position in the family, and so on. Due to the limitation of space, throughout this chapter, only the first component of the analyses in question will be presented and discussed.

3.1 Gender discriminating constellations of meanings: mothers' talk

Table 1 displays the first component of certain relevant features of mothers' questions and their answers to the children. In this table, as in table 2 (in section 5), the semantic features[6] with the initial Q pertain to questions, and those with the letter A refer to the semantic features pertaining to answers. In all mothers asked 2008 questions some features of which formed the input for the analysis in table 1:

Table 1: Attributes of mothers' questions and answers (MQMA)

Question and answer attributes	PCI
Q[confirm]	0.73
A[adequate]	0.73
A[elaborated]	0.67
Q[assumptive]	-0.67
Q[explain]	-0.62
Q[repeat]	-0.59
Q[related]	0.47
Q[prefaced]	0.45
Eigenvalue	3.40
% Variance	34.00

As the table indicates each of the semantic features comprising the cluster identified by this principal component loads criterially (see discussion of PCA in preceding chapters, especially chapters 3–6 of this volume). Analysis of variance of speakers' scores on this PC1 reveals that higher scores on this factor characterise mothers in interaction with their daughters rather than with their sons ($p < .04$). What this PC suggests is that in asking questions mothers of girls will tend to: (i) ask questions which seek a yes/no response Q[confirm]; (ii) not[7] make unspoken assumptions about what the child should know, think or feel Q[assumptive]; (iii) not seek explanations Q[explain]; and (iv) they will not repeat their questions; but (v) they will relate their questions to other messages, thus making its thesis more precise; and (vi) they will present the question as someone's saying, idea, or evaluation Q[prefaced]. In their answering behaviour, these mothers are likely to (vii) provide answers that are A[adequate], which is to say, the answers will tend to address the query point; and (viii) they are quite likely to expand on the answer so that their sayings provide more information than is strictly necessary in view of the query point A[elaborated].

As table 1 shows, a little over a third of the variance in the data is accounted for by this clustering of features. Different semantic orientations (i.e., styles defined in terms of their patterns of meaning) are associated with high and low scoring speakers: high scoring speakers exhibit the kind of behaviour delineated by PC1, while low-scoring speakers exhibit behaviour which would be the reverse of PC1. Although it is difficult to find an extract that is both short enough to be reproduced here and that also displays every feature of the semantic orientation under discussion, some sense of these distinct semantic features can be gathered from reading or listening to segments of discourse. Extract 20 from Donna and her mother is indicative of a high scoring dyad's ways of meaning, while extract 21 from Pete and his mother exemplifies a low scoring dyad's semantic orientation. Segments of these extracts which occur in the mother's turns and illustrate the semantic features relevant to PC1 will be italicised in the mother's discourse, and the relevant semantic feature itself (see table 1) will be indicated in proximity to the items which realise it; note however that sometimes the same message(s) may realise more than one of the semantic features under discussion:

Extract 16

Mother: *do you know who that picture is of?* Q[prefaced]
Donna: my daddy
Mother: no. *looks like your dad, doesn't it*? Q[confirm] but it's not
Donna: who is it? [?daddy]?
Mother: *it is his daddy*. A[adequate] *he'd be your grandfather, if he were alive today* A[elaborated]
Donna: pardon?
Mother: he would be your grandfather if he were alive today your daddy's daddy
Donna: [?his] daddy's daddy?
Mother: *your daddy's father* A[adequate]
Donna: my [?grandma]?
Mother: *your grandfather* A[adequate]
mm *but you don't know him* A[elaborated]
(continuing discourse) *grandma's husband, he's now Martin, isn't he?* Q[confirm]
but he's— she's remarried, I mean.
she's remarried... your father's .. father .. died A[ELABORATED]...
(continuing discourse) *remember we went up to see his grave a little while ago?* Q[related] & Q[confirm] & Q[prefaced] ...
(continuing discourse) *remember .. where he's buried in the cemetery?* Q[related] & Q[confirm] & Q[prefaced] ...
Donna: no ..
Mother: you'd remember if we took you back there, I think
Donna: pardon?
Mother: you'd remember if we took you back there, I think
Donna: where do we have to go to?
Mother: *oh, not very far* .. A[adequate] *just um— remember that park we went to last week to feed the ducks?* Q[confirm] & Q[prefaced] ..
just up from there A[elaborated] & A[adequate]

Extract 17

Mother: *wasn't that a big fishy*? Q[assumptive] & Q[confirm]
Pete: yeah.

Mother: it was a ripper!
Pete: daddy was B
Mother: *will we let him go?* Q[confirm]
Pete: no.
Mother: *why not*? Q[assumptive] Q[explain] he'll die
Pete: yeah we might let him go cause he might die.
Mother: he might die and *he'll miss his— miss his family, won't he?* A[elaborated] & Q[confirm]
Pete: yeah.
Mother: but he's got [?a new family] now though.
Pete: *yeah .. he's got his little friends hasn't he?*
Mother: *yeah* ..A[adequate]

Keeping in mind the ratio of semantic features to the messages, note the absence of Q[explain] and the frequency of Q[confirm] in extract 16. Note also the mother's answer to Donna's clarification seeking question 'My [?grandma]?'. The mother first presents an adequate answer 'Your grandfather'; following this, the remainder of her turn simply elaborates this technically adequate response. Embedded within her [elaborated] answer are further categories of questions: the whole message complex attempts to lead the child slowly to an understanding of the identity of the 'grandfather' in the photograph. The mother's answer thus offers the child information which exceeds both the quantity and the precision explicitly sought by the daughter in her question. In our results, this tendency to attempt precision and detail in giving information is in rapport with the higher frequency of the feature [prefaced]: the two typically co-occur, and this is because of what Whorf would call a 'reactance' between them. A prefaced question seeks to find out someone's point of view – what they said, what they thought, which is indicative of a rhetorical stance in which it is tacitly accepted that others' mental state is un-knowable without precise acts of semiosis (for further discussion, chapter 12 in this volume). For example when Donna's mother asks: 'Do you know who that picture is of?', she is not asking whose picture it is: she is finding out whether her daughter knows – that is to say, her focus is on a detail of her daughter's state of knowledge. The asking of a prefaced question thus acknowledges the separation of individual minds: the speaker implicitly admits to not knowing what the addressee might know, feel or think. This attitude implies in turn that for such speakers verbal interaction is one necessary condition for overcoming the separation of minds: access to other's point of view, their knowledge, memory, opinion etc. can become possible only through verbal construals. There is thus a positive configurative rapport amongst the features [prefaced], [adequate], [elaborated] and [related] [8].

Interestingly, this rapport demands a negation of the feature [assumptive]. In fact, the features [prefaced] and [assumptive] are logically antipathetic: in asking a question with the feature [assumptive], the speaker implies that s/he already knows what the addressee knows, feels, thinks – and this is something that is diametrically opposed to the implication carried by the feature [prefaced]. An [assumptive] question, for example, implies that the answer either *is* or *should be* transparently obvious to both interactants. For example when Pete's mother asks 'Wasn't that a big fishy?', she expects an affirmative response as her message 'It was a ripper' in her next turn shows. And again when she asks 'Why not?', she assumes the reason to be obvious: 'he'll die'. Note that contradicting his earlier answer, the child spells out the position assumed by the mother to be the correct one: 'we might let him go cause he might die'. The posing of an [assumptive] question thus underplays the separation of individual minds: it is as if a community of mind exists between the two which does not depend on discursive resources. Naturally then the feature [assumptive] does not configure at all frequently with the features [elaborated] and/or [related]: the latter are features which capture the expansion of the necessary point(s) of communication so as to give the message(s) greater precision. Our interpretation is supported by PC1 which indicates that speakers who habitually use the features [prefaced] and [elaborated] more frequently, tend also *not* to use the feature [assumptive] as frequently.

The above discussion has identified two contrasting styles, i.e., two distinct semantic orientations in attempting information exchange. We will refer to the first of these which is delineated by PC1 – i.e., the one pertaining to extract 16 – as a style of INDIVIDUAL AUTONOMY[9]: it maximises the separation of individual minds and relies criterially on certain qualities of verbal interaction for bridging that separation. The second kind of semantic orientation – that manifested by extract 17 – is in direct contrast to the first; it displays a higher frequency of the feature [assumptive] and a lower frequency of [*elaborated*] and [*prefaced*]; this is a style of INTERPERSONAL TRUST: it takes for granted a principle of togetherness that need not appear to necessitate verbal interaction for access to a knowledge of other minds.

3.2 Gender and semantic variation in mothers' talk: an interpretation

The analysis of variance on the PC under discussion reveals that the high scoring speakers, i.e. mothers of daughters, tend to employ the style of individual autonomy, whereas, low scoring speakers, i.e., mothers of boys, employ the style of interpersonal trust ($p<.04$). In other words, the behaviours that mothers habitually expose their daughters to – whether consciously or not is beside the point – differ significantly from those they reserve for their sons. This means that the environment of information exchange has a different significance for male and female children: in this same general environment, girls experience a semantic orientation that respects the validity of differences in individual opinions and points of view; if the mother's behaviour is a model, then it schools them into providing detailed information so as to make their intent precise for the listener. Boys, on the other hand, encounter a style where other's point of view can be taken largely as known; where the emphasis is not on providing detailed information since the intents of others may be treated as obvious. It is reasonable to ask what is the significance of the inculcation of these differing perspectives? In answering this question, we will first point out the relevance of this difference to the existing gender ideology before proceeding to place our results in the context of other sociolinguistic studies which report on sociolectal variation correlating with the speakers' sex.

So far as gender ideology is concerned, the style of individual autonomy appears to be a double edged sword. It exposes the female child to an interactive style which obviously acknowledges differences in points of view: arguably such awareness is, on the one hand, the first necessary step toward the ability to make adjustments to the interactive other, to entertain an attitude amenable to negotiation, prepared to meet the other mind half way – in short, to be accommodating. Given the relatively subordinate role of women in our society, this ability to adjust to others' perspectives and to accommodate others has obvious 'virtues'. On the other hand, the awareness of other minds, other points of view, also exerts a semantic pressure whereby certain semantic features are chosen that typically occur in a discursive style with considerable prestige in our community: these are features to do with the detail and precision of information, and the readiness to offer information as if not much can be taken for granted. Interestingly, the semantic style with individual autonomy displays a good deal of resemblance to pedagogic discourse (for discussion chapters 4 and 11 in this volume), which is of course in keeping with the higher value ascribed to the style. That girls are exposed to this style could conceivably bear some relation to the fact that they tend to do better in early schooling. For the past decade we have been searching for an explanation for the relatively higher success rates for young girls as opposed to boys. We are suggesting here that our result might be pointing to one important explanatory factor.

We are saying, then, that the style of individual autonomy is a privileged and privileging sociosemantic variety. In fact, the time has come to reveal that our claim about the prestigious nature of this fashion of meaning is not based *only* on the fact that it shares features with the pedagogically valued style: yes, this fact is important as we have argued above. But for us there is a far more important piece of evidence which carries greater weight: the same statistical analysis firmly supports the view that the semantic orientation mothers employ in questioning and answering their daughters is indeed a socially privileged variety of talk. The scores of subjects on PC1 from table 1 also reveal social class variation in maternal meanings: the pattern of covariance suggests that middle class mothers are more likely to employ the style of individual autonomy than are the working class ones ($p < .002$). On the basis of these results we conclude that (a) girls from the middle class are exposed to a socio-semantic variety characterised by a canonical form of individual autonomy; (b) at the other extreme, working class boys experience a socio-semantic variety characterised by a canonical form of interpersonal solidarity; (c) working class girls experience a socio-semantic variety that in some respects tends to be more like the middle class modes of meaning; and (d) conversely middle class boys experience a sociosemantic variety that in some respects is closer to the working class variety. There has been a suggestion in sociolinguistics that the inclination of the female subjects to use prestige varieties is related to the role of women in upward mobility (Labov 1966a, 1972d; Bernstein 1971a). Our results suggest perhaps that the mechanism whereby this inclination is established could be found in early socialisation patterns such as have been identified here. There is suggestive evidence that early socialisation has such a formative function, that the experience of participating in specific discursive styles does in fact influence the children's own discursive style. This is the theme to which we turn now in the following section.

4 Young children and socio-semantic variation

Although extracts presented in section 2 show that in children's talk there is a fairly keen awareness of gender difference, the interesting fact is that this awareness appears to be restricted only to the elements of *visible* gender discrimination: in their talk children use words whose referential scope encompasses awareness of gender distinction e.g., the distinction between beautiful/handsome, girl/boy etc. (see discussion in section 2). When it comes to the choice of invisible gender-specific constellations of meaning such as we have discussed in the last section with reference to the mothers' discourse, repeated analyses have failed to display *statistically significant* gender variation in children's talk. What is the explanation for this? We offer two possible explanations. Firstly, there is the fact that both boys and girls were speaking to their mothers; so whereas the mothers' addressees – the children – varied by sex, the children's addressees – i.e., mothers – did not do so. For lack of resources, we had to take the decision of excluding fathers from the research. So the data represents children speaking only to their mother. On the assumption that like their mothers children might have displayed semantic variation correlating with the sex of their addressee, it is just possible that our inability to include fathers as subjects in our research explains the absence of the cryptic patterns of gender variation in children's language. This is clearly a speculative explanation.

A second possible explanation may be sought in the maturational level of the children: after all their average age is only three years eight months. The suggestion appears plausible that the children are not yet mature enough to have internalised the cryptotypic ways of creating and maintaining gender differentiation such as discussed with reference to table 1. Perhaps more experience of living is needed before, like their mothers, they too can automatically produce the invisible constellations of meaning that subtly support the gender ideology of their culture. If that is the case, then one might have to conclude that such young children are not likely to display statistically significant sociosemantic variation.

We are however forced to reject this second line of argument. Our analyses have shown that whatever data input displays significant variation by gender *also* displays a variation by social class. Significantly, the reverse is not true: that is to say, there are analyses where the subjects' scores on principal components differentiate them *only* by social class, but not by gender. In fact children's speech is a case in point: it significantly covaries with their social class provenance, but not with their gender identity. To demonstrate this we need to consider the analysis presented in table 2. The data for the analysis in table 2 is taken from the same environment of information exchange, but this time instead of mothers' questions and answers, the input consists of the semantic features of children's questions and answers. As before, only the first principal component will be discussed.

Table 2: Attributes of children's questions and answers (CQCA)

Question and answer attributes	PCI
Q[confirm]	0.60
A[adequate]	0.55
A[elaborated]	0.74
A[responsive]	0.34
Q[assumptive]	-0.51
Q[explain]	0.00
Q[ask]	-0.12
Q[related]	0.63
Q[prefaced]	0.58
Eigenvalue	2.37
% Variance	26.40

The total number of children's questions which formed the basis for the analysis presented in table 2 was 1,350. It will be noted that the semantic features in table 2 closely resemble those of mothers' questions and answers presented in table 1. The semantic features used as input for this analysis are almost identical to those used for the analysis reported in table 1. The differences are (a) that the feature Q[repeat] formed part of the input for the analysis represented in table 1 alone; and (b) that the features Q[ask] and A[responsive] occur in table 2 alone. The semantic feature Q[ask] refers to a non-attitudinal yes/no question e.g., *are you ready?,* which is realised by a polar interrogative (Halliday 1994). In table 2, this feature does not load criterially: in other words, it makes little or no difference to the variation in the data. In the input for table 1, Q[ask] was amalgamated with Q[confirm] which is a relatively grosser category, only one sub-category of which is realised as a polar interrogative[10].

The label A[responsive] is something of a misnomer, since it simply referred to the fact that the addressee of the question had said something which was more like going on talking rather than attending to the question. Thus if we ask what are the environments in which Q[repeat] is at risk of occurring, it is obvious that two such environment would be either one where there was no saying at all, or some saying which, despite the fact that we have called it [responsive] is not really an answer/ reply. Despite these minor differences in the input of the analysis for tables 1 and 2, in all essentials, the style delineated by PC1 in table 2 can be characterised in the same way as that of table 1: it is a style which holds regard for individual autonomy. As in table 1, so also here, high scoring subjects are not likely to ask [assumptive] questions; they are much more likely to ask [prefaced] questions which as we have argued above implies that the high scoring speakers would be inclined to produce elaborations of their messages by relating their questions and replies to other messages thus providing detail and precision to their utterance. This indeed is the case; in fact the highest loading is on the feature A[elaborated]. Note also the greater likelihood of asking yes/no questions, rather than the how/why ones, which also resembles the characterisation for table 1.

The PCA in table 2 accounts for a little over one quarter of the variance in the data while the analysis of variance of speakers' scores on this component reveal that HAP children are much more likely to be high scorers on this PC than the LAP ones ($p < .009$). These results bear a resemblance to those reported with regard to table 1: it would appear that the children have developed a semantic orientation that is highly reminiscent of their mothers' style of meaning; the only difference seems to be that the children are perhaps not as well established in their modes of discourse as their mothers. The difference in the results seems to make sense while supporting the claim of the effectiveness of early socialisation: the children are well on their way to a destination which responds to their family's social positioning; the journey they have to undertake to familiarise themselves with the subcultures of their speech fellowships has already begun.

This result suggests that the absence of gender variation in children's speech cannot be explained by their maturational stage: if they are mature enough to display fairly systematic, sociosemantic variation which correlates with their family's social class position, then surely their maturational stage by itself cannot prevent them from displaying gender based variation. In seeking to explain this situation, it seems more justifiable to refer to the relative importance of the institution of social class in comparison to that of gender. The politico-economic structure of most societies known to us today relies on the institution of social class: as Labov and Bernstein both have remarked early in their writings, social class is, without doubt, the most potent and central element of social organisation. And this observation is even truer today than when Bernstein first raised the issue of his class based theory of code – perhaps because it has become very much more difficult to find simple concrete indices such as the Registrar General's Index of occupations. We pride ourselves on being progressive, democratic, lovers of freedom but the mode of material production in our societies relies on the exploitation of some section of the society somewhere – if not in our own progressive land then in some other country which we describe, with exquisite sensitivity, as 'developing countries'! In any case, the upshot of exploitation is that those invidious inequalities that inhere in our favoured mode of production and distribution continue. Change in the class structure of society would therefore bear highly significant and far reaching consequences for the economic structure of our societies; it would seriously threaten the security of not only the 'ruling class' but many of the social institutions whose management is predicated on the existing class exploitation and in which most members of the society including the authors of this chapter participate one way or another: in a class-based society such as ours, there is no way of living 'outside class'. If the effects of class hierarchisation permeate everything, impinging widely on the life of every speech fellowship and producing forms of interpersonal relations which can only be maintained through symbolic support, then it is not surprising that from an early stage, children become schooled in ways of saying which subtly support the maintenance of existing social class organisation: the sheer ubiquity of the effect of class difference ensures this. By comparison with social class, the hierarchisation of social subjects by reference to their sex is far less central. Its effects perhaps do not impinge on children's life style quite as much. And perhaps this is the main reason that children's speech does not carry evidence of sex based invisible i.e., cryptotypic modes of sociosemantic variation.

We are aware that discourse on the pernicious effects of gender prejudice is a popular topic today; in fact, one's credentials as a progressive and revolutionary person are greatly enhanced by drawing attention to gender-based exploitation; and judging by the number of publications, gender based speech variation is fast becoming an orthodoxy in many enlightened circles. By contrast, as Halliday (1990) has pointed out, drawing attention to social class differences is an unpopular and hazardous enterprise. Going against the popular trends, our explanation might invite criticism both from certain feminist quarters and from those sociolinguists who believe that social class differentiation is a myth perpetuated by certain prejudiced, ill-informed scholars: and that the reflection of social hierarchy resides only in pronunciation, not in what is pronounced. Nonetheless, the explanation we are offering seems to do justice to at least four facts:

(a) that throughout the analyses undertaken in this research (see the chapters in this volume) social class based variation is always prominent;

(b) that in children's speech social class variation is significantly present while gender difference is not;

(c) that young children do display sociolectal variation at the phonological level, thus indicating that they are not impervious to the nature of the language used in their speech fellowships; and

(d) that sociolectal variation at the phonological level covaries with the speakers' class provenance just as we suggest sociosemantic variation does, which is to say, variations that without fail 'reflect social hierarchy' in the speech community as does social class, will be 'picked up' by children who are after all getting schooled by their social environment.

It is true that if social class is defined by reference to such attributes as 'the size of the purse' and the 'nature of the craft', children would have to be regarded as the 'classless' members of our societies – a perspective that has been actually recommended by some sociolinguists as more objective and scientific. As against this rather superficial view of what social class signifies, we may note that in the matter of health, education, nourishment and the quality of access to many social amenities, class affects children as much and as decidedly as it does an enlisted labourer or an executive – in fact much more so than sex or ethnicity, which in themselves have become a lower level indicator for one's social positioning. It is, therefore, hardly surprising that children internalise the grammar of social hierarchy from an early age, and in this internalisation the discourse of the care giver, especially that of the mother, plays a central role.

5 Semantic variation: gender and class

Let us now draw attention to two respects in which our findings complement those reported in the dominant view of sociolinguistics on sex differentiation in language: *first*, studies in dominant sociolinguistics typically report on variables co-varying with speaker's sex whereas our work reports on variables co-varying with addressee's sex; and *secondly*, the nature of the variables differs across the two paradigms. The variables in dominant sociolinguistic studies have generally been phonological. As Saussure pointed out, the relation of phonology to linguistic meaning is purely conventional: phonological patterns simply *express* linguistically formed meaning; they certainly do not *define* them. With respect to such variables, it may be viable to claim as Trudgill (1974) does, that 'using female linguistic variety is as much a case of identifying oneself as female, and of behaving 'as a woman should', as is, say, wearing a skirt'. This explanation is essentially in keeping with the general interpretation of sociolectal variation, which is viewed simply as an indexical phenomenon.

More recently, inspired by the seminal work of Robin Lakoff (1973), scholars have turned to certain grammatical and lexical categories such as forms of intensification, selection of adjectives and so on (see, for example, Lind and O'Barr 1979). While these differences appealing to lexical items are more readily relatable to linguistic meaning, the differentiation is in terms of what may be described as 'isolates'. The kind of semantic variation that we have reported complements these perspectives by focussing on orderly variation in constellations of semantic features, thus showing that variation is a property of every level of linguistic organisation, including the semantic one. Further, in our work this systematic variation in the constellations of meaning is not simply indexical: it is also non-arbitrarily related to ideologies of gender and social class, as our discussion has attempted to show; it also concerns linguistic phenomena which are far below the level of speakers' consciousness. It follows that unlike sociolects, socio-semantic variation such as reported in the previous chapters of this volume and in Cloran (1994, 1999b) and Williams (1995, 2001) etc. cannot be viewed simply as different ways of saying the same thing. Like Whorf's fashions of speaking, semantic variation functions as an important element in the social construction of speaking subjects' consciousness. In our view, this development brings sociolinguistics face to face with the question of the relation of language to social reality: sociolinguistics can be *socio*linguistics only if it respects the nature of the social system as meticulously as it respects the semiotic system. The deeper significance of variation in language can only be revealed from this dual focus. From this point of view, Australian English stands in a homologous relation to the structuration of Australian society[11]: the varieties of Australian English, whatever the linguistic variables by reference to which they are established, are a powerful manifestations of the fact that the Australian society like any other human society is built both on consensus and on conflict.

Notes

1 This paper is co-authored with Carmel Cloran. I am grateful for her permission to include it here.

2 At this point some 700 words concerning the research design were deleted to avoid repetition.

3 Transcription conventions used here are as shown below:

[?abc]	unintelligible speech; nearest best reading based on phonology and context.
[?]	unintelligible; no reading possible.
(ABC)	other than linguistic activities evident from the recording.
Do you?*	the speaker did not allow addressee time to respond to such questions.
******	a portion of the original dialogue is elided due to lack of space.

4 Though we accept that in recent years a great deal of social change has occurred in male and female parents 'sharing' the upbringing of the child, the same cannot be said about other spheres of life in the household.

5 For some details regarding PCA see previous chapters and also Cloran (1989) and Horvath (1985).

6 For some detailed discussion of these features, see previous chapters included in this volume, and Cloran (1994); Williams (1995).

7 Note the minus sign on this and two other features in table 1. The significance of the minus sign has been discussed in earlier chapters (see section 2 of this volume).

8 In this research, the terms [elaborated] and [related] were used interchangeably; the delicate distinction between the two terms had to be ignored because our sample was not large enough to accommodate such detailed analysis. What the two terms have in common is the fact that when either is used, then the thesis of some message is elaborated by relating it to other messages in specific ways so that together the complex achieves the effect of creating greater detail and precision.

9 This style differs only marginally from the one that has identified as *individuated informativeness* (see chapter 5).

10 In order to appreciate the relationship of Q[confirm] and Q[ask] consult the semantic network and discussion in Hasan chapters 3 and 5 of this volume.

11 This comment is a reminder of the fact that the present chapter was produced in the late 1990s in response to an invitation from David Blair and Peter Collins (eds): Focus on Australia, which was to appear in the Series: Varieties of English around the World, Series Editor, Manfred Görlach, publisher John Benjamins of Amsterdam. It so happened that the Series Editor's definition of 'Varieties of English' did not cover either gender or class based socio-semantic variation. The authors thank David Blair and Peter Collins, whose invitation led to further crystallisation of our position.

11 The ontogenesis of decontextualised language: some achievements of classification and framing [2001]

Helen: doesn't matter for you or me to do these [i.e. to wash these dishes. RH]
Mother: no
Helen: because we can do it the right way, God teaches us
Mother: no God doesn't teach us things like that. it's mummy's job to teach you things like that.

(from Hasan 1986a: 144)

Every function in the child's cultural development appears twice: first, on the social level, and later on the individual level; first *between* people (*inter-psychologically*), and then *inside* the child (*intra-psychologically*) ... All the higher functions originate as actual relations between human individuals.

(Vygotsky 1978: 57; emphasis original)

1 Conjectures about decontextualised language[1]

The natural condition for human discourse is to be situation dependent. It is natural both from the point of view of phylogeny and from that of ontogeny. Clearly, it is not possible to cite actual evidence for such language use from early human history, but on the assumption that language grows in the business of living one's life with others, one could reasonably believe this to be the case. Situation dependent discourse, after all, hugs pretty close to the material situational setting in which the interactants find themselves, and on the basis of what is known about the material conditions of social existence for early humans, it does not seem very possible for early language use to have taken any other form. With this close prehension of language and material situation as the defining criterion for context dependent[2] language, its purest condition perhaps is best represented in the initial linguistic processes of infants, especially those at the protolinguistic stage as illustrated by the data presented by Halliday (1975b, 1979b), Painter (1984, 1989) and Torr (1997). But whatever the natural condition of human discourse, whatever the arguments for taking it as the original use of language phylogenetically or ontogenetically, the fact of the matter is that what is remarkably pervasive today is the kind of language use that is known as context independent, disembedded, decontextualised, especially in the sorts of societies spawned by the so-called progressive western world. One might go so far as to say that the very fabric of these societies is woven with decontextualised language use. Thus in the absence of context independent forms of talk, the workings of Bernstein's field of symbolic control would be unimaginable; and Bourdieu's symbolic violence or cultural field would be qualitatively different phenomena. Violence, of course, is not unique to the human species, but the complex modes of exercising violence are certainly unique to it. Humans specialise in subtle ways of exploiting, controlling and claiming power by imposing a particular kind of significance on certain events and actions, and this often calls for the use of decontextualised language just as much as the pursuit of science does.

What might have been the impetus for this change which made context independent language so pervasive? It seems to me that in the battle for survival, somewhere along their history, the species *homo sapiens* chose to use social semiosis rather than bodily change for effecting adjustment to their environment. I would not use the metaphor of *social contract* to describe how this choice might have prevailed, because invoking that metaphor creates more problems than it resolves. I would say, rather, that the early semiotic actions of our ancestors must have possessed an efficacy which argued in favour of the continued use of semiotic action. It is this continued use of language that created the condition whereby the management of environment via semiotic action became a de facto choice: instead of adapting somatically to the environment as other species had done, the species homo sapiens opted for exo-somatic evolution (Vygotsky 1978; Popper 1979) – an evolution which depended not on the body adapting itself physically to the environment but on adapting the environment to the body, underwriting its very obvious weaknesses, and this adaptation of the environment to the human body was achieved by the use of semiotic modalities. Thereafter the continued evolution of decontextualised talk and its pervasiveness became a necessity – a choice that is effectively no longer arbitrary, in the sense that its abandonment would involve a quite improbable turn around of direction for humanity[3]. It is certainly true that such a turn around can come to pass, but it is just as true also that for such a turn around to be propelled into existence, a necessary condition would be the occurrence of some kind of catastrophic event such as a modern day Noah's flood – as a result of global warming, perhaps! On the basis of the behaviour of the pilots of industry and state, it would seem that decontextualised language use is a fact of modern life, and is probably here to stay for the foreseeable future: after all, among other things, decontextualised language is the voice par excellence of official ideology.

Yet the fact remains that the neonate does not come equipped with language of any kind, leave aside language that is context independent. If the natural condition of human discourse is to be context dependent – and this is what children are good at in the very early stages of their life – then the question arises: at what point and by what means might children become inclined to use decontextualised, disembedded language? This is the central issue of my enquiry here. The question is of some interest because as Cloran (1994) points out, scholars such as Bernstein (1971a), Bruner (1970) and Donaldson (1978), amongst others, have cited decontextualised language as essential to the creation of knowledge; it has been claimed that the absence of orientation to such language could be one of the possible reasons for educational failure in some children[4].

To the extent that the above observation is correct, it implies certain things. First, instead of talking about children as a completely homogeneous category which knows no variation, it would be more accurate to say that only some children become inclined to use decontextualised language: these are the children that are likely to be amongst the educationally successful. Secondly, as pedagogic sites, schools themselves could not be said to be uniformly successful in creating the orientation to the use of decontextualised language: this is clear from the fact that the official pedagogic system fails some children. The children whom the system fails are, on this argument, precisely the ones whom it has not managed to initiate into the use of decontextualised language. Third, this situation raises the likelihood that the schools may in fact not be the initial site for the ontogenesis of decontextualised language; that instead of actually creating this inclination, schools may simply make use of it if they find it in their pupils. This would not be surprising since as Vygotsky (1978: 84) points out 'Children's learning begins long before they attend school … Any learning a child encounters in school always has a previous history'. In fact, with specific reference to decontextualised language, Bernstein has argued for nearly half a century now that before children enter the school, the different experiences that they have in their every day life already either predispose them to the 'un-natural' use of decontextualised language, or not, as the case may be: they come to school with distinct orientations. If Bernstein is right, then we should expect to come across examples of both kinds of language in young children's every day talk, and indeed, Cloran's research (1994, 1999b) provides strong indication that a specific category of children do experience decontextualised language at home (see also Williams 1995; Donaldson and chapter 3–6 above). She (Cloran 1999b) has identified the kind of environment in which decontextualised talk between mothers and children typically occurs at home. My main aim here is to use her investigation as a point of departure for moving into a related but somewhat different area. The questions that I am primarily interested in exploring are, first what shape exactly does the ontogenesis of decontextualised language take in the data of naturally occurring everyday talk between some mothers and their children? Secondly, what features of this ontogenesis might be said to attract the children to the continued use of this variety at home? In the course of answering these questions I shall also comment both on the crucial defining criterion of decontextualised talk and on the environment that favours this talk: thus offering further elaboration to Cloran's findings (1994) on this topic. My main hypothesis is that during such talks between mothers and children something happens which is instrumental in creating a mental disposition toward this kind of discourse. In the concluding section of this paper I will look briefly into classroom as the site for the development of decontextualised language.

2 Where, when and how do they learn it?

The mother child dialogues on which the enquiry below is based come from the data of the research described in chapters 3–5 of this volume[5]. Given the conditions in which the interactions between the mothers and their children took place, one would reasonably expect that the mother's language use would be typically context dependent. And so it is – but not all the time, and certainly not to the same extent, for all twenty-four dyads. By way of illustration, here is a dialogue between Carol and her mother. A word first about the background to the extract presented as dialogue 1. Carol, 3 years 6 months old, her little sister, Annie, and the mother are having their snack outside in the garden. Suddenly Carol notices a cat that has wandered into their garden. 'oh a pussy-cat!' says Carol; the mother has also noticed the cat: 'it's up in the tree, isn't it?' she says. Carol and mother discuss how it is alright for a strange cat to appear in their garden; 'we don't mind, do we, mum?'. Carol asks and the mother confirms 'no, we don't'. Carol then goes on to contrast their attitude to cats with that of other people's: they it appears would not like stray cats to come into their gardens. It is at this point that we pick up their dialogue[6]:

Dialogue 1

1 Carol: but sometimes when pussy-cat goes into people's garden some people say 'come back, pussy-cat! come back!'
2 Mother: do they? is that what they do? (AMUSED TONE; MOTHER AND CHILD LAUGH)
3 Carol: mum, do pussy-cats die when people die?
4 Mother: do pussy-cats what, love?
5 Carol: die when people die?

6 Mother: well pussy-cats die when their time comes .. everything dies one day
7 Carol: do dogs? do they one day ?
8 Mother: do what?
9 Carol: do dogs die one day when .
10 Mother: yes, dogs die too .
11 Carol: do fruit die?
12 Mother: fruit dies, yes, in a different sort of way
13 Carol: how?
14 Mother: well see how the fruit up there on the tree's green?
15 Carol: mm
16 Mother: see how down here its gone all yellow and squashy and horrible?
17 Carol: mhhm
18 Mother: that means it's died, its .. well, we don't say (emphasis on 'say') it's died we say its gone bad .
19 Carol: mummy
20 Mother: mm
21 Carol: mum, see where the persimmons have dropped off the tree .. cos um cos they're sick and they've got germs
22 Mother: yes, that's right
23 Carol: they're sick and they've got germs

Probably most readers will agree that the above dialogue makes some use of decontextualised language. Before beginning to look more closely into some of its properties, it would be useful to make one general point. The categories 'context dependent' versus 'context independent', 'embedded' versus 'disembedded' and their other synonyms do not represent an 'all-or-none' affair: there are continuities between the two. One form of this continuity is that these descriptive terms need not apply to the whole of a discourse. Even within the same spatio-temporally located interaction, different parts of the discourse might vary in the extent to which one segment consists of context independent language use and another does not. This situation has been well documented by Cloran (1994, 1999b). But there is another aspect of the continuities between the two, whereby the drawing of clear lines between them is not so easy: I am referring here to the fact that one and the same segment of discourse may display characteristics of both. This calls for a further clarification of the nature of the two varieties. As we continue the examination of the data, we will note that decontextualisation is itself not a uniform phenomenon: there are different degrees of being disembedded, and these differences in ways of being disembedded appear to be significant from the point of view of the child learning how to engage in such discourse. With this brief introduction, I return to dialogue 1 to ask: What continuities and discontinuities do we find here? What are the characteristics of the mother's talk, and what are those of her daughter's? How does this early sortie into decontextualised language occur for Carol? How does it relate to her 'natural' mode of interaction – her discursive *terra firma*, namely situationally dependent talk? I hope that examining these questions might reveal the complexity of what it means to claim orientation to decontextualised talk.

2.1 Continuities between actual and virtual contexts

Elsewhere (Hasan 1984a) I have referred to the discursive theme of the dialogue between Carol and her mother as the discourse of mutability – talk about life and death. But Carol is not really enquiring into mutability as an abstract idea: she is not concerned with the cosmic principle of death as the end of all life; she is concerned rather with the fate of cats. And the idea of the general category 'pussy-cats' itself comes to her mind in the context of talking about '*a* pussy-cat' – the 'real' cat in the here and now of their immediate experience, the cat that had wandered into their garden. It is interesting to note also that before the child raises the question of pussy-cats dying, she introduces the general category 'pussy-cats' as a class of entities that is habitually engaged in familiar everyday activities: pussy-cats come into and go away from people's houses and gardens. In other words, some generalisations based on the actual observation of what cats do are already on the table before we move to the topic of mutability, which in all probability would not be a familiar concept to the child. The child's disembedded discourse, her use of decontextualised language, has employed as its point of departure the discourse that was embedded within the immediate material situation; it relates to a phenomenon that has been physically sensed by the child, and that happens to be an element of her personal experience in the context of this talk. Equally, as the mother attempts to explain the difficult idea of death/perishment as applicable to all organic things, she reaches out to what is actually present in the material situation *the fruit up there on the tree, (the fruit) down here ... all yellow and squashy and horrible .. that means it's died.*

There are thus two critical moments in this discourse – being focused on what is there, and what can be imagined, perhaps as an extension of what is materially present; and I am suggesting that there exists a continuity between these two moments. To comment on the nature of this continuity, I want to introduce two terms, namely: *actual* and *virtual*, which describe the context to which language is referring. I shall say that a context (or some element of it) is actual, if it can be actually, i.e., physically sensed by the interactant(s). For example, *the fruit on the tree* in Carol's garden, and that on the ground *all yellow and squashy and horrible* are instances of reference to actual (elements of) material situational setting, which are thus becoming the relevant context of the text: Carol and her mother both have a bodily experience of these phenomena. By contrast, a context (or some element of it) is virtual, if no possibility exists for experiencing it physically: the phenomena are, in fact, not available to the human senses. A discourse is decontextualised/disembedded not because what it refers to is not physically present to the senses here and now, but because it refers to something that is by its very nature incapable of being present in any spatio-temporal location whatever: it is simply not sens-ible. The virtual context of situation to which some text refers is, then, an entirely text based reality, brought into existence by constitutive verbal action (Hasan 1999). I believe it is important to emphasise here the fact that constitutive verbal action does not always and necessarily create a virtual context of situation: what is critical to the virtual nature of context is its distance from the actual. An actual context is rooted in experience that is essentially sensuous, or sens-ible, irrespective of whether it relates to an immediate situation or one that is displaced as in a narrative of personal experience. When I tell someone what happened to me the other day, my verbal action is constitutive; it re-creates an actual context that actually existed although it is now spatiotemporally displaced. This context, displaced in reality but invoked by constitutive language, is in terms of the distinction I am making here, as actual as an immediate context in which I use my language as an ancillary tool for negotiating the performance of some ongoing physical action such as helping someone wash up. Whether verbal action is ancillary or constitutive, so long as it refers to some actual context one thing is certain: part of the source of my knowledge of the latter type of contexts goes beyond language to other modalities of knowing. Virtual contexts, I am suggesting, differ from both these categories of actual context, the immediate and the displaced. Because virtual contexts are nonmaterial and removed from situational realities, they simply cannot be directly and physically experienced: they are only intellig-ible, not sens-ible. They reside only in a conceptual universe, and consist simply of the said and the imagined. Table 1 summarises these distinctions:

Table 1: A classification of contexts for discourse

<table>
<tr><th colspan="2">Context Type</th><th>verbal action</th><th>speaker's mode</th></tr>
<tr><td rowspan="2">Actual</td><td>immediate</td><td>ancillary</td><td>sensible</td></tr>
<tr><td>displaced</td><td rowspan="2">consitiutive</td><td rowspan="2">intelligible</td></tr>
<tr><td colspan="2">Virtual</td></tr>
</table>

This discussion suggests that for a young child who is as yet an apprentice to a given culture, actual situations are far more accessible than virtual ones. And while much more can be said about the above categories of context, what is relevant here is really this quality of discourse, its capacity to construe a virtual context of situation, that characterises disembedded discourse: this is very much at the heart of the distinction between context dependent and context independent talk. At least some of us become so familiar with virtual contexts that we do not appreciate the strangeness of this universe. For the young child it may be a different experience. We will see how Carol treads hesitatingly as she tries to grasp the elements of this virtual context.

2.2 The cline of de/contextualisation

Cloran (1994, 1999b) set up a cline of decontextualised language. Using her concept of rhetorical unit (henceforth RU), she suggested that if action RU represents the most context dependent language use then the generalisation RU is the most context independent (Cloran 1999b: 37). An example of action RU is 'don't hit her' and of generalisation RU, 'boys don't play with dolls'. Let me begin by considering the category of generalisation, which is akin to what I called principle in the structure of the reasoning game (discussion in chapter 8). Using her metalanguage for the description of RU, Cloran would say that in generalisation, the Central Entity component of the message is a class exhaustive category: it refers not to a specific individual – not to *a* pussy-cat – but to a class 'pussy cats'. At the same time, the Event Orientation of the message is habitual: 'die', not 'has died' or 'is dying' etc. Speaking from observation, there is no doubt that generalisations typically instantiate decontextualised language use. I, however, want to draw attention to a statement such as 'some people say', which to my mind already exemplifies a species of disembedded language although technically speaking it is not a generalisation, since the Central Entity 'some people' refers to a sub-class, not to a whole class, as would 'people'. Relevant to my claim of 'some people say' as already indicating some disembeddedness is the actual versus virtual distinction. The nominal group 'some people' does not refer here to persons in the here and now of the actual immediate situation[7] as it might do in another message such as 'I see some people at the gate'. Instead, it refers to a category of persons that in Whorf's (1956) terms would never form a sensuously apprehended aggregate. It is thus a conceptual construct made possible by language; it has no specific material manifestation, just as most of the situations construed by the language of Metamorphosis or Adventures in the Skin Trade are incapable of having a material manifestation: they will reside in the conceptual universe alone. In one respect, 'some people say' is like 'pussy cats die': the simple present tense in the verb 'say' refers to a habitual and/or timeless event. The time to which a simple present tense refers is, again using Whorf's terminology, not time that is being sensed here and now by the speaker. The simple present tense[8] realising the meaning *habitual* invokes past time, which has been sensed; as well, it invokes future time, which exists as anticipation; and it also invokes present time, which is in the here and now at this very moment of speaking though the occurrence of the event may not be being sensed by the speaker. In simplified language 'says' at once means 'has said, is saying, will say'. The invocation of the past, the future and the present iconically spans all time: it has the effect of bestowing an aspect of timelessness to the event in question. A habitual event is thus an event that defies the boundaries we impose on time: and this too is a conceptual construct made possible by language. It is not a phenomenon that can ever be known as first person sensuous knowledge.

I have deliberately emphasised the sensuous aspect of personal experience to contrast it with the nature of certain forms of knowledge – or information, if you like – that could not be based on bodily experience: bodily experienced phenomena constitute the quintessential context dependent information. One of the things that a generalisation does is to transform categories of referents which could be sensuously apprehended into categories whose referents cannot be sensed: it transports the sens-ible exclusively to the domain of the intellig-ible and that is one reason for maintaining that generalisations typically instantiate disembedded language. But by the same token, any message or RU which is capable of construing the virtual will be, to some extent, a case of disembeddedness. From the point of view under consideration, the further removed the referents of categories from primary, bodily experience, the more decontextualised the information, irrespective of whether or not there is any generalisation involved. It follows that given two or more cases of generalisation, the degree of their disembeddedness need not be the same. So while there is generalisation both in the message 'pussy-cats die' and in 'everything dies one day', nonetheless following the logic of my argument I would maintain that the latter is more decontextualised than the former; and by the same token, the former is more decontextualised than an utterance such as *we don't mind*, on the assumption that 'we' here refers to Carol's immediate family: herself, her parents and her sibling; the Central Entity of this message refers to a tight local group, and the Event refers to a goings-on in which Carol herself would have been implicated. For Carol the message *everything dies one day* is considerably more decontextualised than her own message *we don't mind*. It should be noted in passing that the critical principle underlying variation in the degree of decontextualisation cannot be specified simply in terms of the presence or absence of some lexicogrammatical, *or* semantic *or* contextual category: it must rest on a calibration of all three. The same first person plural pronoun 'we' may refer to the interactants here and now as in 'shall we look at this picture book together', or to a small group well known to the interactants, for example their family, as in Carol's *we don't mind*, or to a group that extends to include friends and or neighbours as in 'we keep our streets clean', or to members of the interactant's 'speech fellowship' to use Firth's (1957) term as in *we don't want to act like those fancy people*, or to the entire human race as in *we owe it to our future generations* ... etc. The referents thus construed discursively are realities of different order. I am suggesting that differences in the orders of reality might be significant at the early stages of learning how to mean disembedded meanings. The more removed from personal experience a category, perhaps the more problematic it is for a very young child from the point of view of understanding its full meaning, and this would naturally mean lack of sure-footedness in building it into one's own discourse. This is evident from Carol's discourse.

2.3 The mastery of disembedded language

The gist of my claim in 2.1–2.2 has been that the stranger, the less familiar the reality being construed, the more decontextualised the message. It follows that the mastery of disembedded language would consist in feeling at home with reality that is not sensuously mediated: this reality is a terrain that is navigated by the intellect alone. The problem that is posed for the child by the incommensurability of the various orders of reality is indicated in how Carol handles the issue of mutability. One way of describing Carol's response to the mother's *everything dies one day* is to say that she is testing the referential scope of *everything*: does the reference of the word extend beyond people to whole other classes of animals such as cats, and dogs? Does it cover in-animate objects: *do fruit die?*. People dying is already a less familiar happening than cats coming and going; but mutability as a superordinate concept which subsumes all change, all perishment, all death is certainly a very remote concept for the child. It is to this high degree of decontextualisation that the mother has moved the discourse by saying that *everything dies one day* and *fruit dies, yes, in a different sort of way*. Note how she attempts to bridge this gap for the child by producing messages that refer to the here and now: the tree in the garden, the fruit on that tree, the colour of that fruit; the fruit on the ground in the garden, the colour of the fruit on the ground; the difference between the colour of the fruit on the tree and that of the fruit on the ground. Sure in the knowledge that all this the child can see, she builds her most abstract claim on it, and goes on to suggest that it is this kind of difference that we refer to as the death of the fruit; more specifically *we say it's gone bad.* The mother's explication is impressive both as a lesson in language and as a lesson in elements of reality: it shows in action the process of conceptualisation as a sociogenetic activity (Vygotsky 1978). Which is not to say that in this one single step Carol will now master the virtual reality construed so carefully by her mother.

Carol enters this virtual universe hesitatingly: note for example the pauses. It is obvious that her navigation of the terrain lacks the assurance the mother had displayed. However, with all the experience of three and a half years of living, Carol can show at least some tentative understanding of organic change. She most probably has knowledge of a particular kind of bodily change that in all likelihood she herself has experienced – having germs, being sick. Carol applies this understanding to the fruit in a halting kind of way: her key to the entry into the remote world of virtual reality is the certainty of the knowledge that most probably she has herself bodily experienced or at least witnessed in person. This halting entry cannot be equated with mastery, though of course it is a significant step in that direction. What is important is the trajectory of her entry into decontextualised forms of discourse.

Again and again, the data of mother child talk shows us evidence of children's halting, hesitating entry into the unfamiliar conceptual universe construed by disembedded language. I present another such example below. In dialogue 2, the mother is trying to get Kristy ready to go to a day-care centre. Kristy is more than reluctant to go: there are tears, tantrums and arguments. Little fights keep erupting between Kristy and her baby sister, Ruth. Much of the mother's energies are devoted to diverting Kristy and to defusing the tension in the air. Through all this she is not only continuing to get Kristy dressed but she is also attending to Ruth. At the point that the following extract begins, the process of dressing Kristy is still continuing:

Dialogue 2a

1 Mother: this tee-shirt? right! we'll have to make you some blouses, won't we?

2 Kristy: yeah then everyday I can wear blouses mummy I think I'm going to get cold today

3 Mother: I have no idea what the weather is going to be like today I'll send your sweatshirt or your cardigan or your jumper or whatever you'd like over too

4 Kristy: I want – I want a short-sleeved cardigan – a long-sleeved one if it goes hot I'll have to wear a short-sleeved one so—**

5 Mother: **yep well see yesterday I thought it was going to be cold and you were really hot by the end of the day so I think the best thing is to put a short-sleeved tee-shirt on you and a cardigan

6 Kristy: yeah I think we don't know what day its going to be

7 Mother: no it's a bit [?] in spring and autumn, isn't it? stand up straight so I can get your duds on in winter it is cold and in the summer it's hot and in the spring and the autumn it's funny
(RUTH IS HEARD CRYING)

8 Mother: oh Ruth .. she's jammed her fingers in the sewing box [? put] her hand on top of the [?lid].. silly monkey!

9 Kristy: silly monkey!

10 Mother: she had her hand in [?the box]

11 Kristy: yeah

12 Mother: and she had the other hand on top pushing it down squashing her hand
(KRISTY LAUGHS)

13 Mother: oh you're a goose Ruth!

14 Kristy: oh you're a goose! do goosies do that?

15 Mother: no, no, but you often call people a goose if they're silly

16 Kristy: hmm

17 Mother: you know if you eat too much I say you're a little pig you're little piggy-wig

18 Kristy: yeah (laughing)

19 Mother: well if people are silly you say 'silly goose' and sometimes you can say they're a donkey (mimicking) you silly donkey!

20 Kristy: silly donkey! (laughs)

21 Mother: and if they are fussy what do you say?* I think you'd say they're a hen .. or a mother hen

22 Kristy: (unintelligible)

23 Mother: you haven't got your panties on, have we? where are they? Goodness me, I put them out there they are! the blue ones

24 Kristy: hello [?fussy hen]

25 Mother: ok Ruth .. we've nearly got Kristy dressed we'll get you dressed after her stand up pet put your hands on my shoulders so you don't fall over

26 Kristy: why is spring and **autumn—

27 Mother: **[?those Kristy's shoes]

28 Kristy: why is spring and autumn um is is funny?

29 Mother: well um it is less predictable you don't really know what it is going to be like

30 Kristy: hmm

31 Mother: in spring the weather is changing from— no I haven't got your [?leg] in .. the weather is changing from cold to hot and in the

autumn the weather is changing from hot to cold and its not just in the middle it seems to um be **colder in the morning
32 Kristy: **hmm
33 Mother: and gets warm later in the day
34 Kristy: yeah why does it?
35 Mother: I don't understand enough about the weather to be able to explain that
(RUTH SCREAMS)

Here the point of departure for the mother's comments on the unreliability of weather in spring and autumn is a practical consideration that has involved Kristy personally: what clothes should the mother send with Kristy so that the daughter would be comfortable, unlike yesterday when she was too hot. So the discourse of weather is initially embedded within something that the child can 'relate to' directly. Note, though, how unsure Kristy's own control of the information concerning weather is as she says (in turn 6) *yeah I think we don't know what day its going to be*. Although talk of weather is interrupted by the discussion of metaphors occasioned by Ruth's antics, Kristy later returns to it (turn 26 onwards) as if she had some inkling of her incomplete understanding of the matter. In response to Kristy's specific questions, the mother elaborates on the 'funniness' of the current weather. As it happens the mother is not able to fully satisfy Kristy's curiosity. But at a later point in the same interaction it becomes obvious that Kristy did not grasp the conceptual world of changing weather even to the extent that the mother was able to explain. As Butt (1989b) comments, what she carries is some vague sense of things being not quite right with regard to mornings, evenings, days and nights – a sense that the uncertain condition of the weather, its 'a-normality', calls for especial consideration. This becomes evident in the segment of the same dialogue presented below as dialogue 2b.

As I pointed out in introducing this interaction, Kristy is quite reluctant to go to the day-care centre. Off and on, throughout this interaction, Kristy has made her disagreement with her mother clear. She has tried to dissuade her mother from sending her there, using all the strategies available to children of her age from tears, to fights with Ruth, to presenting 'rational' reasons, to displaying aggression, but all to no avail[9]. Finally, in a pathetic move, she claims *I want to be a baby* and complains: *I just feel crooked today*. It is at this point that Kristy uses the uncertainties of the weather as presumably her last argument in her battle against being sent to the day-care centre. Here is the relevant segment of the dialogue:

Dialogue 2b

1 Kristy: um I just feel crooked today (COMPLAININGLY)
2 Mother: you just feel crooked?
3 Kristy: I can't help the weather – I don't have the weather – its cold out here in the morning and then it comes hot —
4 Mother: I think you are probably crook just because you have been hanging around the house too long as soon as we get out you'll feel better
5 Kristy: yeah and I don't know what to do (tearful voice)

The longer one stays in official pedagogic sites engaged with the business of re/producing knowledge, the greater grows one's familiarity with disembedded talk, until one comes to take most of its elements for granted. The question of the mastery of concepts such as Kristy and Carol are encountering for the first time in these dialogues does not present itself to us as a problem. Far less are we aware of the fact that our thoughts traffic constantly between the actual and the virtual worlds – that there are continuities between embedded and disembedded language. But the situation is different for children who are just starting off on this journey. On the whole, the children who participated in this research proved themselves impressively competent with language. So their hesitations and their 'peculiar' formulations as they grapple with the virtual world being construed by disembedded discourse is all the more noticeable. Learning how to use disembedded language is in fact learning to come to terms with a new reality; it is learning a new way of engaging with reality that is at best only partly familiar. This learning is something quite hard to accomplish on a piecemeal basis, from nine to five in packages of forty-five minute 'periods' in official pedagogic sites. The children who get oriented to such language under the classroom conditions typically tend to be just those whose life is pervaded with discourse of the kind exemplified in the two extracts above.

2.4 The environment for disembedded talk

This brings me to the last point to be discussed in this section on the ontogenesis of orientation to disembedded talk; the question is: where do the children learn it – those who actually get to do so? What discursive environment might be said to be most hospitable to the ontogenesis of such talk in the home? It is almost impossible to answer this question without appeal to Bernstein's notions of classification and framing, since it is not the 'substantive' nature of the environment which is criterial: disembedded talk may surface and actually establish itself in immediate contexts of different kinds as Cloran (1999b) has demonstrated. But although this can happen in almost any actual immediate context, it does not happen randomly: its establishment is highly selective. The underlying principle guiding this selectivity can be stated very simply and succinctly by reference to Bernstein's concepts of classification and framing, once these concepts are seen within the theoretical framework which gives them their significance. Using these concepts we may very simply claim that the environment hospitable to the ontogenesis of orientation to disembedded talk is furnished by social praxis of the kind that displays relatively weak classification and framing. Underlying this 'simple' statement is a complex situation to which I shall return at the close of this section (see 2.4.2 below); here just a few words on my 'take' on the critical concepts themselves. I see classification and framing as inalienably linked to each other. Classification is a function of power, and framing a function of control to maintain that classification: it is through framing that classification is maintained and altered; and it is one's relation to classification that furnishes the ground for specific forms of framing. Inextricably linked as the concepts are, my focus here will be more on framing though mention of classification will necessarily arise.

Although I believe that Bernstein's account of framing is designed with an eye more to official pedagogic practice than to the local one, it would be nonetheless useful to reproduce the essential account of it here for easy reference (Bernstein 1996: 27):

> Framing is about *who* controls *what*. What follows could be described as the *internal logic* of the pedagogic practice. Framing refers to the nature of the control over:
>
> • the selection of the communication;
>
> • its sequencing (what comes first what comes second);
>
> • its pacing (the rate of expected acquisition);
>
> • the criteria; and
>
> • the control over the social base which makes this transmission possible.
>
> Where framing is strong, the transmitter has explicit control over selection, sequence, pacing, criteria and the social base. Where framing is weak, the acquirer has more *apparent* control (I want to stress 'apparent') over the communication and its social base.

Bernstein points out that the framing values, their strength or weakness, can vary independently for each element of the practice. I will presently touch upon some of these aspects of framing in the dialogues I have presented above. Let me begin here by saying that the Macquarie group of researches[10] on mother child interaction found that mothers varied non-randomly in respect of the strength/weakness of their classification of contexts (Cloran 1994, 1999b; Williams 1995; Hasan 2000): one group of mothers overwhelmingly acted on the principle that contexts must be kept apart, while another overwhelmingly acted on the principle that the natural condition for contexts is to permeate each other. Strong classification of context typically 'goes with' strong framing; conversely weak classification of context, the affirmation of its permeability, goes with weak framing. The dialogues presented in the last section belong to the latter category. I want to say a few words about what weak classification of context means, what is implied in saying that contexts are taken as permeable rather than as binding frames.

Consider dialogues 1 and 2. If we wished to take the entire interaction in which they occur as one unit, how would we describe the context of these interactions? It seems to me that we must invoke some such notion as con/textual shift (Hasan 1999, 2000), or the embedding of one context within another as Cloran puts it (Cloran 1994, 1999b). What I mean by con/textual shift is that on the one hand the speakers are shifting from an ongoing context, they are reclassifying the discursive situation, and on the other hand, the new context to which the shift has been made is still being integrated into the discursive contexts from which the shift is being indicated: every con/textual shift implies a (somewhat) new context with an identity of its own, and at the same time, a context that is contributing to the primary context (for some details see Hasan 1999). Taken together these inter-related contexts succeed in giving the discourse its overall character. So there is reclassification of context and there is integration of the reclassified contexts: both these aspects are important to the progress and character of the discourse[11]. Dialogues 1 and 2 did not begin as an explanation or exposition of any idea. For example, Carol and her mother were engaged in eating snacks; Kristy and her mother were engaged in getting Kristy ready for the day. In these specific respects, both these dialogues are indicative of the sorts of material actions that adults giving care to young children must attend to, and of the fact that at least some of their discourse must be embedded in the here and now of their actual immediate situation: their verbal action must be *ancillary*. But paradoxically precisely because the activities are of this kind – providing food, dressing, playing some game with the child and so on – that is to say, precisely because the action is primarily material (Hasan 1999), the situation becomes a frame in which verbal action can become free to be either ancillary to the activity or to disregard the material action altogether, turning away from it to become a resource for constituting a context that is, as it were, independent of the material situation itself[12]. Germane to this point is the fact that most material activities are capable of being carried out without words, though they are hardly ever accomplished without words when an other is present in the same situation; nonetheless, the potential for the reclassification of context only arises where the on-going verbal action is ancillary: one of the sites where this condition can be found is in talking to very small children while giving them care or playing with them, and so on.

Because material action moves along the temporal axis, because the performance of its stages is visible, and because it has a projected end-point so that the achievement of this goal can be easily ascertained, we may be inclined to prioritise this element of the field of discourse[13]: we may think of the material action as the mother's real agenda; we may say, for example, that what the mother is really doing is dressing the children. But where classification and framing are weak, especially in the environment of local pedagogy, what the mother is really doing on any one occasion may be many things at once. In dialogue 2a, I have deliberately reproduced a segment that goes some way towards illustrating this characteristic. In the first turn of dialogue 2a, which is itself a segment of a longer dialogue, the mother begins with reference to the material action, then there is talk of the uncertainty of weather interspersed with talk of clothing, then we have a lesson in the meaning of metaphors, after which in turn 23, the mother verbally 'returns' to the material activity which had been physically going on all the time any way, but now the verbal action occurs with specific reference to the needs of dressing Kristy: *you haven't got your panties on, have we? where are they? goodness me, I put them out, there they are! the blue ones*, but very soon there is a shift back to talk of weather. There are thus many con/textual shifts throughout this interaction in which the mother's verbal action 'returns' to the material action only to move away from it again. But by far the greater part of this lengthy interaction consists of language that is 'about' things other than getting dressed. What is important here from the point of view of framing is that the movement between contexts, the weaving in and out of contexts, is not unilateral. Throughout this interaction, the shifts are typically construed in partnership with the child as the following discussion documents.

Since local pedagogy is 'segmental', perhaps the aspect of framing concerning sequencing of activities has a different significance here. Note however the sequencing of what happens to Ruth and how the mother 'exploits' it to draw in Kristy into the world of metaphors. And in this connection it is significant that the discourse is provoked by the child's question 'do goosies do that?'. It is difficult to give a good idea of the pacing of discourse without reproducing most of the interaction, but the mother takes time off during the business of dressing Kristy to comfort her, to 'make her feel better', to engage with her reasons for not wanting to go to the day-care centre, to reassure her child that she herself will be back by the time Kristy is supposed to come back home[14]. What can be said and done while Kristy is being got ready to go to the day-care centre is not entirely up to the mother: the child has some say, even if she has no say in the matter of where she would spend that day. The selection of discourse topics is as much Kristy's prerogative as it is the mother's. The discourse between the two is a relatively shared negotiated activity. To be sure, this constantly peripatetic discourse has other purposes than just presenting new information to the child. In a way, the construction of knowledge which entrains the use of decontextualised language plays second fiddle to the mother's primary concern in this interaction. Note that throughout this discourse the mother chooses to develop topics which have the potential of humouring Kristy and diverting her attention from the contentious issue of having to go to the day care centre against her inclination (Hasan 2000, for further discussion in a similar situation). Obviously the mother's relatively weak classification of contexts in no way implies an absence of a specific fixed agenda, which is, as it were, non-negotiable. To this extent, the weakness of the mother's framing would seem to be apparent. In fact it may be true as a general rule that weak framing is simply the ultimate device for disarming opposition by (apparently) entertaining the other's needs. You may describe this situation as showing respect for the other's individuality, but you may equally justifiably describe it as exercising control by stealth – that is to say, invisible control. Once this view is taken, the social universe presents itself as a network of relations defined by various strategies of control. Put more bluntly, the claim I am making is that control is not something that can be elided from the social; it is always present; the question is simply: what is the style of the control? Be that as it may, what is important in the context of this discussion is the fact that decontextualised language typically occurs in the environment of weak framing, and weak framing may imply a readiness to entertain a weak classification of context. The trick is to remember that weak classification and framing are not synonymous with the absence of social power or of control; they are simply indicative of a qualitatively different kind of use of power and a different style of control. This is an important principle to remember in the context of 'progressivist' pedagogy.

2.4.1 Ancillary verbal action and reclassification of context

Above I have suggested that the potential for the reclassification of context only arises where the on-going verbal action is ancillary. I want to emphasise the word 'potential' here, because it is by no means necessary that speakers will be inclined to entertain con/textual shifts, to reclassify their context, whenever the verbal action in the field of discourse is ancillary. The etiology of this inclination and its underlying logic must be traced back by following the workings of Bernstein's theoretical framework, aspects of which will be briefly brought to attention below (see section 2.4.2). But the upshot is that interaction at home between all mothers and children does not uniformly display weak classification and framing of the kind exemplified by dialogues 1 and 2. Below I reproduce segments of a dialogue which is remarkably different from those we have examined so far. This interaction took place at mealtime (like dialogue 1 above) and the recording opens with Karen requesting first some sauce on her food, followed by another request for some lemonade. The mother attends to these requests and reminds Karen of some 'linguistic table manners', asking her to say *please!* and commenting *I didn't hear a thank you from you.* With these niceties observed, we come to the following point:

Dialogue 3a

1	Mother:	come on, eat your tea please .
2	Karen:	could you put some more in there? .
3	Mother:	(warningly) Karen! .. give me it eat your tea
4	Karen:	[?]
5	Mother:	mm?
6	Karen:	[?Put] lemon in it
7	Mother:	well, eat some tea or you don't get nothing
8	Karen:	I see how many [?] There are (KAREN TALKS TO HERSELF AS MOTHER POURS DRINK)
9	Mother:	quick .. want the lid on it?
10	Karen:	no
11	Mother:	come on, eat your tea less drink and more eat .. did you hear what I said Karen?
12	Karen:	mm
13	Mother:	well, do it

As I have pointed out elsewhere (Hasan 2000), here the mother's primary concern is to maintain the boundary of the ongoing context – the context of 'eating your tea': within a dialogue lasting some twenty minutes the mother produced her injunction to 'eat your tea' over twenty times. It is relatively easy to specify the general condition under which – all else being equal – the speakers are able to reclassify their context; it is, however, not easy to say in precise terms where exactly such a shift will actually occur – that is to say, this possibility is not open so long as we focus simply on the nature of the field of discourse (see discussion below in section 4.2.2). There no doubt exists a time and a tide in the affairs of a discourse, which some interactants will grasp thus producing a con/textual shift; but the occurrence of such occasions does not mean that they will be necessarily grasped for this purpose. Here is an example of, as it were, nascent possibility for entertaining a con/textual shift, which the mother, however, does not treat as such:

Dialogue 3b

1 Karen: mummy that haven't got no sauce on it
2 Mother: oh you've got plenty of sauce there now now eat it
3 Karen: on here
4 Mother: oh there's plenty of sauce on your plate Karen you don't need it on every single drop of tea
5 Karen: eh?
6 Mother: you don't need it on every little bit
7 Karen: [? of tea]?
8 Mother: mm
9 Karen: is that [?tea]?
10 Mother: that's sauce
11 Karen: mm hot sauce
12 Mother: no, mint sauce
13 Karen: mince? .. why do you put mince sauce on here for?
14 Mother: 'mint' not 'mince'
15 Karen: mint this mint?
16 Mother: use your spoon or your fork
17 Karen: 'country practice' is on now?
18 Mother: no
19 Karen: 'sons and daughters'?
20 Mother: no, the news
21 Karen: oh .
22 Mother: that's why I said use a spoon .. now sit up and use a spoon

It is not easy to describe the exact delineations of an absence, but that the reclassification of context is noticeably different from that in dialogues 1 and 2 is certainly the case. It seems also not unreasonable to suggest that some of the topics the child raises could have functioned as the point of departure into another context. Karen is probably getting a rise from the mother when she asks 'is that tea?' since the expression 'eat your tea' is fairly common in some communities and the child is bound to have heard it often before. But the mint/mince question, as well as the question of what programmes might be showing on the TV appear to be definite candidates for 'diversion'. The mother, however, displays a single-minded devotion to her own definition of the context: an occasion for tea eating. Whatever does not meet her recognition criteria for the internal attributes of this context she will resist, because the principle on which she is acting is: things must be kept apart. Williams (1995) found that in joint book-reading, a specifiable group of mothers acted in a similar manner: they protected their conception of what counts as book-reading; and they resisted any questions, any comments from the child as a 'distraction' from the business of book-reading. Cloran (1999b) reports similar incidents where the insertion of a putative imaginary context is actively discouraged by some mothers. In dialogue 3, the strength of Karen's mother's framing of the discourse is quite remarkable. Especially the strength of what Bernstein calls the 'social order' becomes evident with segments of the same dialogue such as the following which occurred some ten minutes after the above discussion:

Dialogue 3c

1 Mother:	give me your spoon and I'll feed you, like a big baby come on, baby! give me your spoon
2 Karen:	(in a scandalised tone) no
3 Mother:	well sit up properly and eat your tea ..Karen! (Warning tone)
4 Karen:	I'm falling down (i.e. off the chair)
5 Mother:	you're not falling down
6 Karen:	yes I am, I always fall down .. **I am falling down
7 Mother:	**eat your tea
8 Karen:	I am falling down
9 Mother:	sit up before I get a stick and smack you

Strictly speaking, though, it is not quite correct to say that no contextual shift has occurred in this interaction. It is already obvious from the above extract that the mother is 'escalating' her regulative strategies. Imperceptibly, but surely, the context has moved from one of providing the necessities of tea to the child and of supervising her eating of tea to one of exercising visible control to prevent her from doing things that are just not the right things to do when you are eating your tea. The occasion for nurturing the body becomes the occasion for creating a particular form of personal relation. The mother and daughter half seriously 'threaten' each other with dire actions and some eight minutes later, we encounter the following:

Dialogue 3d

1	Mother:	I'm bigger than you I can hurt more
2	Karen:	and I could too
3	Mother:	no you can't
4	Karen:	yes **I—
5	Mother:	**you are only a little girl who is becoming a very cheeky little girl
6	Karen:	no I not
7	Mother:	and if you don't stop ** it
8	Karen:	**Christine is a naughty girl and spiteful

9 Mother: and so are you, you're a spiteful little girl when you want to be, you can't talk about anybody else, if you don't stop it (i.e. DOING OTHER THINGS THAN EATING) you are going to go into bed and you'll never see anybody cause I won't let you see any of your friends

10 Karen: [?] I will sneak out

11 Mother: no you won't sneak out now sit up on that chair and eat your tea

12 Karen: yes I will (i.e. sneak out)

13 Mother: Karen .. I am not playing games

14 Karen: mum .. oh mummy (cuddling up to the mother)

15 Mother: no go away don't come crawling to me go away go away I don't want you until you sit down and eat your tea .. go away .. go away Karen leave me alone please now sit down and eat your tea I won't talk to you until you eat it no I don't want no cuddles no I don't want a cuddle off of you no, no kisses either no I don't want – oh you kiss me I am not kissing you back .. Karen (WARNING TONE)

16 Karen: it doesn't matter

17 Mother: it will matter in a minute now stop crawling and sit down and eat your tea

I will refrain from making further specific comments about this particular dialogue. It is obvious that the con/textual integration here has what I have called a tone-setting function of a particular kind that borders on the conflictual (Hasan 1999). If invisible control signified by the weaker framing of discourse gives the impression of regard for the unique individuality of the child, visible control which is signified by the stronger framing of social interaction gives the impression of creating a relation of interpersonal dependence. It would be a violence to the mother's intentions and the child's behaviour in dialogue 3a-d to take their mutual threats 'literally': they seems to me to be creating a particular kind of teasing, demanding and controlling relation which differs quite remarkably from the relation that dialogues 1 and 2 might be said to produce. I will return below to the significance of the creation of specific kinds of relation for the ontogenesis of contextualised language.

Our interest in the frequent and varied reclassification of context is because of what it implies for framing; and our interest in weak framing is because its examination permits us to make some generalisations about the ontogenesis of decontextualised language. When reclassification accompanies strong framing, it implies a struggle to maintain the speakers' definition of some class of context: logically in this struggle the participant with greater power will exercise control over the other. This environment typically does not encourage decontextualised discourse; specifically it does not create the higher reaches of disembedded discourse. The highest it goes is the enunciation of communal conventions such as 'don't be silly! boys don't play with dolls' or 'I told you, you don't hit girls', which presents a generalisation but of a different order of abstraction from 'everything dies one day', or 'in the spring the weather is changing from cold to hot and in the autumn the weather is changing from hot to cold'. While the generalisation of the former kind enunciate a code of practical conduct, disembedded language of the latter kind is what 'becomes' the knowledge base of a community, an instrument through which nature and man both can be subjugated or succoured. I am certainly not suggesting that there is nothing more to knowledge than language, but I am claiming that without language it would have been pretty impossible to conserve these other non-language foundations of knowledge for transmission in the community.

2.4.2 Forms of classification and framing and forms of consciousness

We have seen that while it is easy to predict the environment which is potentially hospitable to a switch into decontextualised use of language between mothers and children, it is not possible to specify what turns this potential into a preferred choice on the part of some mothers, but not of others. Simplifying a complex situation I would say that Bernstein's theory explains this situation in a two step process. On the one hand classification and framing enter into a dialectic relation with subjects' social positioning whereby a subject comes to adopt a certain perspective on what counts as legitimate or as an illegitimate category. This perspective informs the subjects' social praxis both from the point of view of recognition and from the point of view of actual participation in that social practice, what Bernstein calls 'realization rules'. On the other hand, participation in social practices is precisely what enters into a dialectic with the subjects' form of consciousness: social subjects are what they do and what they say to and with others. From this point of view, given a subject's social positioning we can infer a range of possible perspectives, and so possible forms of classification and framing practices that will appear desirable and legitimate. By the same token, given the evidence of a subject's habitual social practices we can recover the subject's orientation to certain orders of meaning. Bernstein points out that he uses positioning to 'refer to the establishing of specific relations to other subjects and to the creating of specific relations within subjects' (Bernstein 1990: 13). In other words, to specify where the predisposition for the reclassification of contexts is likely to be found, and where the decisions about the nature of framing come from, we should turn not to the nature of the social action – not to the field of discourse; rather, we should turn to the nature of the social relation being enacted in and through the social action – what is referred to as tenor of discourse in systemic functional linguistics. A particular kind of field offers the potential for the reclassification of contexts: I have argued that the critical properties of this field may be expressed as (i) material action on-going; (ii) verbal action ancillary; and (iii) the sphere of action quotidian (Hasan 1980, 1999). To actually exploit this potential, to actually engage in reclassification of contexts, we need interactants who are given to enacting a certain range of relations with their interactive other. This range of relations inheres in orientation to elaborated code.

The interplay of the material and the semiotic aspects identified as typical of the environment in which decontextualised language can and does occur is important from the point of view of the ontogenesis of this form of discursive behaviour. Earlier I raised the question: why should children continue their engagement in such discourse? A common-sensical answer would be: because children are programmed by nature to wish to learn; because they are curious. But this applies just as much to the children who do not get initiated at home into this kind of discourse and to this particular form of knowledge. In my view the answer to my question is to be found in the material and the semiotic action within the frame of a particular kind of interpersonal relation. The quotidian activities of care givers and children largely tend to centre on the children's needs themselves. The children are being fed, or they are being dressed, in short, they are being looked after physically; this is largely achieved by material action. Secondly, at the same time, they are being attended to intellectually and semiotically with the interaction displaying regard for the child's interests. Not conflict, but cooperation, characterise the interaction where decontextualised talk typically occurs. The bodily satisfaction is thus combined with the satisfaction of companionship. The ontogenesis of decontextualised language becomes associated with the specific characteristics of such relaxed contexts. On the one hand, the weaker framing of the mother willing to reclassifying con/text sets up a tone of mutual negotiation, and on the other hand the satisfaction of primary bodily needs must lead to a feeling of contentment. The instructional discourse of this variety of local pedagogy is then framed within contexts that most probably generate a positive affect in the child, and I speculate that this positive affect plays a crucial part in successfully orienting the children to decontextualised discourse – a form of discourse that I described as essentially un-natural.

3 Decontextualised language and the classroom

As the site for official pedagogic practices, schools and higher educational institutions are where knowledge is re/produced. My concern here is not with how this is done; I wish simply to draw attention to what strikes me as a paradox in the framing of early pedagogic discourse. The data of classroom discourse to which I refer specifically here was collected for my research project from twenty-four schools in and around Sydney, and concerned only the kindergarten class. In fact amongst other things we wished to 'follow' eight of the twenty-four children from phase 1 of the project: we wished to find out if the experience of participating in different kinds of discourse made any systematic difference to how these children acted in the classroom. Each school was recorded on two separate occasions: during the first four weeks of the first year of schooling and during the last four weeks of the same year of schooling. The observations made here are based on the first batch of this data.

Although the strength of framing in classroom discourse can vary as the discussion of progressive and traditional classroom has made abundantly clear, one must pay attention to Bernstein's emphasis on the word apparent (see quote above in section 2.4). When the data of teacher pupil talk was seen side by side with that of mother child talk, what impressed most were the two respects in which it exaggerated maternal behaviour: The semantic orientation of the teachers' talk in the classroom was an exaggerated version of the middle class mothers' semantic orientation (Hasan 1988), while the framing of classroom talk was an exaggerated version of the working class mothers' single minded devotion to one single context. We found that most teachers began with a clear conception of what it was to participate in a teaching learning context, and they exerted themselves to maintain that definition with their young pupils, as early as the second or third week of schooling; and in this connection it is relevant to remember that the KG class is the first real experience of schooling for the five year old children. For example, as one teacher is conducting picture talk, a pupil calls out 'Mummy has got some shells'. But this intervention gets nowhere: like Karen's 'mint/mince' or 'Country Practice/Sons and Daughters' whatever potential the pupil's comment about her mother's shells might have had for a con/textual shift remains unexplored. When someone calls out an answer out of turn, they are either ignored or they're advised 'don't sing out until I call your name'. The regulation of the pupil's conduct is apparently one of the things that children learn pretty early on in the school. Having seen these same children at home with their mothers and in play group, having witnessed their freedom in coming and going, speaking or remaining silent, it comes as a surprise that within a matter of the first couple of weeks of their being at school the children have on the whole already become well schooled in how to conduct themselves. So far as schools are concerned there may be different kinds of reasons for maintaining a stronger classification of the classroom context. First, there is the pressure of time as measured by the curriculum needs, expressed informally as having to 'get through' a certain amount of 'materials'. Mercer (1993) talks also of the fear of being perceived as unable to manage the classroom, which would be a source of serious loss of face. There is also the desirability of 'order': in a class of over twenty pupils, many could wish to claim the privilege of speaking at the same time. But perhaps an important issue centres around the notion of 'self-discipline', an internalisation of standards of conduct as a sign of voluntary control on one's behaviour. Whatever the reason it is clear that children's discourse is being 'ordered' by the teacher[15]. There is no sense at least in my data that the teachers have negotiated with the children the selection of what is being done in the class. The pacing of the discourse is already such that those who get left out could remain out, if not for ever, then certainly for at least an appreciable amount of time. So in many respects then the framing value is strong rather than weak. It was most probably this aspect of class room talk which might have persuaded Edwards (1976) to claim that classroom discourse is oriented to restricted code. Bernstein's description of pedagogic discourse (1990) as a discourse of competencies embedded within the discourse of control clarifies the source of critics' error in equating the framing aspect of classroom discourse with pedagogic discourse as a whole.

So having identified the respect in which classroom discourse presents an exaggerated version of working class mother-child discourse, we turn now to the discourse of competencies. Here, already most teachers are concerned to take the teaching from simple acts of naming, to conjectures, hypotheses, inferential reasoning; in specific subject areas there will be talk of geometrical shapes, forms in nature, and 'language expression', and so on. What is more as I have suggested elsewhere the goal seems to be the achievement of what Bateson (1972b) described as deutero learning: an effort seems to be made to orient children toward such 'desirable' characteristics as objectivity, citation of evidence, argumentation, and logical reasoning. A very simple episode might give some idea: during a picture reading class, the teacher is talking about the picture of a little boy.

Dialogue 4

1	Teacher:	do you think he's having fun?
2	1st pupil:	yes
3	2nd pupil:	mummy's got some shells
4	Teacher:	(ignoring the 2nd pupil) what tells you? What tells you he's having fun? He's enjoying himself?
5	1st pupil:	my brain
6	Teacher:	your brain tells you (dismissive tone)! Well, how can we tell by looking at the picture, that he's enjoying himself, having fun?
7	Pupils:	(many call out together) smile
8	Teacher:	good he's got a smile on his face do you think he'd be enjoying himself if he didn't smile?
9	Pupils:	(many together) no!
10	Teacher:	I don't think so either!

I take this as one insignificant seeming but typical example of an early inculcation of the principle that objective knowledge is superior to subjective knowledge (see also Butt 1989b, Butt and Cloran 1988), and distancing from primary actual experience is what I have suggested above to be the essence of disembedded talk. While the knowledge presented to the children at this stage is 'diluted' for the benefit of their tender years, it is surprising how complex the requirements are and how much is taken for granted by teachers. The projected move of the process of official pedagogy is unmistakably towards disembedded discourse. And yet if my reading of the data of mother child interaction is correct – and I believe it is – then the best environment for learning to use disembedded language is one where a continuity is maintained from the actual to the virtual, from the familiar to the unfamiliar. And the best environment for this tends to be, as I have argued, a social interaction whose framing is relatively weak. With their stronger classification of context and their stronger framing of the discourse, with their greater emphasis on disembedded meanings, their distancing from the personal concerns of the children themselves, it seems very unlikely that schools would provide the best environment for learning how to use such language for those children who do not already possess this expertise to some extent before they enter the school. For the children the question of experiencing any bodily or intellectual satisfaction in classroom discourse is a problem that remains invisible, though it might be one of the most central. Why should a five year old have any interest in finding a single word which refers to what happens to a wound if germs get into it (cf., an example of the construction of knowledge in a language arts classroom)? True that Kristy is riveted by the lesson on the meaning of metaphors (see dialogue 2a), but then her relation to that problem was much more personal, much less an exercise in vocabulary development!

Several years ago in the early 1970s, one heard complaints that there was very little actual data of classroom interaction; with the advent of Sinclair and Coulthard (1975) this situation changed dramatically: now there is perhaps too much data of classroom interaction, but too little theory guiding the examination of that data, and decidedly too little understanding of the significant forms of systematic variation driven ideologically from the experience of living. So it is data that is in search of an exact and thoughtful analysis, which might go beyond the surface manifestations, beyond in fact the somewhat commonsense explanations, to a review which is based on a deeper understanding of the nature of pedagogic discourse, its place in the mis/management of the affairs of humanity, its role in creating both what we cherish, namely, the material and technological advances, the investigation of the new limitless horizons of the virtual world made possible by official pedagogy, and what we, or at least some of us, most abhor, namely, the unequal distribution of our social resources. Is there a field of research here in the linguistics of education which would be served well by paying attention to The Structuring of Pedagogic Discourse?

Notes

1 The major part of the research on which this chapter is based was funded by Macquarie University Grant Scheme and the Australian Research Council Grant, hereby gratefully acknowledged.

2 I wish to acknowledge explicitly here the contribution of Carmel Cloran to this debate. Cloran's discussion (1994, 1999a, 1999b) of the pair of terms *context dependent v. context independent,* and its synonyms within the systemic functional framework remains to date the most careful and detailed account in the field. I would like also to thank her for comments on the first draft of this paper.

3 To claim that the evolution of decontextualised language use is necessary to the exo-somatic evolution of humanity is not to say that as a consequence humanity's relation to natural and social environment could only take the form it has taken in modern industrialised societies; far less does it imply any approval of the form it has taken.

4 For a more detailed discussion of these views, and the controversy surrounding them, see Cloran (1994).

5 Some changes to the original have been made here to avoid repetition.

6 The conventions adopted here for the transcription of the data are presented below.

numbers in 1st column	speaker turn counted afresh for each extract.
(SMALL CAPITALS)	situational comment based on speaker's hearing of the audiotape.
[?go away]	segment not intelligible; best interpretation on the basis of co-text.
[?]	segment unintelligible; no contextual clues for interpretation.
Is it?*	question mark followed by single asterisk shows time was not allowed for a response.
It's for you to—	long dash shows message was not completed.
That's mine ..	dots show longer than usual pause
**	double asterisks paired across contiguous turns show point of overlap in talk.

7 I am ignoring here the use of *some people* to refer coyly to the addressee or to a third party typically a singular who is present in the actual immediate situation; this happens typically in the context of making an adverse statement about the person in question, which is passed off as a non-serious comment by the use of this device while it in fact brings the judgement within the orbit of attention.

8 Again, there are uses of the simple present tense which cannot be treated as habitual. One obvious example of its use is that known as the narrative present. For discussion, see Leech (1987); Halliday (1985a); Quirk, Leech and Svartvik (1985).

9 For a more elaborate discussion of these strategies, see Butt (1989b).

10 The initial research project in this group was directed by me; for her doctoral research, my main co-researcher, Cloran, undertook an investigation of the semantic concept *rhetorical unit* – a major contribution which has made possible the study of reclassification in relation to discursive meanings. Williams conducted a study of joint-book reading; in both these researches the data consisted of mother-child and (KG) teacher pupil interactions. Butt conducted a study of teacher pupil interaction at the primary and secondary levels of education in certain subject areas. These researches, which spanned the period of mid-80s to mid-90s, focussed on context, meaning and discourse and were inspired by the work of Vygotsky, Bernstein and Halliday as well as by the initial sociolinguistic research directed by me at Macquarie University which is reported in the chapters of this volume.

11 In speakers suffering from language disorder, there may be con/textual shift but no con/textual integration.

12 For a more detailed discussion of these issues, see Hasan (1999).

13 I use the term *field* here as it is used in systemic functional linguistics to refer to one parameter of the context of situation within which discourse is said to embedded. It should not be confused with *field* as in Bernstein or in Bourdieu, which is more like *domain* in sociolinguistics.

14 Other parts of this dialogue, including those where Kristy is wailing and 'whingeing' or having fisty-cuffs with her little sister, are discussed in Butt (1989b) and Hasan (2000).

15 In pointing out this fact, I am not making a value judgement. While the evaluation of these practices is necessary, here my purpose is simply to describe, to record what we found.

12 The world in words: semiotic mediation, tenor and ideology [2004]

1 Introduction

It has been customary to talk about children's language development by focusing on children – by asking what words and structures they can produce or comprehend at any particular stage of their biological development. If adults are mentioned, this is typically in relation to what specific realisation of some linguistic elements they model for the young learners[1]: the mastery of language as an autonomous system is what language development has largely been about. A significant advance took place, when in his case study of one child's language development, Halliday (1969b, 1973a, 1974a, 1975b) ignored the exclusive preoccupation with linguistic form, focused on the functions of language in children's life, and demonstrated the critical contribution of social interaction to their language development. But while both Halliday and colleagues, replicating his research (e.g. Painter 1984; Torr 1997)[2] have emphasised the importance of children's *meaning group* (Halliday 1975b), the dominant focus of research, even here, has remained on what the children said when, where, and how rather than on the significance of the sayings of the adults with whom the children interact[3].

These comments are not intended as a critique but as a brief account of the state of the art: Focus on the speaking subject's language is understandably the central concern in the study of language development. Nonetheless, it is well to remember that speakers do not speak just because they happen to have language. Saying is activated by speakers' perception of their social context, which implies the development of a near automatised mode of engaging with the socially fashioned universe. Underlying the spoken words are speakers' evaluations, beliefs, desires and intentions: their consciousness and social identity is intimately implicated in their acts of meaning. The development of language and social identity are not two separate processes: they are, in fact, deeply intertwined, each responding to the changing state of the other. This suggests a multiplicity of facets in learning how to mean, and Halliday (1980) has identified three of these facets as *learning language, learning through language and learning about language*. The aim of this chapter is to highlight the most fundamental kind of learning children do *through language*, with specific emphasis on the systematic variation in what they learn. I will argue that this variation correlates with their location in the typical modern societies with which we are most familiar today (Hasan 1989, 1992a, 1992b; Cloran 1994, 1999a, 2001; Williams 1995, 1999, 2001). Related to this is a subsidiary aim: to briefly identify the areas where systemic functional linguistics (SFL) needs to develop in order to account for these patterns of variability.

Attention to this kind of learning is important because arguably such learning contributes to the formation of mental dispositions, which is likely to colour every social action that children will participate in for a substantial part of their growing years, sometimes, perhaps, throughout their life. I will examine some adult-child casual conversations as this constitutes the major site for such learning. In their sayings, adults model more than words, structures and pronunciation: in fact, they define, at least initially, the child's world, giving it the power of 'reality' and the attraction of new possibilities open to exploration. This defined world is fashioned in the image of the adult world, clearly a necessary requirement for acculturation. In the literature on language development, children are treated as 'culturally neutral', but cultural neutrality is, in fact, just a brief episode in their life; they very soon become 'culturally specific'. The development of their consciousness begins with the internalisation of the world they live in – a process initiated in early infancy (Trevarthen 1974; Brazelton, Koslowski and Main 1974; Bateson 1975; Halliday 1973a, 1975b; Reddy, Hay, Murray and Trevarthen 1997). Reality is kaleidoscopic, and different representations of the world are construed by persons in different social locations (Bernstein 2000). In this construal, all semiotic modalities are active; language, however, plays a crucial role, and in a very important sense, young children's world is in the words they encounter in early life.

2 On learning through language: the meaning of semiotic mediation

The usefulness of language in learning is hardly ever questioned, but in most approaches to cognition/mental development, the idea of language itself tends to be somewhat questionable. Language is assigned a passive role by being treated as a relay system for individual's thoughts and experiences, as if thoughts exist, and experience takes shape independently of language. Rejecting this approach, I adopt the SFL perspective, where language has the active power of construing experience through meaning (Halliday and Matthiessen 1999; Bernstein 1971a), and so, of playing a crucial role in the formation of consciousness. This perspective was eloquently argued by Vygotsky (1962, 1978) in his powerful theory of the role of semiotic mediation in the development of 'higher mental functions'[4]. The term 'semiotic' obviously encompasses all modalities for meaning, though in his own investigation, Vygotsky singled out language as the most important modality in the making of human mind. In this chapter, I use 'semiotic mediation' to mean 'semiotic mediation by means of the modality of language'. Language is singled out here as the most relevant modality for three reasons:

1) this is in keeping with the dominant Vygotskian practice;
2) theories of the co-genesis of language and human mind (Deacon 1997; Greenfield 1997; Boncinelli 2001) provide evidence for the crucial role of language in the development of mind; and
3) the aim of this chapter is to foreground what children learn by engaging in discourse with adults; and the predominant modality employed in discourse is language. Whatever the contribution of the other modalities to discourse, language has to be viewed as the most indispensable in this context, thus making semiotic mediation by means of language central to the concerns of this chapter.

The semiotic activity of discourse mediates meaning, and Vygotsky (1978) convincingly argued the essential connection between linguistic meaning and mental development as for example in his discussion of concept formation. This Vygotskian theme resonates well with Halliday's expression 'learning through language'. If the mediation of meaning is the basis for the internalisation of concepts, and if meaning is mediated wherever the cultural practice of discourse occurs, it follows that discourse of any order is a site for the semiotic mediation of culturally based mental activity: the question is simply what it is that might be mediated in different kinds of discourses.

This interpretation gives the concept of semiotic mediation a breathtaking scope (Hasan 2002a), covering both mundane knowledge mediated in language use in everyday life and esoteric knowledge, mediated typically in specialised discourses of official pedagogy. But in the writings of Vygotsky and his colleagues, as well as in contemporary discussions and applications of the theory, the scope of semiotic mediation has been rather restricted: the concept is typically used to indicate its active power in mental activities specifically relevant to official pedagogic practices[5] – a limited interpretation, not free of problems (Hasan 1992a, 1995b, 2002a). If semiotic mediation is instrumental in the development of mental functions as Vygotsky claimed, then being based in discourse, it cannot be specialised to the construal of educational knowledge alone: it must construe other kinds of knowledge as well, since human discourse spans a vast area of experience. Significantly, the arguments for rejecting this limited though dominant interpretation of semiotic mediation are implied in Vygotsky's own writings. Vygotsky recognises two general categories of mental function: 'elementary', rooted in the biogenetic line of development, and 'higher', based in the social line of development, i.e., 'sociogenetic', which are logically semiotically mediated. Sociogenetic/higher mental activity 'breaks away from biological development and creates new forms of *culturally based* psychological processes' (Vygotsky 1978: 40; emphasis mine, *RH*). But, clearly, culturally based psychological processes are not limited to mediating only technical/ scientific concepts, or 'logical' thinking as in solving syllogistic puzzles, tests that Luria's Uzbek subjects failed (Luria 1976). The primary function of semiotic mediation in the life of young humans is to enable the internalisation of cultural designs essential to everyday living (Hasan 2002a). They must learn to recognise ways of being, doing and saying prevalent in their meaning group, their own speech fellowship, so as to act and to anticipate others' actions and reactions, something without which the easy automatised flow of everyday life can not be maintained. The primary achievement of semiotic mediation – both chronologically and logically – is the construal of such mundane knowledge, which is without doubt sociogenetic. It is irrelevant that educational systems either ignore such knowledge or render it unrecognisable as knowledge through their exotic theorisation. What matters is that (i) mundane knowledge is sociogenetic; (ii) so has to be semiotically mediated; and (iii) involves culturally based higher mental functioning (Hasan 1992c). Wertsch (1985b: 25) cites four distinguishing criteria of higher mental functions, derived from Vygotsky's writing:

1) shift of control from environment to the individual, that is, emergence of voluntary regulation;
2) the emergence of conscious realisation of mental process;
3) the social origins and the social nature of higher mental functions; and
4) the use of sign to mediate ... [them].

Clearly, mundane knowledge does possess the last two characteristics: its nature and origin are unquestionably social: since it is not inherited, it must clearly be semiotically mediated. But what about the first two? Because our daily life is not a series of random events, it follows that the mental activities for bringing them about must involve the emergence of voluntary regulation; and while their 'conscious realisation' would require some effort, this is hardly different from many specialised activities, such as multiplication, spelling, or even concept definition. From this point of view, Luria's Uzbek subjects were just as capable of higher mental functions, as the hypothetical schoolboy in Vygotsky's examples: the difference was not that the Uzbek peasant was stuck at the biogenetically based elementary mental functioning, while the schoolboy had moved on to the sociogenetic, i.e., culturally based higher mental functions; what differentiated them is the *kind* of cultural knowledge they had experienced, internalised and considered relevant, as Luria rightly pointed out: given their life experience, they had developed different 'habits of the mind', different forms of consciousness.

It is important to dissociate the process of semiotic mediation as such from that which it mediates: just as it is important to dissociate the valuation of different categories of knowledge from the objective basis for the categorisation of knowledge itself. There may or may not be good reasons for attaching high value to cognitive functions such as the formation of technical concepts, logical thinking, problem solving, inferential reasoning and other such activities highly prized in the world of academic knowledge. However, this cannot be taken as the sum-total of higher consciousness, although this is how the cognitive sciences conceptualise 'cognition'. By consciousness/mental disposition I mean nothing less in this chapter than 'mind' as Greenfield (1997) defines it – a 'personalised brain' whose unique character in each individual is fashioned by their unique experience of living. Since experience of living forms the basis of commonsense knowledge, the beginnings of the internalisation of such knowledge would offer the primary manifestations of the development of a child's mind[6]. Bernstein (e.g. 1971a, 2000) argued that the inclination to learn exotic, disembedded knowledge presupposes a sense of its relevance on the learners' part: to succeed in this enterprise, they must have already acquired a favourable mental disposition, which itself is fashioned in the experience of everyday life (Hasan 2002a, 2002b). This is not to claim that specialised, uncommon-sense knowledge is irrelevant to mental development; simply that it is secondary in terms of the child's history, and thus contingent on the already established mental disposition. Cognitive studies claim to be concerned with mental development, but judge 'cognition' by the mastery of secondary, specialised knowledge, which is just one aspect of human mind. Ironically, despite its narrower focus, cognition has, metaphorically speaking, hi-jacked the study of consciousness/mind, so that discussions of mental development turn into studies of the mastery of esoteric knowledge, witness much of neo-Vygotskian literature. Even the term 'learning' has become largely synonymous with the mastery of elements of educational knowledge. In fact, it is almost impossible to discuss any other kind of internalisation as an act of conceptualisation, or of mental development.

3 Naturally occurring discourse and semiotic mediation

The revival of Vygotskian perspectives on mental development has foregrounded the role of the social in making human minds. The cultural basis of semiotic mediation suggests that while an individual's mind is his/her own 'personalised brain', the process of personalisation entails interpersonal relations: as Vygotsky (1978: 57) pointed out, in the development of higher mental functions 'an interpersonal process is transformed into an intrapersonal one'. The definition of self is forged in interaction with others. The crucial part played in this process by semiotic mediation is most clearly manifested in unself-conscious discourse: it is here that interpersonal relations are semiotically created, maintained and changed. The situation is inherently complex: discourse is necessary for semiotic mediation to occur, but semiotic mediation is necessary for the formation of interpersonal relations which, in their turn, crucially influence the course of the development of interaction, thus affecting the outcome of the ongoing semiotic mediation. This is most evident in discourse with young children, still apprentices to their culture: naturally occurring everyday talk between mothers and children offers a rich resource for studying the semiotic mediation of emerging minds and personalities. This is so because young children tend mostly to talk with adults – the younger the child, the truer this observation – and, in the nature of things, the interacting adult tends to be some kind of care giver, a role still typically assigned to mothers. Below I present a brief account of such an investigation. The design of this research[7] has been described in previous chapters (especially chapters 3–5). The present chapter will focus on the management of context by adults in such discourse.

4 The potential of everyday talk: indications from mother-child dialogues

Many human activities are, in principle, capable of being undertaken without the intervention of talk. However, in practice, *material action* i.e., physically carried out action and *verbal action* i.e., language use, often co-occur. The specific configuration of these two kinds of human actions is significant to the character of on-going talk. Sometime the verbal action is *ancillary* to the material action; sometimes it has nothing much to do with it, but is, instead, *constitutive* of an entirely different activity, which can run alongside the material action without the latter significantly affecting the course of the former (Hasan 1999)[8]. Many of the activities of giving care to children are of this kind: they can be conducted, at least partially, without the assistance of language thus creating a site where constitutive verbal action becomes possible: while getting the child a snack or dressing her to go out, a mother can talk of almost anything depending on her disposition and the child's willingness to engage in that discourse. Certainly there are some restrictions on what can be talked about, e.g., the child's age and the mothers' preoccupations with the material action, but the most decisive factor in determining the character of the discourse appears to be the mothers' mental disposition. What she talks of and how she manages her discourse – what Bernstein (1996) called the classification and framing of discourse – has a flow-on effect on the kind of knowledge semiotically mediated. Here are two extracts from the data to illustrate this point.

Extract 1[9]

01 Mother	now Stephen, do you want a sandwich for lunch?
02 Stephen	yes
03	and some passionfruit
04 Mother	and some passionfruit
05	where is the passionfruit?
06 Stephen	um .. um the passionfruit is um .. um [?]
07	do you know where the passionfruit is?
08 Mother	no
09	you were walking around with it
10	what did you do with it?
11 Stephen	I don't remember
12 Mother	is it on the table?
13 Stephen	let me see .. it's under the table
14 Mother	under the table!
15 Stephen	yes .
16	here it is
17 Mother	ok .. right .. peanut butter sandwich?
18 Stephen	yeah .
19 Mother	you go to the table
20	and I'll bring it in .
21	there aren't many passionfruit out there at the moment
22 Stephen	why?
23 Mother	because .. passionfruit usually come
24	when it's warm
25	here, you sit here in nana's seat
26 Stephen	**whyc
27 Mother	**I'll put –
28 Stephen	why does nana like to sit here?

29 Mother	I'll put –
30	oh it's easy for her to get up
31	if she's sitting there ..

Extract 2 [10]

32 Mother:	come on, eat your tea please .
33 Karen:	could you put some more in there? .
34 Mother:	(warningly) Karen! .
35	give me it
36	eat your tea
37 Karen:	[?]
38 Mother:	mm?
39 Karen:	[?put] lemon in it
40 Mother:	well, eat some tea
41	or you don't get nothing
42 Karen:	I see how many [?] there are (talks to herself as mother pours drink)
43 Mother:	quick .
44	want the lid on it?
45 Karen:	no
46 Mother:	come on, eat your tea
47	less drink
48	and more eat .
49	did you hear what I said Karen?
50 Karen:	mm
51 Mother:	well, do it

[30 messages excluded from analysis here at this point]

81 Karen:	mummy that haven't got no sauce on it
82 Mother:	oh you've got plenty of sauce there now
83	now eat it
84 Karen:	on here
85 Mother:	oh there's plenty of sauce on your plate Karen
86	you don't need it on every single drop of tea
87 Karen:	eh?
88 Mother:	you don't need it on every little bit
89 Karen:	[? of tea]?
90 Mother:	mm
91 Karen:	is that [?tea]?
92 Mother:	that's sauce
93 Karen:	mm hot sauce

94 Mother: no, mint sauce
95 Karen: mince? .
96 why do you put mince sauce on here for?
97 Mother: 'mint' not 'mince'
98 Karen: mint
99 this mint?
100 Mother: use your spoon or your fork

Extract 1 begins with ancillary verbal action (1–20): language is used here to assist the material action of getting Stephen's lunch organised; but the mother's verbal action becomes informing as she chats with Stephen (21–31); this *informative episode*[11] presents Stephen the possibility of learning about 'passionfruit season' (21–24) and the 'logic in Nana's preference' for a particular chair (26–31). *An informative episode is construed by constitutive verbal action which offers the addressee the potential of internalising some element(s) of knowledge, irrespective of the domain to which the knowledge belongs.* In 1, the knowledge pertains to everyday living and appears in sharp contrast to classroom discourse, especially if compared with 'presentation' lessons which introduce to pupils concepts from specialised domains of knowledge, supposedly for the first time (Butt 2000). However, the boundary between the two categories of knowledge is permeable, as Extract 3 shows:

Extract 3

1 Mother: when you plant seeds from mandarins or oranges
2 sometimes you get very strange fruit
3 or sometimes you don't get much fruit at all
4 so you have to plant a tree that's been grafted – that's been stuck on
5 they're special trees that they make
6 by sticking one tree to another tree
7 Stephen: how do they stick it?
8 Mother: well, I think they cut it in a special way
9 they cut them in a special way
10 and they put them together
11 and then they bind stuff around the outside
12 to hold them together
13 till they grow together ..
14 they eventually grow together the same way as when – ..
15 if you cut yourself
16 the skin grows together again, doesn't it?
17 the two pieces of skin grow together again
18 well, the tree – the two bits of the tree grow back too

Like official pedagogic discourse, informative episodes in everyday talk give information in an explicit way. In other words, the semiotic mediation is *explicit* in both cases (Hasan 2002a): where at least one of the participants is conscious of the concepts being presented. Further, the information in such episodes is not tied to any immediate practical goal. The latter feature draws them closer to official pedagogic discourse which foregrounds *decontextualised language* (Bernstein 1971a; Cloran 1994; Donaldson 1978). However, as shown in the previous chapter, in everyday discourse, decontextualisation is often tempered by relating the information to the child's direct experience; extract 3 is a good example: here the mother relates the process of grafting trees to Stephen's physical experience, which helps make it intelligible for him (15–18). But for this, 3 could easily have been taken as a 'lesson' for young learners on an aspect of horticulture. The episode here is also fairly 'sustained', with 'grafting' elaborated at some length. The quality of sustaining a topic is essential to official pedagogy; however, in local pedagogy the construal of knowledge is fragmented, and the sustaining of topic occurs selectively, as illustrated by extract 2.

The general context for extract 2 is largely the same as for Extract 1, though the mother's repeated injunctions indicate that the meal is well past the preparation stage. The physical activity, i.e., the material action, appears to be uppermost in the mother's mind: for her, this is primarily an occasion for 'eating tea'. Of the mother's 24 messages, 12 revolve around 'eat your tea'; 7 control Karen's eating in other ways; two are paralinguistic; only 3 may be said to belong to a (minimal) informative episode, as indicated in table 1.

Table 1: One mother's construal of meal time context

Eat your tea	Further points of control	Informative episode
come on, eat your tea please (32)	mm (38)	that's sauce (92)
Karen, give me it, eat your tea (34-6)	quick! Want the lid on it? (43-4)	no, mint sauce (94)
well, eat some tea, or you don't get nothing (40-1)	oh, you've got plenty of sauce there now (82)	'mint', not 'mince' (97)
come on, eat your tea, less drink, and more tea, did you hear what I said (46-9)	oh, there's plenty of sauce on your plate, Karen; you don't need it on every single drop of tea (85-6)	
well, do it (51)	you don't need it on every bit (88)	
now eat it (83)	mm (90)	
	use your spoon or your fork (100)	

It might be thought that in this dialogue there was no opening for engaging in chat; but openings in dialogues are often made: one seizes the moment, the stray word, and takes off from there. For example, much could have been made of Karen's puzzlement: *is that [?tea]?* (91), but Karen's mother simply says *that's sauce* (92). This certainly gives information which identifies an object, and though the object is present in the context, the identification goes beyond the moment, as does the more specific information in her further corrective comments *no, mint sauce* (94) and *'mint', not 'mince'* (97). Establishing connection with the addressee's context is typical to the initiation of decontextualised discourse in some mother's talk: by making use of generalisations and explanations, mothers provide information which transcends spatio-temporal boundaries, but this topic itself invariably arises from something right there in the immediate situation. Viewed from this point of view, the informative episode in Extract 2 is not sustained: in fact, it could hardly be more minimal; and while it offers the possibility of internalising some knowledge, the knowledge consists of a category label. This minimal informative episode in the talk (91–100) presents at least three occasions for sustained informing action, as is clear from Karen's puzzled questions. If Karen's mother does not make use of this possibility, it is because her view of 'what goes' in this context renders such verbal action irrelevant. The analysis of her discourse with her child elsewhere shows that she habitually maintains strong classification of contextual boundaries: for her, meal times are for eating meals, bath times are for bathing (see chapter 7), and bed times for being in bed, not for doing anything else (discussion chapter 8). By contrast, Stephen's mother's classification of context is considerably weaker. Far from a random phenomenon, this difference between the two mothers is indicative of an orderly variation. Cloran (1994, 1999a) found that LAP mothers were relatively less likely to sustain topics long enough to allow explicit construal of concept(s). The implication is that children in the HAP social location will have participated more often in discourses that are much closer to the official instructional discourse.

One might be tempted to conclude that the difference between the two groups of children lies in what they know, i.e., the content of their knowledge. At one level this is true. At a deeper level, though, more crucial differences are being mediated: in experiencing different fashions of speaking (Whorf 1956), the two groups will form different mental habits, different orders of relevance, and in the end, through these ways of saying and meaning different conceptions of their own identities will have been mediated. To substantiate this large claim, I will examine some other patterns in child-adult discourse. These patterns are made up of semantic features, each of which by itself might appear quite insignificant, but in combination with others they become powerful indicators of habitual ways of meaning. These ways of meaning mediate more than 'meets the ear'.

Extract 4

1 Karen:	how did you get that?**
2	you didn't get out of [?]
3 Mother:	I walked over
4	and got it
5	didn't you see me?
6 Karen:	nup
7Mother:	you must be blind

Extract 5

1 Mother:	d'you love daddy?..
2	d'you love daddy?
3 Julian:	mm (affirmative)
4 Mother:	d'you love Rosemary?
5 Julian:	no
6 Mother:	why don't you love Rosemary? (Julian laughs)
7	why don't you love Rosemary? (Julian continues to laugh)
8 Mother:	you're a [?rat-bag] (realises child was teasing)
9 Julian:	I do
10 Mother:	[?]
11 Julian:	who else do you want me to love?

In extract 4, the mother's question *didn't you see me?* (5) is realised by a negative interrogative; and this is a pretty obvious fact. Such questions have the semantic feature [assumptive] and questions with this attribute typically imply the speaker already knows what the answer should be. Here, the assumed answer is something like *yes I saw you go out*. Failing to give this answer Karen is told *you must be blind* (7), implying *otherwise you would have seen me go out*. One might object that this appears to be too subtle an interpretation for a small child of this age. But extract 5 presents evidence to the contrary, for here Julian's *who else do you want me to love?* (11) has to be understood something as follows: *I infer from your question that you believe I should love Rosemary; so I wonder who else you think I ought to love*, which shows that Julian had got the point of *why don't you love Rosemary* (6,7). So, the habitual use of [assumptive] questions implies the belief on the part of the enquirer that s/he knows the addressee's mental map – what the addressee should be able to see or hear, how they should react to persons, objects and events, what they should know or believe to be the case. This suggests that most probably there exists a presupposition of close resemblance between the speaker's and addressee's mental life. Since, in this view, the other's mind is an open book, the need to 'reach the other' verbally is less urgent: under these conditions, verbal communication may appear less relevant. Contrast this semantic feature with another called [prefaced]: the two are diametrically opposed.

Extract 6

1 Mother: can you try and remind me to ring Pam this afternoon?
2 Kristy: mm [=yes]
3 why?
4 Mother: I'm going to ask her if she'll mind you one night next week
5 Kristy: mm
6 Mother: 'cause I'm going out to dinner with some of the ladies from the playgroup
7 because Sue is leaving
8 Kristy: pardon?*
9 pardon?
10 Mother: I'm going out with some of the ladies
11 because Sue is leaving
12 Kristy: mm
13 Mother: did you know that they are going to leave?
14 Kristy: no
15 Mother: they've been building a house
16 Kristy: mm
17 Mother: oh they haven't been building it
18 somebody else has been building it for them
19 and it's nearly finished
20 and they're going to move to their house in May
21 Kristy: why in May?
22 Mother: they're going to wait until the end of the school term
23 Kristy: mm
24 Mother: because Cathy goes to school now
25 and then she will change to her new school after **the holidays
26 Kristy: ** mm
27 Mother: if they'd moved earlier
28 she'd only go to the new school for a week or two
29 and then they'd have holidays you see
30 it would mess it up a bit for her

The mother's question *did you know that they are going to leave?* (13) has the semantic feature [prefaced], realised by a variety of projected interrogative. This question differs importantly from *are they going to leave?* The latter asks about the state of the world: is something about to happen in it or not;

the former asks about the addressee's state of knowledge: *do you or don't you know something*. [Prefaced] questions clearly imply that unlike the asker of the [assumptive] question, the speaker here does not assume knowledge of the addressee's mental map. The habitual use of the feature [prefaced] carries the implication that individual participants are unique; their sensations, reactions, knowledge or belief cannot be taken for granted: there is little or no assumption of similarity in the mental life of the interactants. Logically, then, such speakers would be quite unlikely to ask [assumptive] questions. It is in this sense that these two semantic features are diametrically opposed. But there is more to this story. Semiotic action is extraordinarily complex, and particularly so at the level of meaning, because most semantic features carry an intricate web of presuppositions and implications. The interpretation of utterances consists in 'reading' the meanings that are explicitly construed, as well as inferring the implied ones. I use the features [prefaced] and [assumptive] to develop this observation.

A necessary presupposition for smooth and continued semiotic interaction, e.g., everyday talk, is the existence of shared knowledge between the interactants. With the habitual use of [assumptive], the source of such knowledge is expected to lie in resembling selves; by contrast, the negation of this expectation is a condition for the habitual use of [prefaced]. This poses a problem: how to counteract the absence of shared knowledge? One possible solution is to make sayings such that they render the required information accessible. These contextual pressures, which arise from the speakers' conception of their social relation to the other, activate the choice of linguistic devices for elaboration. One such device is the semantic feature [related]. Messages with the feature [related] amplify the meaning of the message(s) to which they are related by making them more precise or by developing some aspect of their meaning. A good example is the mother's answer to Kristy's *why in May?* (21). It begins with *they're going to wait until the end of the school term* (22). She could have stopped there, but she goes on to produce six more [related] messages (24–25; 27–30), which develop the first message in her answer to make explicit the reasoning that supports Cathy's parents' decision to leave in May at the end of the school term (22) (chapter 5 for discussion). Further, if verbal communication is viewed as essential to meaning sharing, this calls for attention to other's sayings. In the present context, this means not ignoring questions, but being [responsive] to them, and providing [adequate] answers by addressing the question's query point. So the habitual use of the semantic feature [prefaced] is highly likely to 'attract' a cluster of other semantic features, namely, [related] messages, [responsive], and [adequate] answers. Since the feature [assumptive] is diametrically opposed to [prefaced], the cluster of semantic features the former attracts is highly likely to be the converse of that just discussed. With less value attached to language as a means of sharing knowledge, attending to the other's discourse is not an imperative: questions can be ignored; their meaning need not be amplified; answers could be minimal rather than detailed; so the feature [related] would be highly *unlikely* to occur under those conditions.

I have thus identified two clusters of semantic features; each has as nucleus either the semantic feature [prefaced] or [assumptive] which acts as the pivot, attracting other semantic features. The clustering together of 'sympathetic' elements around one nucleus is not unique to the semantic level. At the lexico-grammatical level, strong lexical nodes act as a 'magnet' for specific collocates. The node's inner nature supports predictions about what will go with what. The same is true of semantic features: a strong 'semantic node' will attract other predictable semantic features. Just as lexical clusters have become visible through large scale analysis of lexis, so various semantic clusters have emerged from the statistical results of the semantic analysis of a large amount of data in my research. This analogous pattern is not surprising given the solidary relation between wording and meaning. It is worth emphasising that the semantic nodes and the clusters they attract are important for the deep understanding of a discourse because they relate directly to the construal of context – a theme to which I will return in discussing the results of the semantic analysis. More specifically, the clusters under focus are relevant to the construal of the contextual component 'tenor'. Table 2 displays the result of the analysis of over 2000 questions that mothers asked their children, and their own answers to the children's questions:

Table 2: Attributes of mothers' questions and answers (h > l: $p < .0003$)

Question and answer attributes	**PCI**
Q[*prefaced*]*	0.69
A[*related*]*	0.68
A[*responsive*]*	0.67
Q[*related*]*	0.65
A[*adequate*]*	0.56
Q[*assumptive*]*	0.52
Q[confirm]	0.37
Q[ask]	0.21
Q[explain]	0.32
Eigenvalue	2.72
% Variance	30.20

(H > L: $p < .0003$)

The major contribution to the statistically highly significant semantic variation between the groups HAP (dominating) and LAP (dominated) is made by the

the semantic features marked with an asterisk; the remaining features, due to their low loading, are relatively irrelevant in the context of questions and answers. The foregrounded features are precisely the ones that make up the clusters discussed above. Note the negative loading of feature [assumptive], implying that high scoring subjects are highly unlikely to display it in their discourse. The feature [prefaced], by contrast, has the highest loading: the high scoring subjects are highly likely to have this feature in their discourse. Further, [related] questions/answers are highly likely in their discourse, and they are very likely to provide [responsive], [adequate] answers. Since the choice of the feature [assumptive] has a significance diametrically opposed to [prefaced], this implies mothers habitually using the feature [assumptive] are very unlikely to display the feature [related]; instead of being responsive to the questions, they are likely to ignore the questions and inclined to provide either minimal or inadequate answer.

But what have the above results to do with children's language development, or with the emergence of their identities, or with the formation of consciousness, i.e., their internalisation of the world they live in? As a short answer, see table 3, with the PCA result of children's questions and answers with the same semantic features as input:

Table 3: Attributes of children's questions and answers (h >l: p<.009)

Question and answer attributes	**PCI**
A[*related*]*	0.74
Q[*related*]*	0.63
Q[*confirm*]*	0.60
Q[*prefaced*]*	0.58
A[*adequate*]*	0.55
Q[*assumptive*]*	0.51
A[responsive]	0.34
Q[ask]	0.12
Q[explain]	0.00
Eigenvalue	2.37
% Variance	26.40

(H > L: p < .009)

That the two groups of children are following the maternal trend in ways of meaning to a significant extent is quite obvious. The realisational relation of semantics and lexicogrammar would argue that adults' talk has contributed to the development of both their ways of saying and of meaning. As to the shaping of their social identities, the results suggest that the presuppositions and assumptions found in their mothers' discourse are becoming relevant to children's discourse as well, who unmistakably indicate the same attitude to the other. It seems reasonable to suggest that maternal ways of asking and answering questions are significant in positioning children as discursive partners. In the dominating HAP group children are given greater discretion, treated as partners – individuals with equal rights. These perceptions become a part of their mental disposition, setting up expectations of discursive rights and obligations: in chapters 5 and 10 I have referred to the mental disposition thus produced as *individuated informativeness*. In the dominated LAP group, the maternal discourse positions children as not yet mature, therefore needing supervision. It would be in accordance with this view to give them less discretion: they are not so much equal partners in discourse as needing to be guided into appropriate forms of behaviour considered legitimate by the mother. At the same time, with the assumption of an intuitive knowledge of the other's mental map, there is an absence of social distance between them, which encourages a disposition of *personal trust*. Interpersonal relations thus assume greater significance than 'objective' information, which is so highly valued in the life of the privileged.

In view of these interpretations, the clusters of semantic features identified above are best seen as *formative motifs*[12]: their function is to play a role in forming identities and social relations. A *formative motif is a cluster of semantic features which are related to each other by a logic that underlies their configurative rapport*[13]. Such clusters are made up of meanings that are held together by a logical necessity, each cluster being built around one strong node, which bears some contextual presupposition giving rise to a set of implications. For a cluster to function as a formative motif, it acts not just as some localised meanings – e.g., the meaning of items such as *did you know, do you think, do you remember* – that are relevant but rather what is implied by their use as [preface]: it is the implied meanings that appear to be most relevant to a semantic cluster's capacity to function as a *formative motif*. The occurrence of the cluster in the discourse is typically prosodic: all relevant features of a cluster cannot be found in the same or even contiguous message(s); the elements of the cluster are dispersed throughout the discourse; they have no syntagmatic order. These characteristics of the semantic cluster have important consequences. The prosodic realisation of the clusters makes them invisible, and their role in the mediation of social identities and mental dispositions calls for a deep understanding of the nature of semiotic acts. This means that formative clusters are a means of *invisible semiotic mediation*, where interactants are very rarely, if ever, aware of the nature of what their discourse is mediating, even though the significance of some feature may be recognised. Julian, for example, recognises the implication of his mother's [assumptive] question, but it is highly unlikely that she sees it as part of a device capable of acting on her elaboration of information at some point in the discourse, or that such sayings play a crucial role in the formation of Julian's consciousness. So far as speakers are concerned, the very presence of *formative motifs* in their own discourse may never rise to the level of awareness. In their habitual use of the clusters of semantic features speakers' are not aware of doing anything special, extraordinary or noteworthy any more than they are aware of the patterns of wording relevant to the 'configurative rapport' when they use expressions such as *three days* and *a stick of butter* (cf. Whorf 1956): all they are doing is, simply speaking their social location, and their ideological stance – their unselfconscious, everyday casual discourse is a 'natural' expression of who they are, what their relation to the interactant is, and what they consider relevant.

It remains now to add a brief word about the relation between what I have called *informative episode* and *formative motifs*. These are not two physically separate phenomena: as the indicators of the speaker's ideological stance, *formative motifs* have a pervasive effect on the classification and framing of the discourse. Underlying the sustained *informative episodes* is the cluster of semantic features with the nucleus [prefaced], which functions as a *formative motif*, mediating an orientation to *individuated informativeness*. Return, for example, to the sustained form of *informative episodes* which mediate knowledge of some kind explicitly. The mothers producing such episodes, where knowledge, concepts, reasoning are laid out in front of the child – often in response to the child's question as for example in 3 or 6 – do not just make information accessible; they are also engaged in the semiotic mediation of a mental disposition, a social identity, even if they do not know they are doing this. The experience of receiving sustained explicit information in emotionally supportive environments develops in these children an orientation toward decontextualised knowledge. It becomes an aspect of their mental disposition, colouring their mental activities. This achievement of *invisible semiotic mediation* is likely to be far more significant in the life of these children than the actual elements of knowledge acquired through *explicit semiotic mediation* in the early years. Knowledge is a replaceable commodity, and is easily replaced every day: Santa Claus is fact one day, fiction the next; but the mental disposition and the sense of social identity that the adult's discourse develops in the child is something that requires extraordinary circumstances to diverge from its established course. The study of children's development thus takes us to their experiences, which invariably involve adults. And in the wake of the adults come issues associated with living in society. This, in today's world, often means pluralistic societies, where hierarchies, inequalities and differentiation are the other face of belonging to a particular group. To the extent that semiotic mediation is culturally based, it cannot be impervious to these social/cultural phenomena.

5 Tenor and the mediation of mental disposition: concluding remarks

The last section has attempted to present the complex nature of the interplay between social relations, semantic characteristics of discourse, and the working of semiotic mediation. The results in tables 2 and 3 indicate that the critical principle for explaining the orderly variation in the management of discourse is the social positioning of the speakers. The expression *social positioning of speaker* takes us to the notion of tenor in SFL's theorisation of context. This theory is rich and possesses the potential of throwing light on the processes that lead to the co-genesis of language and society. This is not to say that the details of such an enterprise have been fully worked out, but certainly at an abstract level a framework has been produced which lays the foundation of such description. This is evident from a consideration of figure 1 reproduced from Halliday (1999: 8).

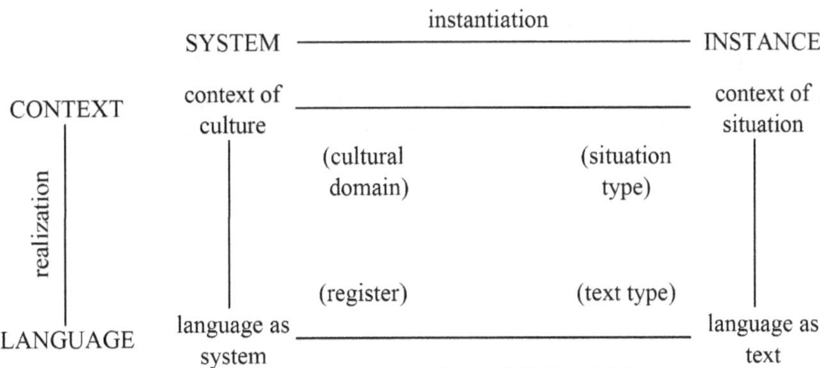

Figure 1: Language and context; system and instance

Note: Culture instantiated in situation, as system instantiated in text.

Culture realised in/construed by language; same relation as that holding between linguistic strata (semantics: lexicogrammar: phonology: phonetics).

Cultural domain and register are 'sub-systems': likeness viewed from 'system' end.

Situation type and text type are 'instance types': likeness viewed from 'instance' end.

But when it comes to details of description, the relationships that are formulated in the greatest detail in SFL are those towards the right margin of the figure. In particular, the theory tells us a good deal more about context of situation than about context of culture. If context of situation is to context of culture as text is to the system of language, then by analogy, so far as context theory in SFL is concerned it is the theory of text, without an ability to show its relation to the theory of language system, which is clearly far from desirable. In other words, the specific ways that cultural preoccupations are construed by the system of language is an issue much in need of deeper exploration.

In the description of context of situation, three aspects have been long recognised in SFL (Halliday, Macintosh and Stevens 1964): (i) Field, i.e., social action: what is going on?; (ii) Tenor, i.e., social relation: who is taking part in the goings on?; and (iii) Mode, i.e., social contact: how the speaker and the addressee encounter each other, both materially and semiotically? All three are relevant to the nature and management of the discourse, but tenor, i.e., social relation is perhaps the most important component in understanding the relevance of social positioning to semiotic mediation. I see social positioning with its intimate relation to ideological stance as a powerful concept for linking tenor in the context of situation to the most fundamental principles for the organisation of societies in the context of culture. 'Ideology' as Bernstein (1996: 30) tells us, 'is a way of establishing relations. *It is not a content, but a way in which relationships are made*' (my emphasis, RH). It is their ideological stance that makes the mothers in the reported research view the contexts the way they do, the way they establish their relationship with their child; the organisation and character of their discourse, i.e., the details of their social practice, are a realisation of who they are, and how their own personal identities were formed. But in the current state of the development of context theory it is not at all obvious how these relations can be described. SFL needs to develop a principled way of describing the instance – i.e., the context of situation – in such a way that it becomes evident what the underlying system is like. Admittedly, the description of culture as system is not an element of the study of the nature of language. My concern is not with arid field demarcations, but rather with how to describe context of situation in a way that sheds light both on the similarities and differences between contexts such as those relevant to extract 1 and 2; or those on the basis of which the occurrence of a particular formative motif may be predicted. The solution to these problems needs much time and effort; it is nonetheless an urgent requirement for a model whose object of study is *language as social semiotic*.

Notes

1 For some examples, see Beveridge (1982).

2 See the contributions of Halliday, Matthiessen, and Painter in Williams and Lukin (2004) for a more detailed account of aspects of the SFL approach to language development. See also Halliday (2003) for further information.

3 More accurately, Painter (1989, 1999) did go beyond words and sentences into the adults' role in modelling genres (1989) as well as in the development of children's cognitive abilities (1999). I will comment later on the popular conceptualisation of the term 'cognitive', a central aspect of which to my understanding is the main concern of Painter (1999).

4 Higher mental functions are sometimes also called 'higher consciousness' (cf. Vygotsky (1978).

5 In his writing on infants learning to mean, Vygotsky (1962, 1978) indicates the power of this concept, e.g., in his discussion of how, through semiotic mediation, the infant comes to recognise a specific physical action, not as mere bodily movement, but as 'gesture', a particular semiotic device for signaling an intersubjective meaning.

6 Lave (1997) has highlighted some crucial differences between knowledge acquired in the living of life and the disembedded knowledge of designed instruction.

7 Funding by the Australian Research Council and Macquarie University Research Grant Scheme is gratefully acknowledged. Note certain segments have been deleted at this point to avoid too much repetition.

8 An account of the analysis of human action relevant to discourse organisation is presented in Hasan (1999) and Butt (2008b). Comments on human action types in this chapter are based on Hasan (1999, especially the systemic choices as shown in figure 3).

9 For a discussion of larger portions of the dialogue to which extract 1 belongs, see Cloran (1999b). Transcription conventions are shown below:

number in 1st column	indicates message number in this extract;
(?I wasn't)	segment unintelligible; enclosed is best guess on the basis of context and co-text;
**no	double asterisk paired across contiguous turns show point of overlap;
you didn't –	dash indicate message was left incomplete;
didn't you?*	question followed by a single asterisk indicates response time was not allowed;
(?)	this segment was unintelligible; no clues to help interpretation;

[PETE CRIES]	situational information based on recorded information.
let me see...	dots indicate longer pause than expected in ongoing speech tempo

10 The full dialogue to which this extract belongs is found in Hasan (2000).

11 I have referred to this way of talking as the *informative mode* (Hasan 2002b). On reflection, *informative episode* may be better, since 'mode' could be confused with 'mode of discourse', appearing closer to 'contact' (Hasan 2001) than to the characterisation of a discursive segment.

12 Hasan (2000b) refereed to this as *formative mode*; *formative motif* is preferred to avoid confusion with mode as in mode of discourse.

13 I use *configurative rapport* with apologies to Whorf (1956) in a different context from his to convey the meaning that there is a 'natural' prehension in the terms of the cluster.

References

Abercrombie, D. (1965) *Studies in Phonetics and Linguistics*. London: Oxford University Press (Language and Language Learning, 10).

Alatis, J. E. (1993) (ed.) *Language, Communication and Social Meaning: Georgetown University Round Table Conference on Languages and Linguistics 1992*. Washington, DC: Georgetown University Press.

Ammon, U., Dittmar, N. and Mattheier, K. J. (eds) (1987) *Soziolinguistiks/ Sociolinguistics: An International Handbook of the Science of Society, Vol 1*. Berlin: Walter de Gruyter.

Antilla, A. (2002) Variation and phonological theory. In J. K.Chambers, P. Trudgill and N. Schilling-Estes (eds).

Antilla, R. (1989) *Historical and Comparative Linguistics*. Amsterdam: John Benjamins.

Apple, M. W. (ed.) (1982) *Cultural and Economic Reproduction in Education: Essays on Class, Ideology and the State*. London: Routledge and Kegan Paul.

Ash, S. (2002) Social class. In J. K. Chambers, P. Trudgill and N. Schilling-Estes (eds).

Ashworth, E. (1973) *Language in the Junior School*. London: Edward Arnold.

Atkinson, P. (1985) *Language, Structure and Reproduction: an Introduction to the Sociology of Basil Bernstein*. London: Methuen.

Austin, J. L. (1980) *How to Do Things with Words*. Revised ed., edited by J. O. Urmson and M. Sbisá. Oxford: Oxford University Press. 1st published, 1962.

Bailey, C. J. N. and Shuy, R. W. (eds) (1973) *New Ways of Analysing Variation in English*. Washington, DC: Georgetown University Press.

Baker, G. P. and Hacker, P. M. S. (1988) *Wittgenstein: rules, grammar and necessity: Volume 2 of an Analytical Commentary on the Philosophical Investigations*. London: Blackwell.

Bar-Hillel, Y. (1970) Argumentation in pragmatic languages. In *Aspects of Language: essays and lectures on philosophy, linguistic philosophy and methodology of language* 206–21. Amsterdam: North-Holland Publishing Company.

Barwise, J. and Perry, J. (1983) *Situation and Attitudes*. Cambridge, Mass.: MIT Press.

Barwise, J. (1988) On the circumstantial relation between meaning and content. In U. Eco, M. Santambrogio and P. Violi (eds).

Barwise, J. (1989) *The Situation in Logic*. CSLI Lecture Notes 17. Stanford: Center for the Study of Language and Information.

Bateson, G. (1972a) *Steps to an Ecology of Mind*. New York: Ballantine Books.

Bateson, G. (1972b) The logical categories of learning and communication. In Bateson, 1972a.

Bateson, G. (1979) *Mind and Nature: A Necessary Unity*. New York: Bantam Books.

Bateson, G. (1987) Men are grass: metaphor and the world of mental process. In W. I. Thompson (ed.) *Gaia: a Way of Knowing*. Great Barrington: Lindisfarne Press.

Bayley, R. (2002) The quantitative paradigm. In J. K. Chambers, P. Trudgill and N. Schilling-Estes (eds).

Benson, J. D. and Greaves, W. S. (eds) (1985) *Systemic Perspectives on Discourse, Volume 1: Selected Theoretical Papers from the 9th International Systemic Workshop*. Norwood, N. J.: Ablex.

Benson, J.D., Cummings, M. J. and Greaves, W. S. (eds) (1988) *Linguistics in a Systemic Perspective*. Amsterdam: John Benjamins.

Berger, P. L. and Luckman, T. (1971) *The Social Construction of Reality*. Harmondsworth: Penguin.

Bernstein, B. (1971a) *Class Codes and Control, Vol 1: Theoretical Studies toward a Sociology of Language*. London: Routledge and Kegan Paul.

Bernstein, B. (1971b) A sociolinguistic approach to socialization: with some reference to educability. Reprinted in J. J. Gumperz and D. Hymes (eds) 1972.

Bernstein, B. (1971c) Social class, language and socialization. In A. S. Abramson et al. (eds) *Current Trends in Sociolinguistics, Vol 12*. The Hague: Mouton. Repr. In Bernstein 1971a.

Bernstein, B. (ed.) (1973) *Class Codes and Control, Vol 2: Applied Studies towards Sociology of Language*. London: Routledge & Kegan Paul.

Bernstein, B. (1975a) *Class, Codes and Control, Vol 3: toward a Theory of Educational Transmission*. London: Routledge & Kegan Paul.

Bernstein, B. (1975b) On the classification and framing of educational knowledge. In R. Brown (ed.) *Knowledge, Education, and Cultural Change*. Tavistock Publications. 1st printed in Bernstein 1971a. Revised edition, reprinted in Bernstein 1975a)

Bernstein, B. (1982) Codes, modalities and processes of cultural reproduction: a model. In M. W. Apple (ed.). Reprinted in revised form in Bernstein 1990.

Bernstein, B. (1986) On pedagogic discourse. In J. G. Richardson (ed.) *Handbook of Theory and Research in the Sociology of Education*. New York, Greenwood Press. Reprinted in revised form in Bernstein 1990.

Bernstein, B. (1987a) Social class, codes and communication. In U. Ammon, N. Dittmar and K. J. Matthier (eds). Reprinted in revised form in Bernstein 1990.

Bernstein, B. (1987b) Elaborated and restricted codes: an overview 1958–85. Occasional Papers No 2. Amsterdam: Amsterdam University Centre for Race and Ethnic Studies. Revised version, reprinted in Bernstein 1990.

Bernstein, B. (1990) *The Structuring of Pedagogic Discourse, Vol IV: Class, Codes and Control*. London: Routledge.

Bernstein, B. (1996) *Pedagogy, Symbolic Control and Identity: Theory, Research, Critique.* London: Taylor & Francis.

Bernstein, B. (2000) *Pedagogy, Symbolic Control and Identity: Theory, Research, Critique.* Oxford: Rowan and Littlefield (2nd edi. revised).

Berry, M. (1981) Systemic linguistics and discourse analysis: a multilayered approach to exchange structure. In M. Coulthard and M. Montgomery (eds) *Studies in Discourse Analysis*. London: Routledge and Kegan Paul.

Berry, M. (1982) Review of Halliday 1978. *Nottingham Linguistic Circular* 11: 64-94.

Beveridge, M. (ed.) (1982) *Children Thinking through Language*. London: Arnold.

Biber, D. (1988) *Variation Across Speech and Writing*. Cambridge: Cambridge University Press.

Boas, F. (1911) Introduction to the Handbook of American Indian Languages. Vol 40.1, Bulletin of the Bureau of American Ethnology. Washington, DC: Smithsonian Institution. Reprinted in C. I. J. Stuart (ed.) *Report of the Fifteenth Annual Round Table Meeting on Linguistics and Language Study* (Monograph Series in Language and Linguistics 17).

Boncinelli, E. (2001) Erasmus lecture: brain and mind. *European Review* 9 (4): 389–398.

Bottomore, T. B. and Rubel, M. (eds) (1976) *Karl Marx: Selected Writings in Sociology and Social Philosophy*. Harmondsworth: Penguin. 1st published 1958; 1st Penguin edition 1963.

Bourdieu, P. (1977) *Outline of a Theory of Practice.* Translated by R. Nice. Cambridge: Cambridge University Press.

Bourdieu, P. (1990) *The Logic of Practice.* Translated by R. Nice. Cambridge: Cambridge University Press.

Bourdieu, P. (1991) *Language and Symbolic Power*. Translated by G. Raymond and M. Adamson, edited by J. B. Thompson. (1st Paper back edition). Cambridge: Polity Press.

Brazelton, T. B., Koslowski, B. and Main, M. (1974) The origins of reciprocity: the early mother-infant interaction. In M. Lewis and L. A. Rosenblum (eds) *The Effects of the Infant on Its Caregiver*. New York: Wiley.

Brown, P. and Levinson, S. (1983) *Politeness: Some Universals in Language Usage*. Cambridge: Cambridge University Press.

Brown, R. and Lenneberg, E.H. (1954) A study in language and cognition. *Journal of Abnormal and Social Psychology* 49(3).

Bruner, J. S. (1970) *Poverty and Childhood.* Detroit: Merril-Palmer Institute.

Bűhler, K. (1990) *Theory of Language: The Representational Function of Language*. Translated by D. F. Goodwin. Amsterdam: Benjamins. 1st published, Jena: Gustav Fisher Verlag,1934.

Bullowa, M. (ed.) (1979) *Before Speech: The Beginning of Interpersonal Communication*. Cambridge: Cambridge University Press.

Burton, D. (1983) I think they know that: aspects of English language work in primary classrooms. In M. Stubbs and H. Hillier (eds).

Butler, C. S. (1985) *Systemic Linguistics: Theory and Application*. London: Batsford Academic.

Butler, C S. (1988) Politeness and the semantics of modalized directives. In J. D. Benson, M. J. Cummings and W. S. Greaves (eds).

Butt, D. (1983) Ideational meaning and the mirror of nature. Paper presented at the Eighth Congress of the Applied Linguistics Association of Australia, La Trobe University, Melbourne.

Butt, D. (1984) *To Be without a Description of to Be: the Relationship between Theme and Lexicogrammar in the Poetry of Wallace Stevens*. Unpublished Doctoral dissertation, Sydney: Dept of English and Linguistics, Macquarie University.

Butt, D. (1989a) *Talking and Thinking: the Patterns of Behaviour*. Oxford: Oxford University Press.

Butt, D. (1989b) The object of language. In R. Hasan and J. R. Martin (eds).

Butt, D. (2000) Critical abstractions and rhetoric: the latent order of pedagogic discourse. In D. Butt and C. M. I. M. Matthiessen, *The Meaning Potential of Language: Mapping Meaning Systemically*. Department of Linguistics: Macquarie University, Sydney. Mimeo.

Butt, D. (2008a) The robustness of realizational systems. In J. J. Webster (ed.) *Meaning in Context:Sstrategies for Implementing Intelligent Applications of Language Studies*. London: Continuum.

Butt, D. (2008b) *Parameters of Context: On Establishing the Similarities and Differences between Social Processes*. Department of Linguistics: Macquarie University, Sydney. Mimeo.

Butt, D. and Cloran, C. (1988) Language and the transition from home to school. In Gerot et al. (eds).

Chambers, J. K. and Trudgill, P. (1980) *Dialectology*. Cambridge: Cambridge University Press.

Chambers, J. K., Trudgill, P. and Schilling-Estes, N. (eds) (2002) *The Handbook of Language Variation and Change*. London: Blackwell.

Chloupek, J., Nekvapil, J. et. al. (eds) (1987) *Reader in Czech Sociolinguistics*. Amsterdam: Benjamins.

Chomsky, N. (1965) *Aspects of the Theory of Syntax*. Cambridge, MA: MIT Press.

Christie, F. (1988) The construction of knowledge in the junior primary school. In Gerot et al. (eds).

Christie, F. (1989) Language development in education. In R. Hasan and J. R. Martin (eds)

Cloran, C. (1987) Negotiating new contexts in conversation. *Occasional Papers in Systemic Linguistics, Vol 1*. Nottingham University.

Cloran, C. (1989) Learning through language: the social construction of gender. In R. Hasan and J. R. Martin (eds).

Cloran, C. (1994) *Rhetorical Units and Decontextualization: an Enquiry into some Relations of Context, Meaning and Grammar. Monograph in Systemic Linguistics, No 6.* Nottingham: Department of English Studies, Nottingham University.

Cloran, C. (1995) Defining and relating text segments: subject and theme in discourse. In R. Hasan and P. H. Fries (eds).

Cloran, C. (1999a) Context, material situation and text. In M. Ghadessy (ed.).

Cloran, C. (1999b) Contexts for learning. In F. Christie (ed.) *Pedagogy and the Shaping of Consciousness: Linguistic and Social Factors*. London: Cassell.

Cloran, C. (2001) Socio-semantic variation: different wordings, different meanings. In L. Unsworth (ed.) *Researching Language in Schools and Communities: Functional Linguistic Perspectives* 152–83. London: Cassell.

Cloran, C., Butt, D and Williams, G. (eds) (1996) *Ways of Saying, Ways of Meaning: Selected Papers of Ruqaiya Hasan.* London: Cassell.

Cohen, J. L. (1981) Can human irrationality be experimentally demonstrated?, *The Behavioural and Brain Sciences* 4: 317–370.

Cole, M. (1976) Foreword. In. Luria, A. R, *Cognitive Development*. Cambridge, MA: Harvard University Press.

Connell, R. W. (1977) *Ruling Class, Ruling Culture: Studies of Conflict, Power and Hegemony in Australian Life*. Cambridge: Cambridge University Press.

Connell, R. W. (1983) *Which Way is Up? Essays on Class, Sex and Culture.* Sydney: Allen and Unwin.

Connell, R. W. (1988) Social power, language and education. In Gerot et al. (eds).

Crystal, D. (ed.) (1991) *A Dictionary of Linguistics and Phonetics*, 3rd edition. Oxford: Oxford University Press.

Cummins, R. (1989) *Meaning and Mental Representation.* A Bradford Book. Cambridge, Mass.: MIT Press.

Damasio, A. (2000) *The Feeling of What Happens: Body, Emotion and the Making of Consciousness*. London: Vintage.

Daneš, F. (1987) On Prague School functionalism in linguistics. In Dirven and Fried (eds).

Davidse, K. (1987) M. A. K. Halliday's functional grammar and the Prague School. In Dirven and Fried (eds).

Deacon, T. (1997) *The Symbolic Species: the Co-Evolution of Language and the Human Brain*. London: Penguin.

Dearden, R. F., Hirst, P. H. and Peters, R. S. (1972) (eds) *Education and the Development of Reason.* London: Routledge & Kegan Paul.

Derrida, J. (1974) *Of Grammatology*. Translated by G. C. Spivak. Princeton: The Johns Hopkins University Press.

Dirven, R. and Fried, V. (eds) (1987) *Functionalism in Linguistics. LLSEE Vol 20*. Amsterdam: Benjamins.

Dittmar, N. (1976) *Sociolinguistics: a Critical Survey of Theory and Application.* London: Edward Arnold.
Donaldson, M. (1978) *Children's Minds*. London: Fontana.
Douglas, M. (1975) In the nature of things. In *Implicit Meanings: Essays in Anthropology*. London: Routledge & Kegan Paul.
Dressler, W. U. (ed.) (1978) *Current Trends in Text Linguistics*. Berlin: Walter de Gruyter.
Dunbar, R. I. M. (1996) *Grooming, Gossip and the Evolution of Language*. London: Faber and Faber.
Dunbar, R. I. M. (2003) The social brain: mind, language and society in evolutionary perspective. *Annual Review of Anthropology* 32: 163–81.
Durkheim, E. (1964) The Division of Labour in Society. Translated by G. Simpson. New York: The Free Press.
Eco, U., Santambrogio, M. and Violi, P. (eds) (1988) *Meaning and Mental Representations*. Bloomington: Indiana University Press.
Edelman, G. M. and Tononi, G. (2000) *Consciousness: How Matter Becomes Imagination.* London: Penguin Books.
Edwards, A. D. (1976) *Language in Culture and Class*. London: Heinemann.
Elshtain, J. B. 1981. *Public Man, Private Woman.* Oxford: Martin Pobertson.
Fairclough, N. 1989. *Language and Power*. London: Longmans.
Fauconnier, G. (1988) Quantifications, roles and domains. In U. Eco, M. Santambrogio and P. Violi (eds).
Fawcett, R. P., Halliday M. A. K., Lamb, S. M. and Makkai, A. (eds) (1984) *The Semiotics of Culture and Language Vol 1: Language as Social Semiotic*. London: Frances Pinter.
Firth, J. R. (1935) The technique of semantics. *Transactions of the Philological Society*. Reprinted in J. R. Firth, 1957.
Firth, J. R. (1950) Language and personality in society. *The Sociological Review 42*. Reprinted in J. R. Firth, 1957.
Firth, J. R. (1957) *Papers in Linguistics* 1934–1951. London: Oxford University Press.
Fishman, J. A. (ed.) (1968) *Readings in the Sociology of Language*. The Hague: Mouton.
Fodor, J. D. (1977) *Semantics*. New York: Crowell.
Foley, J. A. (ed.) (2004) *Language, Education and Discourse: Functional Approaches*. London: Continuum
Friedrich, P. (1980) Linguistic relativity and the order-to-chaos continuum. In J. Maquet (ed.) *On Linguistic Anthropology*. Malibu, CA: Undena Publications.
Gardin, B. and Marcellesi, J. B. (1987) The subject matter of sociolinguistics. In U. Ammon, N. Dittmar and K. J. Matthier (eds).
Gerot, L., Oldenburg (Torr), J. and van Leeuwen, T. (1988) *Language and Socialization: Home and School. Proceedings from the Working Conference on Language in Education.* Sydney: Macquarie University.

Giddens, A. and Held, D. (eds) (1982) *Classes, Power and Conflict: Classical and Contemporary Debates*. London: Macmillan.
Gleick, J. (1987) *Chaos: Making a New Science*. Cardinal: Sphere Books.
Goffman, E. (1967) *Interaction Ritual: Essays on Face to Face Behaviour*. New York: Anchor Books.
Goffman, E. (1983) *Forms of Talk*. Philadelphia: University of Pennsylvania Press.
Goody, E. N. (ed.) (1978) *Questions and Politeness: Strategies in Social Interaction*. Cambridge: Cambridge University Press.
Greenfield, S. (1995) *A Journey to the Centres of the Mind: Toward a Science of Consciousness*. New York: W. H. Freeman & Co.
Greenfield, S. (1997) *The Human Brain: a guided tour*. London: Weidenfield and Nicolson.
Gregory, M. (1967) Aspects of varieties differentiation. *Journal of Linguistics* 3(2): 177–98
Gumperz, J. (ed.) (1982a) *Language and Social Identity*. Cambridge: Cambridge University Press.
Gumperz, J. (1982b) *Discourse Strategies*. Cambridge: Cambridge University Press.
Gumperz, J. J. and Hymes, D. (eds). (1986) Directions in Sociolinguistics: The Ethnography of Communication. London: Blackwell. 1st published New York: Holt, Rinehart and Winston, 1972.
Guy, G. R. (1988) Language and social class. In F. J. Newmeyer (ed.).
Habermas, J. (1970a) Towards a theory of communicative competence. *Inquiry* 13: 360–75.
Habermas, J. (1970b) On systematically distorted communication. *Inquiry* 13: 205–18.
Habermas, J. (1984) *The Theory of Communicative Action, Vol 1: Reason and the Rationalization of the Society.* London: Heinemann.
Halliday, M. A. K. (1961) Categories of the theory of grammar. *Word* 17(3): 242–92. Reprinted in J. J. Webster (ed.) *The Collected Works of M. A. K. Halliday, Vol 1: On Grammar*. London: Continuum 2002.
Halliday, M. A. K. (1967) *Intonation and Grammar in British English* (Janua Linguarum Series Practica 48). The Hague: Mouton.
Halliday, M. A. K. (1966–68) Notes on theme and transitivity in English. *Journal of Linguistics*. 3; 3.1; 4. Reprinted in J. J. Webster (ed.) *The Collected Works of M. A. K. Halliday, Vol. 7: Studies in English Language*. London: Continuum, 2005.
Halliday, M. A. K. (1968) Users and uses of English. In J. A. Fishman (ed.). 1st published as chapter 4 in Halliday, McIntosh and Strevens 1964; reprinted in J. J. Webster (ed.) *The Collected Works of M. A. K. Halliday, Vol. 10: Language and Society*. London: Continuum, 2007.

Halliday, M. A. K. (1969a) Options and functions in the English clause. *Brno Studies in English* 8. Reprinted in J. J. Webster (ed.) *The Collected Works of M. A. K. Halliday, Vol. 7: Studies in English Language.* London: Continuum 2005.

Halliday, M. A. K. (1969b) Relevant models of language. *The State of Language, Special Issue of Educational Review* 22(1): 26–73. Birmingham: University of Birmingham. Reprinted in J. J. Webster (ed.) *The Collected Works of M. A. K. Halliday, Vol. 4: The Language of Early Childhood.* London: Continuum 2003.

Halliday, M. A. K. (1970) Language structure and language function. In J. Lyons (ed.) N*ew Horizons in Linguistics* 140–65. Harmondsworth: Penguin. Reprinted in J. J. Webster (ed.) *The Collected Works of M. A. K. Halliday, Vol 1: On Grammar*. London: Continuum 2002.

Halliday, M. A. K. (1973a) *Explorations in the Functions of Language*. London: Edward Arnold.

Halliday, M. A. K. (1973b) Towards a sociological semantics. In Halliday 1973a. Reprinted in J. J. Webster (ed.) *The Collected Works of M. A. K. Halliday, Vol. 3: Language and Linguistics*. London: Continuum 2003.

Halliday, M. A. K. (1974a) A sociosemiotic perspective on language development. Bulleting of the School of Oriental and African Studies, 37(1): 98–118. Reprinted in J. J. Webster (ed.) *The Collected Works of M. A. K. Halliday, Vol. 4: Language of Early Childhood.* London: Continuum 2003.

Halliday, M. A. K. (1974b) *Language and Social Man*. (Schools Council Programme in Linguistics and English Teaching: Papers Series II, Vol 3). London: Longman. Reprinted in J. J. Webster (ed.) *The Collected Works of M. A. K. Halliday, Vol 10: Language and Society*. London: Continuum 2007.

Halliday, M. A. K. (1975a) Language as social semiotic: towards a general sociolinguistic theory. In A. Makkai and V. B. Makkai (eds) *The First LACUS Forum* 17–46. Columbia, SC: Hornbeam Press. Reprinted in J. J. Webster (ed.) *The Collected Works of M. A. K. Halliday, Vol 10: Language and Society*. London: Continuum 2007.

Halliday, M. A. K. (1975b) *Learning How to Mean: explorations in the development of language*. London: Edward Arnold. Reprinted in J. J. Webster (ed.) *The Collected Works of M. A. K. Halliday, Vol 4: The Language of Early Childhood*. London: Continuum 2003.

Halliday, M. A. K. (1975c) Sociological aspects of semantic change. In L. Heilmann (ed.) *Proceedings of the Eleventh International Congress of linguists* (ed.): Bologna: Il Mulino. Reprinted in J. J. Webster (ed.) *Collected Works of M. A. K. Halliday, Vol 10: Language and Society*. London: Continuum 2007.

Halliday, M. A. K. (1976a) Anti-languages. *American Anthropologist*. 78 (3): 570–84. Reprinted in J. J. Webster (ed.) *Collected Works of M. A. K. Halliday, Vol 10: Language and Society*. London: Continuum 2007.

Halliday, M. A. K. (1976b) *System and Function in Language: Selected Papers*, edited by Gunther R Kress. London: Oxford University.

Halliday, M. A. K. (1977) Text as semantic choice in social context. In T. A. van Dijk and J. S. Petőfi (eds) *Grammars and Descriptions*. Berlin: Walter de Gruyter. Reprinted in J. J. Webster (ed.) *Collected Works of M. A. K. Halliday, Vol 2: Linguistic Studies of Text and Discourse*. London: Continuum 2002.

Halliday, M. A. K. (1978) *Language as Social Semiotic: the Social Interpretation of Language and Meaning*. London: Arnold.

Halliday, M. A. K. (1979a) Modes of meaning and modes of expression: types of grammatical structure and their determination by different semantic functions. In D. J. Allerton, E. Carney and D. Holdcroft (eds) *Function and Context in Linguistic Analysis*. Cambridge: Cambridge University Press. Reprinted in J. J. Webster (ed.) *Collected Works of M. A. K. Halliday, Vol 1: On Grammar*. London: Continuum 2002.

Halliday, M. A. K. (1979b) One child's protolanguage. In M. Bullows (ed.) *Before Speech: the beginning of interpersonal communication*. Cambridge: Cambridge University Press. Reprinted in J. J. Webster (ed.) *Collected Works of M. A. K. Halliday, Vol 4: The Language of Early Childhood*. London: Continuum 2003.

Halliday, M. A. K. (1980) Three aspects of children's language development: learning language, learning through language, learning about language. In Y. Goodman, M. M. Haussler and D. M. Strickland (eds) *Oral and Written Language Development: impact on schools*. (Proceedings from the 1979–1980 Impact Conferences) International Reading Association and National Council of Teachers of English 7–19. Reprinted in J. J. Webster (ed.) *Collected Works of M. A. K. Halliday, Vol 4: The Language of Early Childhood*. London: Continuum 2003.

Halliday, M. A. K. (1984a) Language as code and language as behaviour: a systemic functional interpretation of the nature and ontogenesis of dialogue. In R. P. Fawcett, M. A. K. Halliday, S. M. Lamb and A. Makkai (eds) *The Semiotics of Culture and Language, Vol 1*. London: Frances Pinter. Extracts in J. J. Webster (ed.) *Collected Works of M. A. K. Halliday, Vol 4: The Language of Early Childhood*. London: Continuum 2003.

Halliday, M. A. K. (1984b) On the ineffability of grammatical categories. In A. Manning, P. Martin and K. McCalla (eds) *The Tenth LACUS Forum*. Columbia: Hornbeam Press. Reprinted in J. J. Webster (ed.) *Collected Works of M. A. K. Halliday, Vol 1: On Grammar*. London: Continuum 2002.

Halliday, M. A. K. (1985a) *An Introduction to Functional Grammar*. London: Edward Arnold. Revised 2nd edition, 1994.

Halliday, M. A. K. (1985b) Context of situation, Chapter 1 in Halliday and Hasan, 1985.

Halliday, M. A. K. (1987) Language and the order of nature. In N. Fabb, D. Attridge, A. Durant and C. McCabe (eds) *The linguistics of Writing: Arguments between Language and Literature* 135–54. Manchester: Manchester University Press. Reprinted in J. J. Webster (ed.) *Collected Works of M. A. K. Halliday, Vol 3: On Language and Linguistics*. London: Continuum 2003.

Halliday, M. A. K. (1988b) On the language of physical science. In M. Ghadessy (ed.) *Registers of Written English: Situational Factors and Linguistic Features* 162–78. London: Frances Pinter. Reprinted in *The Collected Works of M. A. K. Halliday, Vol 5: The Language of Science.* London: Continuum, 2004.

Halliday, M. A. K. (1988c) Language and socialization: home and school. In Gerot et al. (eds). Reprinted in J. J. Webster (ed.) *The Collected Works of M. A. K. Halliday, Vol 9: Language and Education*. London: Continuum, 2007.

Halliday, M. A. K. (1990) New ways of meaning: a challenge to applied linguistics. *Journal of Applied Linguistics* 6: 7–36. Greek Applied Linguistics Association. Reprinted in J. J. Webster (ed.) *Collected Works of M. A. K. Halliday, Vol 3: On Language and Linguistics*. London: Continuum 2003.

Halliday, M. A. K. (1992a) How do you mean?, In M. Davies and L. Ravelli (eds) *Advances in Systemic Linguistics: recent theory and practice* 20–35. London: Pinter. Reprinted in J. J. Webster (ed.) *Collected Works of M. A. K. Halliday, Vol 1: On Grammar*. London: Continuum 2002.

Halliday, M. A. K. (1992b) The act of meaning. In J. E. Alatis (ed.) *Language Communication and Social Meaning: Georgetown University Road Table on Language and Linguistics 1992.* Washington, DC: Georgetown University Press. Reprinted in J. J. Webster (ed.) *Collected Works of M. A. K. Halliday, Vol 3: On Language and Linguistics*. London: Continuum 2003

Halliday, M. A. K. (1996) On grammar and grammatics. In R. Hasan, C. Cloran and D. Butt (eds) *Functional Descriptions: Theory in Practice.* Amsterdam: Benjamins. Reprinted in J. J. Webster (ed.) *The Collected Works of M. A. K. Halliday, Vol 1: On Grammar*. London: Continuum 2002.

Halliday, M. A. K. (1999) The notion of 'context' in language education. In Ghadessy (ed.) 1st published in T. Lê and M. McCausland (eds) *Language Education: interaction and development* 1–26. Launceston: University of Tasmania. Reprinted in J. J. Webster (ed.) *Collected Works of M. A. K. Halliday, Vol 9: Language and Education.* London: Continuum 2007.

Halliday, M. A. K. (2003) *Collected Works of M. A. K. Halliday Vol 4: the Language of Early Childhood.* J. J. Webster (ed.). London: Continuum.

Halliday, M. A. K. (2004a) *Collected Works of M. A. K. Halliday Vol 5: The Language of Science.* J. J. Webster (ed.). London: Continuum.

Halliday, M. A. K. (2004b) Grammar as the driving force from primary to higher-order consciousness. In G. Williams and A. Lukin (eds).

Halliday, M. A. K. (2008) *Complementarities in Language*. Beijing: Commercial Press.

Halliday, M. A. K. and Fawcett, R. P. (eds) (1987) *New Developments in Systemic Linguistics Vol 1: Theory and Description*. London: Frances Pinter.

Halliday, M. A. K., Gibbons, J. and Nicholas, H. (eds) (1990) *Learning, Keeping and Using Language, Vol 1: Selected Papers from the 8th World Congress of Applied Linguistics*. Amsterdam: Benjamins.

Halliday M. A. K. and Hasan, R. (1976) *Cohesion in English*. London: Longmans.

Halliday, M. A. K. and Hasan, R. (1985) *Language, Context and Text: aspects of language in a social-semiotic perspective*. Geelong, Vic: Deakin University Press. Reprinted: Oxford: Oxford University Press 1989.

Halliday, M. A. K. and Martin, J. R. (eds) (1981) *Readings in Systemic Linguistics*. London: Batsford.

Halliday, M. A. K. and Martin, J. R. (1993) *Writing Science: Literacy and Discursive Power*. London: Falmer Press

Halliday, M. A. K. and Matthiessen, C. M. I. M. (1999) *Construing Experience through Meaning: a Language Based Approach to Cognition*. London: Cassell.

Halliday, M. A. K. and Matthiessen, C. M. I. M. (2004) *An Introduction to Functional Grammar*. 3rd edition. London: Arnold.

Halliday, M. A. K., McIntosh, A. and Stevens, P. (1964) *The Linguistic Sciences and Language Teaching*. London: Longman.

Harris, R. (1987) *Reading Saussure: A Critical Commentary on the Cours de Linguistique Générale*. London: Duckworth.

Hasan, R. (1973a) Code, register and social dialect. In B. Bernstein (ed.) *Class, Codes and Control, Vol 2: Applied Studies toward a Sociology of Language* 253–92. London: Routledge and Kegan Paul. Reprinted in Hasan, 2005.

Hasan, R. (1973b) *Measuring the Length of a Text*. Sydney: Macquarie University. Mimeo.

Hasan, R. (1978) Text in the systemic functional model. In W. U. Dressler (ed.).

Hasan, R. (1979) On the notion of text. In J. S. Petofi (ed.) *Text vs. Sentence. Basic Questions of Textlinguistics. Papers in Textlinguistics* 20(2). Hamburg: Helmut Buske.

Hasan, R. (1980) What's going on? A dynamic view of context in language. In J. E. Copeland and P. W. Davies (eds) *The Seventh LACUS Forum* 106–21. Columbia: Hornbeam Press. Reprinted in C. Cloran, D. Butt and G. Williams (eds) *Ways of Saying, Ways of Meaning: selected papers of Ruqaiya Hasan*. London: Cassell 1996.

Hasan, R. (1983) *A Semantic Network for the Analysis of Messages in Everyday Talk between Mothers and Their Children*. Department of Linguistics: Macquarie University, Sydney. Mimeo.

Hasan, R. (1984a) What kind of resource is language? *Australian Review of Applied Linguistics* 7(1): 57–85. Reprinted in C. Cloran, D. Butt and G. Williams (eds).

Hasan, R. (1984b) The nursery tale as a genre. *Nottingham Linguistic Circular* 13: 71–102. Special Issue on Linguistics edited by B. Margaret, M. Stubbs and R. Carter. Nottingham: Nottingham University Press. Reprinted (abridged) in Cloran, Butt and Williams (eds).

Hasan, R. (1984c) Ways of saying: ways of meaning. In R. P. Fawcett, M. A. K. Halliday, S. M. Lamb and A. Makkai (eds) *The Semiotics of Culture and Language, Vol 1: Language as Social Semiotic.* London: Frances Pinter. Reprinted in C. Cloran, D. Butt and G. Williams (eds).

Hasan, R. (1984d) Coherence and cohesive harmony. In J. Flood (ed.) *Understanding Reading Comprehension* 181–219. Newark: International Reading Association.

Hasan, R. (1985a) The identity of the text. Chapter 6, in M. A. K. Halliday and R. Hasan 1985.

Hasan, R. (1985b) The texture of a text. Chapter 5, in M. A. K. Halliday and R. Hasan 1985.

Hasan, R. (1985c) The Structure of a text. Chapter 4, in M. A. K. Halliday and R. Hasan 1985.

Hasan, R. (1985d) Lending and borrowing: from grammar to lexis. In J. E. Clark (ed.) *The cultivated Australian: festschrift in honour of Arthur Delbridge* 55–67. Hamburg: Helmut Buske.

Hasan, R. (1985e) Meaning, context, and text: fifty years after Malinowski. In J. D. Benson and W. S. Greaves (eds).

Hasan, R. (1985f) *Linguistics, Language and Verbal Art.* Geelong, Vic: Deakin University Press.

Hasan, R. (1986a) The ontogenesis of ideology: an interpretation of mother child talk. In T. Threadgold, E. A. Grosz, G. Kress and M. A. K. Halliday (eds) *Semiotics Ideology Language* 124–44. Sydney, Sydney Association for Studies in Society and Culture (Sydney Studies in Society and Culture Volume 3). Reprinted in Cloran, Butt and Williams (eds) 1996. Reprinted in Hasan 2005.

Hasan, R. (1986b) *Offers in the Making: a systemic functional approach.* Mimeo: Macquarie University (Department of Linguistics).

Hasan, R. (1986c) The implications of semantic distance for language in education. In Anvita Abbi (ed.) *Studies in Bilingualism.* New Delhi: Bahri Publications. 1st presented to the 10th International Congress of Anthropological and Ethnological Sciences, held December 1978, Mysore, India.

Hasan, R. (1987a) The grammarian's dream: lexis as most delicate grammar. In M. A. K. Halliday and R. P. Fawcett (eds). Reprinted in Cloran, Butt and Williams (eds).

Hasan, R. (1987b) Directions from structuralism. In N. Fabb, D. Attridge, A. Durant and C. McCabe. (eds). Manchester: Manchester University Press.

Hasan, R. (1987c) Reading picture reading: invisible instruction at home and in school. Proceedings of the 13th Conference of the Australian Reading Association. Sydney, July 1987. (no Editor, no Publisher, no Date).

Hasan, R. (1988) Language in the processes of socialisation: home and school. In J. Oldenburg, T. van Leeuwen and L. Gerot (eds). [Chapter 4, this volume].

Hasan, R. (1989) Semantic variation and sociolinguistics. *Australian Journal of Linguistics* 9(2): 221–76. [Chapter 5, this volume].

Hasan, R. (1991) Questions as a mode of learning in everyday talk. In Thao Lê and Mike McCausland (eds) *Language Education: Interaction and Development* 70–119. Launceston: University of Tasmania. [Chapter 6, this volume].

Hasan, R. (1992a) Meaning in socilinguistic theory. In K. Bolton and H. Kwok (eds) *Sociolinguistics Today: International Perspectives* 80–119. London: Routledge. [Chapter 7, this volume]

Hasan, R. (1992b) Rationality and everyday talk: from process to system. In J. Svartvik (ed.) *Directions in Corpus Linguistics: proceedings of Nobel Symposium 82, Stockholm, 4–8 August 1991* 257–307. Berlin: Walter de Gruyter. [Chapter 8, this volume]

Hasan, R. (1992c) Speech genre, semiotic mediation and the development of higher mental functions. In M. A. K. Halliday and F. C. C. Peng (eds) *Language Sciences* 14(4): 489–528. (Special Issue: Current Research in Functional Grammar, Discourse and Computational Linguistics with a Foundation in Systemic Theory. Reprinted in Hasan, 2005.

Hasan, R. (1993) Contexts for meaning. In J. E. Alatis (ed.). [Chapter 9, this volume].

Hasan, R. (1994) Situation and the definition of genre. In A. D. Grimshaw (ed.) *What's Going on Here? Complementary Studies of Professional Talk.* Norwood, NJ: Ablex.

Hasan, R. (1995a) The conception of context in text. In P. H. Fries and M. Gregory (eds). *Discourse in Society: systemic functional perspectives (Meaning and Choice in Language: Studies for Michael Halliday).* Norwood, NJ: Ablex.

Hasan, R. (1995b) On social conditions for semiotic mediation: the genesis of mind in society. In A. R. Sadovnik (ed.) *Knowledge and Pedagogy: the Sociology of Basil Bernstein* 171–196. Norwood, NJ: Ablex. Reprinted in Hasan, 2005.

Hasan, R. (1996) Semantic networks: a tool for the analysis of meaning. In C. Cloran, D. Butt and G. Williams (eds),1996.

Hasan, R. (1998) The disempowerment game: Bourdieu and language in literacy. *Linguistics and Education* 10(1). Reprinted in Hasan, 2005.

Hasan, R. (1999) Speaking with reference to context. In M. Ghadessy (ed.).

Hasan, R. (2000) The uses of talk. In S. Sarangi and M. Coulthard (eds) *Discourse and Social Life* 28–47. London: Pearson Education. Reprinted in Hasan, 2005.

Hasan, R. (2001) Wherefore context? The place of context in the system and process of language. In S. Z. Ren, W. Gutherie and I. W. Ronald Fong (eds) *Grammar and Discourse: Proceedings of the International Conference on Discourse Analysis* 1–21. Macau: Universidad de Macau.

Hasan, R. (2002a) Semiotic mediation and mental development in pluralistic societies: some implications for tomorrow's schooling. In G. Wells and G. Claxton (eds) *Learning for Life in the 21st Century: Socio-Cultural Perspectives on the Future of Education.* Oxford: Blackwell. Reprinted in Hasan, 2005.

Hasan, R. (2002b) Ways of meaning, ways of learning: code as an explanatory concept. *British Journal of Sociology of Education* 23(4): 537–548. Reprinted in Hasan, 2005.

Hasan, R. (2003) Globalization, literacy and ideology. *World Englishes* 22(4).

Hasan, R. (2004a) Analysing discursive variation. In L. Young and C. Harrison (eds) *Systemic Functional Linguistics and Critical Discourse Analysis.* London: Continuum.

Hasan, R. (2004b) Reading picture reading: a study in ideology and inference. In J. A. Foley (ed.). Reprinted in Hasan, 2005.

Hasan, R. (2005) *Language, Society and Consciousness: Collected Works of Ruqaiya Hasan Vol 1.* Edited by J. J. Webster. London: Equinox.

Hasan, R. and Cloran, C. (1990) A sociolinguistic interpretation of everyday talk between mothers and children. In M. A. K. Halliday, J. Gibbon and H. Nicholas (eds) *Learning, Keeping and Using Language Volume 1: selected papers from the 8th World Congress of Applied Linguistics, Sydney 16–21 August 1987* 67–100. Amsterdam: Benjamins. [Extended version reprinted as Chapter 4, this Volume].

Hasan, R., Cloran, C. and Butt D. (eds) (1996) Functional Descriptions: Theory in Practice. Amsterdam: Benjamins.

Hasan, R and Fries, P. H. (eds) (1995) *On Subject and Theme: a discourse functional perspective.* Amsterdam: Benjamins.

Hasan, R. and Martin, J. R. (1989) (eds) *Language Development: learning language, learning Culture. Meaning and Choice in Language: Studies for Michael Halliday.* Norwood, NJ: Ablex.

Hasan, R. Matthiessen, C. M. I. M. and Webster, J. J. (eds) *Continuing Discourse on Language Vol 2.* London: Equinox

Heilman, L. (ed.) (1975) *Proceedings of the Eleventh International Congress of Linguists.Held in Bologna, Italy 28 Aug – 2 Sept 1972.* Bologna: Il Mulino.

Hill, J. H. (1985) Is a sociolinguistics possible? A review article. *Comparative Studies in Society and History* 27(3): 461–71.

Hjelmslev, L. (1961) *Prolegomena to a Theory of Language*. Translated by F. J. Whitfield. Wisconsin: University of Wisconsin Press. 1st published 1953.

Holmes, J. (1988) Of course: a pragmatic particle in New Zealand women's & men's speech. *Australian Journal of Linguistics* 8(1): 49-74.

Horvath, B. M. (1985) *Variation in Australian English: the sociolects of Sydney*. Cambridge: Cambridge University Press.

Hudson, R A. (1980) *Sociolinguistics*. Cambridge: Cambridge University Press.

von Humboldt, W. (1971) Linguistic Variability and Intellectual Development, Translated by G C Buck and F A Raven. Philadelphia: University of Pennsylvania Press. 1st published 1836 in German by the Royal Society of Sciences in Berlin.

Hymes, D. (1962) The ethnography of speaking. In T. Gladwin and W. C. Strutevant (eds) *Anthropology and Human Behaviour*. Washington, DC: Anthropological Society of Washington. Reprinted in J. A. Fishman (ed.)

Hymes, D. (1967) Models of the interaction of language and social setting. *Journal of Social Issues* 23(2): 8–28.

Hymes, D. (1971) Sociolinguistics and the ethnography of speaking. In E. Ardener (ed.) *Social Anthropology and Linguistics. Association of Social Anthropologist, Monograph 10*. London: Tavistock.

Hymes, D. (1993) Inequality in language: taking for granted. In J. E. Alatis (ed.).

Jackendoff, R. (1988) Conceptual semantics. In U. Eco, M. Santambrogio and P. Violi (eds).

Jarvie, I. C. (1976) Toulmin and the rationality of science. In R. S. Cohen, P. K. Feyerabend and M. W. Wartofsky (eds) *Essays in Memory of Imre Lakatos* 311–33. Dordrecht: D Reidel Publishing Company.

Kappagoda, A. (2005) What do people do to know? In R. Hasan, C. M. I. M. Matthiessen and J. J. Webster (eds) *Continuing Discourse on Language Vol 1*. London: Equinox.

Kekes, J. (1979) Rationality and the social sciences [review article]. *The Philosophy of Social Science* 9(1): 105–13.

Kempson, R. M. (1977) *Semantic Theory*. London: Cambridge University Press.

Klein, N. (2007) *The Shock Doctrine: the rise of disaster capitalism*. London: Allen lane (Penguin Books).

Klemperer, V. (1975) *The Language of the Third Reich*. Translated by M. Brady). London: Continuum.

Knorr-Cetina, K.D. (1981) Introduction: the micro-sociological challenge of macro-sociology: towards a reconstruction of social theory and methodology. In K. D. Knorr-Cetina and A. V. Cicourel (eds) *Advances in Social Theory and Methodology: toward an integration of micro-and-macro-sociologie*s. London: Routledge & Kegan Paul.

Kwok, H. and Bolton, K. (eds) (1992) *Sociolinguistics Today: International Perspectives*. London: Routledge & Kegan Paul.

Labov, W. (1966a) *The Social Stratification of English in New York City.* Washington, DC: Centre for Applied Linguistics.

Labov, W. (1966b) The linguistic variable as a structural unit. *Washington Linguistic Review* 3: 4–22.

Labov, W. (1968) The reflection of social processes in linguistic structures. In J. A. Fishman (ed.) *Readings in the Sociology of Language*. The Hague: Mouton.

Labov, W. (1969) The logic of nonstandard English. *Georgetown Monographs on Language and Linguistics*, Vol 22. Washington, DC: Georgetown University Press.

Labov, W. (1972a) *Sociolinguistic Patterns*. Oxford: Basil Blackwell.

Labov, W. (1972b) The study of language in its social context. In Labov 1972a.

Labov, W. (1972c) The social motivation of a sound change. In Labov 1972a.

Labov, W. (1972d) *Language in the Inner City: Studies in the Black English Vernacular*. Philadelphia: University of Pennsylvania Press.

Labov, W. (1972e) The transformation of experience in narrative syntax. In Labov 1972d.

Labov, W. (1973) The boundaries of words and their meanings. In C. J. N. Bailey and R. W. Shuy (eds) *New Ways of Analysing Variation in English.* Washington, DC: Georgetown University Press.

Labov, W. (1978a) Where does the sociolinguistic variable stop? A response to Beatriz Lavandera. *Working Papers in Sociolinguistics* 44. Austin, Tex.: Southwest Educational Development Laboratory.

Labov, W. (1978b) Crossing the gulf between sociology and linguistics. *The American Sociologist* 13.

Labov, W. (1980) *Locating Language in Time and Space*. New York: Academic Press.

Labov, W. (1987) The overestimation of functionalism. In R. Dirven and V. Fried (eds) *Functionalism in Linguistics*. Amsterdam: Benjamins.

Labov, W. and Fanshel, D. (1977) *Therapeutic Discourse: psychotherapy as conversation.* New York: Academic Press.

Labov,W. and Weiner, E. J. (1977) Constraints on the agentless passive. University of Pennsylvania: Manuscript.

Lakoff, R. (1973) Language and women's place. *Language and Society* 2: 45–79.

Lavandera, B. R. (1978) Where does the sociolinguistic variable stop? *Language in Society* 7: 171–83.

Lavandera, B. R. (1988) The study of language in its socio-cultural context. In Newmyer (ed.).

Lave, J. (1997) What's special about experiments as contexts for thinking. In M. Cole, Y. Engeström and O. Vasquez (eds) *Mind, Culture and Activity: Seminal Papers from the Laboratory of Human Cognition* 57–69. Cambridge: Cambridge University Press.

Le Page, R.B. and Tabouret-Keller, A. (1985) *Acts of Identity: creole-based approaches to language and ethnicity.* Cambridge: Cambridge University Press.

Leech, G. N. (1983) *Principles of Pragmatics*. London: Longman.

Leech, G N. (1987) *Meaning and the English Verb*. London: Longman.

Lehman, W. P. and Malkiel, Y. (eds) (1968) *Directions from Historical Linguistics: A Symposium*. Austin, Texas: University of Texas Press.

Lemke, J. L. (1984) *Semiotics and Education.* Toronto Semiotic Circle Monographs. Working Papers and Pre-publications 1984.2. Toronto: Victoria University.

Lenneberg, E.H. (1975) Language and cognition. In D. D. Steinberg and L. A. Jakobovits (eds), *Semantics*. Cambridge: Cambridge University Press.

Leont'ev, A.N. (1981) The problem of activity in psychology. In J. W. Wertsch (ed.) *The Concept of Activity in Soviet Psychology*. Sharpe Inc. Publisher.

Levinson, S. (1983) *Pragmatics*. Oxford: Oxford University Press.

Lieberson, S. (1966) Explorations in sociolinguistics. *Sociological Inquiry* 36: 2.

Lind, E. A. and O'Barr, W. M. (1979) The social significance of speech in the courtroom. In H. Giles and R. St Clair (eds) *Language and Social Psychology*. Oxford: Basil Blackwell.

Lock, A. (ed.) (1978) *Action, Gesture and Symbol: the Emergence of Language*. London: Academic Press.

Lukes, S. (1974) *Power: a Radical View*. London: Macmillan.

Luria, A R. (1976) *Cognitive Development: its Cultural and Social Foundations.* (translated by M. Lopez-Morillas and L. Solotaroff, edited by M. Cole). Cambridge, MA: Harvard University Press.

Lyons, J. (ed.) (1970) *New Horizons in Linguistics*. Harmondworth: Penguin.

Mackay, R.W. (1974) Conceptions of children and models of socialization. In R. Turner (ed.) *Ethomethodology*. Harmondsworth: Penguin.

Maley, Y. and Hahey, R. (1991) Presenting the evidence: construction of reality in court. *International Journal for Seniotics of Law* 4(1): 3–17.

Malinowski, B. (1923) The problem of meaning in primitive languages.In Supplement 1 to C. K. Ogden and I. A. Richards (eds) *The Meaning of Meaning.* London: Kegan Paul.

Malinowski, B. (1935) An ethnographic theory of language. Part IV in *Coral Gardens and Their Magic, Vol 2*. London: Allen & Unwin.

Mann, W. C. and Thompson, S. A. (1987) Rhetorical structure theory: description and construction of text structures. In G. Kempen (ed.) *Natural Language Generation: New Results in Artificial Intelligence, Psychology and Linguistics* 85–95. Dordrecht: Martinus Nijhoff.

Markova, I. (1988) A three step process as a unit of analysis in dialogue. In I. Markova and K. Foppa (eds) *The Dynamics of Dialogue* 129–146. New York: Harvester.

Marshall, G., Rose, D., Newby, H. and Vogler, C. (eds) (1988) *Social Class in Modern Britain*. London: Unwin Hyman.

Martin, J. R. (1985) Process and text: two aspects of human semiosis. In J. D. Benson and W. S. Greaves (eds).

Martin, J. R. (1987) The meaning of features in systemic linguistics. In Halliday & Fawcett (eds).

Martin, J. R. (1988) Secret English: discourse technology in a Junior Secondary school In L. Gerot, J. Oldenburg and T. van Leeuwen (eds), *Language and Socialisation: home and school.* Sydney: Macquarie University.

Martin, J. R. (1991) Intrinsic functionality: implications for contextual theory. *Social Semiotics* 1(1): 99–162. Sydney: Sydney University Publication.

Martin, J. R. (1992) *English Text: System and Structure*. Amsterdam: John Benjamins.

Martin, J.R., Wignell, P., Eggins, S. and Rothery, J. (1988) Secret English: discourse technology in a junior secondary school *143–173*. In Gerot et al. (eds).

Marwick, B. (2005) The interpersonal origins of language: social and linguistic implications of an archaeological approach to language evolution. *Linguistics and the Human Sciences* 1(2): 197- 224.

Marx, K. and Engels, F. (1985) *The German Ideology*, Part One (edited and introduction by C. J. Arthur). London: Lawrence and Wishart. 1st published 1970.

Mathesius, V. (1964) On the potentiality of the phenomena of language. In J. Vachek (ed.) *A Prague School Reader in Linguistics*. Bloomington: Indiana University Press. 1st published in Czech in 1911.

Matthiessen, C. M. I. M. (1991) Language on language: the grammar of semiosis. *Social Semiotics* 1.2: 61-111.

Matthiessen, C. M. I. M. (1992) Intrerpreting the textual metafunction. In M. Davies and L. Ravelli (eds) *Advances in Systemic Linguistics: recent theory and practice*. London: Frances Pinter.

Matthiessen, C. M. I. M. (2004) The evolution of language: a systemic functional exploration of phylogenetic phases. In G. Williams and A. Lukin (eds).

Mattheissen, C. M. I. M. (2007) The architecture of language according to systemic functional theory: developments since the 1970s. In R. Hasan, C. M. I. M. Matthiessen and J. J. Webster (eds).

Matthiessen, C. M. I. M. and Nesbit, C. (1996) On the idea of theory-neutral description. In R. Hasan, C. Cloran and D. G. Butt (eds).

Matthiessen, C. M. I. M. and Thompson, S. A. (1989) The structure of discourse and subordination. In J. Haiman and S. A. Thompson (eds) *Clause Combining in Grammar and Discourse* 275–329. Amsterdam: John Benjamins.

McLellan, D. (1975) *Marx. Fontana Modern Masters Series*. Glasgow: Fontana/ Collins.

McMahon, A. M. S. (1994) *Understanding Language Change*. Cambridge: Cambridge University Press.

McMurty, J. (1999) *The Cancer Stage of Capitalism*. Sterling,VA: Pluto Press.
Mead, G. H. (1934) *Mind, Self and Society: from the standpoint of a Social Behaviourist*. Edited by C. W. Morris. Chicago: Chicago University Press.
Medawar, P. (1982) *Pluto's Republic*. Oxford: Oxford Univesriy Press.
Mercer, N. (1993) *The Guided Construction of Knowledge: Talk among Teachers and Learners*. Adelaide: Multilingual Matters.
Miller, M. (1987) Argumentation and cognition. In M. Hickman (ed.) *Social and Functional Approaches to Language and Thought* 225–49. Boston: Academic Press.
Milroy, L. (1980) *Language and Social Networks*. Oxford: Blackwell.
Mitchell, T. F. (1957) The language of buying and selling in Cyrenaica: a situational statements. Hesperis. Reprinted in *Principles of Firthian Linguistics*. 1975. London: Longman.
Nesbitt, C. and Plum, G. (1988) Probabilities in a systemic functional grammar: the clause complex in English. In R. P. Fawcett and D. J. Young (eds) *New Developments in Systemic Linguistics Volume 2: Theory and Applications*. London: Frances Pinter.
Newmeyer, F. J. (ed.) (1988) *Language: the Socio-cultural Context. Volume IV of Linguistics: The Cambridge Survey*. Cambridge: Cambridge University Press.
Nisbett, R. and Ross, L. (1980) *Human Inference: Strategies and Shortcomings of Social judgment*. Englewood Cliffs, NJ: Prentice-Hall.
Overton, W. F. (1990) Competence and procedures: constraints on the development of logical reasoning. In W. F. Overton (ed.) *Reasoning, Necessity, and Logic: Developmental Perspectives* 1–44. Hillsdale, NJ: Lawrence Erlebaum Associates.
Painter, C. (1984) *Into the Mother Tongue: a Case Study in Early Language Development*. London: Frances Pinter.
Painter, C. (1989) Learning language: a functional view of language development. In R. Hasan and J. R. Martin (eds).
Painter, C. (1999) *Learning through Language in Early Childhood*. London: Continuum.
Painter, C. (2004) The 'interpersonal first' principle in child language development. In G. Williams and A. Lukin (eds).
Patten, T. (1988) *Systemic Text Generation as Problem Solving*. Cambridge: Cambridge University Press.
Peirce, C. S. (1955) *Philosophical writings of Peirce*. (Selected and edited by J. Buchler). New York: Dover.
Peters, R. S. (1972) Reason and passion. In R. F. Dearden, P. H. Hirst and R. S. Peters (eds).
Petőfi, J. S. (ed.) (1979) *Text vs Sentence: Basic Questions of Text Linguistics*. (First and Second Parts.) Hamburg: Helmut Buske.
Piaget, J. (1960) *Language and Thought of the Child*. London: Routledge and Kegan Paul.

Plum, G. and Cowling, A. (1987) Social constraints on grammatical variables: tense choice in English. In R. Steele and T. Threadgold (eds) *Language Topics: Essays in Honour of Michael Halliday, Vol 2*. Amsterdam: John Benjamins.

Pole, D. (1972) The concept of reason. In R. F. Dearden, P. H. Hirst and R. S. Peters (eds).

Pollner, M. (1974) Mundane reasoning. *Philosophy of Social Science* 4: 35–54.

Popper, K. R. (1979) *Objective Knowledge: an evolutionary approach*. Revised edition. Oxford: Clarendon Press. 1st published 1972.

Popper, K. R. and Eccles, J. C. (1977) *The Self and its Brain*. London: Routledge & Kegan Paul.

Poulantzas, N. (1981) Social class and the state. In T. Bottomore (ed.) *Modern Interpretations of Marx*. London: Basil Blackwell.

Quirk, R., Leech, G. N. and Svartvik, J. (1985) *A Comprehensive Grammar of the English Language*. London: Longman.

Reddy, V., Hay, D., Murray, L. and Trevarthen, C. (1997) Communication in infancy: mutual regulation of communication in infancy. In G. Brenner, A. Slater and G. Butterworth (eds) *Infant Development: recent advances*. London: Psychology Press.

Robinson, W. P. and Rackstraw, S. J. (1972) *A Question of Answers, Vols 1 & 2*. London: Routledge & Kegan Paul.

Robinson, W P. (1979) Speech markers and social class. In K. R. Scherer and H. Giles (eds).

Romaine, S. (1982a) *Sociohistorical Linguistics: its status and methodology*. Cambridge: Cambridge University Press.

Romaine, S. (ed.) (1982b) *Sociolinguistic Variation in Speech Communities*. London: Arnold.

Romaine, S. (1984) On the problem of syntactic variation and pragmatic meaning in sociolinguistic theory. Folia Linguistica xviii.3-4: 409–37 The Hague, Mouton.

Rosen, C. and Rosen, H. (1973) *The Language of Primary School Children*. Harmondsworth: Penguin.

Rosen, H. (1972) *Language and Class: a critical look at the Theories of Basil Bernstein*. Bristol: Falling Well Press.

Sankoff, G. (1973) Above and beyond phonology in variable rules. In C. J. Bailey and R. Shuy (eds) *New Ways of Analyzing Variation in English*. Washington, DC: Georgetown University Press.

Santambrogio, M. and Violi, P. (1988) Introduction. In U. Eco, M. Santambrogio and P. Violi (eds) *Meaning and Mental Representations* 3–22. Bloomington: Indiana University Press.

Sapir, E. (1921) *Language: an introduction to the study of speech*. New York: Harcourt, Brace and Co.

Sapir, E. (1944) Grading: a study in semantics. *Philosophy of Science* 11: 93-116. Reprinted in D. G. Mandelbaum (ed.) *Selected Writings of Edward Sapir on Language, Culture and Personality*. Berkeley: University of California Press (1951).

de Saussure, F. (1966) *Course in General Linguistics*. Translated by W. Baskin. New York: McGraw-Hill.

Schank, R. and Abelson, R. (1977) *Scripts Plans Goals and Understanding: an enquiry into human knowledge structures*. Hillsdale, NJ: Lawrence Erlbaum.

Scherer, K. R. and Giles, H. (eds) (1979) *Social Markers in Speech*. Cambridge, Cambridge University Press.

Schilling-Estes, N. (2002a) Investigating stylistic variation. In J. K. Chambers, P. Trudgill and N. Schilling-Estes (eds).

Schilling-Estes, N. (2002b) What is 'style'? In J. K. Chambers, P. Trudgill and N. Schilling-Estes (eds).

Searle, J. R. (1969) *Speech Acts: an essay in the philosophy of language*. London: Cambridge University Press.

Sells, P. (1985) *Lectures on Contemporary Syntactic Theories: an introduction to government-binding theory, generalized phrase structure grammar, and lexical functional grammar*. Stanford: CSLI.

Shuy, R, Wolfram, W. and Riley, W. K. (1967) *A Study of Social Dialects in Detroit.* Final Report, Project No. 6-1347. Washington, DC: Office of Education.

Sinclair, J. M. (1987) Introduction. In *Collins COBUILD English language dictionary*. London: Collins.

Sinclair, J. M. (1991) Shared knowledge. In J. E. Alatis (ed.) *Linguistics and Language Pedagogy: the state of the art. Georgetown University Round Table on Languages and Linguistics 1991* 489–500. Washington, DC: Georgetown University Press.

Sinclair, J. M. and Coulthard, M. (1975) *Towards an Analysis of Discourse: the English used by teachers and pupils.* London: Oxford University Press.

Stich, S. P. (1990) Rationality. In D. N. Osherson and E. E. Smith (eds) *An Invitation to Cognitive Science Vol 3: Thinking*. Cambridge, MA: MIT Press.

Stubbs, M. (1983) What is to be done? Theory or practice – problem of resource? In M. Stubbs and H. Hillier (eds), *Readings on Language, Schools and Classrooms: contemporary sociology of the school*. London: Methuen.

Swann, B. (ed.) (1983) *Smoothing the Ground.* Berkeley: University of California Press.

Thibault, P. J. (1997) *Re-reading Saussure: the dynamics of sign in social life.* London: Routeldge.

Thibault, P. J. (2004) *Agency and Consciousness in Discourse: Self-Other Dynamics as a Complex System.* London: Continuum.

Torr, J. (1997) *From Child Tongue to Mother Tongue: a Case Study of Language Development in the First Two and a Half Years.* Monograph in Systemic Linguistics No. 9. Nottingham: Department of English Studies, University of Nottingham.

Toulmin, S. E. (1958) *The Uses of Argument.* Cambridge: Cambridge University Press.

Toulmin, S. E. (1972) *Human Understanding: Vol 1.* Princeton, NJ: Princeton University Press.

Trevarthen, C. (1974) Conversations with a two-month old. *New Scientist* 62: 230–5.

Trevarthen, C. and Hubley, P. (1978) Confidence, confiding, and acts of meaning in the first year. In A. Lock (ed.).

Trudgill, P. (1974) *Sociolinguistics: an introduction.* Harmondworth: Penguin

Trudgill, P. (ed.) (1978) *Sociolinguistic Patterns in British English.* London: Edward Arnold.

Trudgill, P. (1983) *On Dialect: social and geographical perspectives.* Oxford: Blackwell.

Tucker, G. H. (1998) *The Lexicogrammar of Adjectives: a systemic functional approach to lexis.* London: Cassell.

Turner, G. J. (1973) Social class and children's language of control at age five amd seven. In B. Bernstein (ed.) *Class, Codes and Control Vol 2: Applied Studies towards a Sociology of Language.* London: Routledge & Kegan Paul.

Turner, G. J. and Mohan, B. (1970) *A Linguistic Description and Computer Program for Children's Speech.* London: Routledge & Kegan Paul.

Turner, G. J. and Pickvance, R. E. (1973) Social class differences in the expression of uncertainty in five year old children. In B. Bernstein (ed.) *Class, Codes and Control Vol 2: Applied Studies Towards a Sociology of Language.* London: Routledge & Kegan Paul.

Turner, P. R. (ed.) (1982) *Bilingualism in the Southwest.* Tuscon: University of Arizona Press. (Revised 2nd edition).

Ventola, E. (1987) *The Structure of Social Interaction: a Systemic Approach to the Semiotics of Service Encounters.* London: Frances Pinter.

Vološinov, V. N. (1973) *Marxism and the Philosophy of Language.* Translated by L. Matjeka and I. R. Titunik. Cambridge, MA: Harvard University Press.

Vygorsky, L. S. (1962) *Thought and Language.* Translated and edited by E. Hanffman and G. Vakar. Cambridge, MA: Harvard University Press.

Vygotsky, L. S. (1978) *Mind in Society: the development of higher psychological processes.* Edited by M. Cole, V. John-Steiner, S. Scribner and E. Souberman. Cambridge, MA: Harvard University Press.

Vygotsky, L.S. (1981) The genesis of higher mental functions. In J. V. Wertsch (ed.) *The Concept of Activity in Soviet Psychology.* Armonk, NY: M. E. Sharp.

Wason, P. C. and Johnson-Laird, P. N. (eds) (1968) *Thinking and Reasoning.* Harmondsworth: Penguin.

Wason, P. C. and Johnson-Laird, P. N. (1972) *Psychology of Reasoning: structure and content.* London: B. T. Batsford.

Weiner, E. J. and Labov, W. (1983) Constraints on agent-less passive. *Australian Journal of Linguistics* 19(1): 29–58.

Weinreich, U., Labov, W. and Herzog, M. I. (1968) Empirical foundations for a theory of language change. In W. P. Lehman and Y. Malkiel (eds) *Directions for Historical Linguistics: A Symposium.* Austin: University of Texas Press.

Wells, G. (1977) Language use and educational success: An empirical response to Joan Tough: The development of meaning. *Research in Education* 18. (Quoted from Osser, H. (1983) Language as the instrument of school socialization: an examination of Bernstein's thesis. In B. Bain (ed.) *The Sociogenesis of Language and Human Conduct.* New York: Plenum Press.

Wells, G. (1981) *Learning through Interaction: the Study of Language Development. (Language at Home and at School, 1).* Cambridge: Cambridge University Press.

Wells, G. (1985) *Learning through Interaction: Language Development in Pre-School Years.* Cambridge: Cambridge University Press.

Wertsch, J. V. (1985a) *Culture, Communication and Cognition: Vygotskian Perspectives.* Cambridge, Cambridge University Press.

Wertsch, J. V. (1985b) *Vygotsky and the Social Formation of Mind.* Cambridge, Mass.: Harvard University Press.

Wexler, P. (1982) Structure, text and subject. In M. W. Apple (ed.).

Whorf, B L. (1956) *Language, Thought and Reality: selected writings of Benjamin Lee Whorf.* Edited and introduced by J. B. Carroll. Cambridge, MA: The MIT Press.

Wierzbicka, A. (1984) Cups and mugs: lexicolocy and conceptual analysis. *Australian Journal of Linguistics* 4(2): 205–56.

Williams, G. (1992) *Sociolinguistics: a sociological critique.* London: Routledge.

Williams, G. (1995) *Joint Book-Reading and Literacy Pedagogy: a socio-semantic interpretation.* Unpublished Ph D Dissertation. Sydney: School of English, Linguistics & Media, Macquarie University (Available as CORE Volume 1(19): 3 and Volume 2(20): 1).

Williams, G. (1999) Preparing for school: developing a semantic style for educational knowledge. In F. Christie (ed.) *Pedagogy and the Shaping of Consciousness: linguistic and social processes* 88–122. London: Cassell.

Williams, G. (2001) Literacy pedagogy prior to schooling: relations between social positioning and semantic variation. In A. Morais, I. Neves, B. Davies and H. Daniels (eds) *Towards a Sociology of Pedagogy: the contribution of Basil Bernstein to research* 17–45. New York: Peter Lang.

Williams, G. and Lukin, A. (eds). (2004) *The Development of Language: Functional Perspectives on Species and Individuals.* Londom: Continuum.

Wittgenstein, L. (1958) *Philosophical Investigations*. Translated by G. E. M. Anscombe. Oxford: Blackwell. 2nd edition. 1st published, 1953.
Wootton, A. J. (1974) Talk in the homes of young children. *Sociology* 8.

Index

www.ingramcontent.com/pod-product-compliance
Lightning Source LLC
LaVergne TN
LVHW010443080826
844660LV00026B/1200